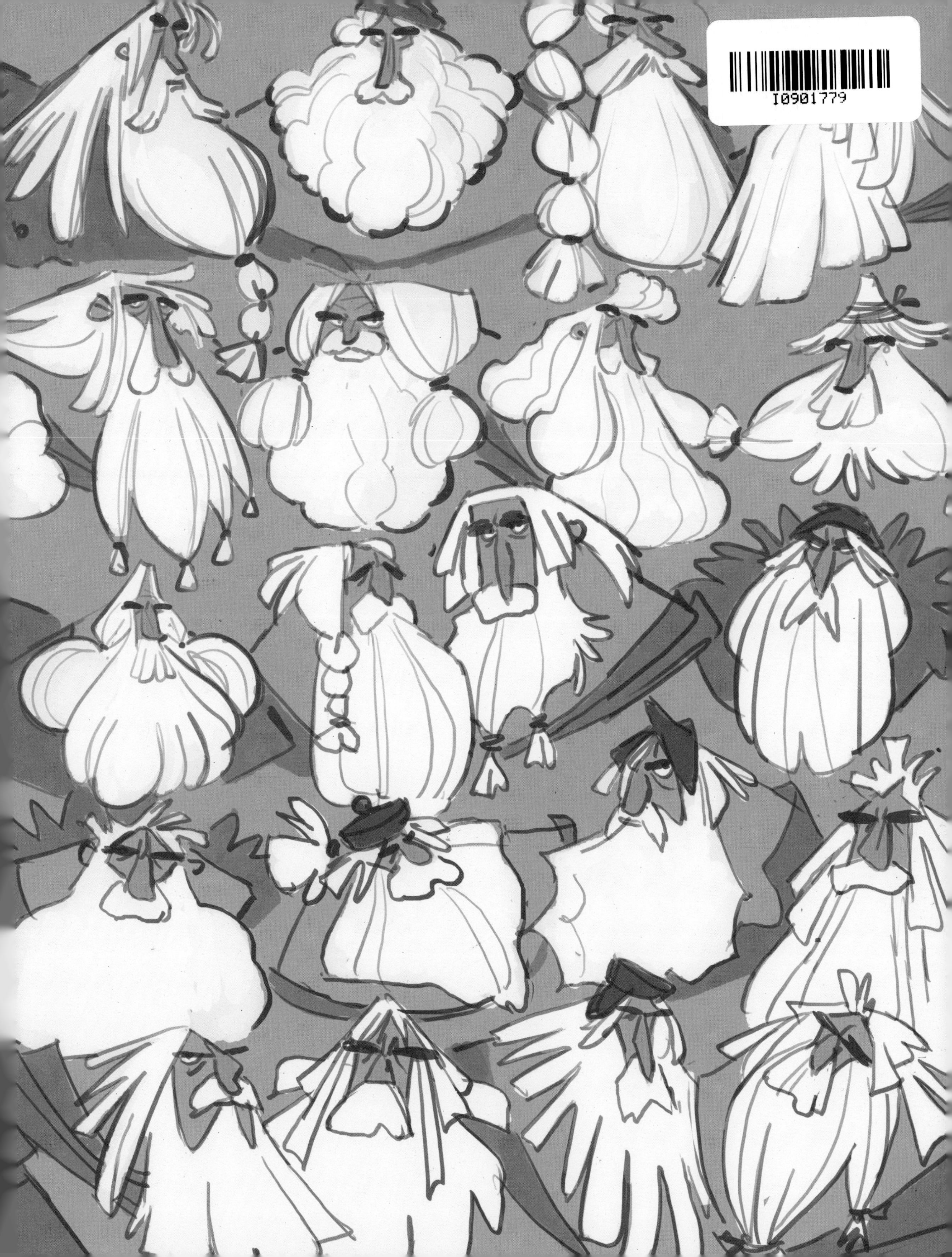

Klaus

KLAUS

THE ART OF THE MOVIE

ISBN: 9781789093124

Published by Titan Books
A division of Titan Publishing Group Ltd.
144 Southwark St.
London
SE1 0UP

FIRST EDITION: NOVEMBER 2019
7 9 10 8 6

DID YOU ENJOY THIS BOOK?

We love to hear from our readers. Please e-mail us at: readerfeedback@titanemail.com or write to Reader Feedback at the above address.

To receive advance information, news, competitions, and exclusive offers online, please sign up for the Titan newsletter on our website: www.titanbooks.com

A CIP catalogue record for this title is available from the British Library.

Printed in China

Klaus

THE ART OF THE MOVIE

FOREWORD BY JAMES BAXTER
WRITTEN BY RAMIN ZAHED

TITAN BOOKS

Contents

Foreword

"I'm not trying to bring traditional animation back, I'm trying to bring it forward." That's how Sergio Pablos explained to me his reasons for pursuing the gorgeous and utterly unique visual style on display in his movie *Klaus*. I first met Sergio during the production of Disney's *The Hunchback of Notre Dame* in 1995, when I was supervising the animation for Quasimodo. He is an immensely talented character animator, but what I was unaware of back then was that he is also an immensely talented storyteller and filmmaker. When Sergio started pursuing a directing career, we had always maintained a casual assumption that I might be a small part of whatever project he managed to get off the ground, especially if that meant doing some hand-drawn animation. So it was with great satisfaction and joy that I was able to contribute some animation to *Klaus*.

What every great animated film has at its core is a great story, and *Klaus* takes us on a wonderful and unexpected ride through some familiar territory. It's a Christmas story, but one like you've never seen before, told through the eyes of some fantastic characters – some of them quirky, some stoic, some crazy, some cute, but all contributing to a tale of real emotion and heart. Once you have a great story, the task becomes designing the world and the look of the characters, and the designers for *Klaus* have created a world where the shapes and colors contribute to the emotion of the story. You feel the cold through the sharp lines of the trees and the warmth of the firelight through the colors reflected in the characters' eyes. It is at once dimensional and graphic, a feeling only possible if you draw it by hand, and that's part of why it is so appealing to me.

Something Sergio and I have in common is that we are both ardent devotees of this medium. Even though much of computer generated animation is spectacular, tactile, appealing, and immersive; for us, nothing compares to the feeling of seeing a drawing come to life. When I see a drawing spring to life, it fills me with joy. The mere fact that animation extends beyond the simulation of reality – it lives, breathes, and feels – is magical.

The incredible team of artists and technicians at Sergio's Madrid-based SPA Studios have pushed the boundaries of what feature-length, hand-drawn animation is commonly assumed to be: namely, line and simple color shapes. By combining new technology with traditional artistry, they have managed to make it possible for the painterly and textured feel of visual development art to finally reach the screen as fully realized, lush, hand-drawn animation. Attempts at this in the past have usually succumbed to various concessions, like limiting the number of drawings or keeping it contained to a short sequence. But now it seems all bets are off.

Animation is going through an interesting time right now. With the new tools available in the animator's toolbox, a filmmaker no longer has to settle for what a certain technique will produce on screen. Rather they only have to answer the question, "What do I want this film to look like?" and the appropriate tools can be found to fulfill that vision. As you will discover in these pages, the vision for *Klaus* is a thing of beauty, filled with caricature, humor, grace, and emotion. Sergio and *Klaus* are bringing traditional, hand-drawn animation forward.

JAMES BAXTER

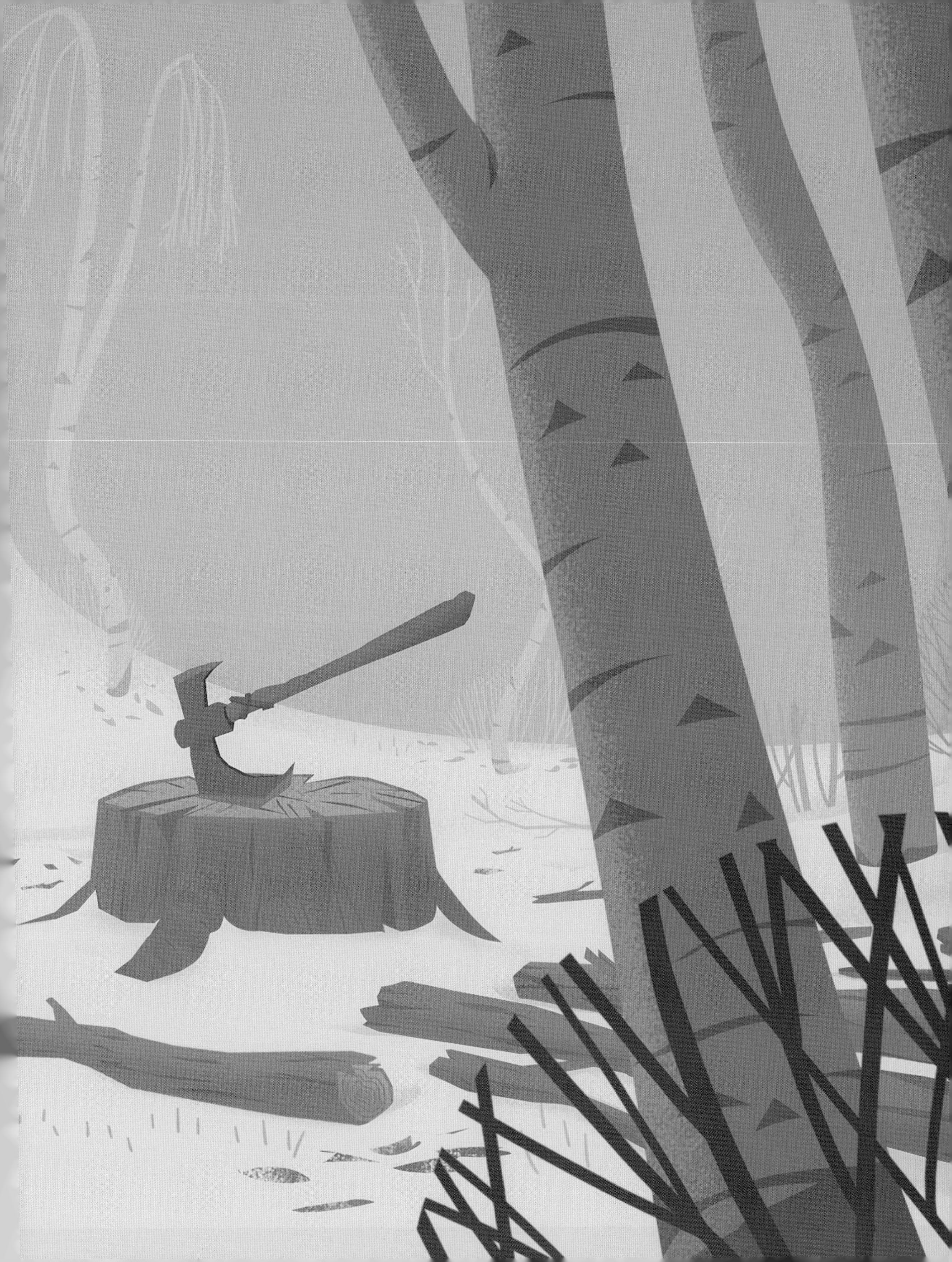

Introduction

CREATING *KLAUS*

Great inspiration for animated movies can arrive from the most unexpected sources. Just ask *Klaus'* writer-director Sergio Pablos, who decided to investigate interesting origin stories of a variety of characters after seeing Christopher Nolan's 2005 movie *Batman Begins*.

"I really liked the way Nolan took the lore of an outdated character and made it relevant for modern audiences with *Batman Begins*," says the Spanish-born founder and CEO of Madrid's Sergio Pablos Animation (SPA Studios). "I thought it would be an interesting exercise to do a similar thing for popular characters from literature, folk tales, and history. I considered characters like Dracula and Napoleon but, when I arrived at Santa Claus, I was surprised to discover that he didn't have one single, widely accepted origin story. It was a mix of religion, tradition, and lore, and each country had a different idea about

THIS PAGE: Jesper explores Klaus' workshop for the first time – final render.

NEXT PAGE: Early concept for Jesper by Sergio Pablos.

NEXT SPREAD: Early artwork by Pascal Campion, showing Klaus and Jesper.

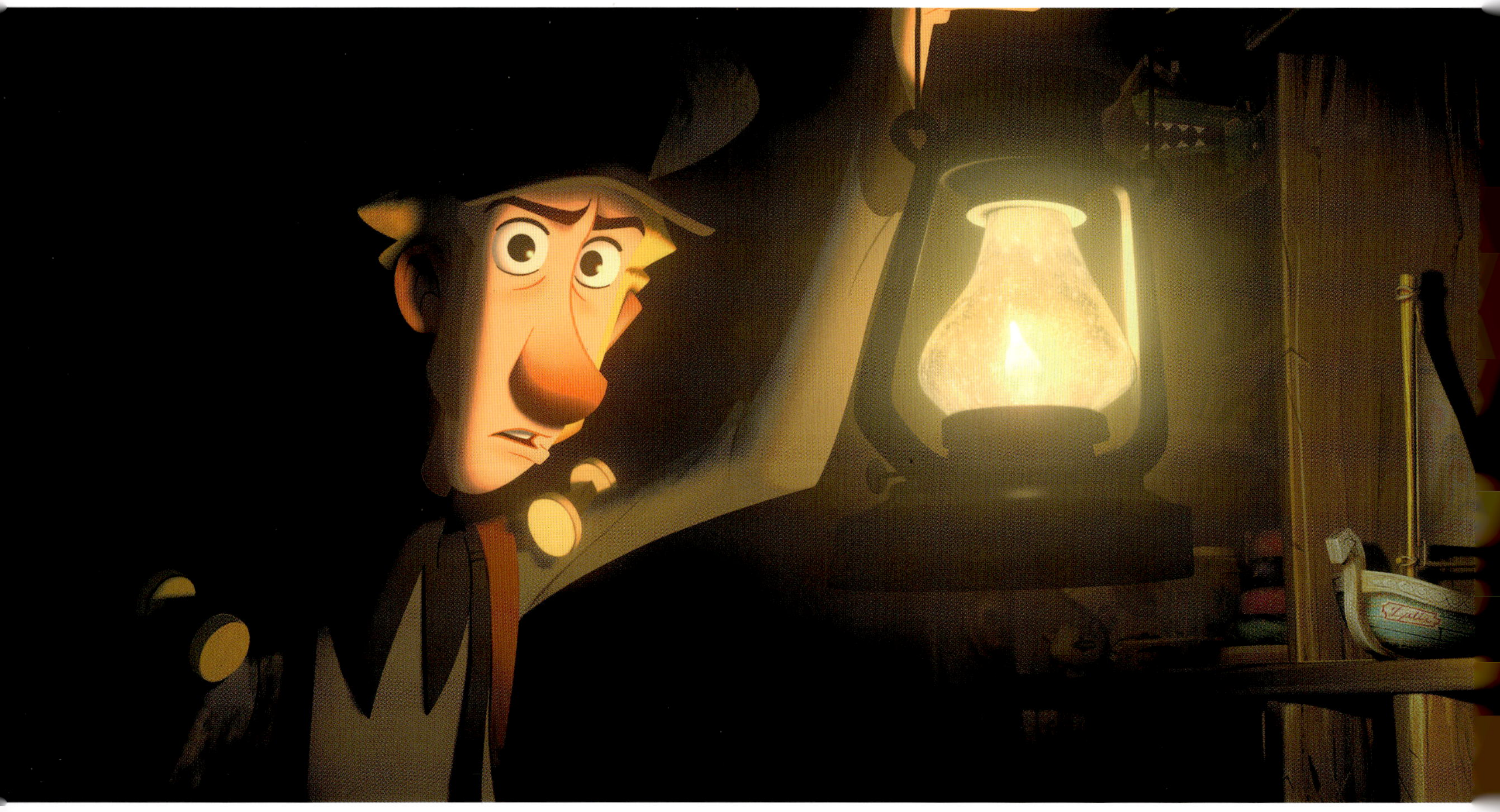

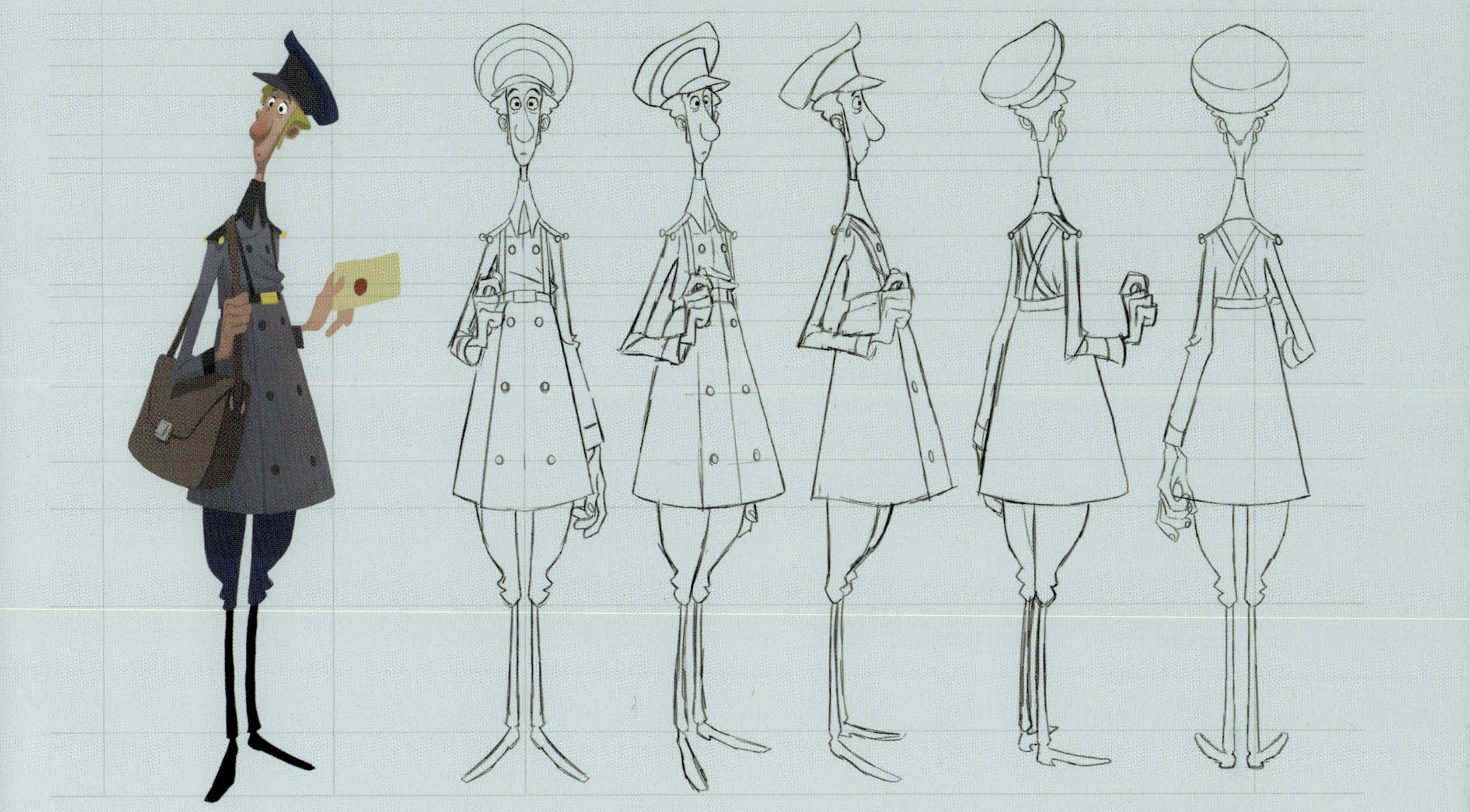

him. So I felt that we had this great opportunity to try and fill in that missing chapter for him. And, if we could do it with a good dose of humor and heart, we might be able to create a true Christmas classic."

Producer Marisa Roman recalls the early beginnings of the highly original *Klaus*, Pablos' directorial debut. "Sergio was keen on exploring the period before this character became Santa Claus," she says. "He created a universe around this man, and came up with this world little by little – what did he believe in, what time period would be best for this story, which country, etc. He also needed another character like Jesper, the postman, to bring this story to life."

What was important to Pablos was avoiding all the clichés and overly sentimental approaches that we sometimes see in stories about Christmas. "Santa is a symbol of altruism," he explains, "so the idea of having a selfish character, who is doing everything for his own gain, but inadvertently creates the legend of Santa Claus, worked very well. It was that irony that attracted me to the story and made me realize that we could build an interesting animated movie around it."

The Barcelona-born Pablos, who was an animator on such Disney films as *The Hunchback of Notre Dame* and *Hercules*, and supervising animator on *Tarzan* and *Treasure Planet*, is best known as co-creator of the global blockbuster *Despicable Me*, and has also worked on features such as *Rio*, *Nocturna*, and *Smallfoot*, the latter of which he originated the content for. He says one of his most important goals was to create a movie that not only looked unique, but also had its own sense of storytelling and tone. "It was very important to me that the film did not feel like it could have come out of any other studio, and that it had its own personality without losing the broad appeal that's expected from a high-end holiday film."

As the film's acclaimed producer Jinko Gotoh (*The Little Prince*, *The LEGO Movie 2: The Second Part*, *Finding Nemo*) points out, "One of *Klaus*' major themes is the value of selflessness. That's a universal theme that I think anyone in any age group can understand. What's so beautiful about this is that, even though the movie is a Christmas story, it centers on such a powerful, universal theme that everyone can identify with."

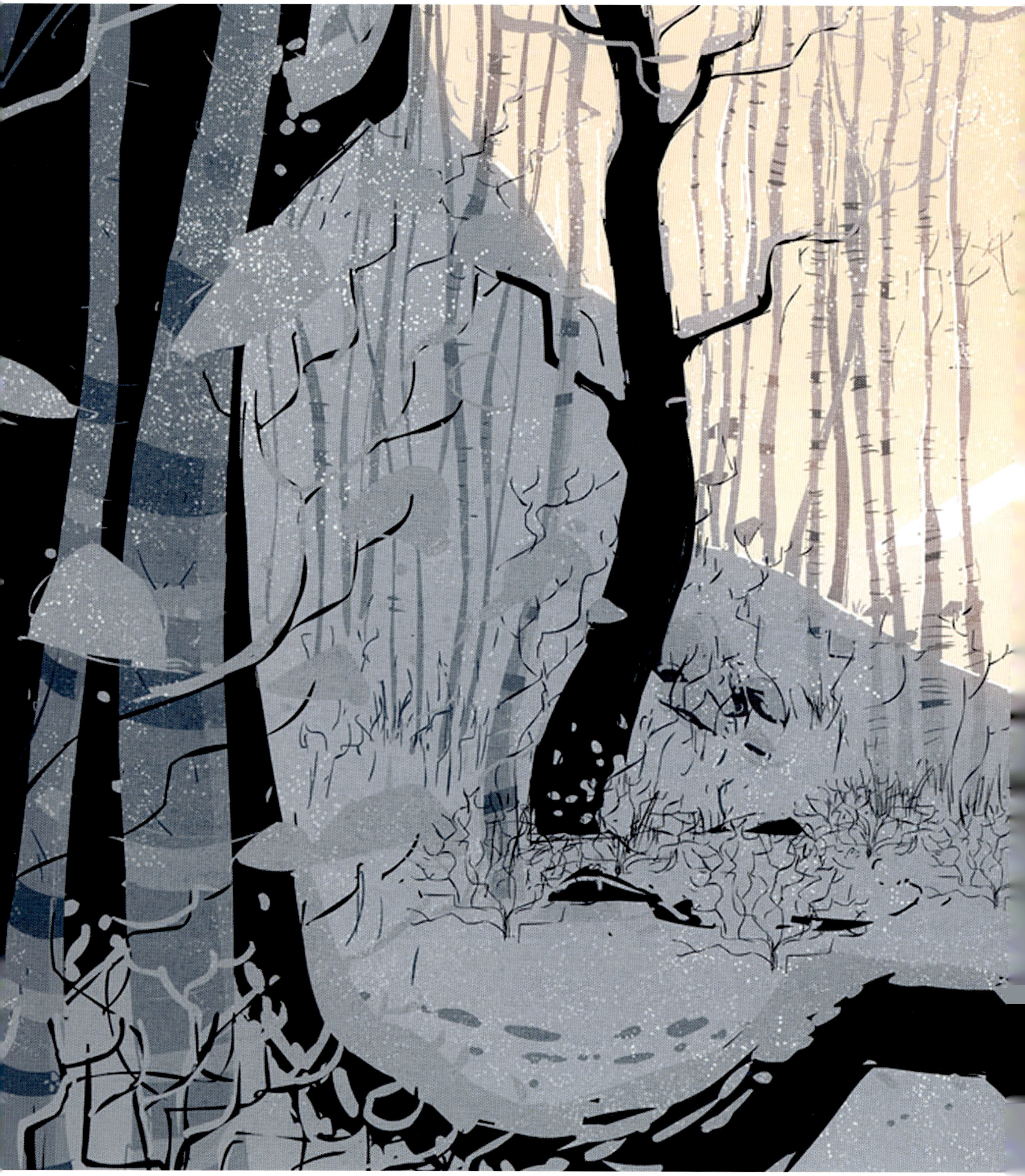

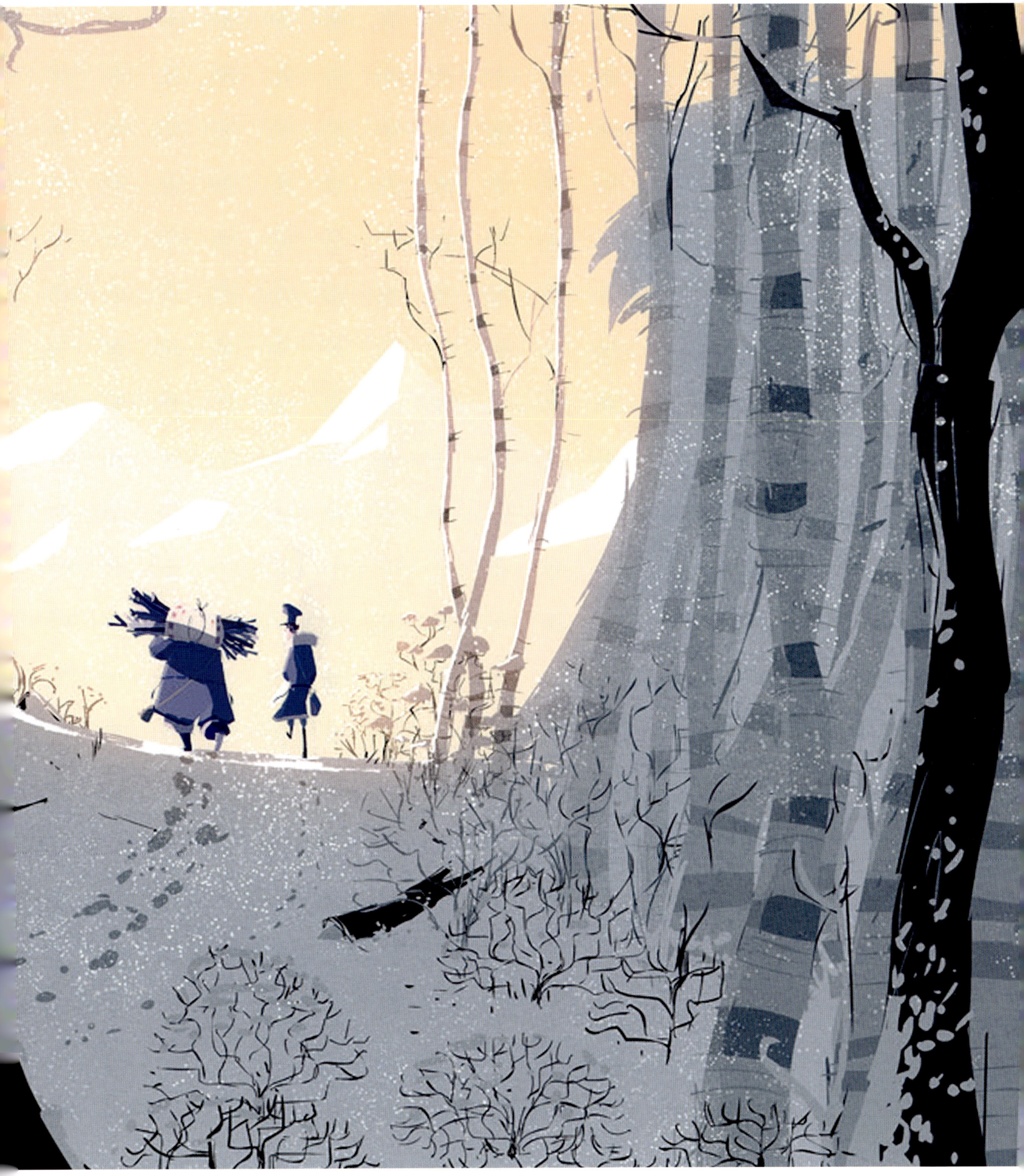

Among Pablos' most important decisions regarding *Klaus* was to launch it as a state-of-the-art, traditionally animated movie, unlike any of the other projects coming out of the major studios these days. "As someone who's always looking for the next great animated film idea, I've come to learn that these ideas have a strong voice when it comes to what they want to be," he explains. "If you learn to listen, you'll find that some ideas clearly lend themselves more to CGI, some to live action and, every now and then, you come across an idea that clearly would benefit from the organic quality that only traditional animation can bring. This was the case with *Klaus*."

Many of the artists and animators working on *Klaus* point out that what really sets the movie apart is how all the key elements are integrated together to work in service of the story. As lead animator Alfredo Cassano mentions, "We have 2D and 3D elements, and the background paintings all perfectly blend in a way that, if you pause the frame, you won't be able to tell them apart. It really helps the storytelling, so the viewer won't get distracted by the technique."

Cassano, whose many credits include the acclaimed features *Song of the Sea* and *The Secret of Kells*, says it's been wonderful to work on a movie where all the drawings – even the in-betweens – have been done by hand. "I believe it's a technique that needs to be kept alive," Cassano says. "It actually ages much better than 3D animation. If you look at CG-animated movies from 20 years ago, they don't look as amazing as they did at the time. But if you look at some of the traditionally animated classics, they are still as beautiful as they were when they were first released. So we hope that *Klaus* will remind people of the power of traditionally animated movies."

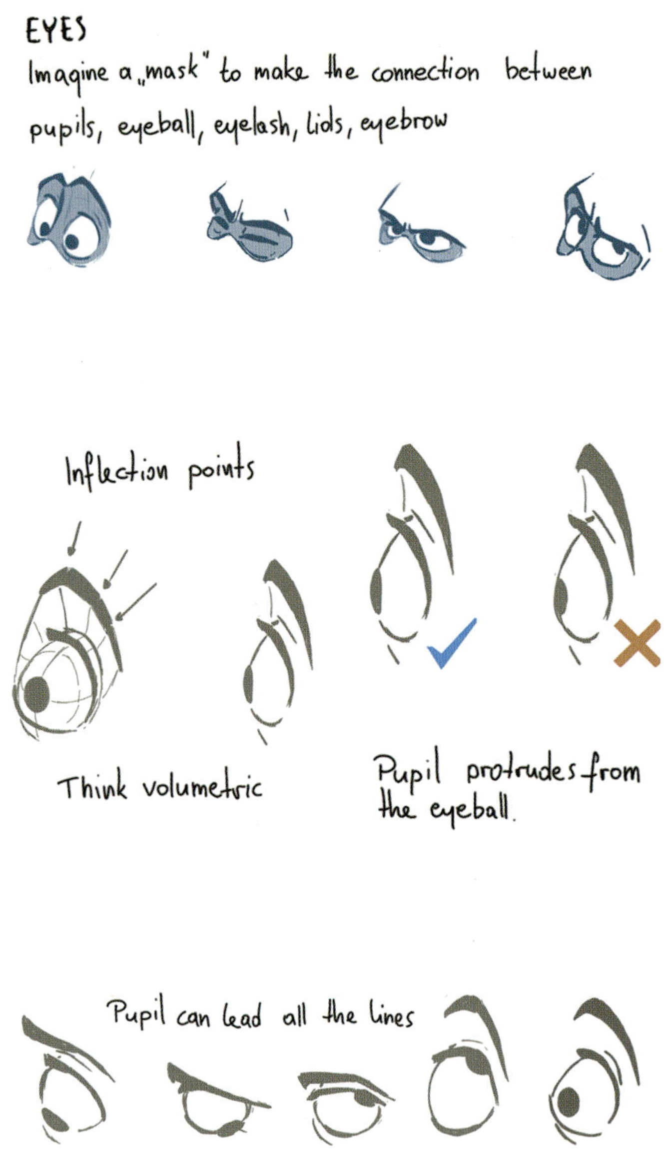

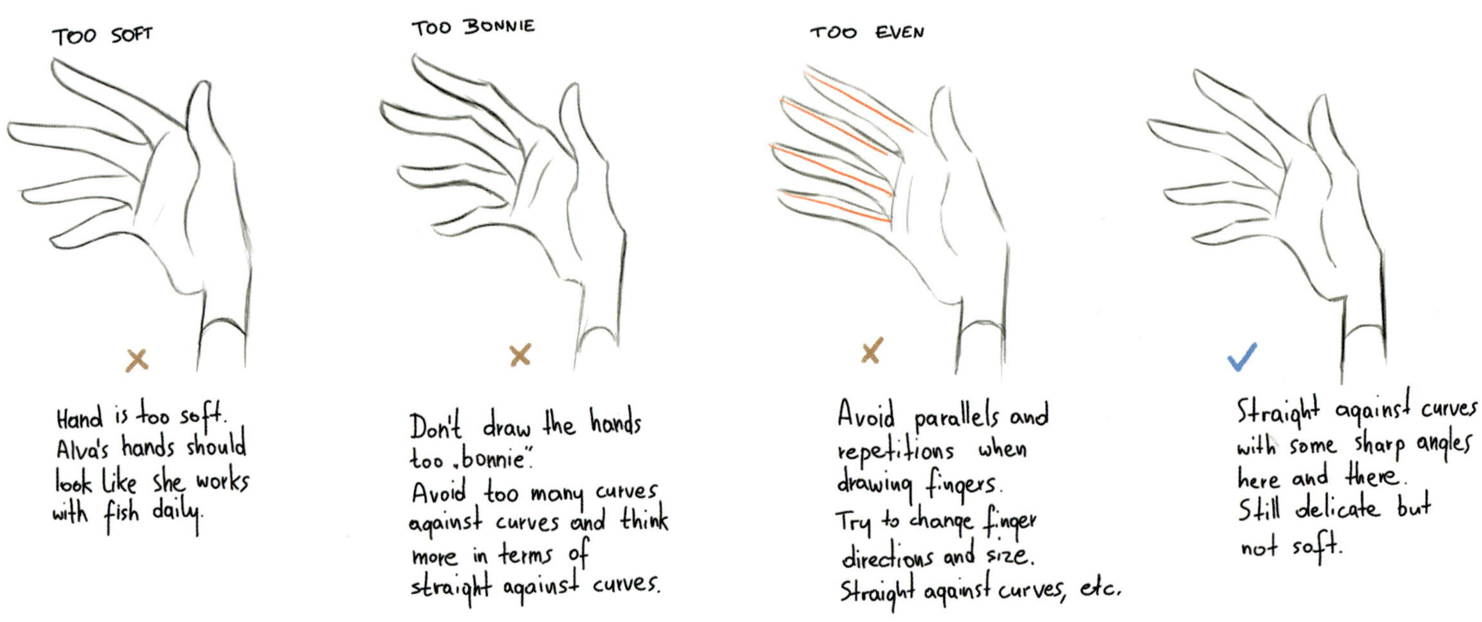

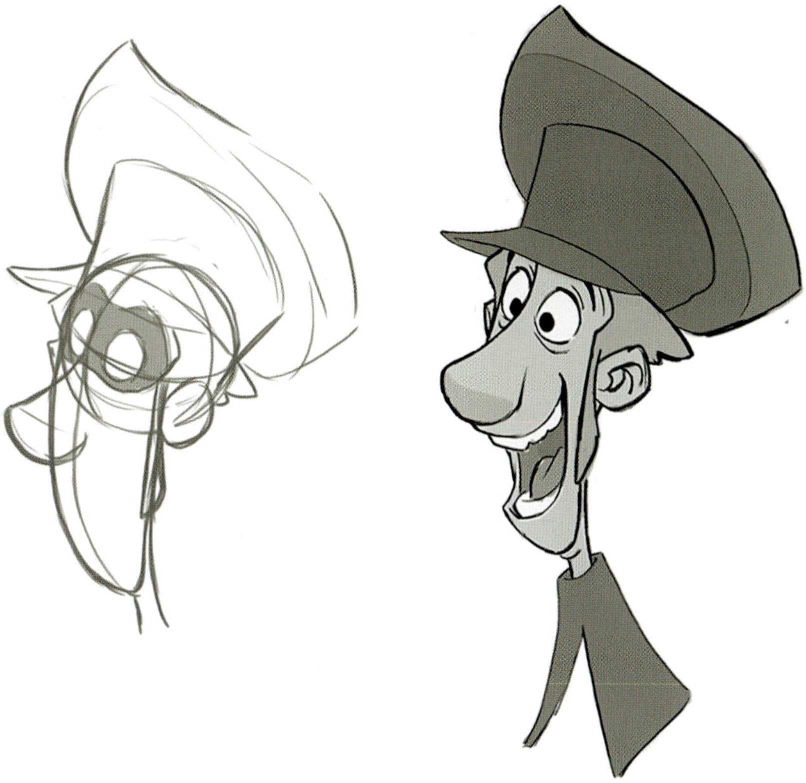

> "What's so beautiful about this is that, even though the movie is a Christmas story, it centers on such a powerful, universal theme that everyone can identify with."
>
> *Jinko Gotoh, Producer*

THIS SPREAD: Animation tips by Yoshimichi Tamura and Sergio Martins.

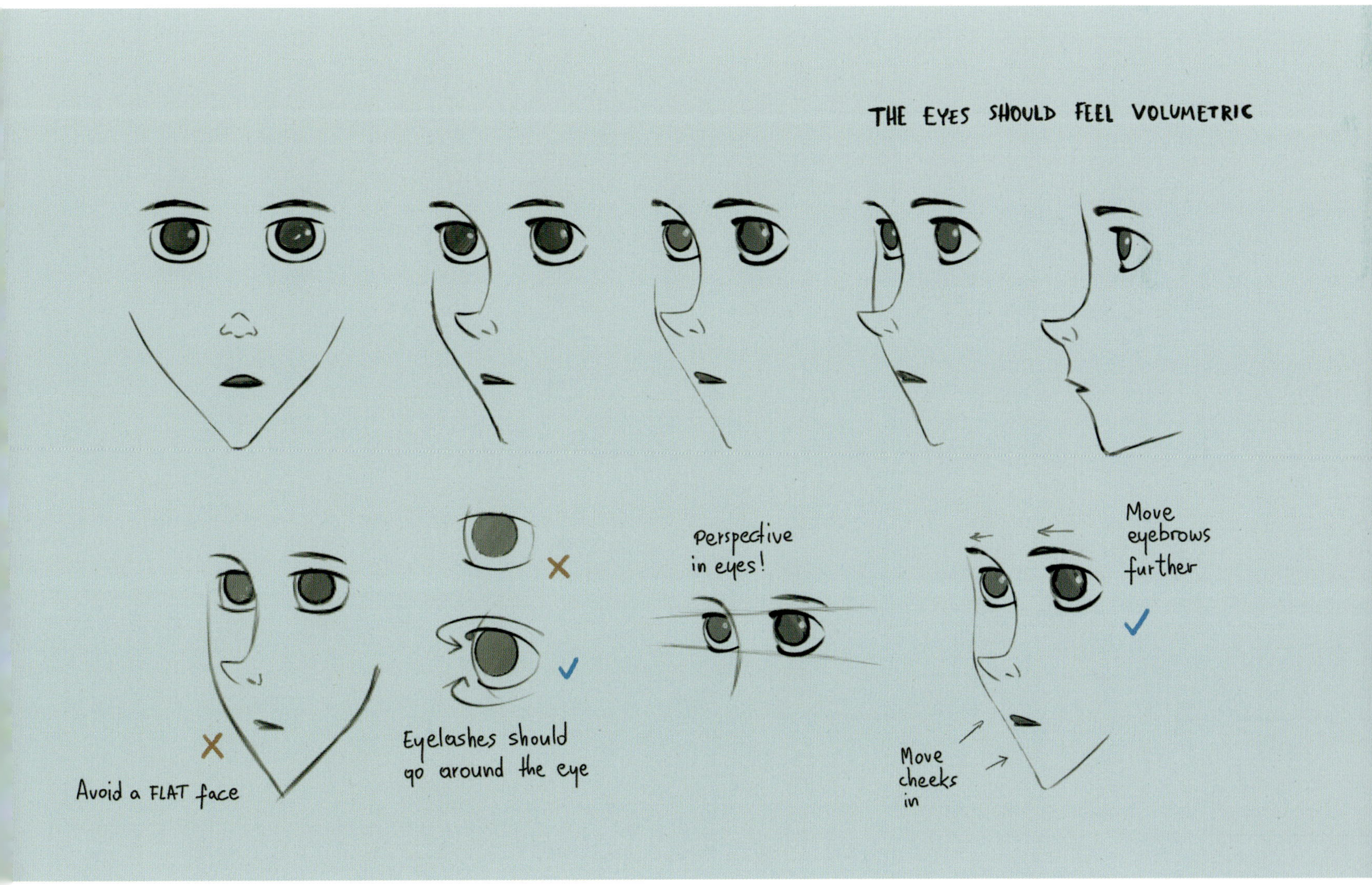

One of the key qualities that makes *Klaus* stand out among other traditionally animated features is its meticulous and varied approach to lighting. As production designer Marcin Jakubowski explains, "Every frame of the film's animation is crafted by the artists, but *Klaus* looks different because we developed a new technique to put the light on the characters. In other traditionally animated movies, the characters are just flat cels that sit on top of the fully rendered backgrounds, and they often don't match. We were able to apply light on top of the characters, which creates the sensation of volume and also helps integrate the characters with the backgrounds entirely."

Furthermore, Jakubowski says the new lighting and shading tools allowed the artists to better incorporate shadows, bouncing light, ambient light from the sky, and even translucency on the characters' skin throughout the movie.

Head of lighting Florian Aupetit says the general aesthetics of the project reminded him of book illustrations. "It's a bit like watching a book with very, very nice illustrations. We are watching these amazing drawings move and come to life. We are not used to seeing this level of detail in the lighting and backgrounds of a traditionally animated movie."

He adds, "We made some very bold decisions in lighting. For example, if a character was in the shadows, we could lose him completely. But if it served the story, then it would be fine. It's common to see characters that are all very well lit in animated movies, but we want characters to belong to their environments. We were striving for balance between the art direction, design, lighting, and all the other elements."

BELOW: An early design for Klaus by Torsten Schrank.

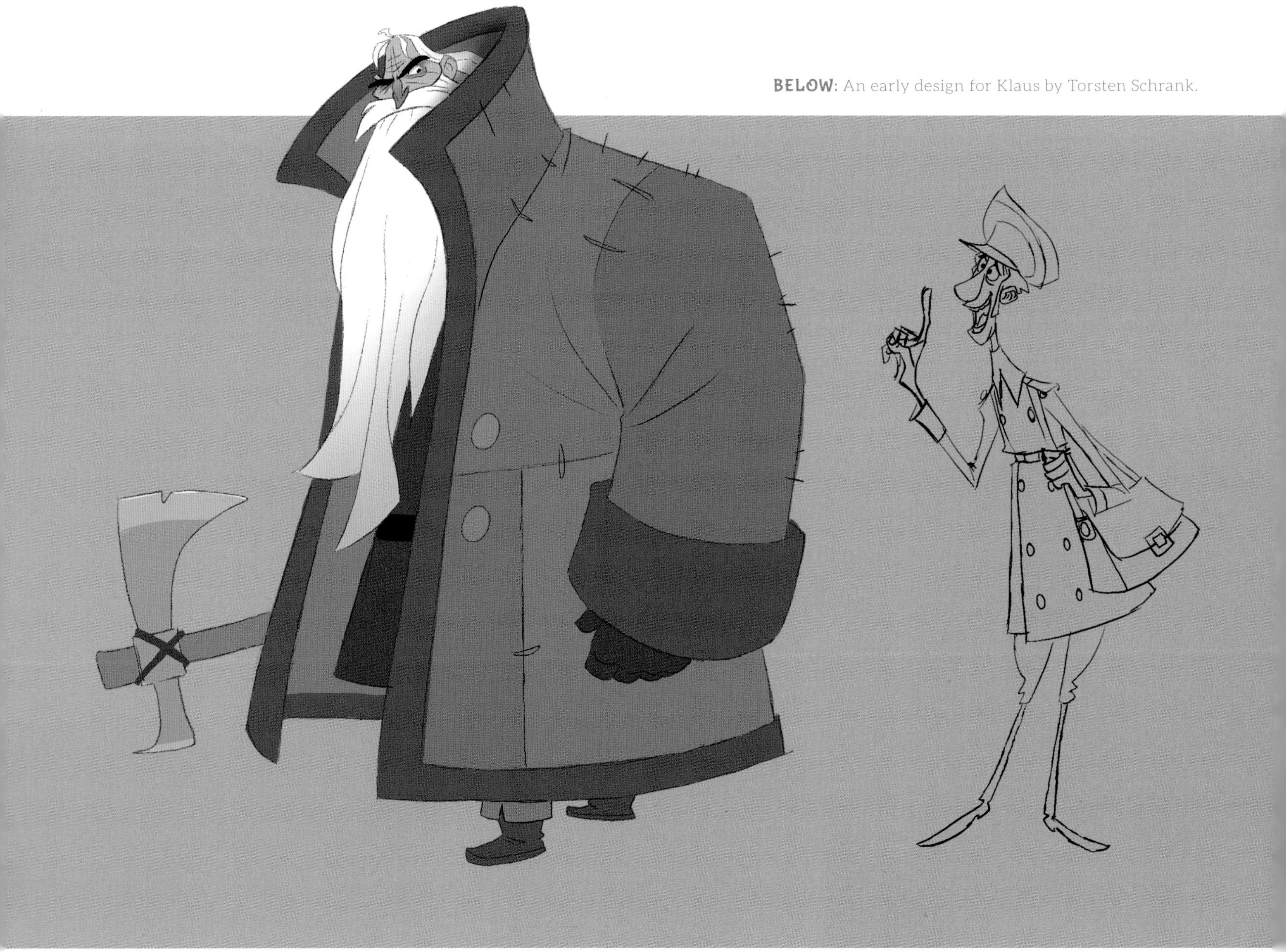

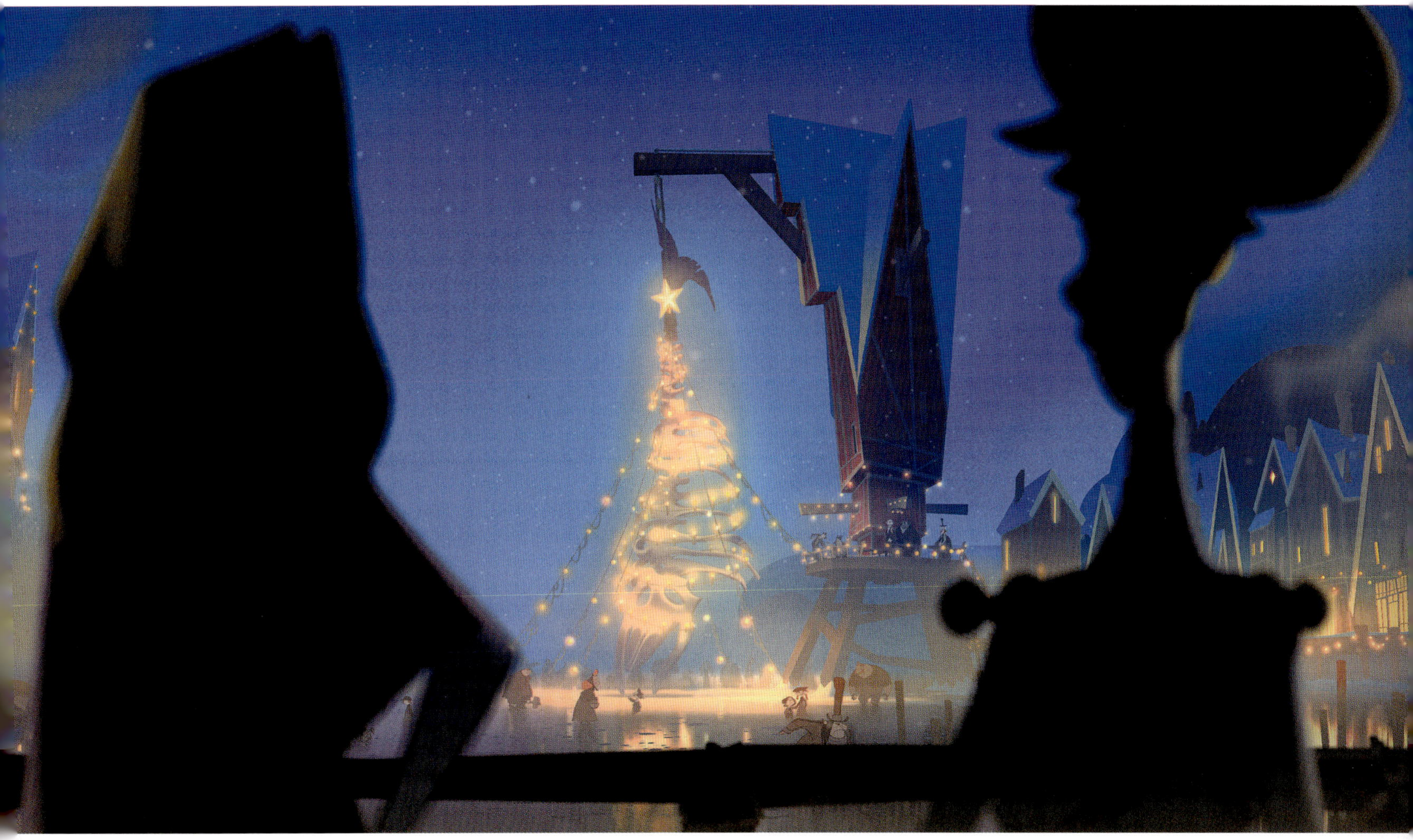

"Every frame of the film's animation is crafted by the artists, but *Klaus* looks different because we developed a new technique to put the light on the characters."

Marcin Jakubowski, Production Designer

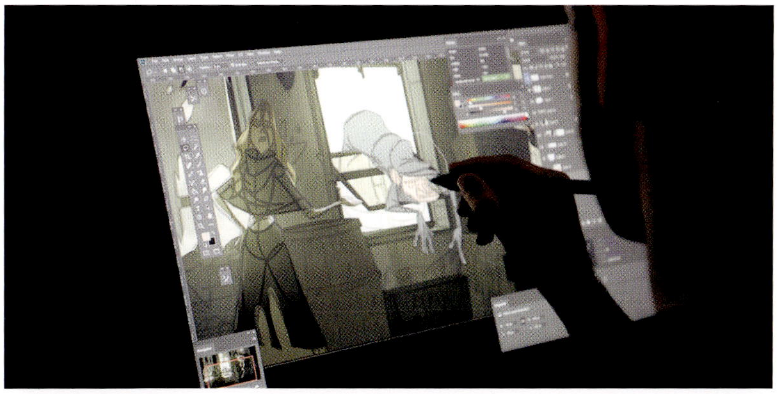

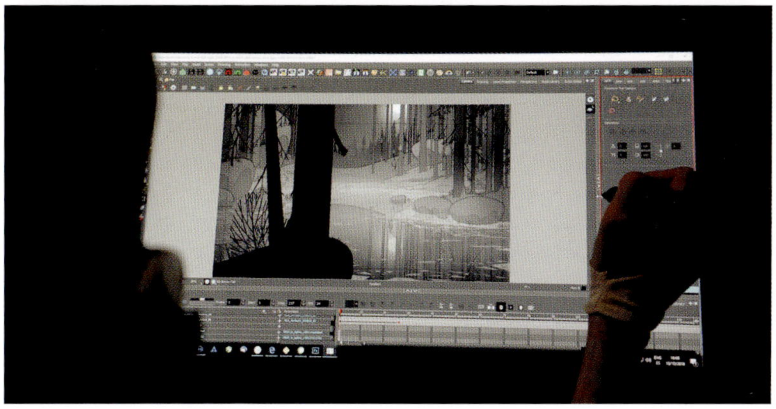

ABOVE: Concept art by Henrik Evensen.

RIGHT: SPA's artists working on the film.

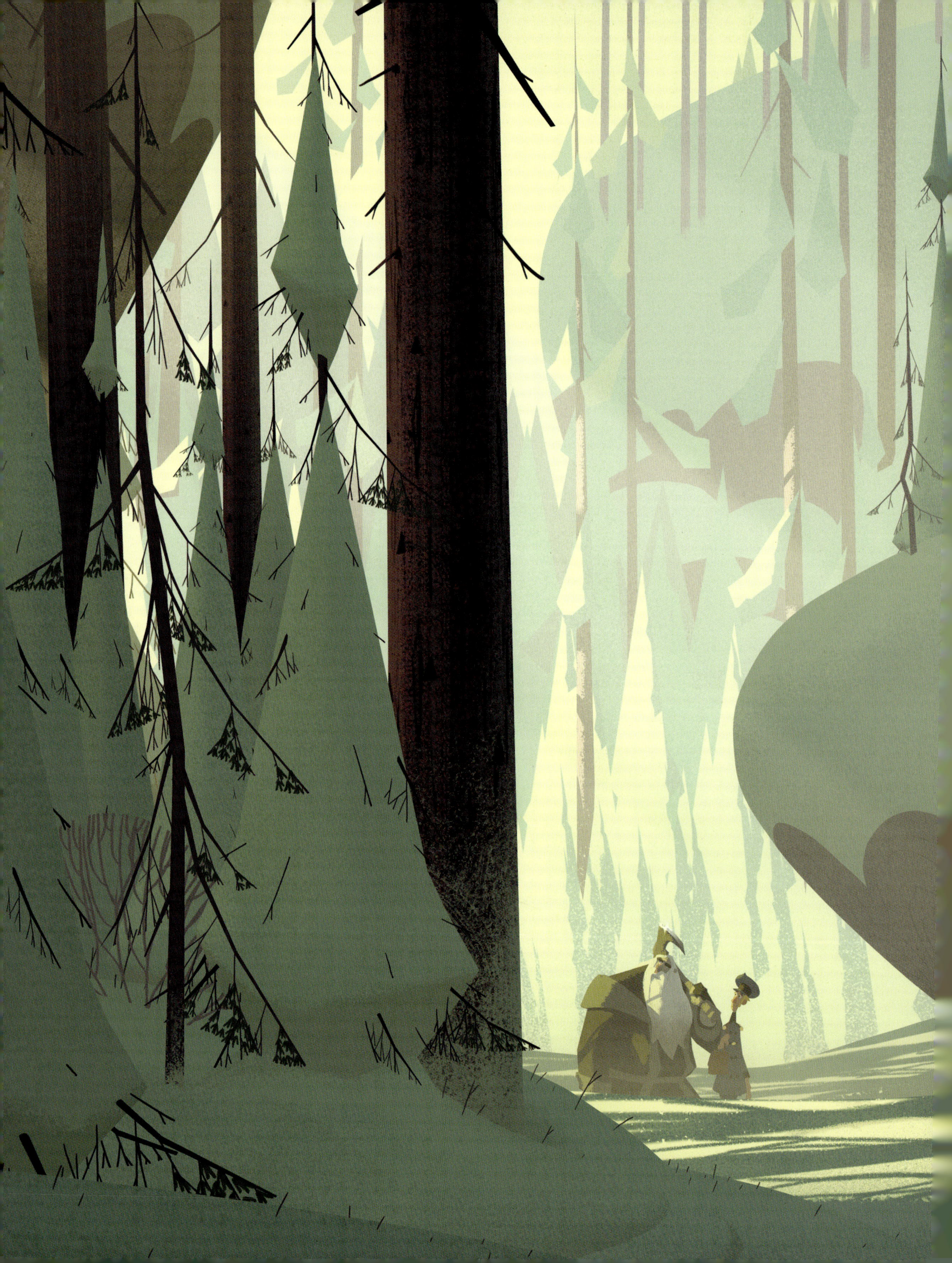

An Unlikely Duo

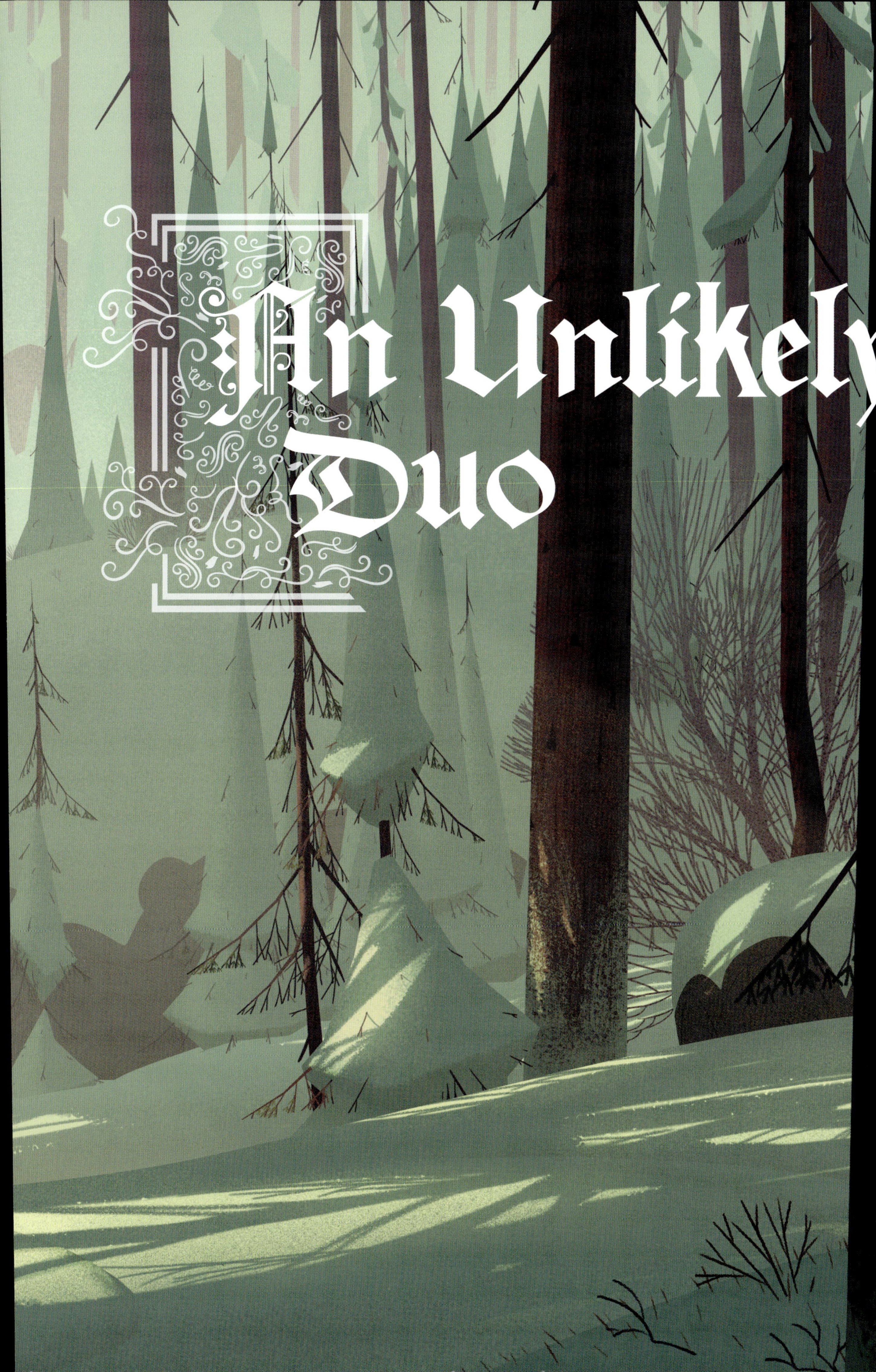

Jesper

THE RELUCTANT POSTMAN

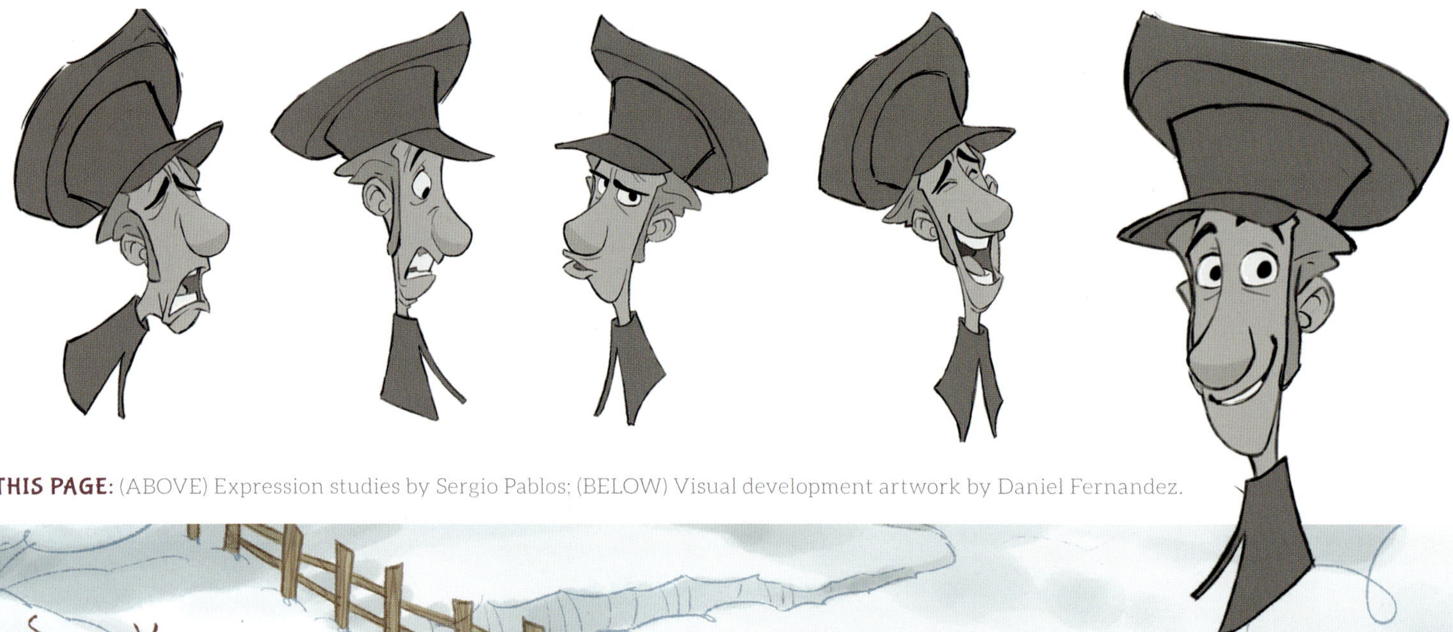

THIS PAGE: (ABOVE) Expression studies by Sergio Pablos; (BELOW) Visual development artwork by Daniel Fernandez.

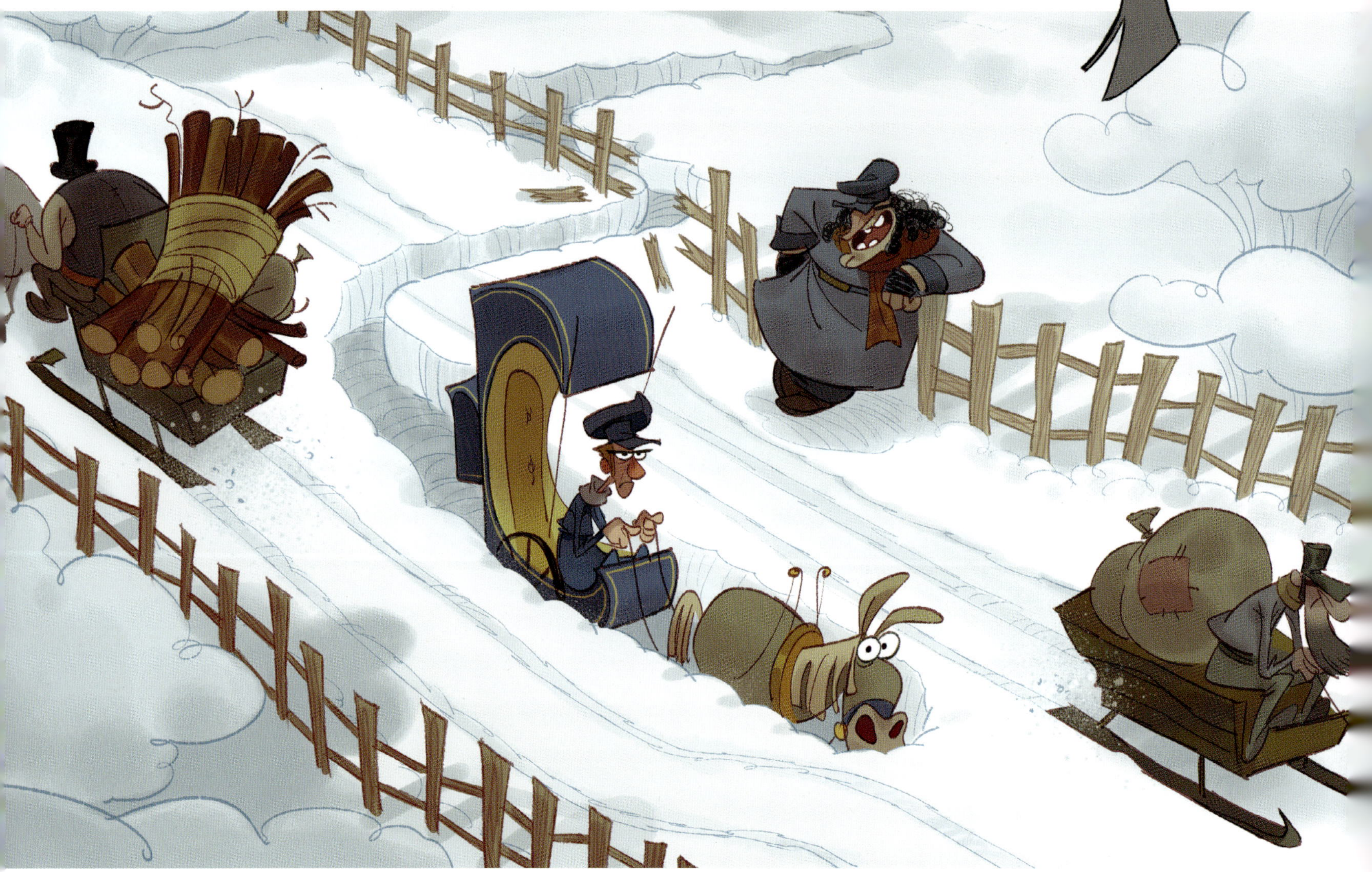

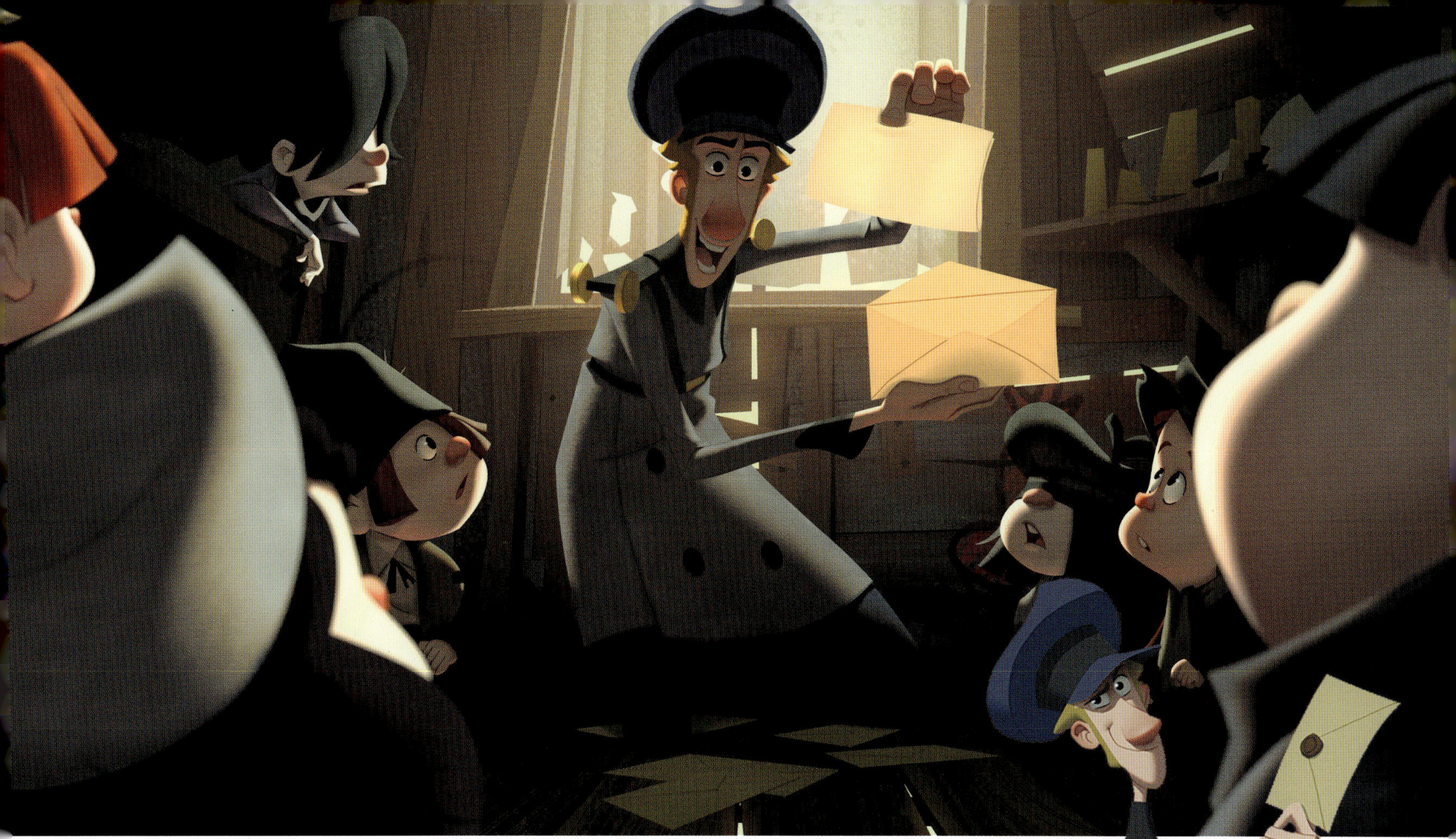

To enrich the narrative dynamic of the movie, Pablos set out to tell the story of *Klaus* as seen through the eyes of a young, callow postman-in-training. "Jesper is essentially a funny caricature of the stereotypical millennial that we have put in the 18th century," says the writer-director. "He is a kid who's been benefiting from his family's wealth all his life. He has this scheme of getting kicked out of his father's Royal Postal Academy. Then he finds himself in the middle of nowhere in Scandinavia and has to find a way to get the people of the town to write letters. His motivation is purely selfish, but he doesn't realize that he's actually transforming the town and, in the process, is transforming himself as well. He [learns to understand] the real power of selfless giving."

In terms of the character's design, Pablos says he thought of Jesper as a typical, lanky guy. "I worked for eight years at Disney, so that graphic style has become part of my own personal style," he says. "I was fortunate to have [lead character designer] Torsten Schrank working with us, because he is a great designer who can handle a character from the concept stage to the final look. He can also take existing material and come up with new ideas to make the designs adapt to the needs of the story."

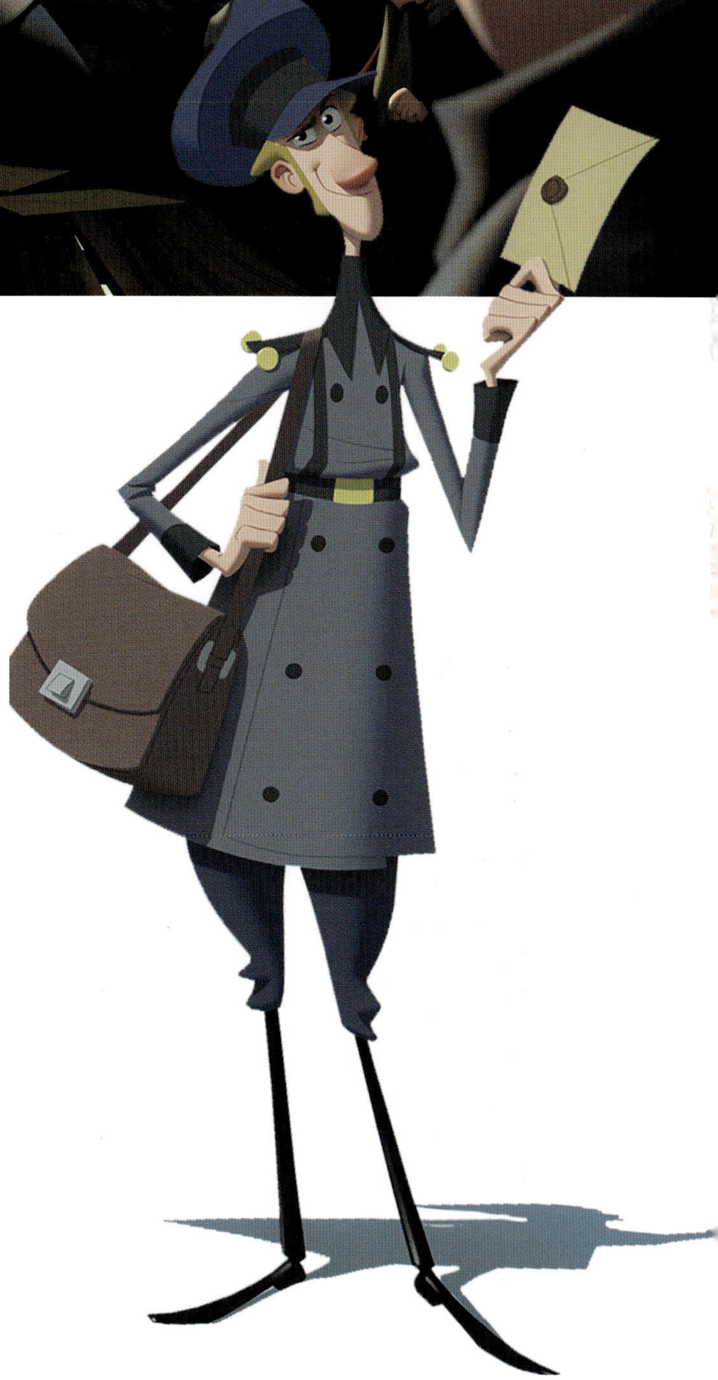

THIS PAGE: Final renders of Jesper.

PREVIOUS SPREAD: Concept art by Szymon Biernacki.

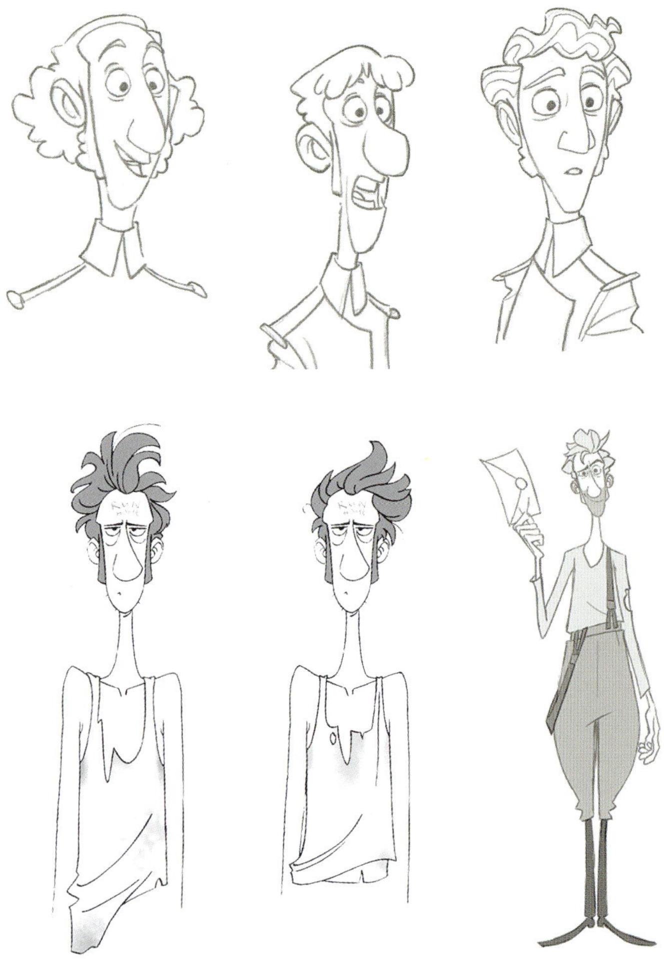

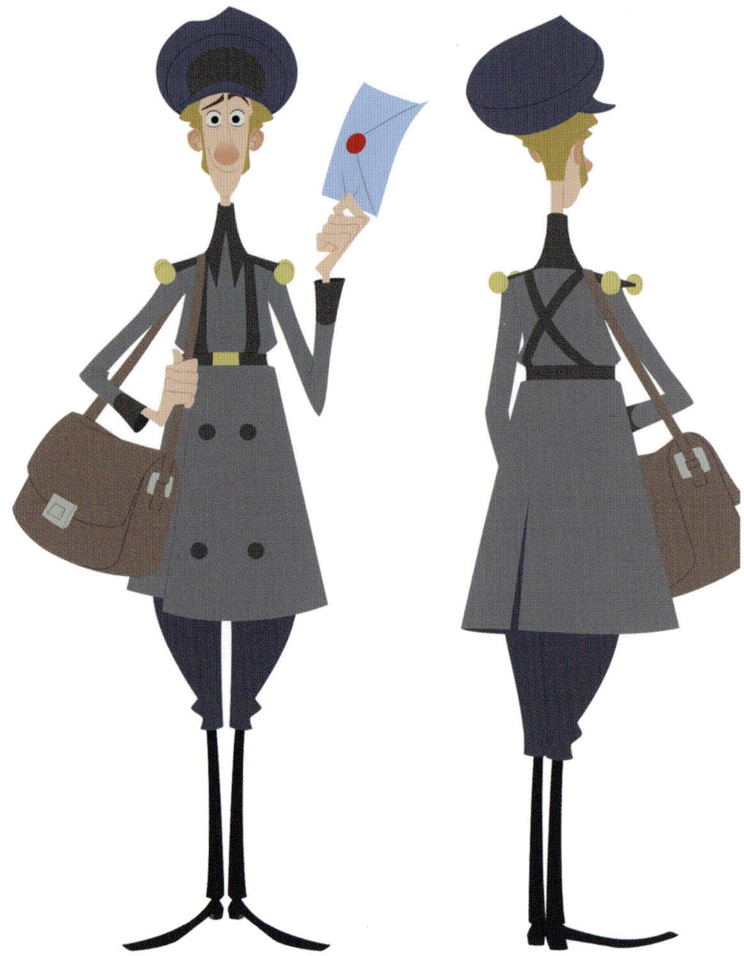

THIS PAGE: (TOP) Various sketches and designs; (BOTTOM) Final render of Jesper.

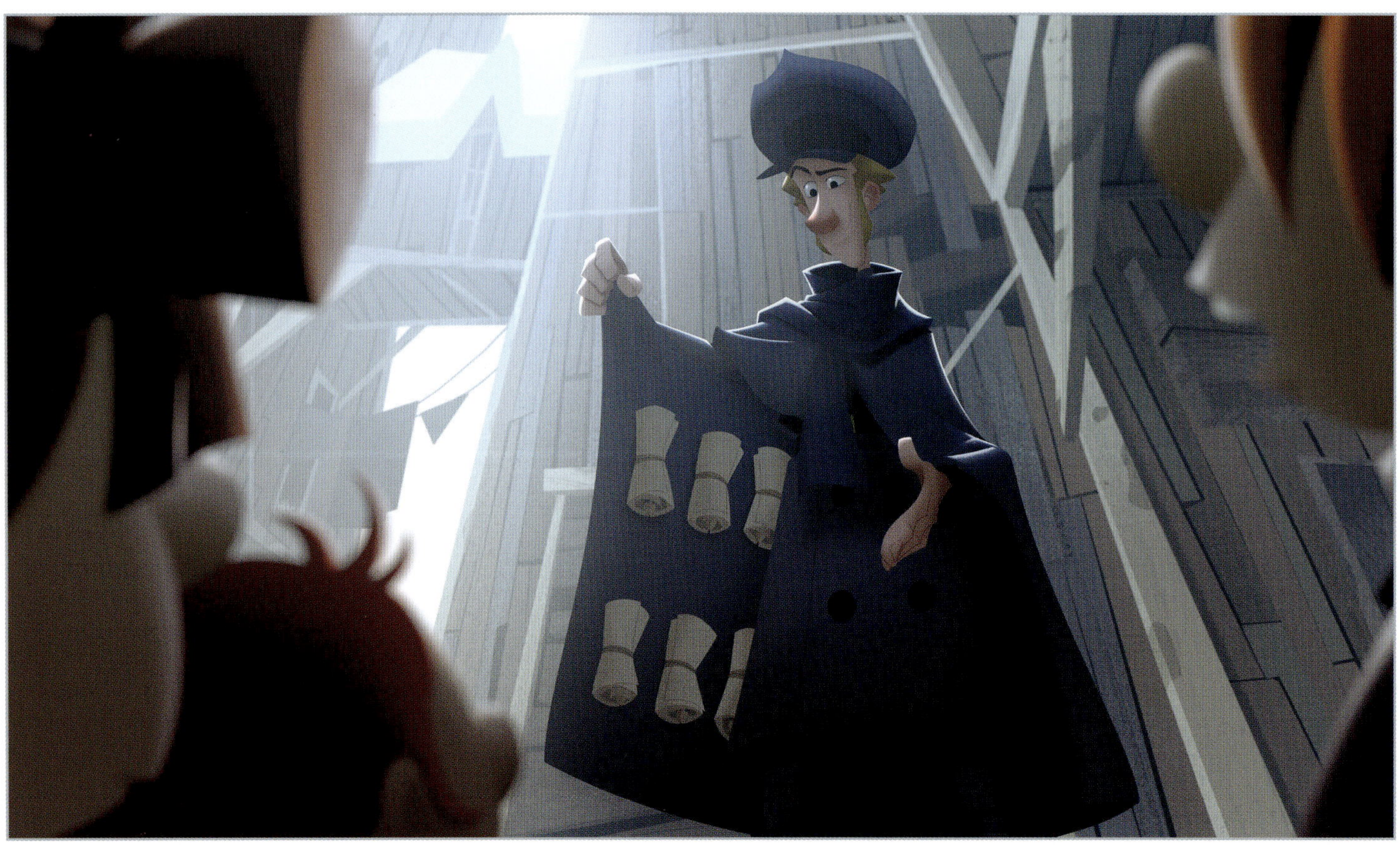

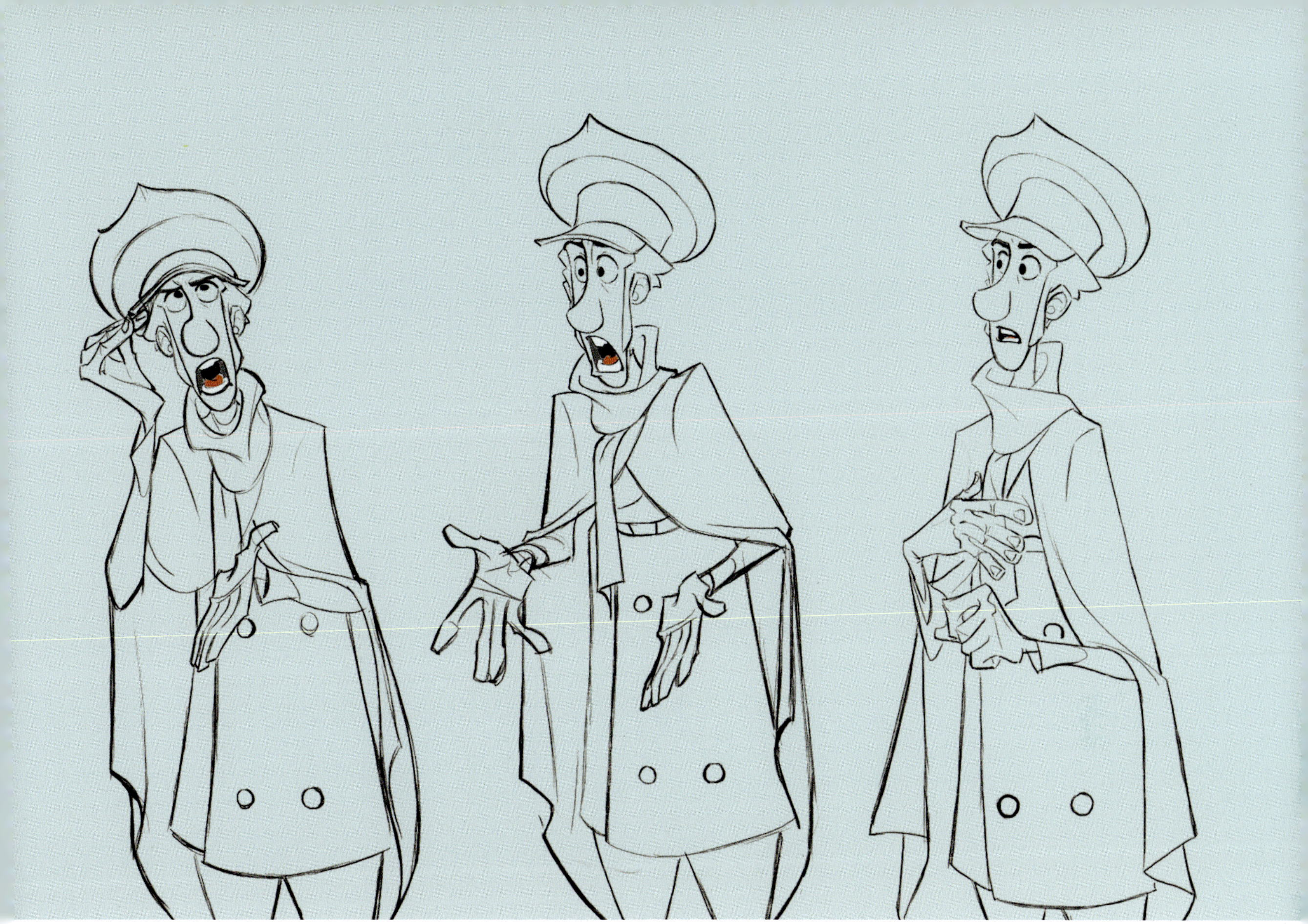

To voice Jesper, the director searched for an actor who could make the audience care about him and follow him on his journey, even though he starts out as a selfish and lazy young man. "It's quite a challenge to have a central character who starts out as a jerk, and then has to redeem himself," explains Pablos. "The audience may end up thinking of them as unlikable, and may never fully be in his or her corner. So we had to find someone who was able to have the right approach to this character, and we were very lucky to have Jason Schwartzman in this role. He made it all work, because you begin by hating him, then you love to hate him, and finally you get to love to love him."

Pablos says Schwartzman was so good at inventing perfect improvised lines for the character that they ended up with a lot of additional dialog. "I would say that only about forty percent of Jesper's lines ended up as they had been scripted. Most of it was improvised on the spot," he admits.

THIS PAGE: Animation keys by Yoshimichi Tamura.

NEXT SPREAD: Concept art by Marcin Jakubowski and Sergio Pablos.

"Jesper's personality undergoes a significant development in the story. The challenge here was to find the right balance of cartoony and semi-realistic elements in order to give the animators the opportunity to serve this wide range of acting possibilities."

Torsten Schrank, Character Designer

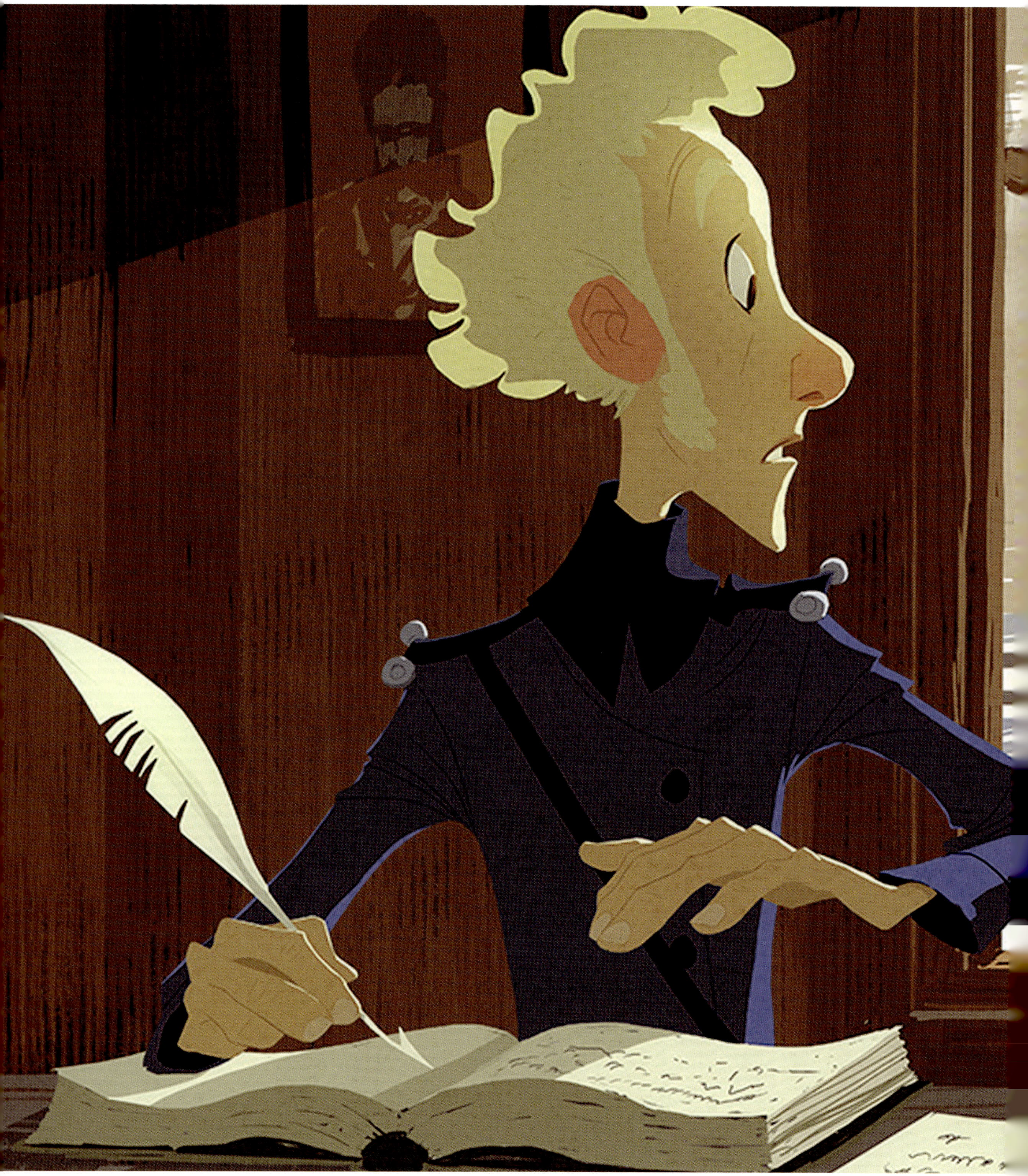

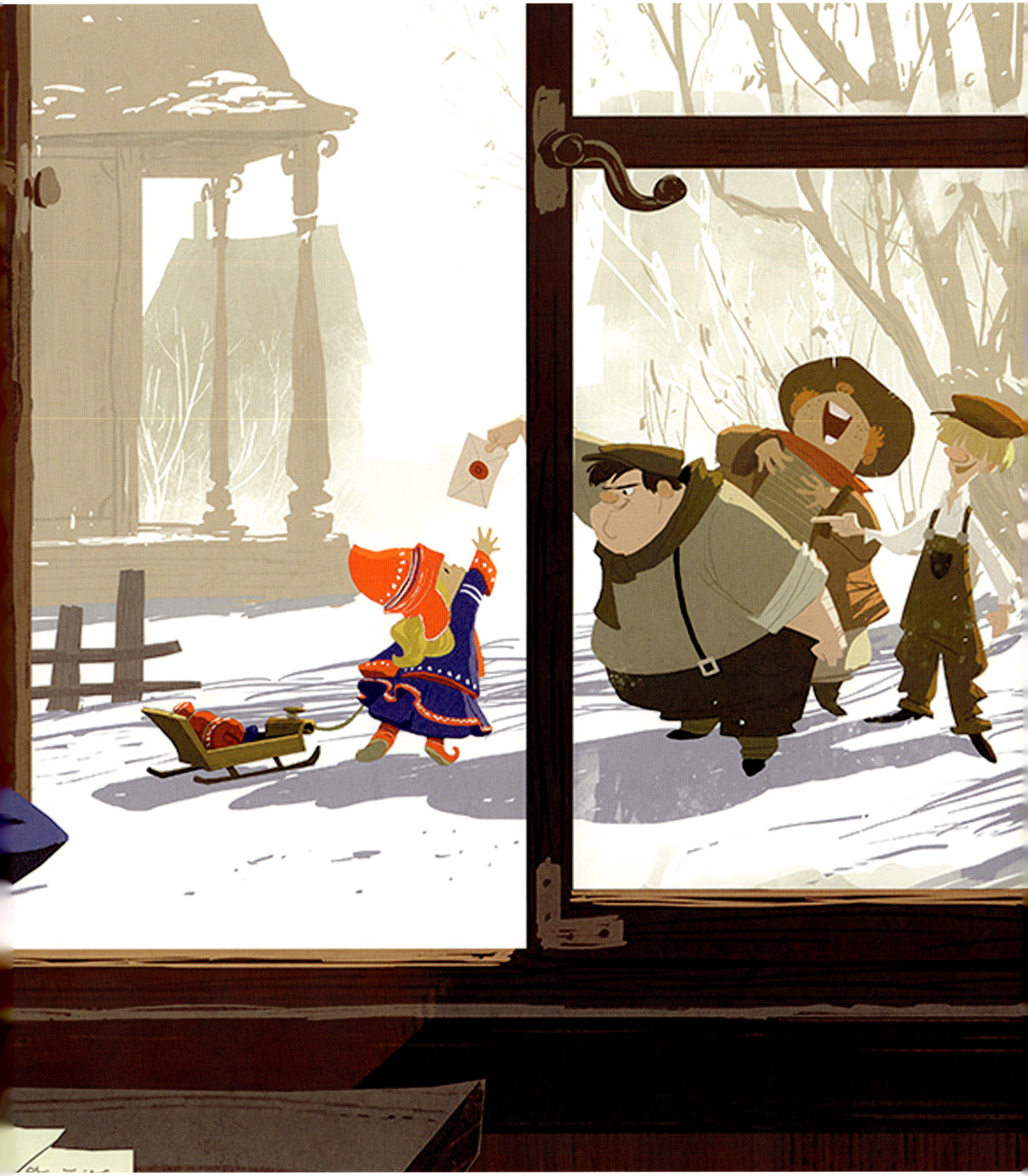

Klaus

THE WOODSMAN

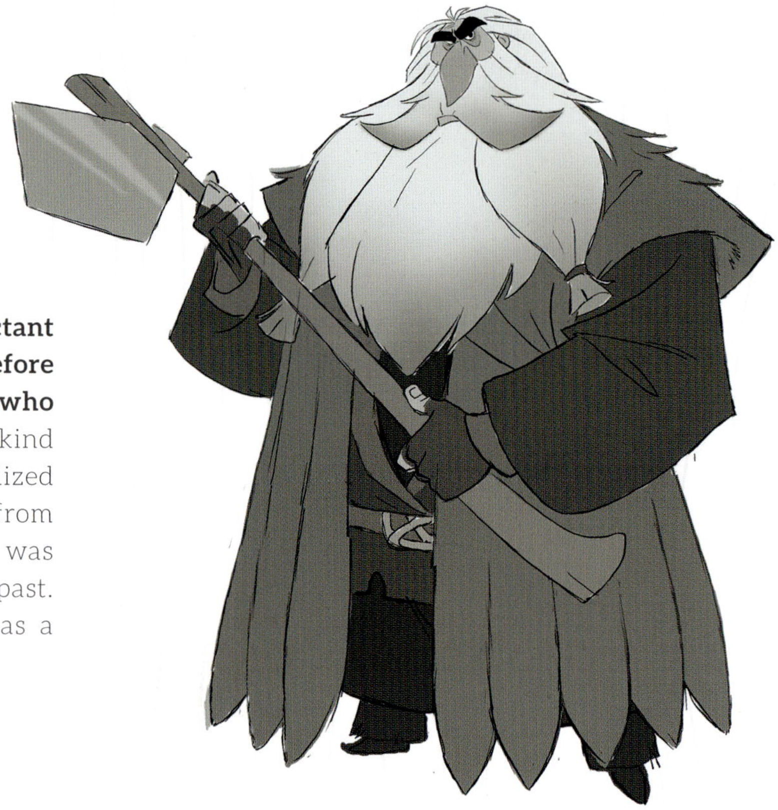

The character of Klaus, the intimidating and reluctant toymaker, went through several iterations before Pablos came up with the enigmatic character who anchors the movie. "In the early stages, Klaus was a kind and giving man from the beginning, but we quickly realized that this wouldn't work, because he had nowhere to go from there," explains the director. "What we ended up doing was presenting him as someone who has had a traumatic past. We don't know exactly what happened to him but, as a result, he has isolated himself from the world.

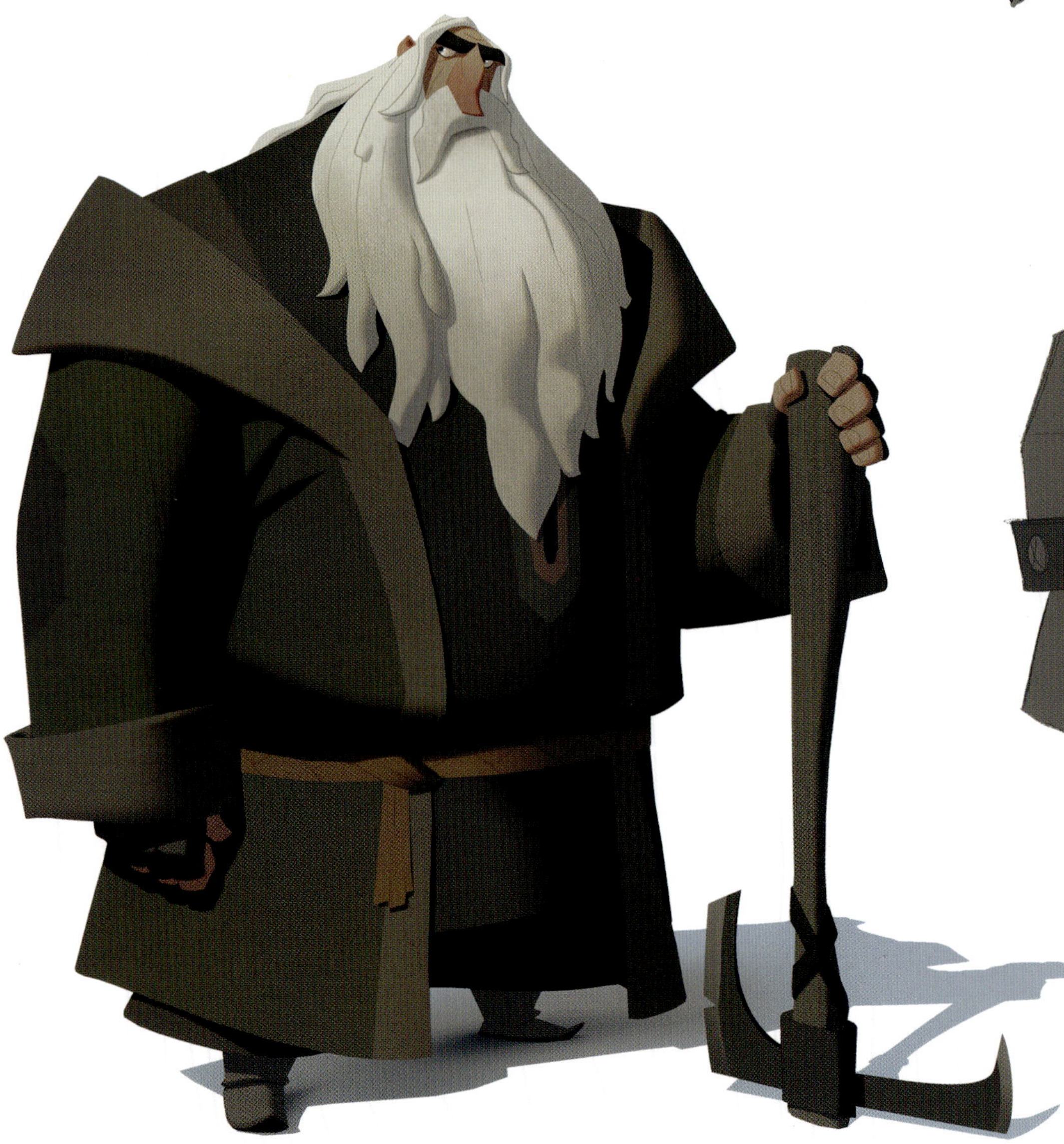

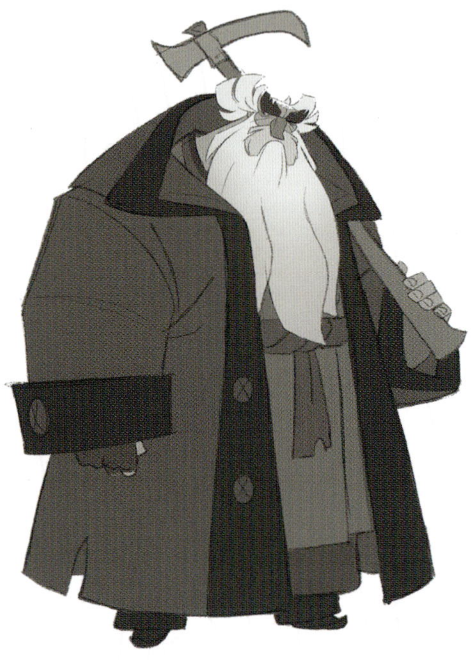

THIS PAGE: Character explorations by Torsten Schrank.

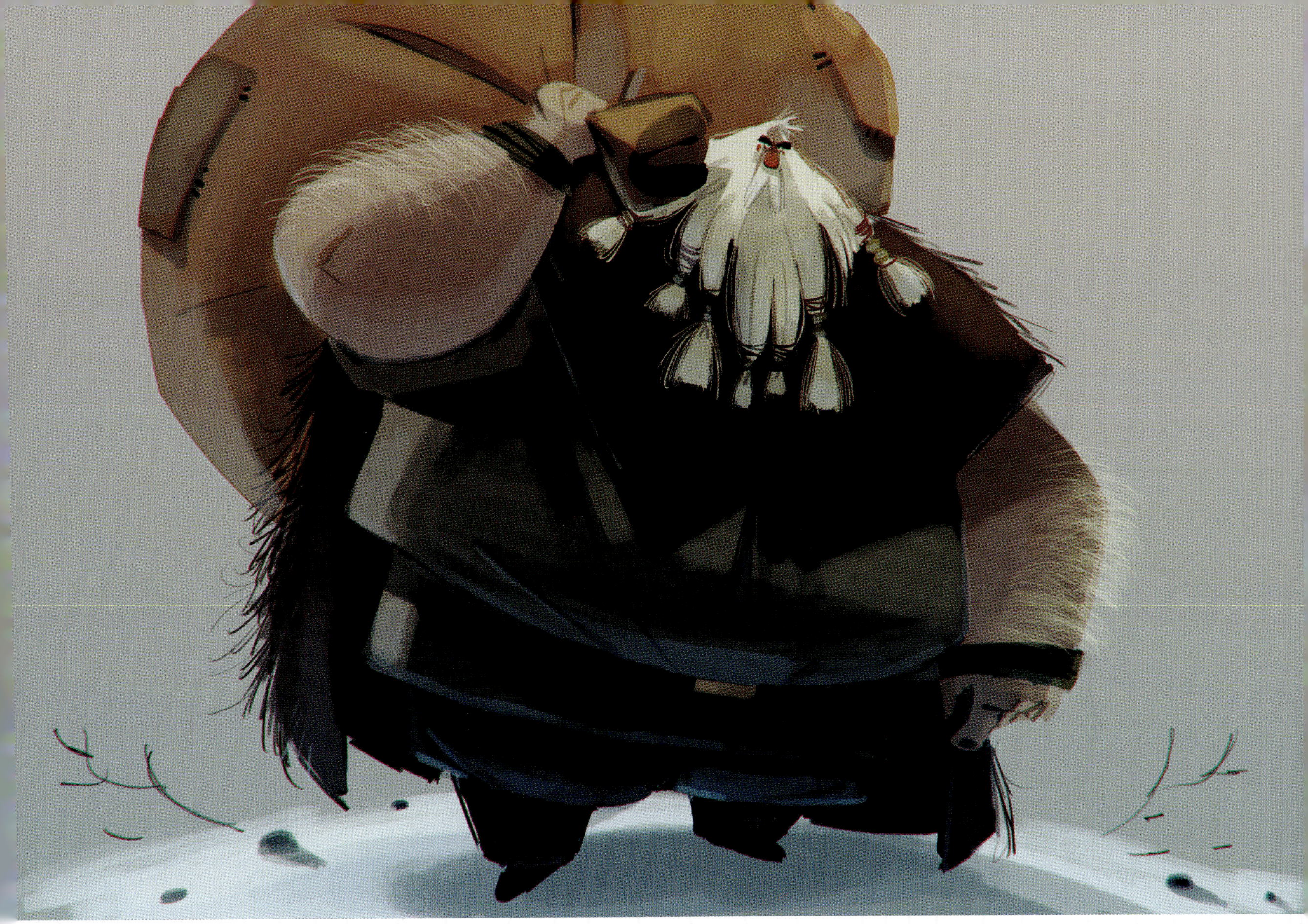

"He has been alone for so long that he has lost touch with social conventions. He can't even carry a normal conversation and can't relate to people at all."

When it came to the design and animation of Klaus, Pablos wanted to make sure he was depicted as a fear-inducing character at first. "We wanted to do away with the notion of Santa Claus as a jolly old man and take it in the complete other direction," he says. "The first time we see Klaus, we wanted him to be quite scary. He is carrying an axe, and you can easily see him as an axe murderer in a slasher movie. He should be scary and Jesper should be terrified. The audience may be unsure, and asking themselves, 'Why is this guy so far from Santa?' That's why it would be interesting to see him gradually come out of his shell, talk about his past, and change to become the Santa that everyone knows and loves."

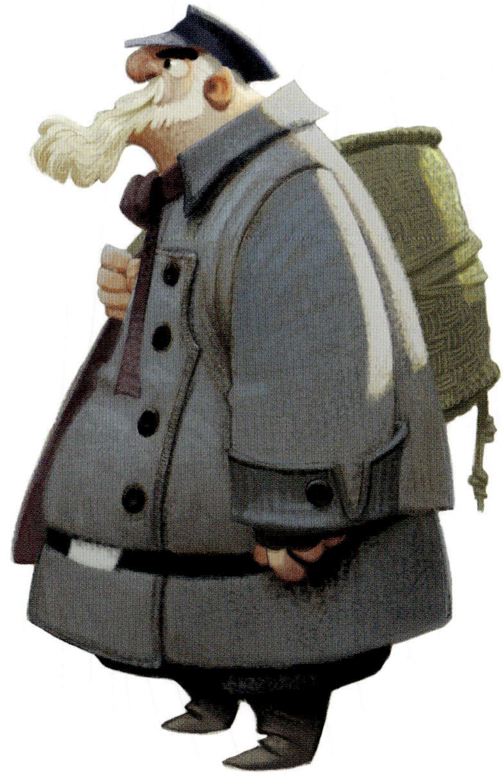

THIS PAGE: (TOP) Character exploration by Daniel Fernandez; (BOTTOM) Early design by Sergio Pablos.

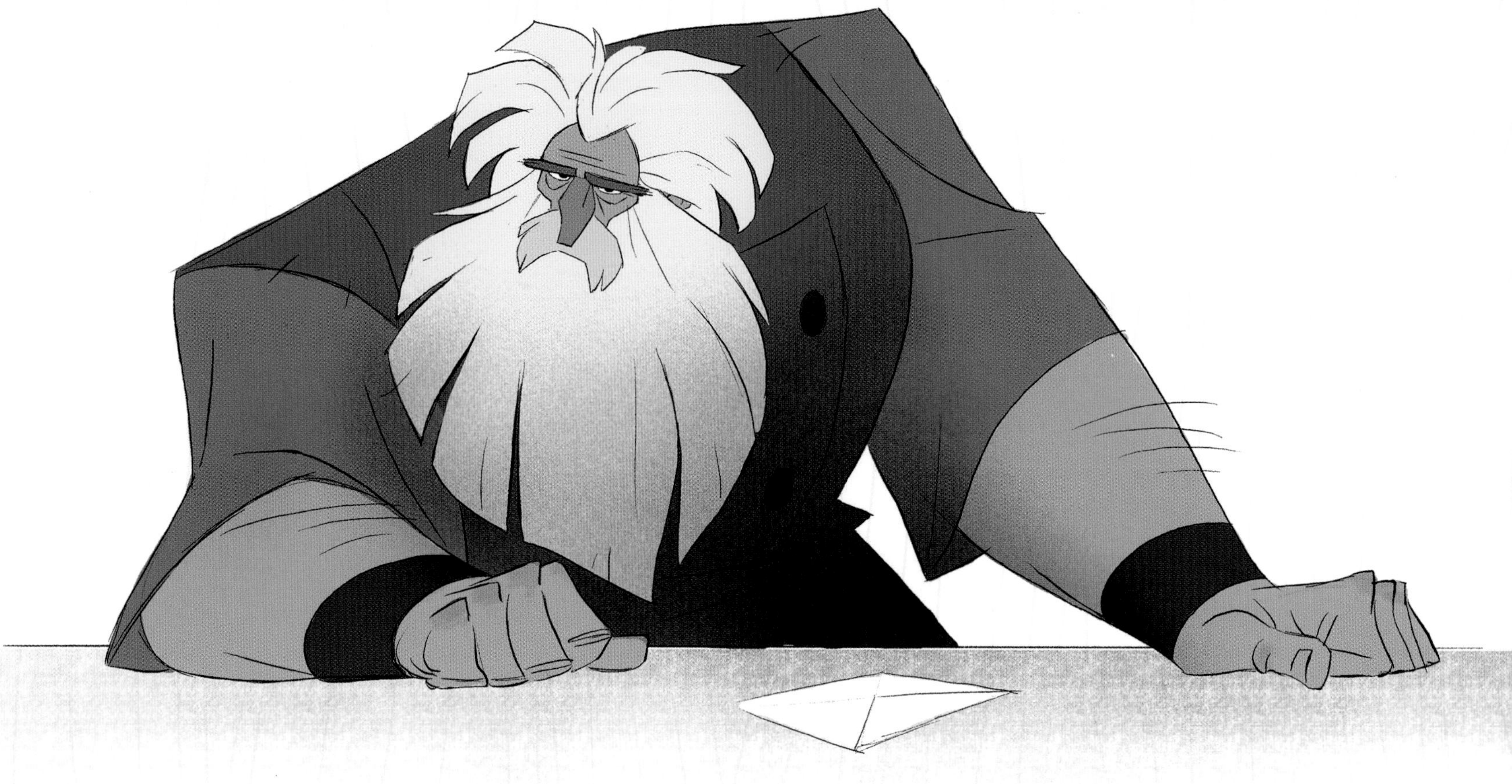

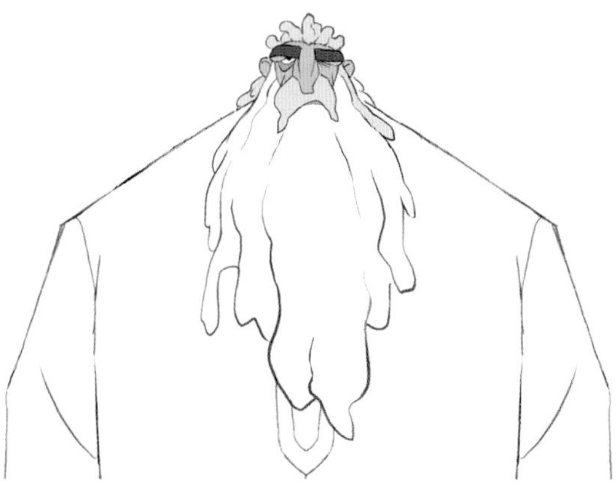

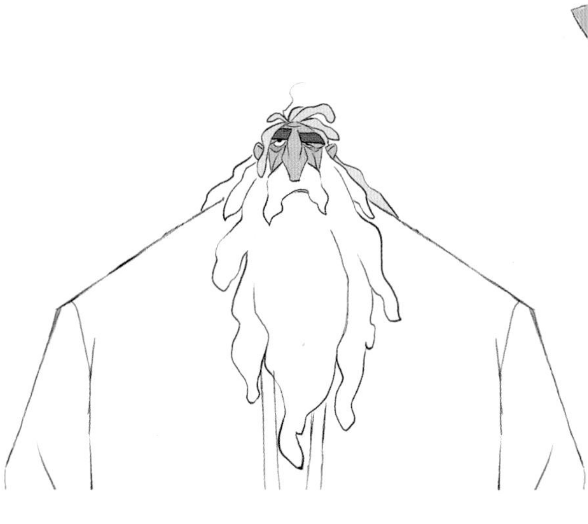

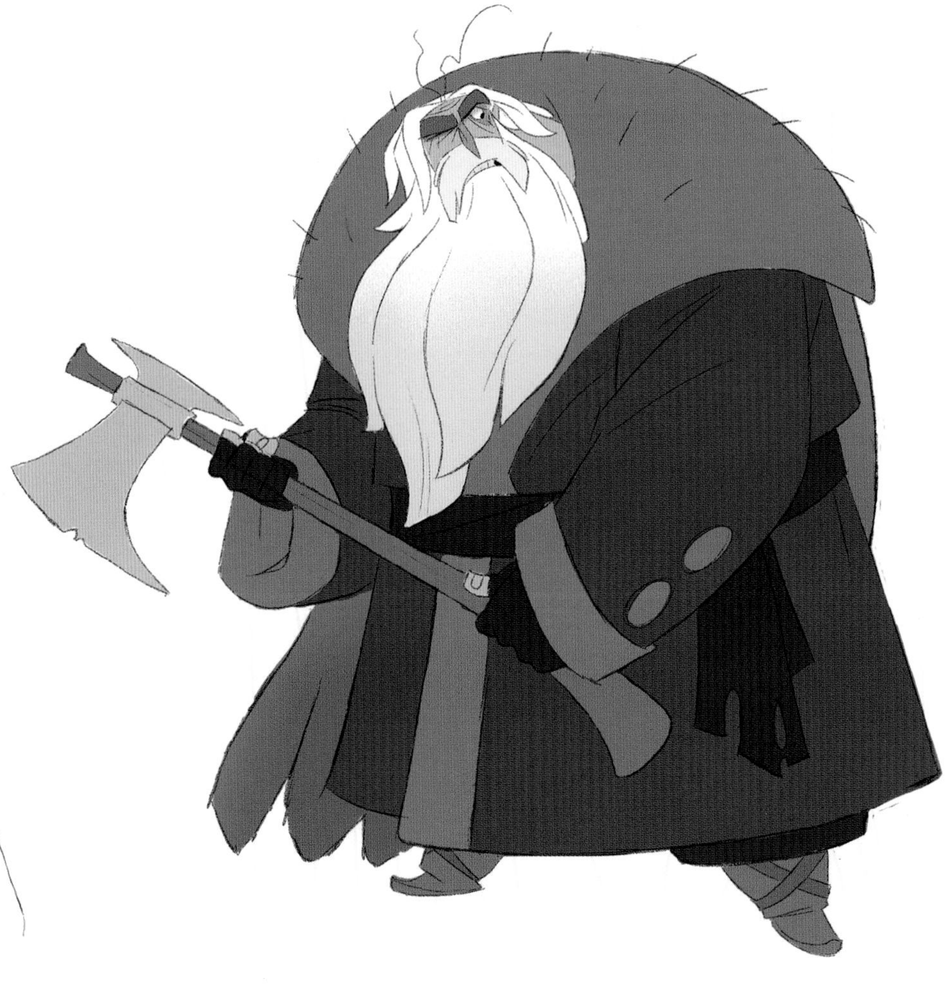

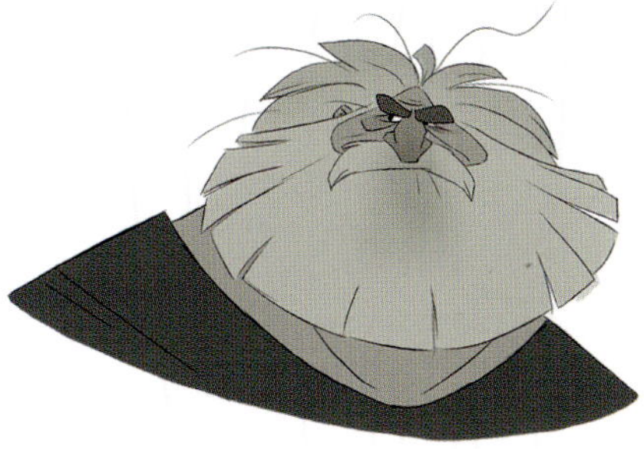

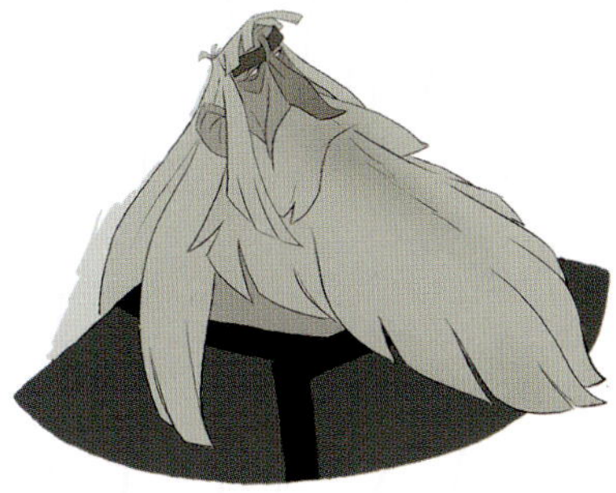

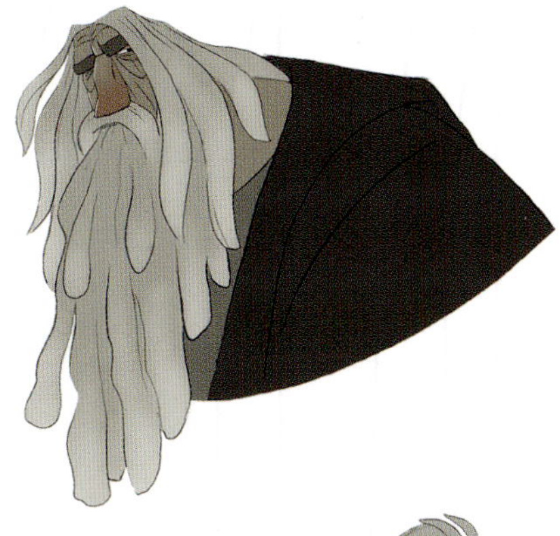

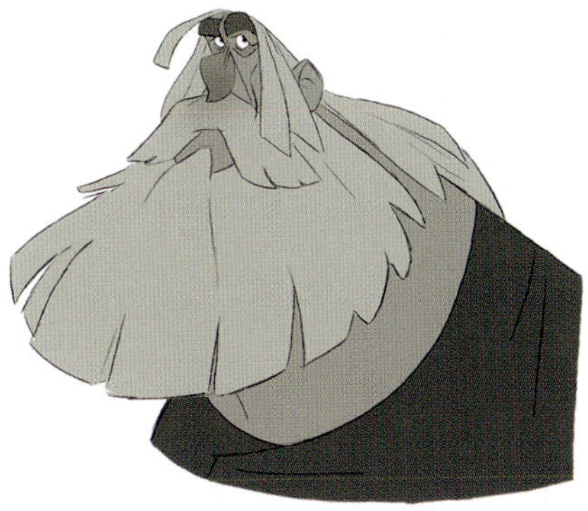

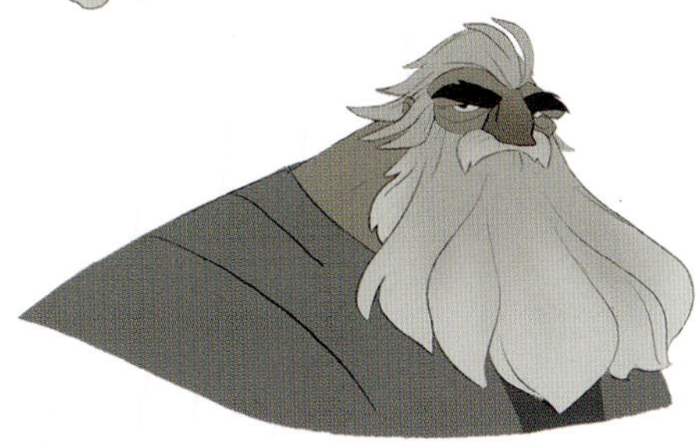

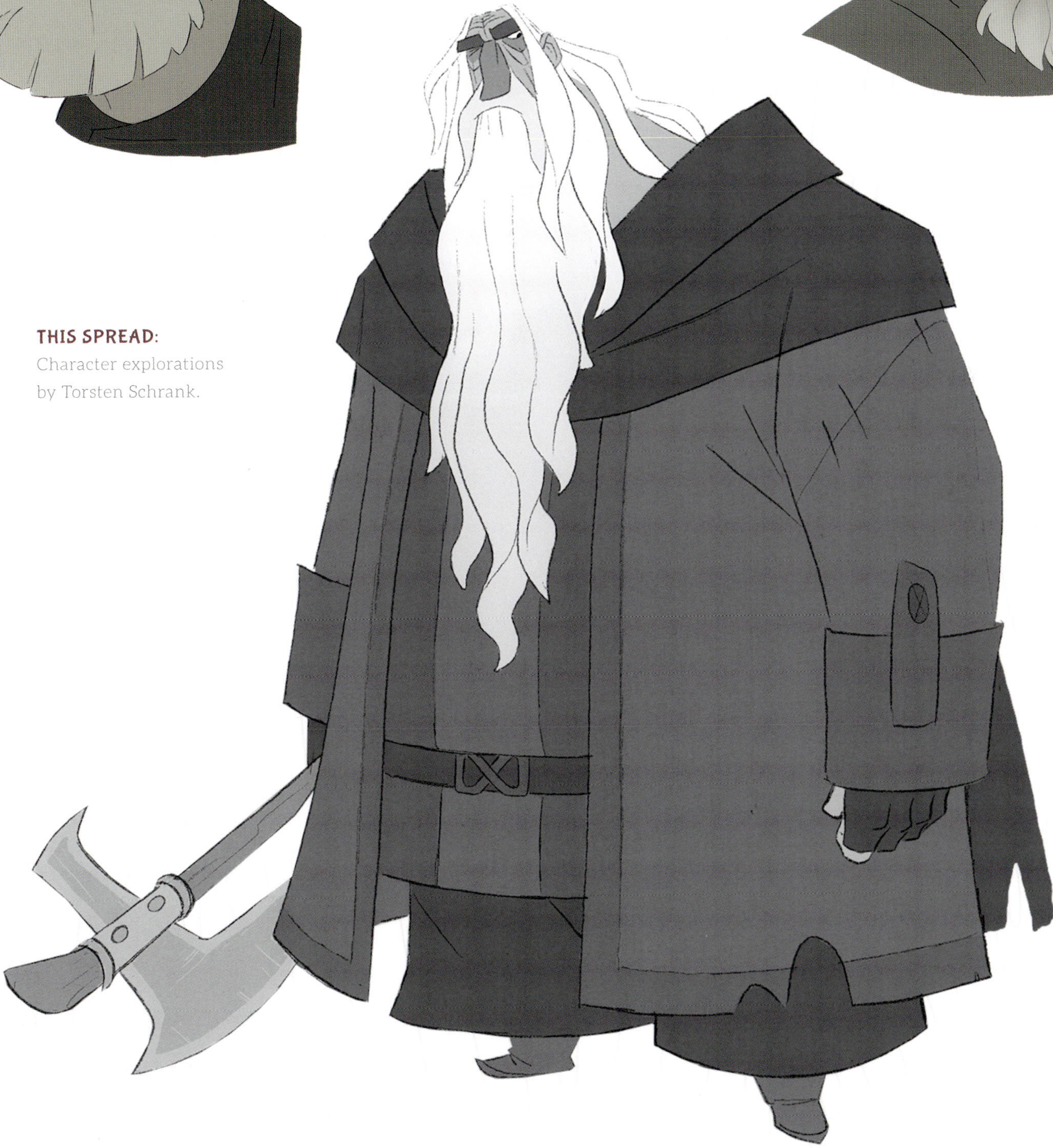

THIS SPREAD:
Character explorations by Torsten Schrank.

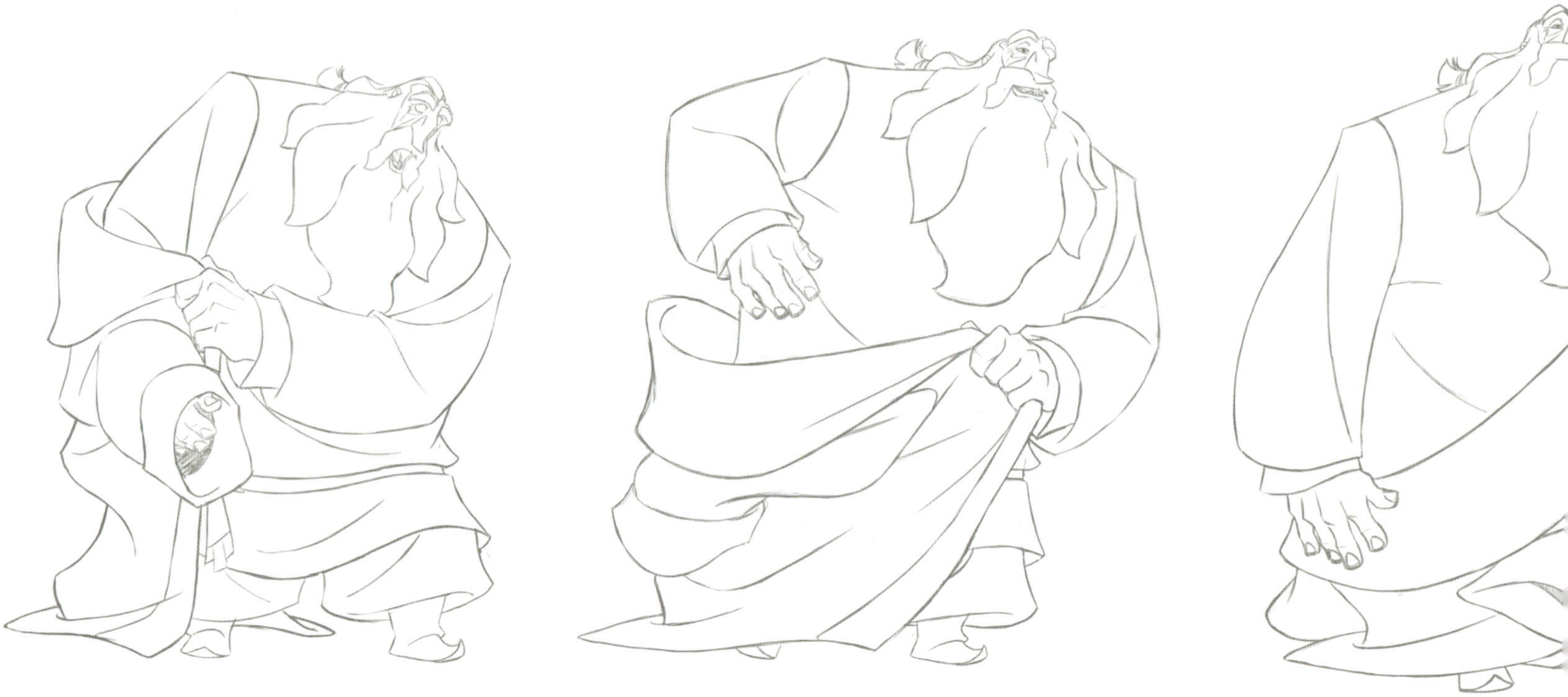

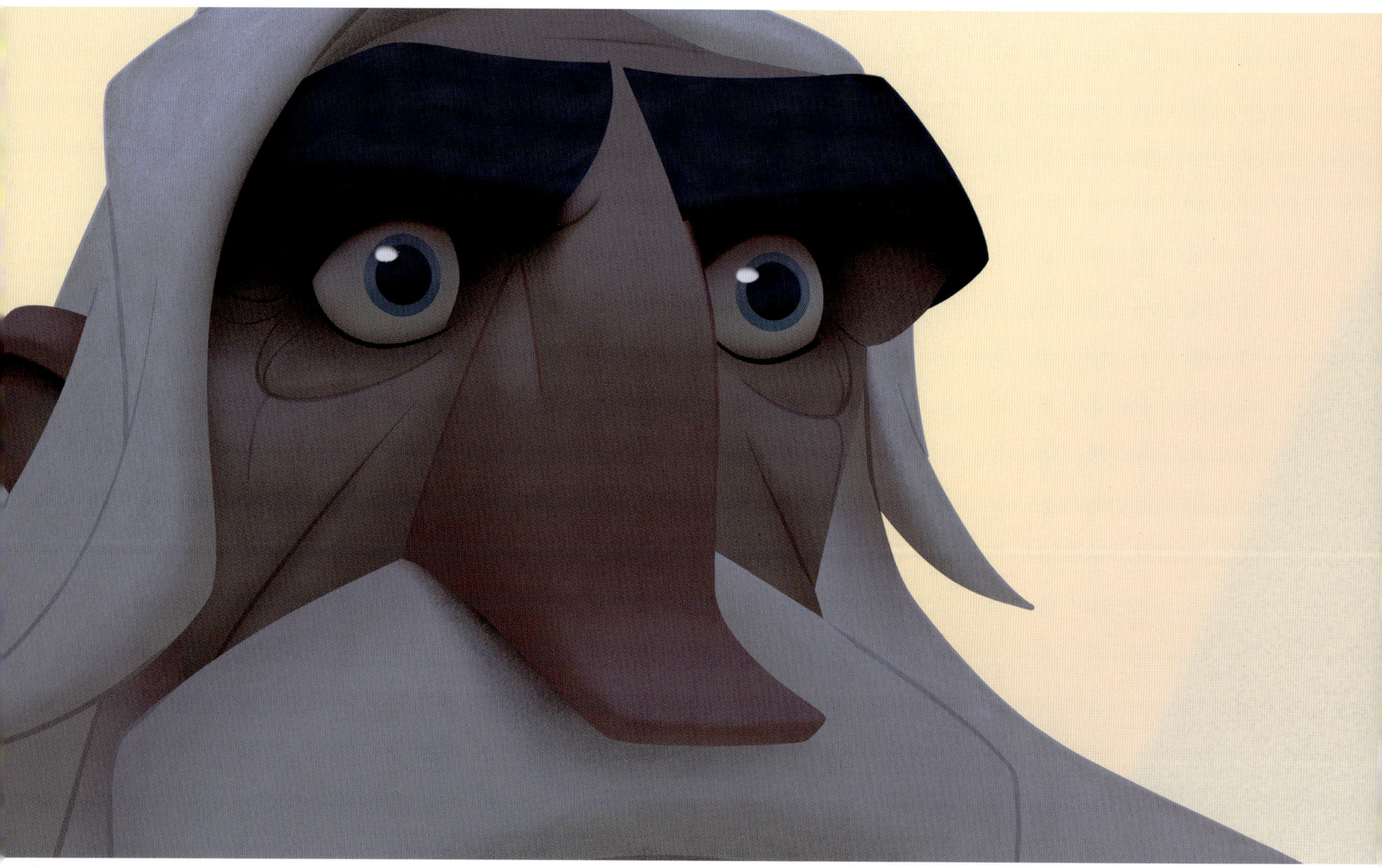

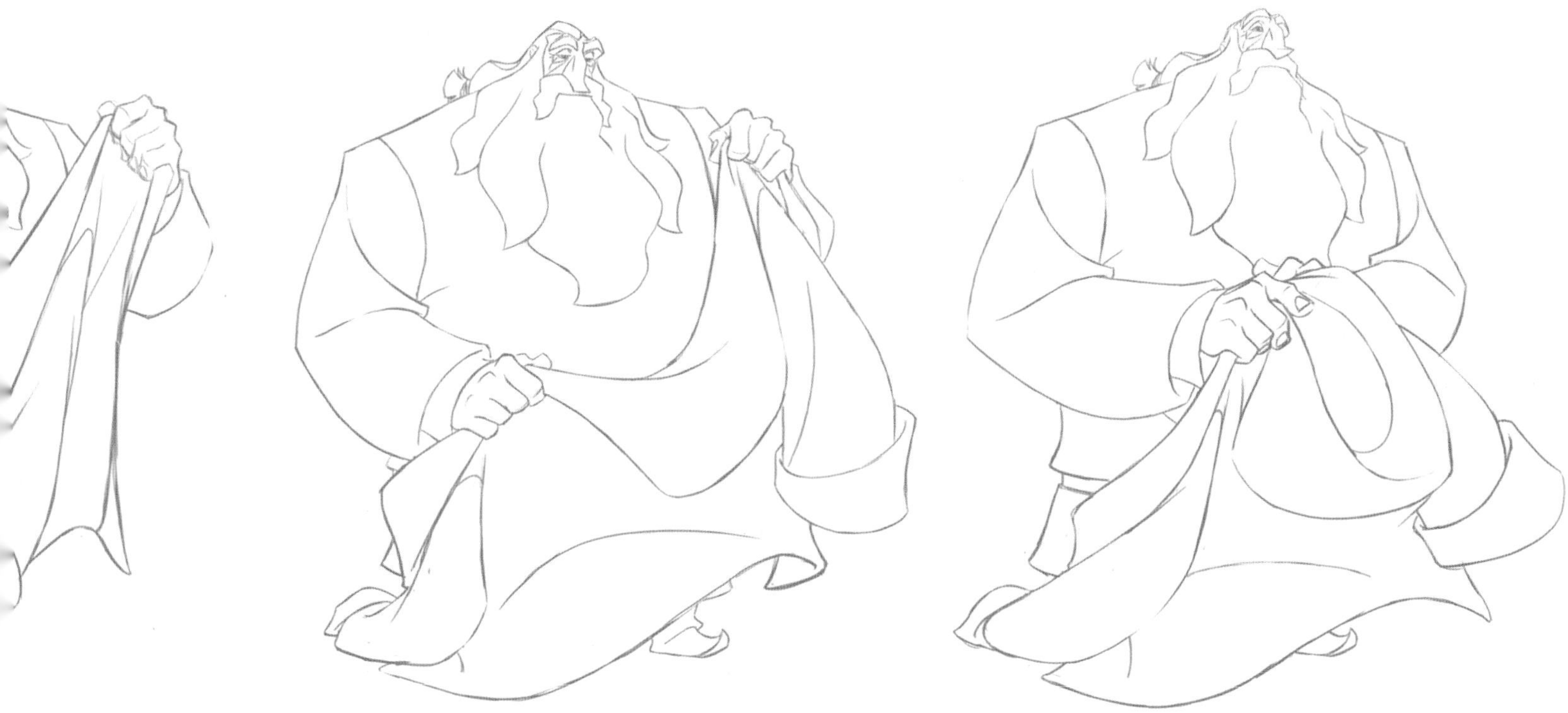

As lead character designer Torsten Schrank explains, the team at SPA had already produced a lot of designs for the proof-of-concept trailer for the movie. "The challenge was to find the right spark in the existing concept sketches," he recalls. "Sergio encouraged me to start from scratch again. We knew that Klaus should be a big guy (not fat) with an impressive, intimidating structure. Sergio was looking for someone who hides a story behind his big beard and long hair. It was really clear that we didn't want to follow the generic look for Santa Claus. Pictures of big, older men with long, felted beards, as well as actors like Sam Elliott, or Sean Connery in *Medicine Man*, were some of our inspirations."

Schrank started with more cartoony versions of Klaus, but then fine-tuned it for a more mature, serious look until he came up with the one sketch that had the right look in his eyes. "That sketch was the spark we were looking for," he notes. "Then, for his legendary red suit, I looked at the colorful and unique traditional costumes of the Saami people [the native inhabitants of the northern parts of Norway, Sweden, Finland, and the Murmansk Oblast of Russia]."

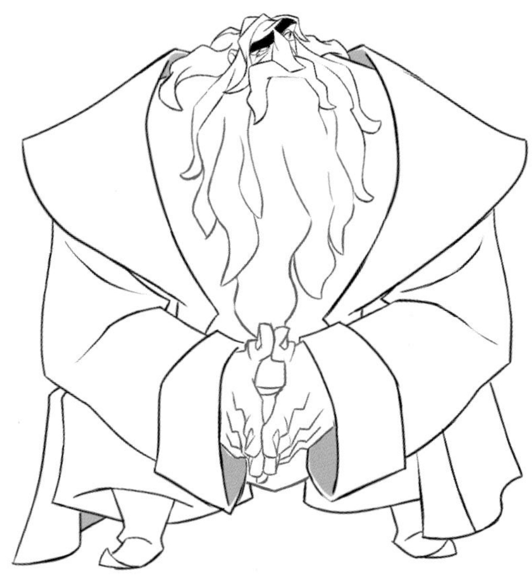

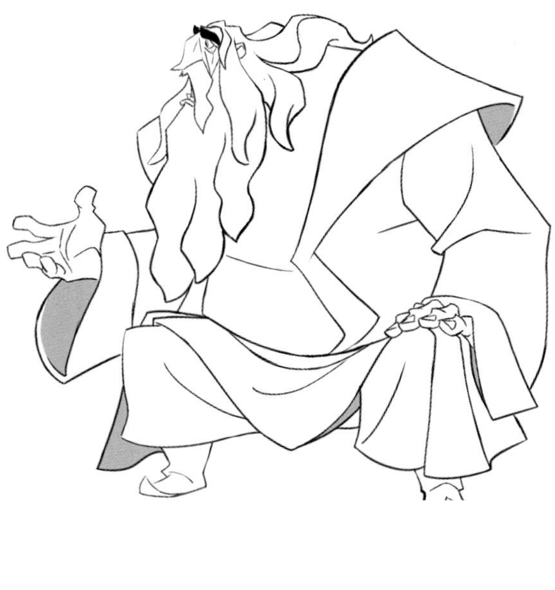

ABOVE: Animated sequence by animation supervisor Victor Ens.

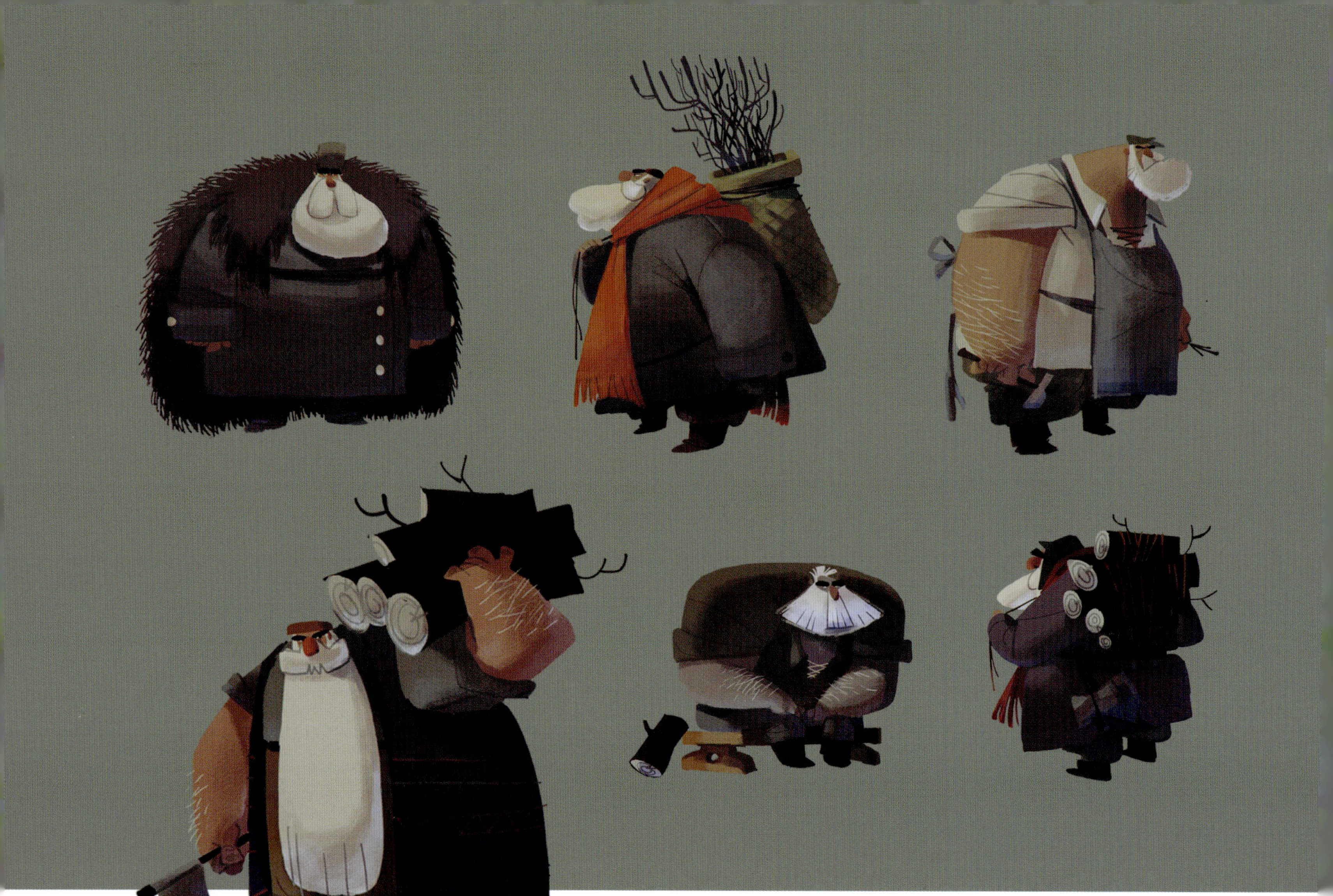

THIS SPREAD: Character explorations by Daniel Fernandez, Victor Ens, and Torsten Schrank.

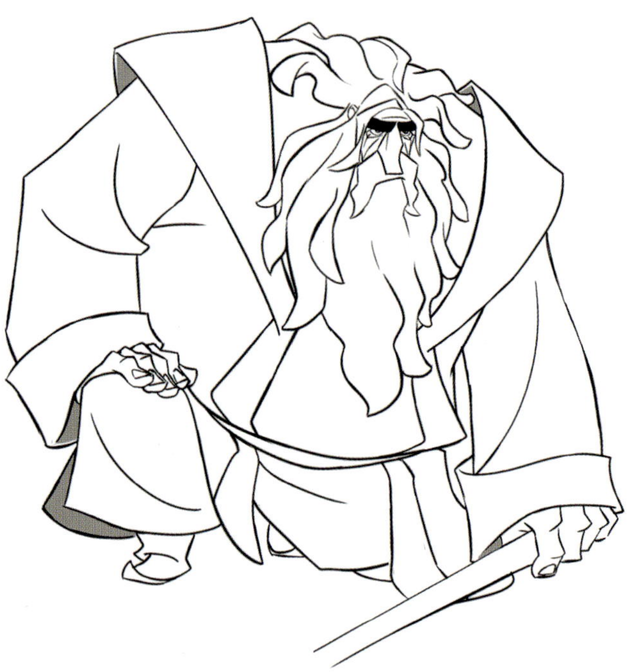

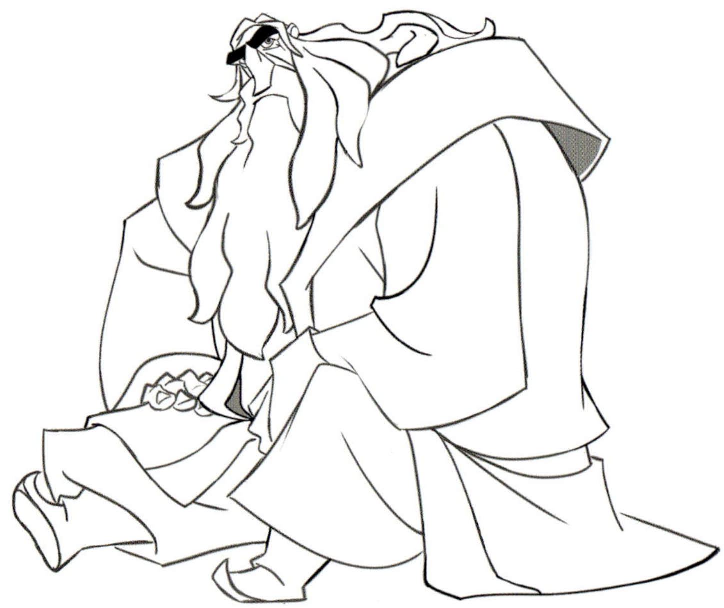

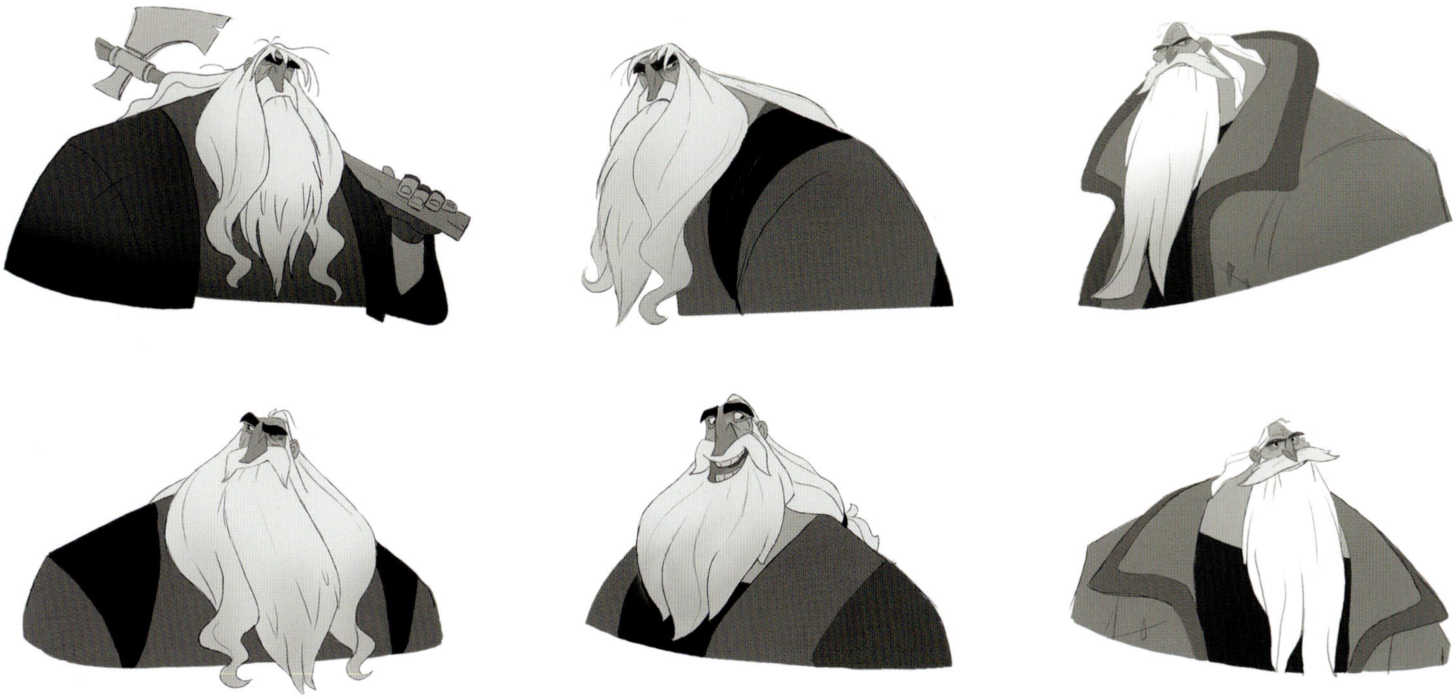

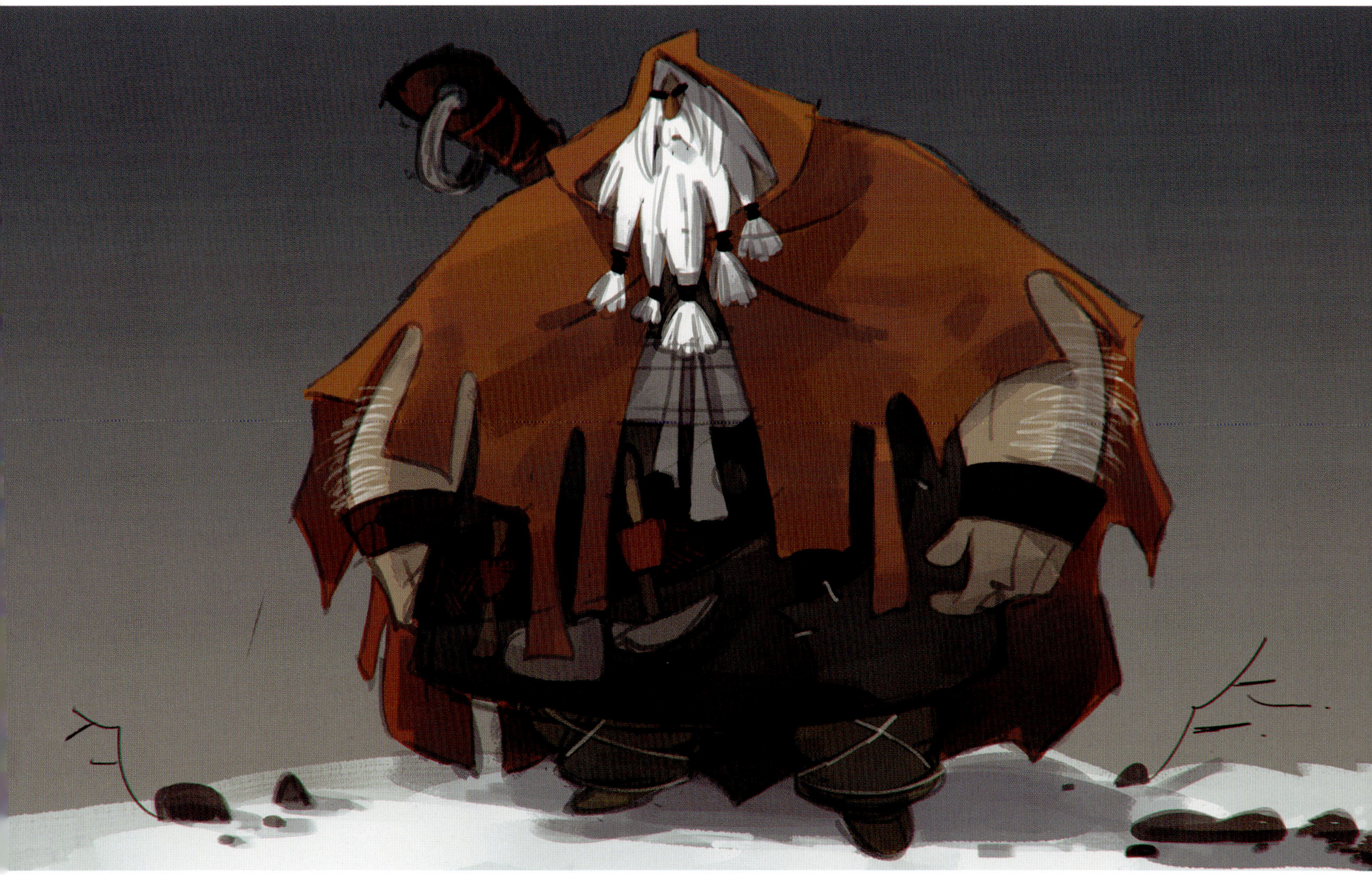

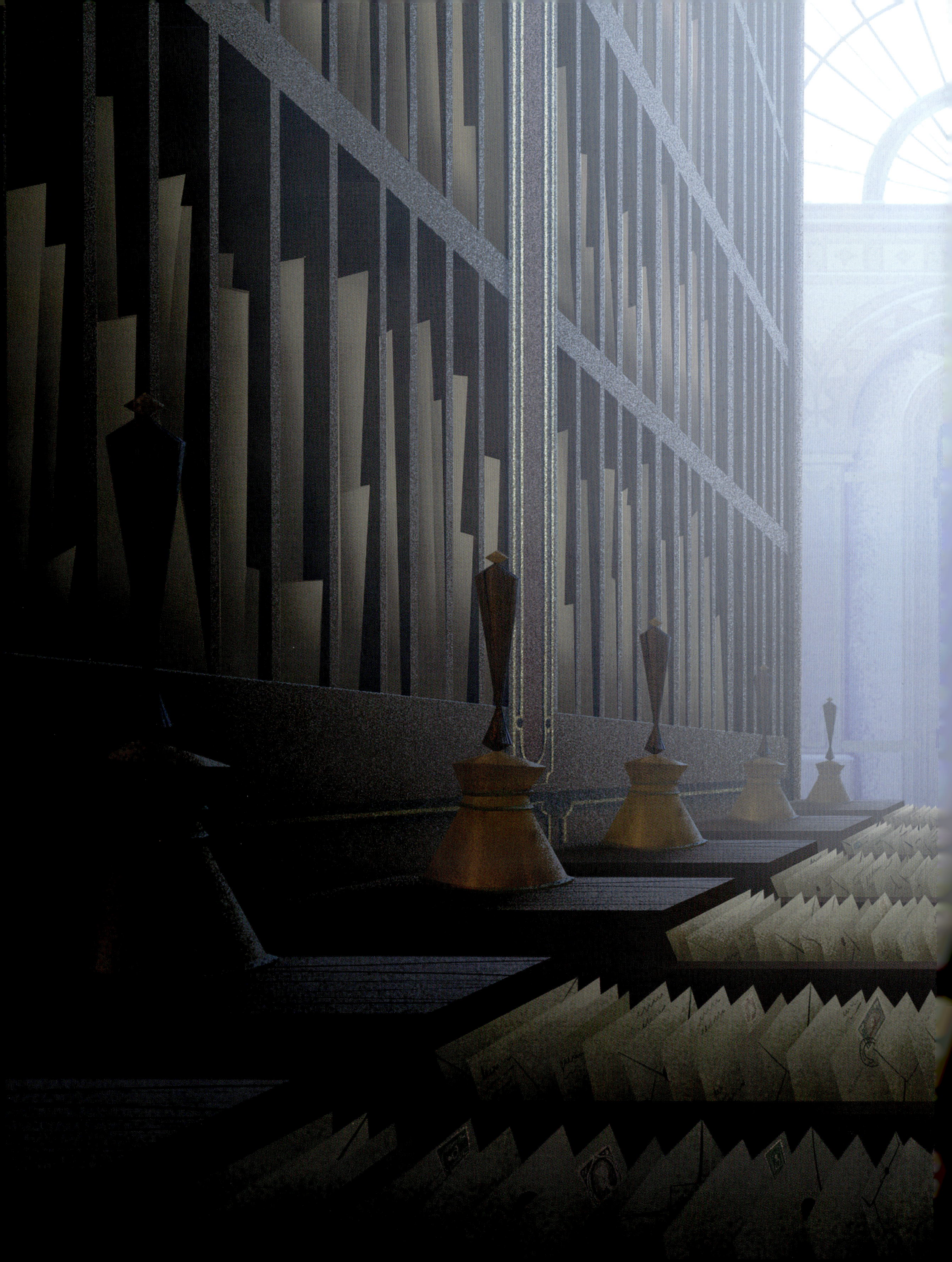

You've Got Mail

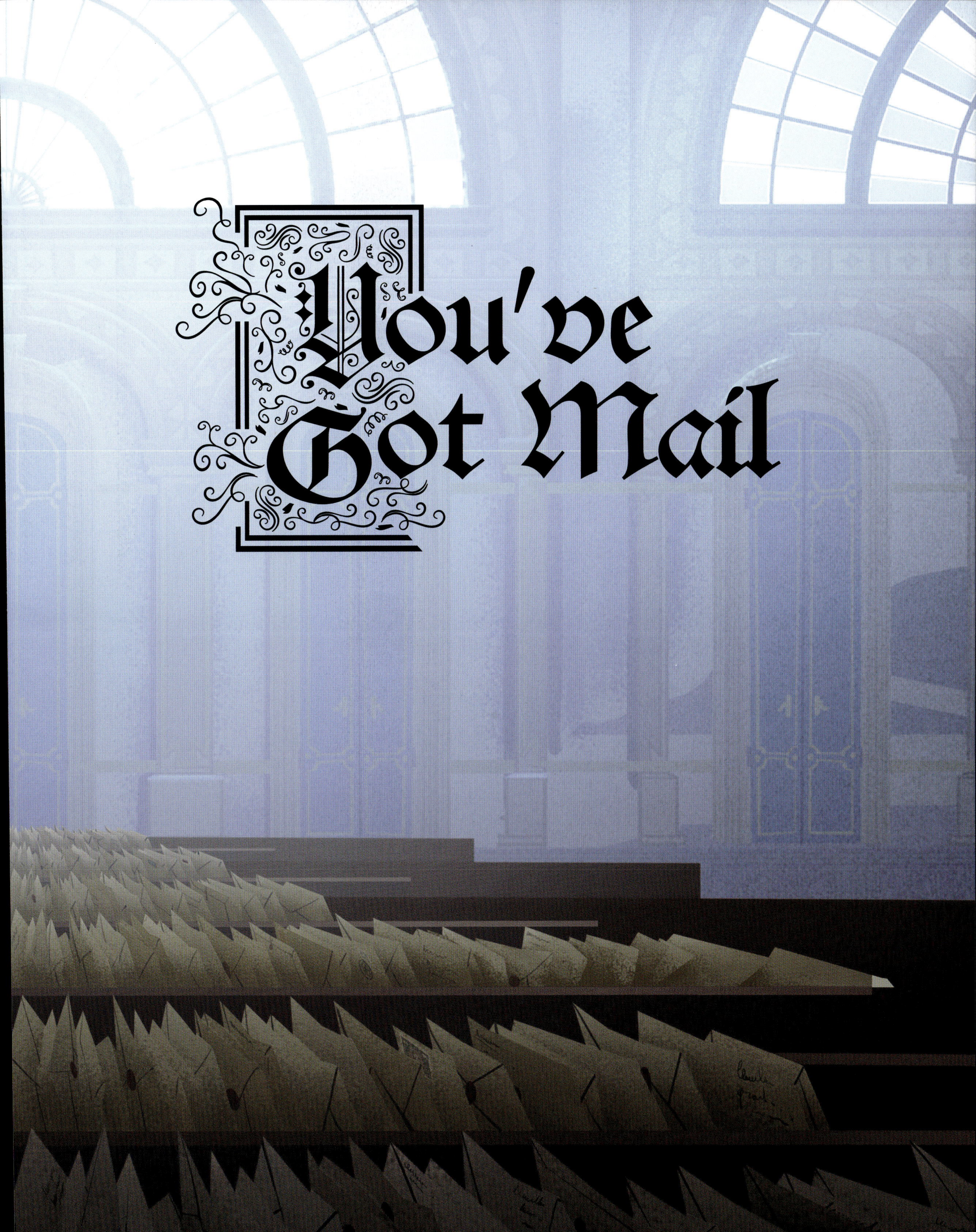

Postal Academy

THE BEGINNING OF A JOURNEY

We first get to meet Jesper as he's confronted by a drill sergeant in the Postal Academy. This austere facility was designed to contrast heavily with Jesper's selfish and feeble personality. As production designer Marcin Jakubowski explains, "The Academy is all about discipline, purpose, and efficiency, so we illustrate that using simple visual symbols. The architectural elements are vertically elongated. They're spaced evenly to evoke the feeling of order and repetition. These elongated shapes, towering over Jesper, imply power and importance. These simple rectangular objects are solid and minimalistic, but the modest décor adds dignity to the overall impression of the Academy."

PREVIOUS SPREAD: Background by Gabriel Gomez.

THIS PAGE: The Royal Postal Academy is the picture of splendor, its bright colors and smooth lines providing a stark contrast to the grim palette and jagged edges of Smeerensburg.

NEXT PAGE: Layout and background by Gabriel Gomez.

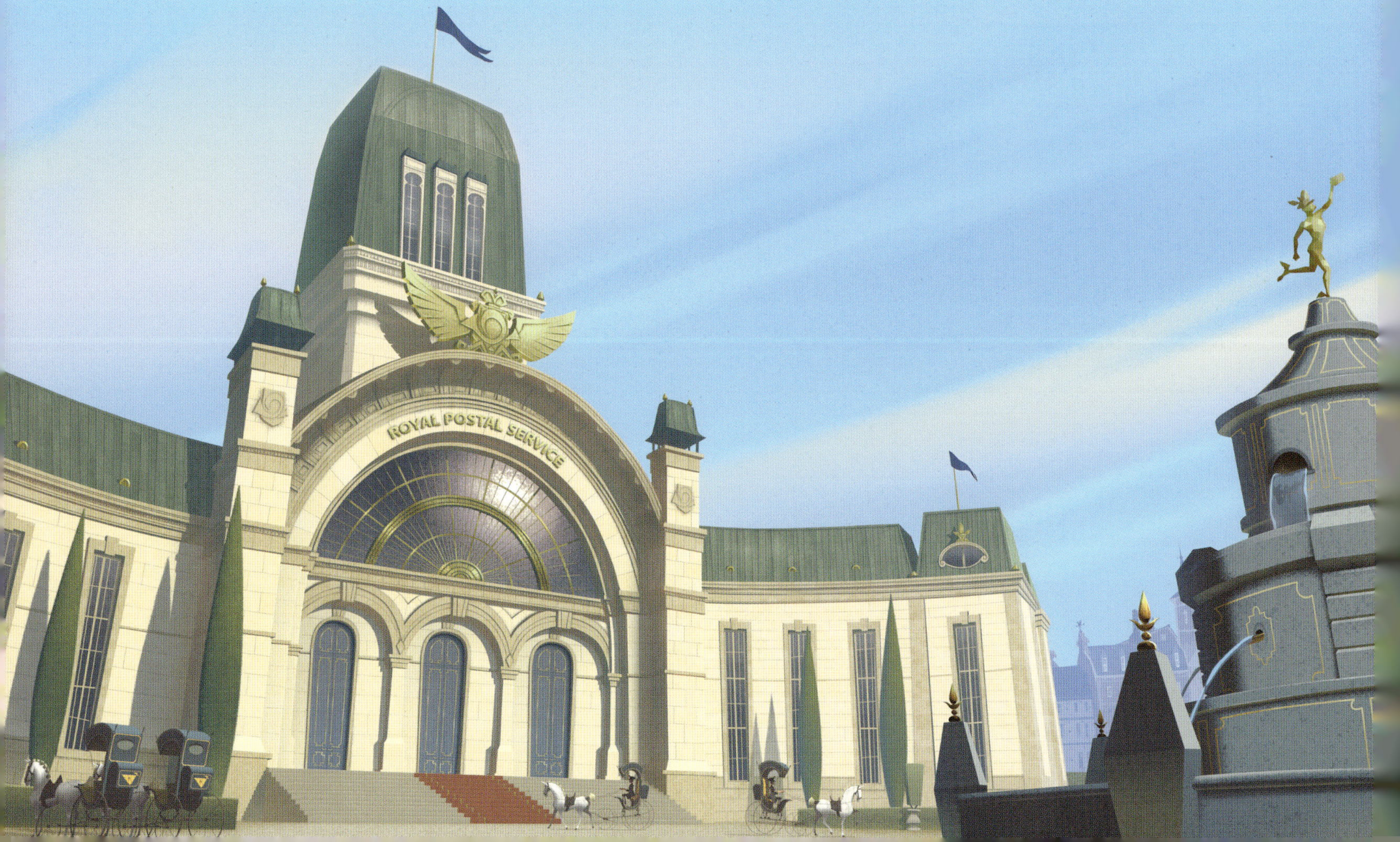

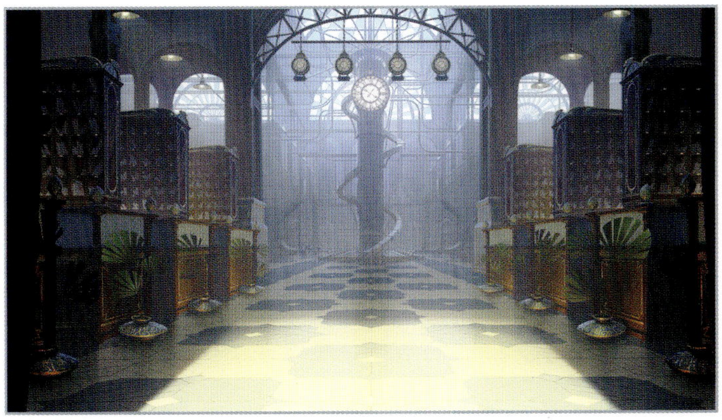

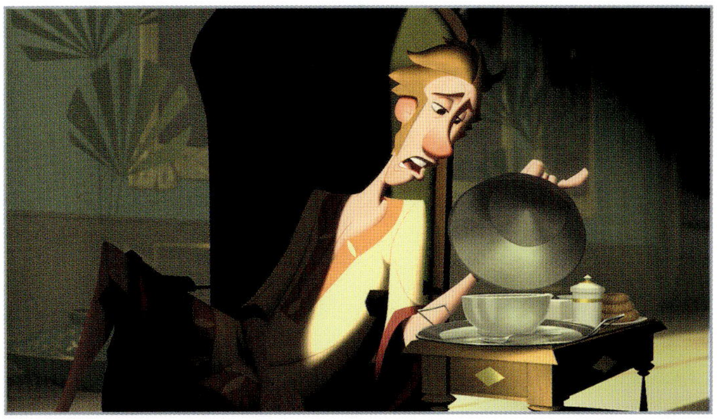

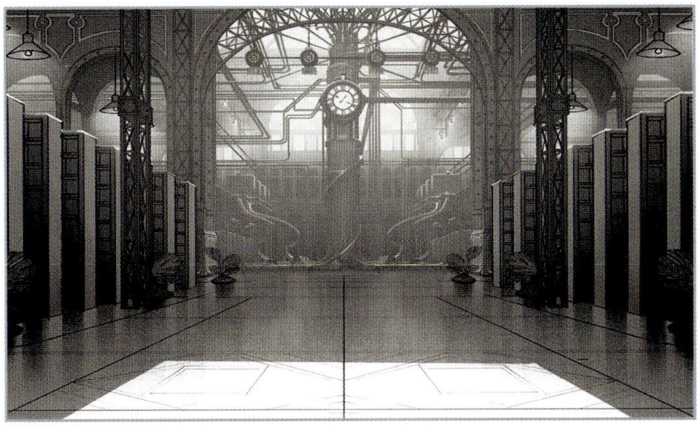

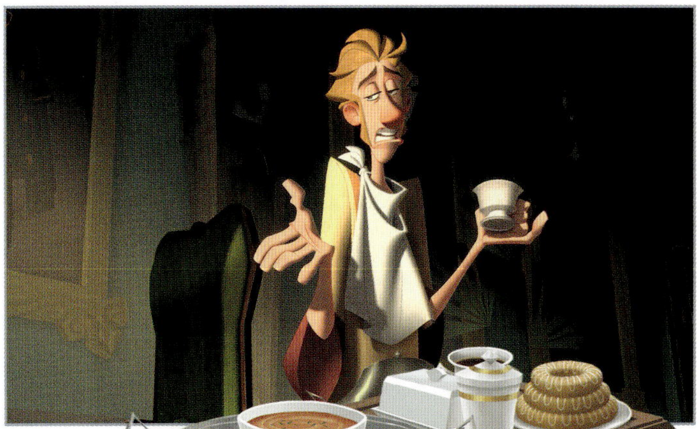

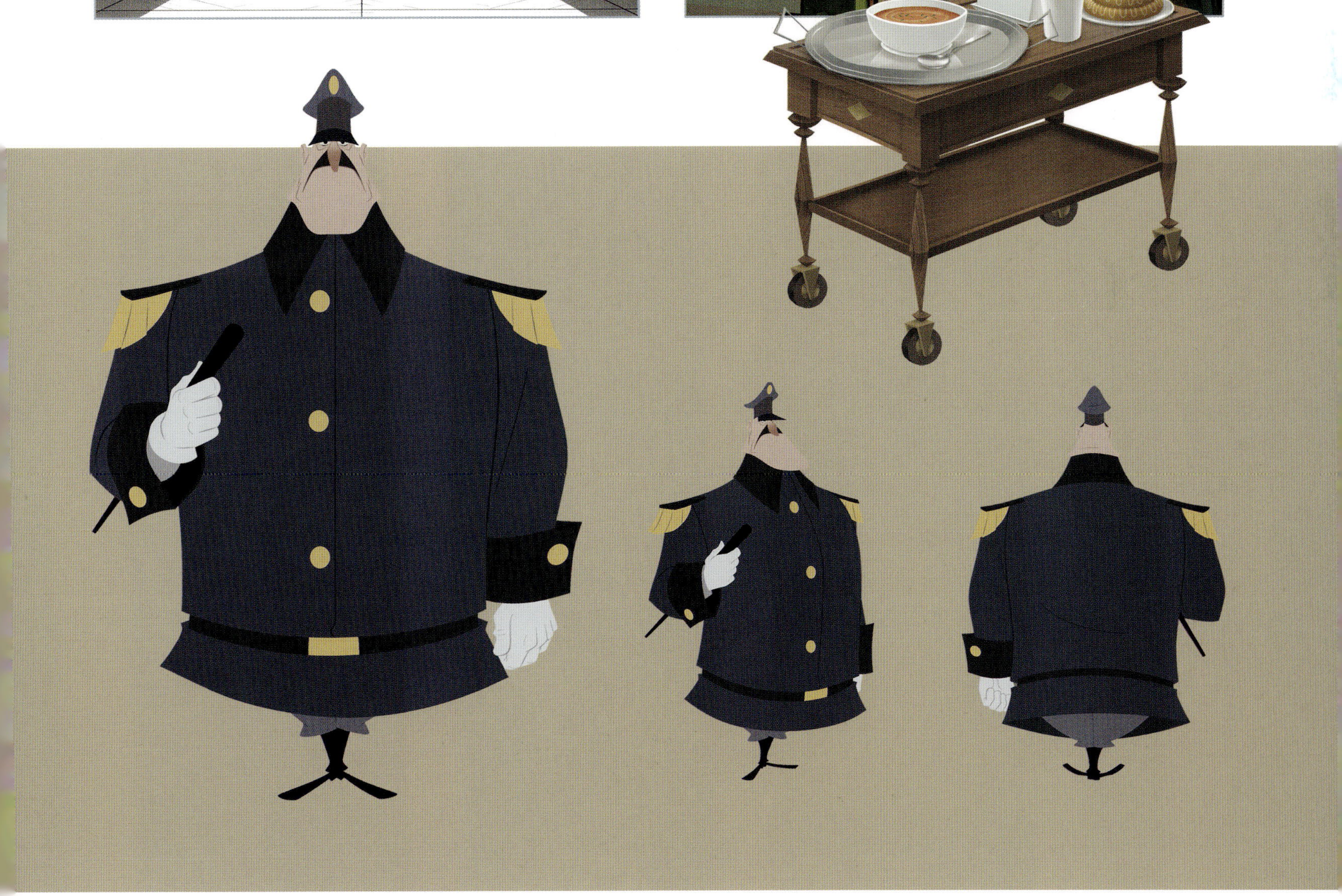

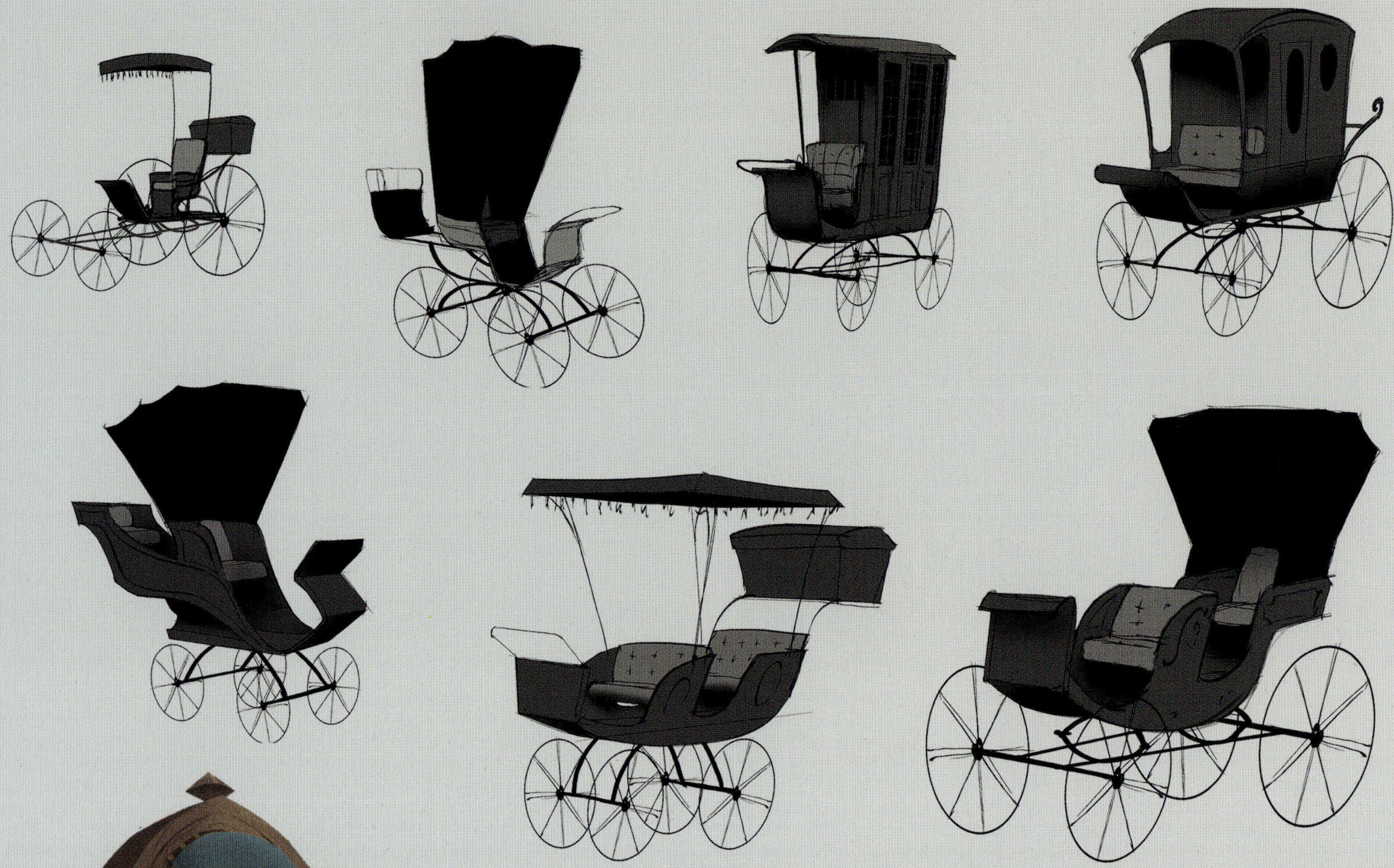

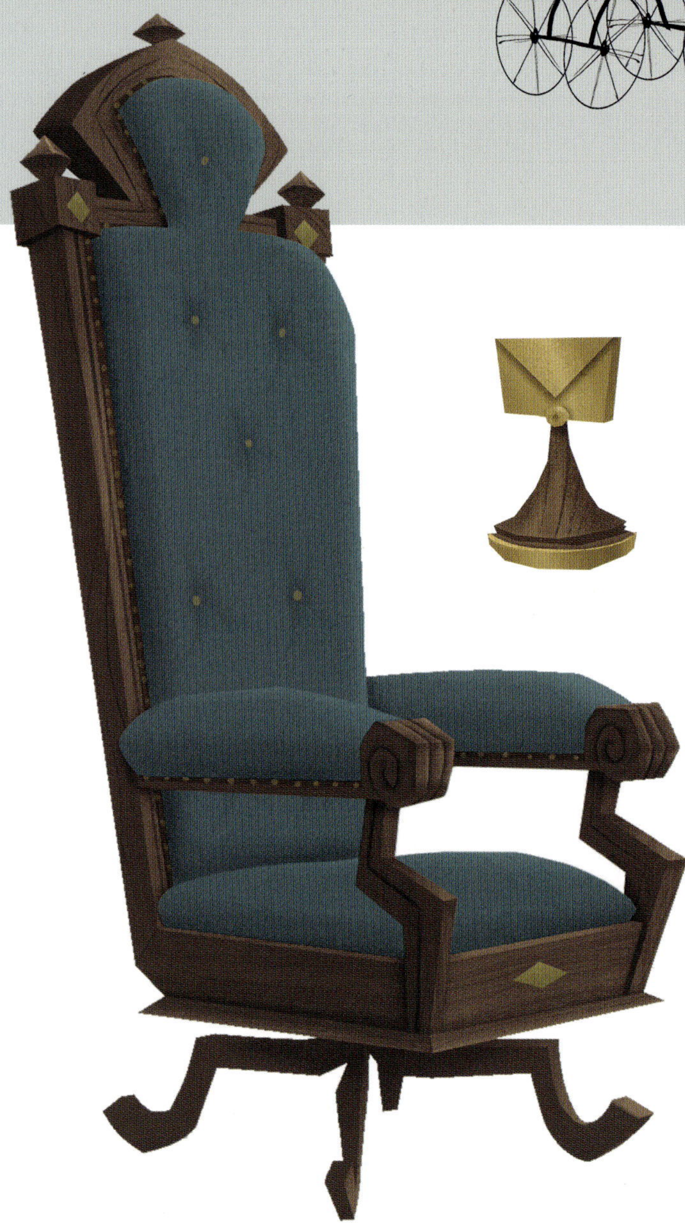

"What sets *Klaus* apart from other animated movies is that it's a combination of quality animation, stylistic illustration, and the treatment and design of a Hollywood movie. I have never worked on a project where these three worlds have come together in this way before."

Adam Parker,
Head of Compositing

ABOVE: Car explorations by Szymon Biernacki.

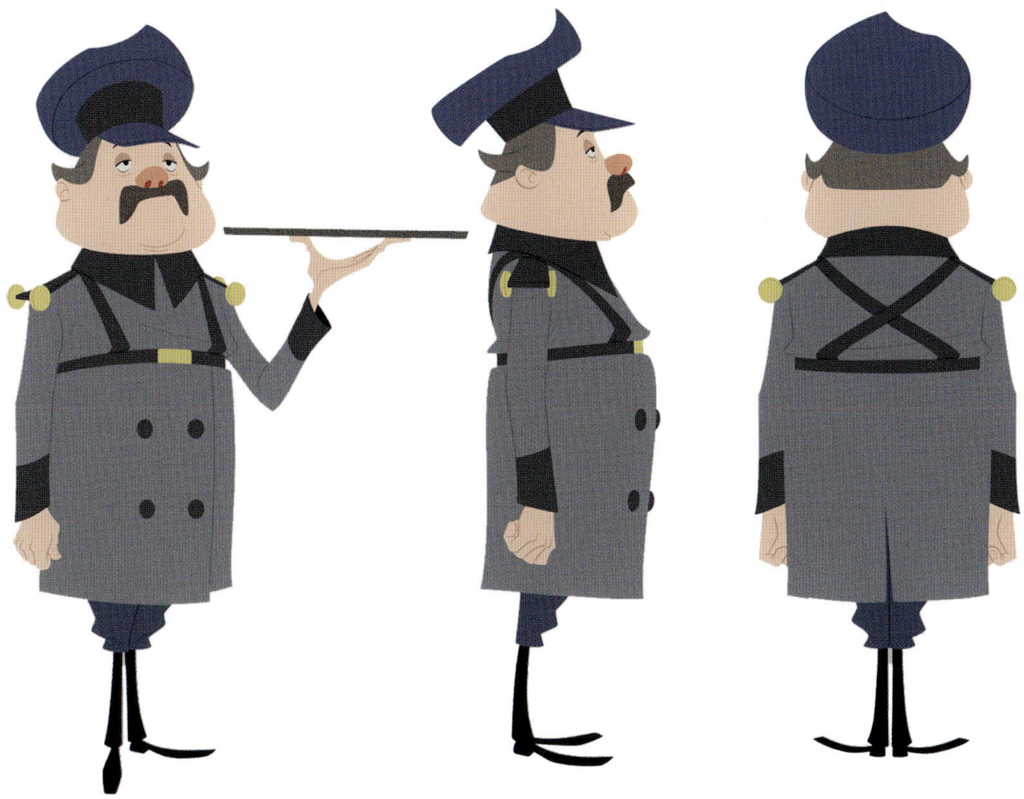

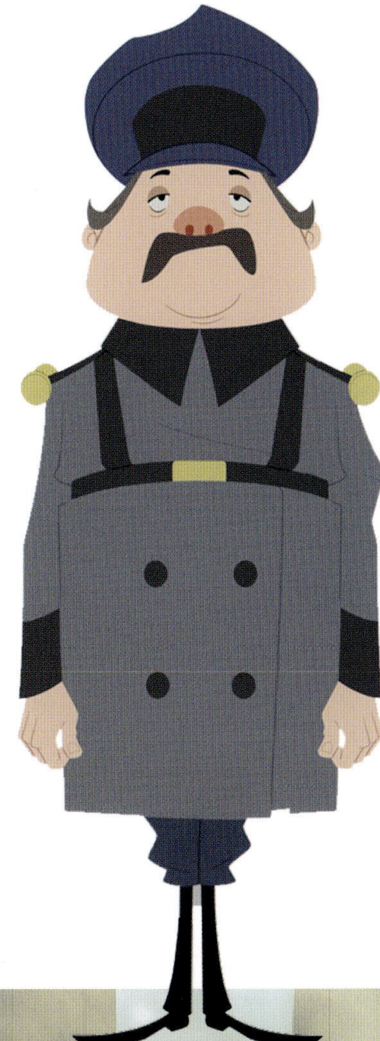

THIS PAGE: (TOP) Character design for the Postal Academy clerk by Torsten Schrank; (BOTTOM) Final render of Jesper in his postal classes.

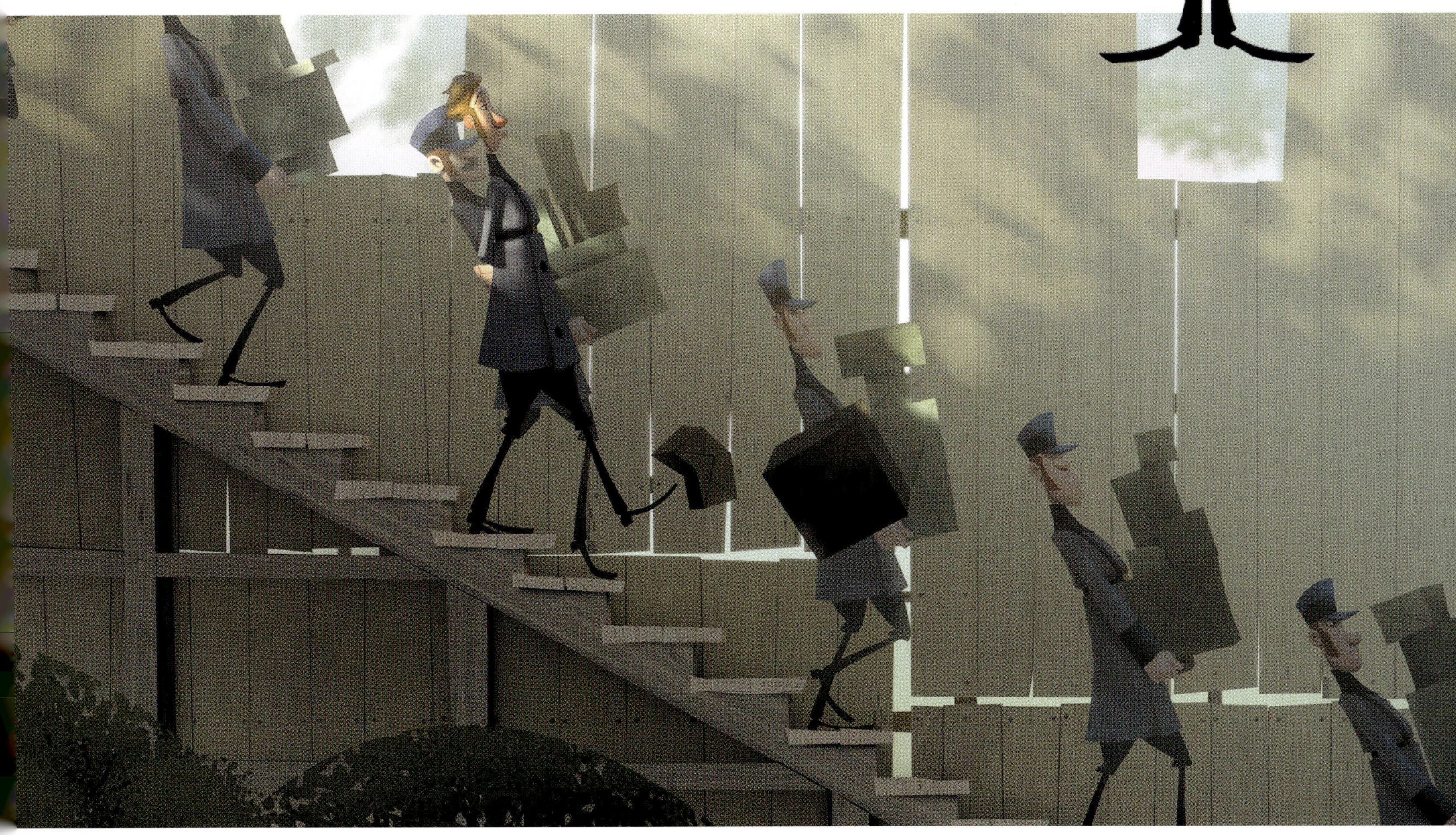

Postmaster

JESPER'S FATHER

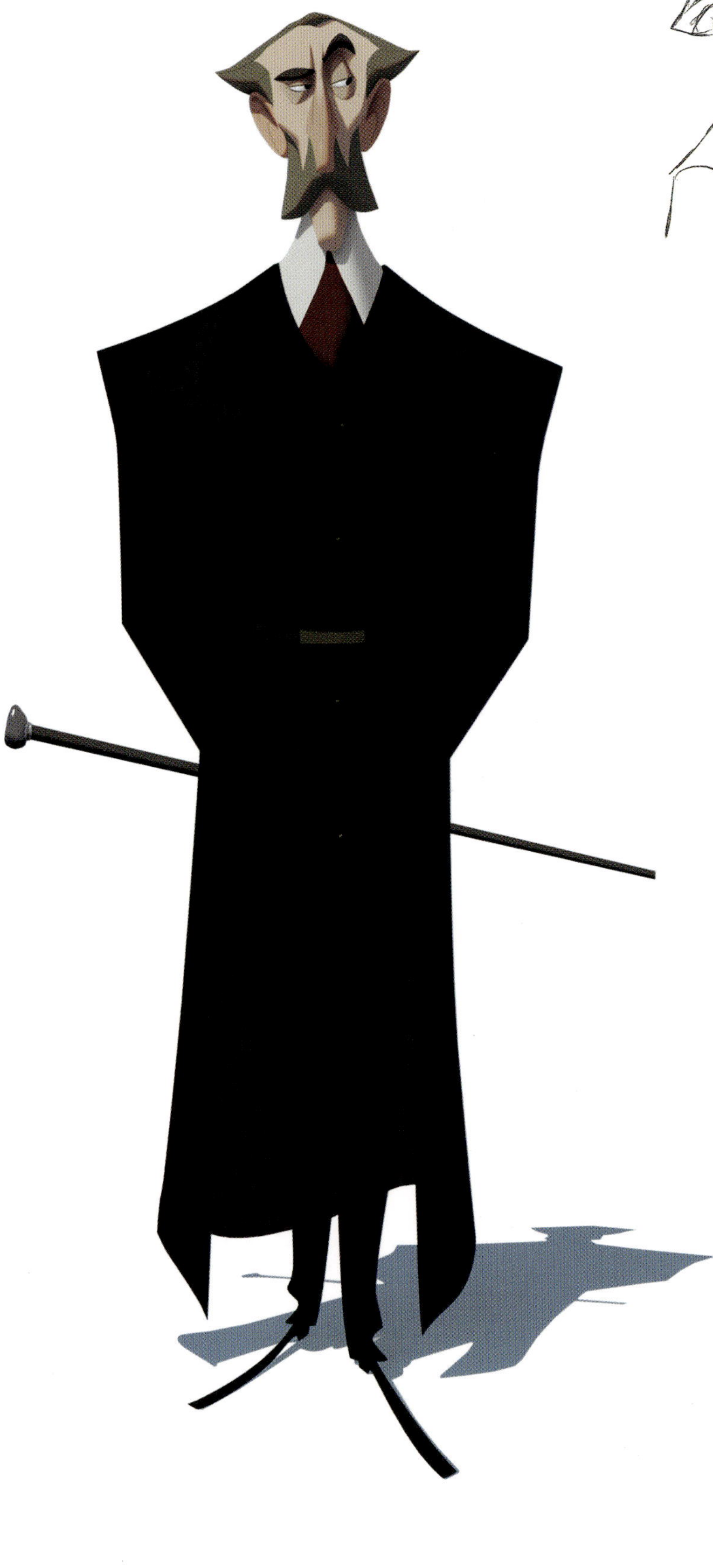

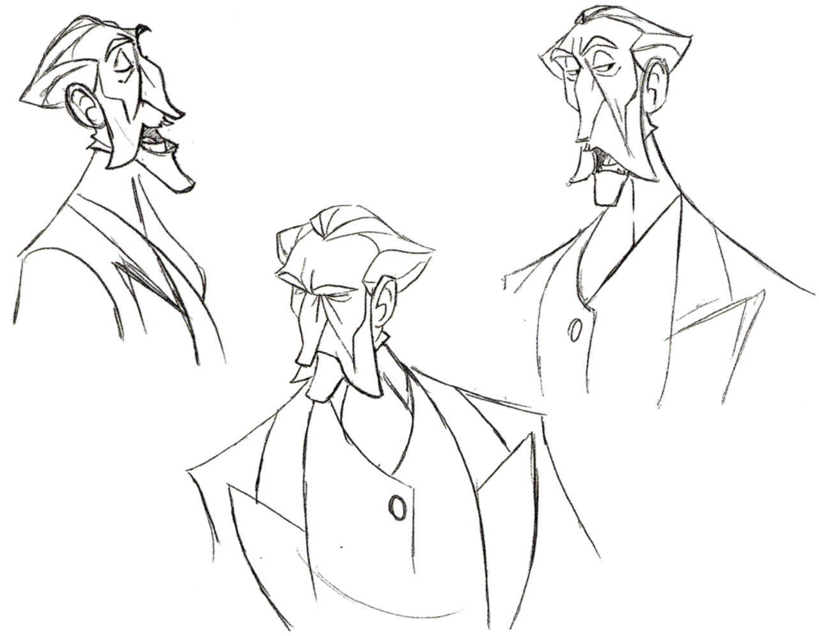

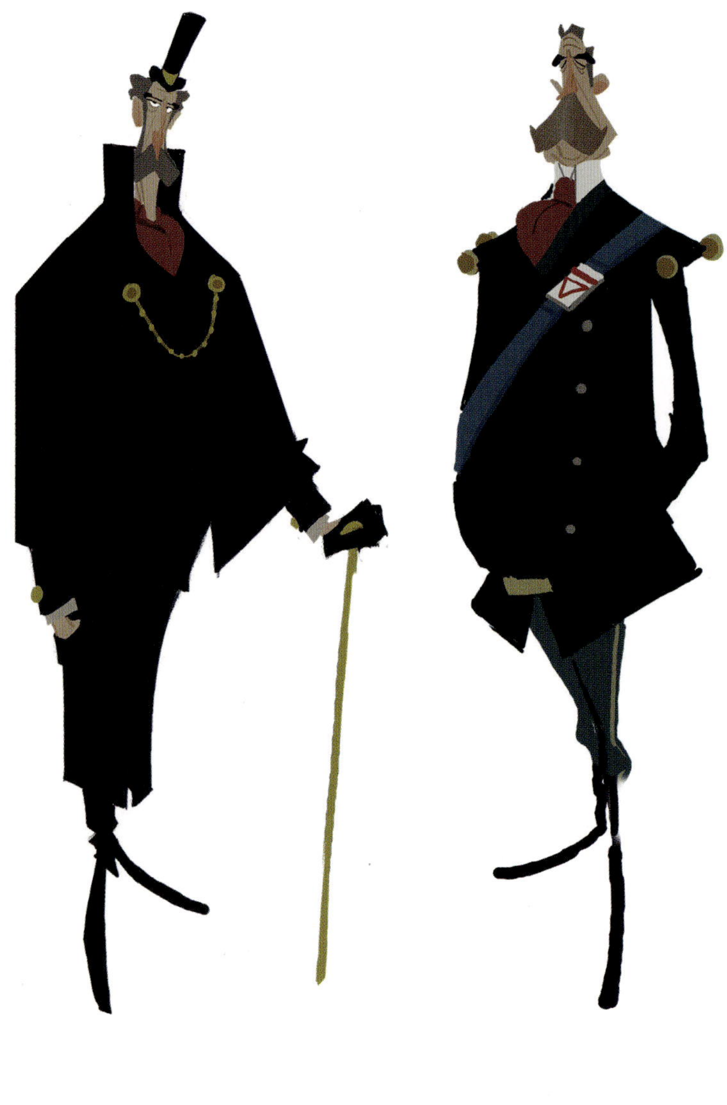

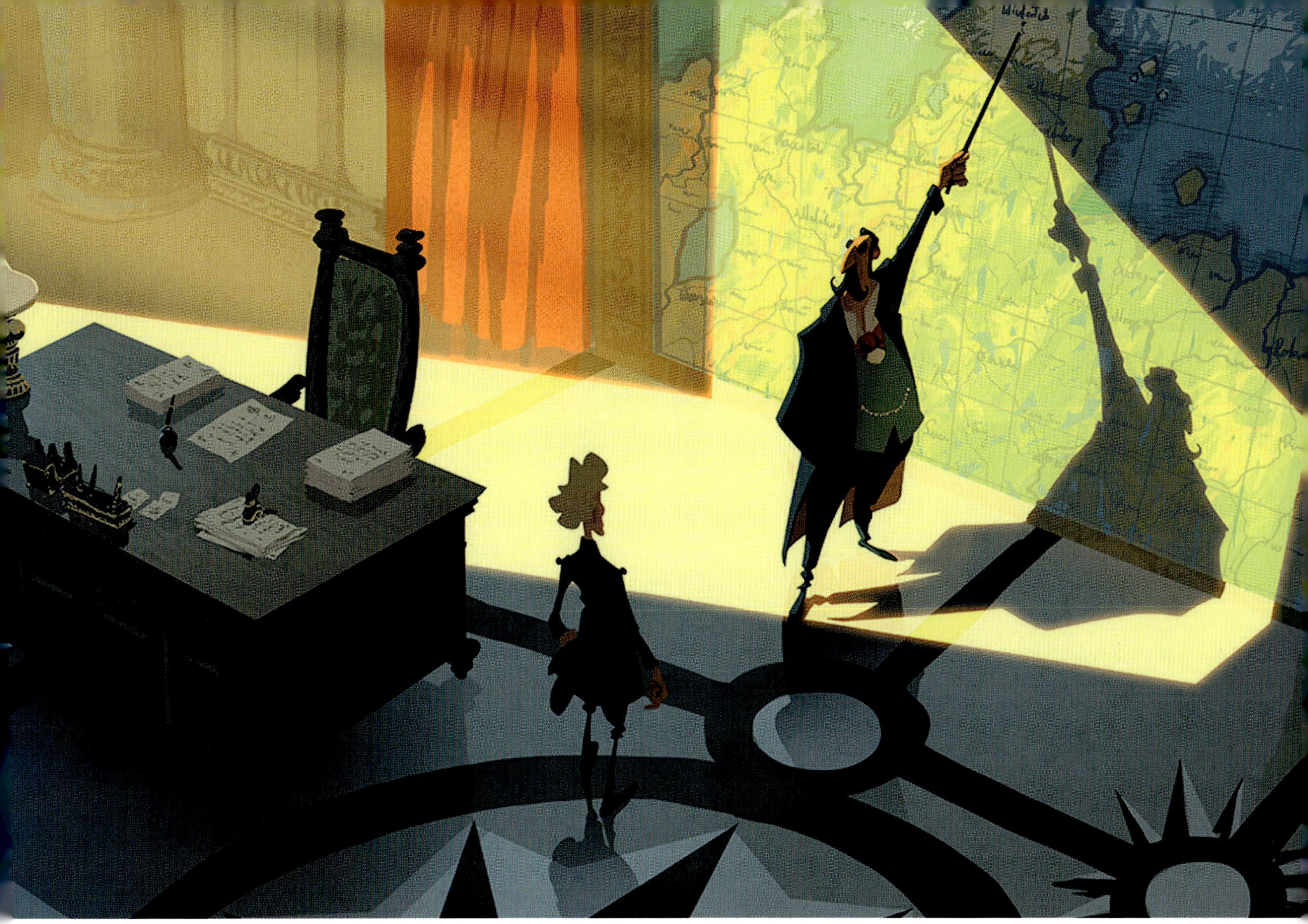

THIS SPREAD: (TOP RIGHT) Concept art by Marcin Jakubowski and Sergio Pablos; (REST OF SPREAD) Character explorations by Torsten Schrank, Charlie Bonifacio, and Daniel Fernandez.

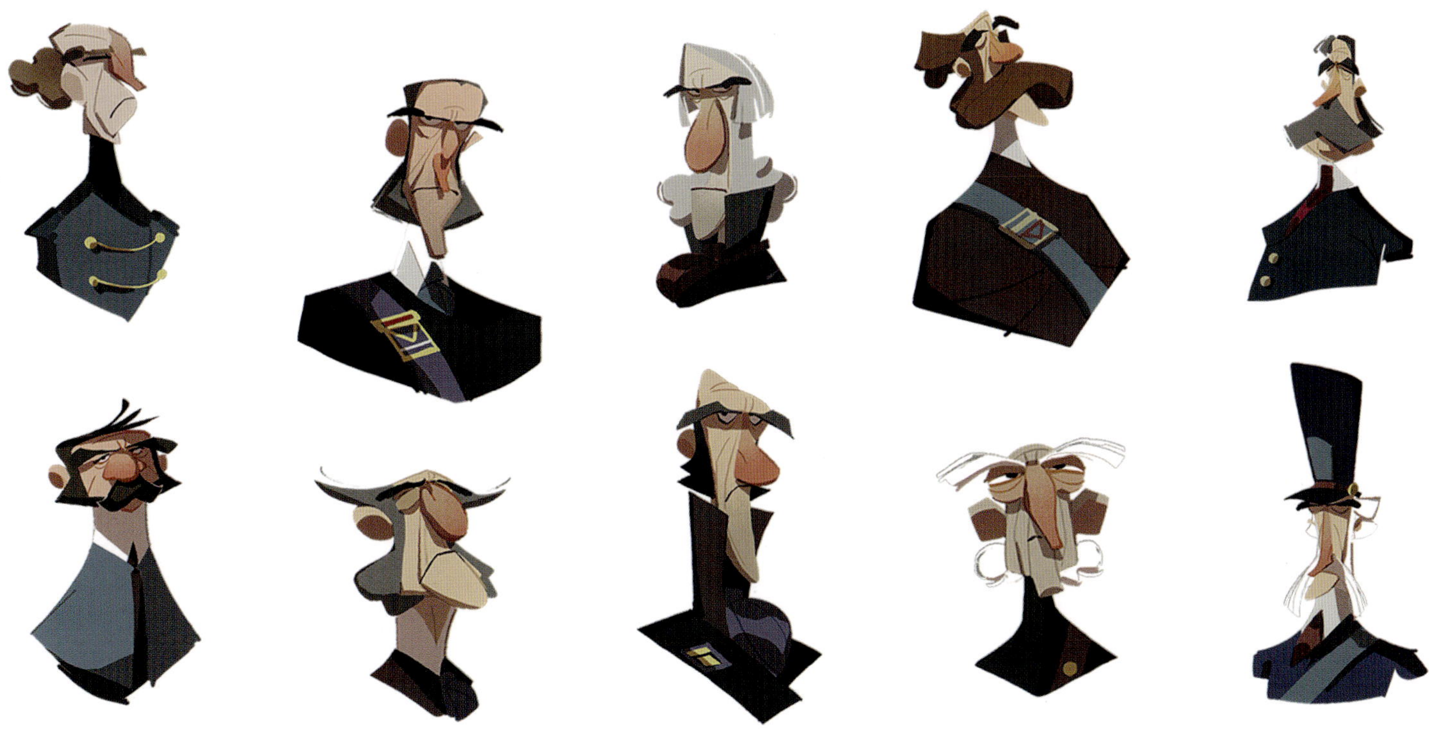

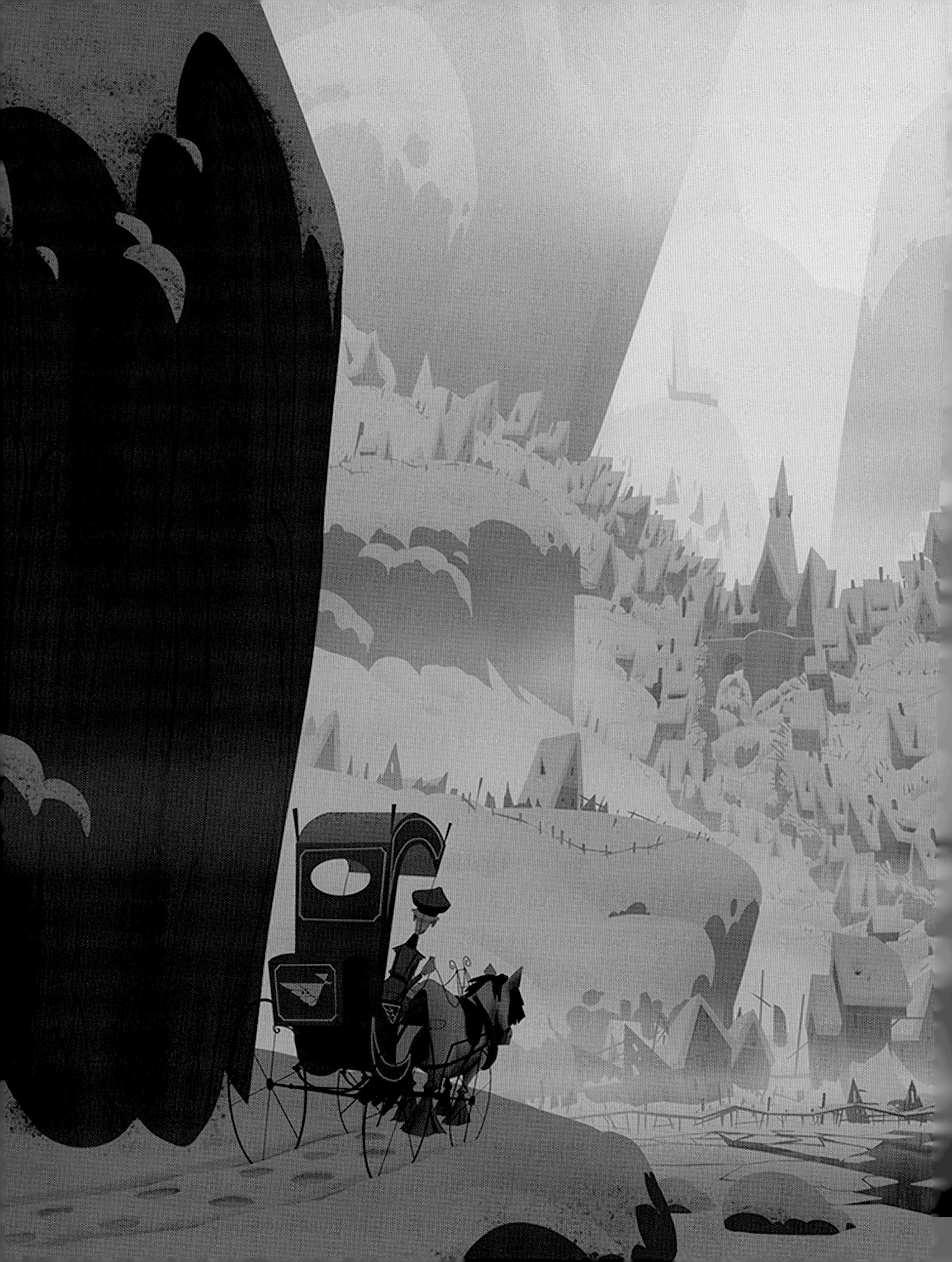

Way to Smeerensburg

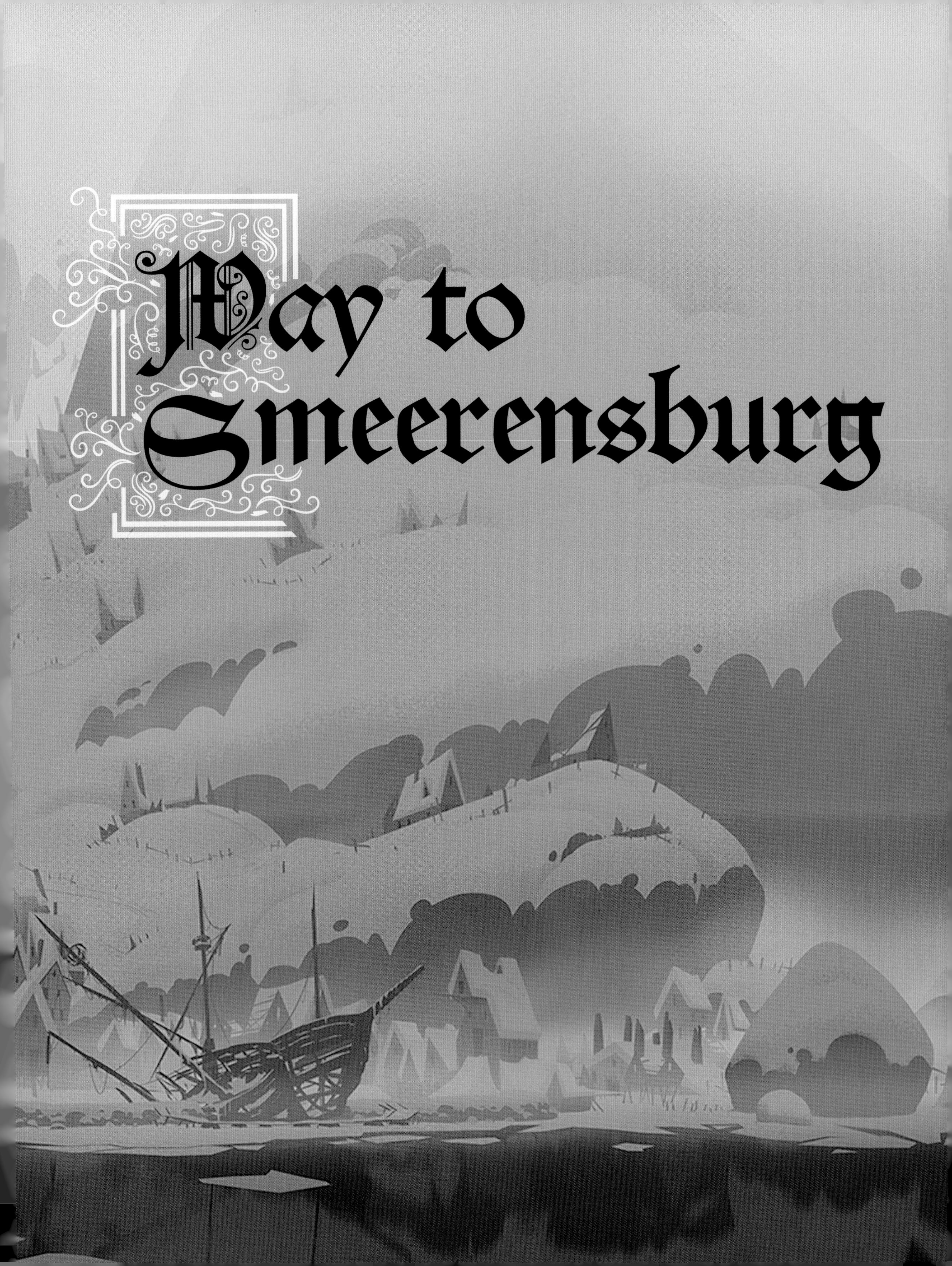

Jesper's Journey

FROM ISAKSDAL TO SMEERENSBURG

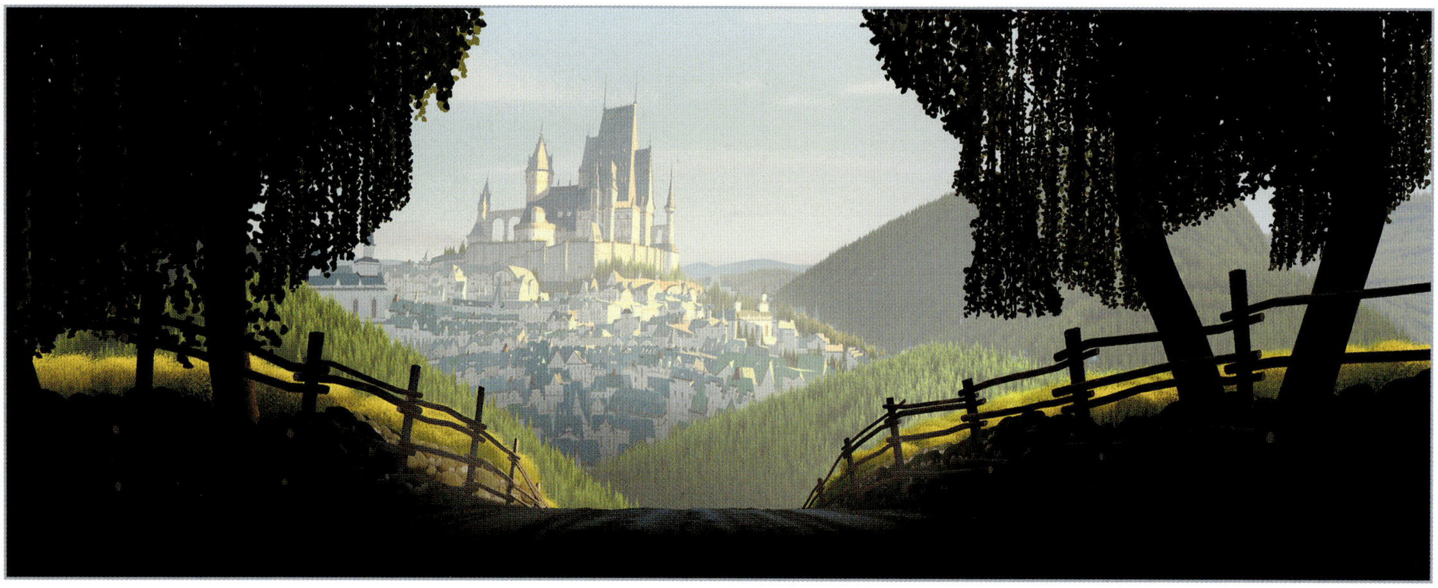

PREVIOUS SPREAD: Concept art by Szymon Biernacki.

THIS PAGE: (TOP) Final background by Henrik Evensen; (BOTTOM) Concept art by Marcin Jakubowski.

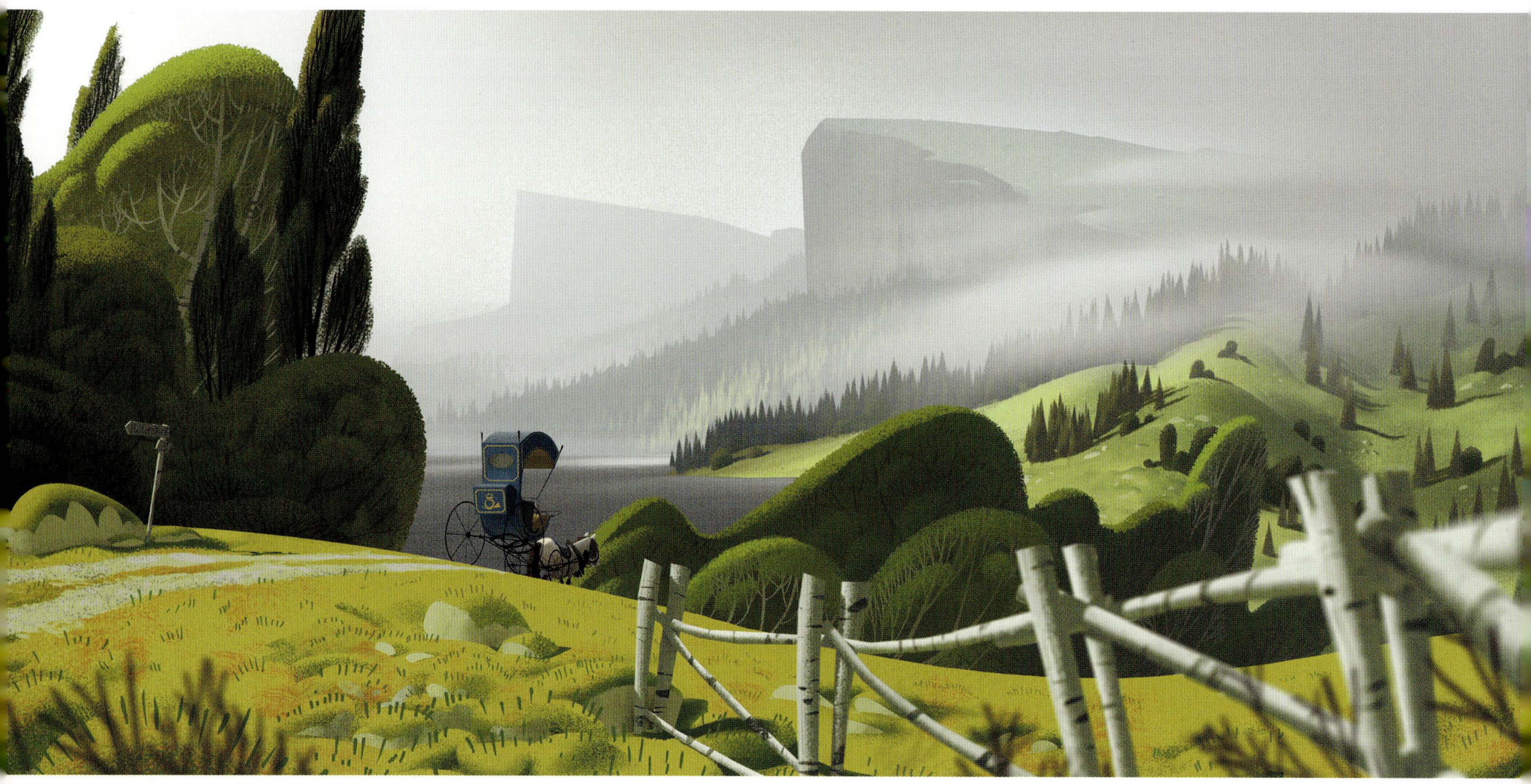

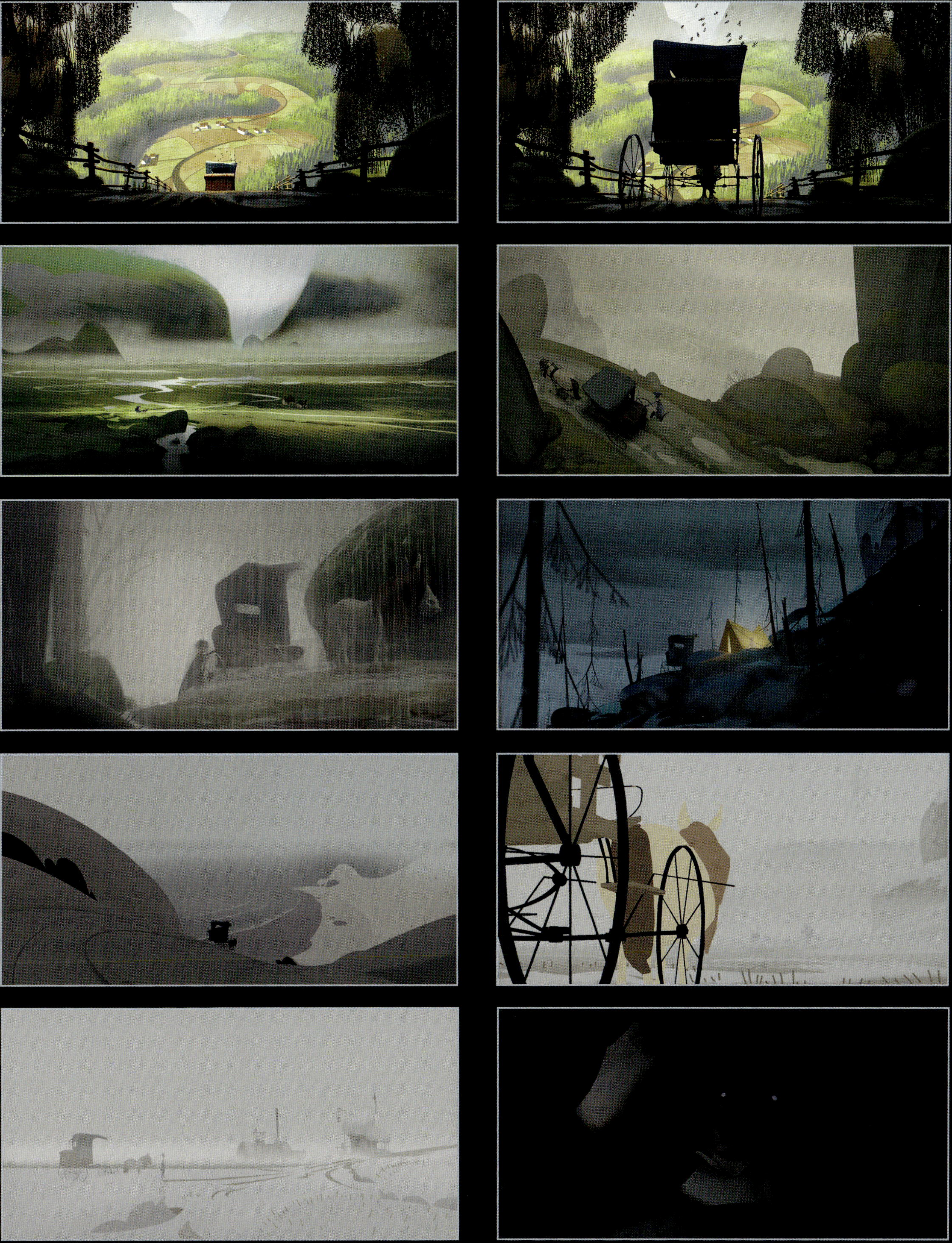

THIS PAGE: Color keys by Daniel Merchán Ruiz and Samuel Smith.

NEXT SPREAD: Concept art by Pascal Campion.

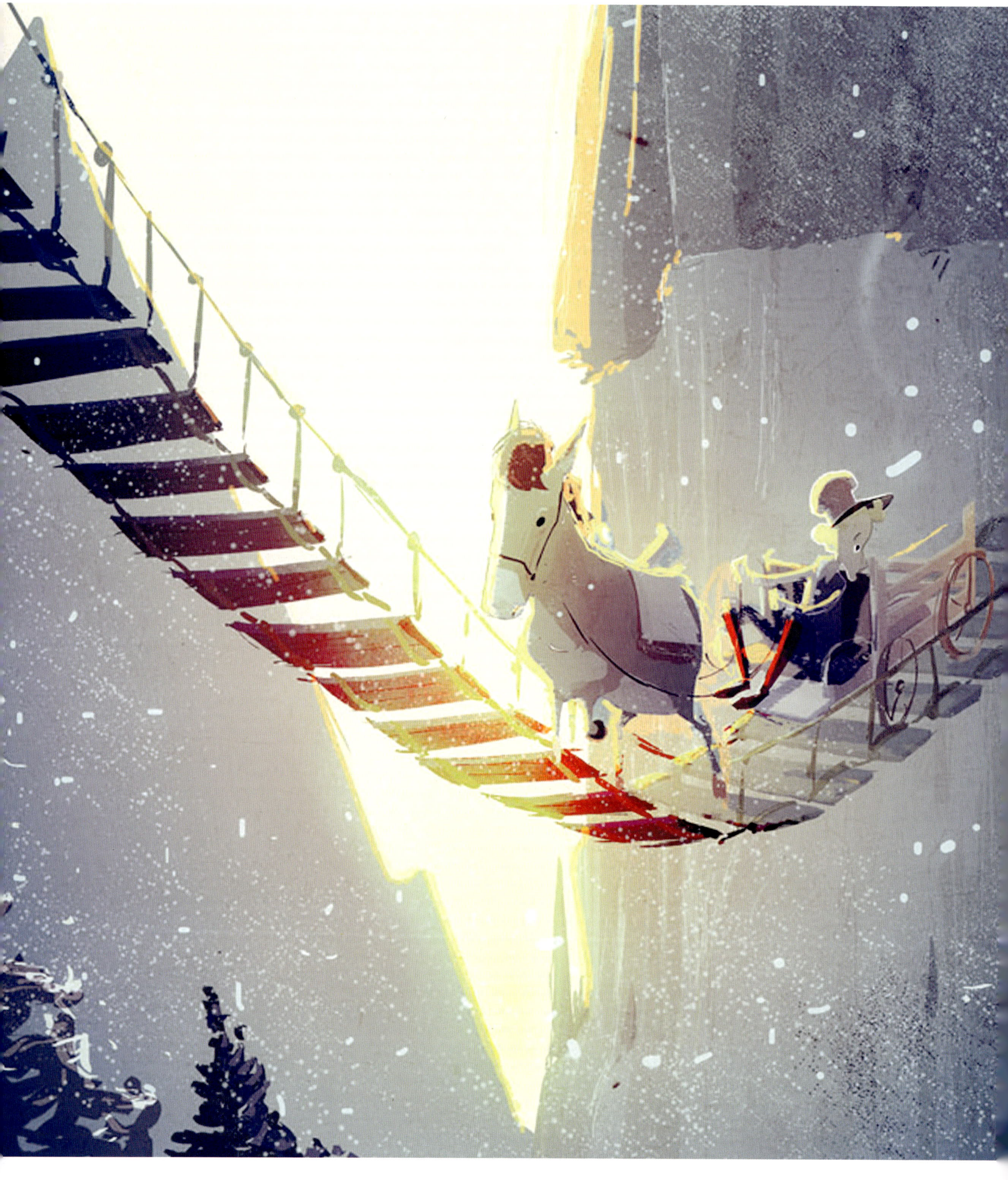

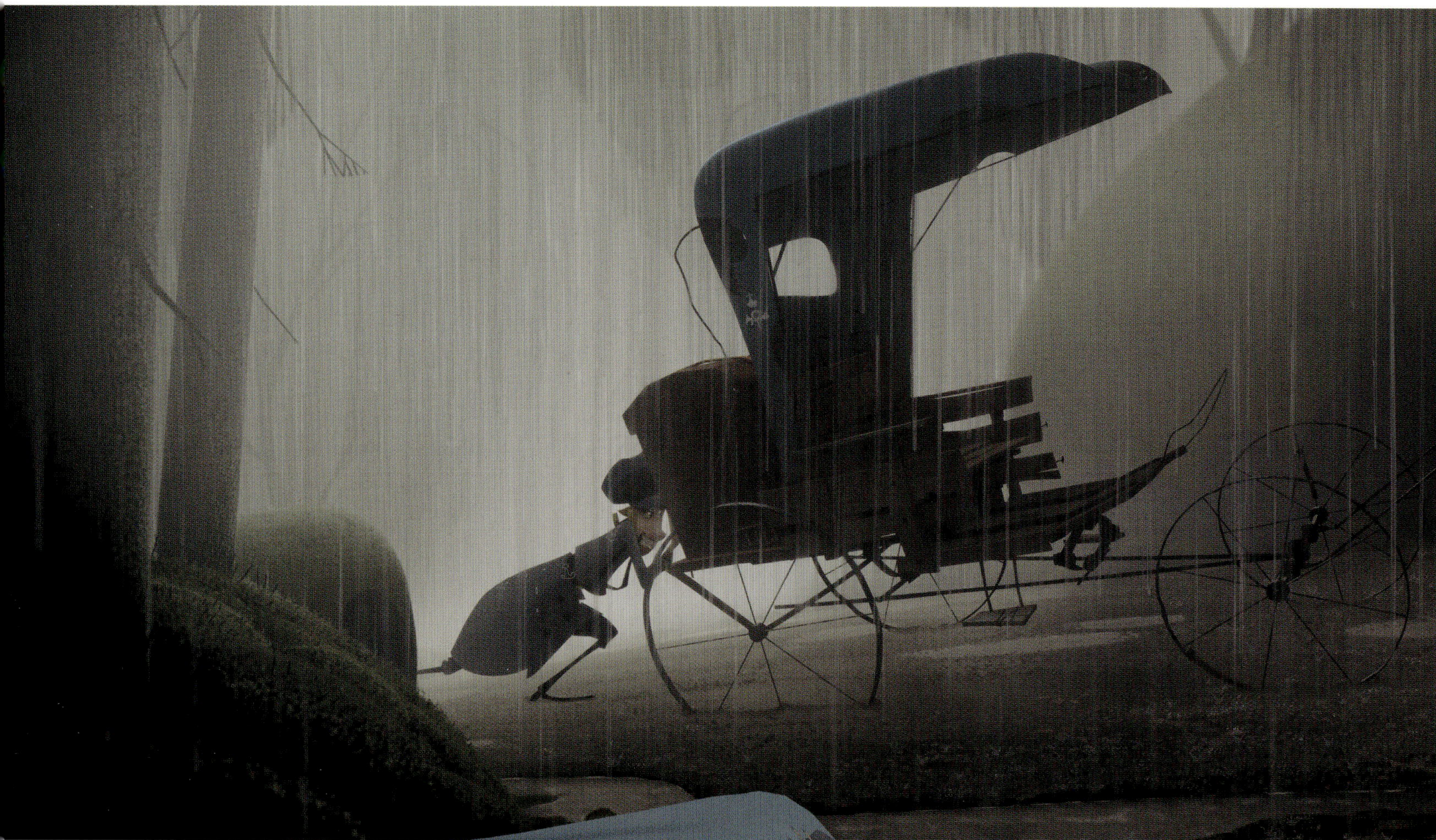

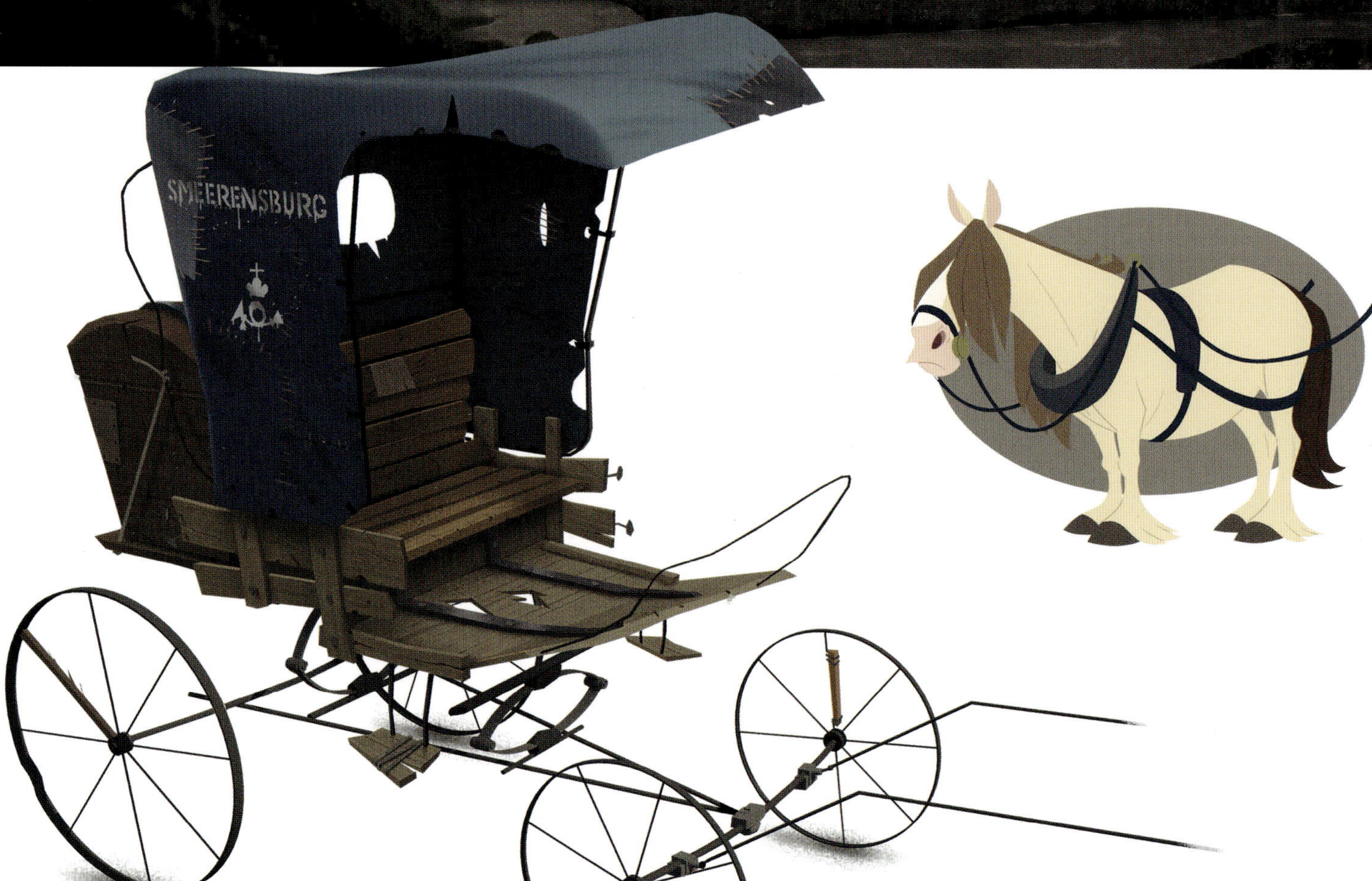

THIS PAGE: Jesper's cart designs by Krzysztof Roslan.

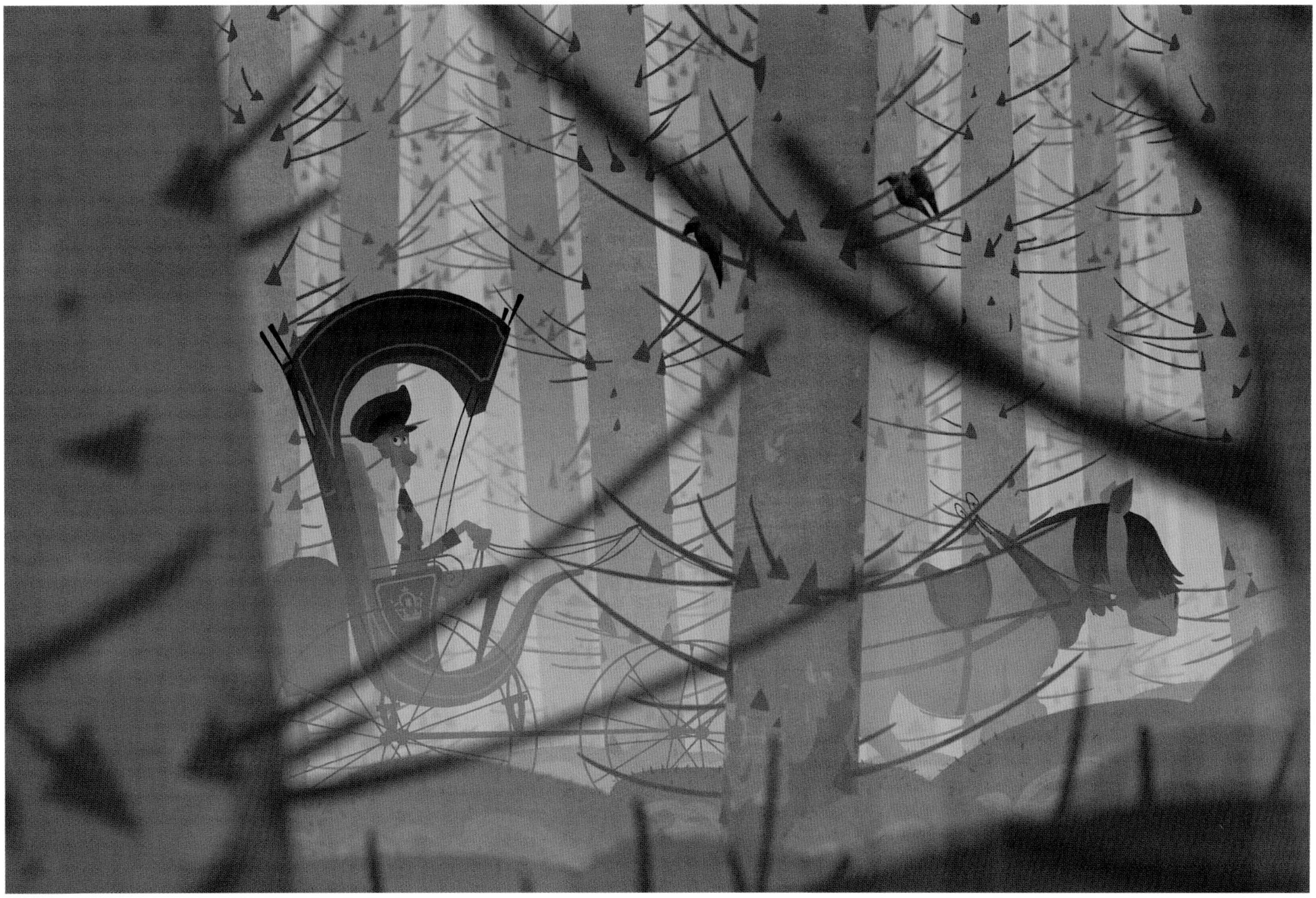

THIS SPREAD: (TOP RIGHT) Concept art by Szymon Biernacki; (BOTTOM) Jesper's cart designs by Krzysztof Roslan.

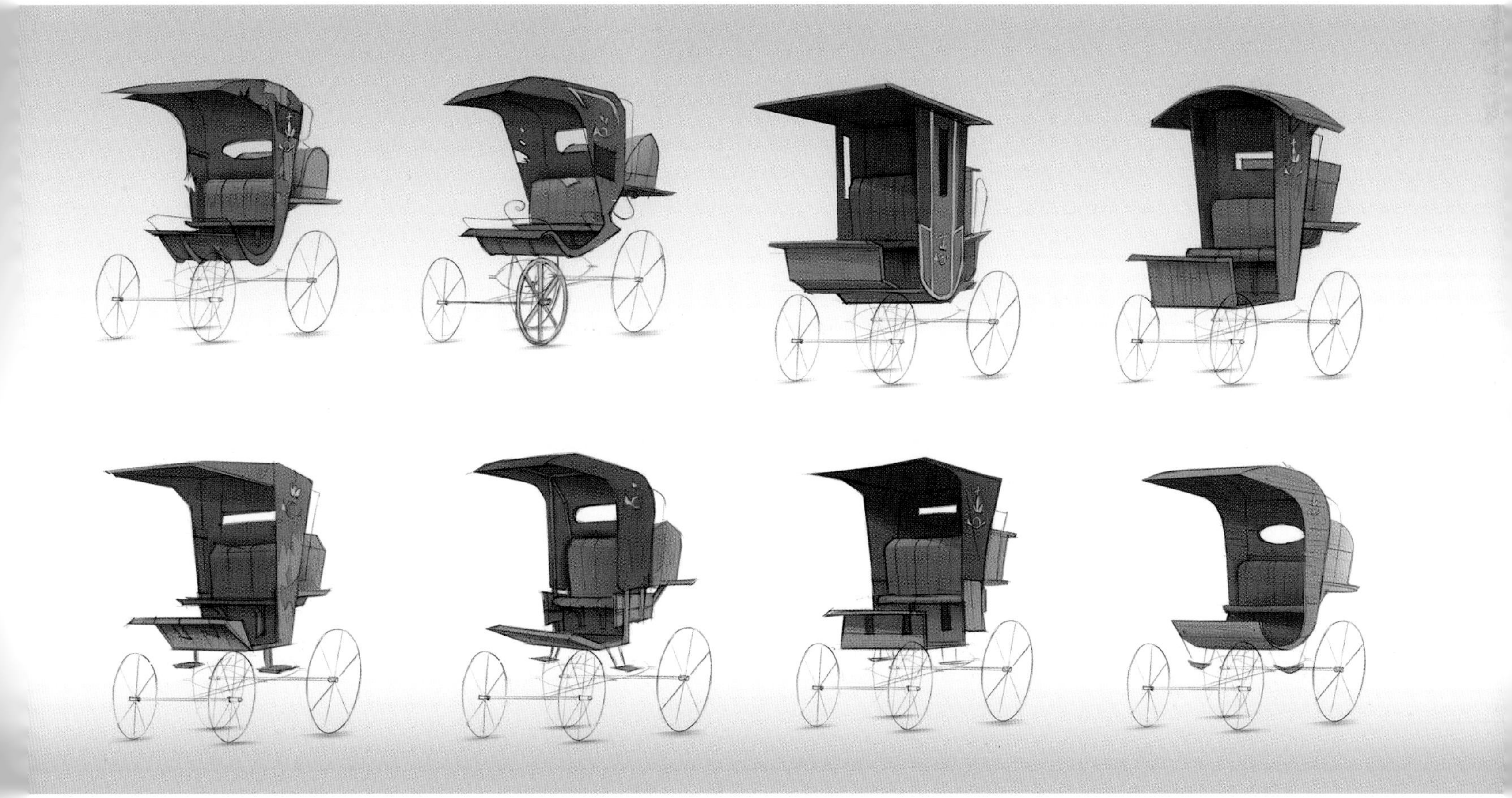

Mogens

THE FERRYMAN

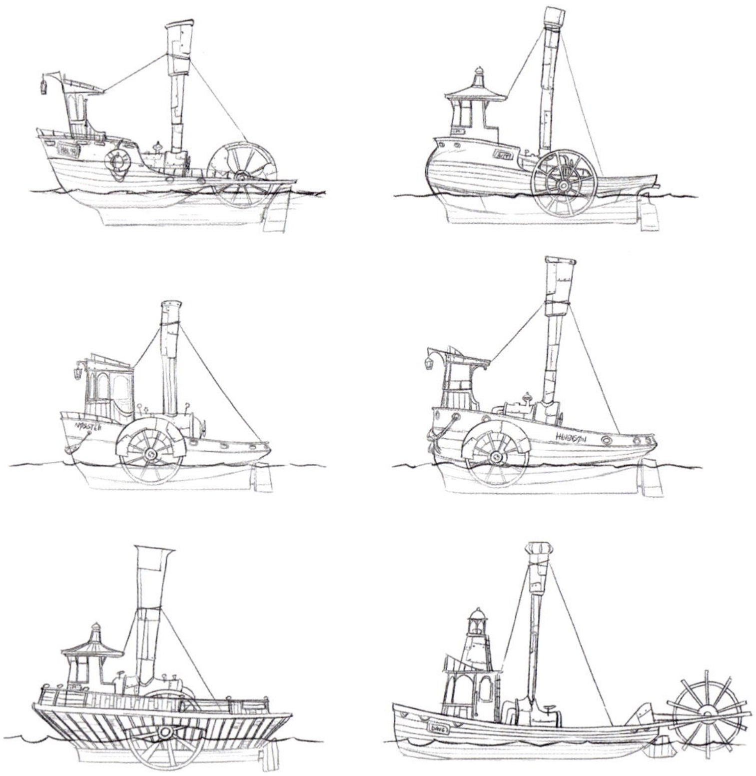

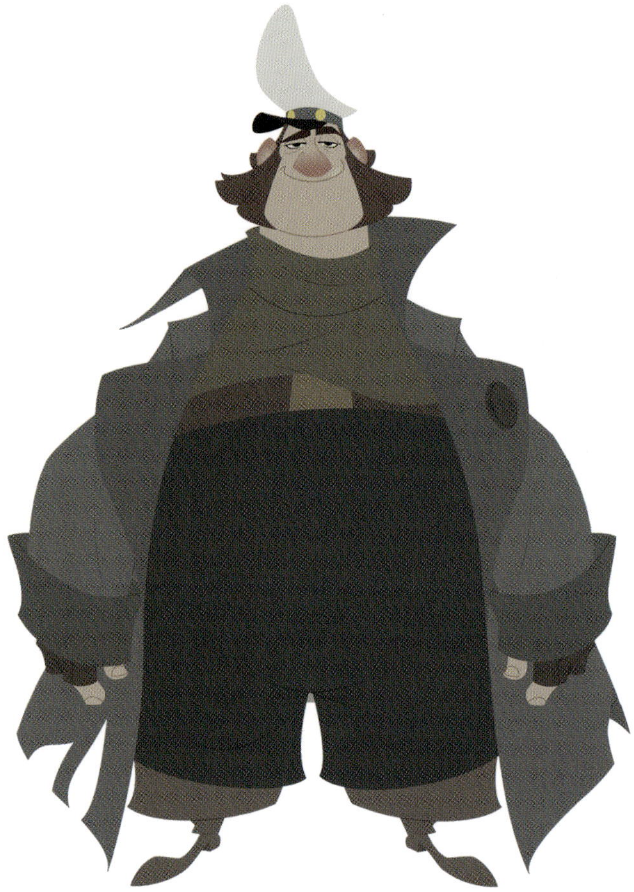

ABOVE: Ferry studies by Meryl Franck.

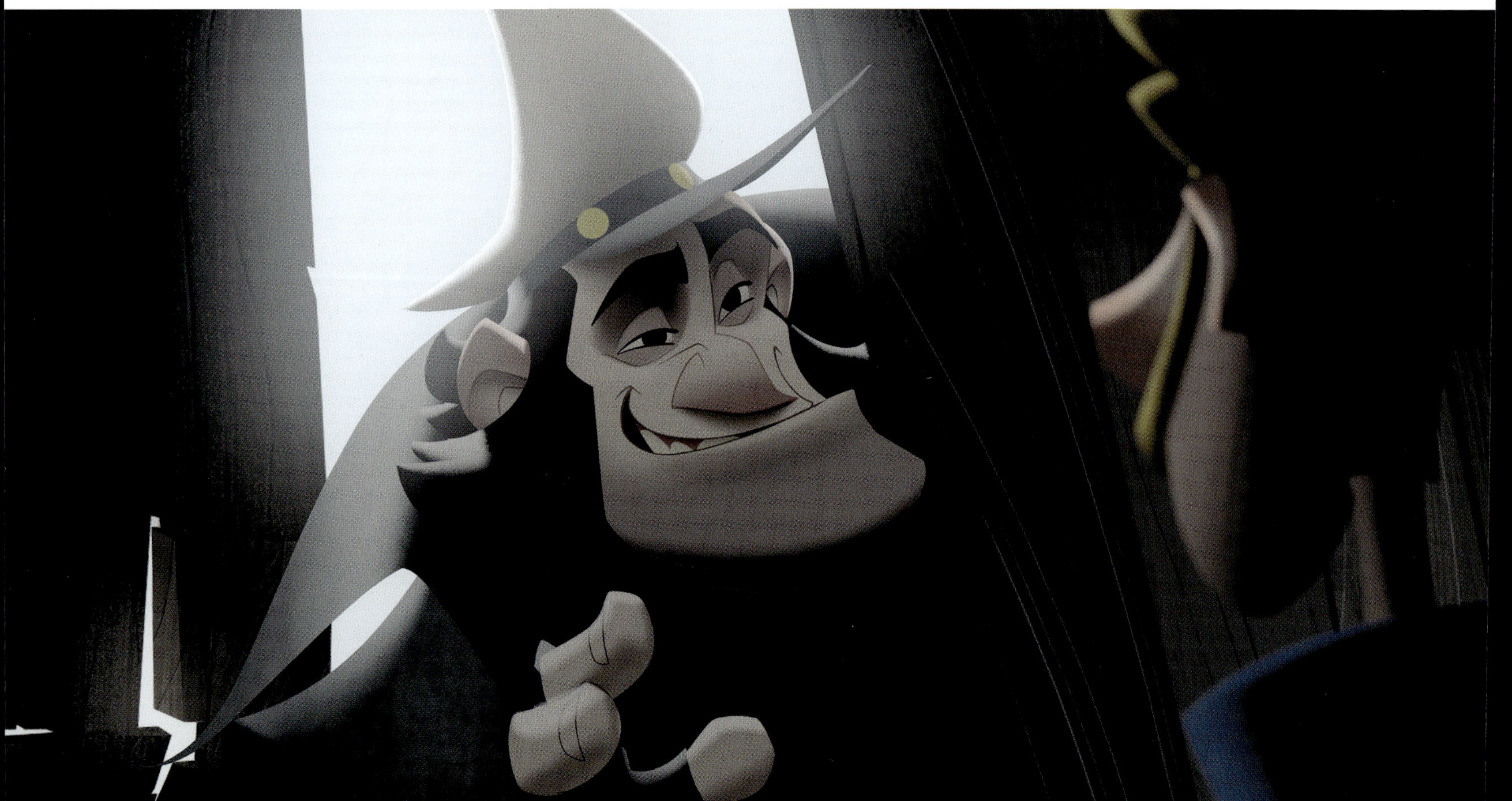

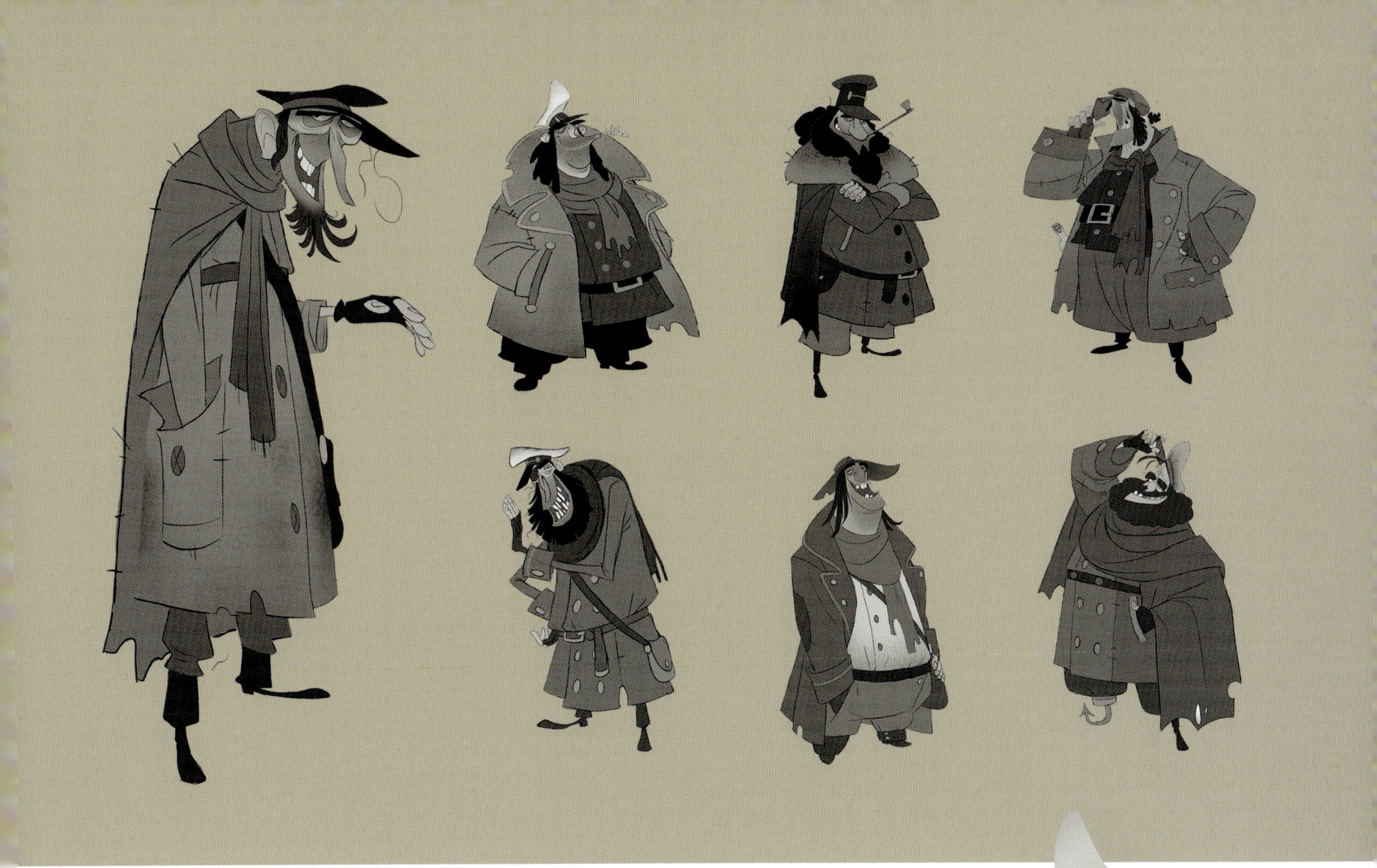

An intriguing character who ferries our hero from the mainland to Smeerensburg and back, Mogens also acts as his foil. As lead animator Matt Williames points out, he is a sarcastic, careless man who uses his humor to keep people at a distance. "We don't know where he came from or where he's going," says Williames, whose many animation credits include *Mary Poppins Returns*, *The Princess and the Frog*, and *Curious George*. "He's always after the next pleasurable thing, and we really don't know why he loves to see others fail, perhaps because his dreams were not realized and he is embittered."

Just like Jesper, Mogens finds himself changed by the final scenes of the movie. He is caught by surprise when he feels a certain kinship towards the postmaster, and he uses his typical sarcasm to guilt trip Jesper's father into letting his son stay.

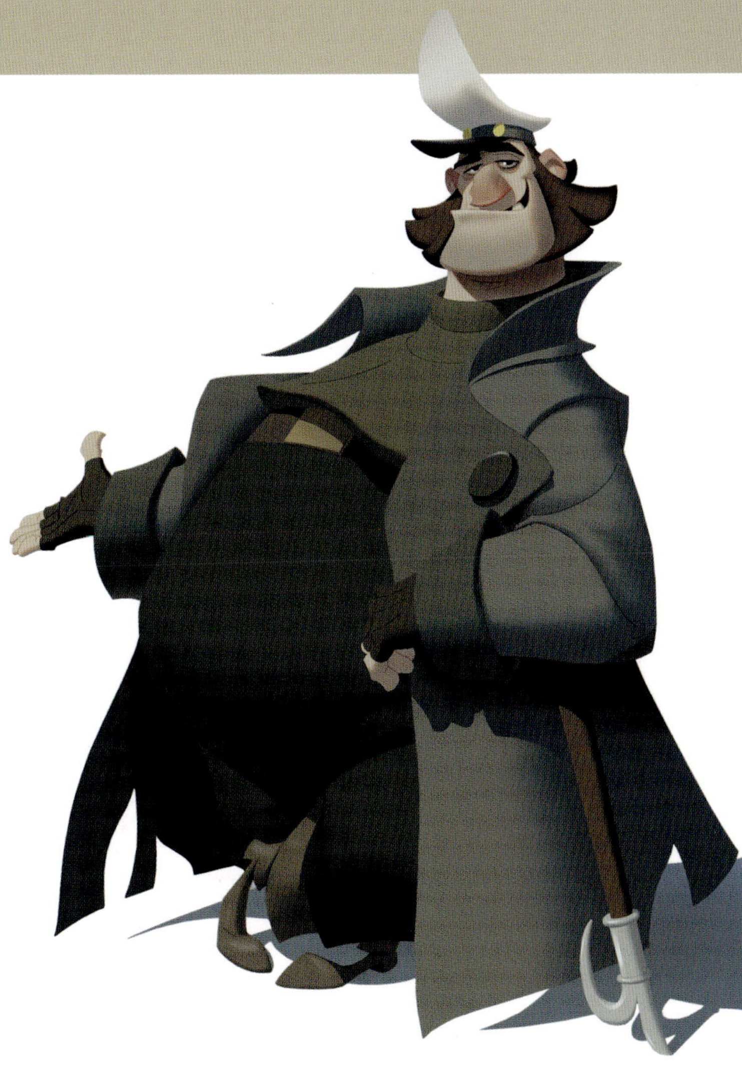

TOP: Character studies by Torsten Schrank.

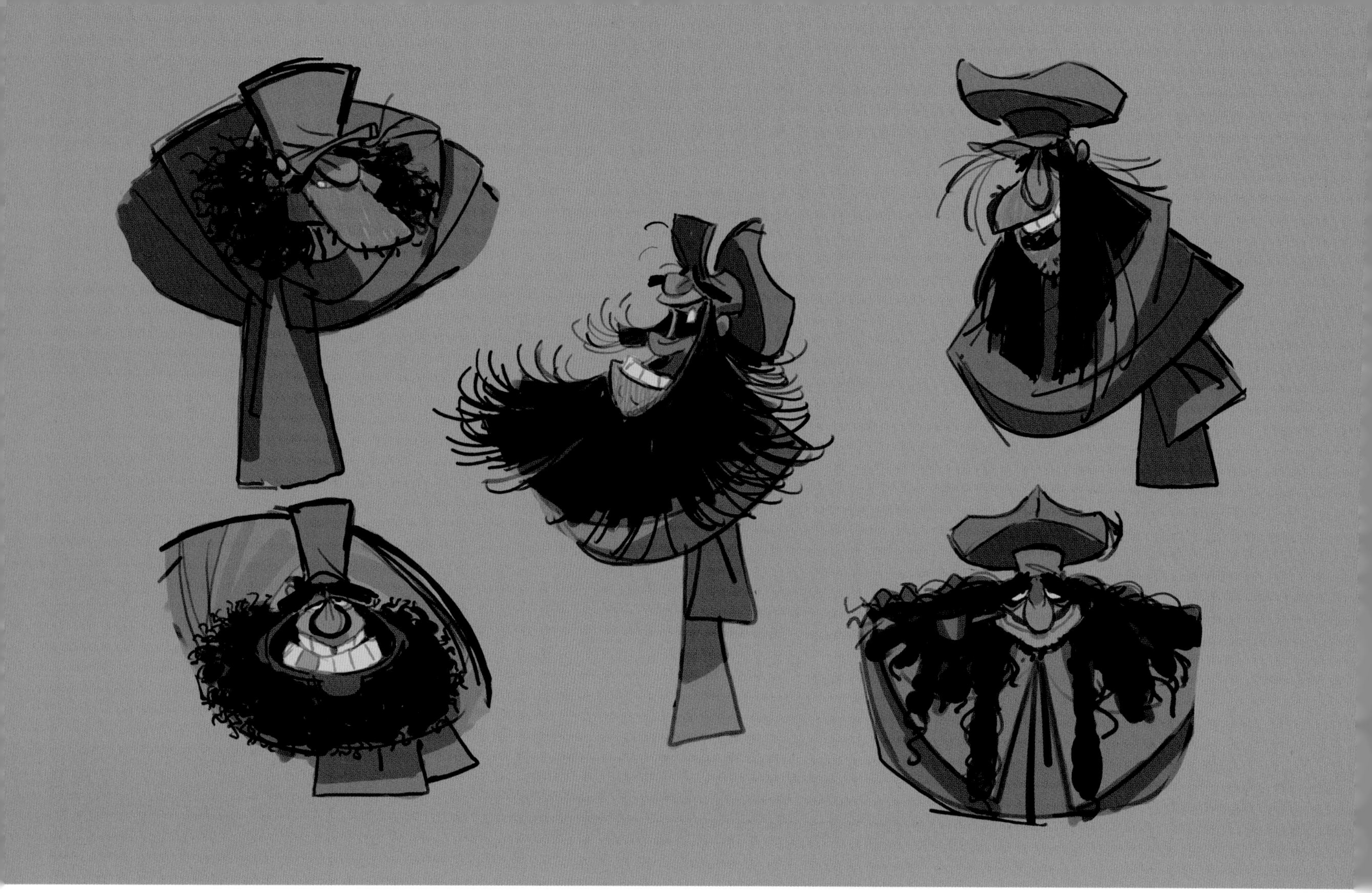

THIS PAGE: (TOP) Early concepts by Daniel Fernandez; (BOTTOM) Ferry design by Marcin Jakubowski.

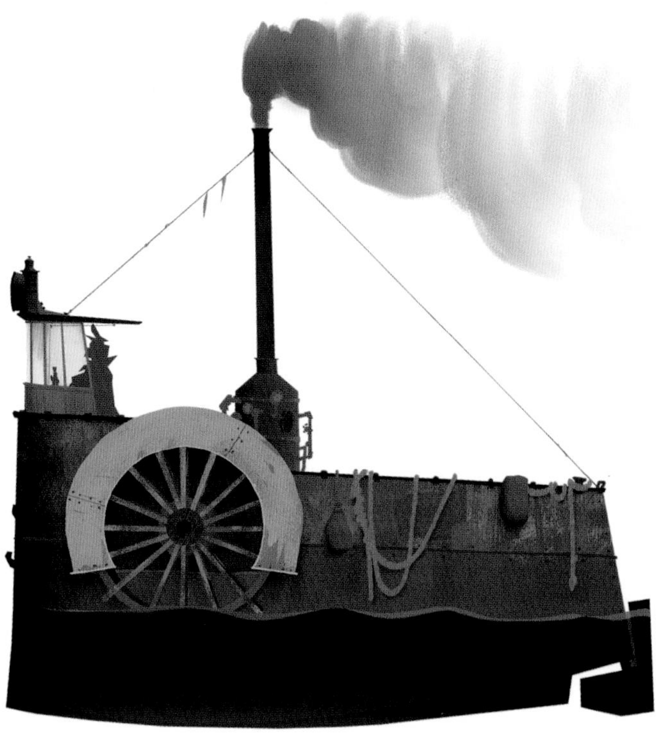

According to Williames, the design of the character was also influenced by his key character traits. "We thought of him as a crooked character, and that's why we often see him leaning or bent over," the animator explains. "He is insincere, so he often has one eye closed. When he moves, he often leads with his groin. That's something I designed for the character to suggest that he lives for the pleasures of life. He has one snaggletooth, and you can tell he doesn't take care of himself. There are two tufts of semi-beard on his face. He wears an old seafaring sweater and is missing a button on his overcoat."

Although actor Norm Macdonald was cast after the character had been designed, Williames says he fit the visuals perfectly. "Macdonald can order a menu, and it will still sound funny," he mentions. "The voice needed to have a sarcastic edge to it. The lines would be funny because of his personality. Yet something happened to Mogens along the way that hardened his heart. We also wanted to show that Jesper could have become just like Mogens if he hadn't met Klaus. By the end of the movie, Mogens also realizes that what he wanted was pleasure, but what he needs is to care about somebody."

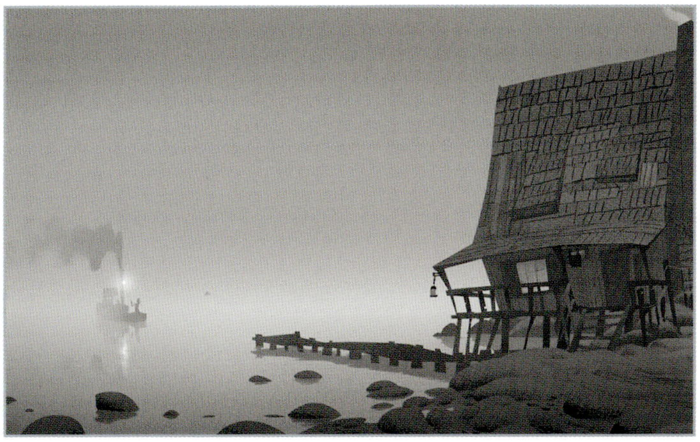

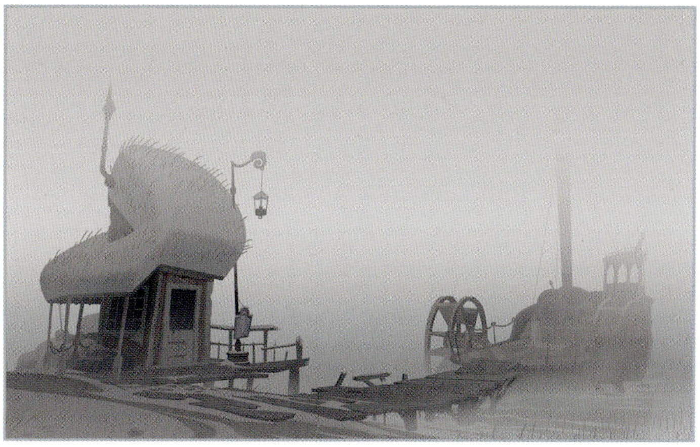

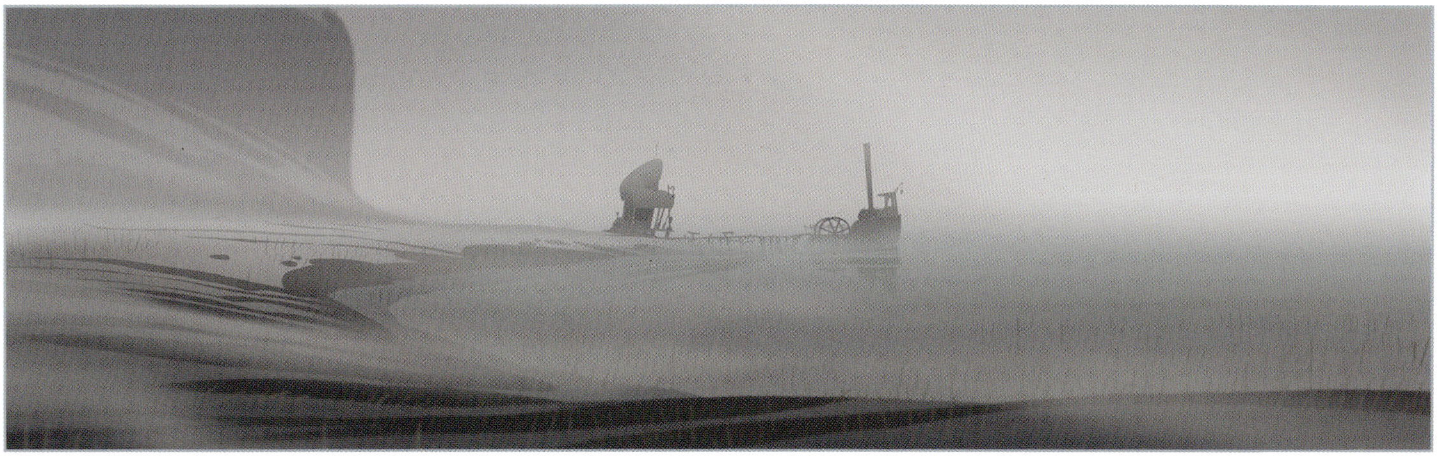

THIS PAGE: (TOP) Location studies by Meryl Franck and Marcin Jakubowski; (BOTTOM) Early concepts by Daniel Fernandez.

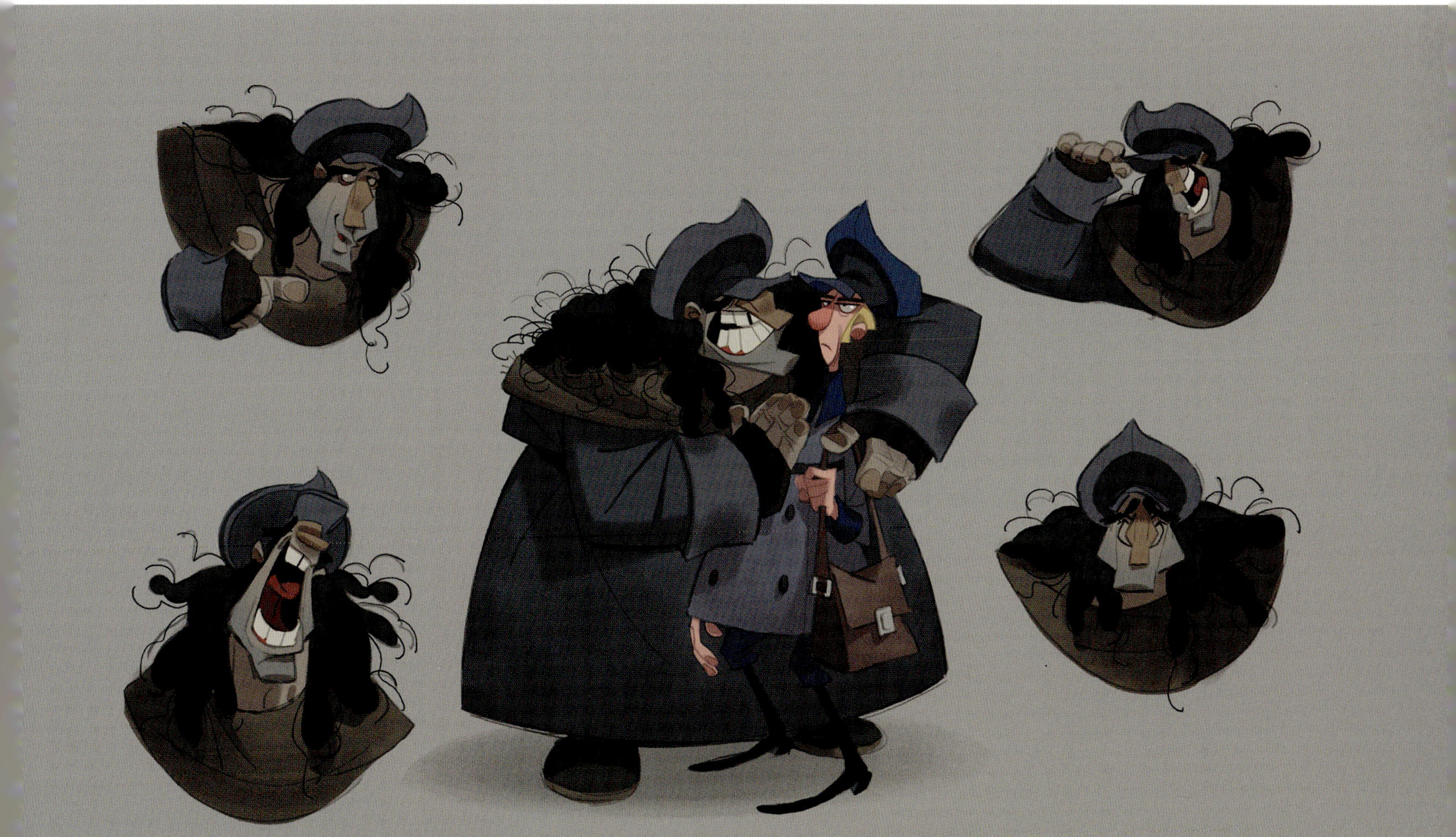

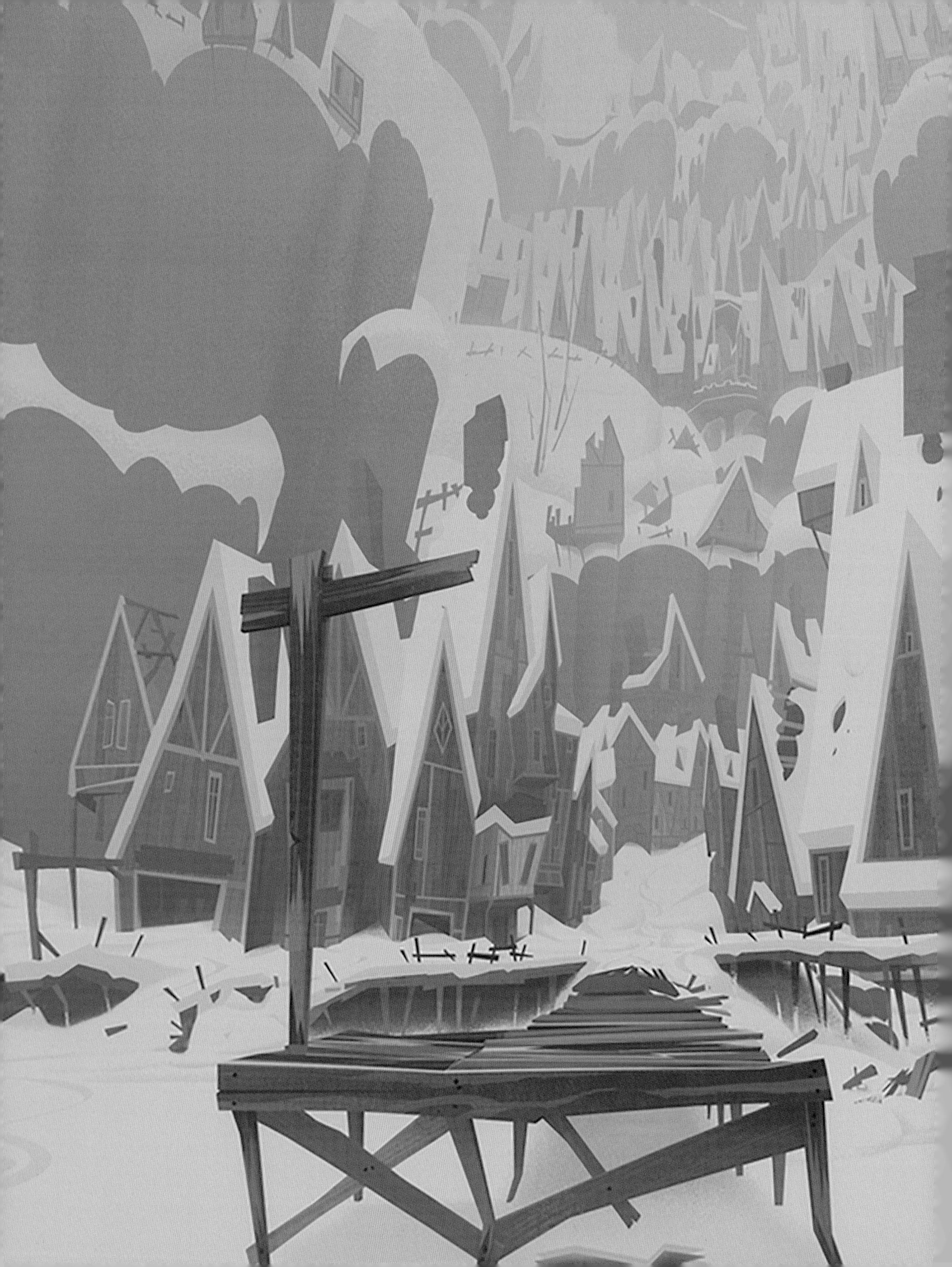

A Town Divided

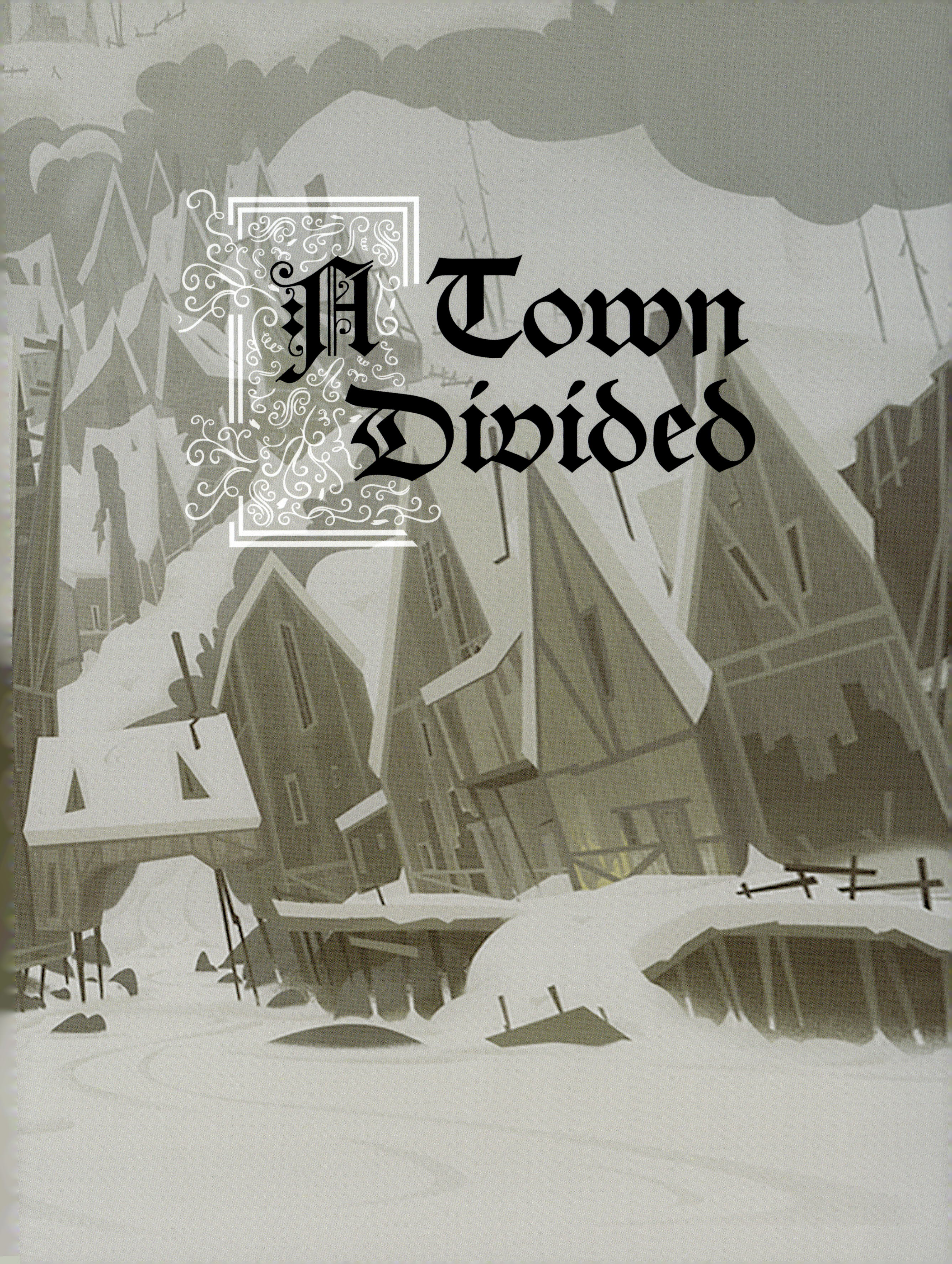

Smeerensburg

IN THE BEGINNING

The remote, snow-covered town of Smeerensburg has to be one of the most memorable locations for an animated movie in recent years. Located somewhere at the edge of Scandinavia, this is where Jesper's father sends him to teach him a lesson and prepare him for the real world.

Pablos was adamant that the movie's location be deeply rooted in the real world. So he went online and began intensive research on the northernmost human settlements in history. "I always try to find a semblance of reality behind the locations," he explains. "Our movie is a fantasy, but we want to be truthful to the origins of our story. I wanted a place that no longer existed, and I found a whaling post in Northern Scandinavia, which was once a prosperous town, but is now a pile of rocks."

PREVIOUS SPREAD: Concept art by Henrik Evensen.

THIS PAGE: Concept art by Marcin Jakubowski.

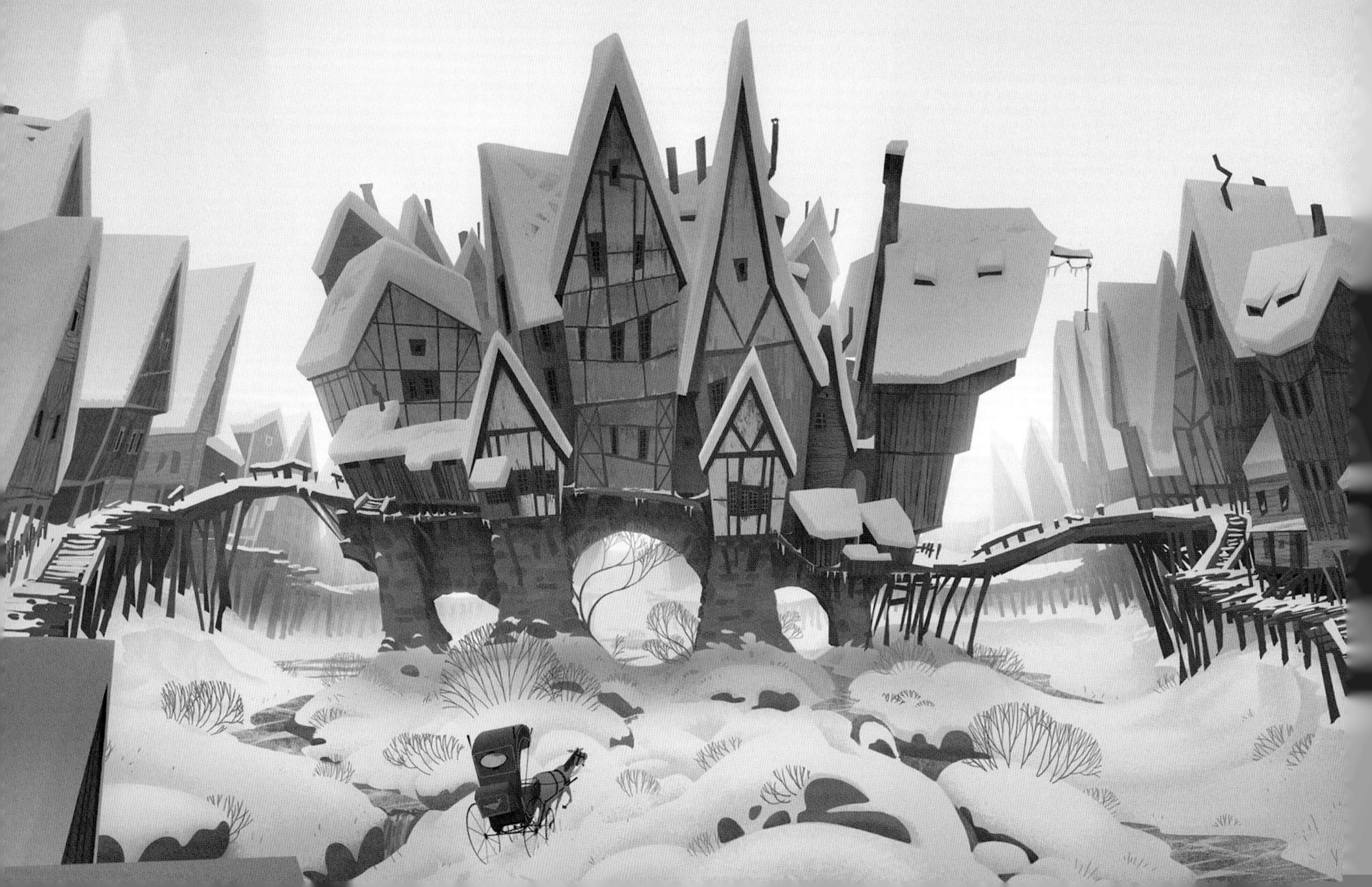

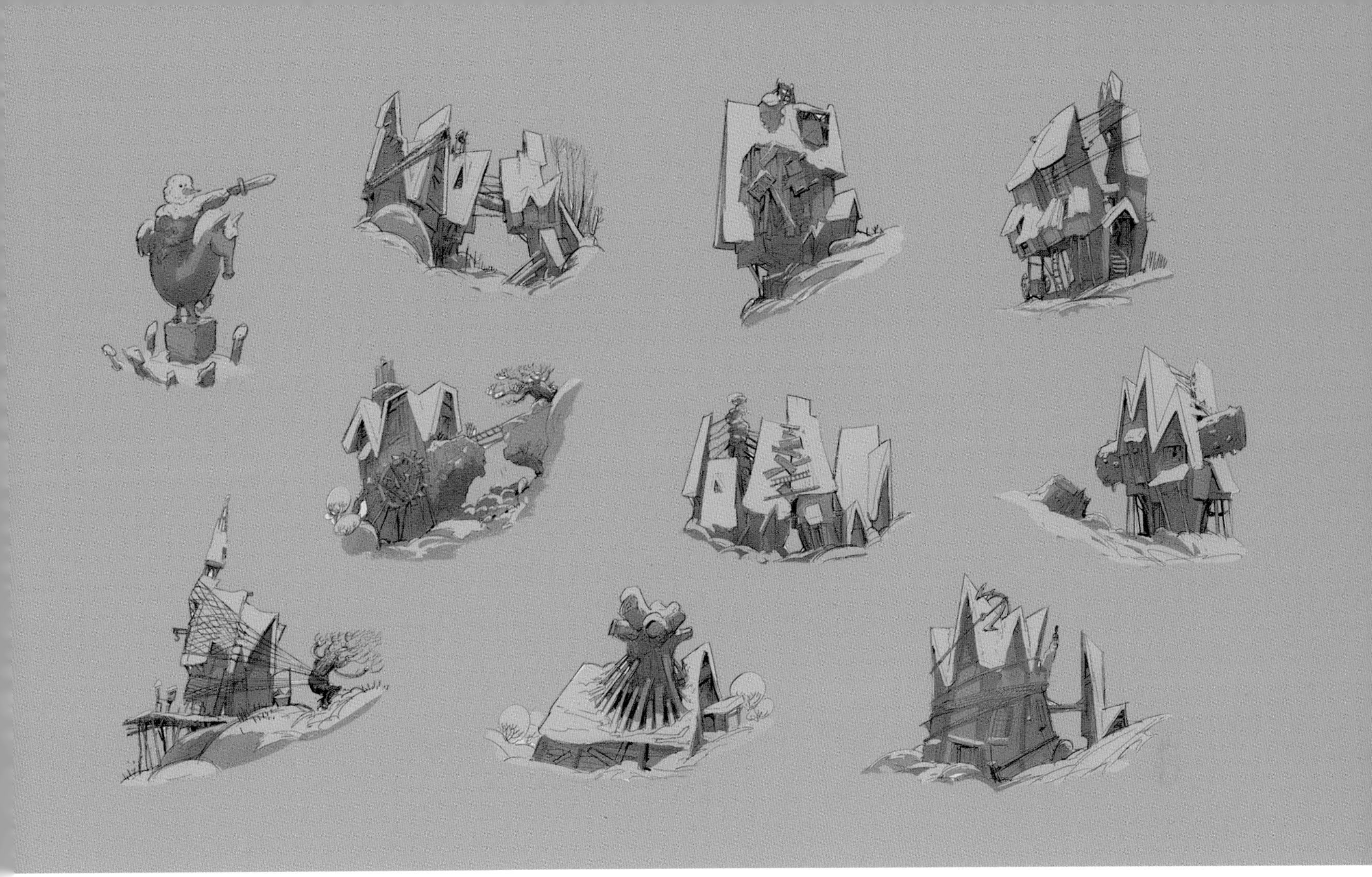

THIS PAGE: Location studies by Tobi Trebeljahr, Thibaut Denise, Henrik Evensen, and Arthus Pilorget.

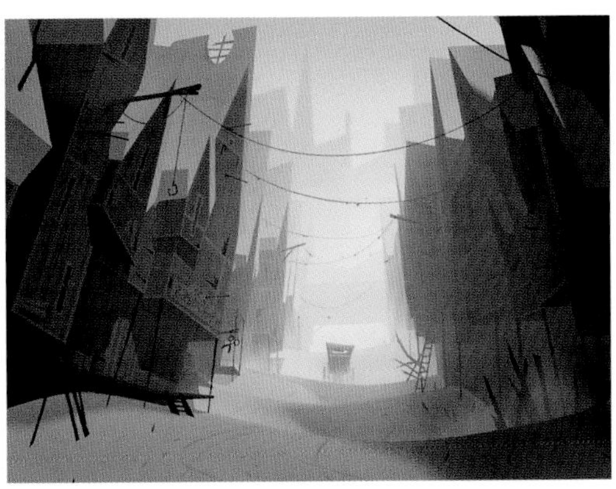

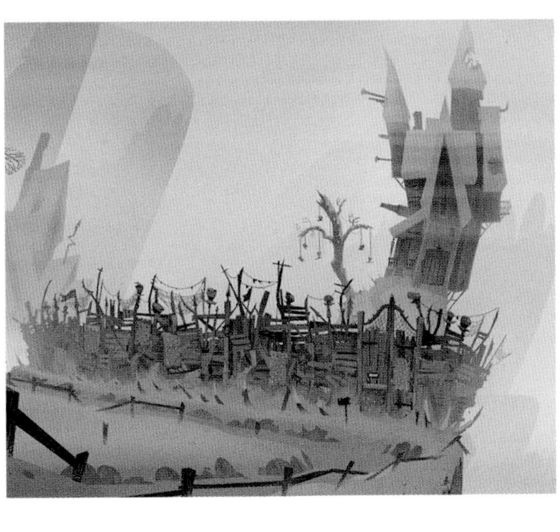

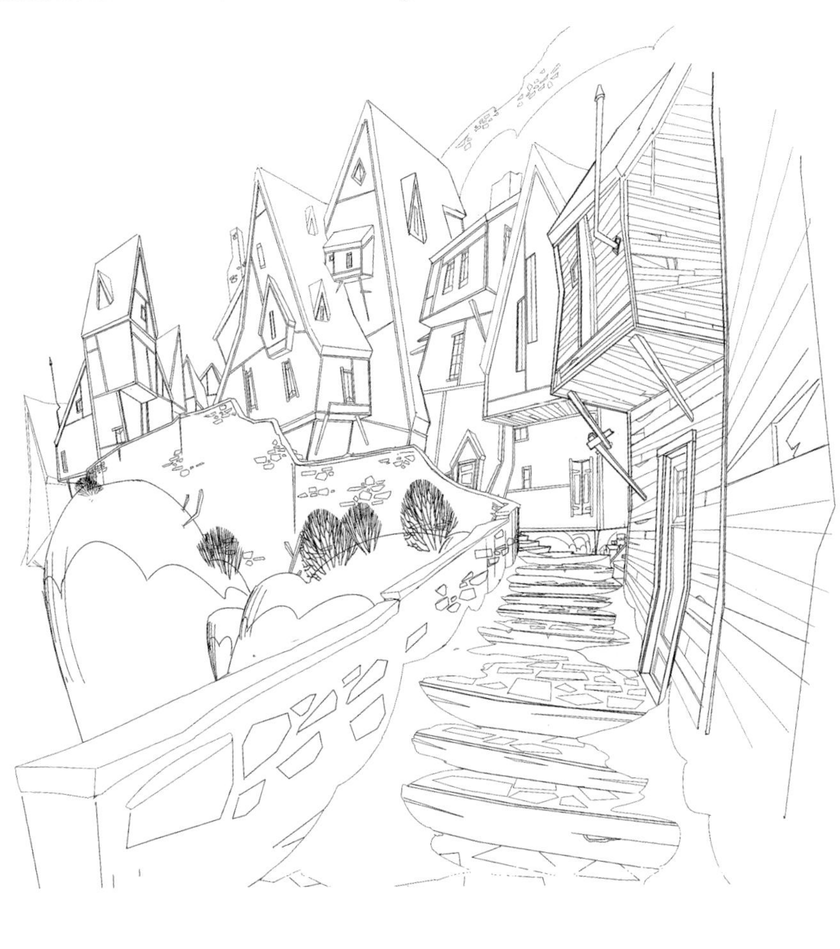

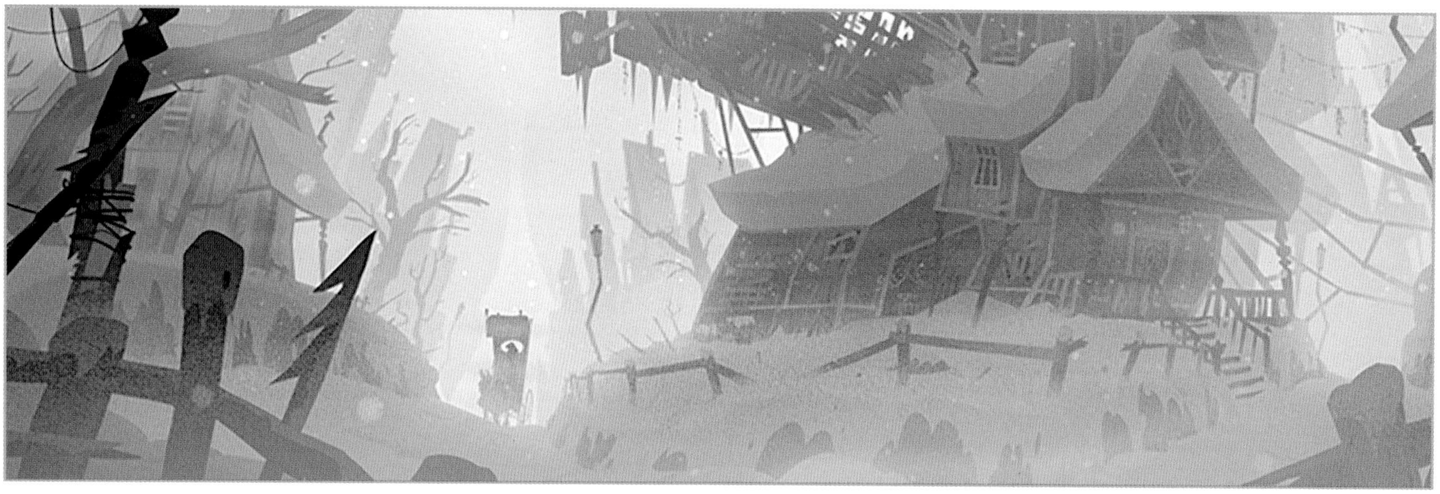

TOP: Artwork by Tobi Trebeljahr.
ABOVE: Artwork by Arthus Pilorget.

BELOW: Artwork by Marcin Jakubowski.

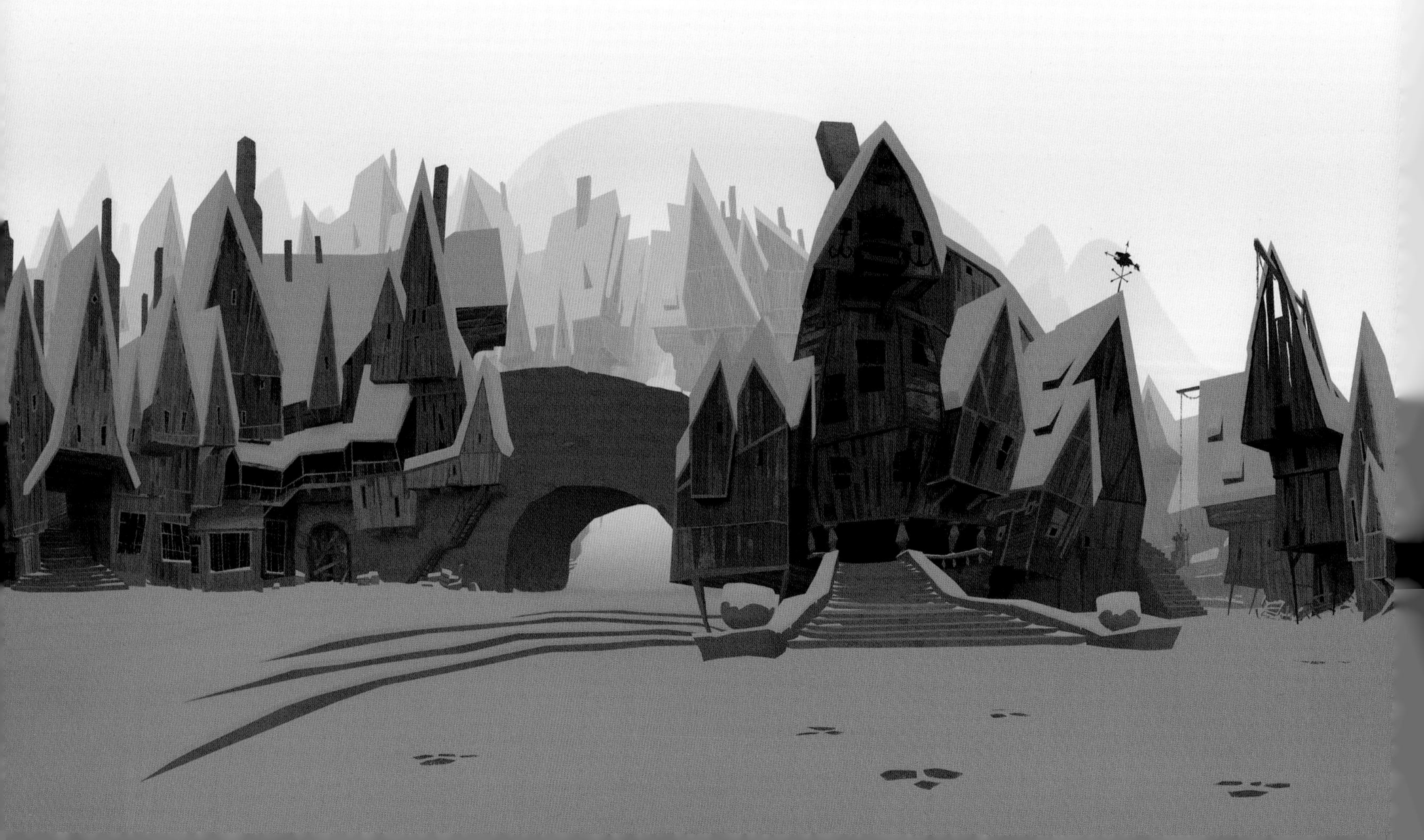

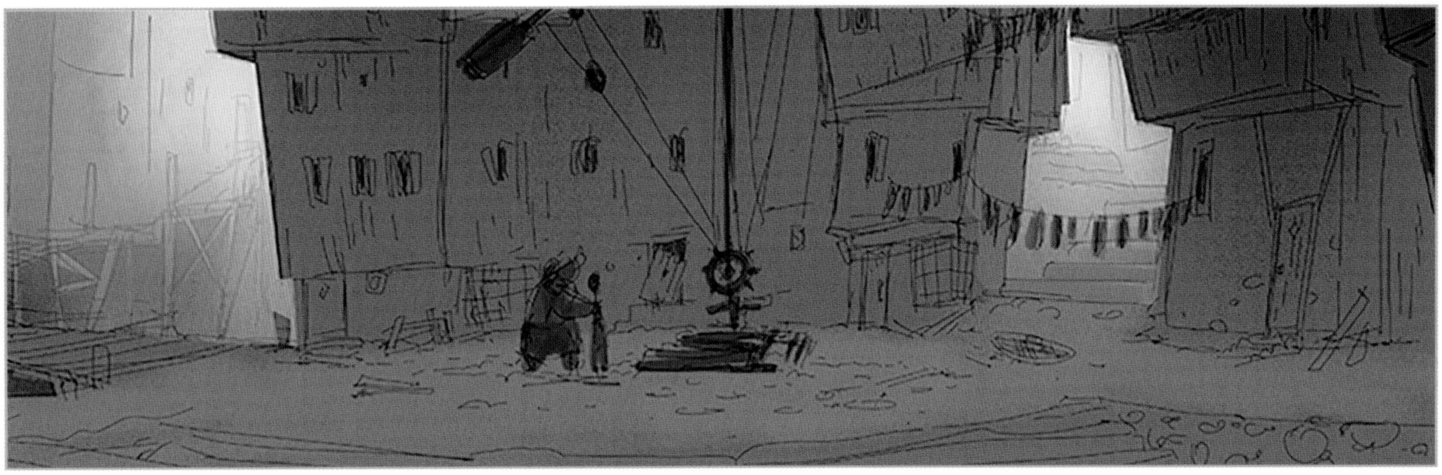

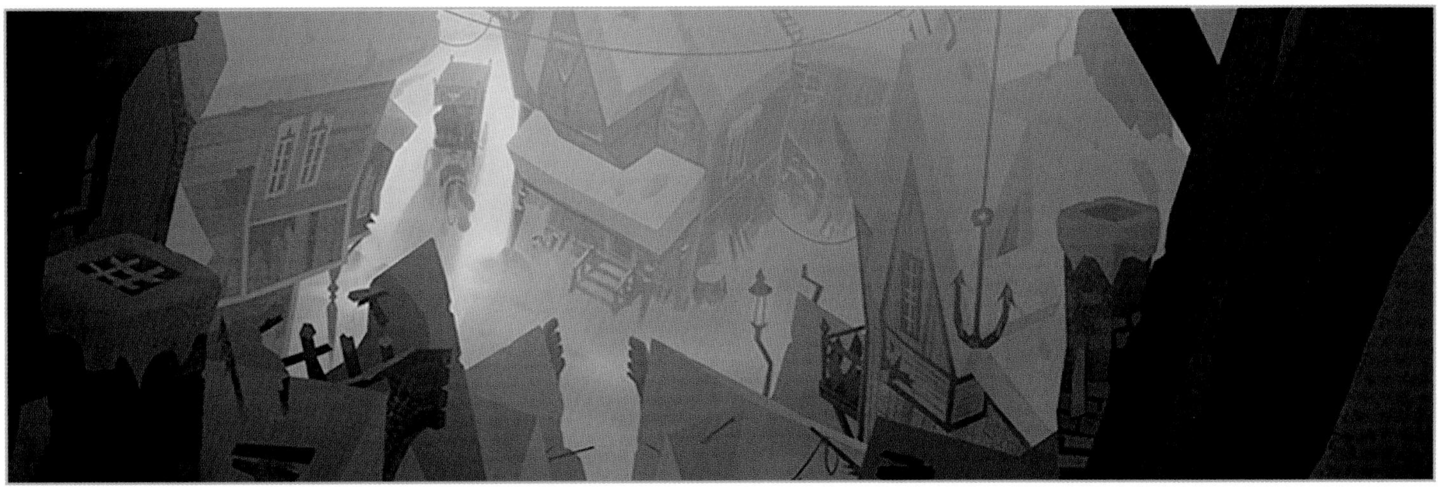

TOP: Artwork by Marcin Jakubowski.
ABOVE: Artwork by Arthus Pilorget.

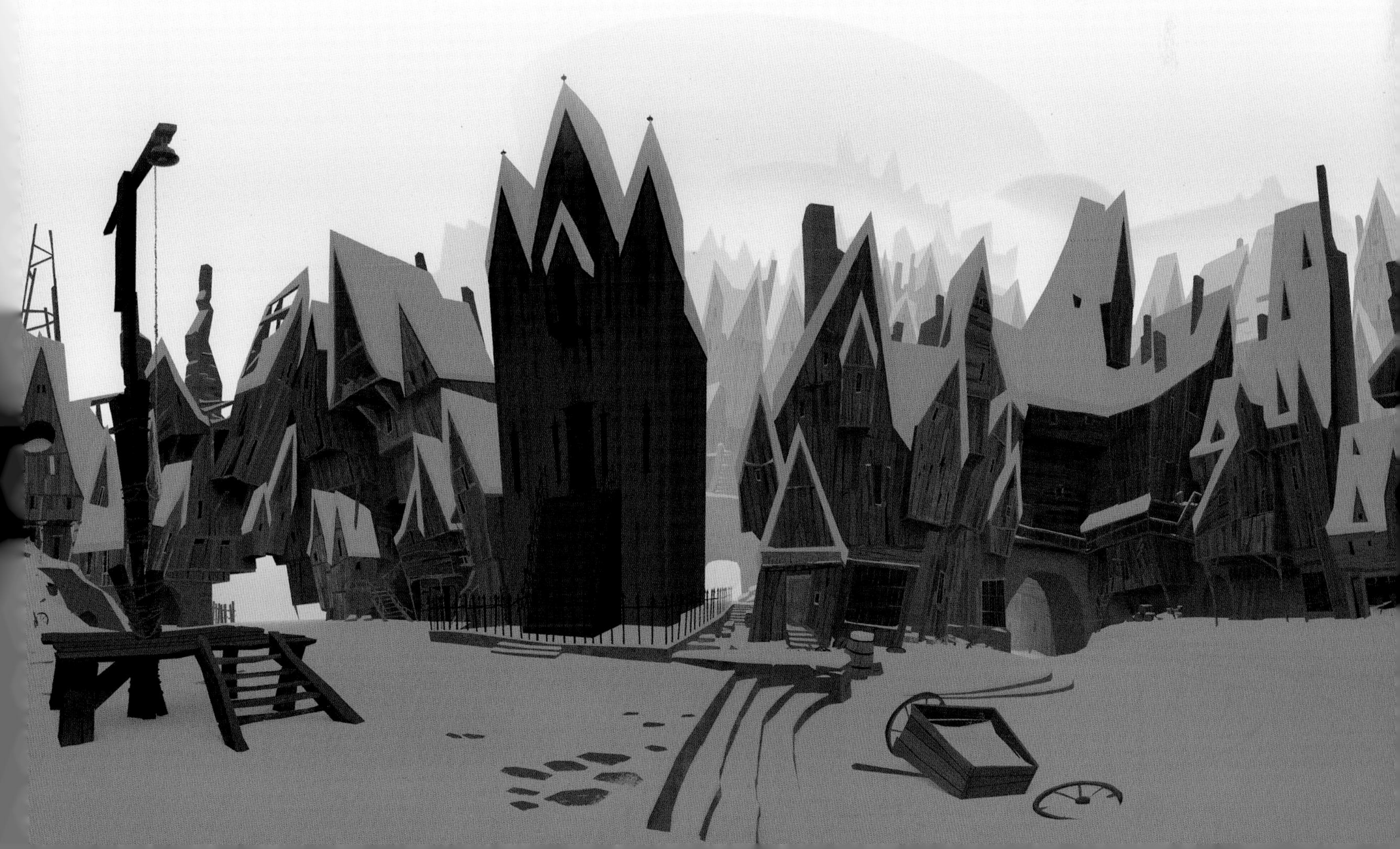

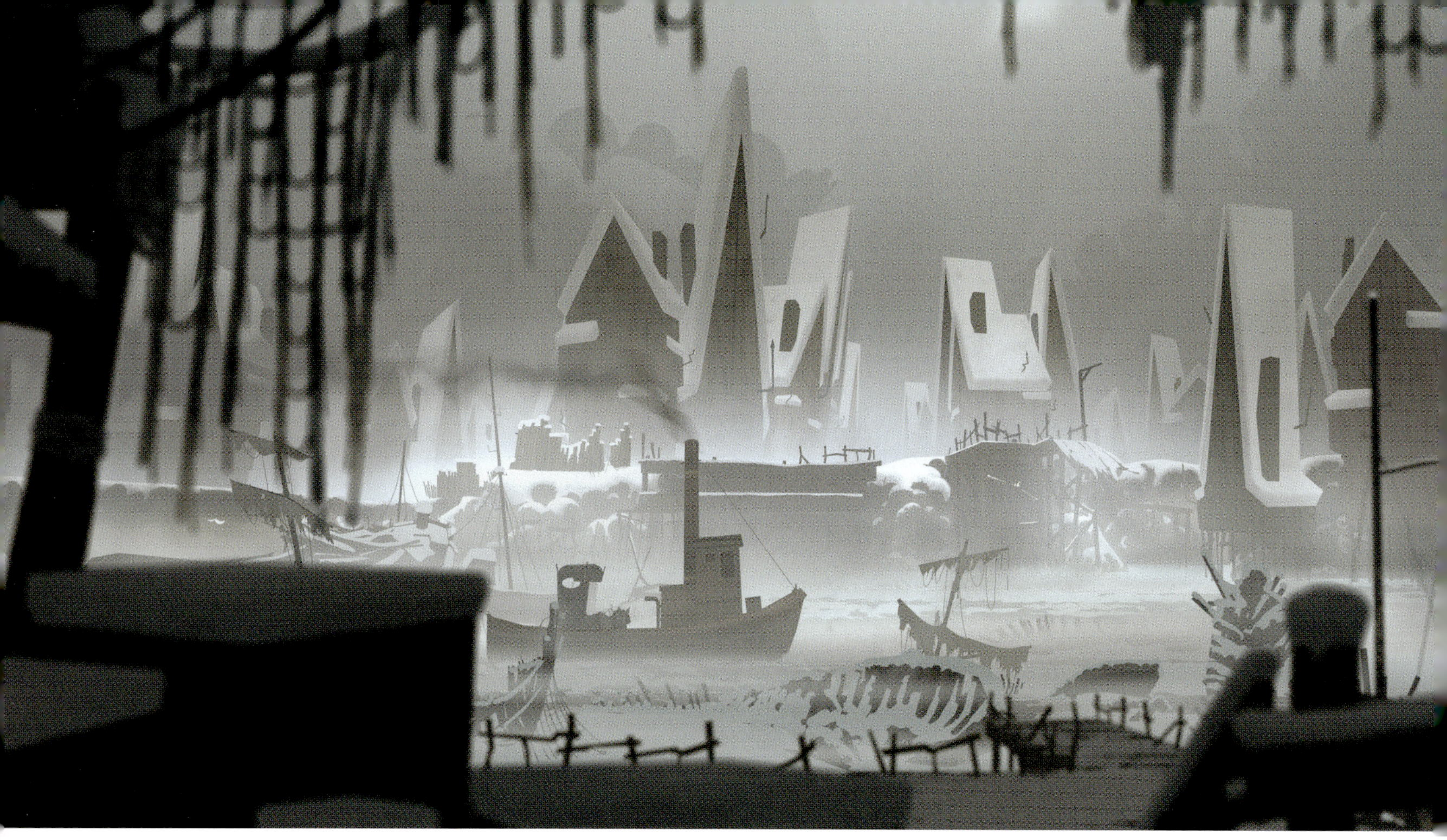

THIS PAGE: Concept art by Henrik Evensen.

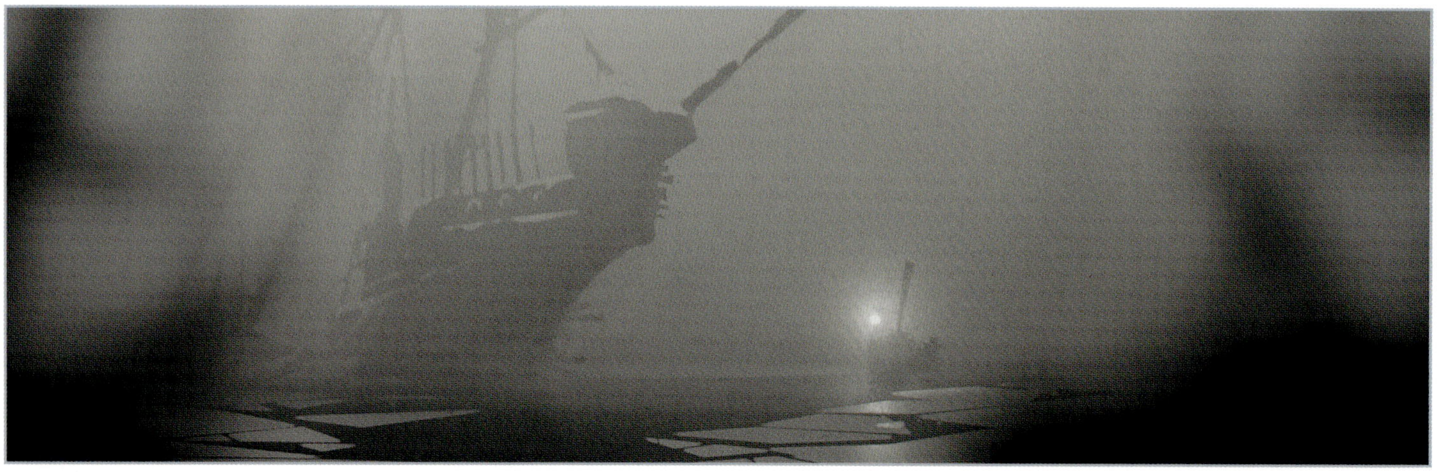

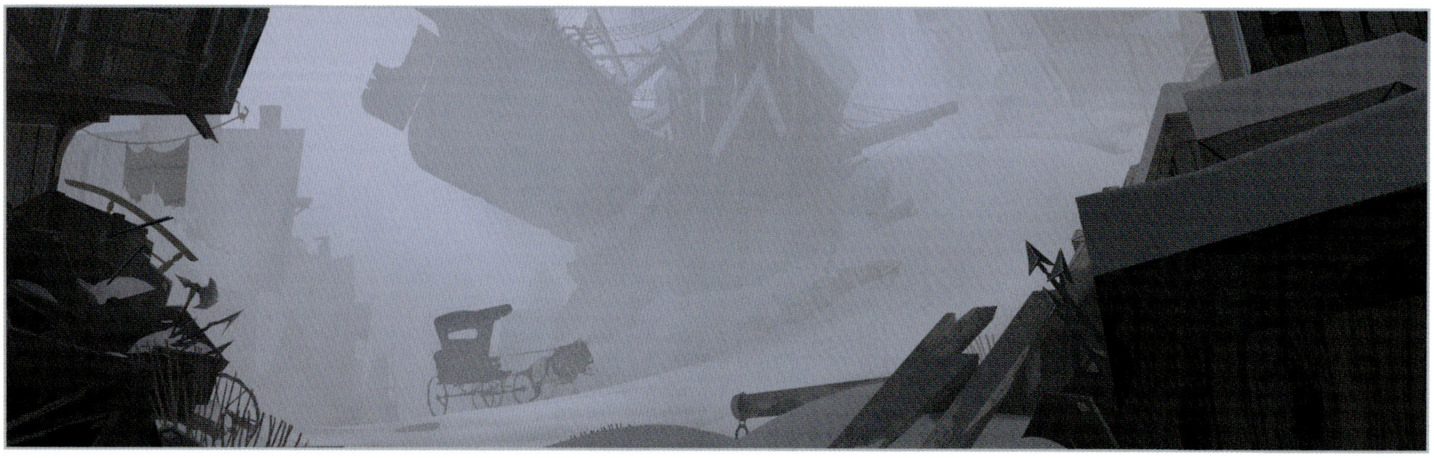

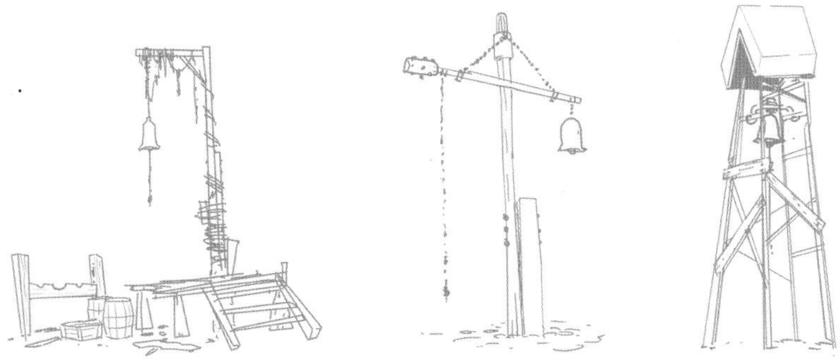

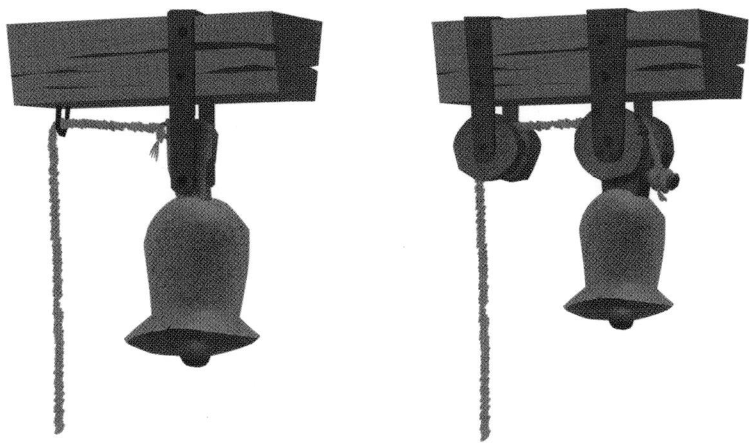

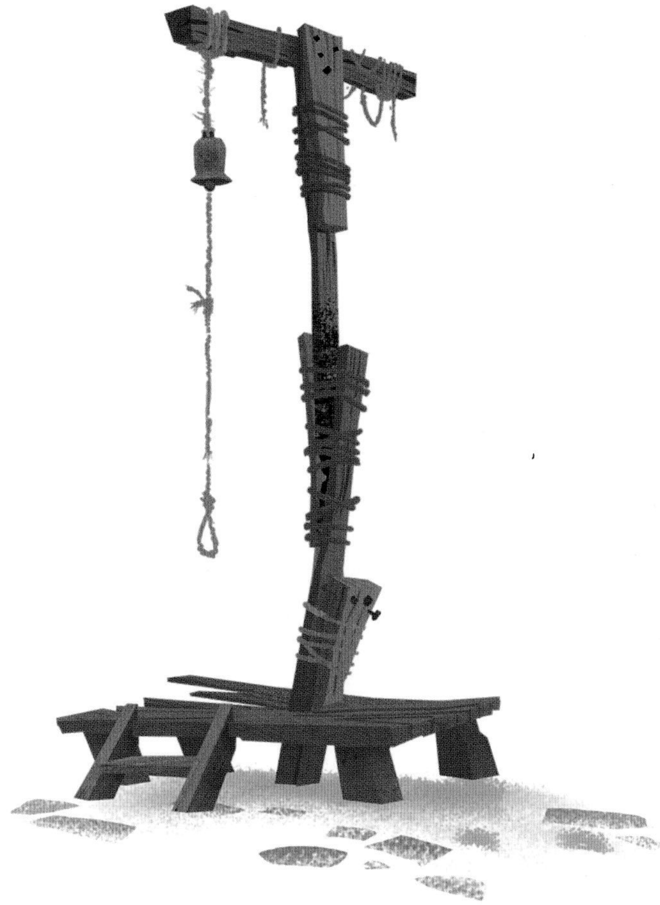

Something about the name 'Smeerensburg' just sounded right to Pablos, taken from a real-life town, Smeerenburg, in Svalbard (though he chose to add the 's', to avoid too many similarities). Head of backgrounds Gabriel Gomez says the vast Nordic exteriors and stark, snow-covered territories were some of his favorite things to paint on the project. "Our art directors, Marcin and Szymon, did a wonderful job of preparing it for us, not only creating the whole style, but also gathering lots of photos of light, colors, snow, and Nordic decorations and designs," he recalls. "We found inspiration from artists such as Carl Larsson and his *aquarelles* of everyday Scandinavian life of the era."

Head of light and shadow Florian Aupetit says the landscape was also inspired by the paintings of Joaquín Sorolla, Petrus van Schendel, and Rembrandt. He also cited the stark visuals of Francis Ford Coppola's *Apocalypse Now* and the acclaimed TV series *Breaking Bad* as points of reference for the team.

As production designer Szymon Biernacki explains, "When Jesper moves to Smeerensburg, he discovers that it's a hostile environment for him. We looked at many Nordic towns in Norway, Sweden, and Iceland. We wanted to get the right feel for the environment there."

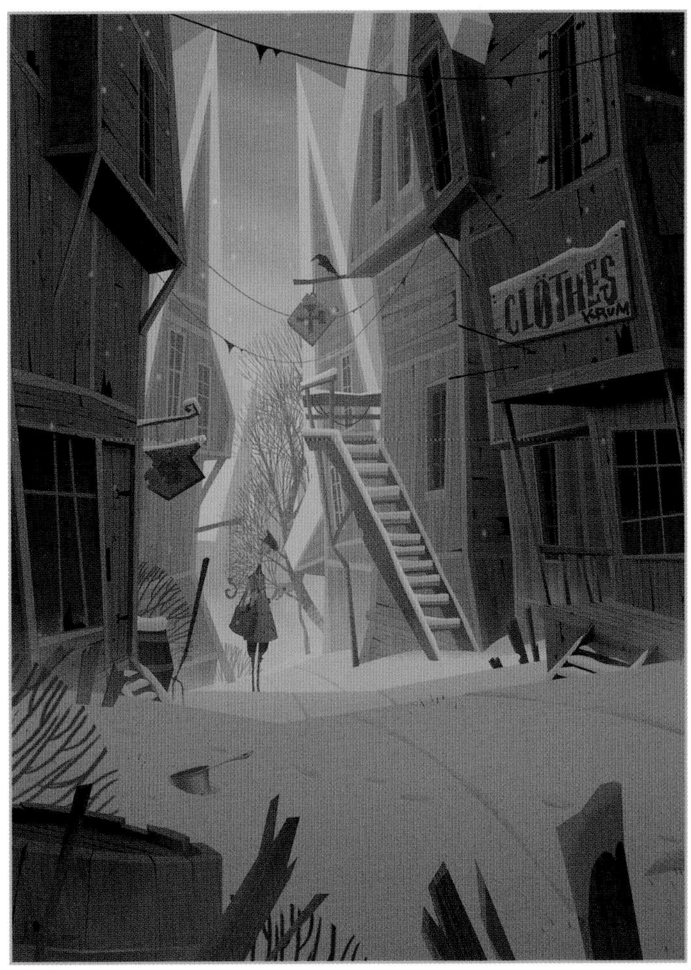

THIS PAGE: (TOP) Artwork by Marcin Jakubowski; (BOTTOM) Artwork by Thibaut Denise.

Post Office

The post office is described as the punchline to the joke of Jesper's surreal arrival in town. "We wanted to create a place that was a caricature of a real post office," says production designer Szymon Biernacki. "It has nothing to do with the prestige and power of the Royal Postal Service and it is on the opposite end of the spectrum from the world that Jesper grew up in."

The residents of Smeerensburg don't care about sending letters, and the post office reflects their lack of respect towards the institution. "The building looks more like a barn, and it has been taken over by chickens, which have made the letter cabinet their home," says Biernacki. "There's no real furniture – the makeshift desk is actually an old door supported by crates and a barrel, and the bed is an old sleigh with a dirty mattress on top. The building has surrendered to the elements. The whole building has tilted because of the snow that has been pushing against it for years. Our goal was to create a place that would reflect the hopeless task that Jesper has ahead of him."

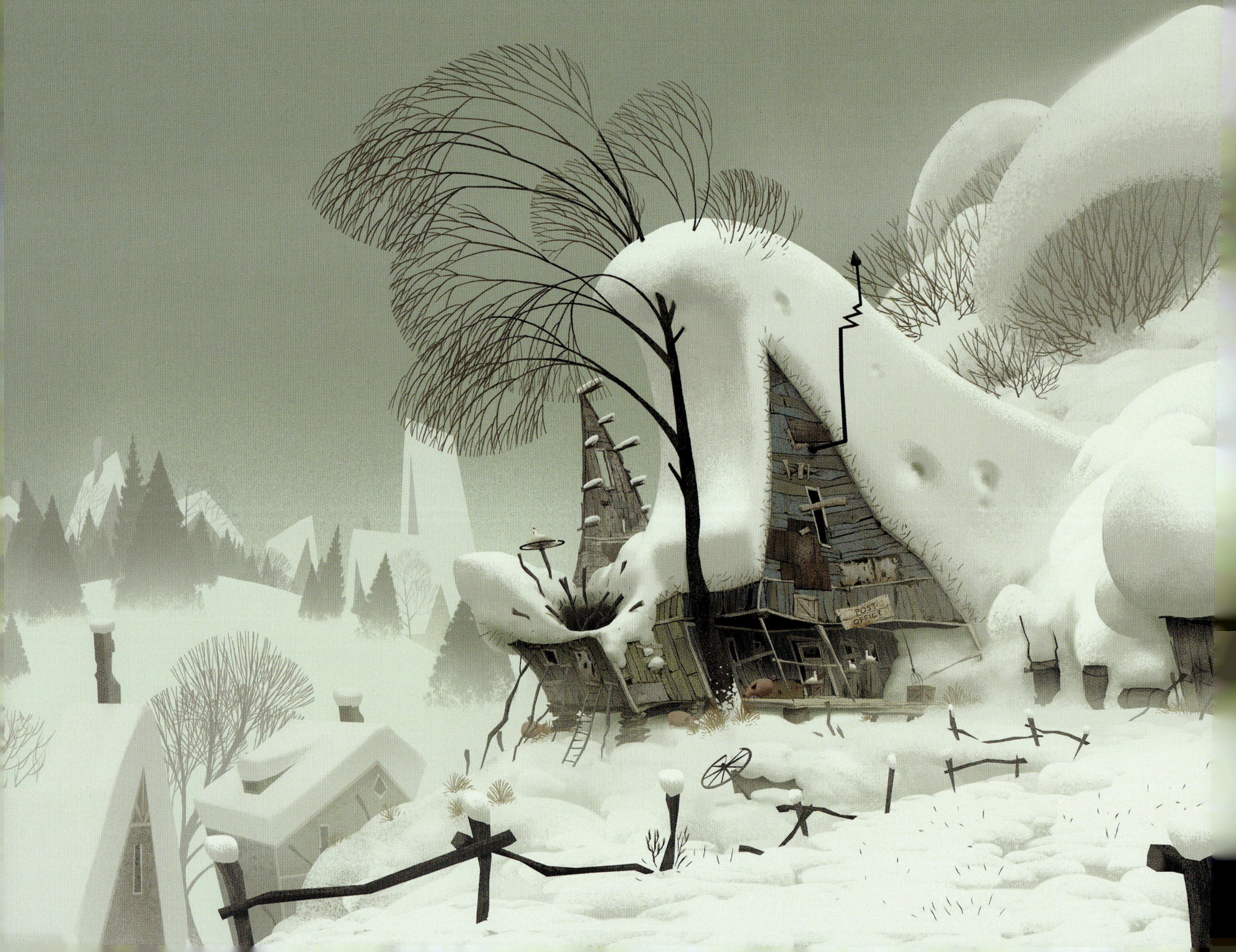

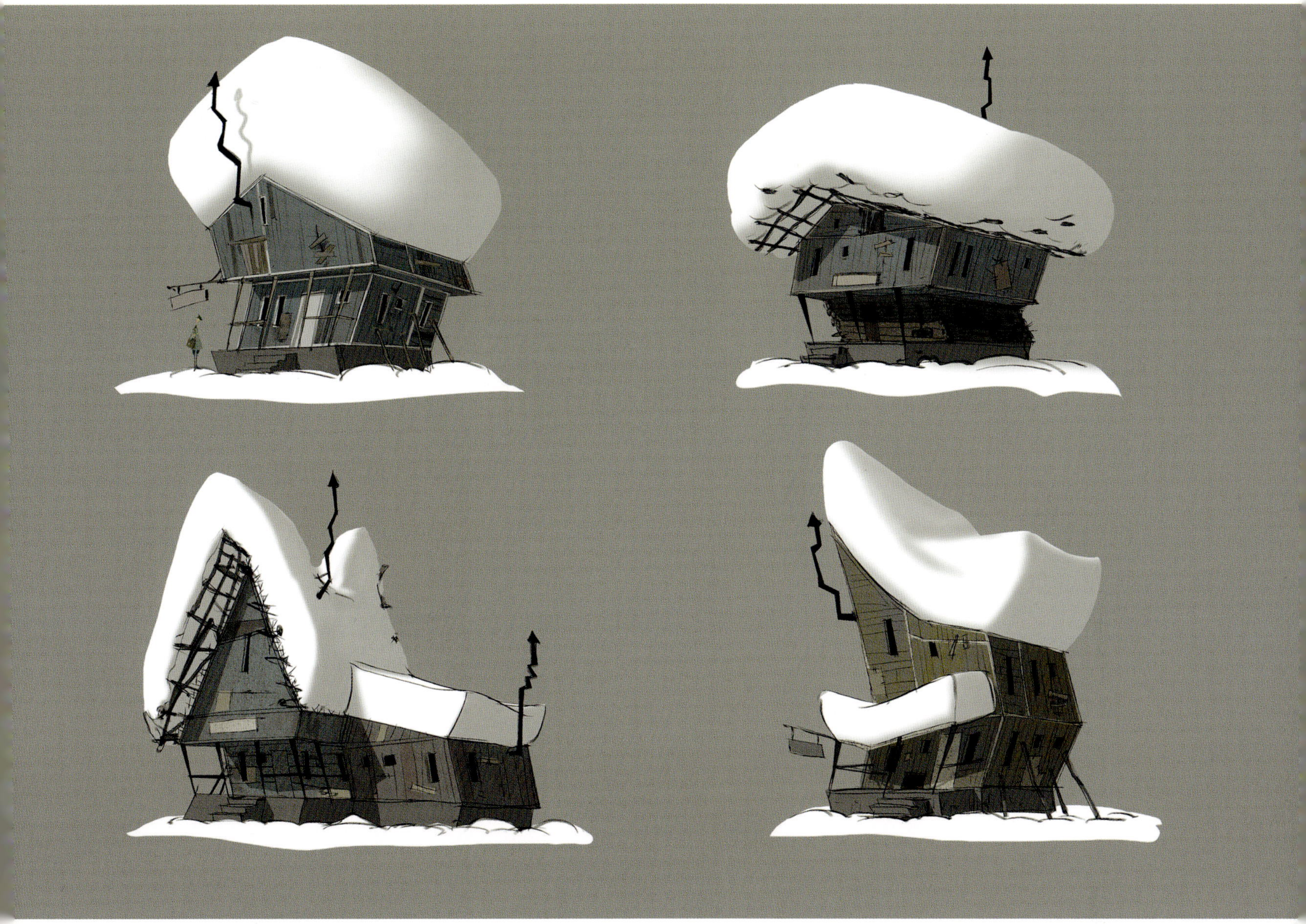

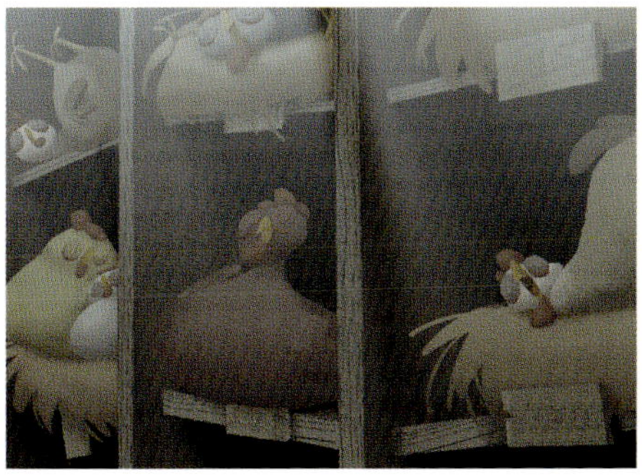

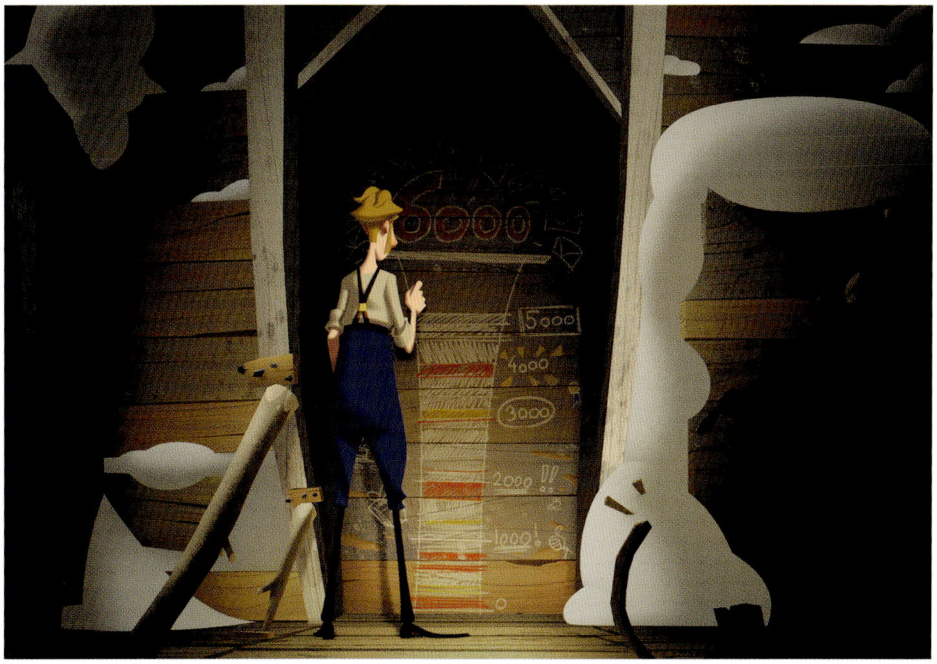

PREVIOUS PAGE: Concept art by Szymon Biernacki.

TOP: Early explorations by Szymon Biernacki.

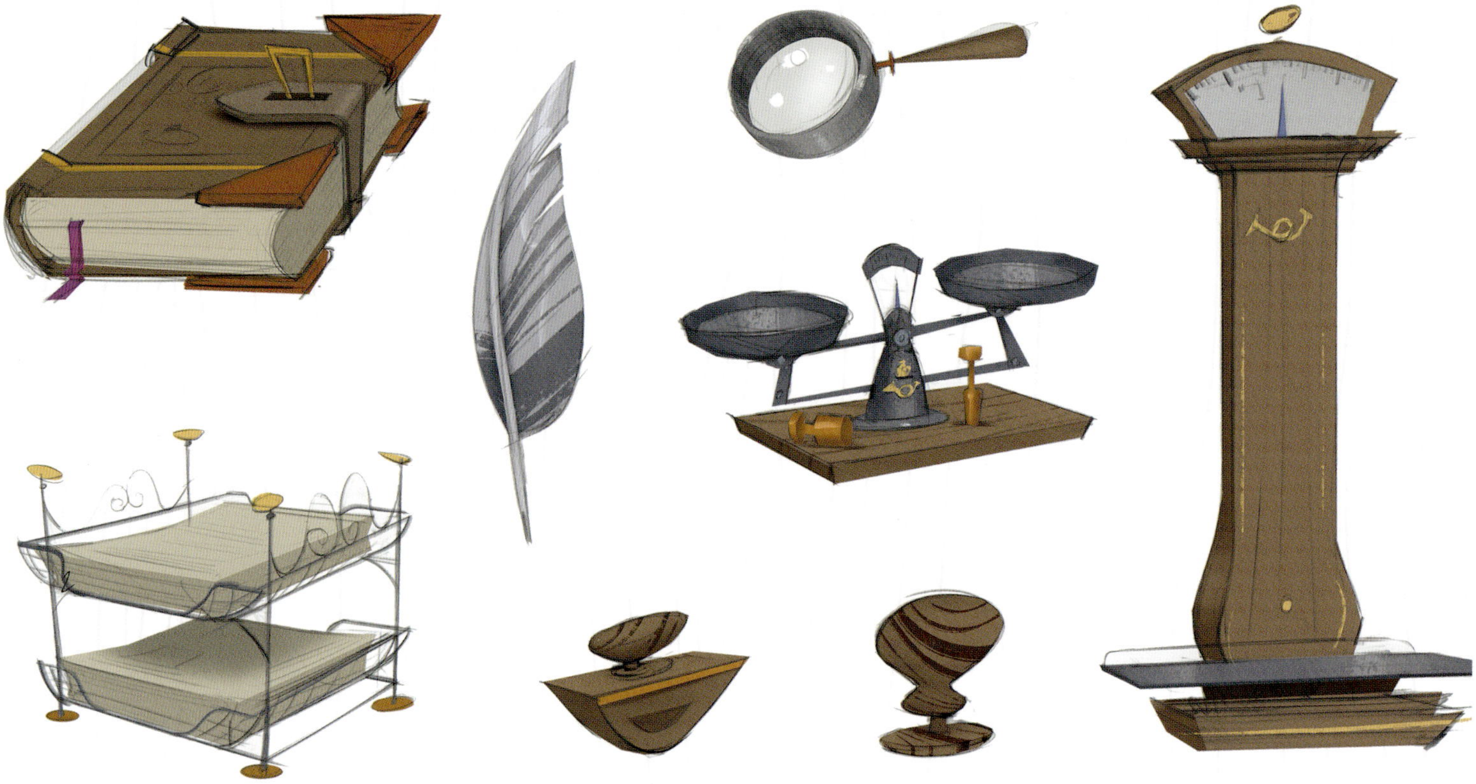

THIS PAGE: (TOP) Artwork by Krzysztof Roslan; (BOTTOM) Concept art by Szymon Biernacki.

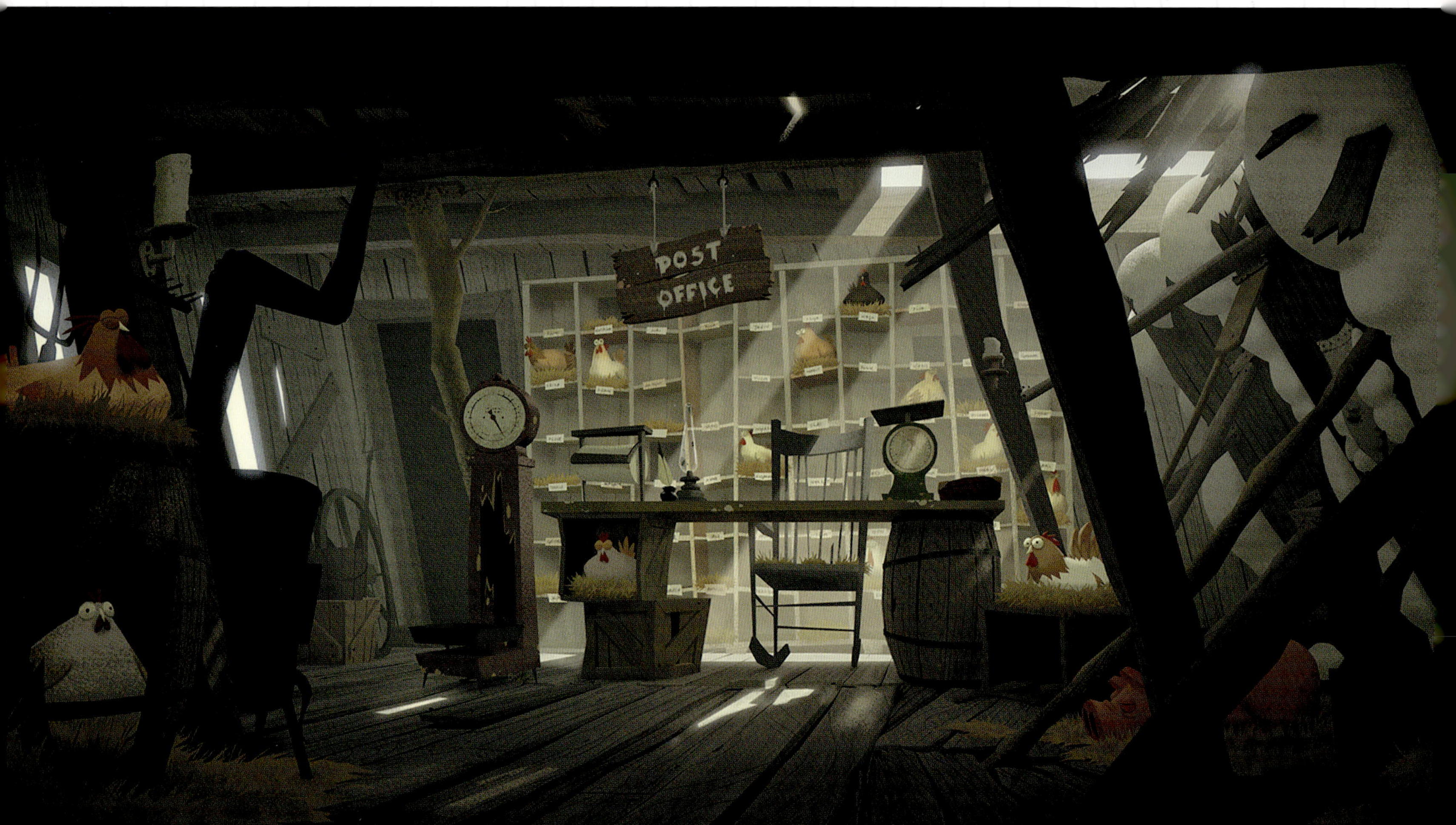

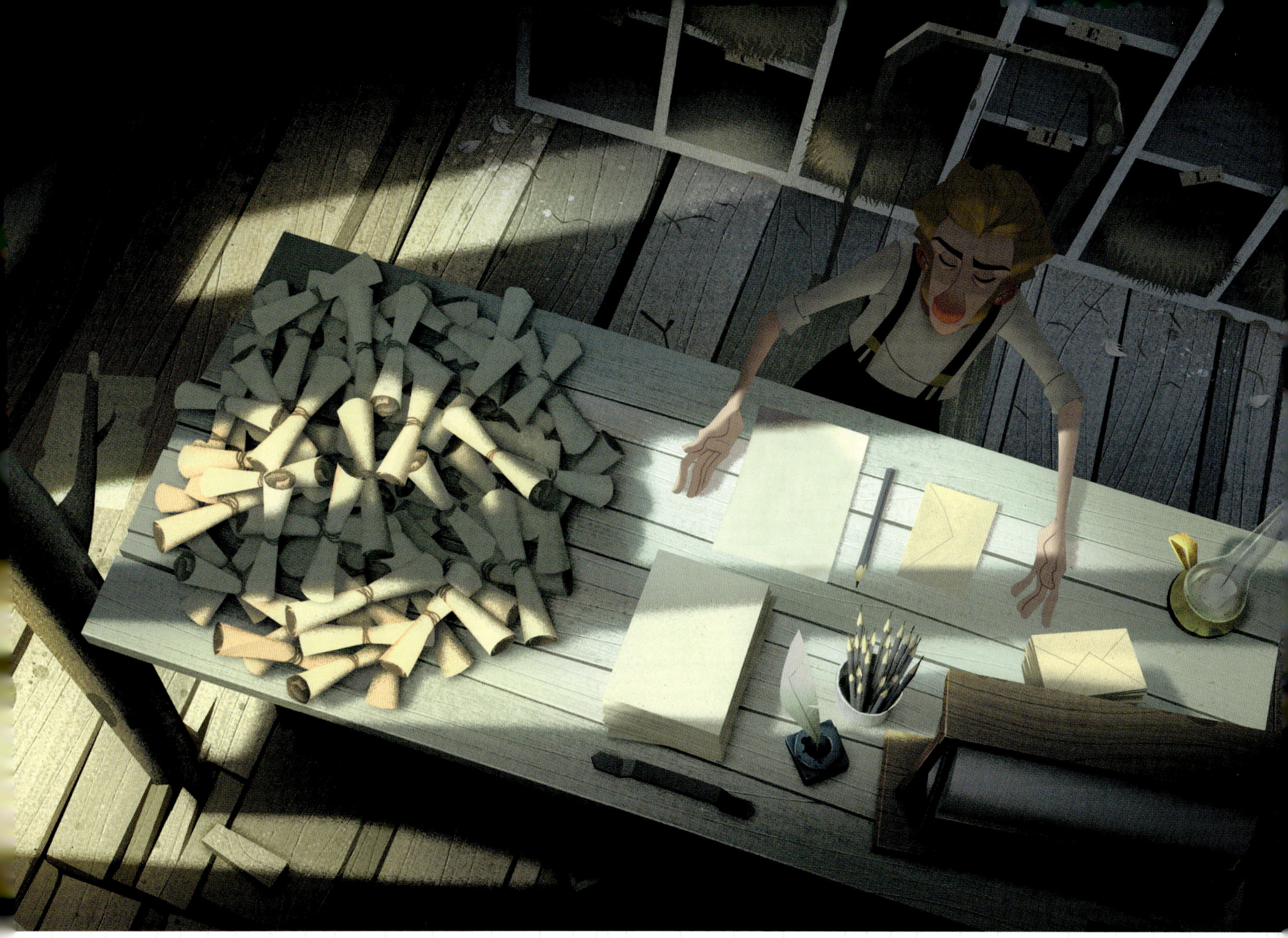

BELOW: Artwork by Krzysztof Roslan.

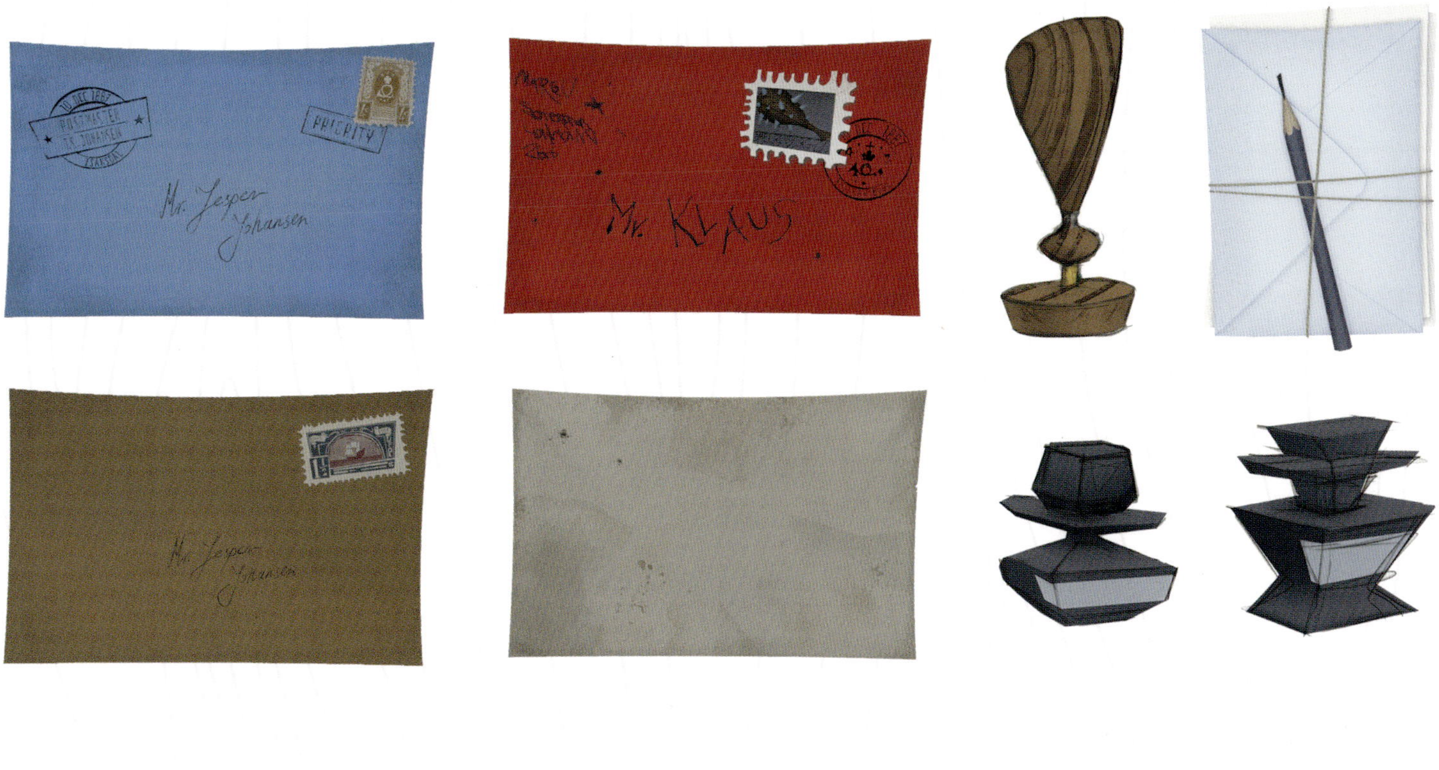

Alva

TEACHER TURNED FISHMONGER

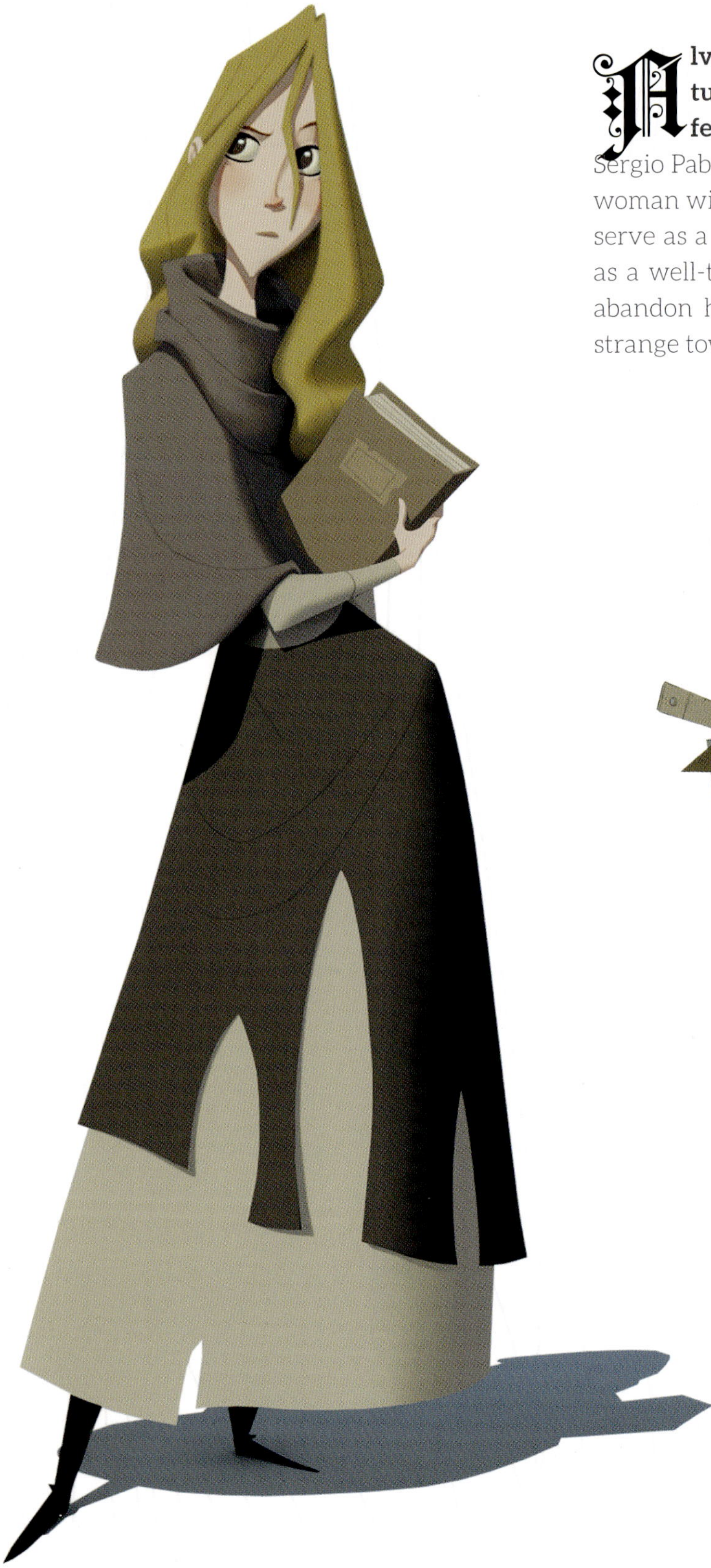

Alva, Smeerensburg's disappointed schoolteacher-turned-fishmonger, must be one of the most interesting female characters in recent memory. Writer-director Sergio Pablos says it was important to him that they had a strong woman with an important part to play in the film who didn't just serve as a love interest for Jesper. The designers envisioned her as a well-to-do, educated young woman who has had to slowly abandon her goals after the harsh realities of life in this very strange town overwhelmed her.

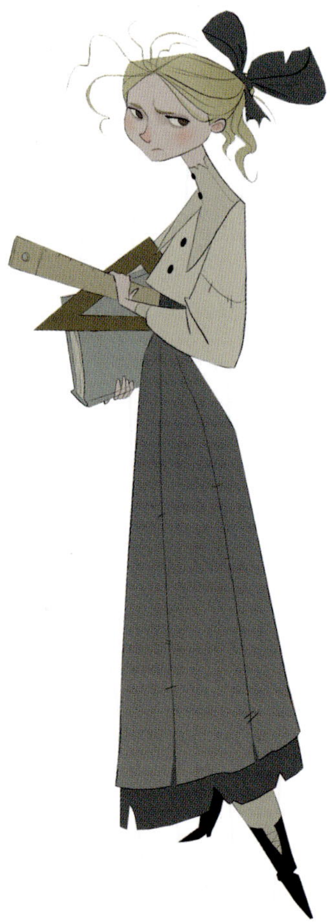

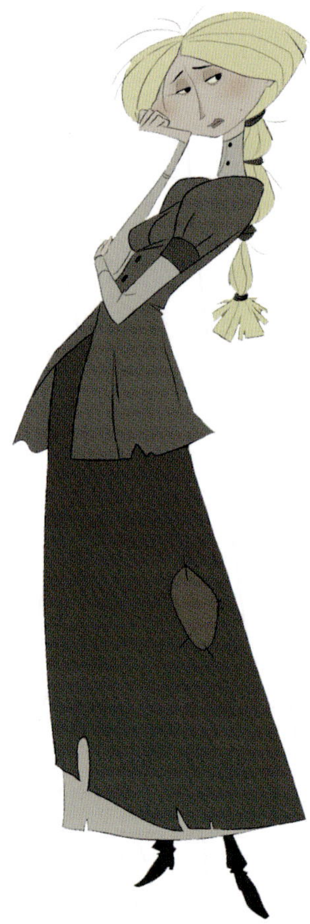

THIS PAGE: Early designs for Alva by Torsten Schrank.

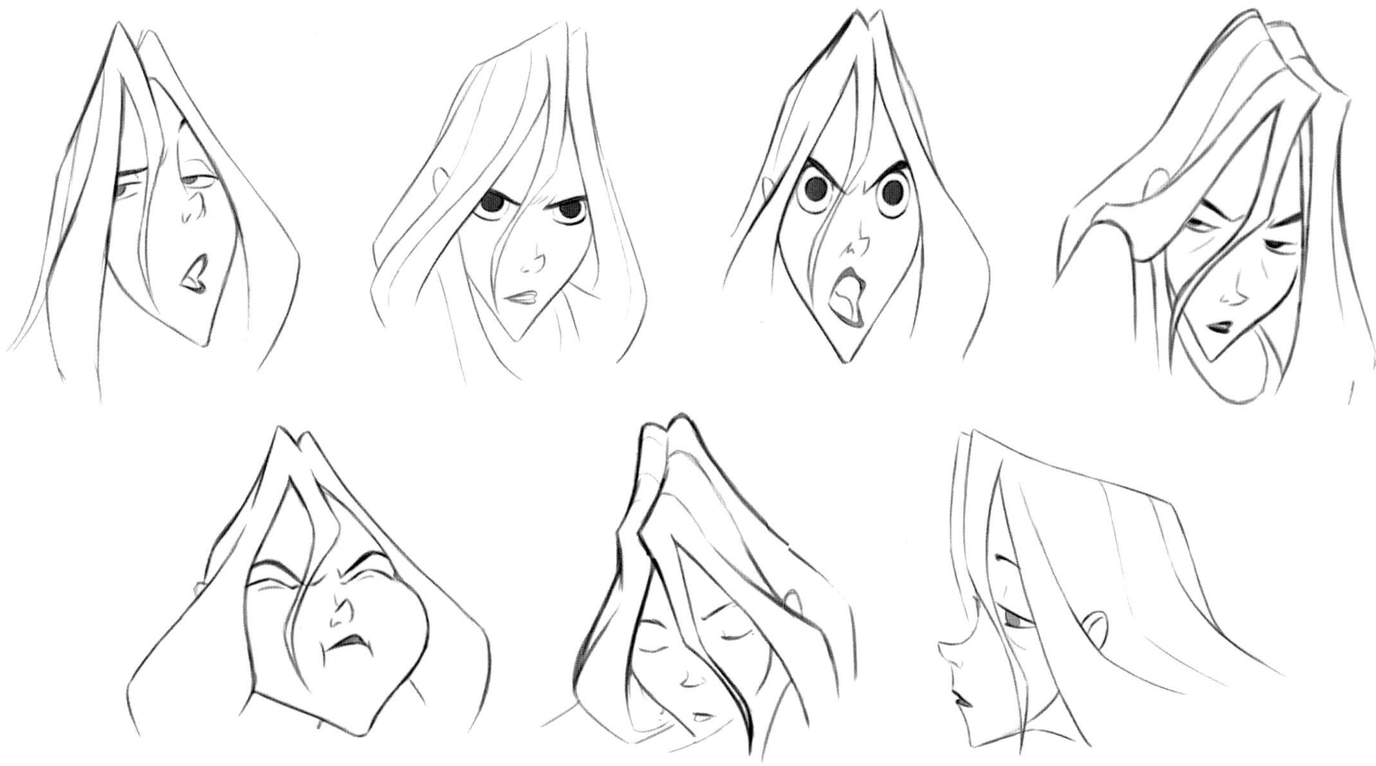

THIS PAGE: Animation key frames by Sergio Martins.

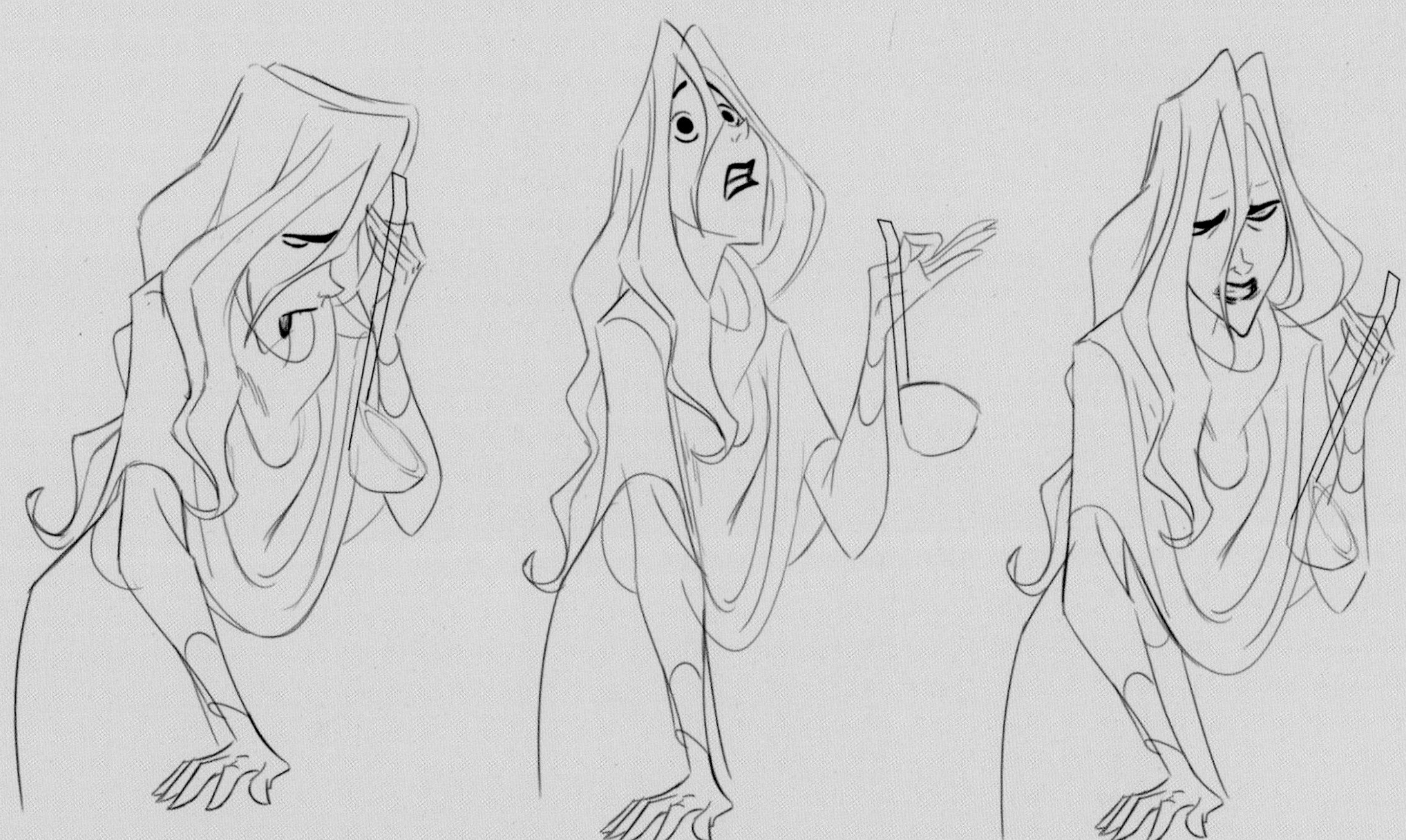

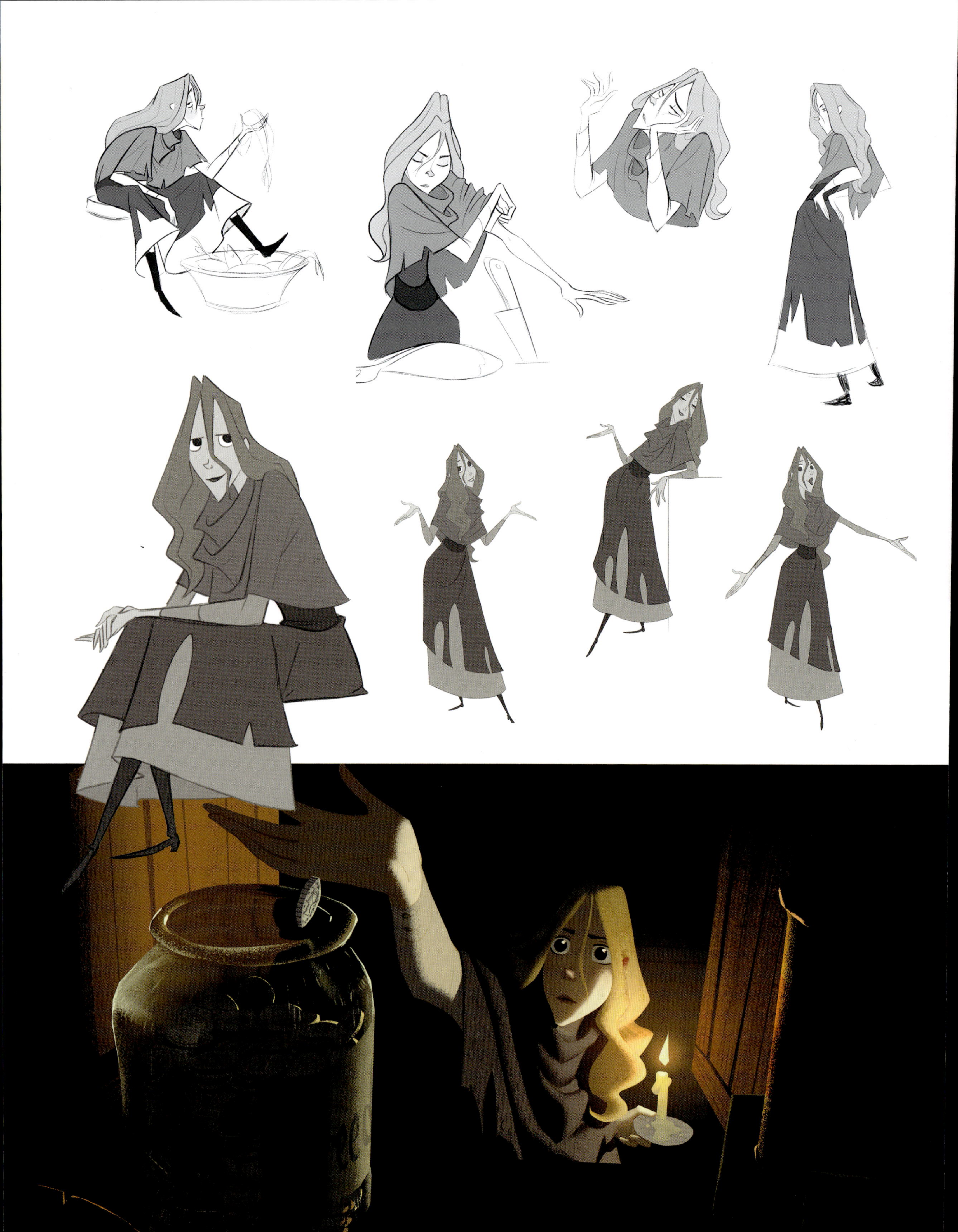

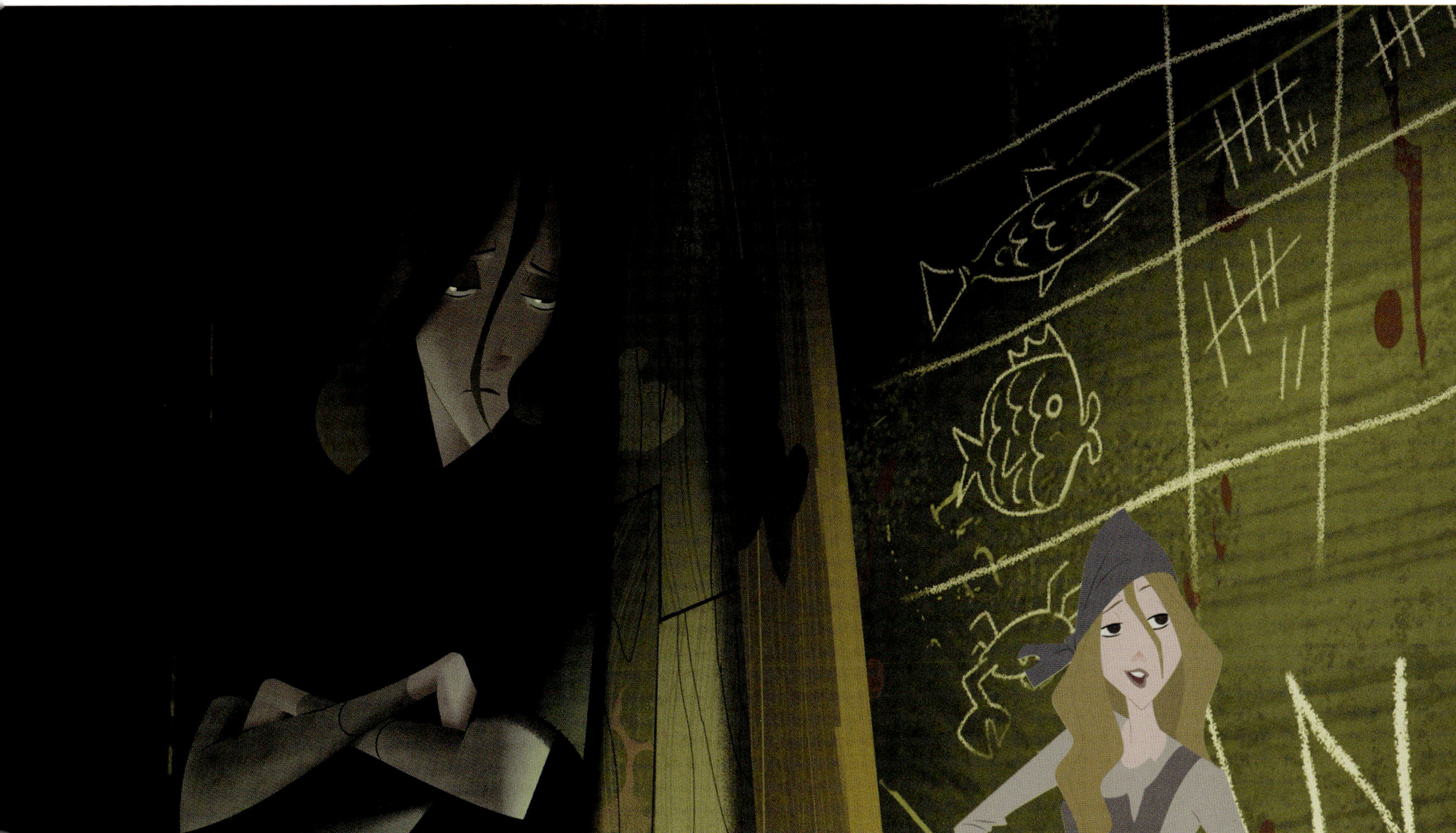

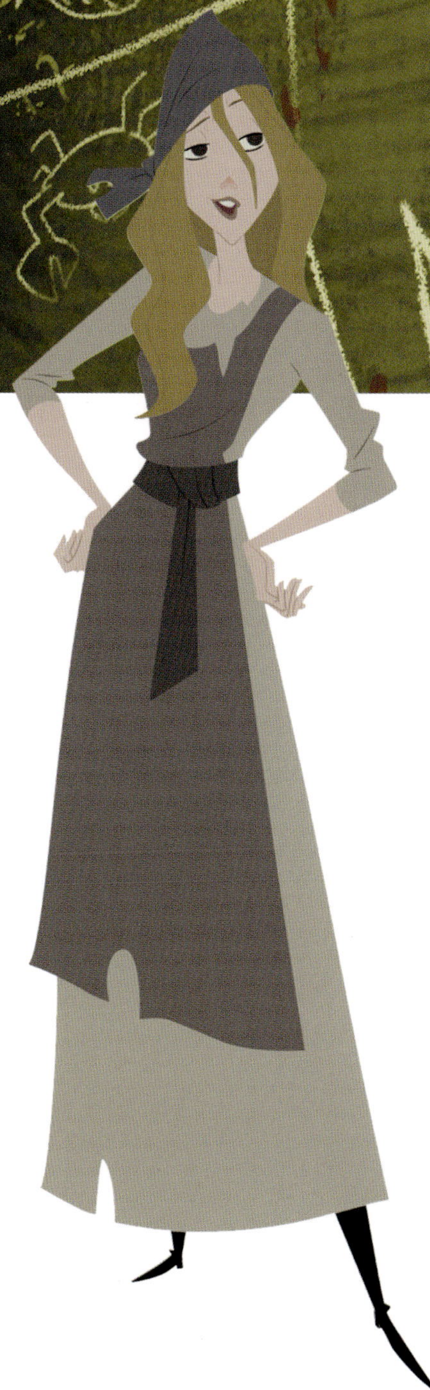

"She is essential to the plot, as she's a teacher who has given up on her dreams of teaching, so she is putting all her efforts into getting out of this town," Pablos explains. "When Jesper's actions result in children coming to school to learn how to write letters, that rekindles her love for teaching."

Pablos says having actress Rashida Jones involved in the film was a huge asset to the authenticity and believability of Alva as a well-rounded character. "Rashida was great at bringing lots of texture to the character," he notes. "It was a huge advantage to have her in the room, because she's also a great writer. She would come up with far more natural and in-character solutions so, when I had to do a rewrite, I understood Alva a lot better because of her input."

Looking back, Pablos says Alva is one of his favorite characters in the whole movie. "It's just very interesting to see how she needs to re-evaluate all her values again and return to what inspired her in the beginning... Her story is quite powerful."

PREVIOUS PAGE: (TOP) Character attitude exploration by Sergio Martins and Torsten Schrank; (BOTTOM) Early artwork by Marcin Jakubowski and Juan Pablo Navas.

School

SCHOOL TURNED FISH SHOP

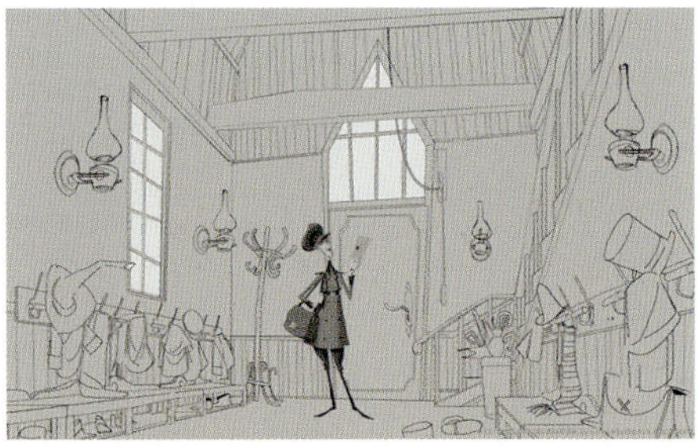

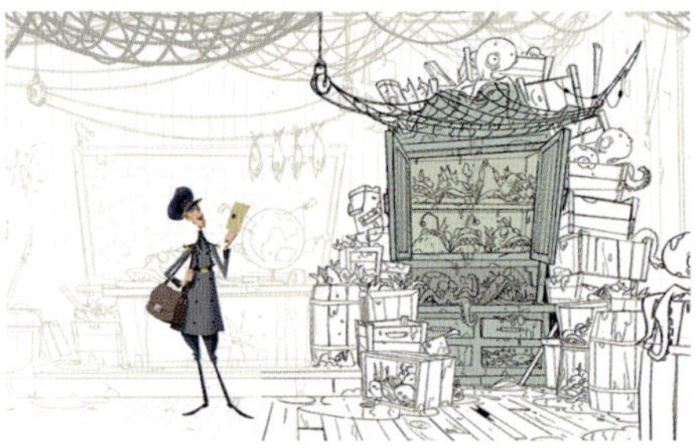

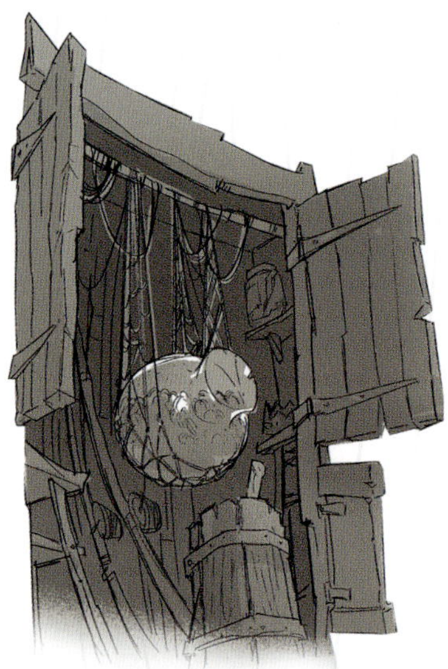

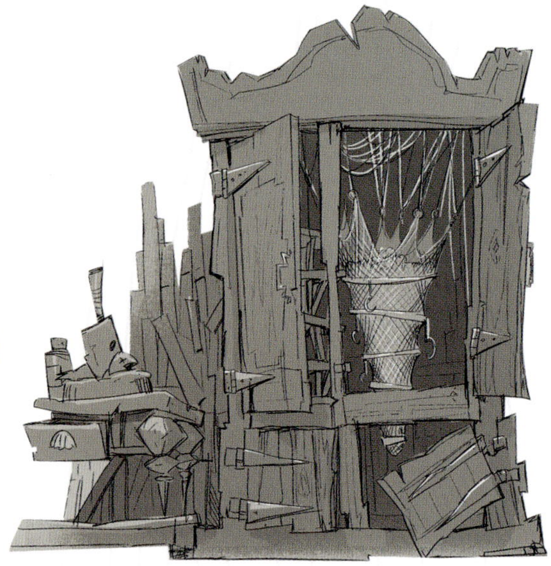

ABOVE: Sketches of the fish shop by Arthus Pilorget and Tobi Trebeljahr.

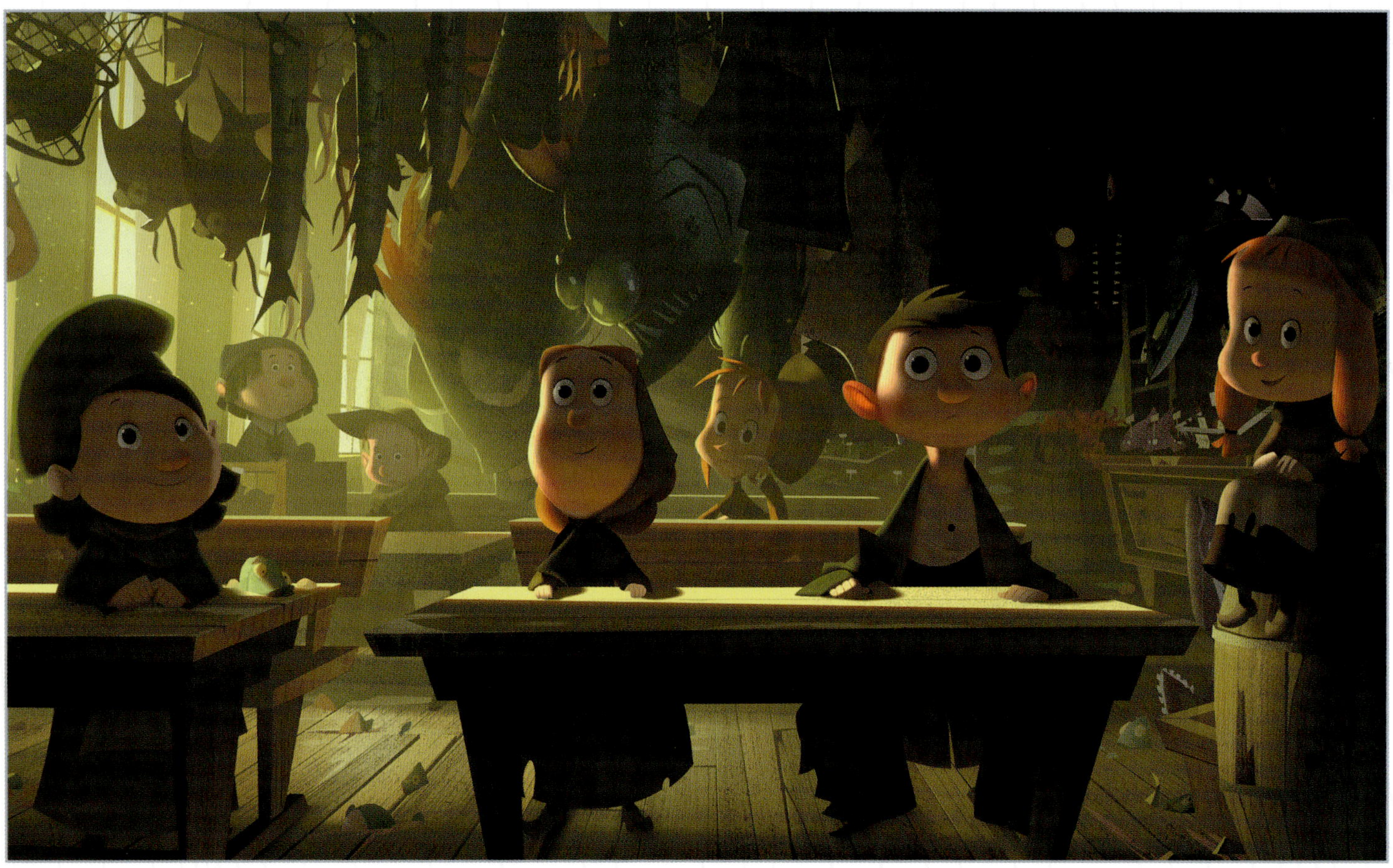

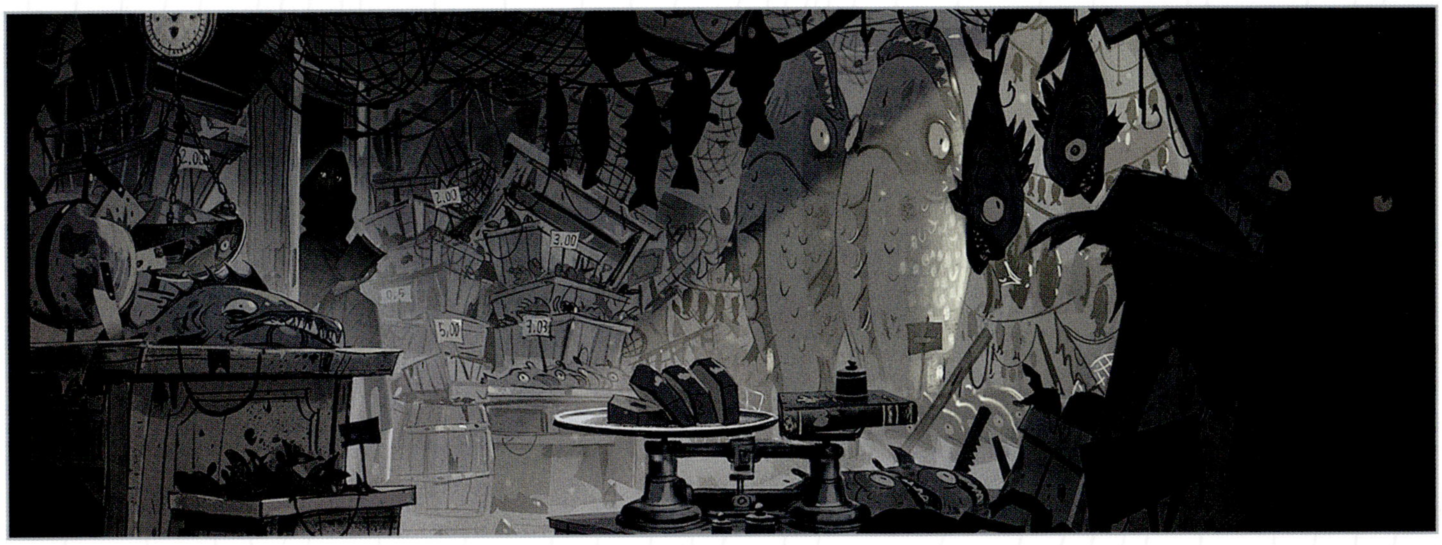

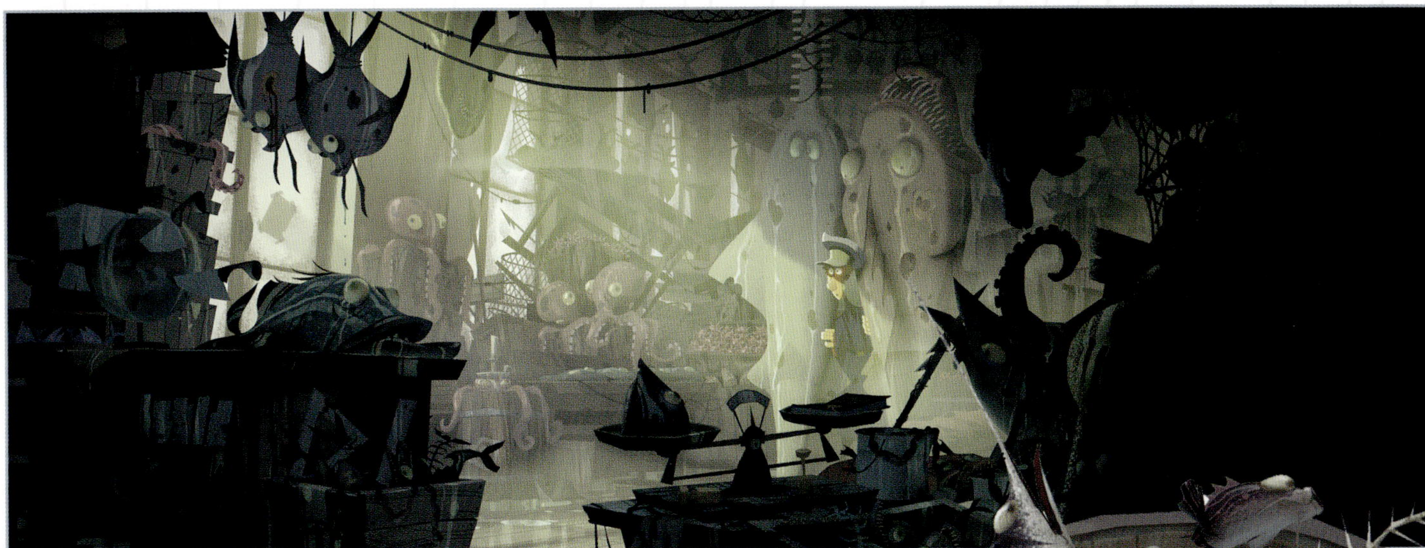

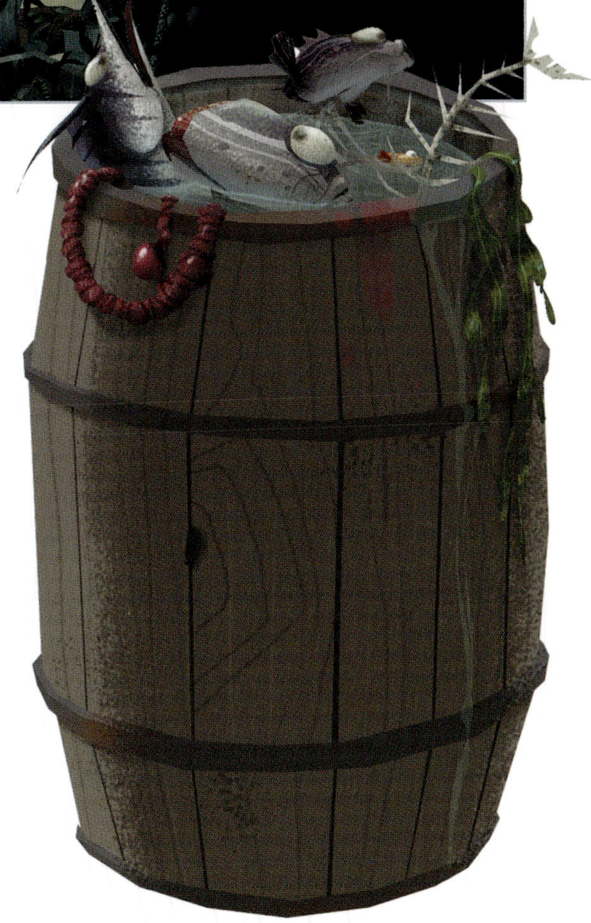

When Jesper first enters Alva's schoolhouse, which has been converted into a fish shop, he is shocked by how cramped and cluttered it is. What used to be a schoolhouse now has barrels crammed everywhere and, as is described in the script, Jesper has to navigate through "a labyrinth of rotting fish hanging from lines." The sorry state of the building is a great reflection of Alva's abandoned hopes and dreams.

Production designer Marcin Jakubowski explains, "Jesper is escaping the mayhem of the town, where everyone is fighting, and he believes that he has found a safe zone in this school."

The design team didn't want the audience to know immediately that the fish shop used to be a schoolhouse. "We wanted the history to be revealed to Jesper as we went along," says Jakubowski. "The key words for us were dense, humid, and cluttered. We wanted to really show the suffocating humidity hanging in the air, and our characters are traveling through this environment. Light is filtered here with different angles. We can see the delicate glow, but it's a very rich, monochromatic palette."

THIS PAGE: Concept art by Arthus Pilorget.

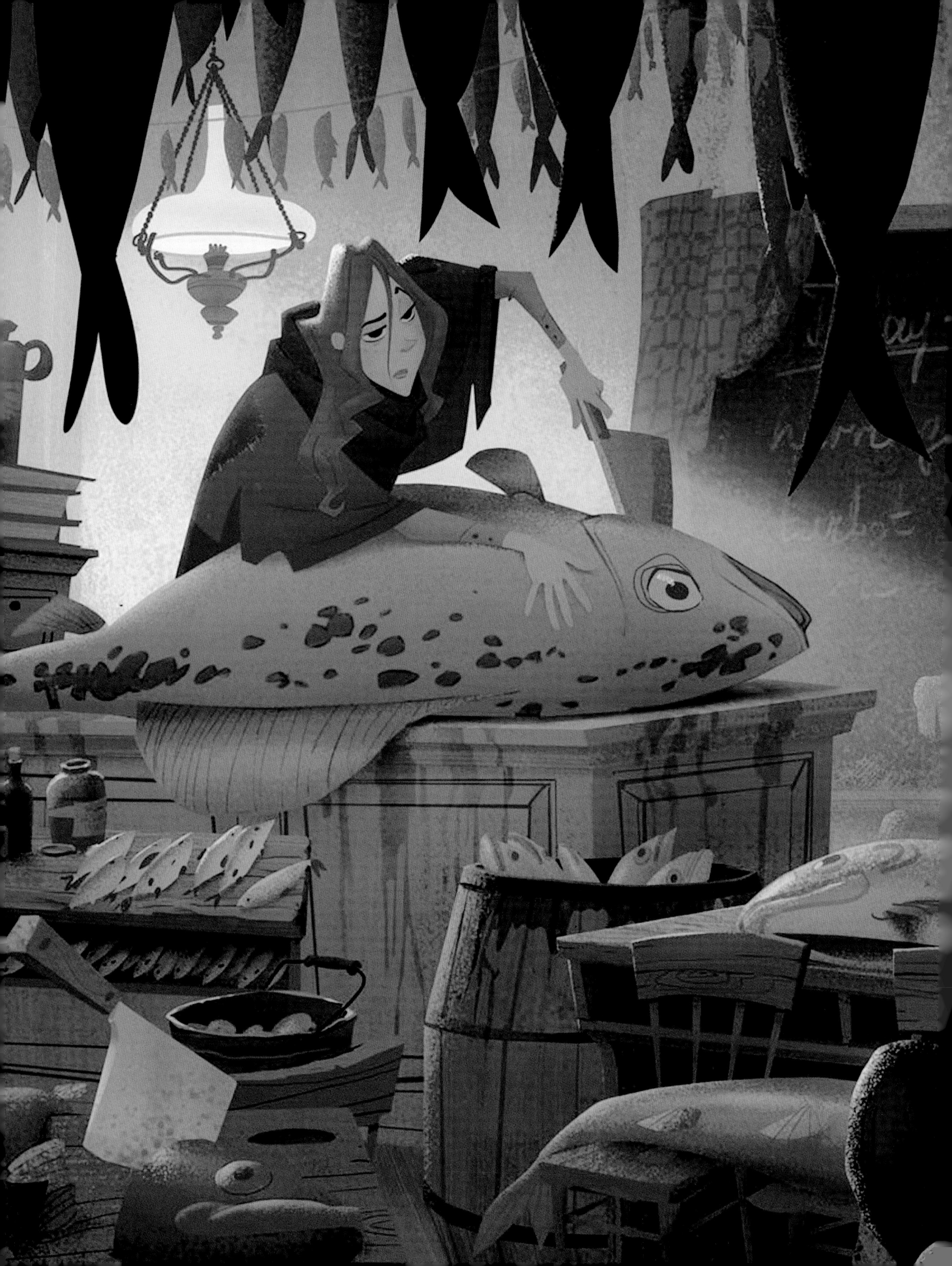

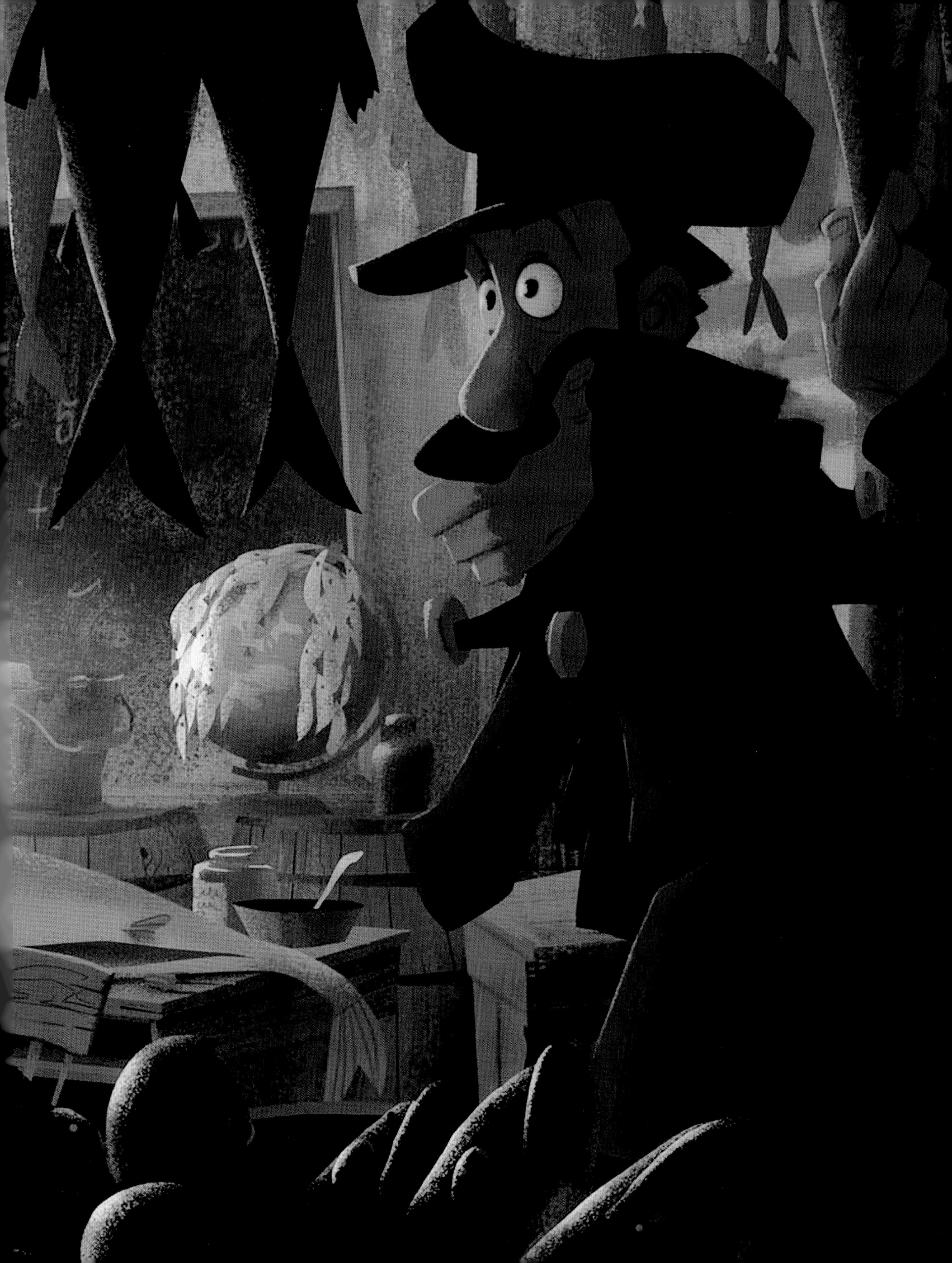

Clans at War

THE ELLINGBOES AND THE KRUMS

Echoing legendary warring clans like the Hatfields and the McCoys, *Klaus* has the Krums and the Ellingboes, who bring a lot of color and humor to the mix. Sergio Pablos says, initially, he was thinking about rival Viking families, but then found himself leaning more towards modern-day soccer hooligans as inspiration.

"The conflict and sense of hatred towards each other doesn't make any sense, and it's all about what others have done in the past," explains Pablos. "When we were designing the clans, the easy route would have been to split them up, but we wanted them to be all mixed up: everyone has a neighbor they hate."

In terms of their overall design, the Ellingboes are rounder and shorter, while the Krums are straighter and more elongated. Also, the Krums are more puritanical in nature, so they wear more black and white colors, while the Ellingboes are depicted in earth tones. According to Pablos, even their houses follow the same design and color principles. "There is an underlying class difference as well, but we don't really get to it in the movie. There are just hints there for the audience to pick up, so they are easily distinguished from each other!"

PREVIOUS SPREAD: Artwork by Marcin Jakubowski and Juan Pablo Navas.

BELOW: Krums and Ellingboes, showing the subtle differences in character design. Artwork by Daniel Fernandez.

NEXT PAGE: Artwork by Tobi Trebeljahr.

NEXT SPREAD: Concept art by Daniel Fernandez.

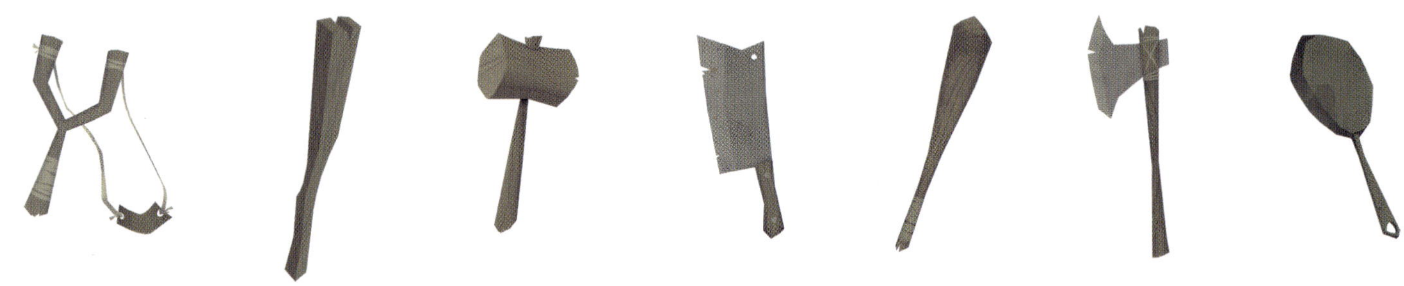

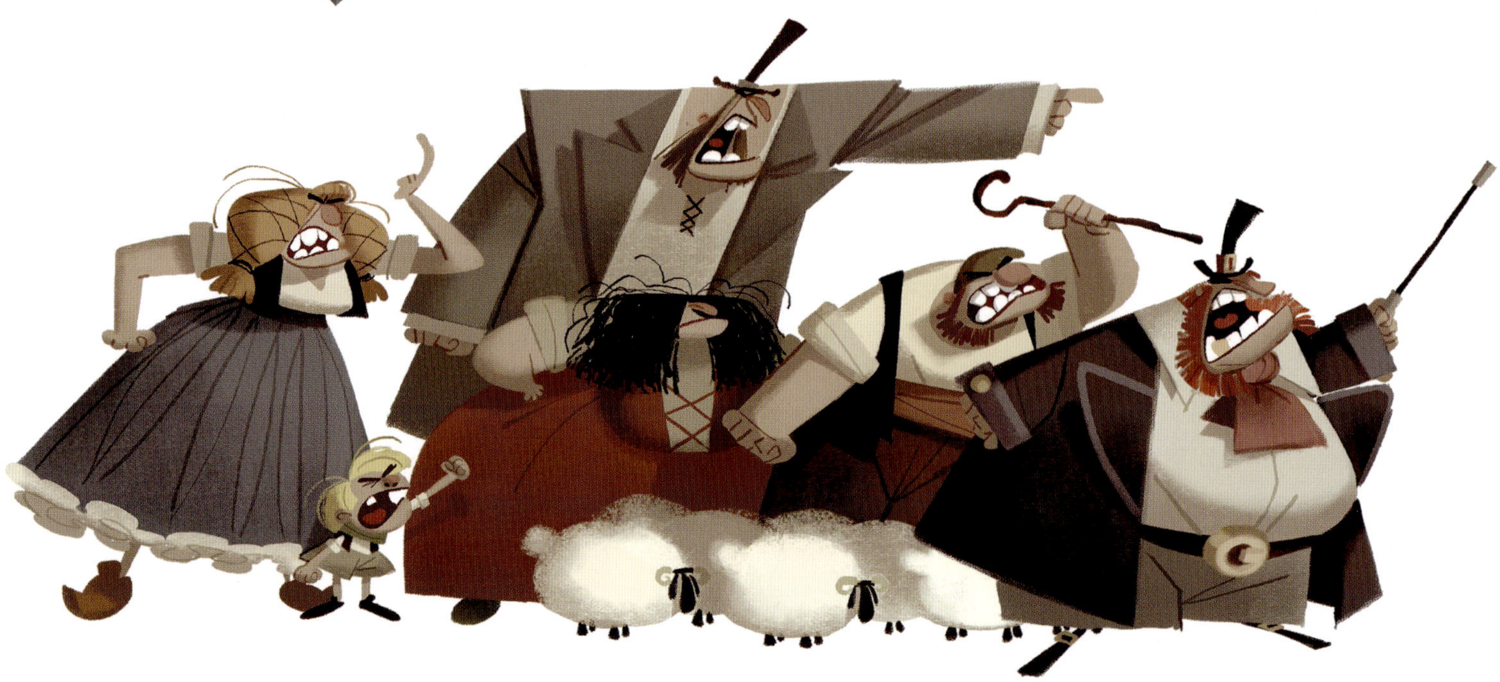

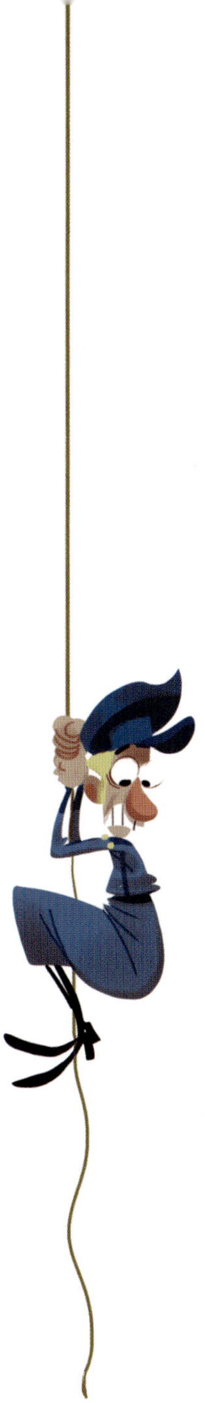

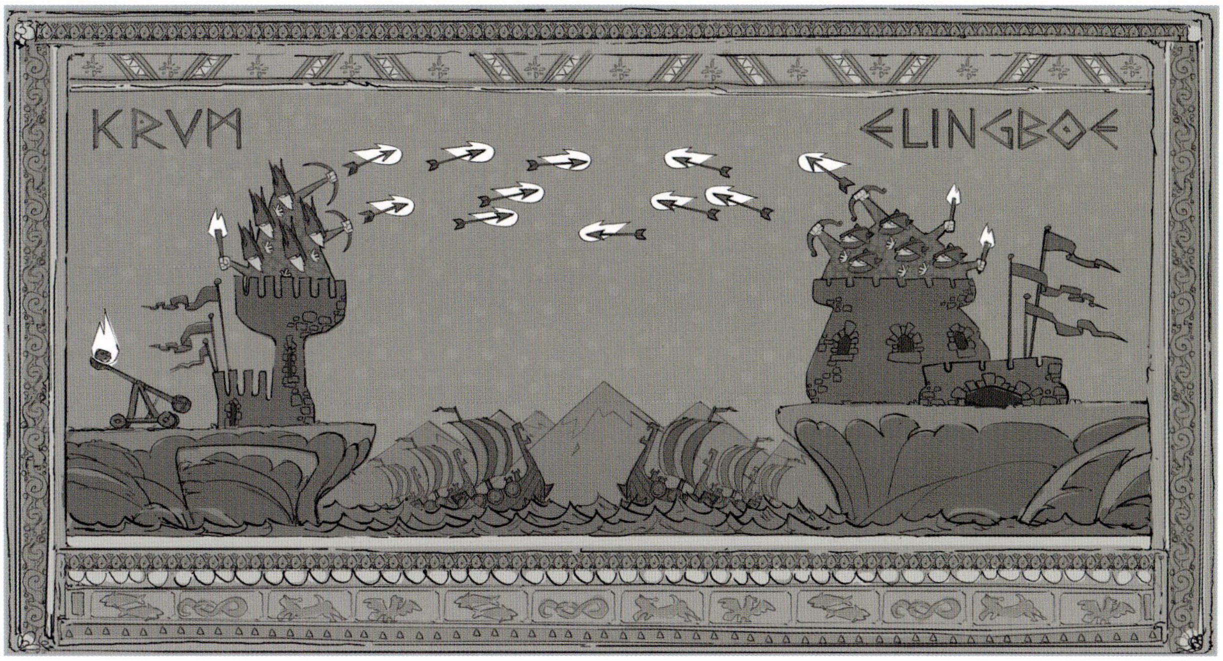
KRVM
ELINGBOE

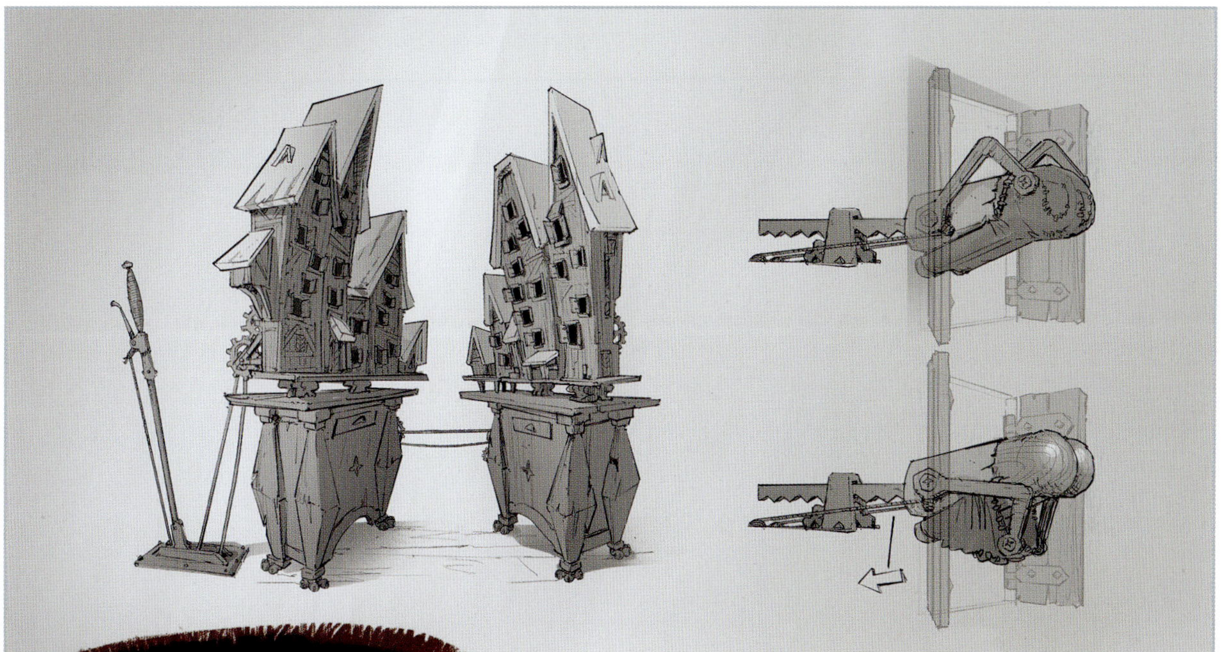

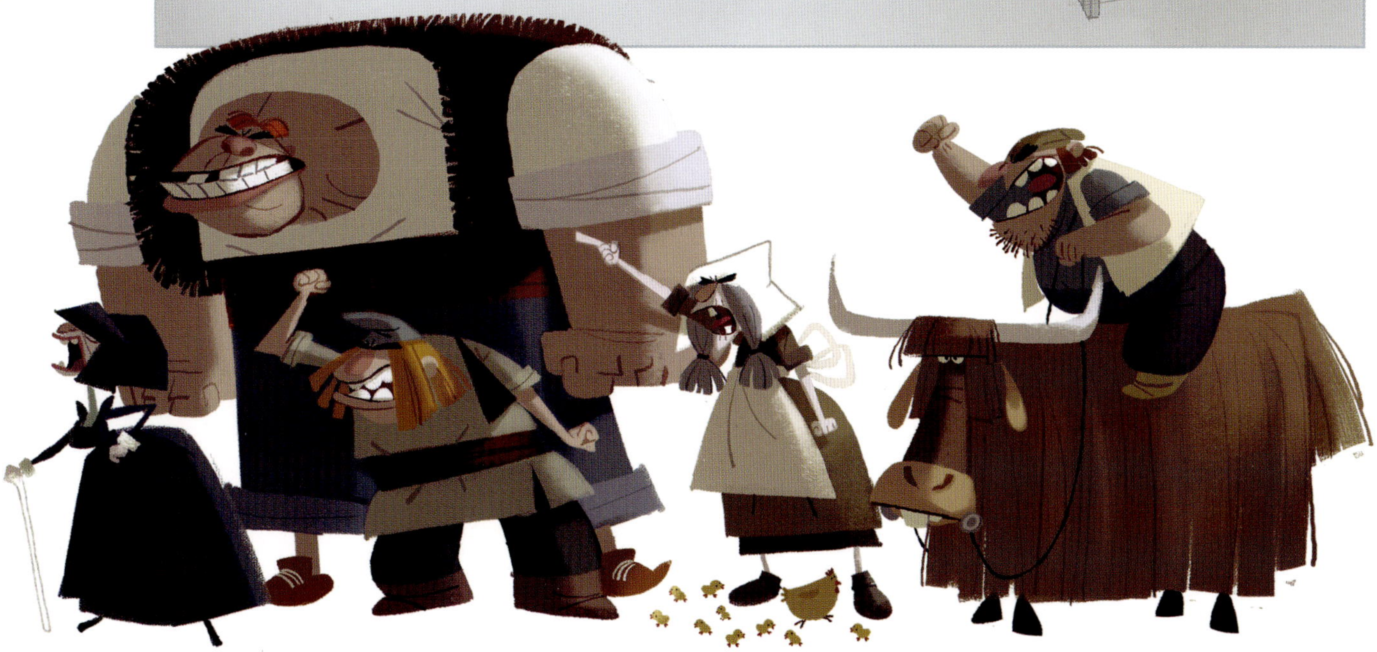

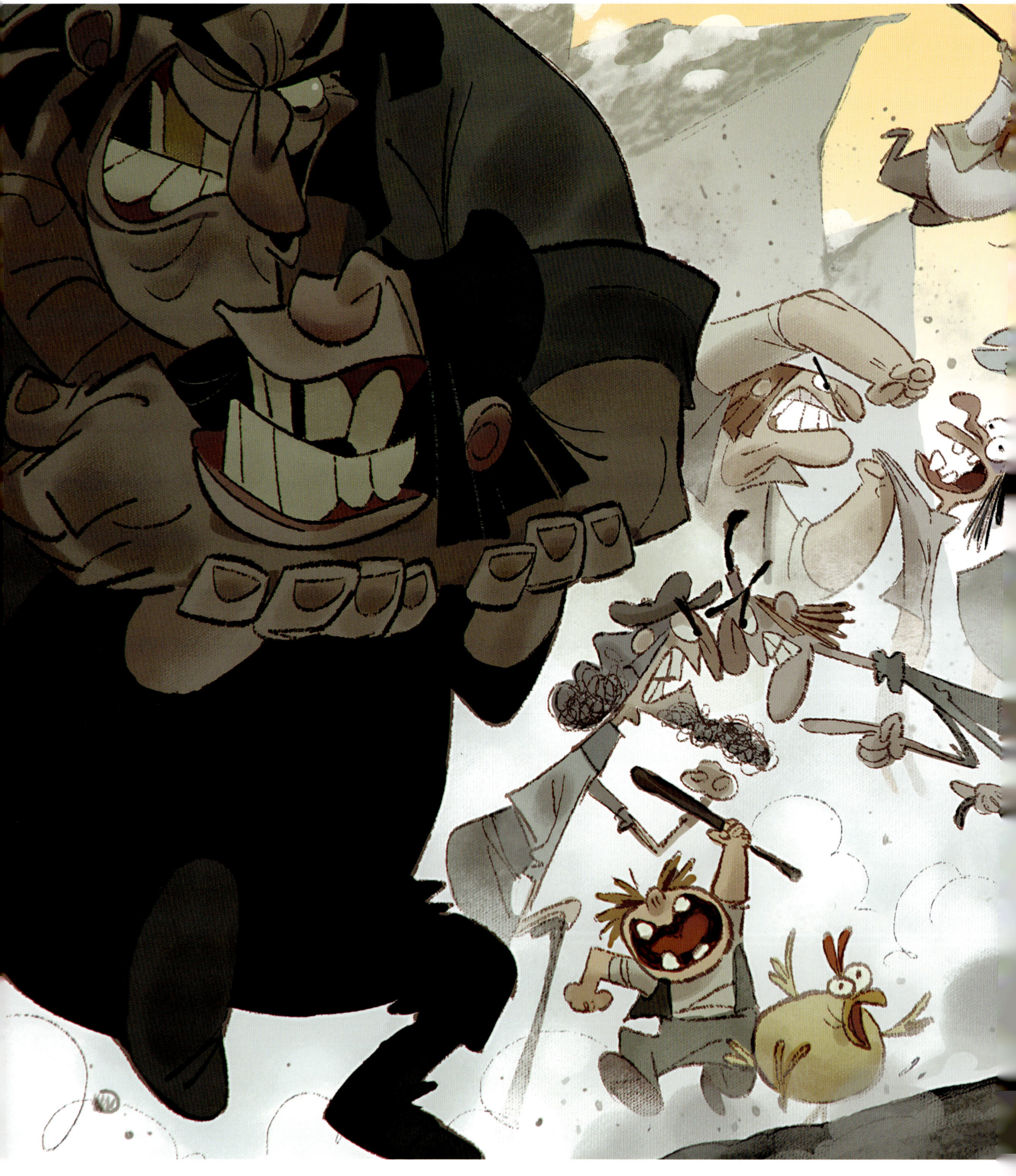

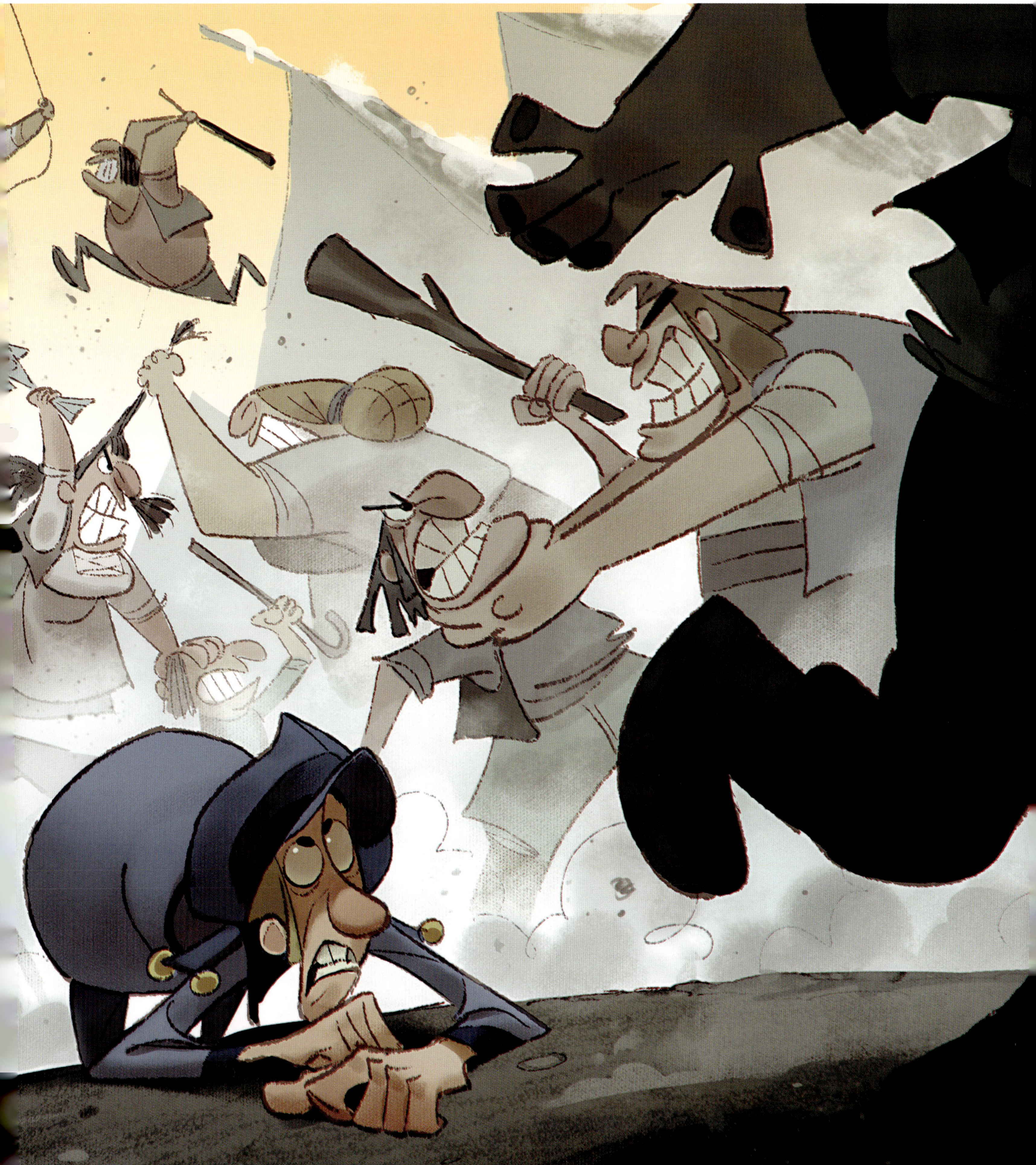

Children of Smeerensburg

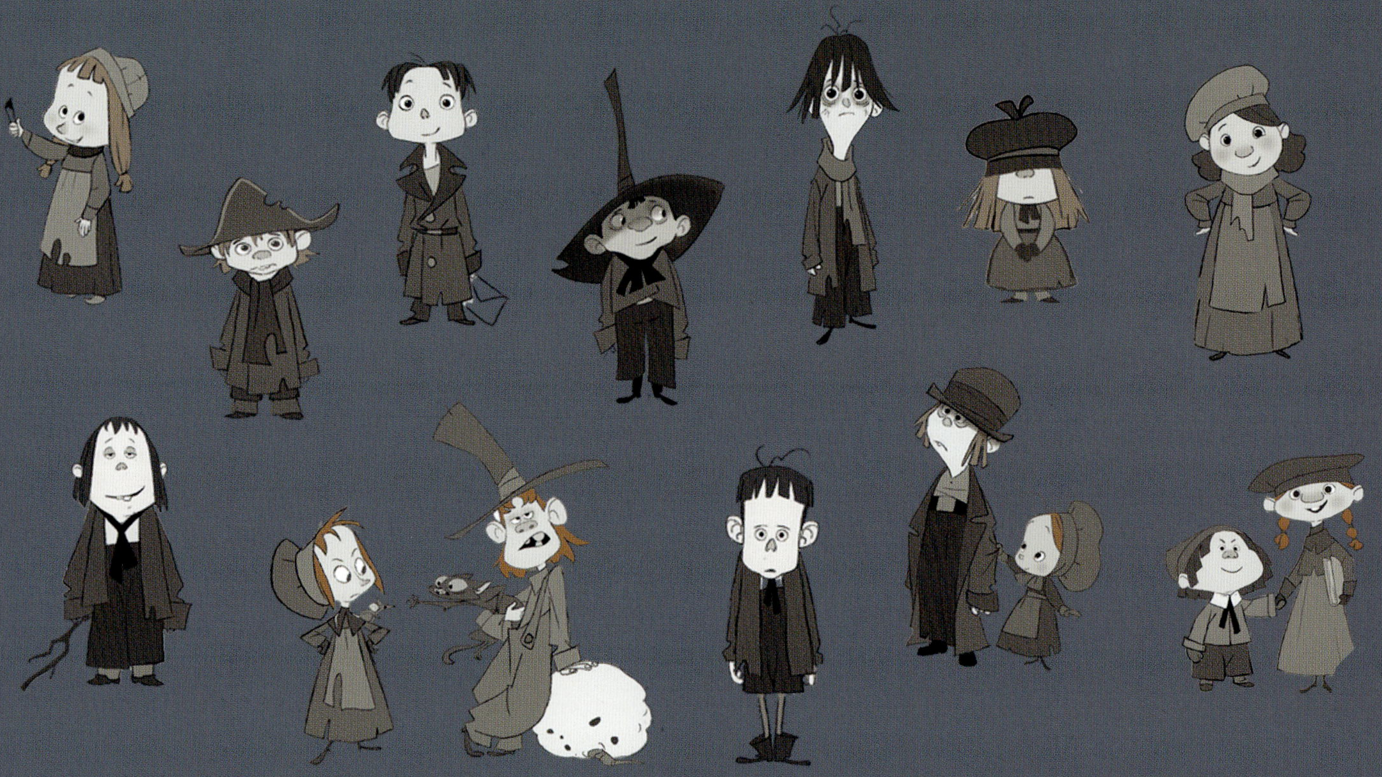

THIS PAGE: (TOP) Artwork by Torsten Schrank; (BOTTOM) Artwork by Daniel Fernandez.

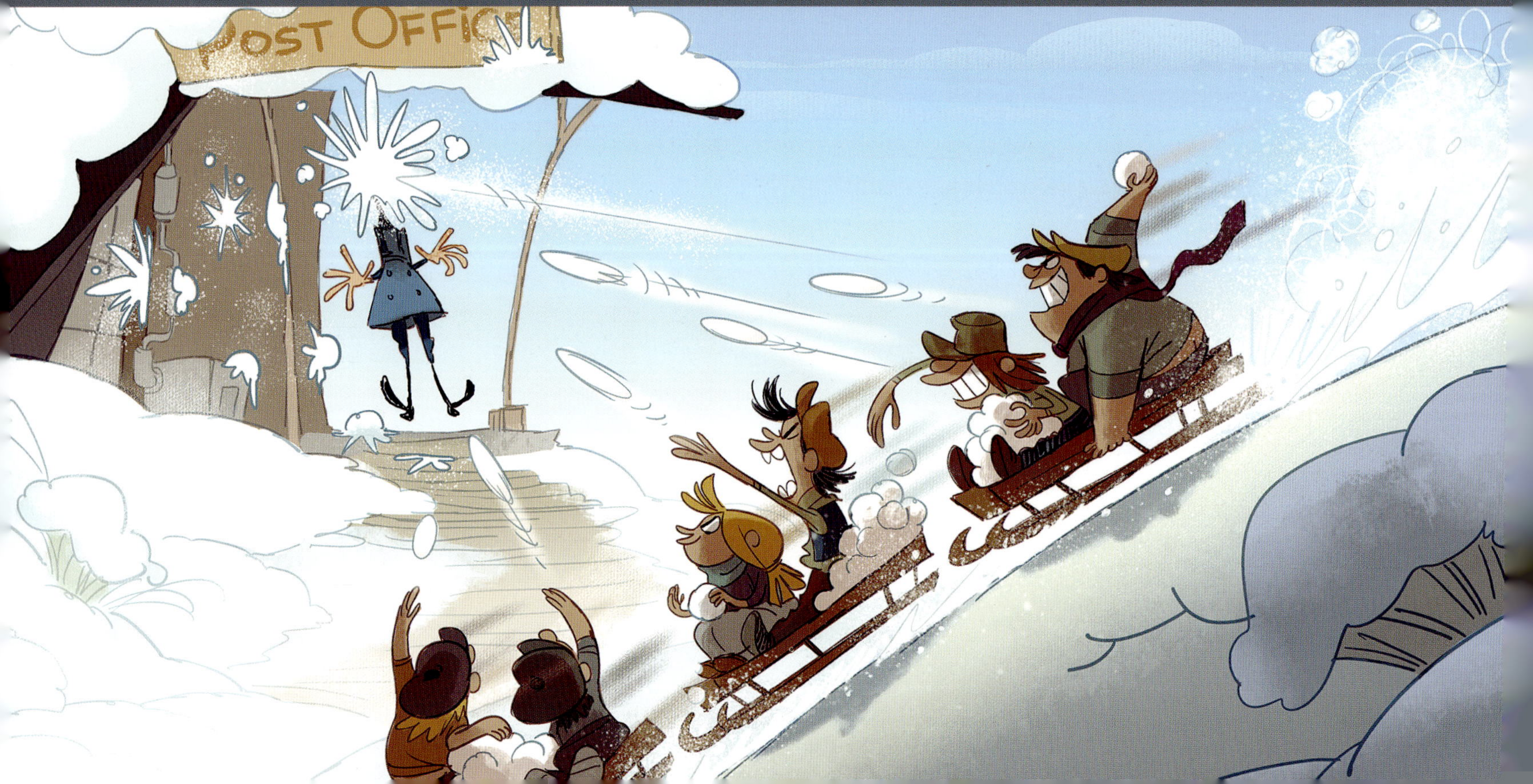

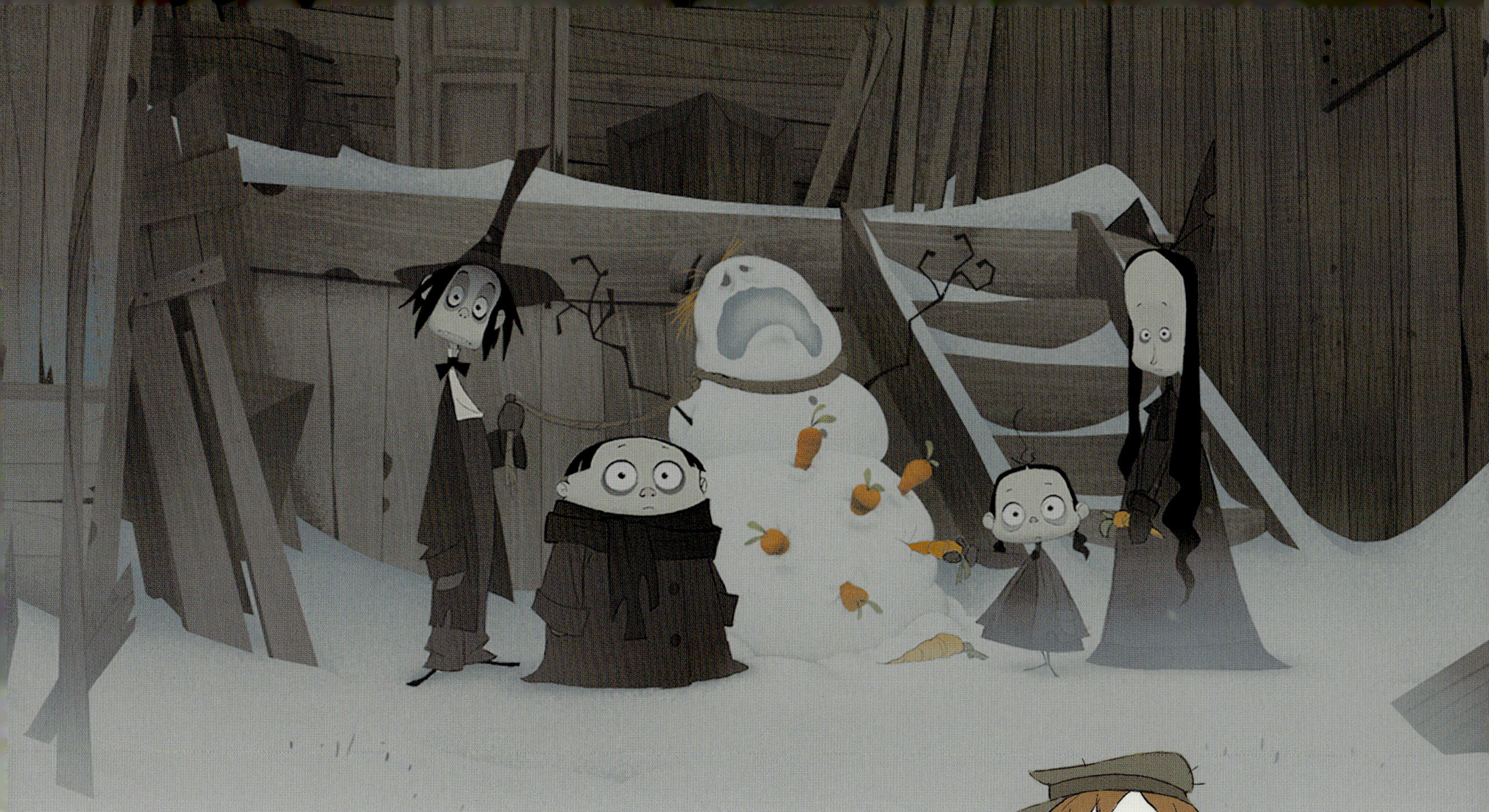

THIS PAGE: (TOP) Artwork by Thibaut Denise; (BOTTOM) Character exploration by Torsten Schrank.

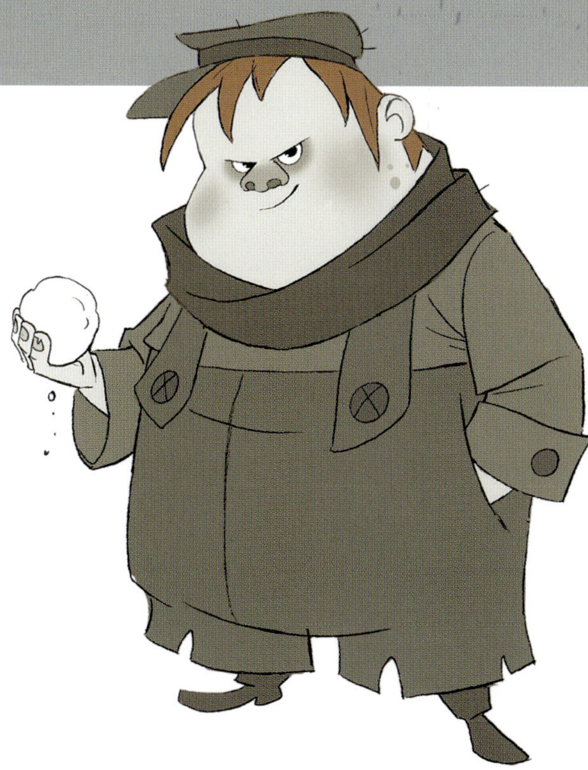

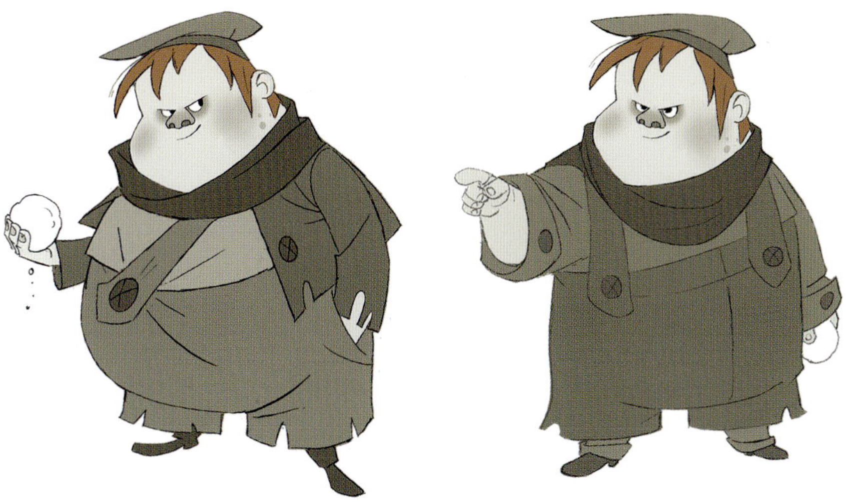

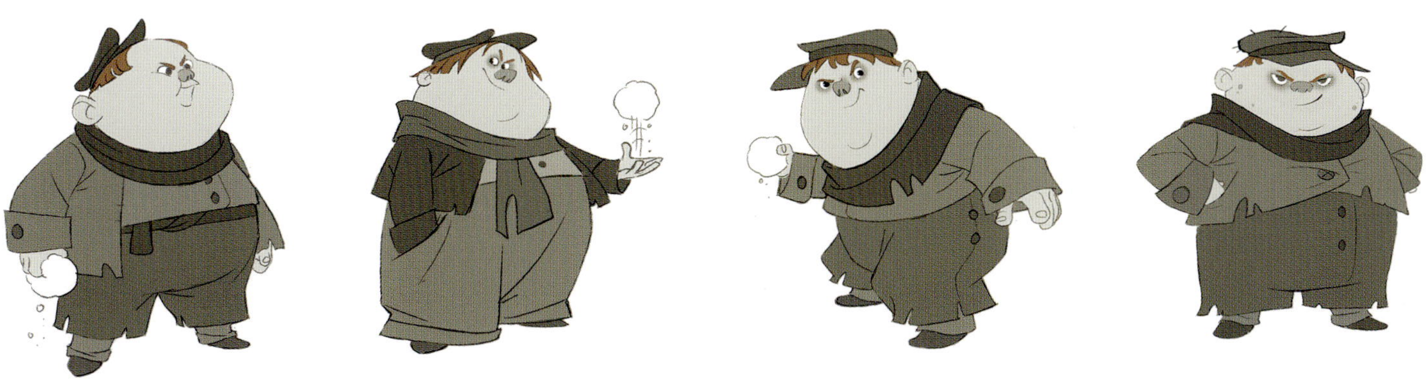

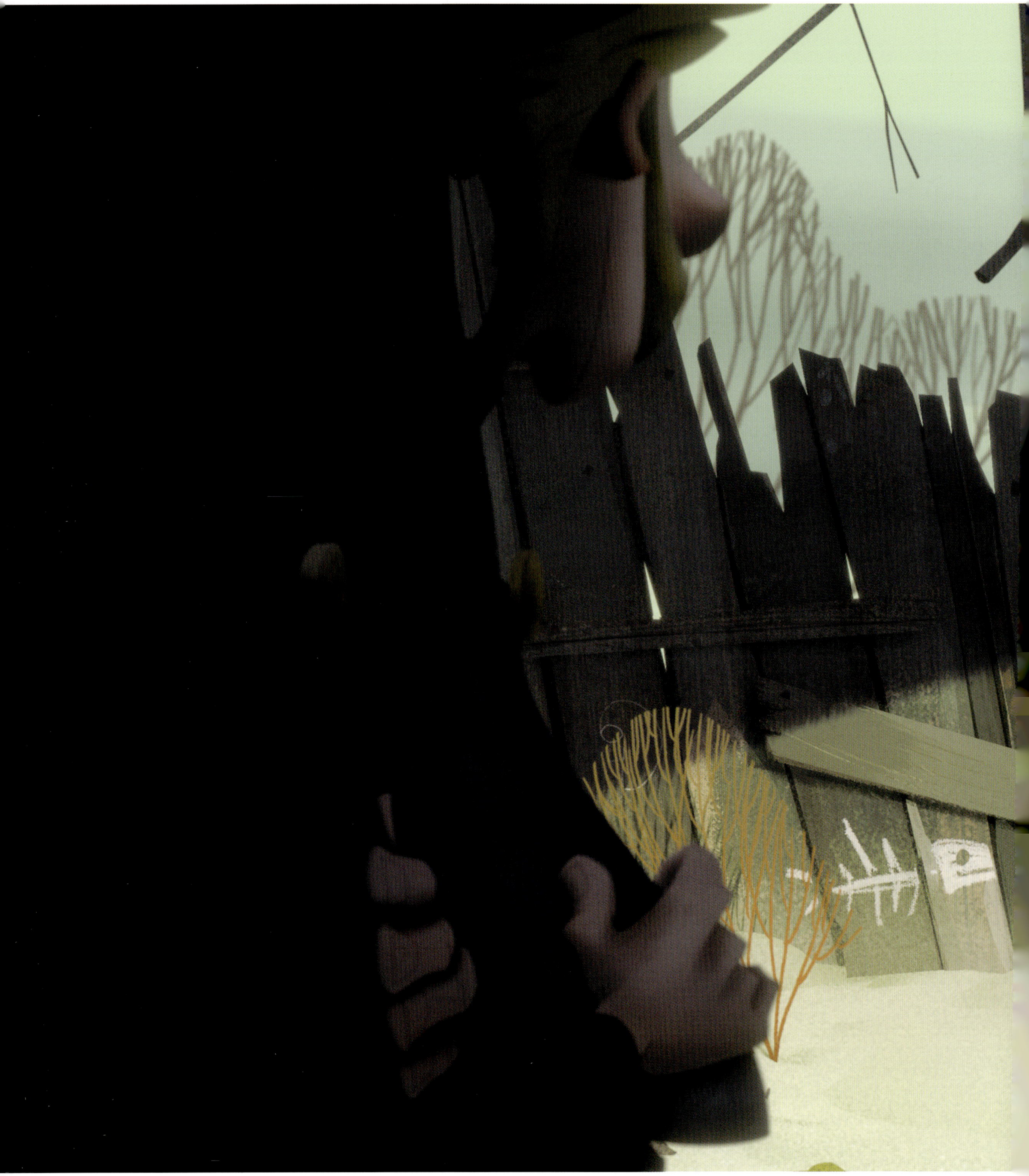

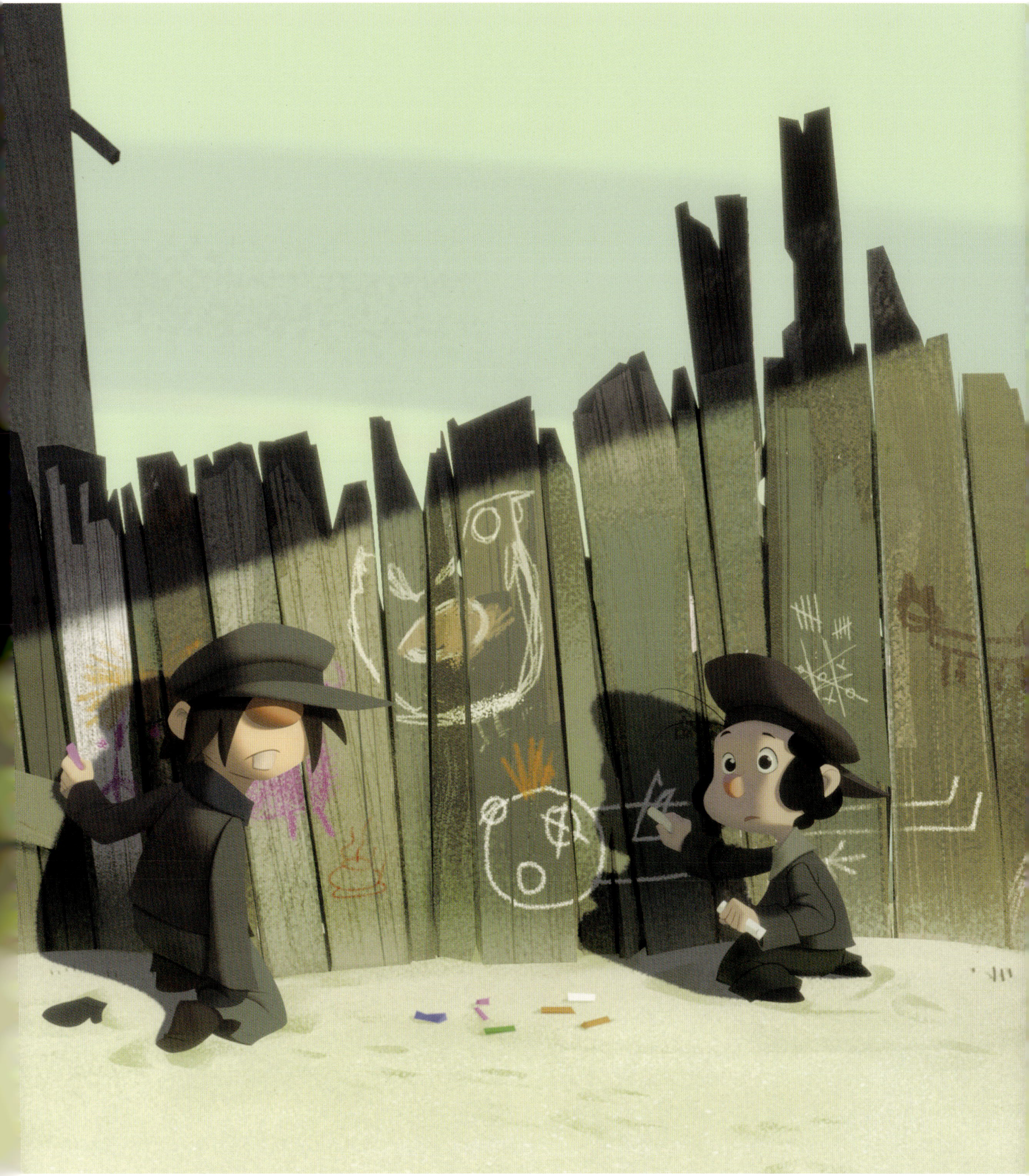

The Krums

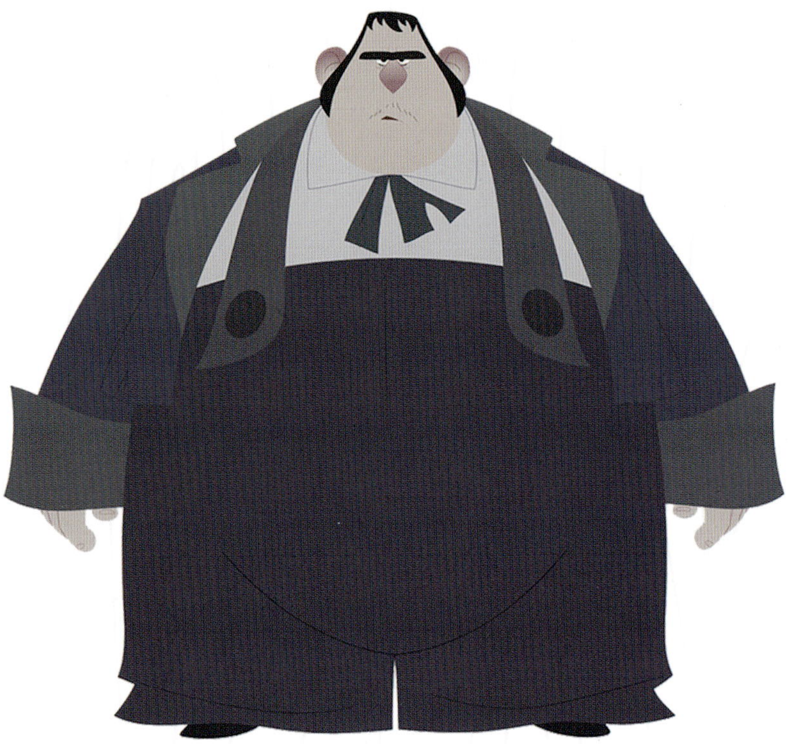

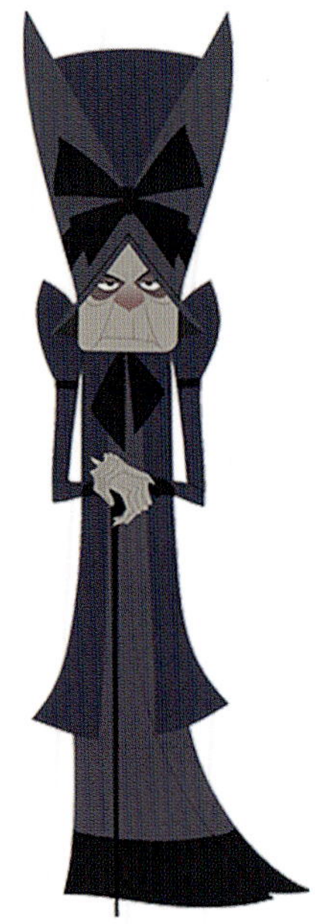

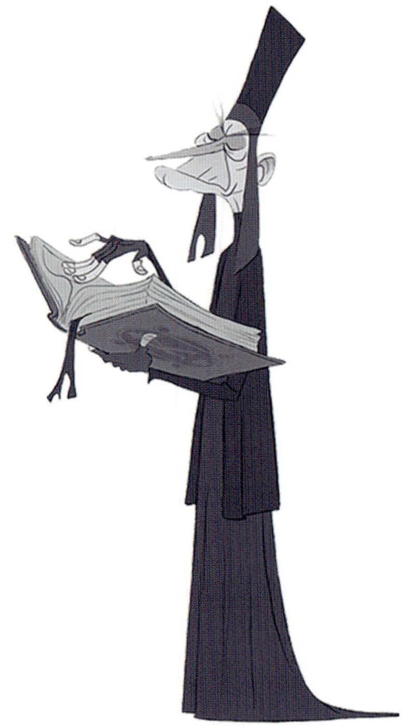

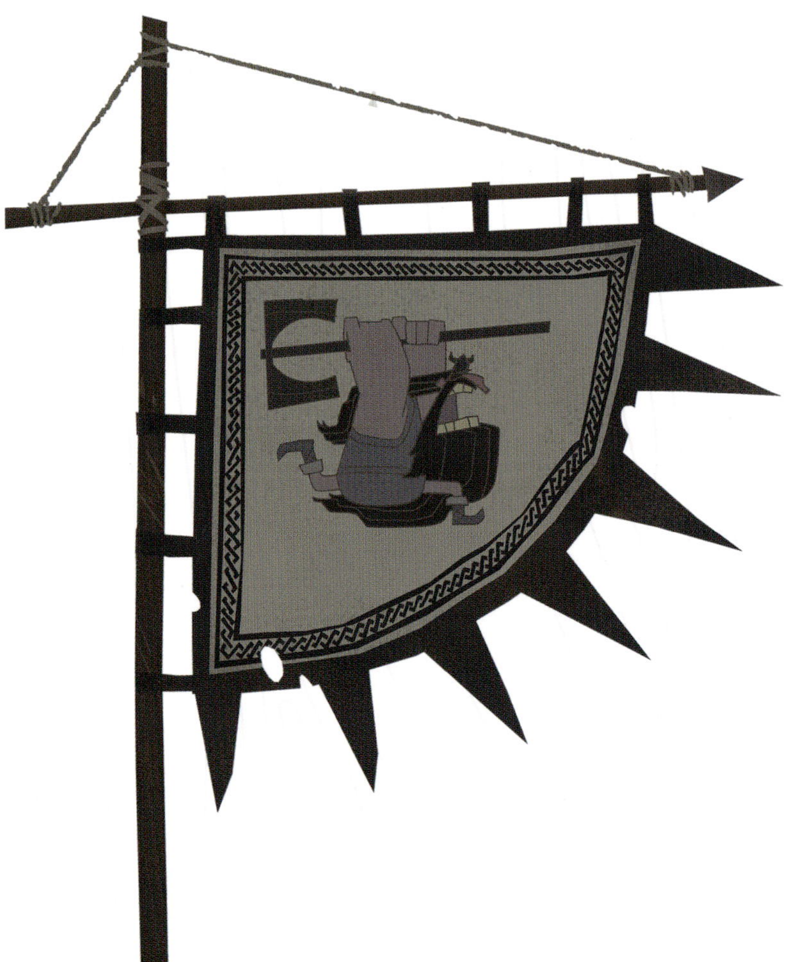

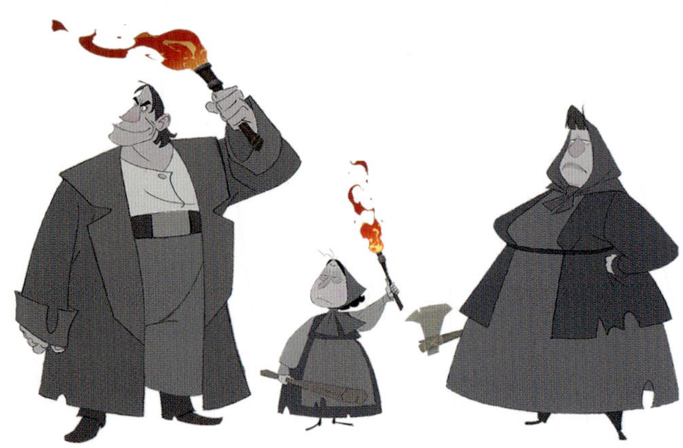

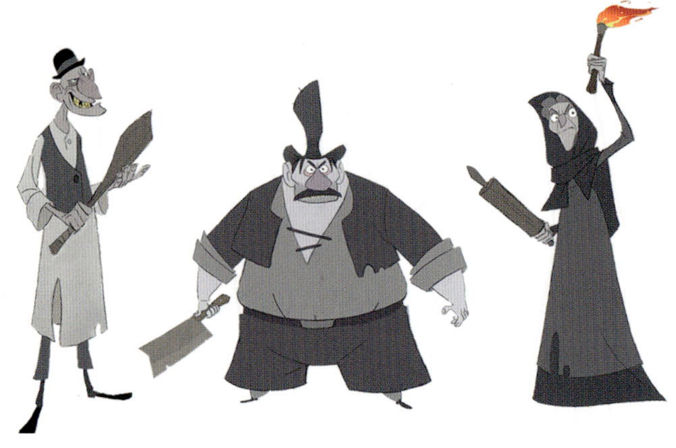

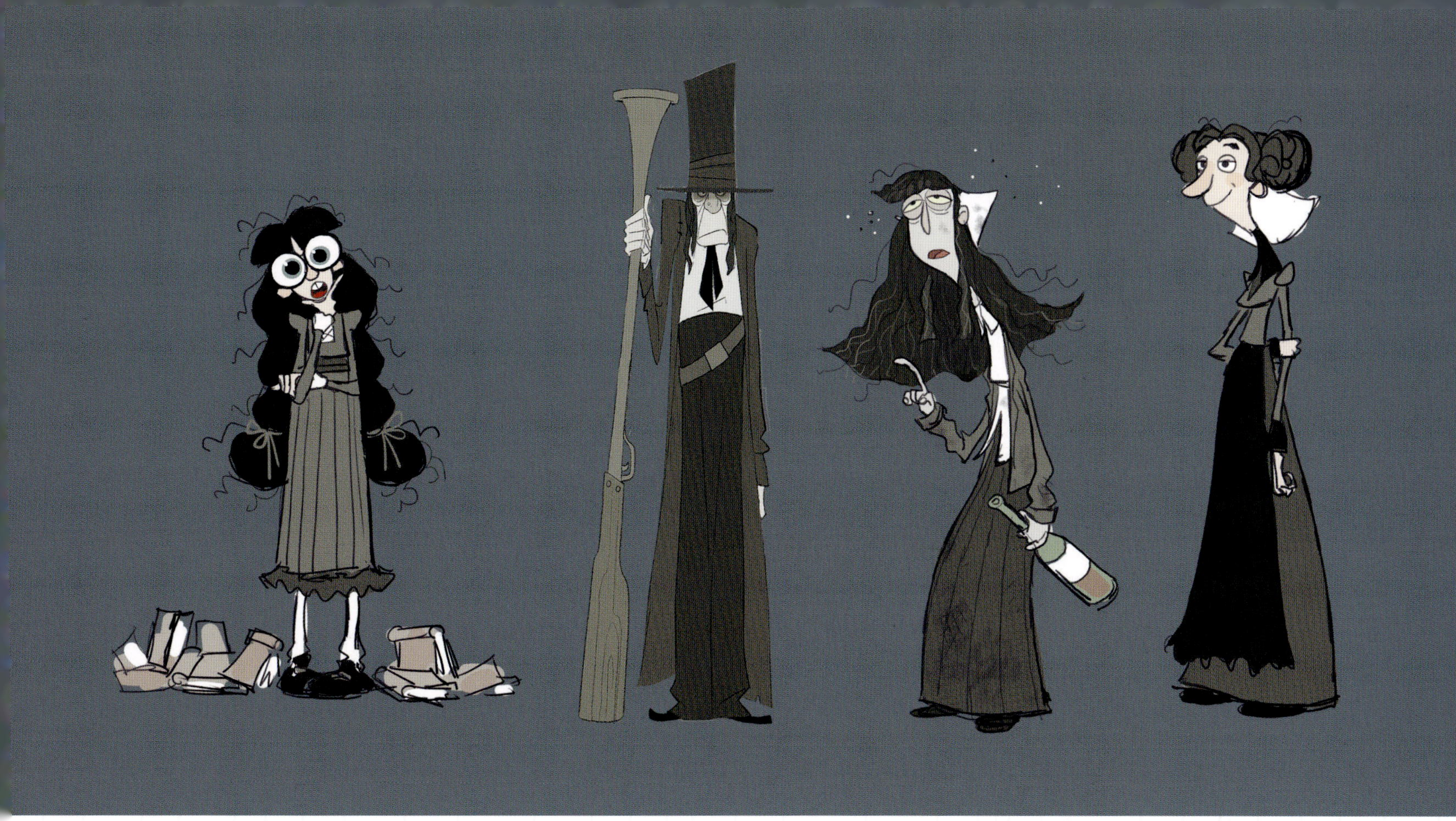

THIS SPREAD: Artwork by Torsten Schrank and Daniel Fernandez.

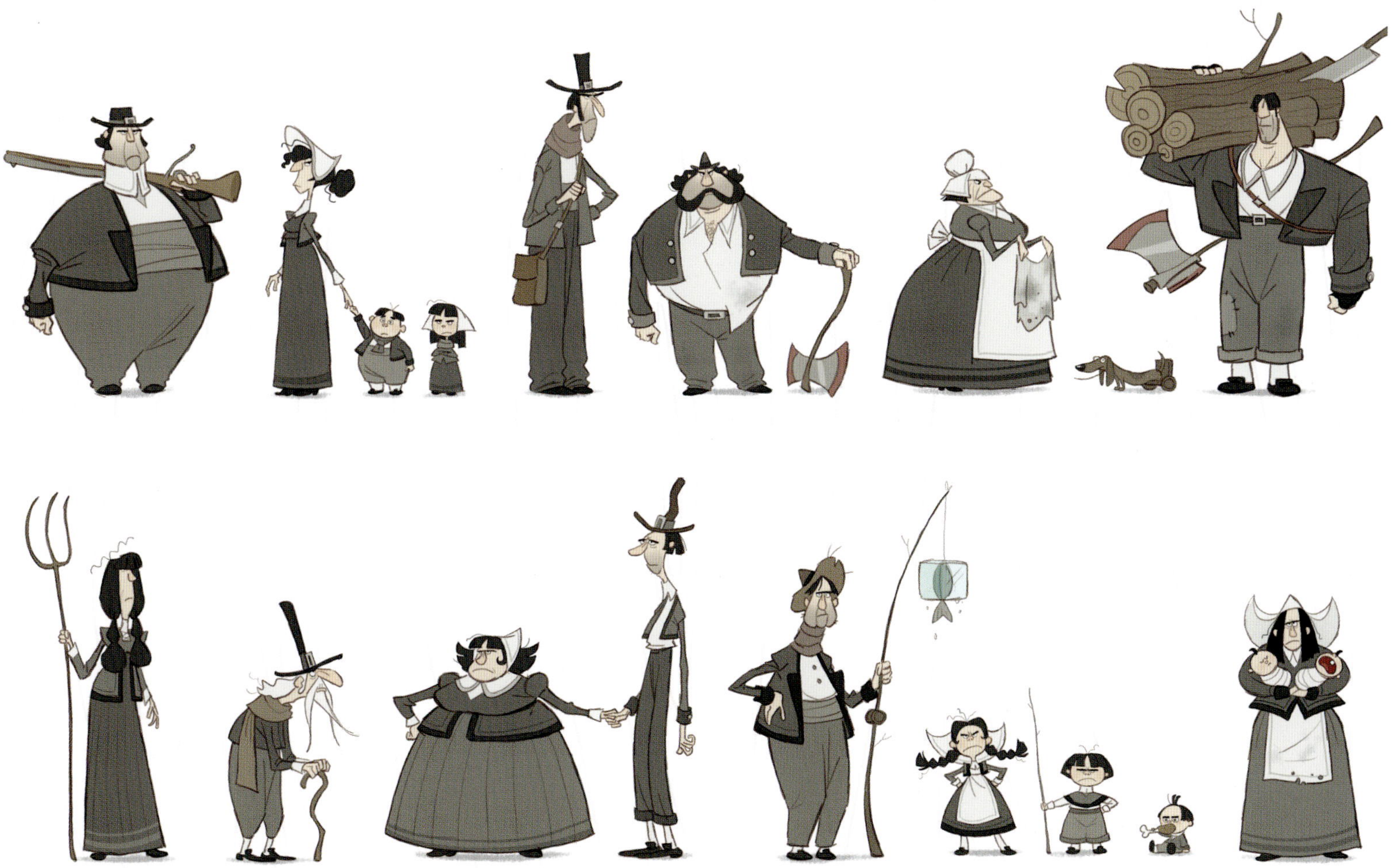

Mrs. Krum

Sergio Pablos says he never thought of Joan Cusack when he was writing the part of Mrs. Krum but, because he had been a huge fan of the actress for a very long time, he really wanted her to be involved in the movie. "She came in, and she has this ability to go from very small to quite huge," the director says. "She has such an amazing range, which allowed the character to have a lot to play with. That's why the animators [had] a blast with this character!"

Supervising animator Charlie Bonifacio adds, "The designs of some of the characters, like the two clan leaders, have evolved a little bit to make them more flexible, especially that of Mrs. Krum. Originally, she was designed as this craggy old lady, but then, when we had Joan Cusack as the voice actress, we made her more flexible and a lot more dynamic. The change came more in the way we posed her, and the way we visualized her felt more dynamic."

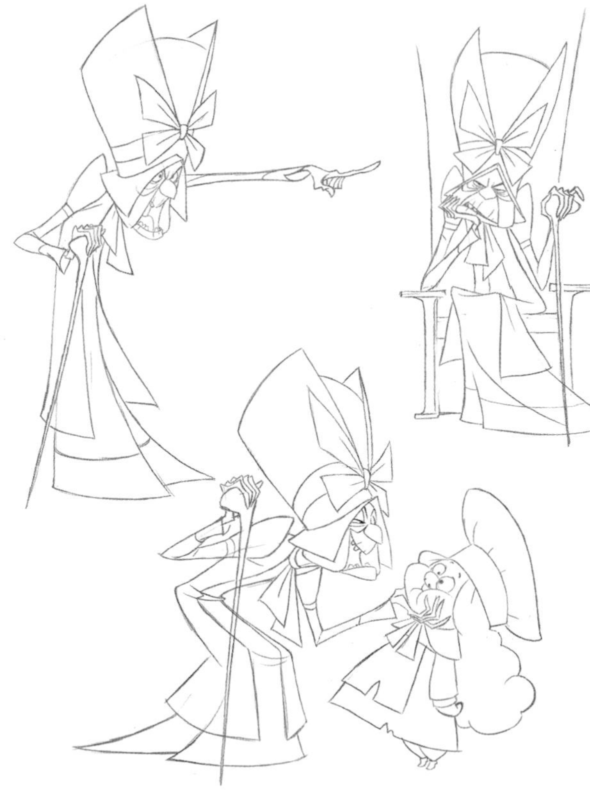

THIS SPREAD: Character exploration by Torsten Schrank and Daniel Fernandez.

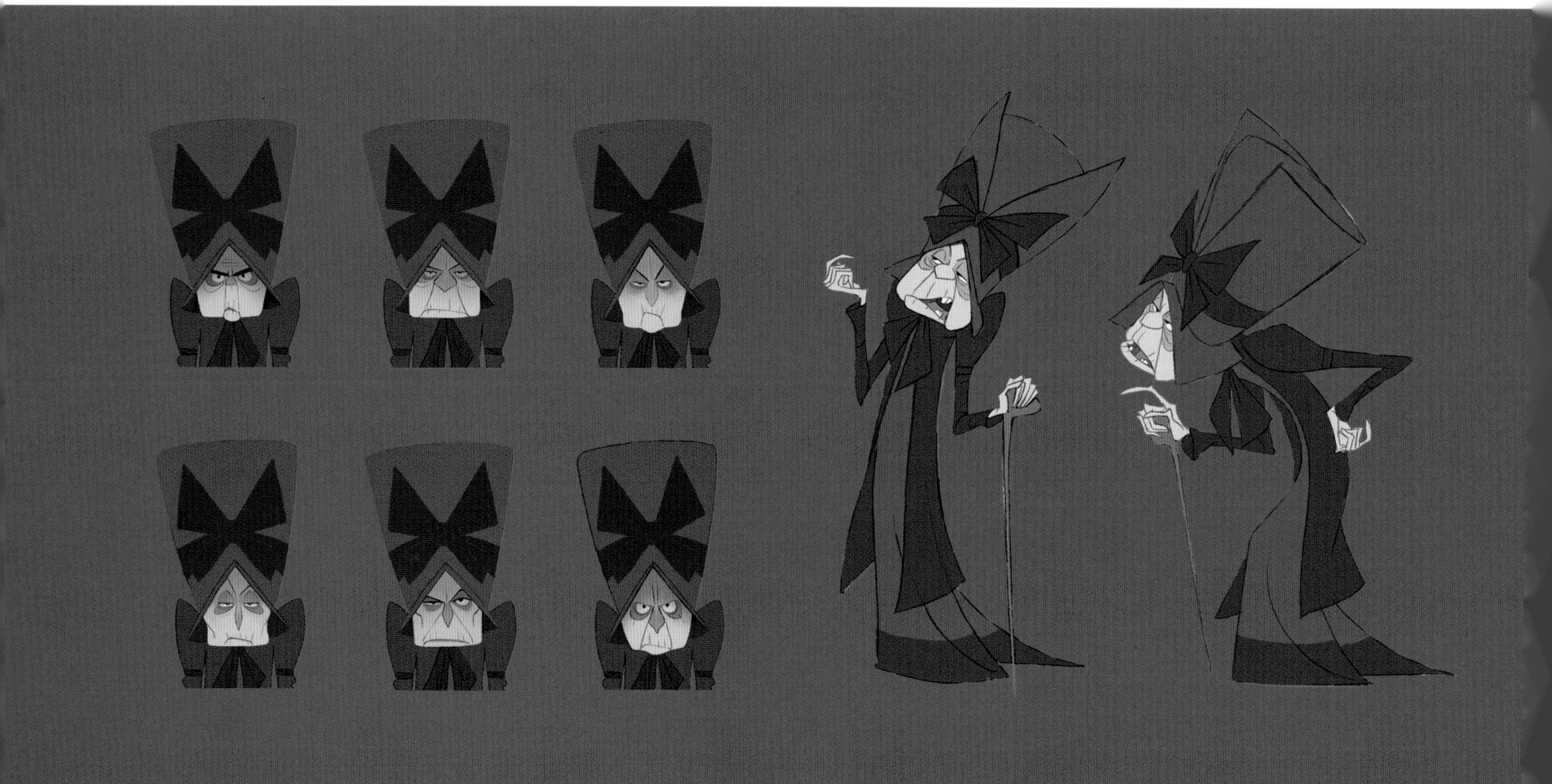

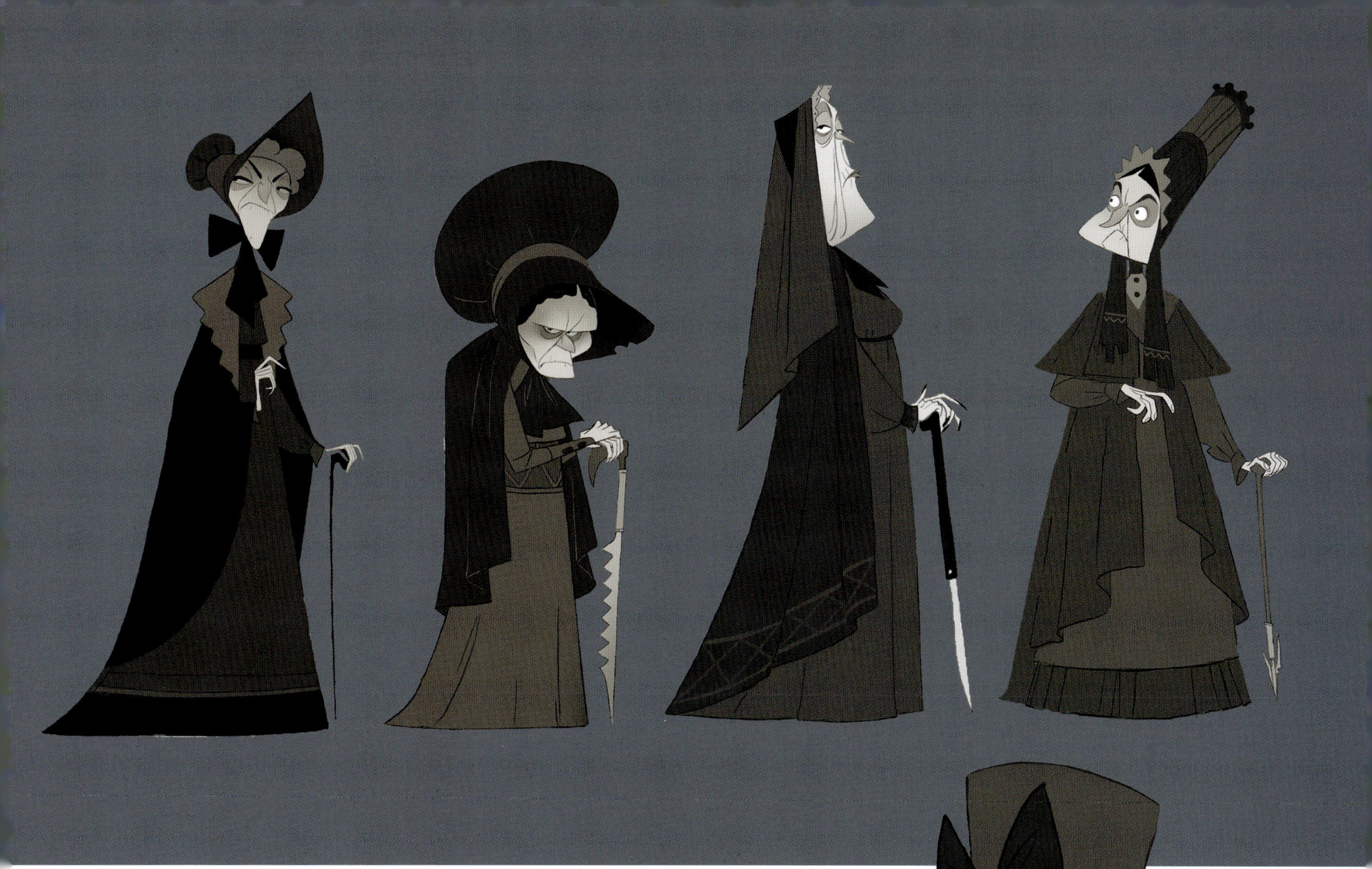

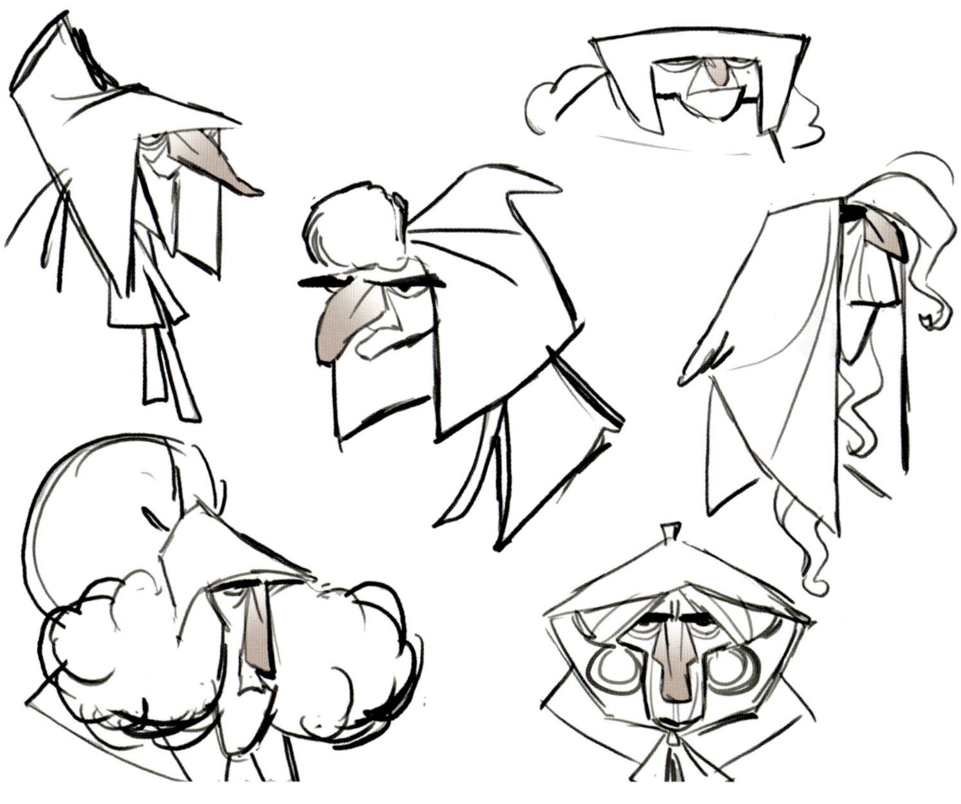

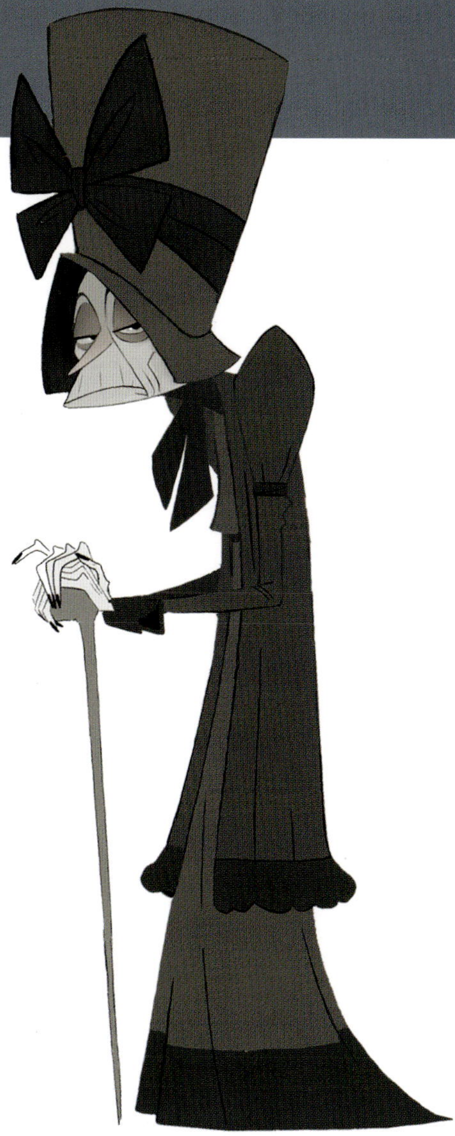

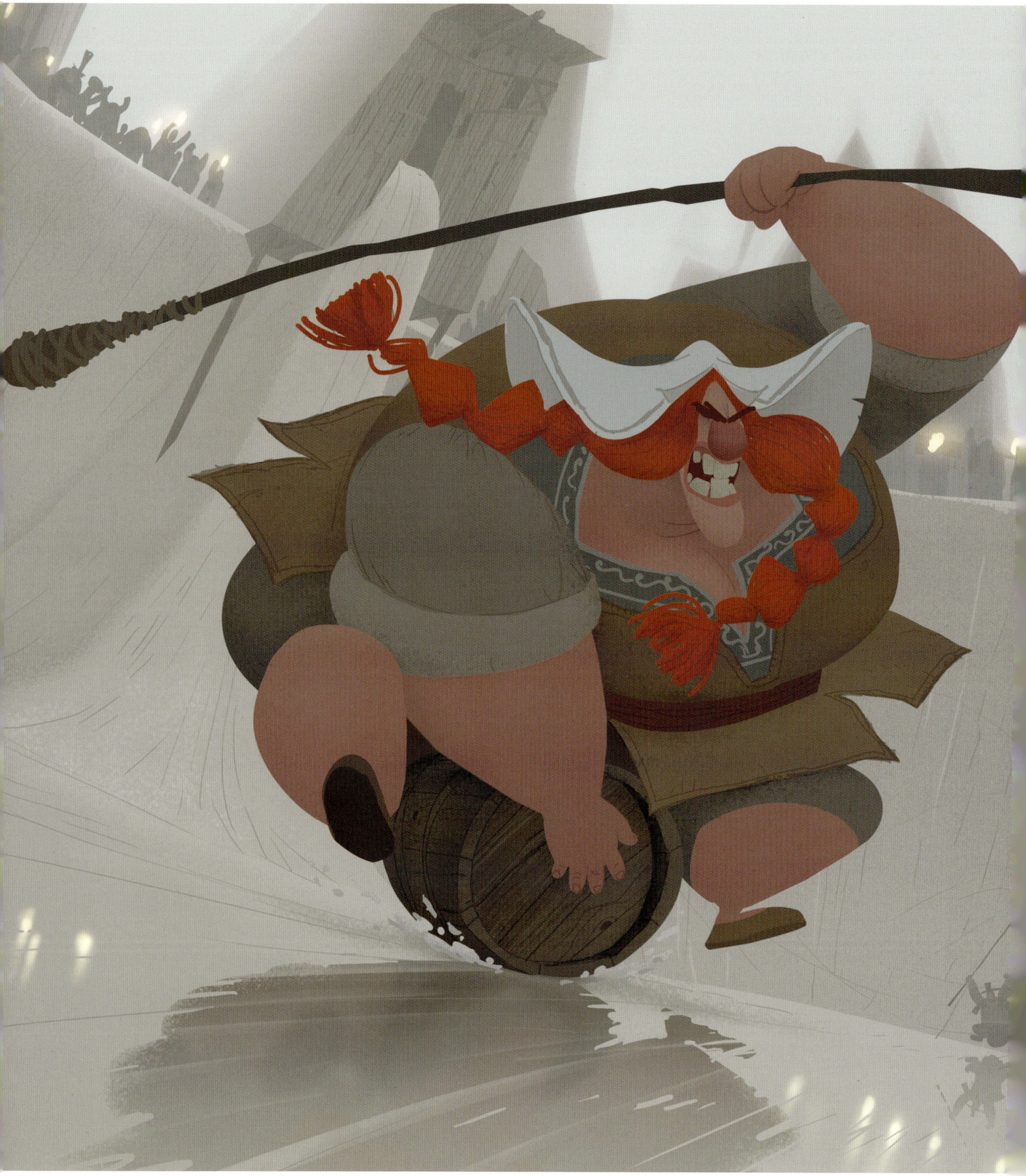

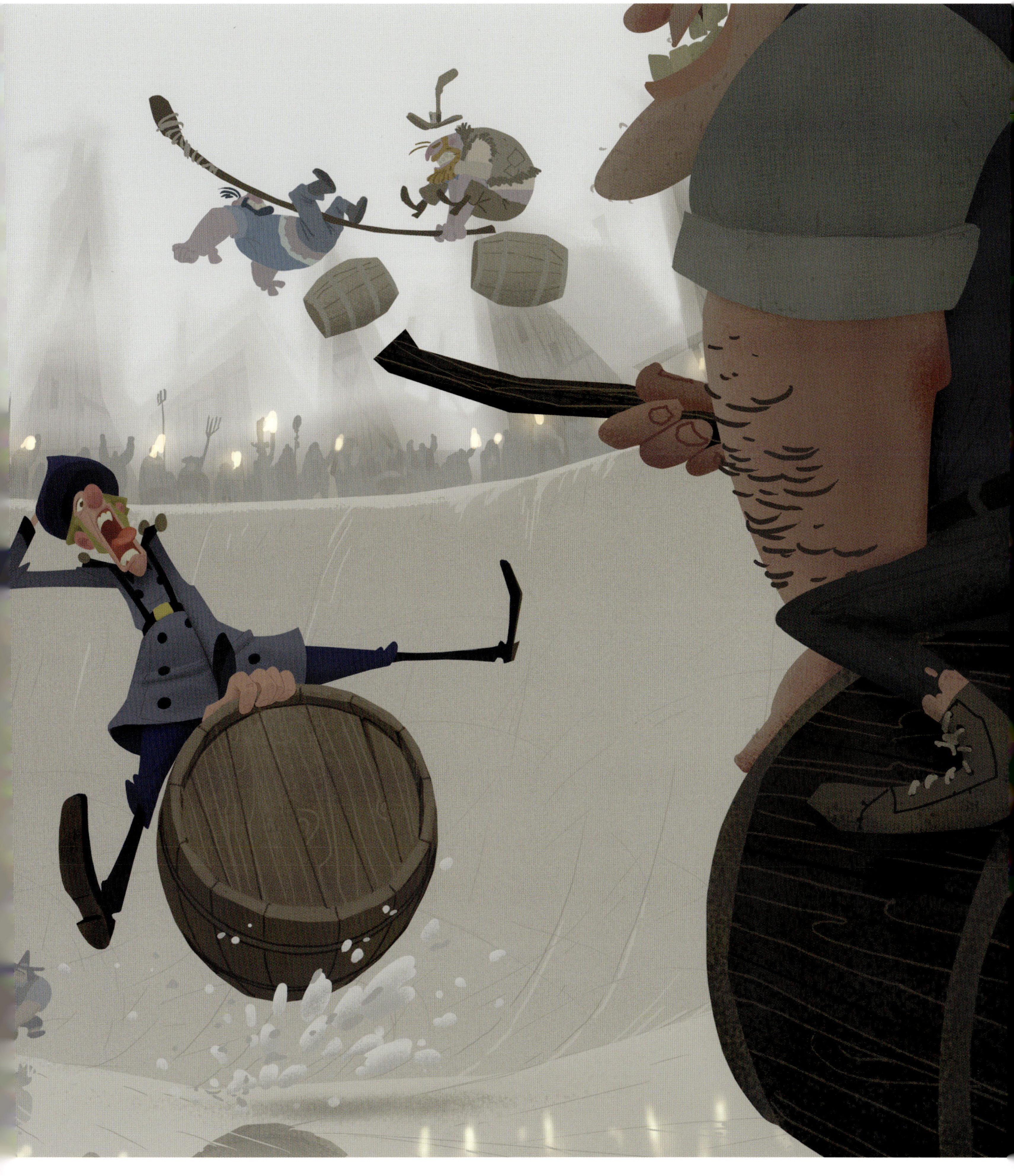

The Ellingboes

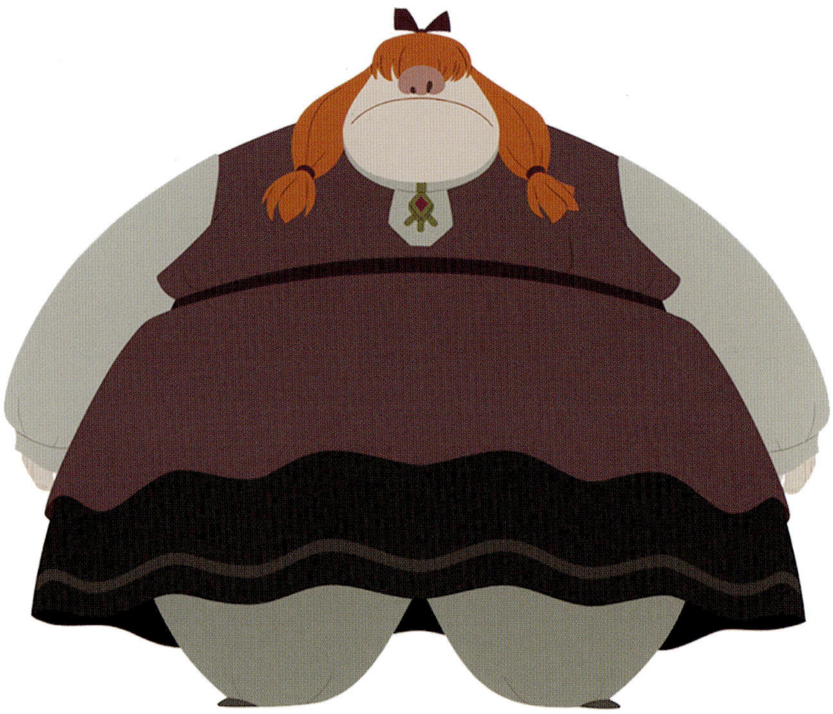

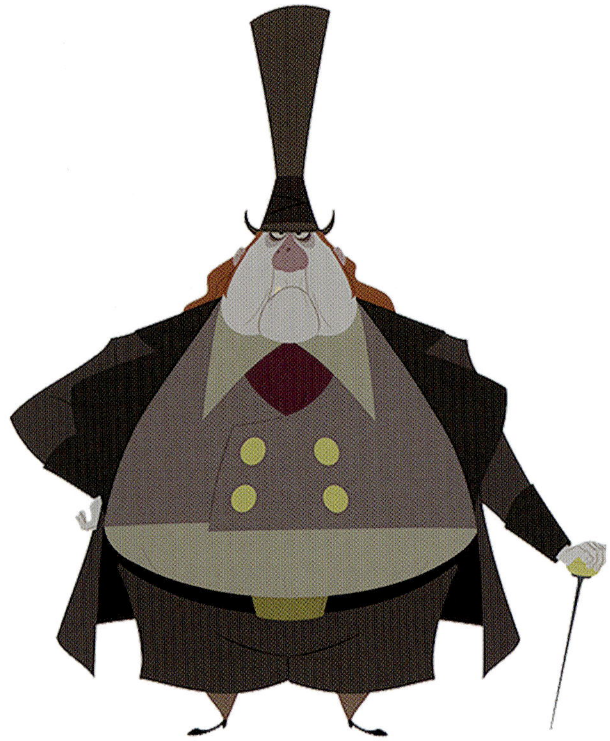

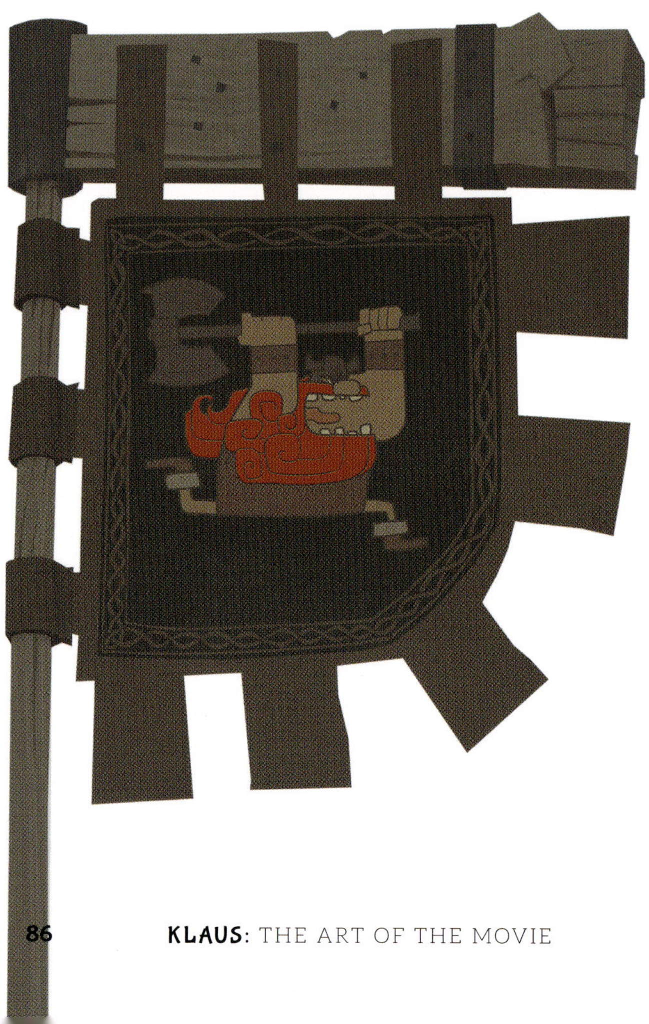

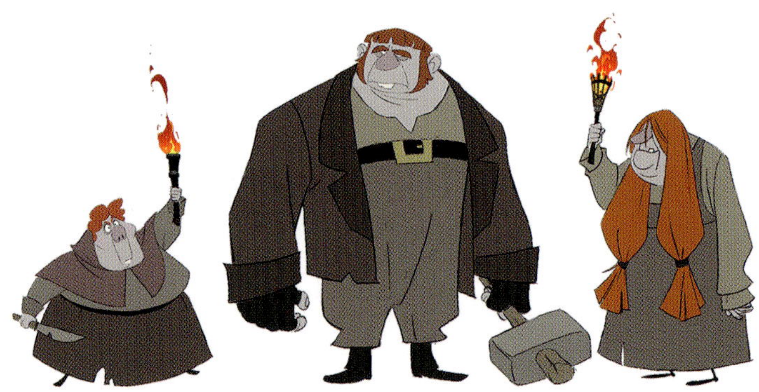

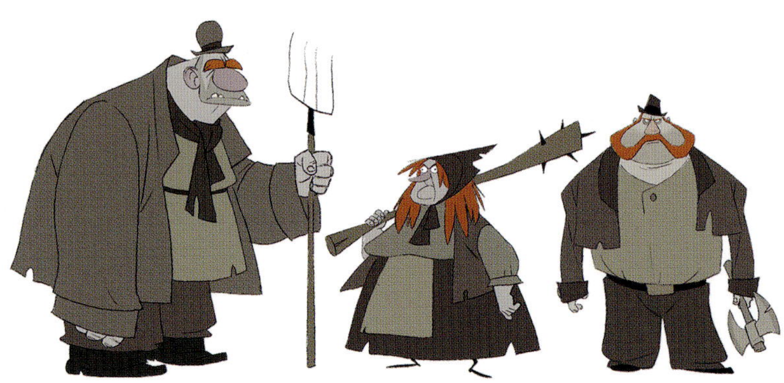

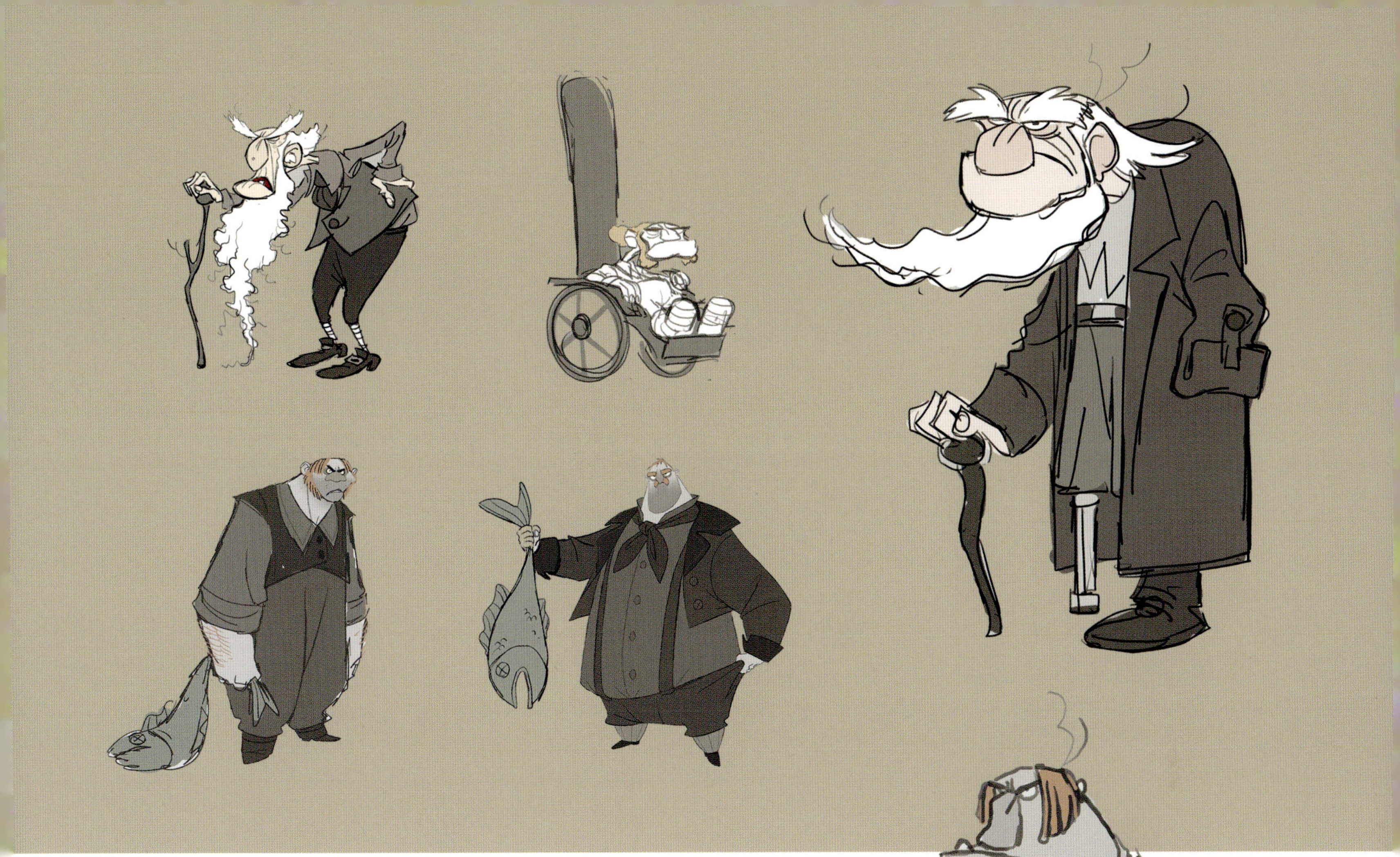

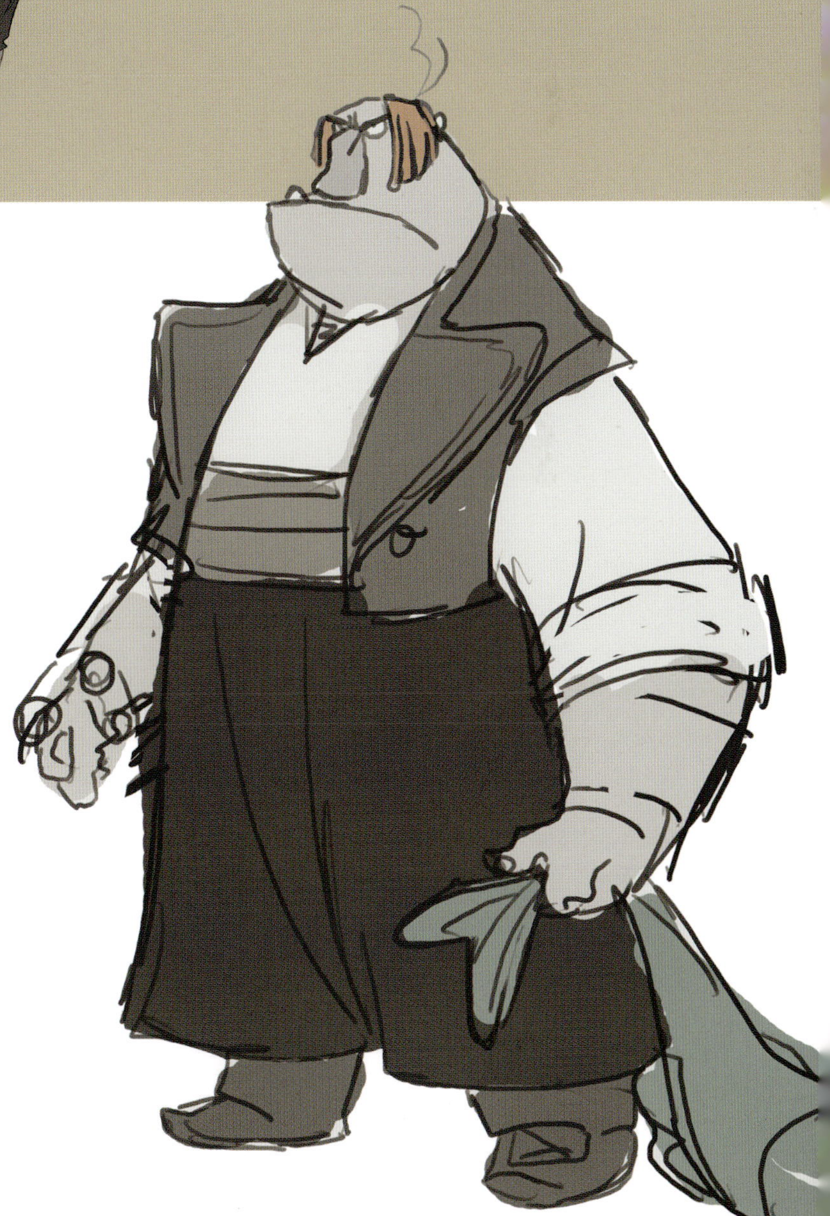

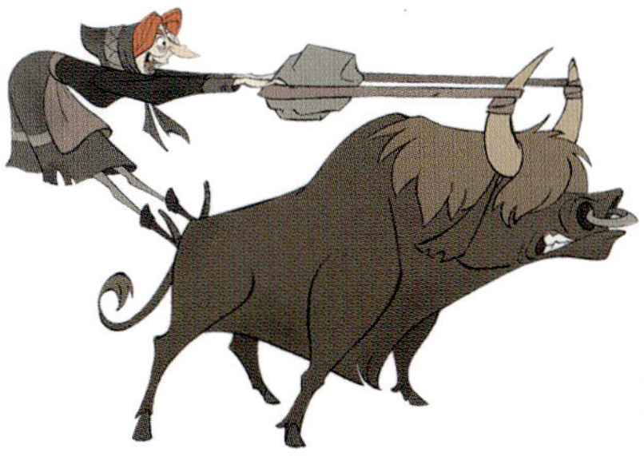

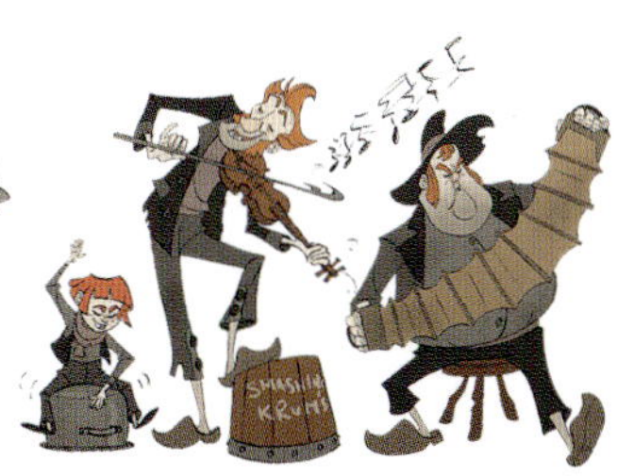

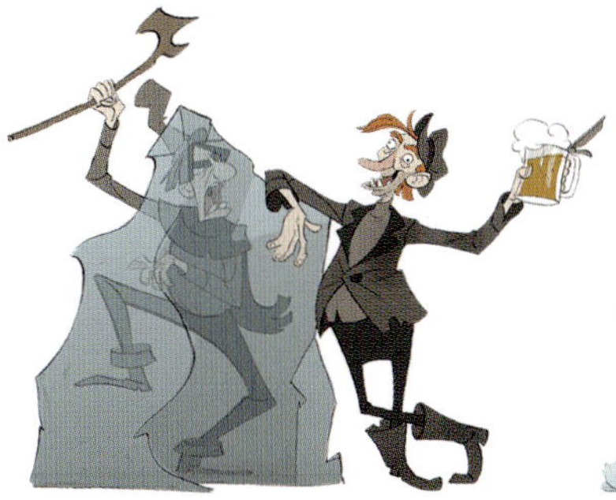

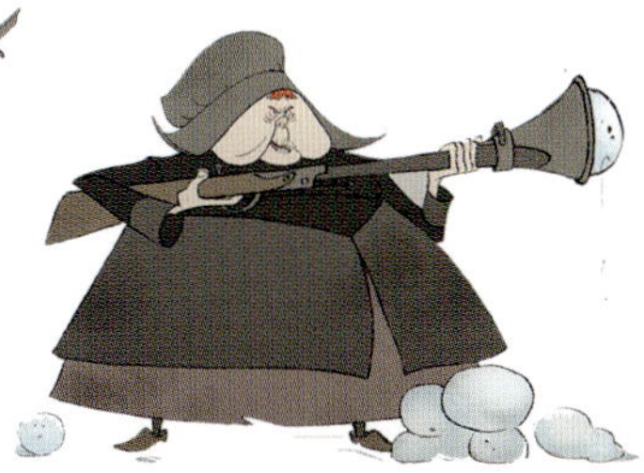

PREVIOUS SPREAD: Concept artwork by Marcin Jakubowski and Juan Pablo Navas.

THIS SPREAD: Artwork by Torsten Schrank and Daniel Fernandez.

Mr. Ellingboe

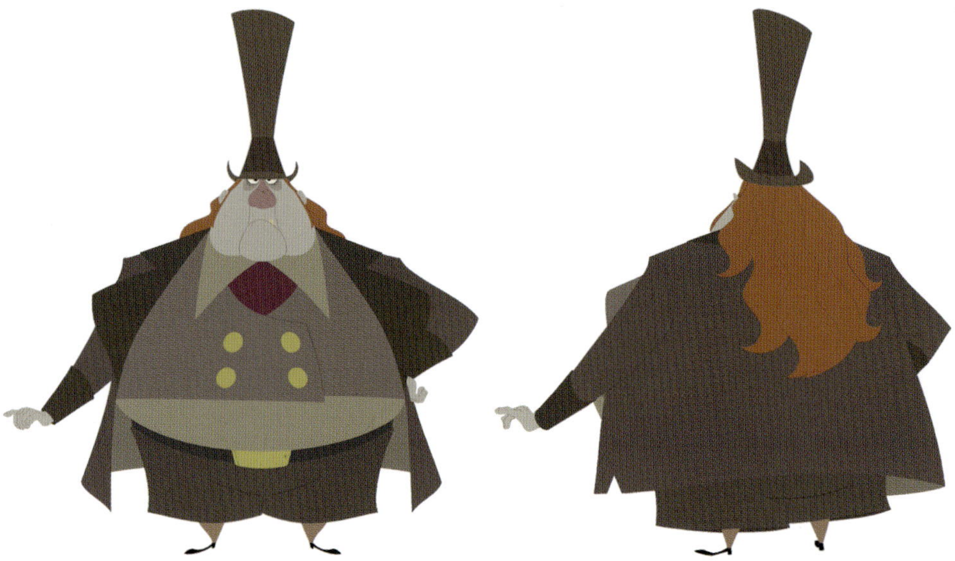

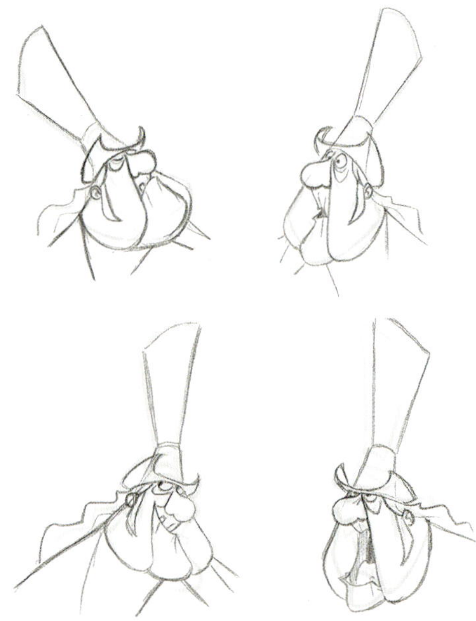

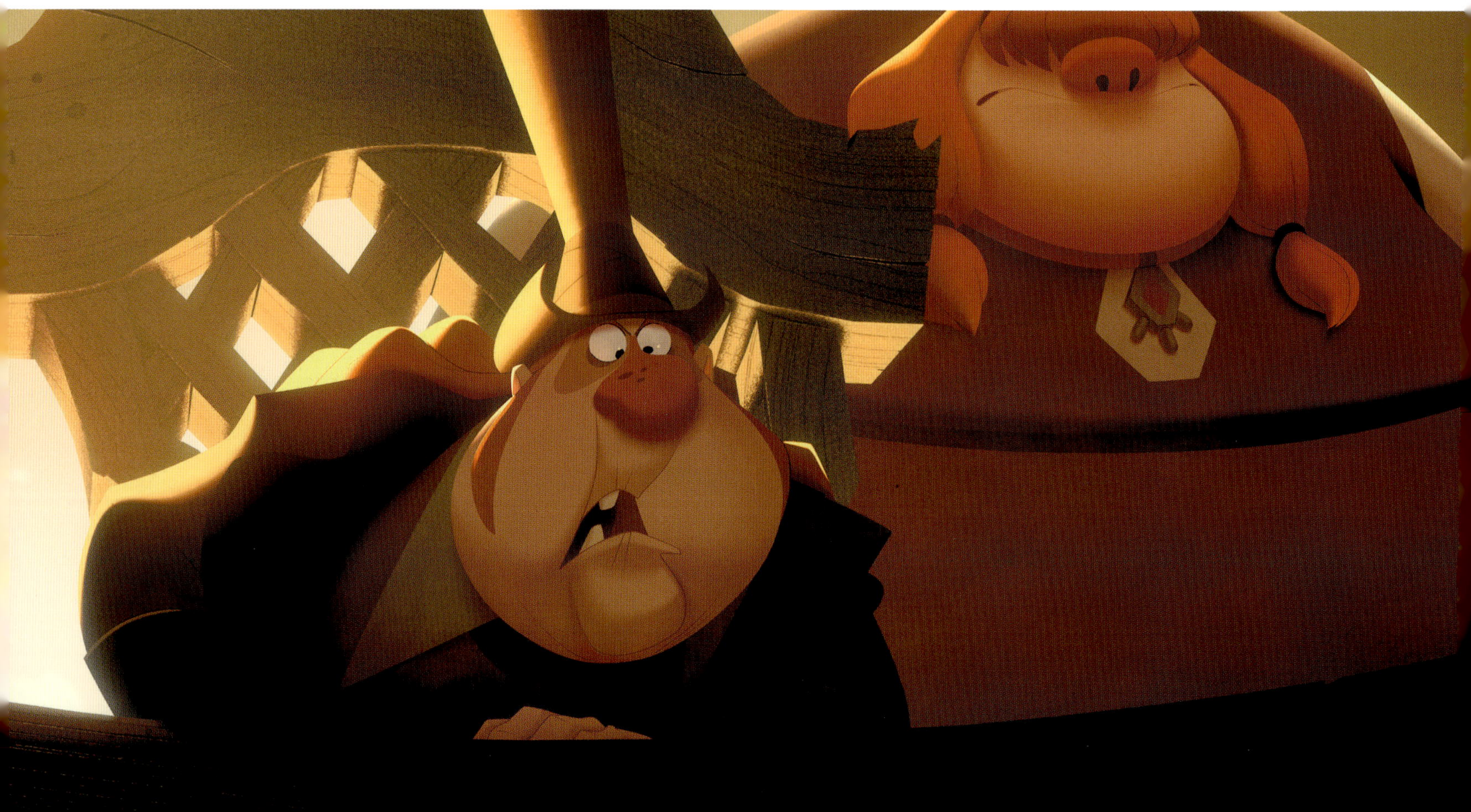

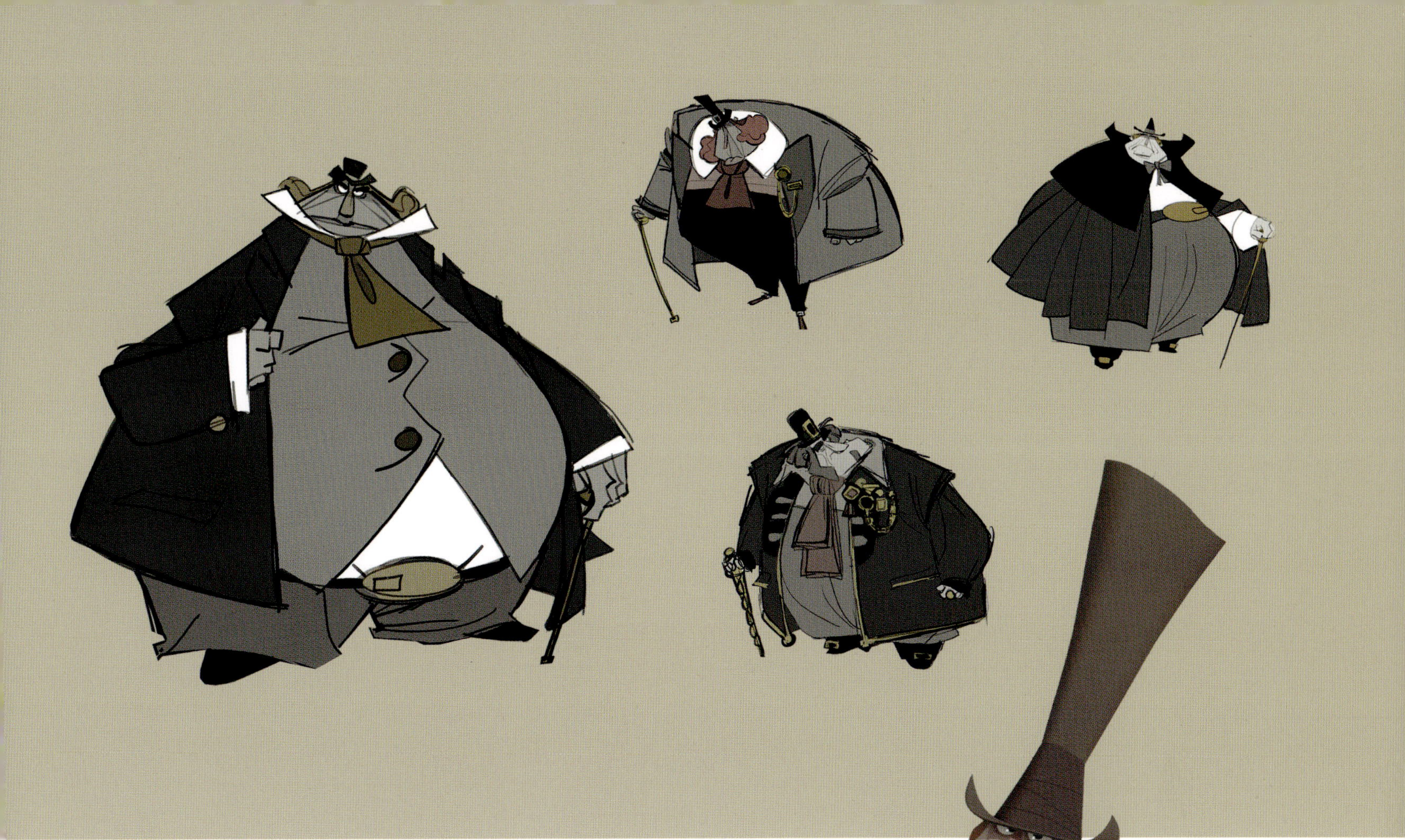

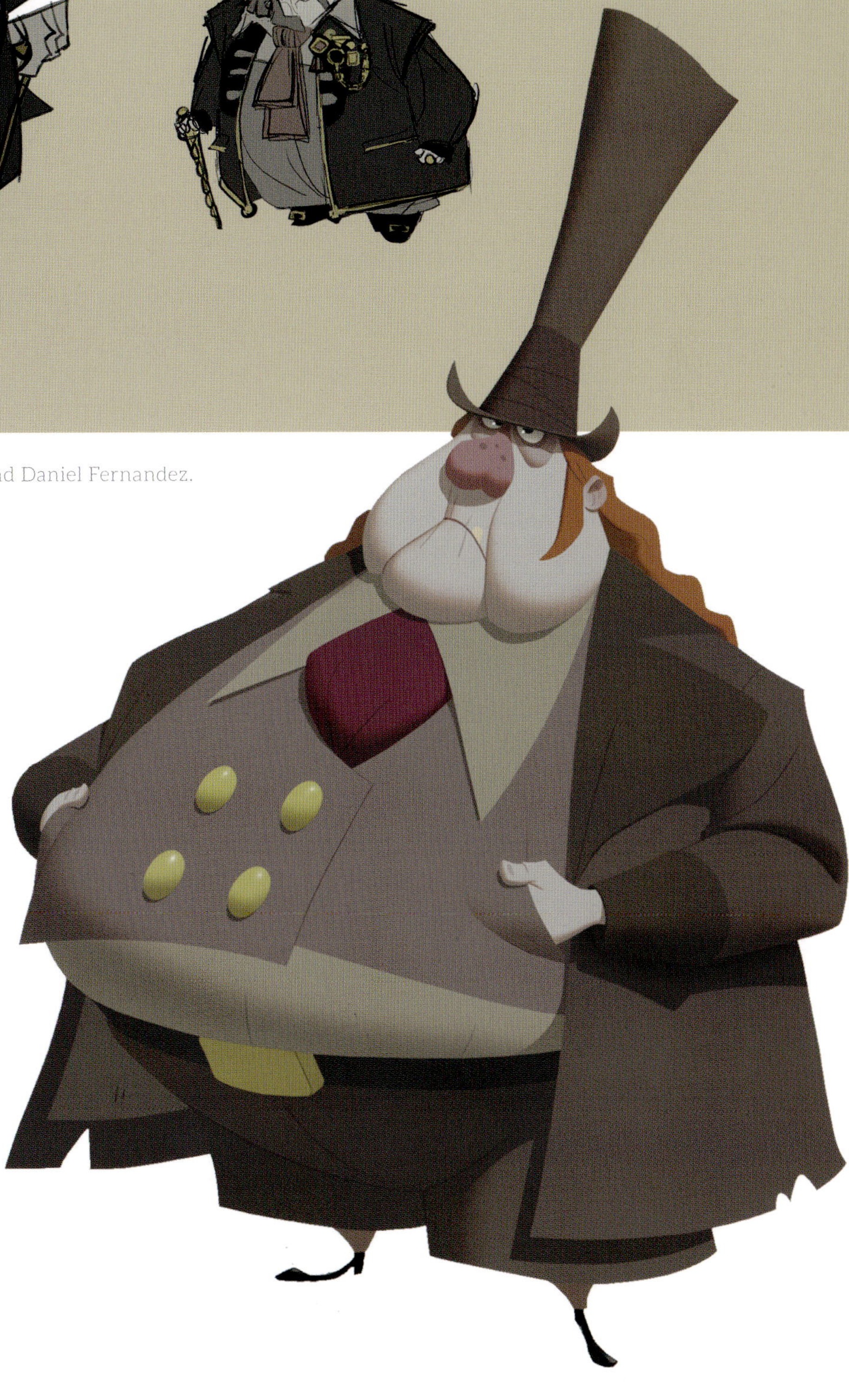

THIS SPREAD: Character design by Torsten Schrank and Daniel Fernandez.

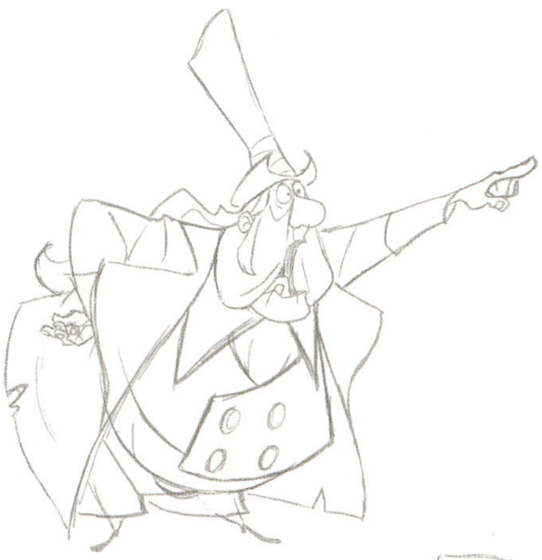

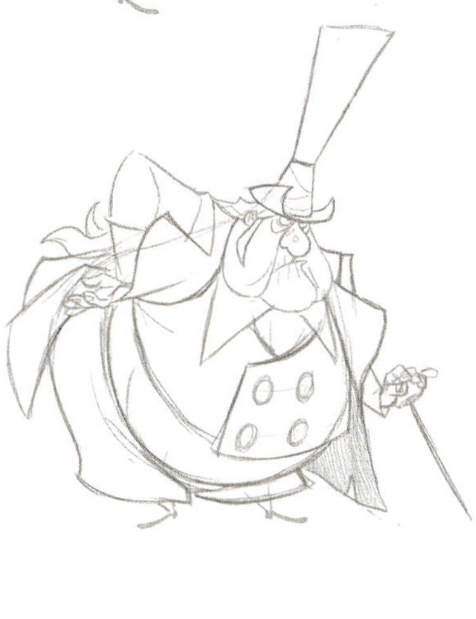

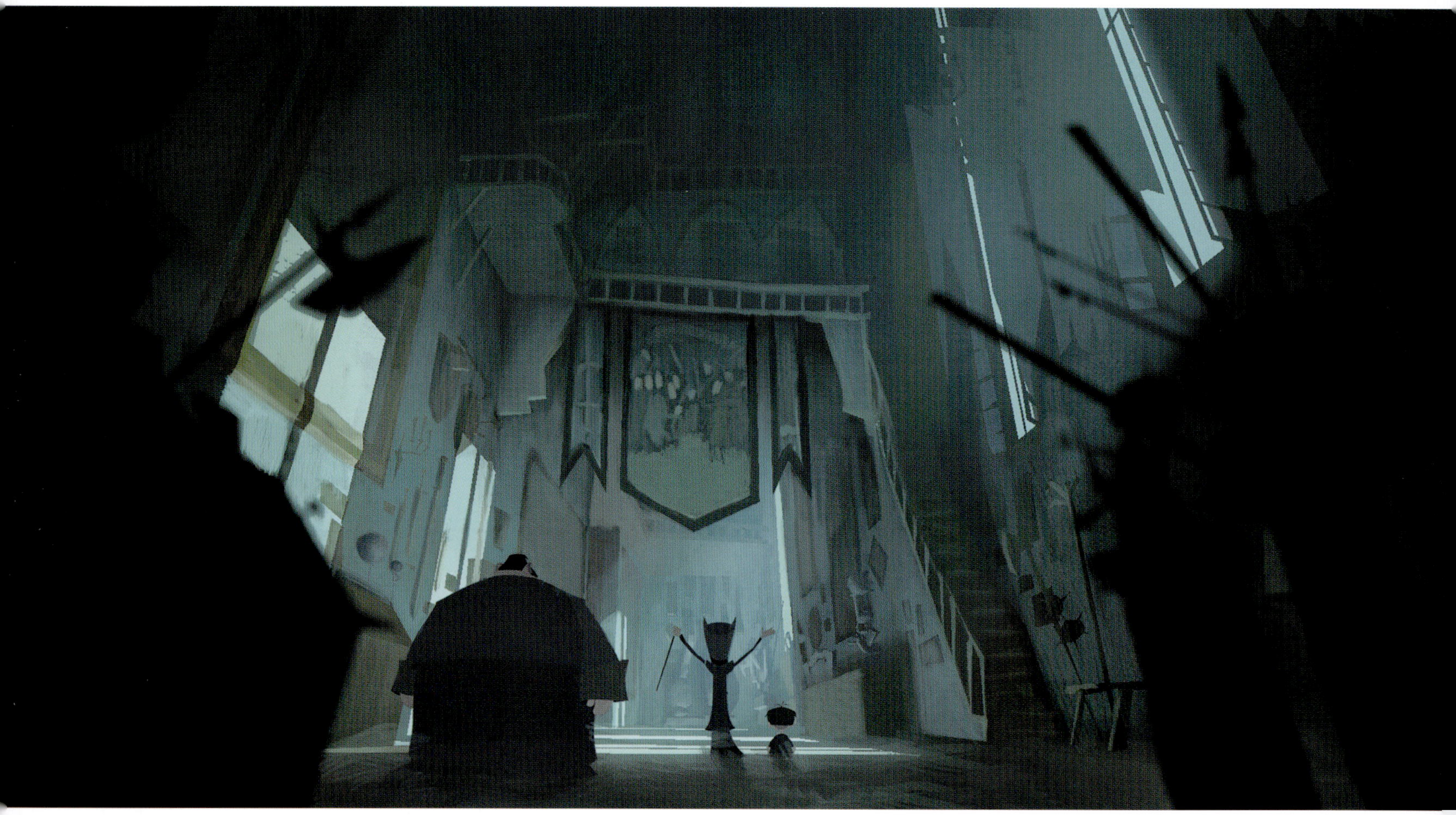

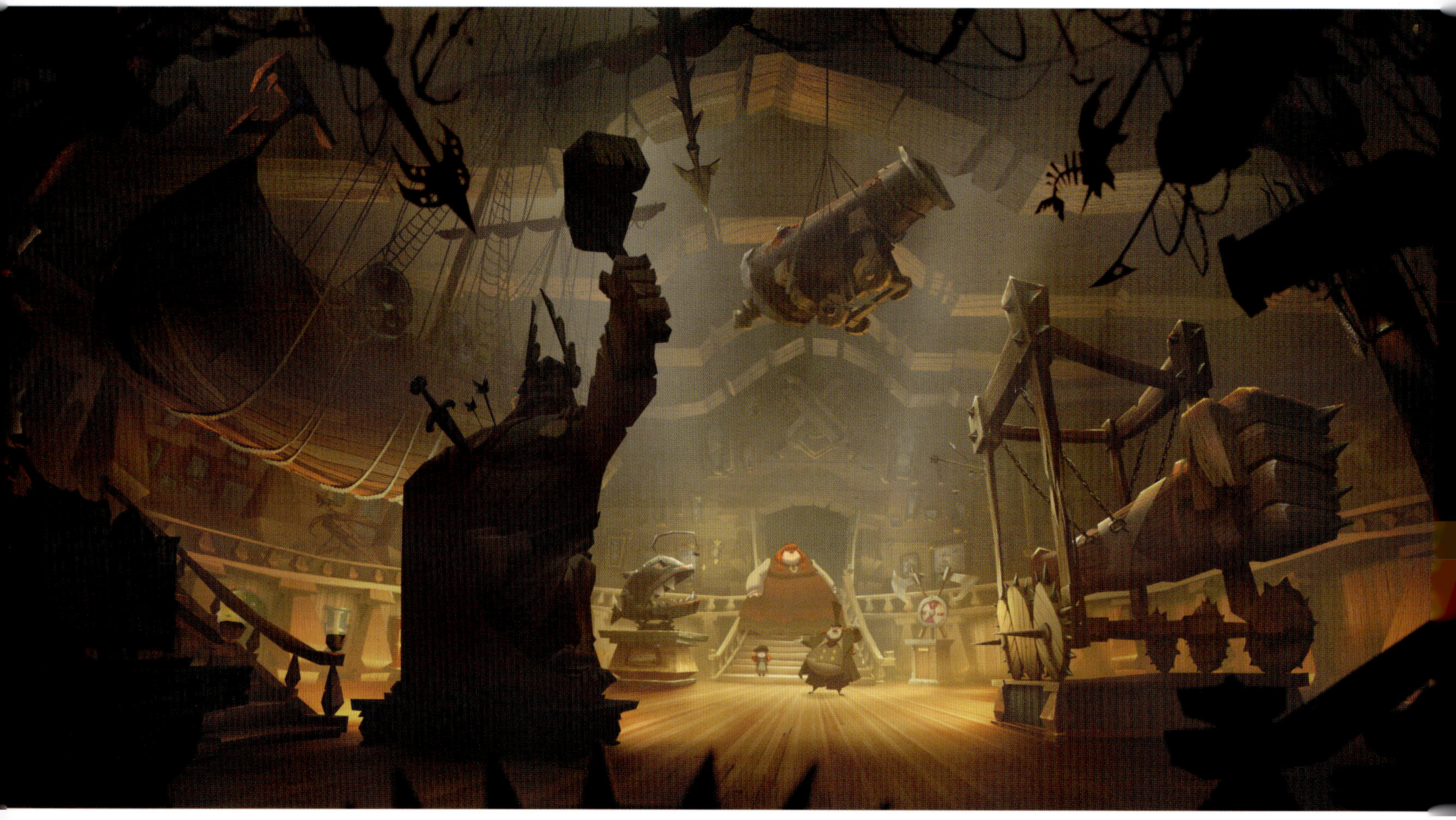

Mrs. Krum and Mr. Ellingboe's houses were designed with the looks of their owners in mind. The Krum house is tall and thin, while the Ellingboe manor is shorter and broader. The dark palette of the Krums and the earthy tones of the Ellingboes are also seen in the designs of their homes.

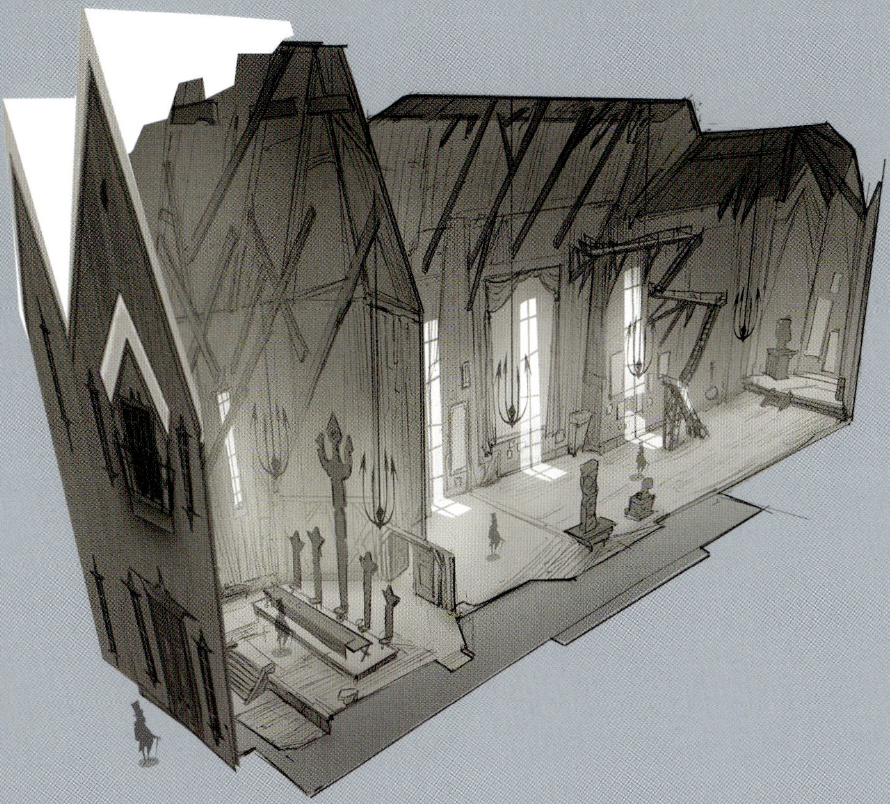

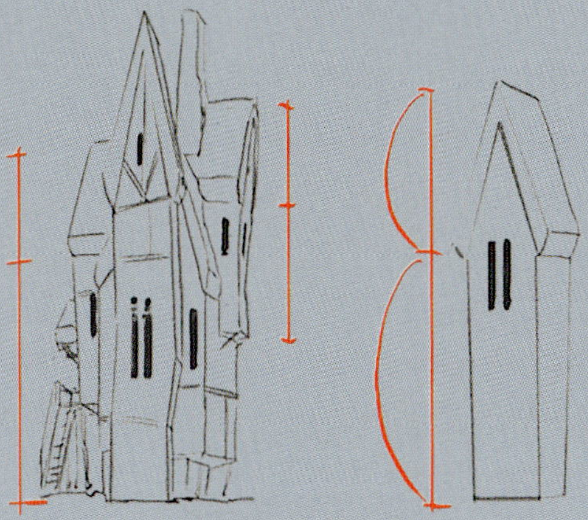

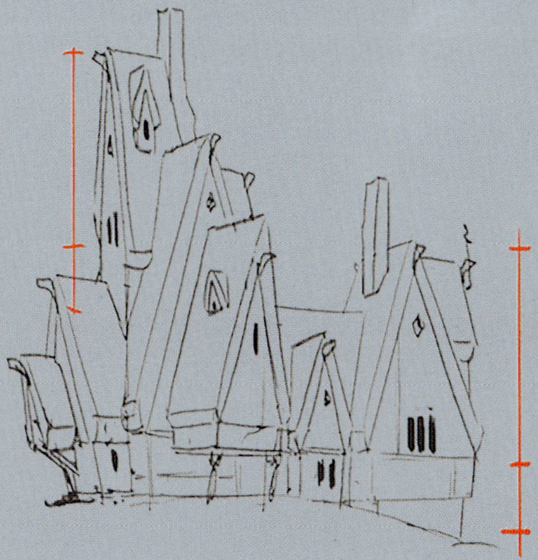

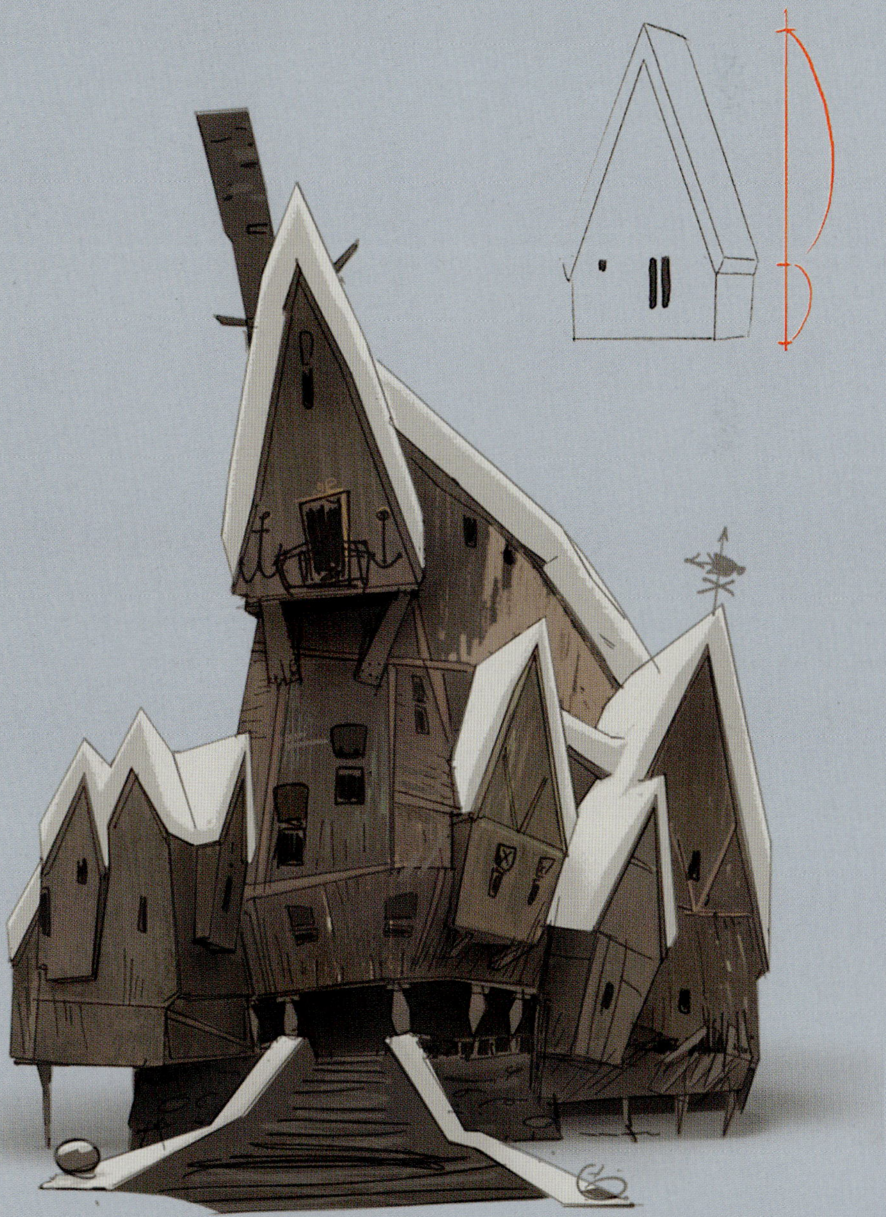

PREVIOUS PAGE: Final frames of the Krum and Ellingboe houses.

RIGHT: (TOP RIGHT) Mrs. Krum's house concept art by Tobi Trebeljahr; (BOTTOM RIGHT) Mr. Ellingboe's house concept art by Marcin Jakubowski; (TOP LEFT) Krum house sketches by Szymon Biernacki; (BOTTOM LEFT) Ellingboe house sketches by Szymon Biernacki.

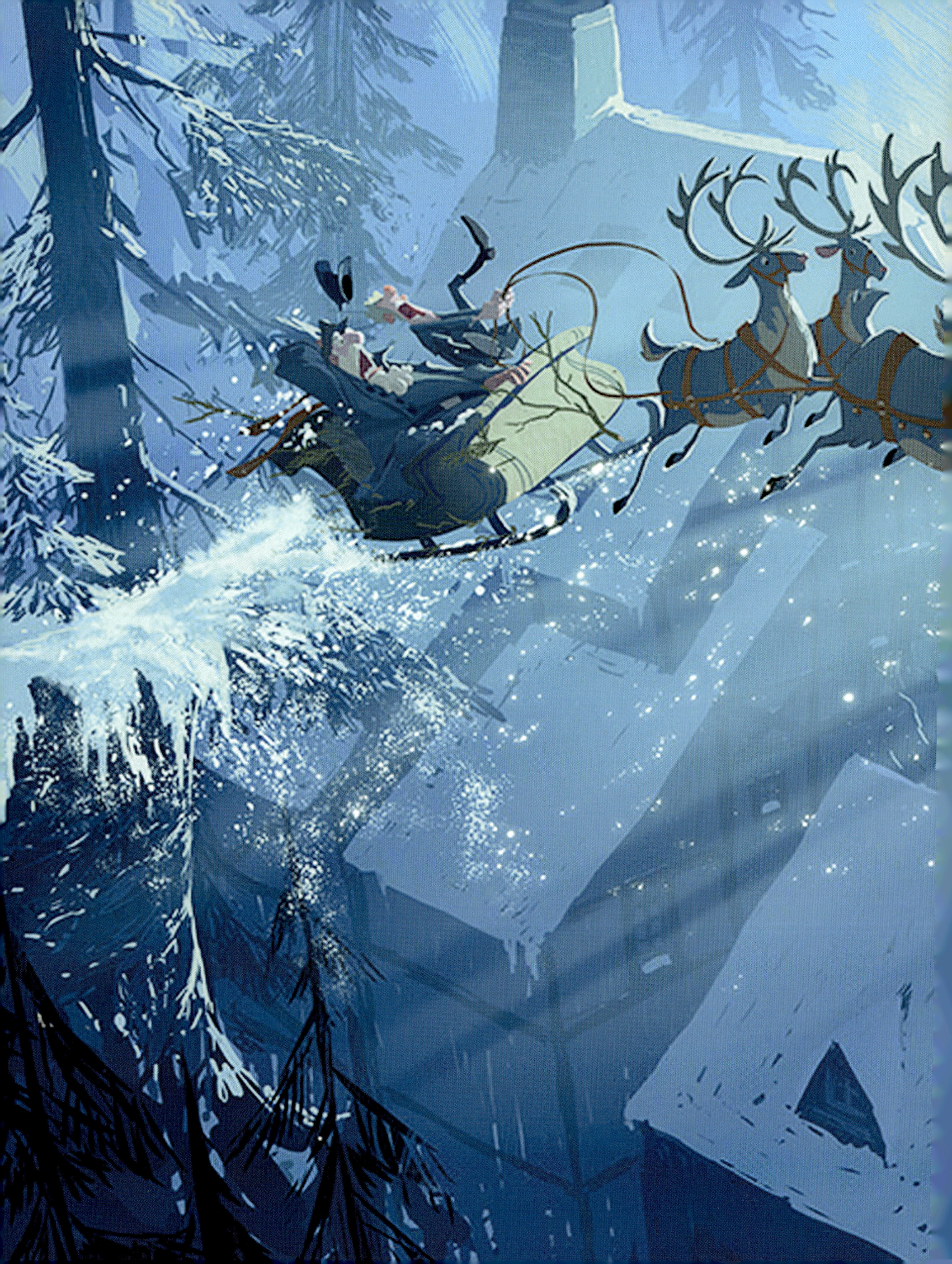

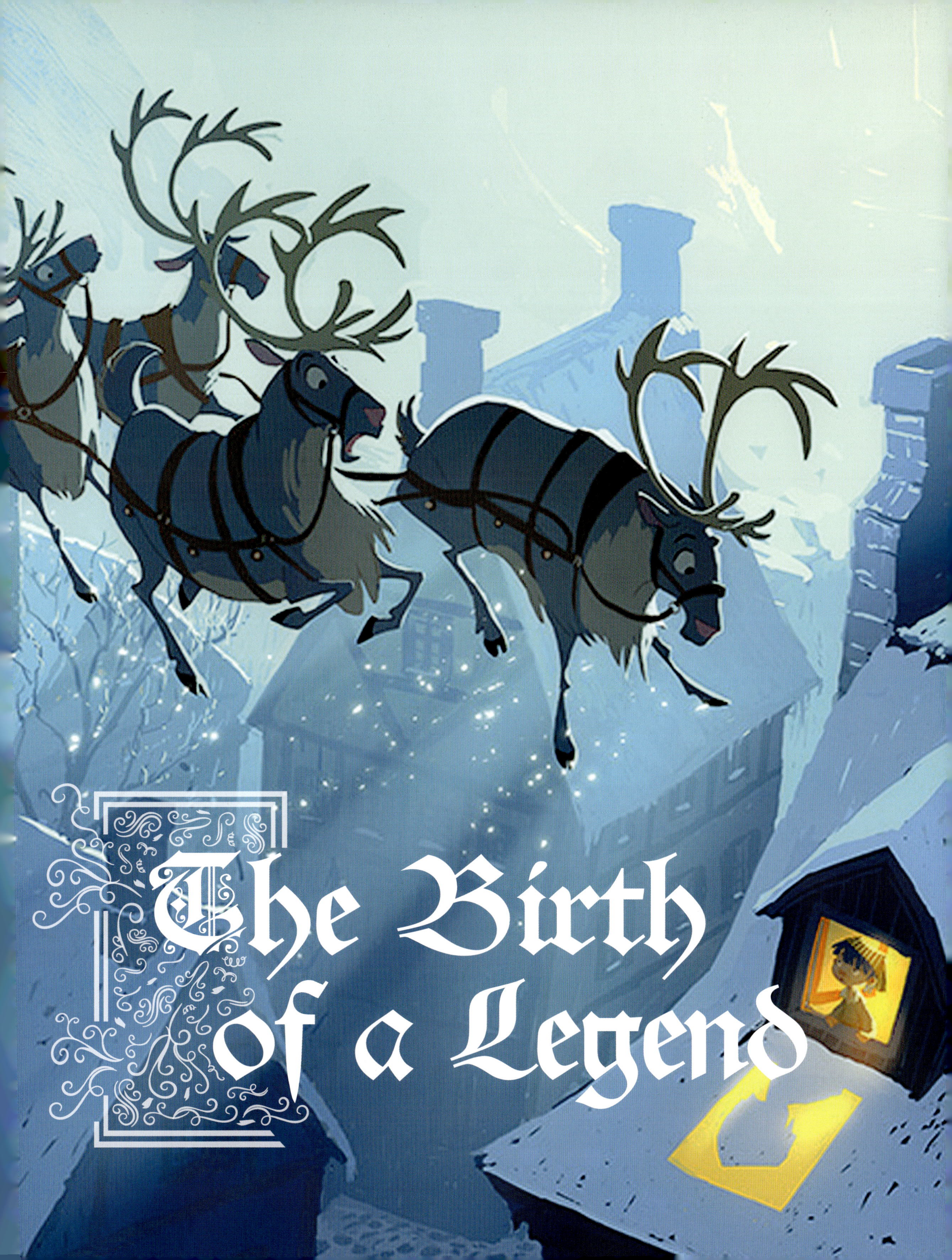

The Birth of a Legend

Klaus' Barn

THE WOODSMAN'S COTTAGE

Just as Smeerensburg's atmosphere changes as Klaus becomes part of the community, Klaus' barn also shifts its general ambience as the movie progresses. "The buildings are in harmony with nature; they're covered in snow and blend softly with the majestic forest around," says production designer Marcin Jakubowski. "We wanted to convey the sense that Klaus is someone who has a deep love for his craft, through carvings, painted decorations, and the toys he has around him. In a way, he is quite connected to the land and his culture – his home's designs are influenced by Viking-era style architecture."

PREVIOUS SPREAD: Concept art by Marcin Jakubowski and Sergio Pablos.

THIS PAGE: The exterior of Klaus' barn as we first see it, quiet and foreboding.

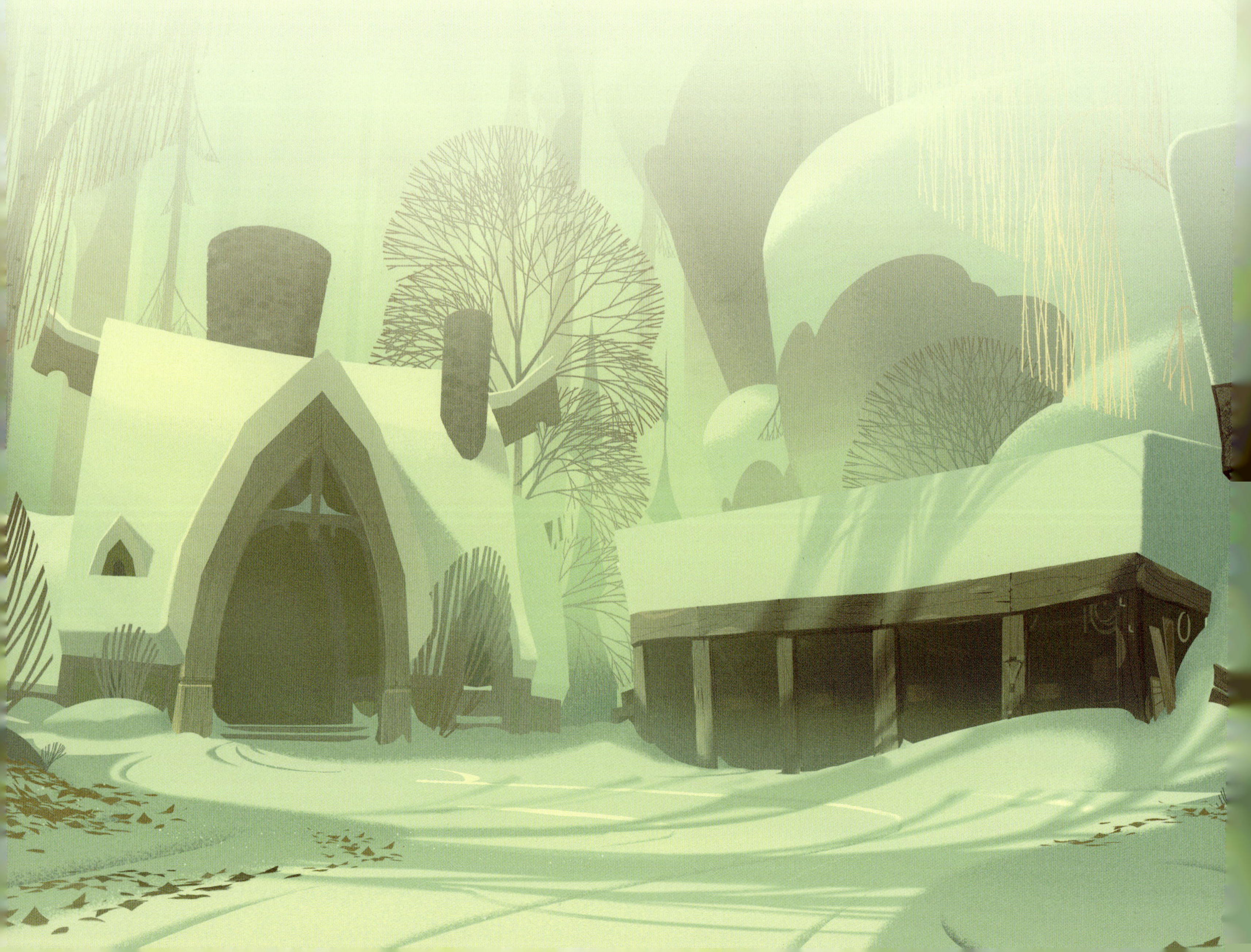

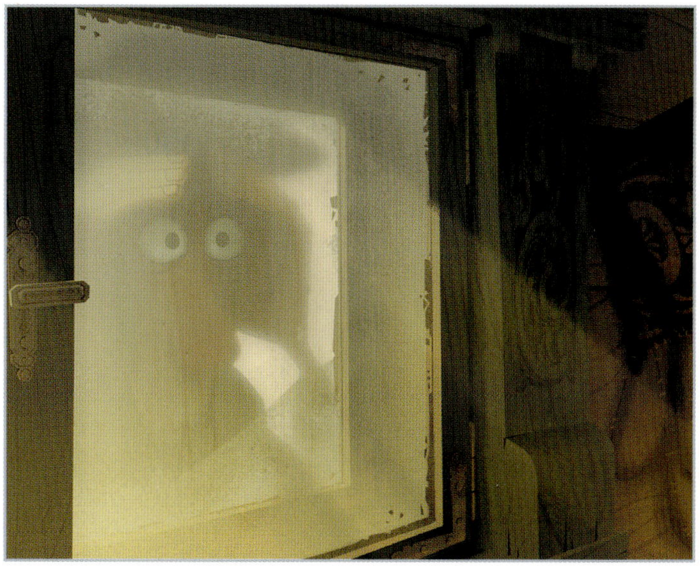

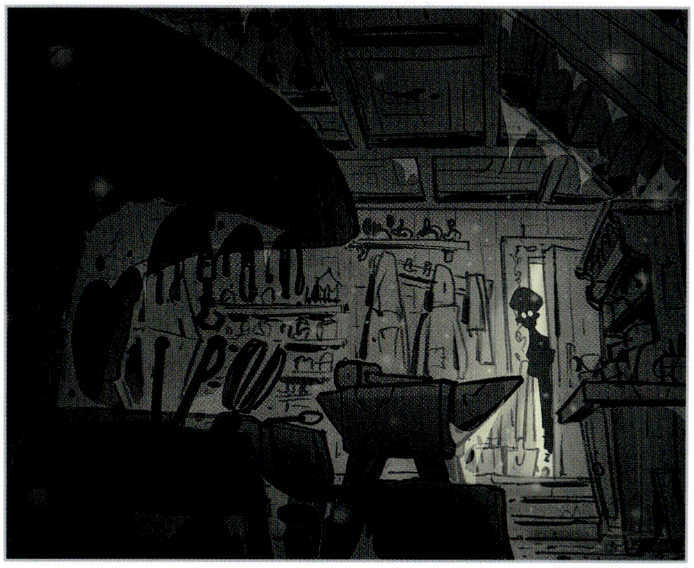

ABOVE: Artwork by Arthus Pilorget.

BELOW: Artwork by Kevin Le Moigne.

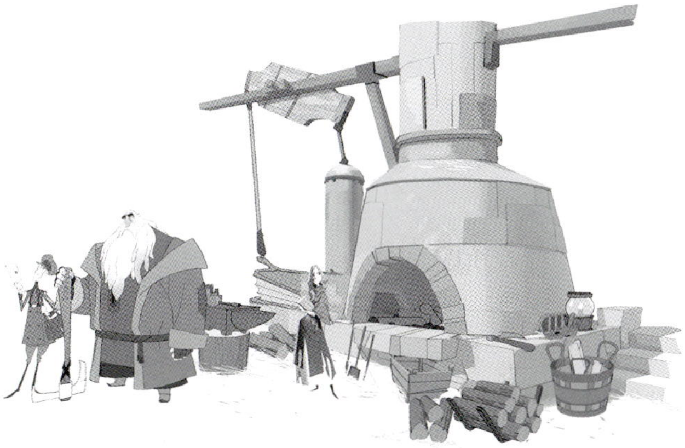

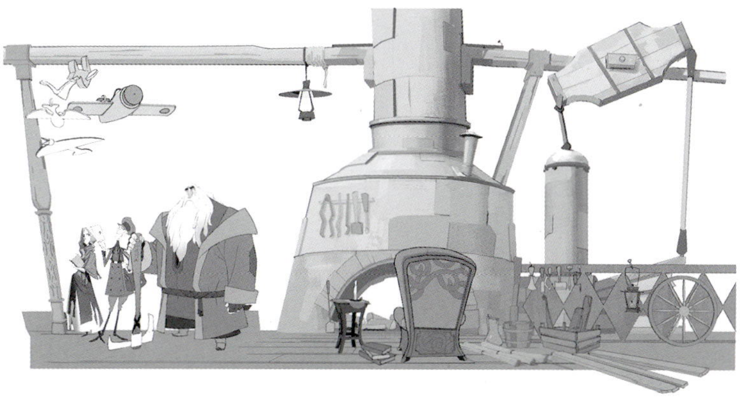

BELOW: Artwork by Arthus Pilorget.

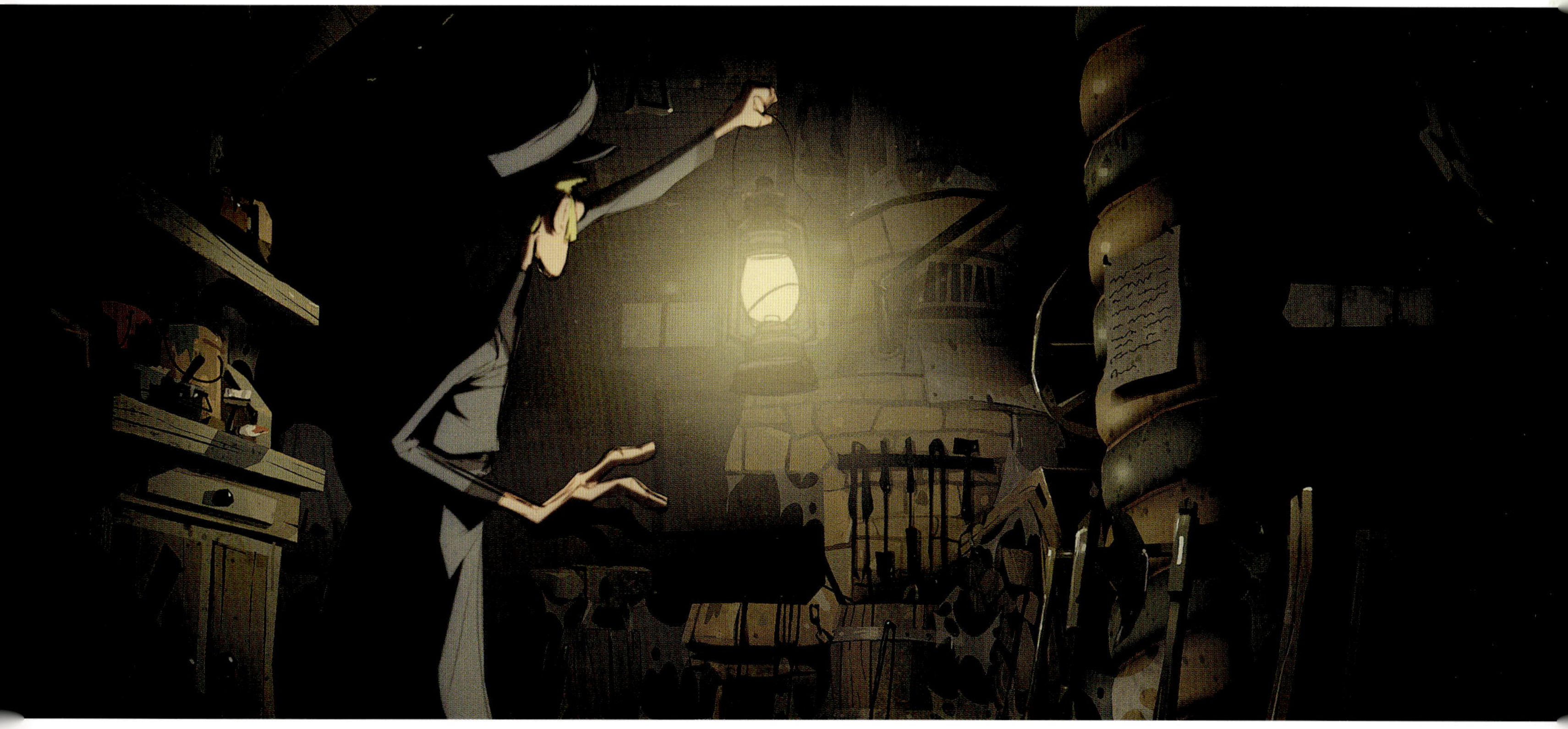

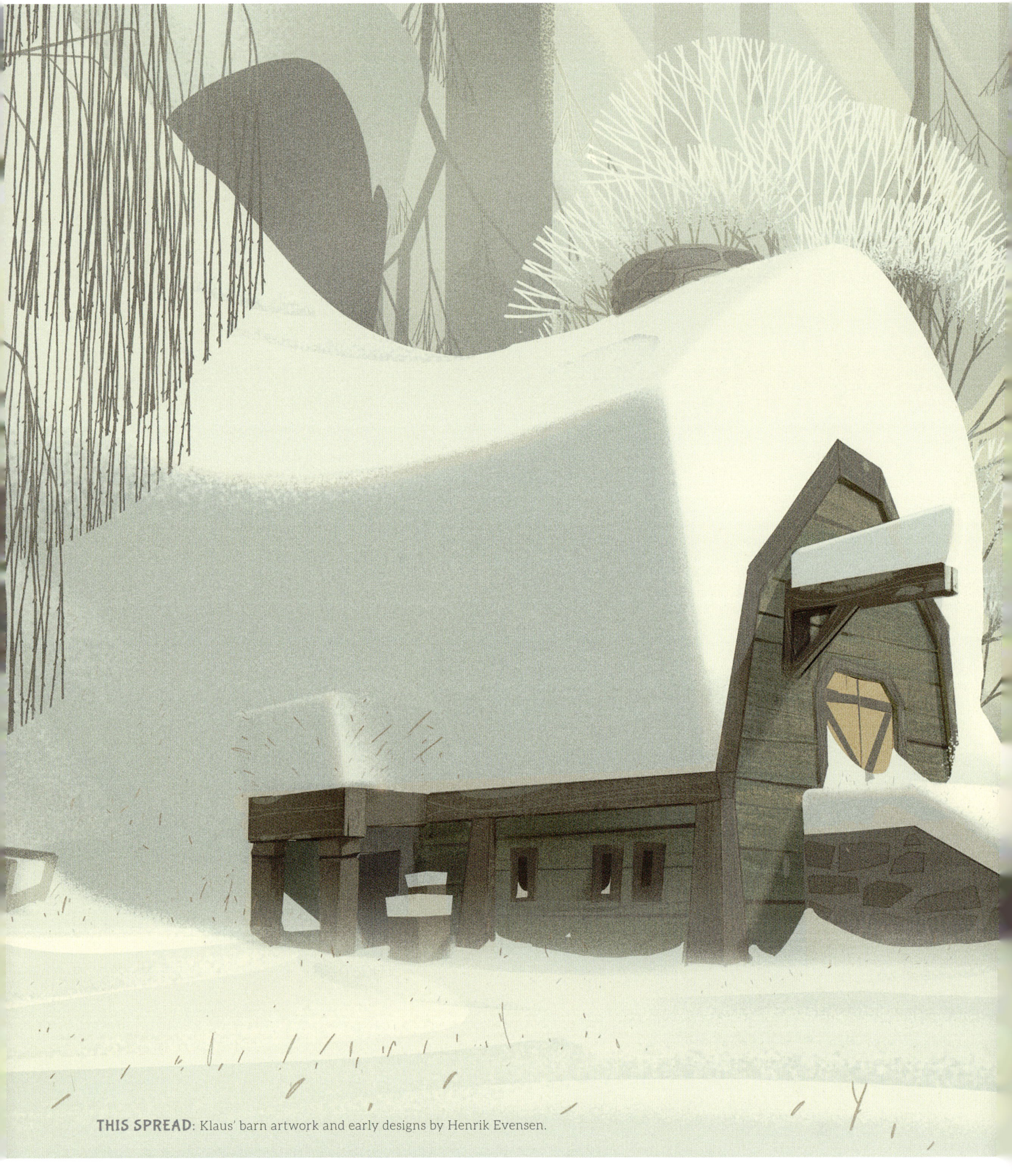

THIS SPREAD: Klaus' barn artwork and early designs by Henrik Evensen.

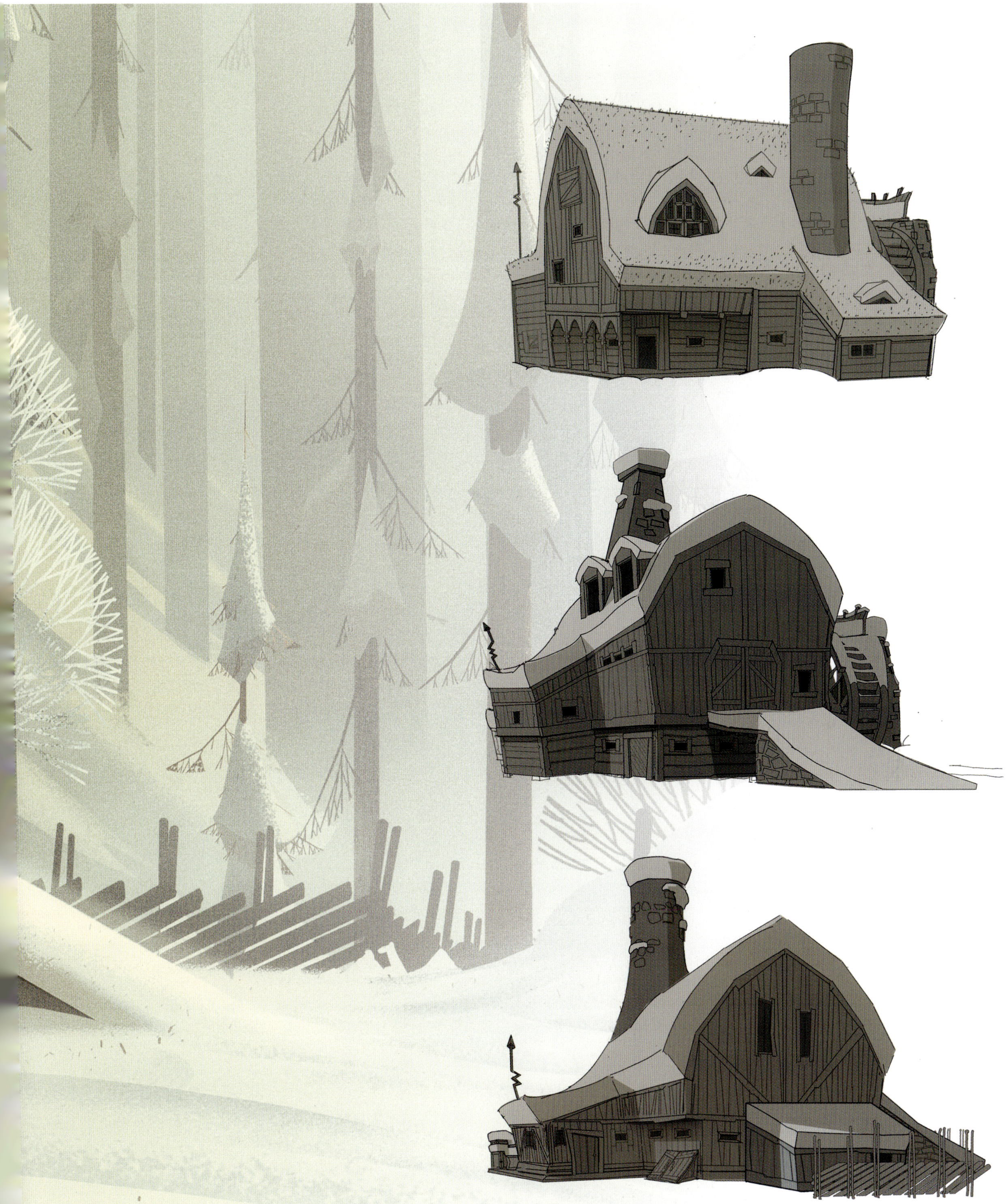

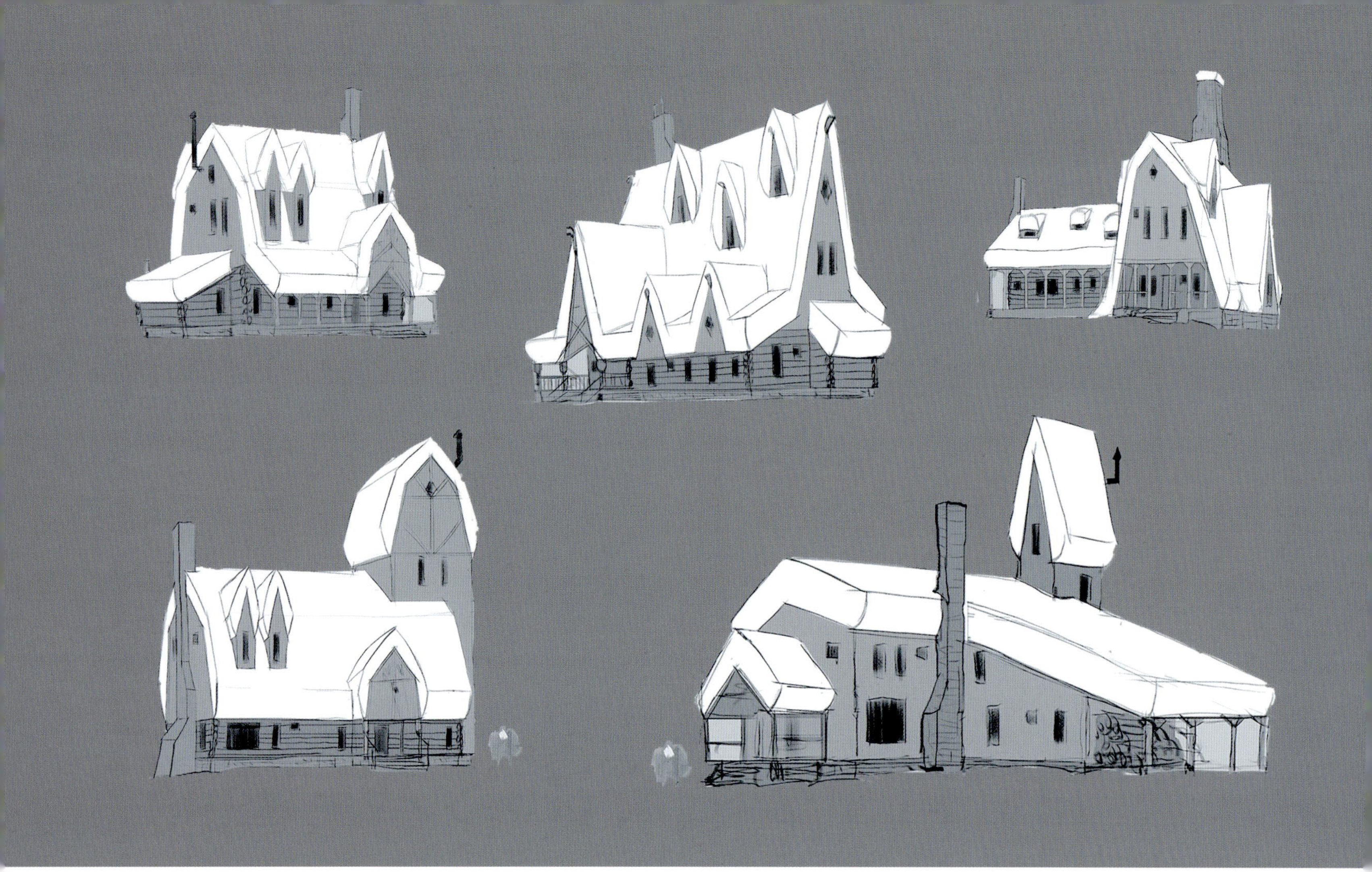

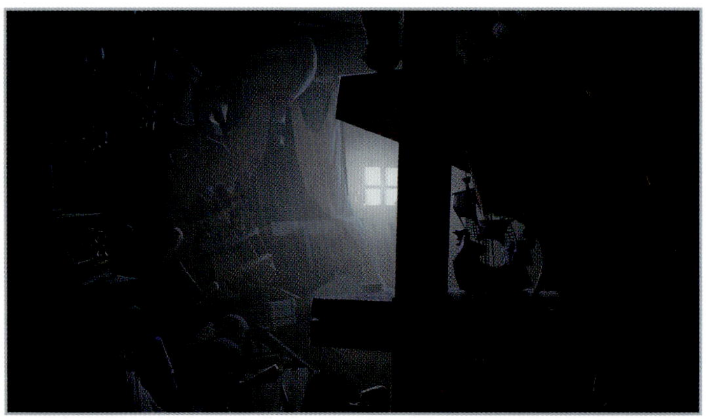

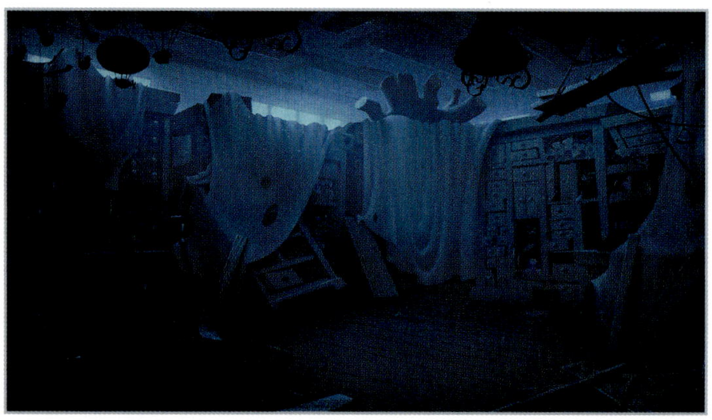

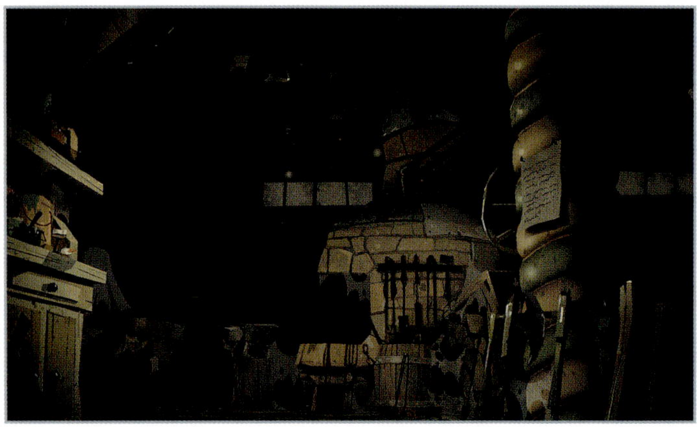

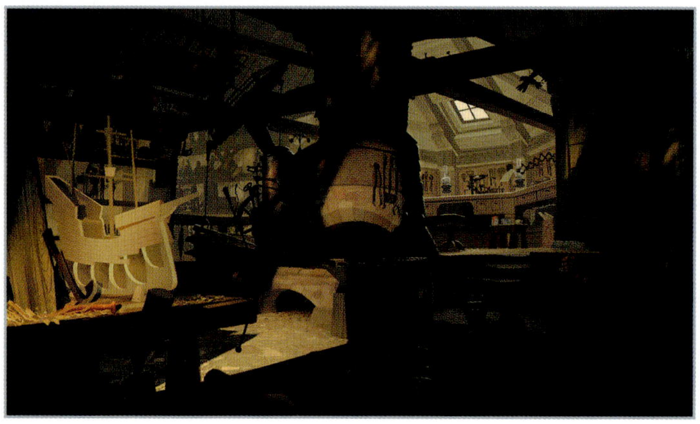

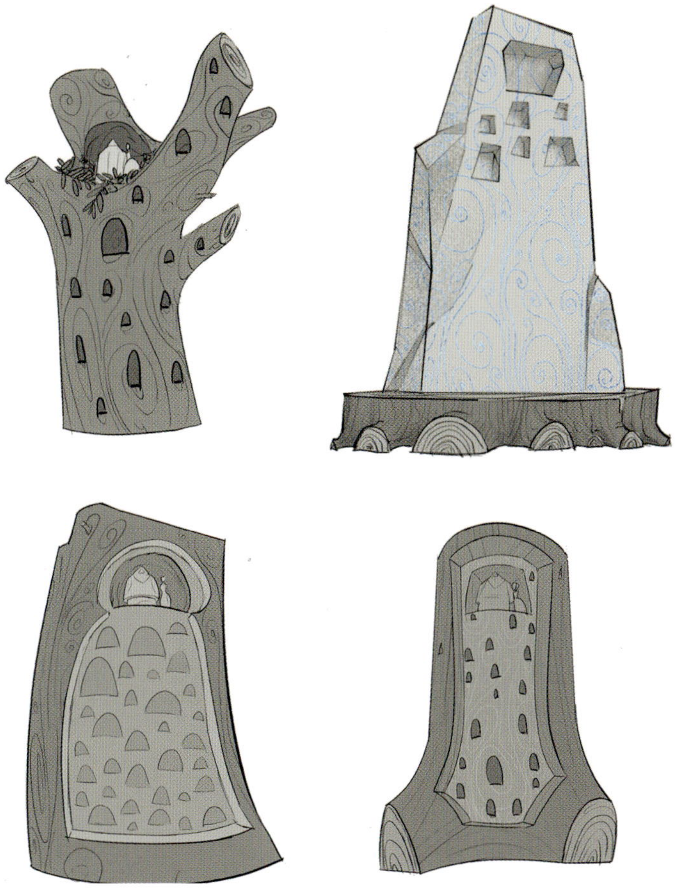

"The 2D animation process is very similar to what it used to be in the 60s or 70s. Of course, we can now save the drawings in the computer instead of shooting them with film and camera. But we are literally doing every drawing by hand, including the in-betweens."

Alfredo Cassano, Lead Animator

PREVIOUS PAGE: Artwork by Szymon Biernacki.

THIS PAGE: Artwork by Gabriel Gomez.

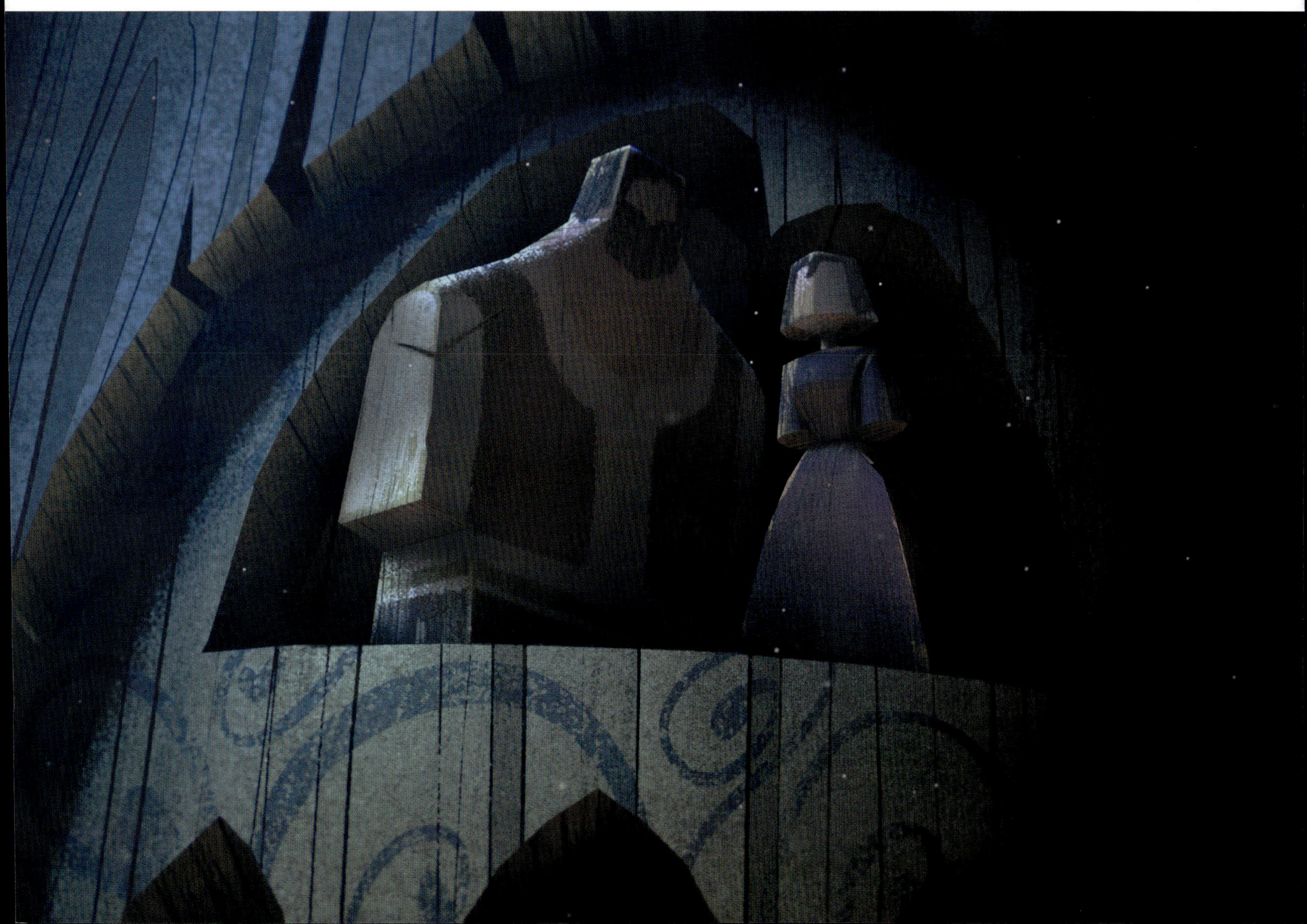

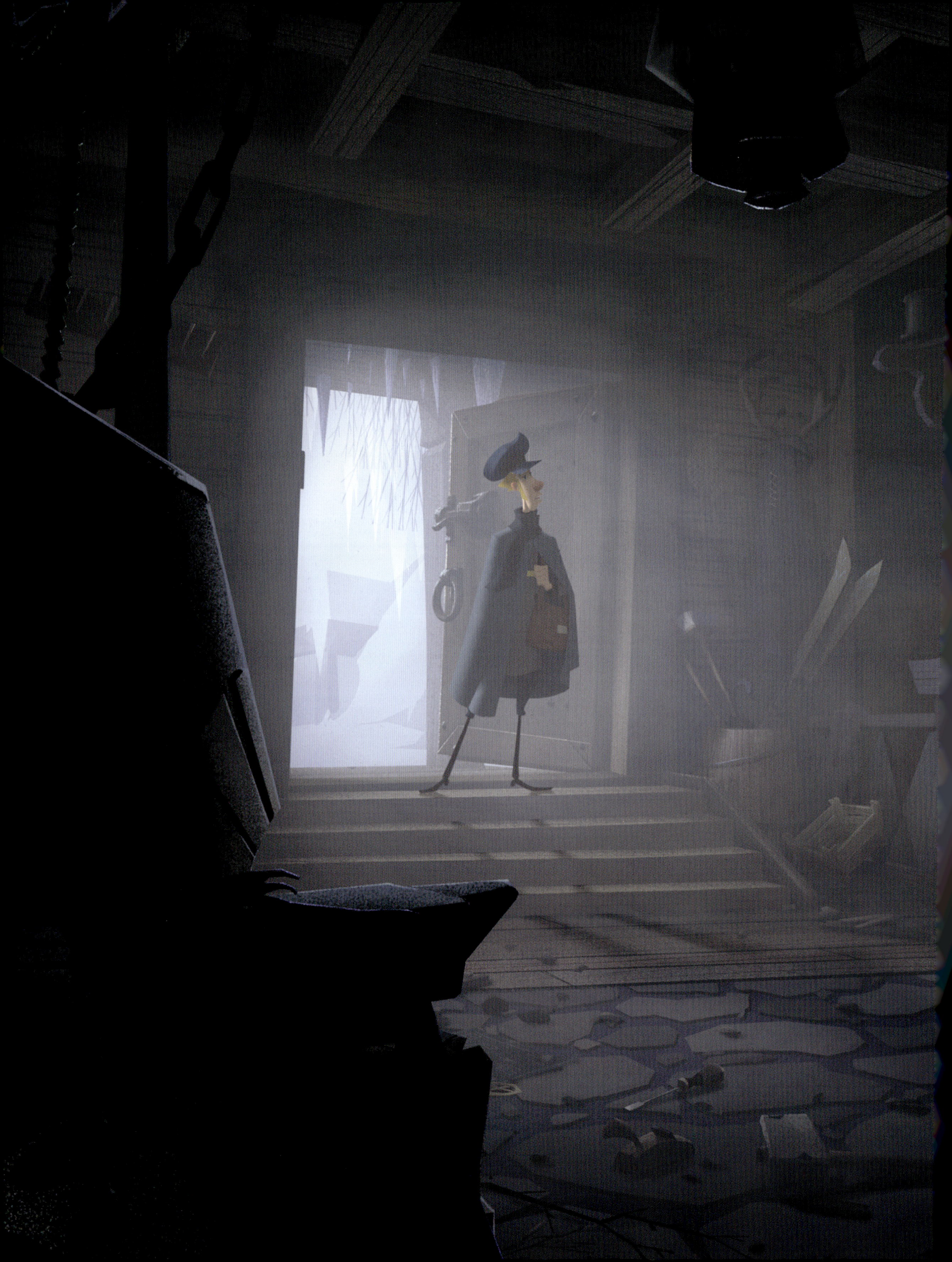

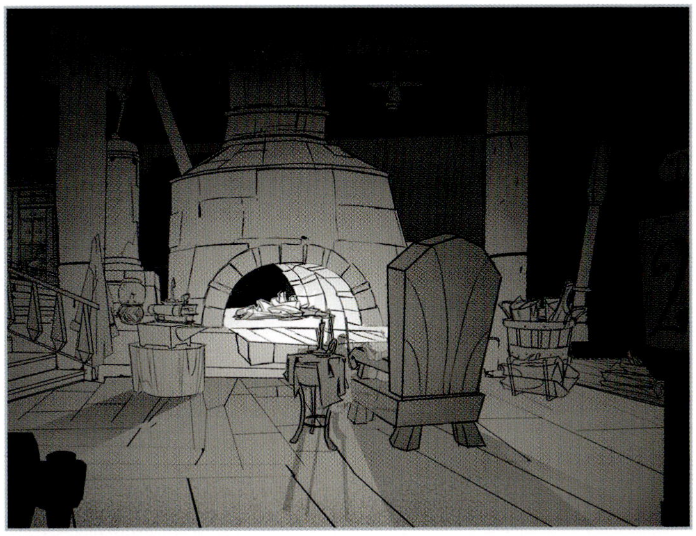

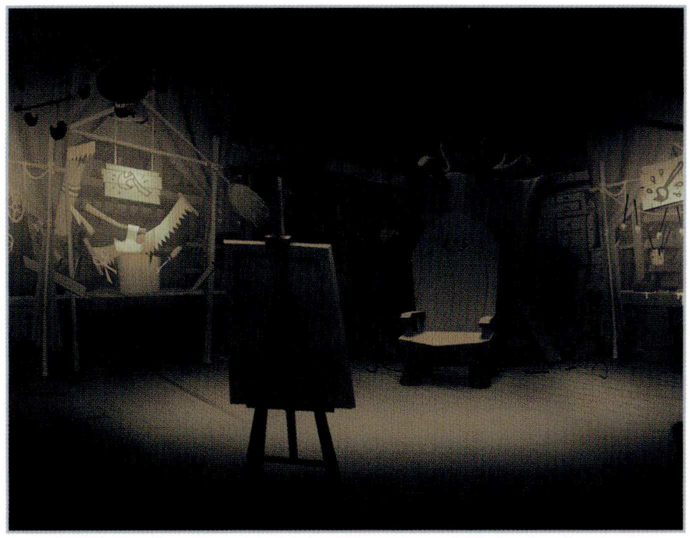

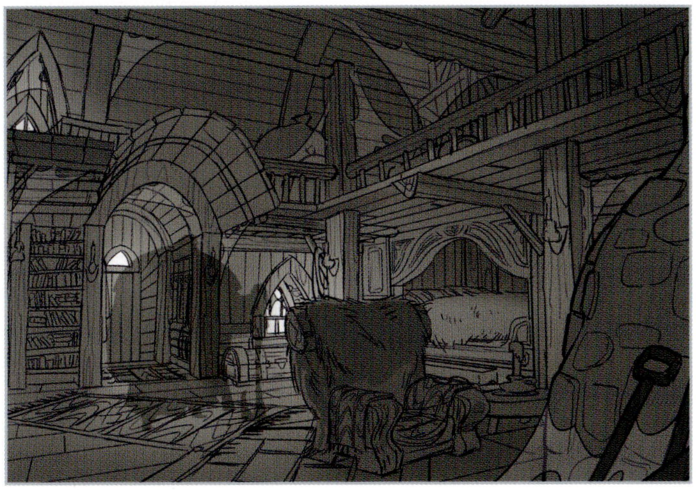

Klaus' home contrasts with Smeerensburg, which is dry and removed from any culture or history – apart from that of the feuds between the clans. His house has a thick, stable construction with a low center of gravity. "These design principles were accentuated to create a subtle feeling of stability, in contrast to rickety Smeerensburg," says Jakubowski. "This is a place where Jesper finally finds something solid in his life."

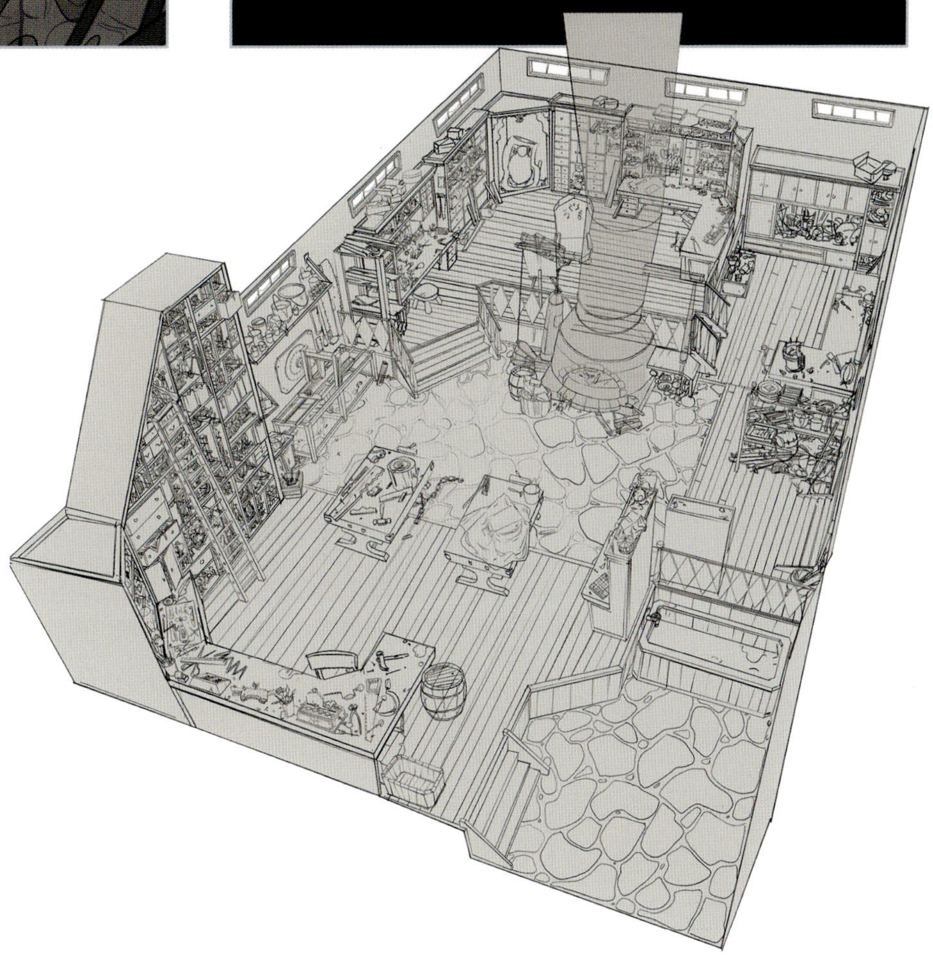

THIS PAGE: Sketches and artwork of the interior of Klaus' barn by Clement Dartigues, Thibaut Denise, Meryl Franck, and Gabriel Gomez.

Klaus

THE TOYMAKER

To voice Klaus, the production reached out to Oscar-winning character actor J.K. Simmons (*Whiplash*), who is best known to animation lovers as the voice of Kai in *Kung Fu Panda 3*, Ford Pines in *Gravity Falls*, and Tenzin in *The Legend of Korra*. As Pablos recalls, "Having him voice the character was a no-brainer. The minute his name popped up, I knew that he was the right man for the part. His voice is loud and scary when it needs to be, and sweet and charming when it's required. He is such a professional that he always asks the right questions, and he always nails it on the first take. Of course, since we were paying him by the hour, we made him do it a few more times – just to be safe!"

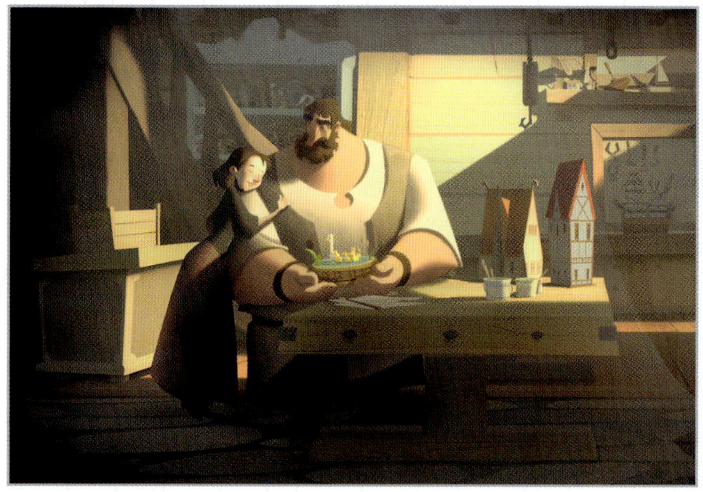

THIS PAGE: Prop designs by Andres Arcos and Krzysztof Roslan.

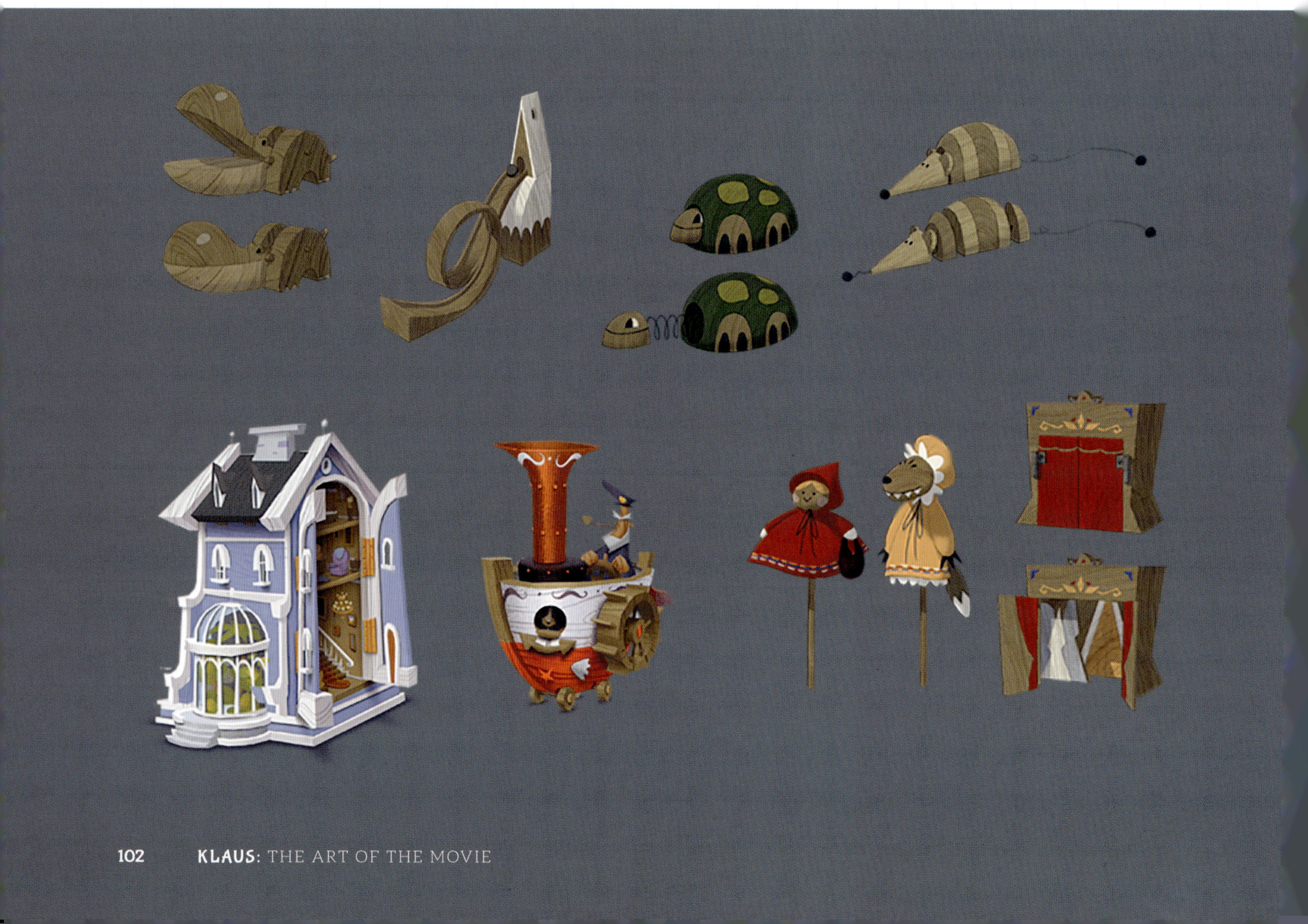

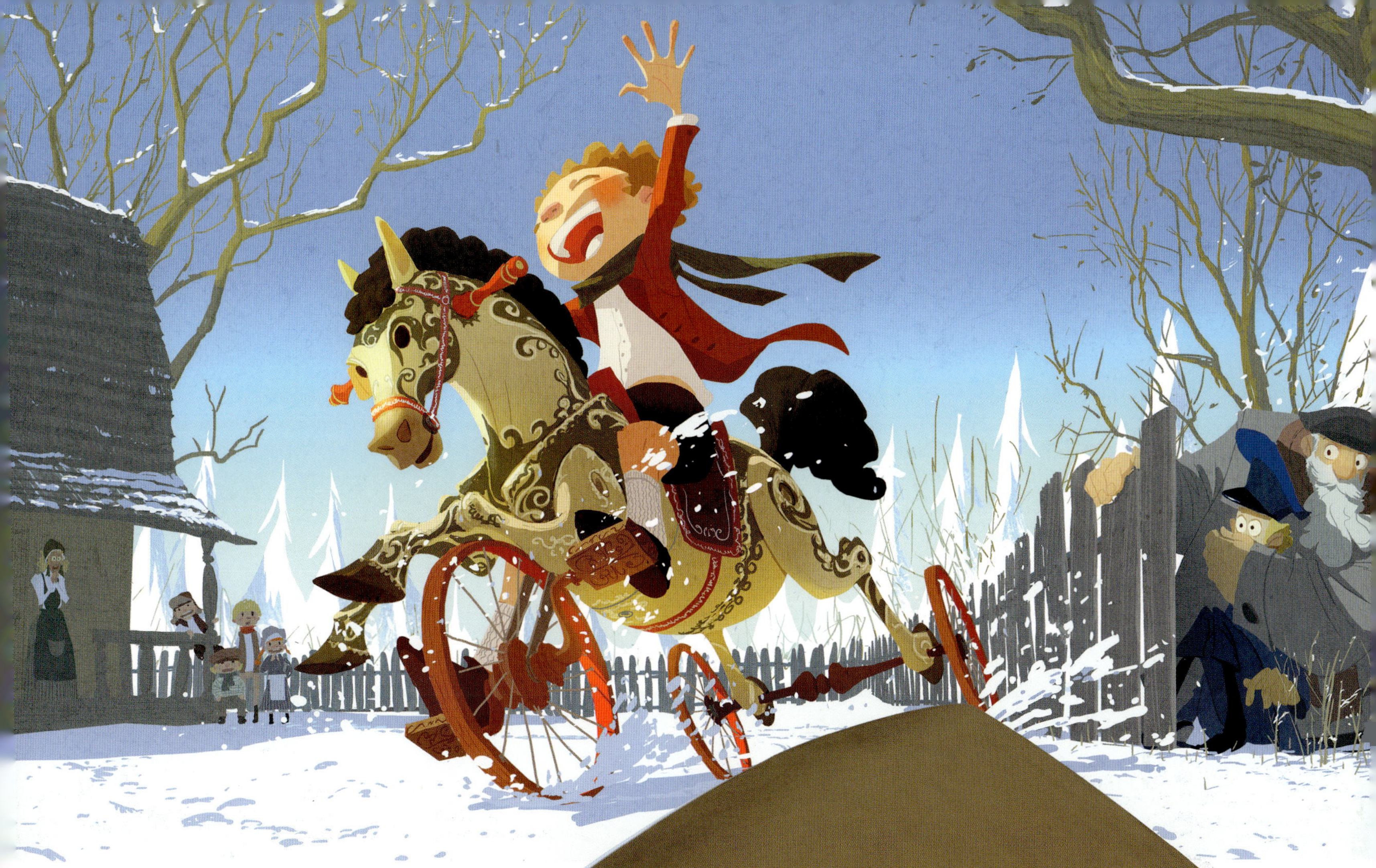

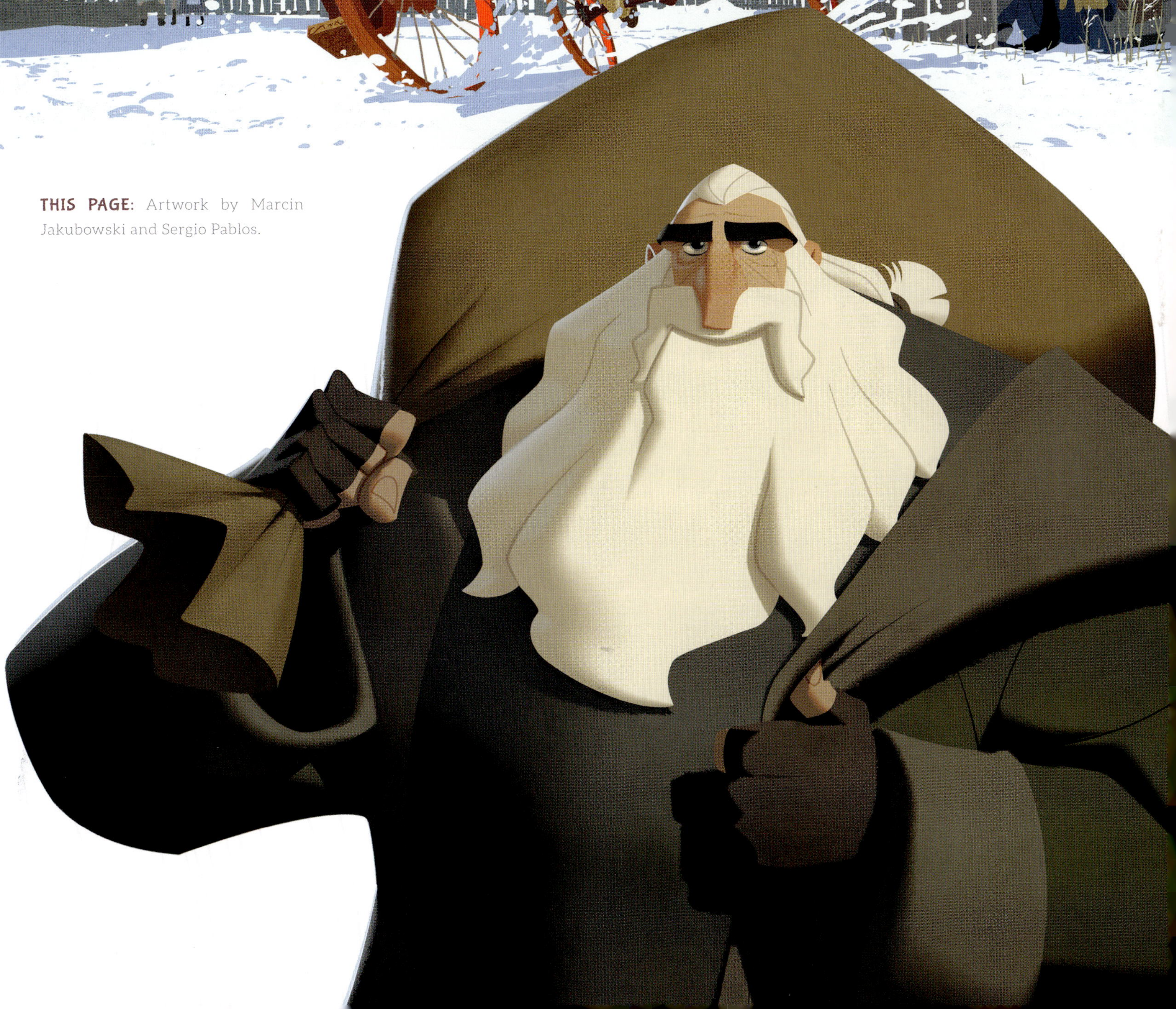

THIS PAGE: Artwork by Marcin Jakubowski and Sergio Pablos.

Lydia

THE GUIDING FORCE

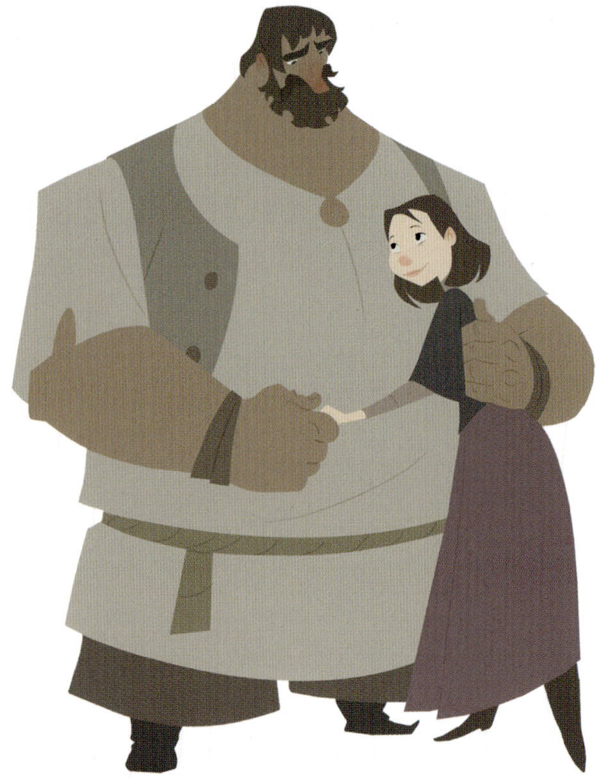

Although the audience never really gets to see Lydia, Klaus' wife, except in short flashbacks, her presence is felt throughout the movie. As Pablos explains, "We find out that what made Klaus step away from the world was the tragic loss of his wife. Our story isn't about magic, but it's about how we get to the magical part of the legend. In a way, the movie is a prequel to the legend of Santa Claus, which we all know."

But the story needed a device that hinted at the presence of magic, or an otherworldly force that guides Klaus. "You can feel Lydia's spirit in the form of the wind that blows through the scene and rustles the leaves and moves the bird perches," Pablos explains. "It's Lydia who shows him the right path, even if it means listening to Jesper, who might sound like a jerk! It's the guiding force of his lost wife that allows him to transcend and become the magical legend we are all familiar with."

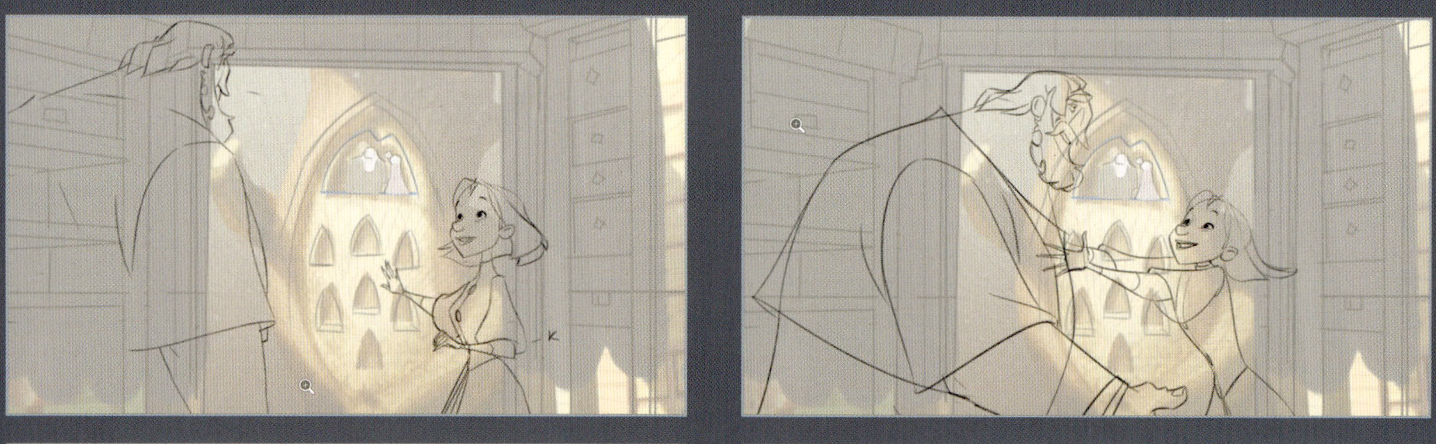

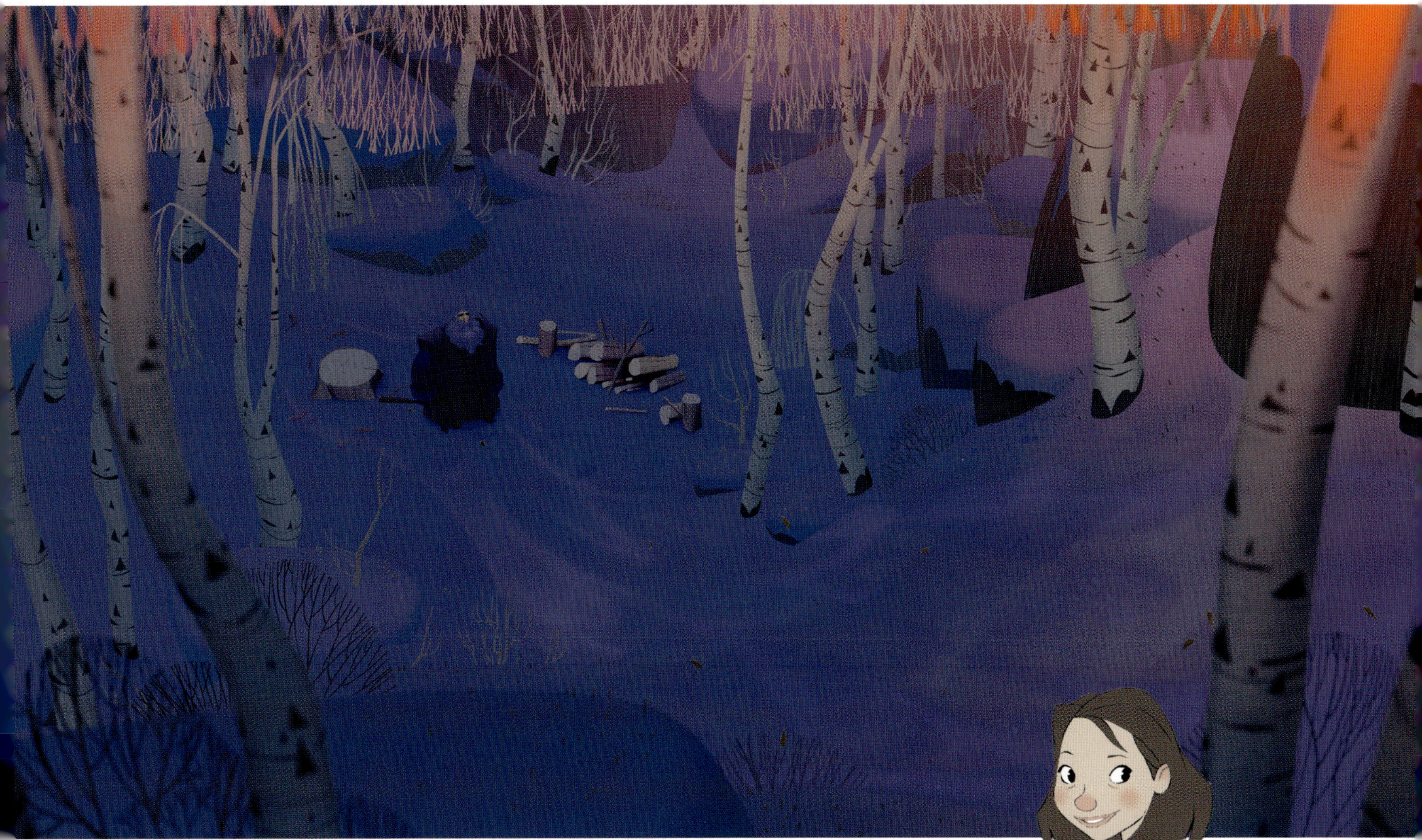

THIS SPREAD: Character designs by Torsten Schrank and animation by Cécile Carre.

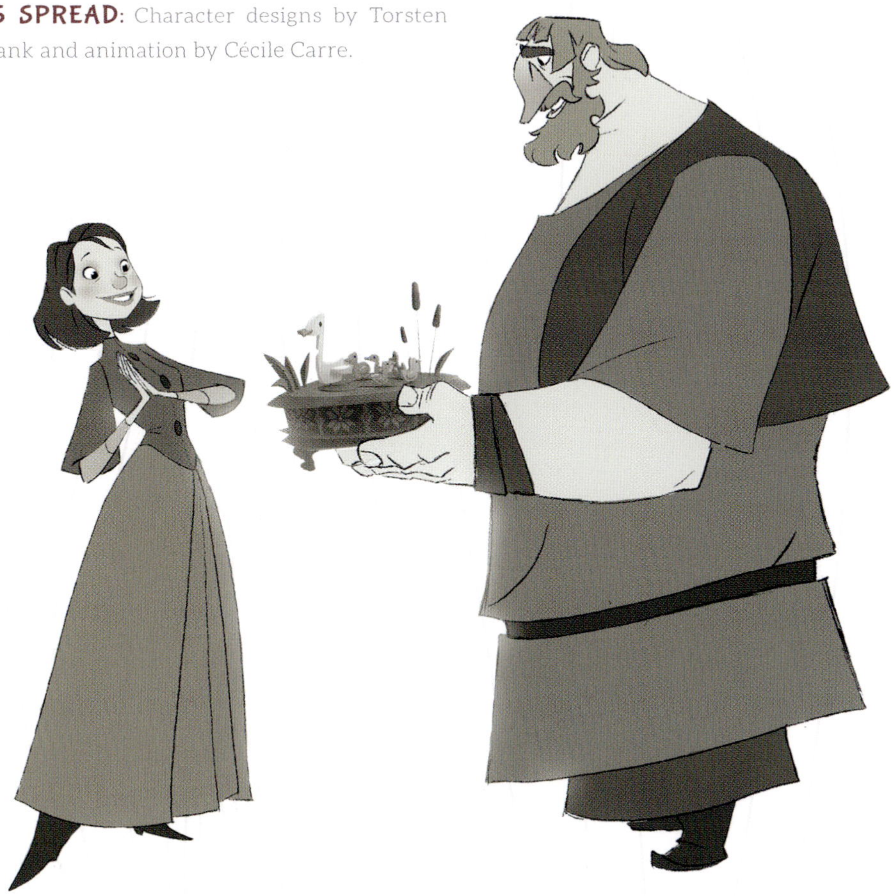

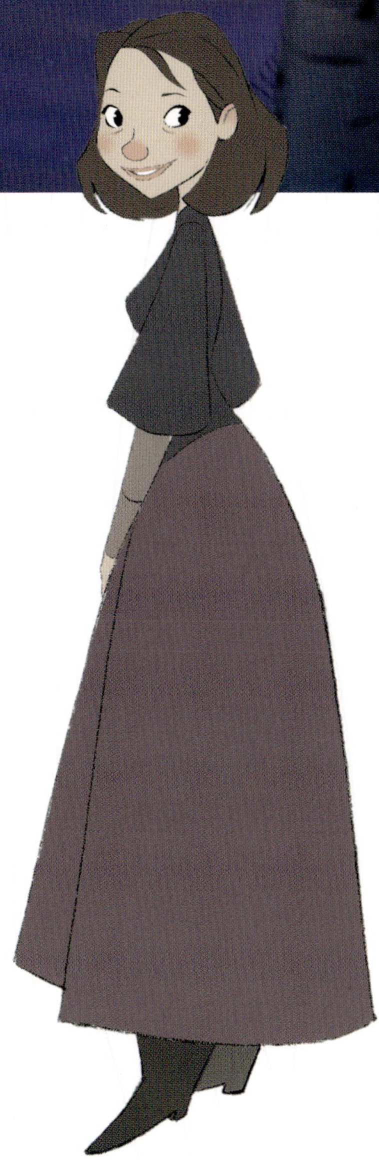

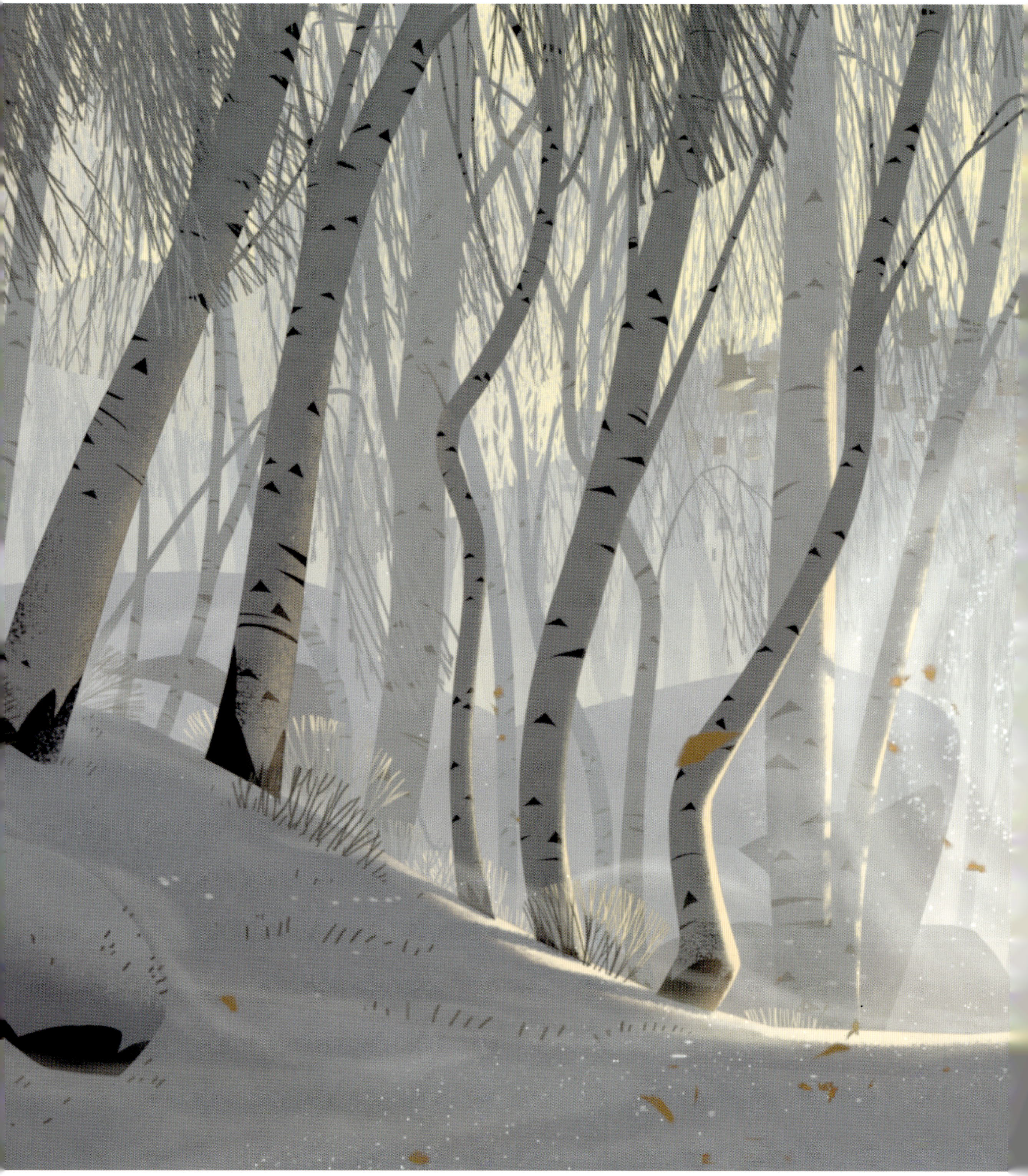

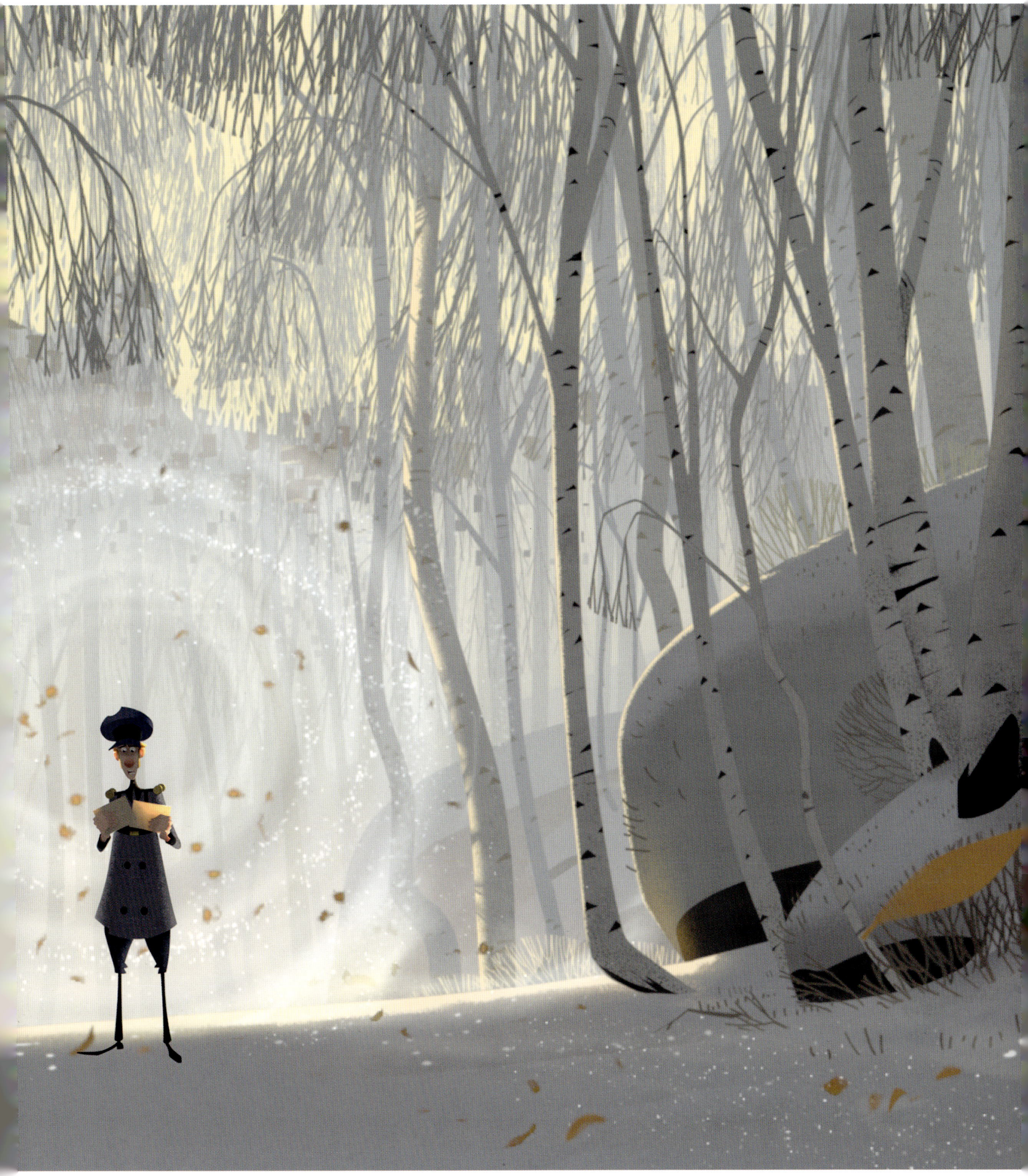

Reindeer

AND OTHER ANIMALS

A major design decision that has been consistently carried out throughout the movie is the way that animals are depicted. Sergio Pablos wanted the dogs, horses, reindeer, and other beasts to act like their counterparts in the real world. "We didn't want sentient animals," he mentions. "We wanted our animals to be consistent with this real environment we had created. So that's why our reindeer don't smile or act like sidekicks!"

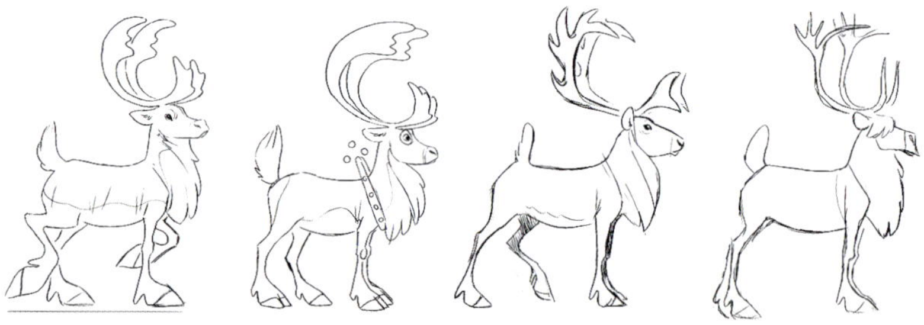

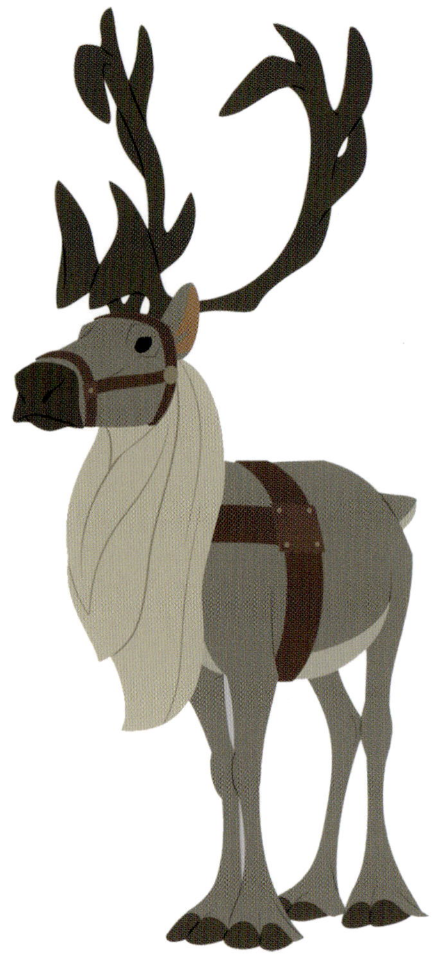

BELOW: Artwork by Daniel Fernandez.

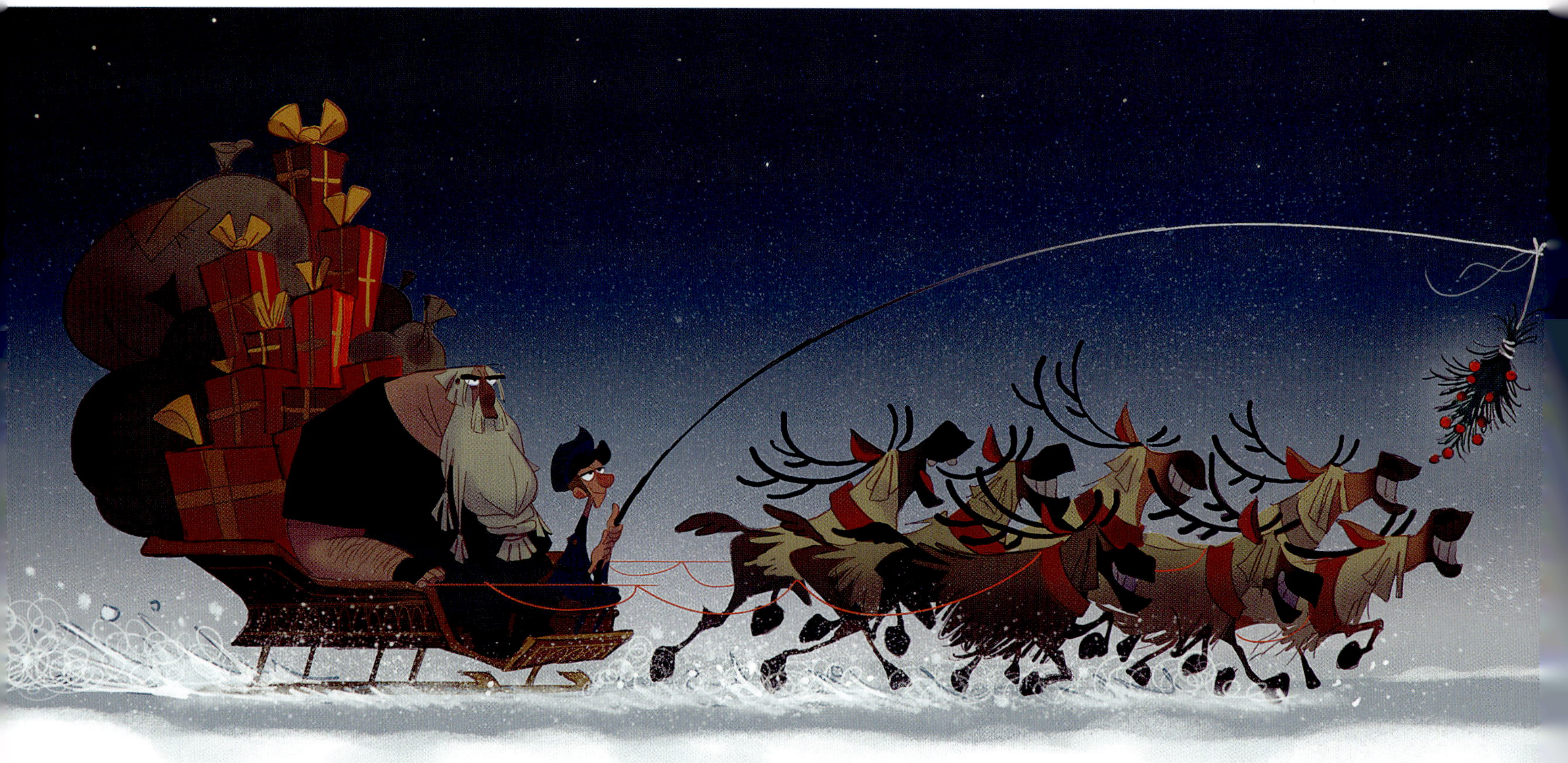

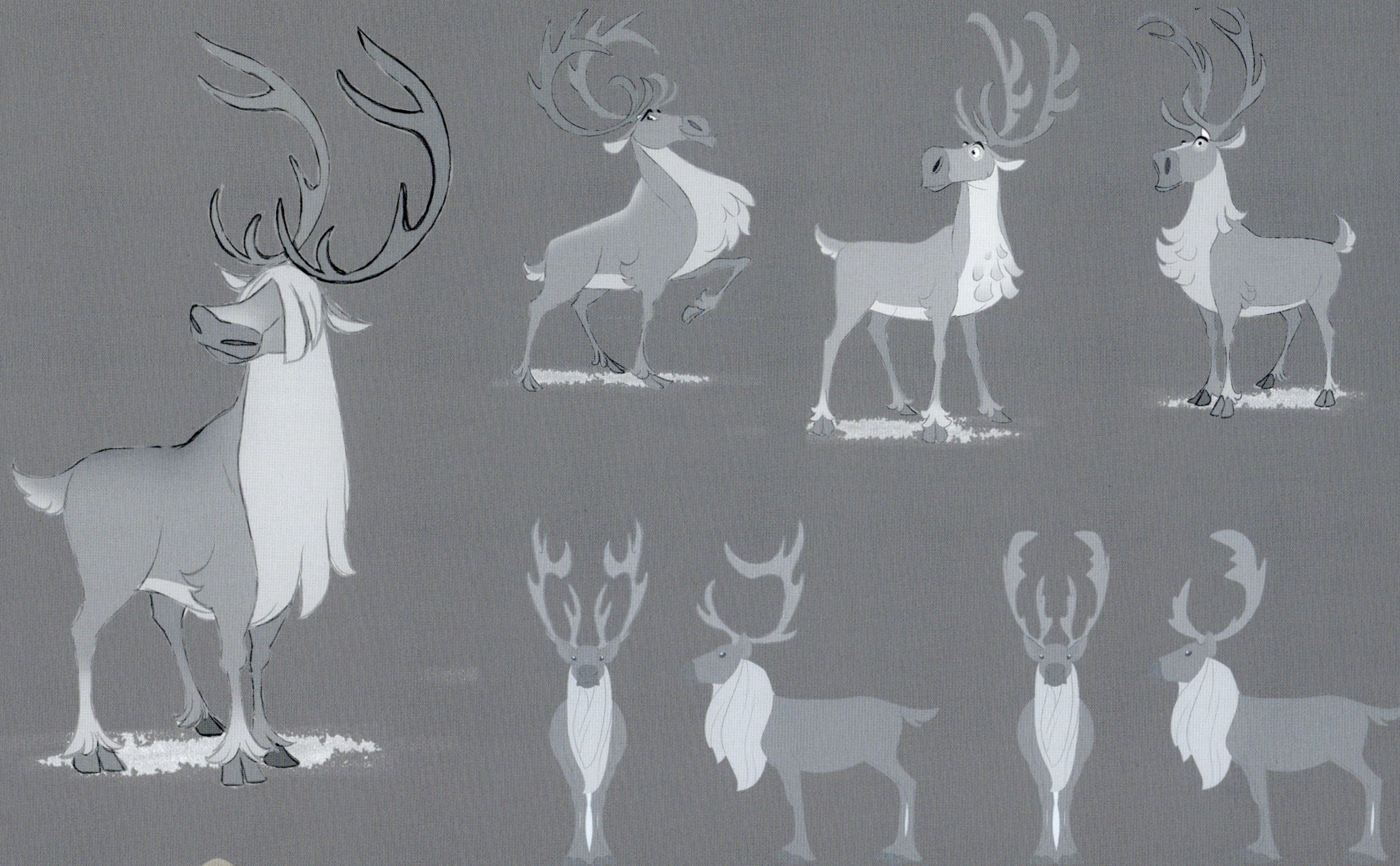

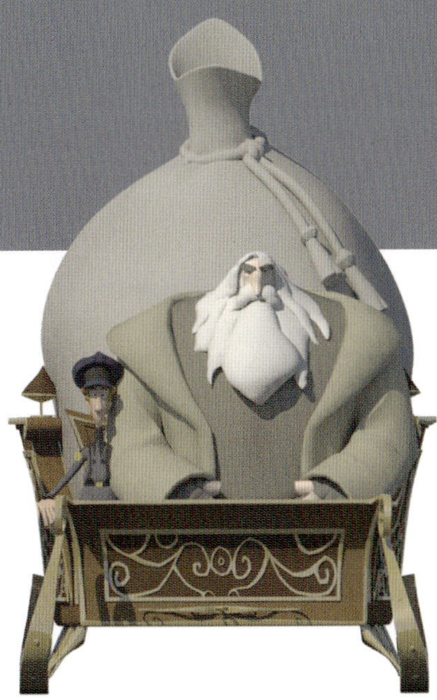

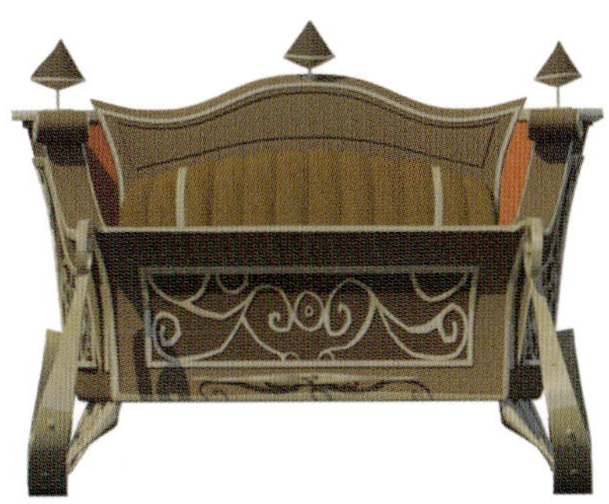

THIS SPREAD: Reindeer designs by Torsten Schrank and Fernando Moro.

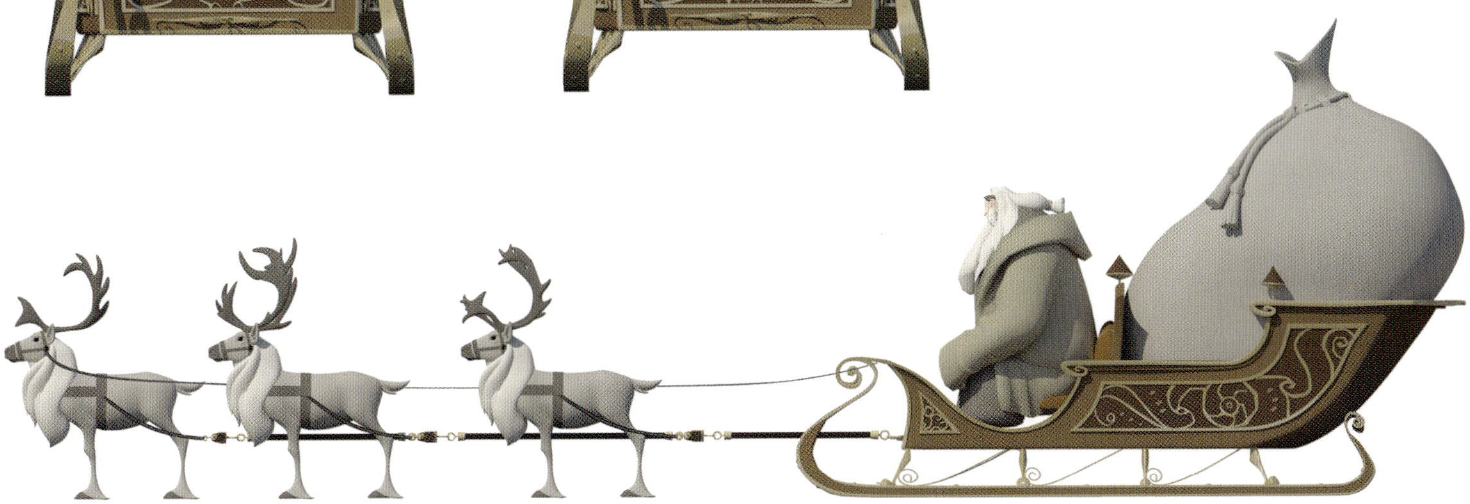

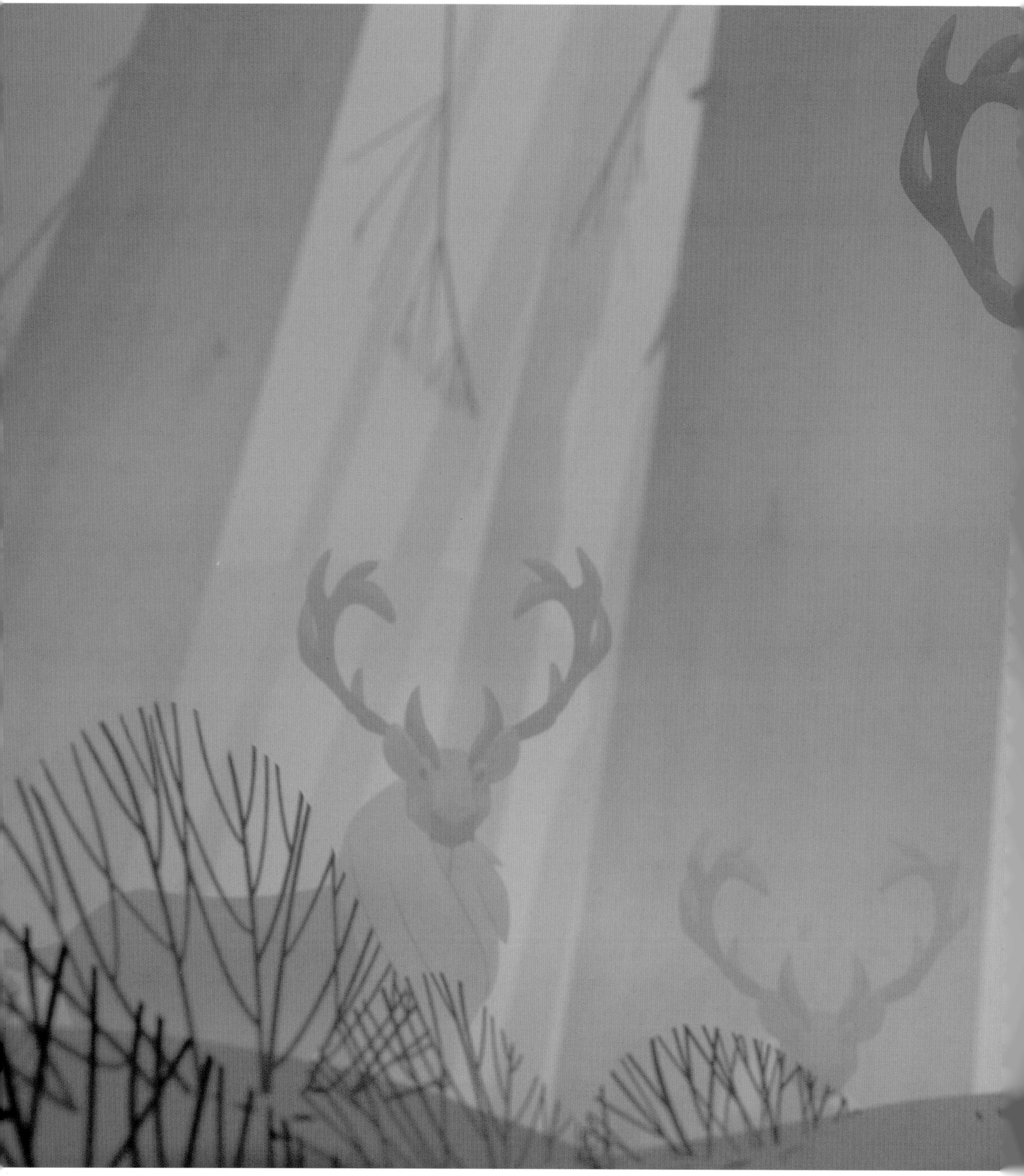

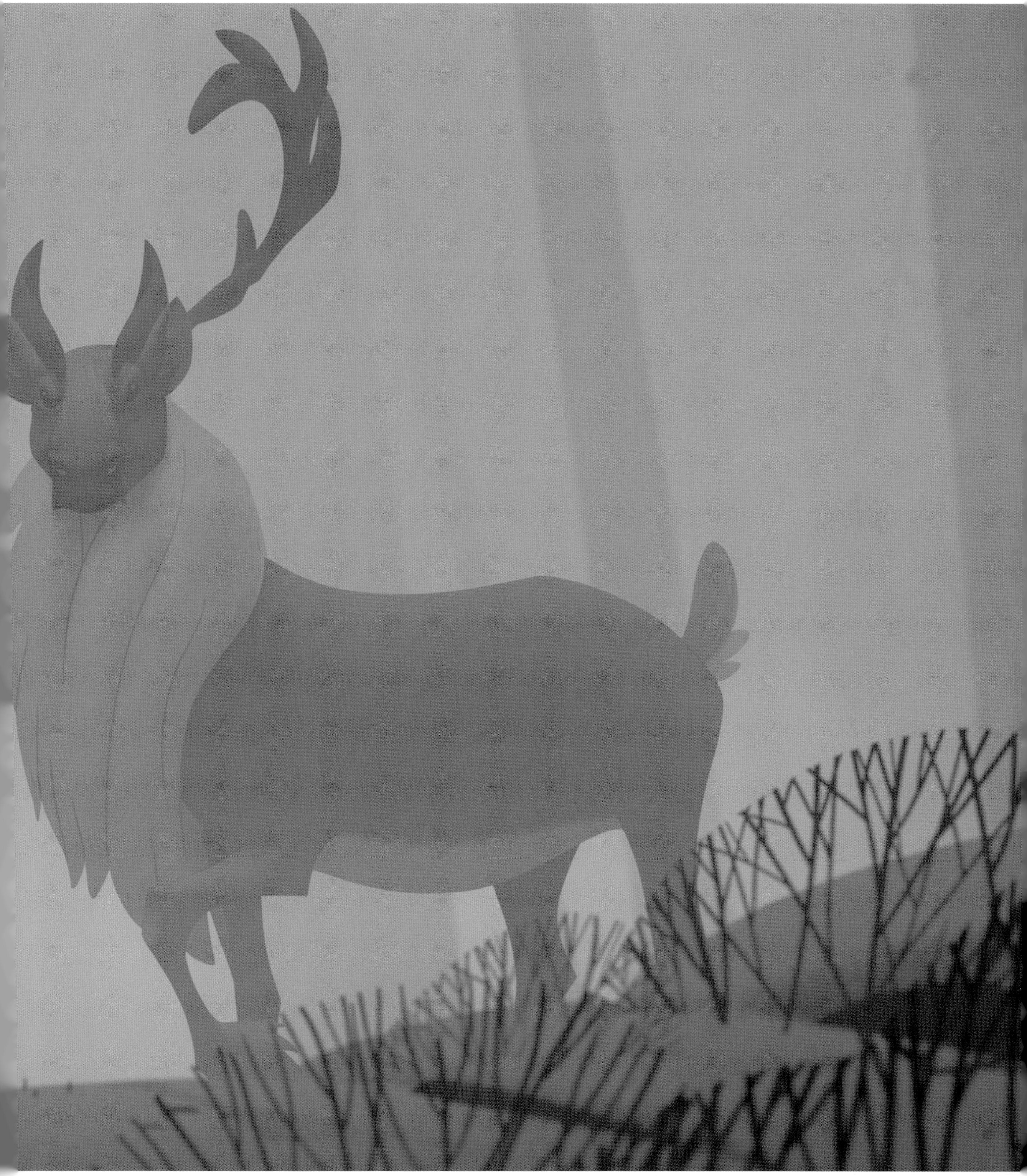

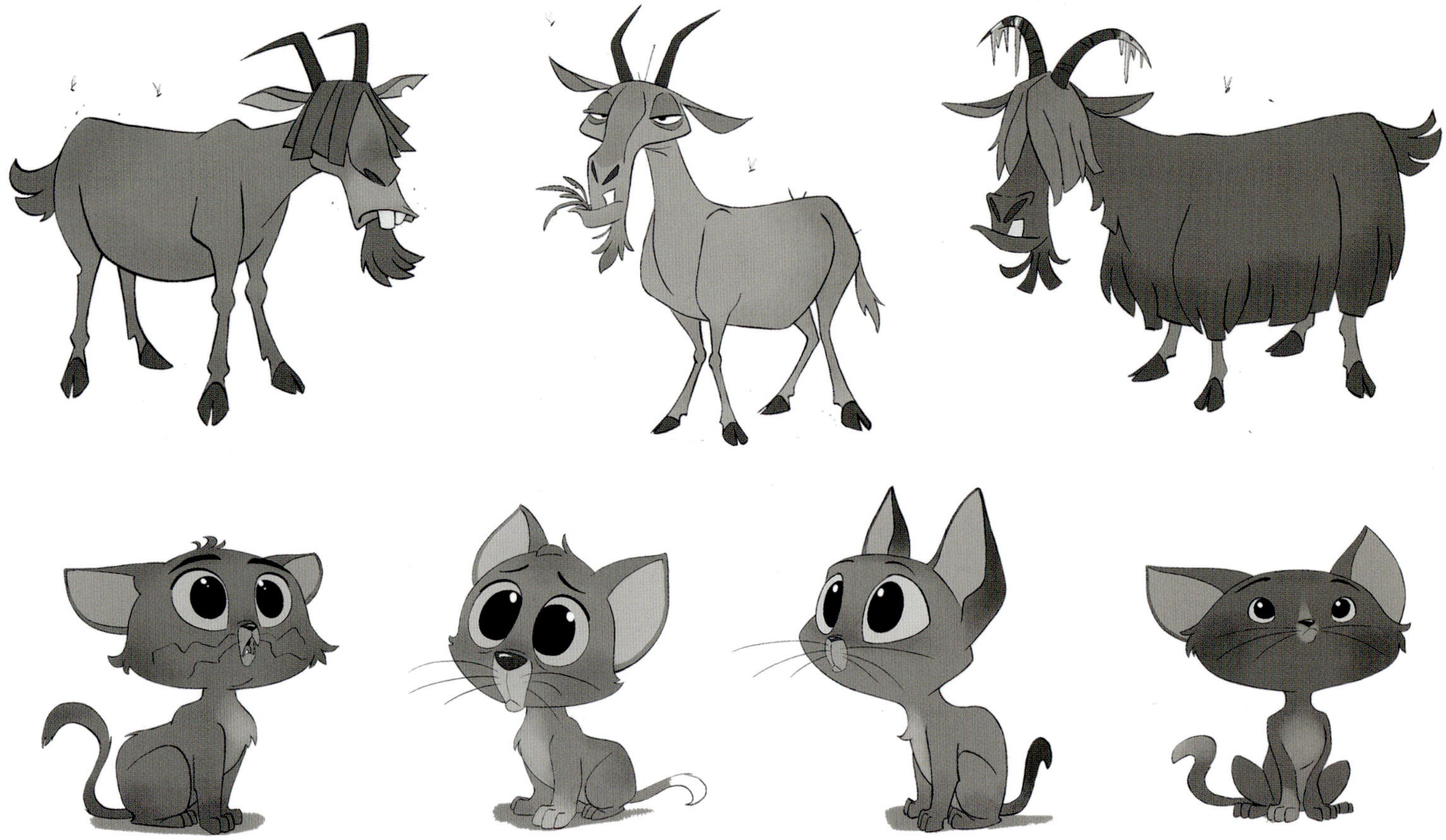

THIS SPREAD: Animal exploration by Torsten Schrank, Marta Andreeva, and Daniel Fernandez.

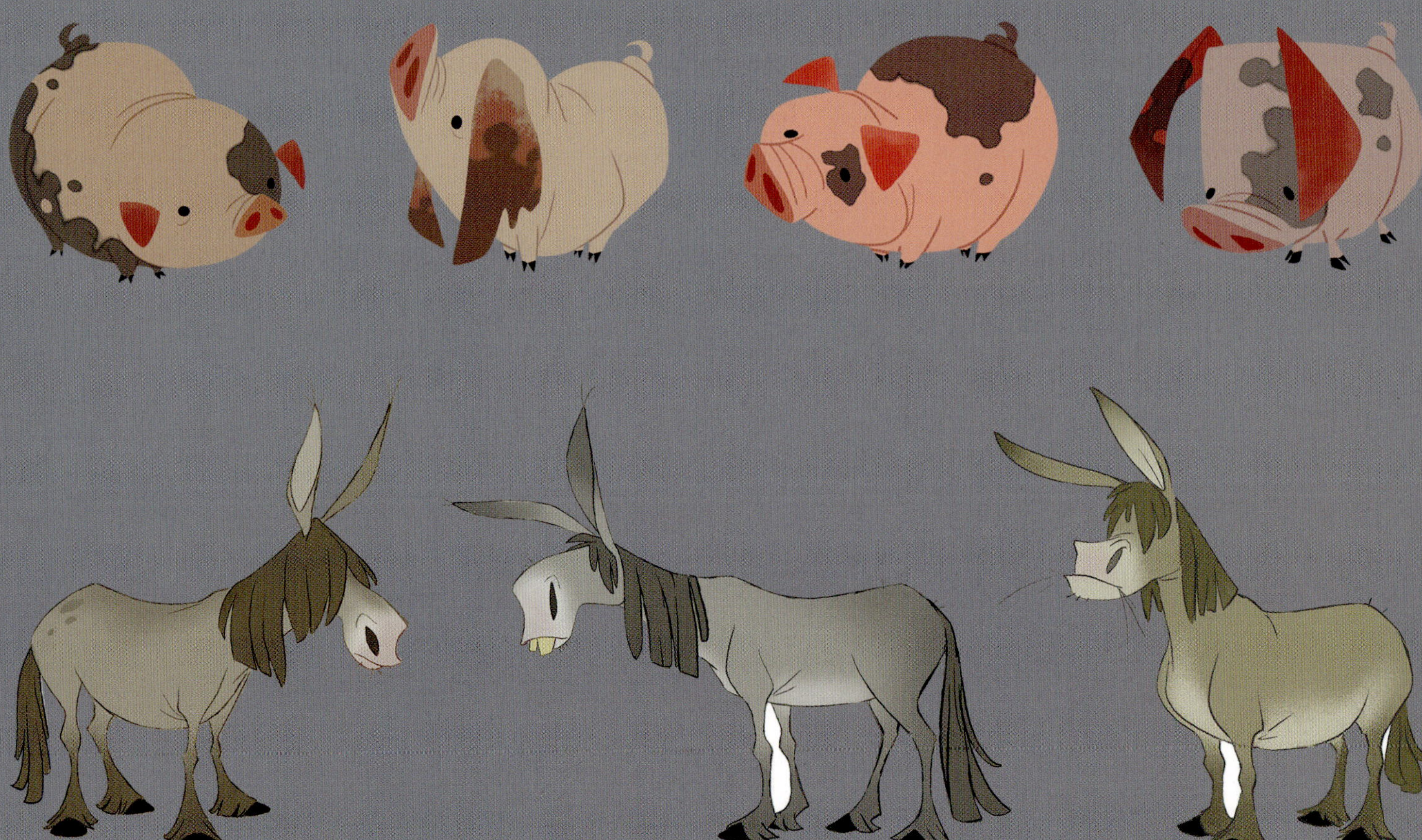

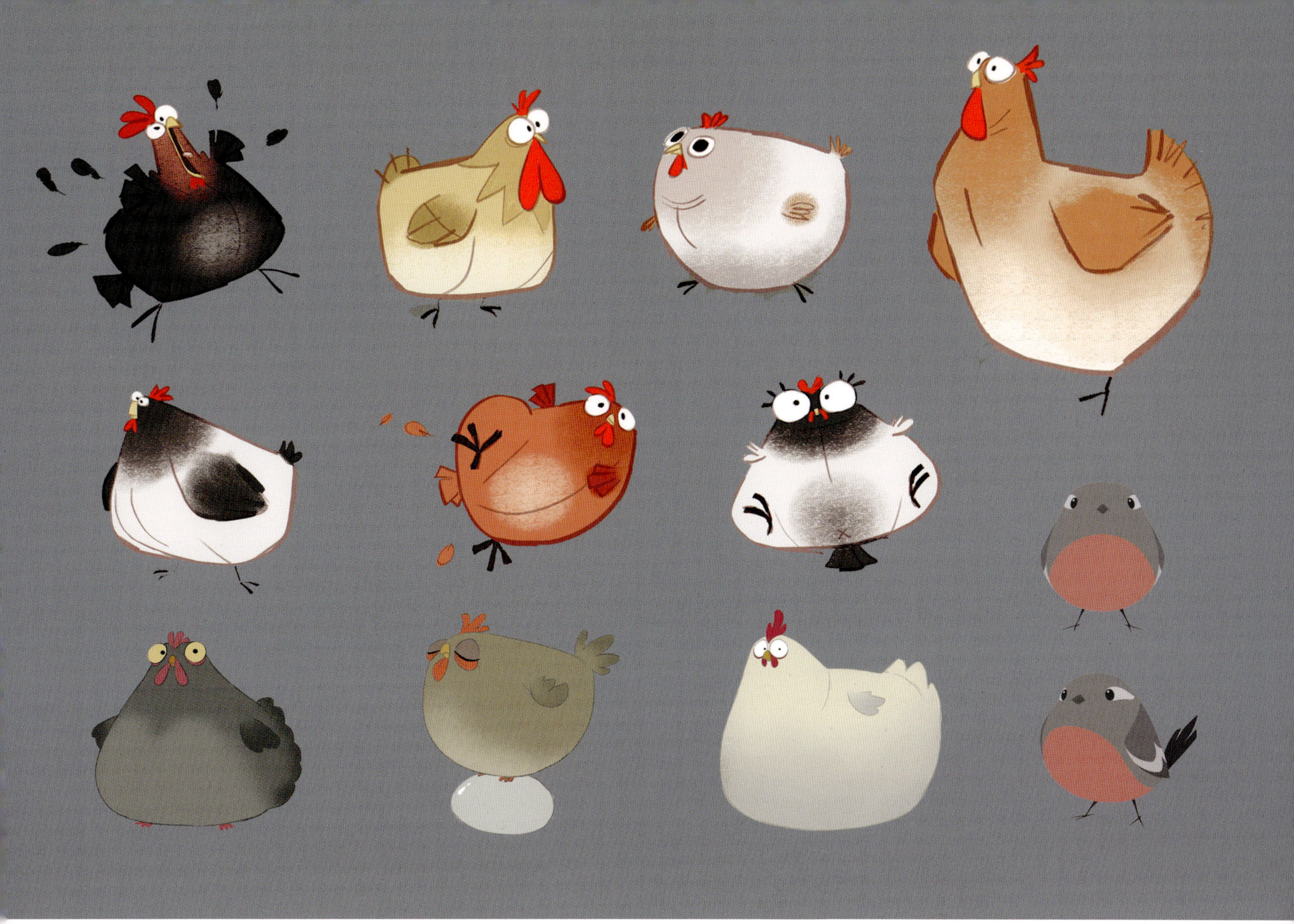

NEXT SPREAD: Artwork by Arthus Pilorget.

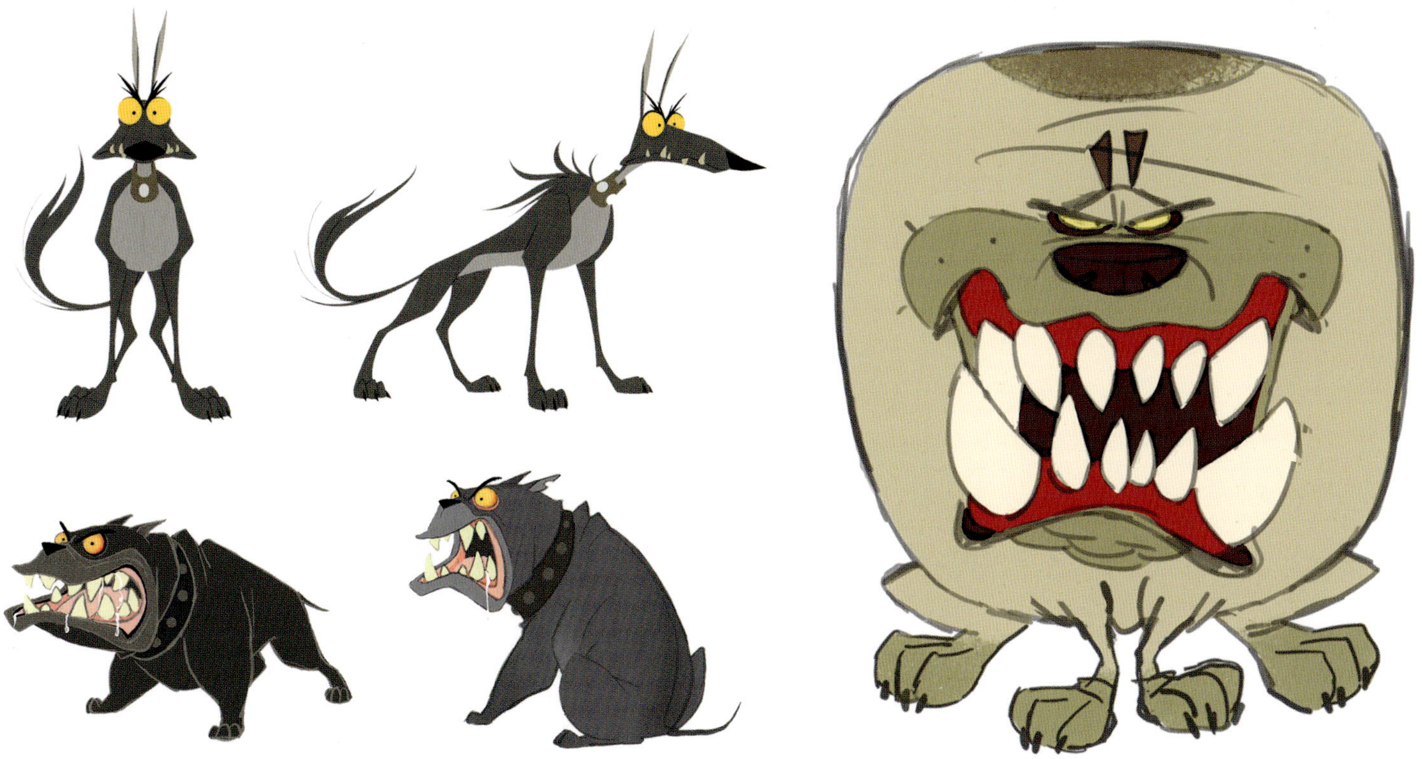

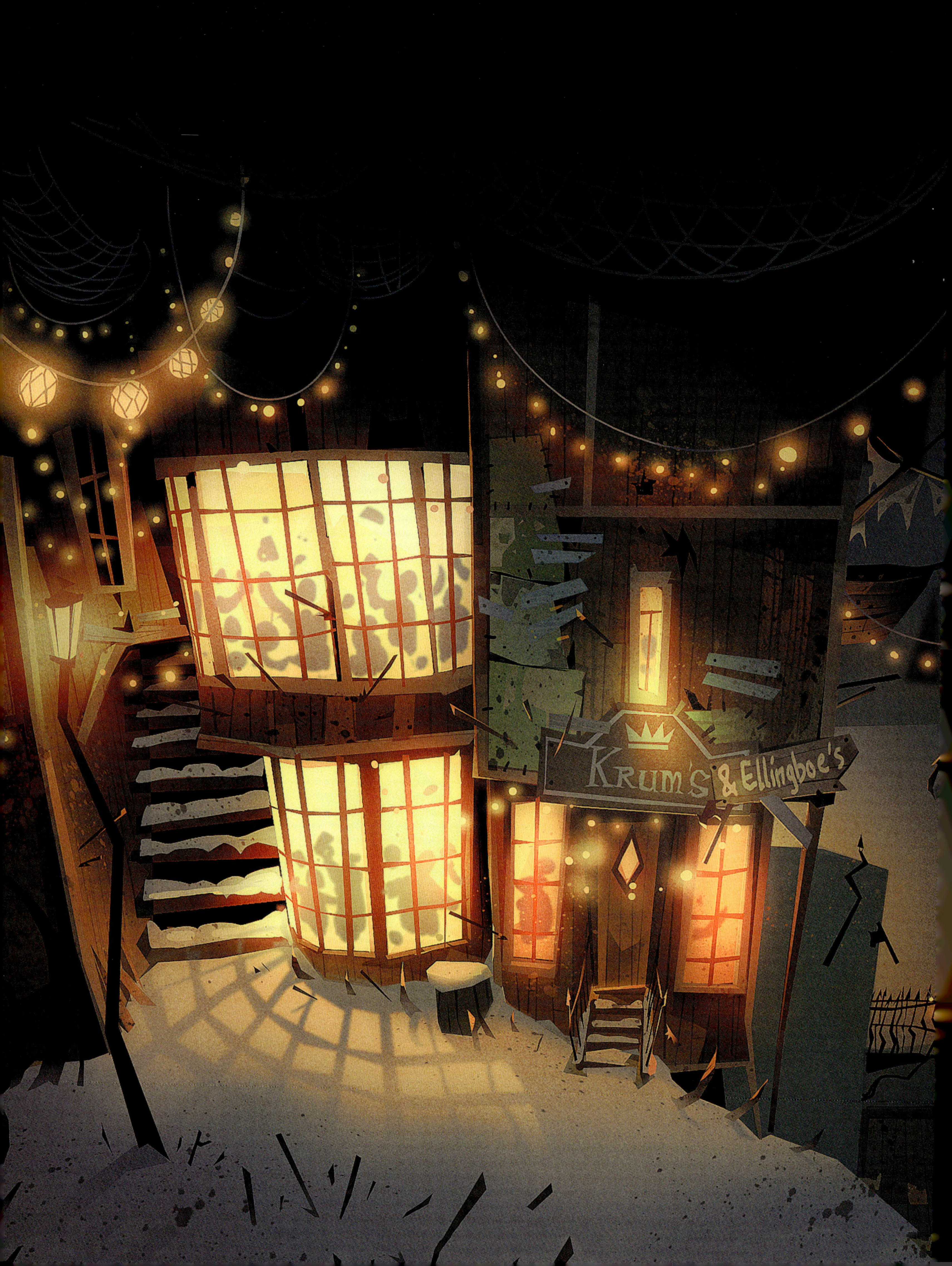
Krum's
& Ellingboe's

Finding the Christmas Spirit

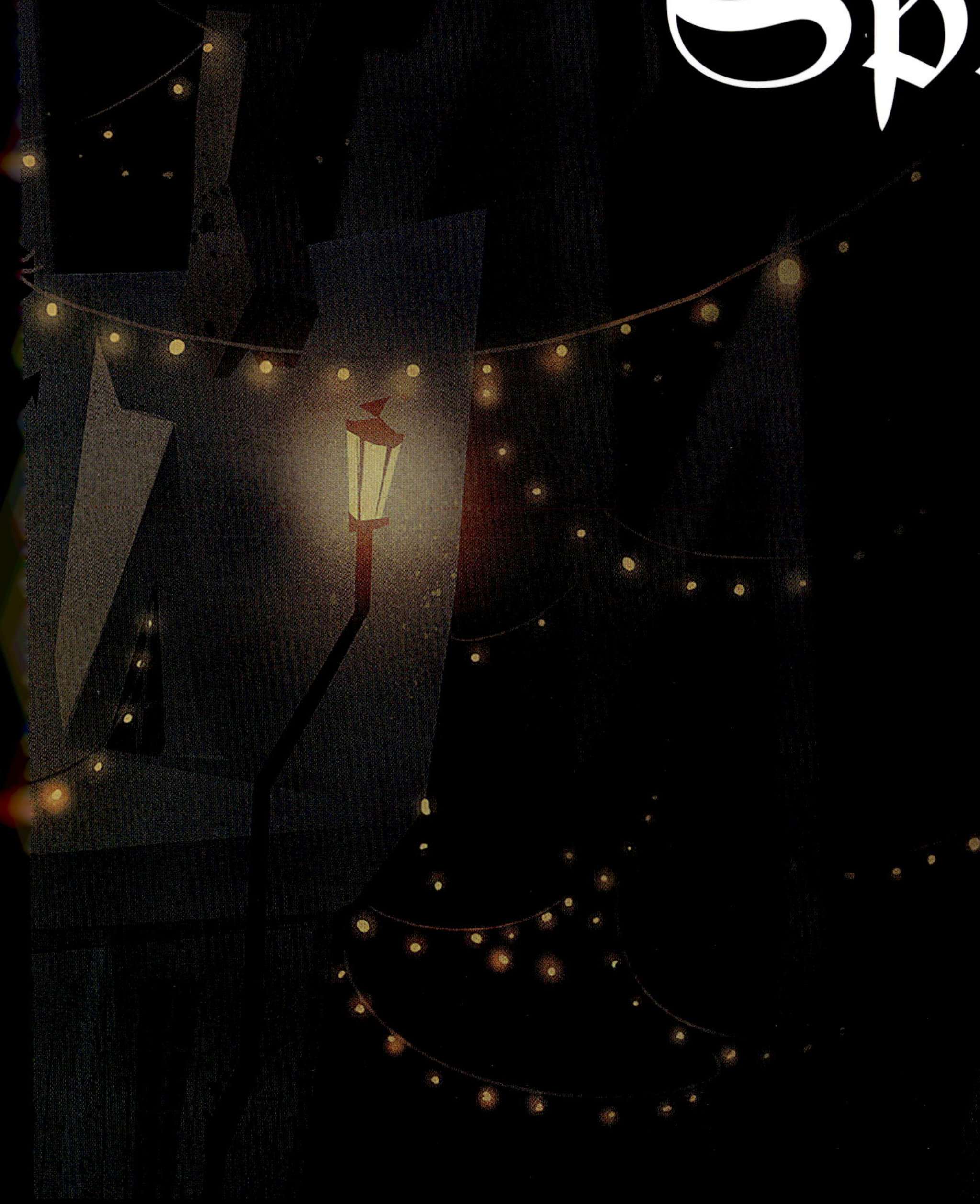

The First Gift

A BOY AND HIS FROG

Although this sequence happens months before the arrival of Christmas, it represents the first delivery of a holiday gift. "One of our challenges was to create a mood that would be scary for Jesper as he delivers the package," says production designer Szymon Biernacki. "Yet we also needed to quickly shift into an intimate and magical setting for the boy that discovers the toy."

Another big challenge was the toy itself. The artists had to come up with a design that would be more than just a toy. "It had to feel almost alive, but still look like a mechanical contraption," says Biernacki. "The design had to be appealing from all angles, and the animators had to be able to move it around in a way that looked like it had a will of its own. We ended up working back and forth with Torsten Schrank to arrive at a design that we felt would satisfy all those needs."

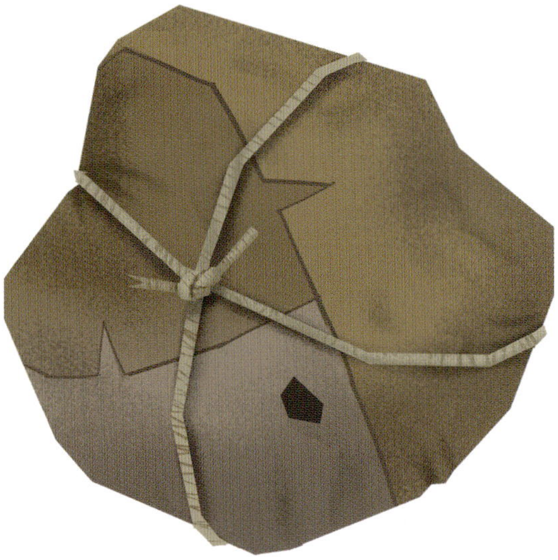

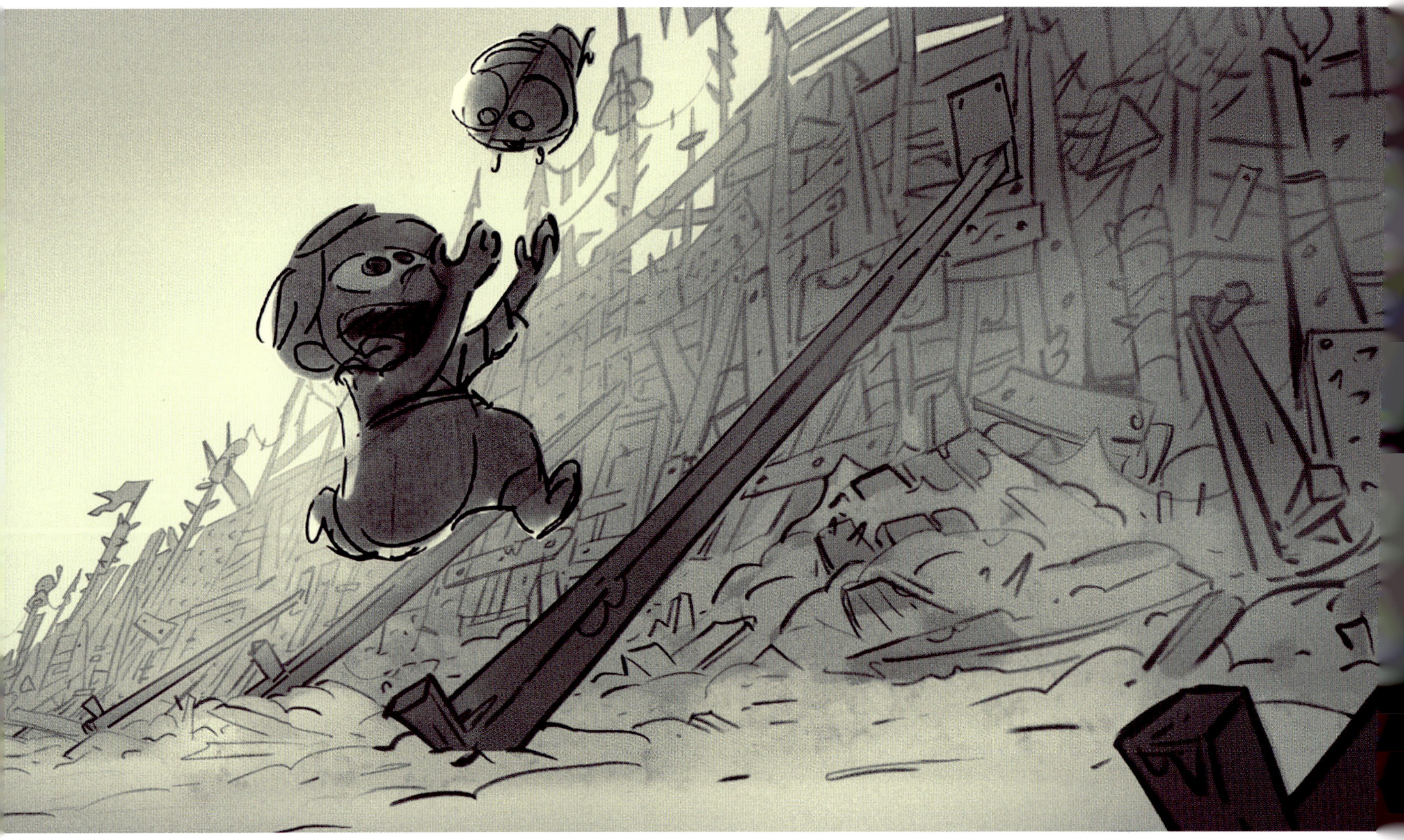

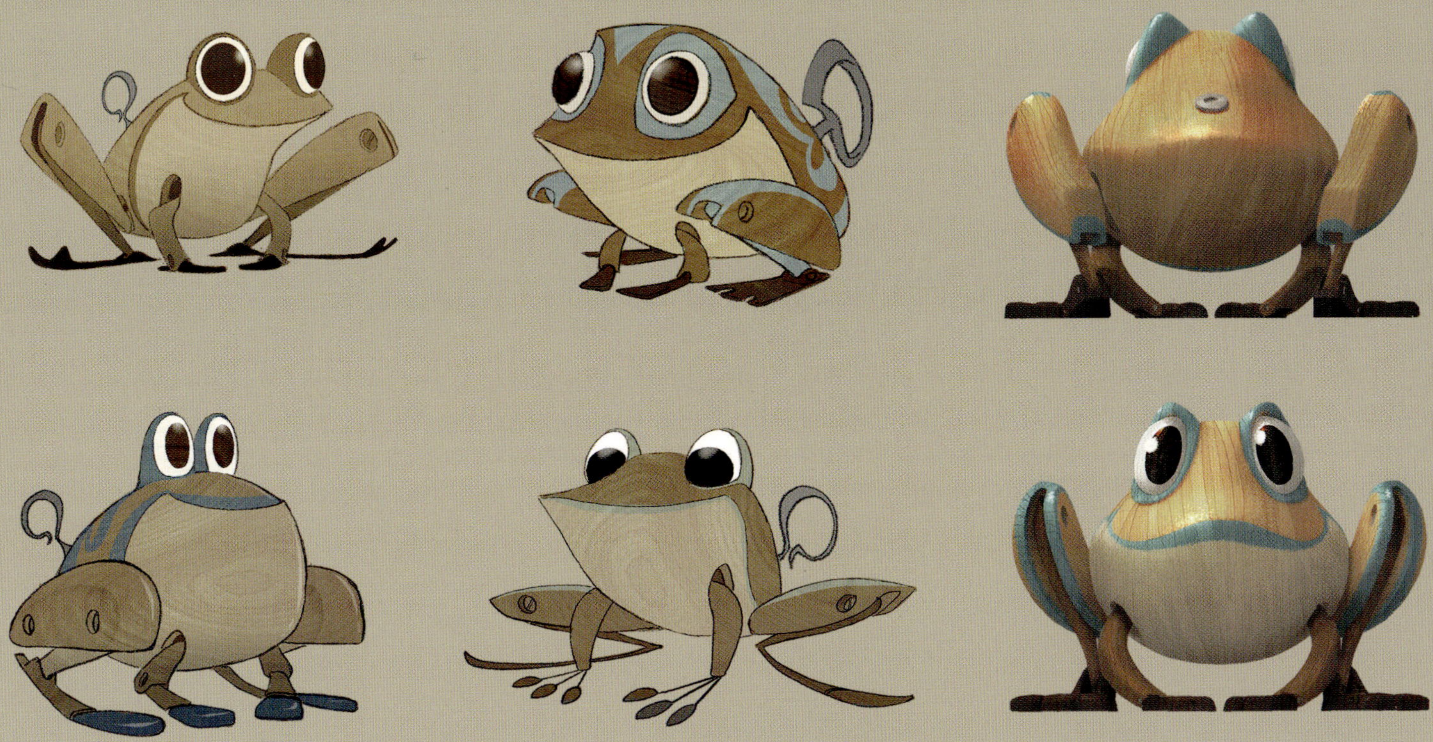

PREVIOUS PAGE: Artwork by Arthus Pilorget.

THIS PAGE: (TOP) Designs by Torsten Schrank; (BOTTOM) Drawing designs by Arthus Pilorget.

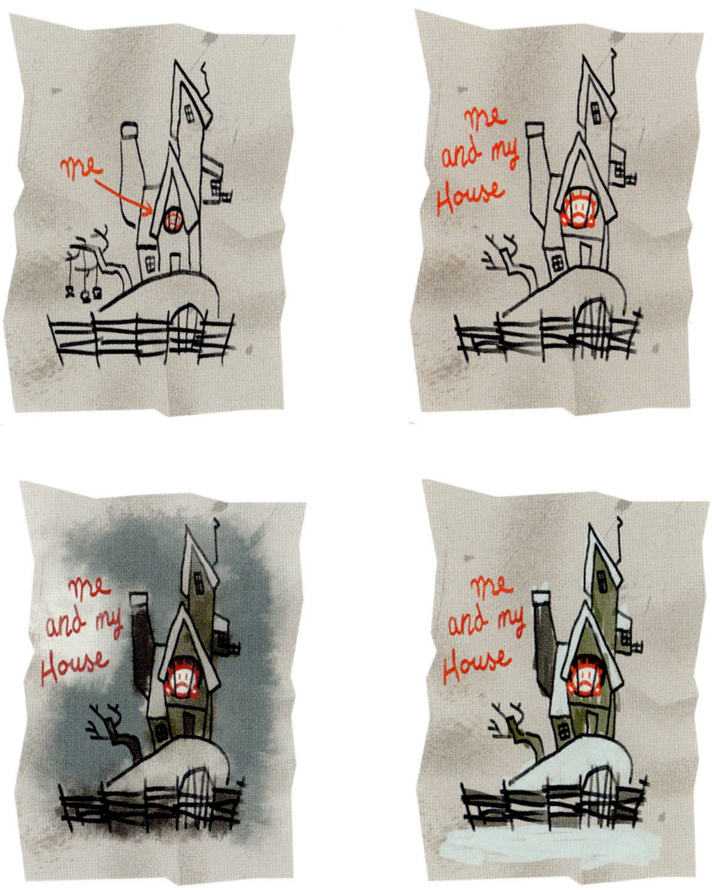

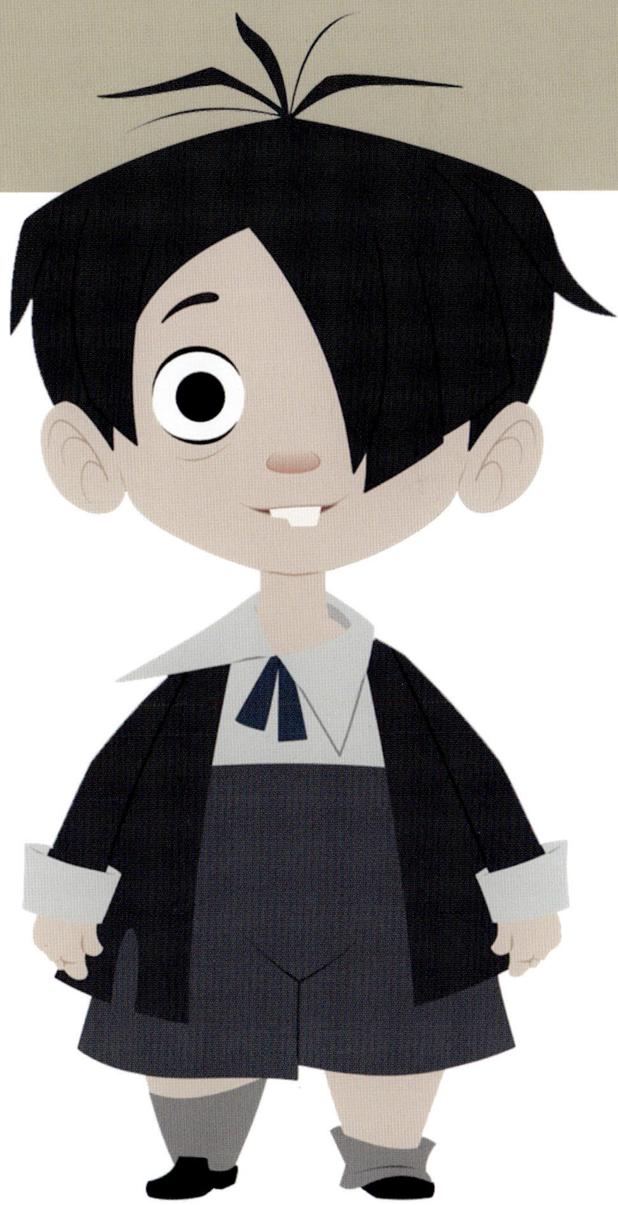

Transformation

DESIGNING A CHANGING TOWN

One of the key artistic directions the movie follows is how the town's buildings stand in contrast with the harsh, snow-covered environments of the north. As art director Szymon Biernacki points out, the world outside the town is usually just rocks, snow, and very little vegetation. "The houses look like wooden hats stuck on top of everything," he says. "They don't feel like they really belong there. Also, they all have this primitive shape, like a box with a triangular roof. That's why we tried to emphasize those shapes and amplify them to create an environment that feels hostile and unwelcoming."

THIS PAGE: (TOP) Artwork by Arthus Pilorget; (BOTTOM) Transformation guide by Marcin Jakubowski.

NEXT PAGE: Artwork by Kevin Le Moigne.

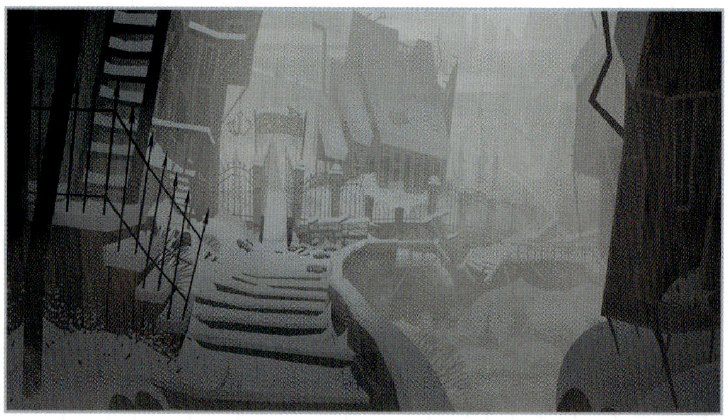

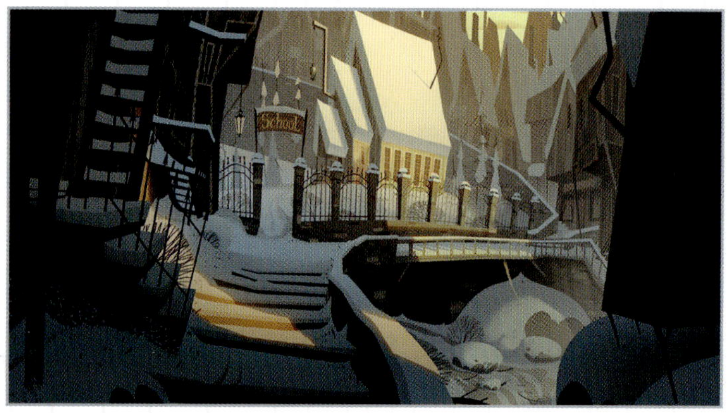

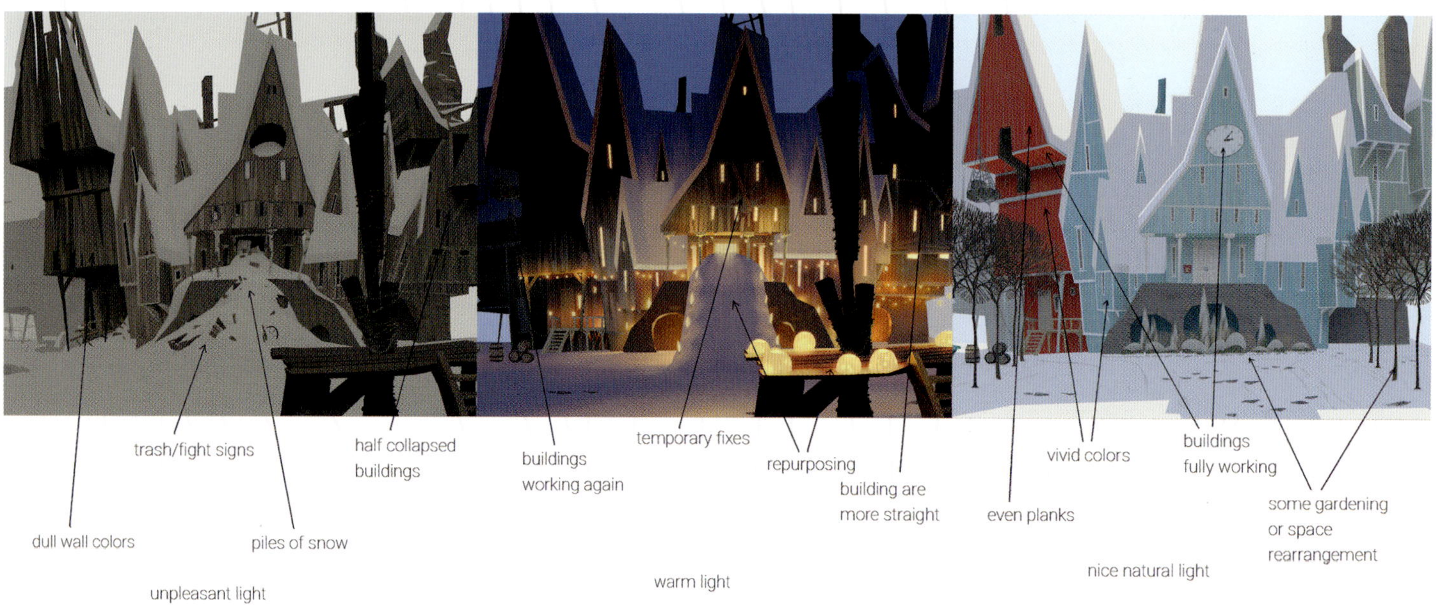

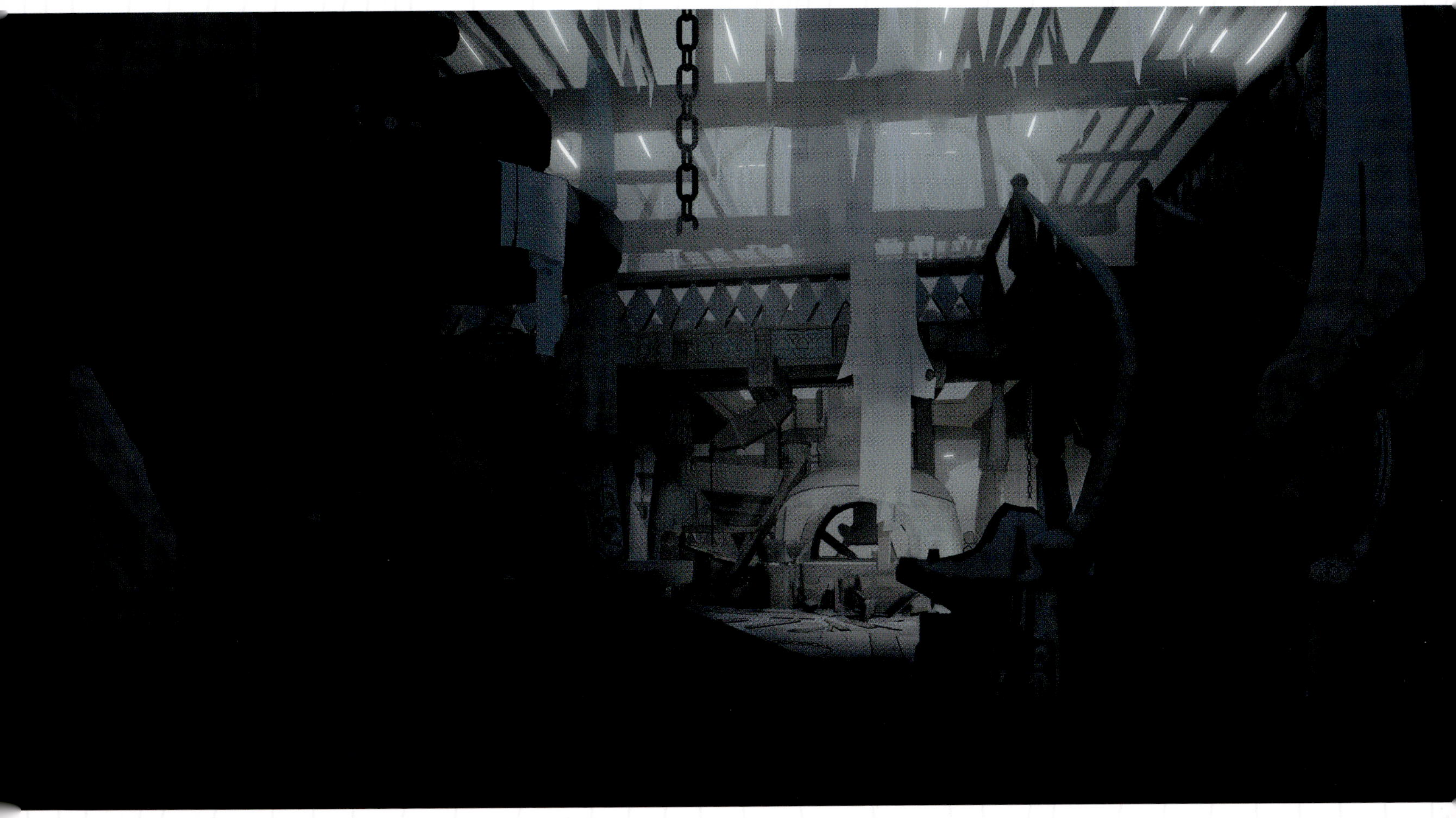

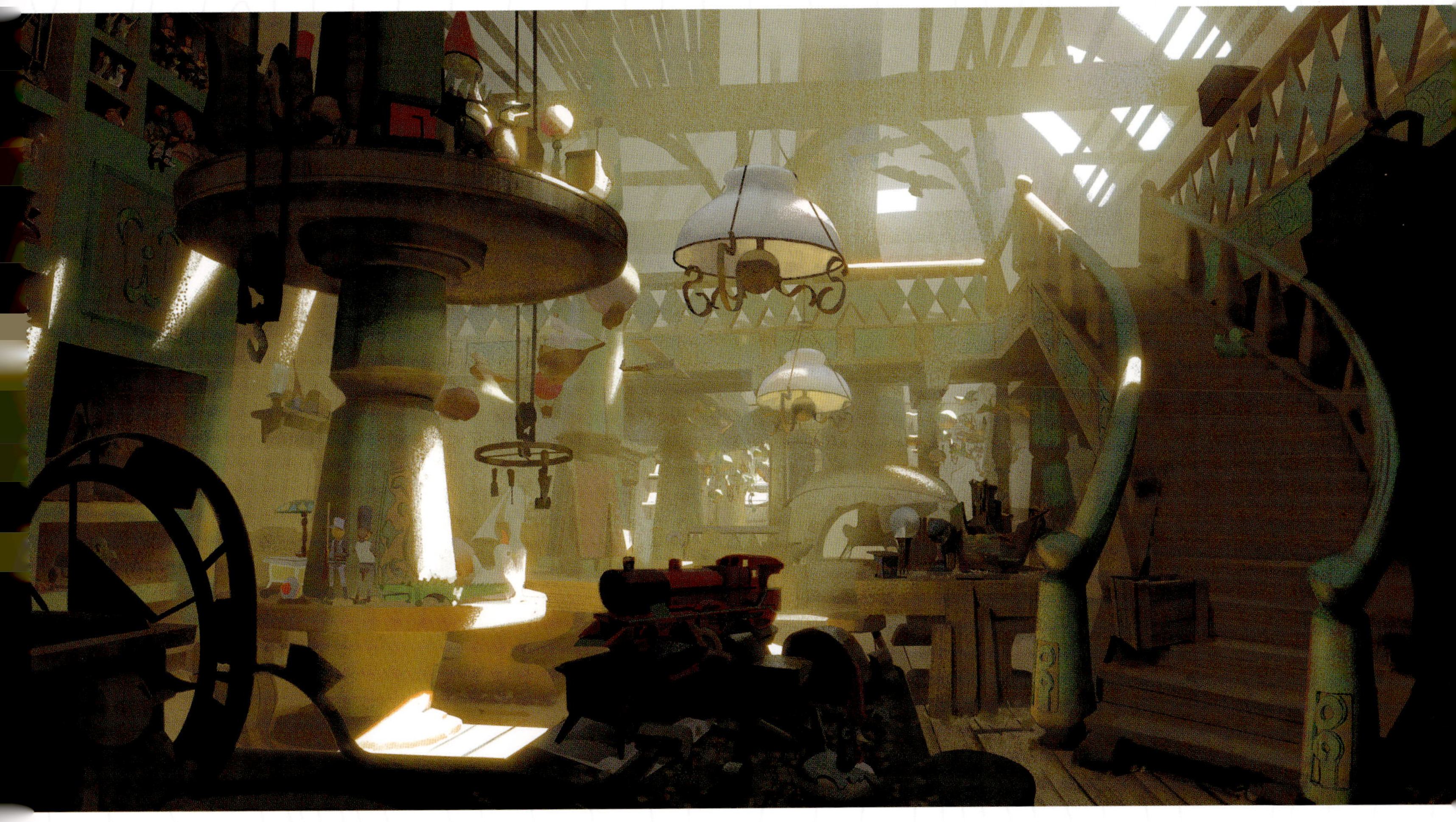

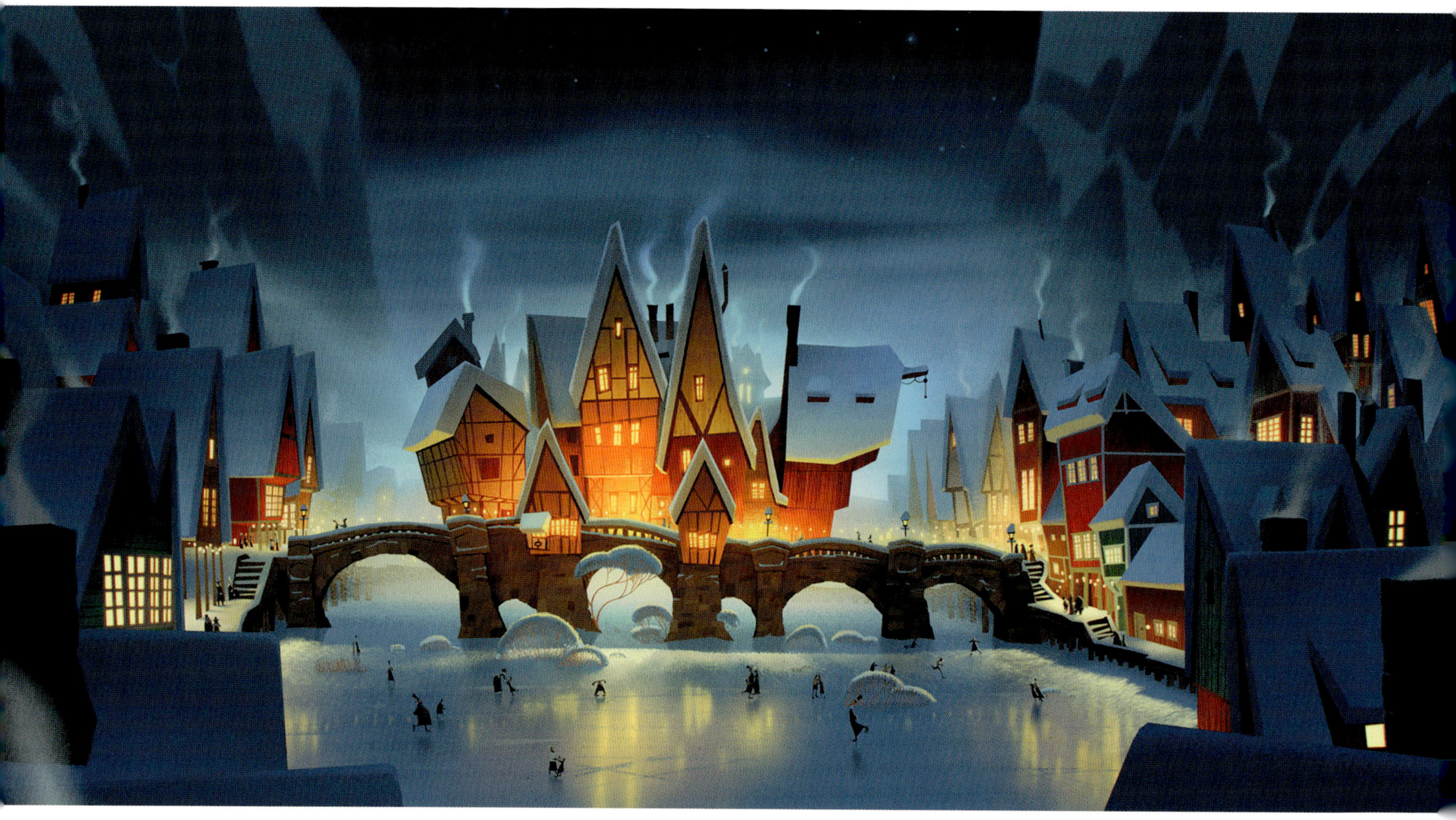

THIS PAGE: Artwork by Marcin Jakubowski.

NEXT SPREAD: Artwork by Marcin Jakubowski.

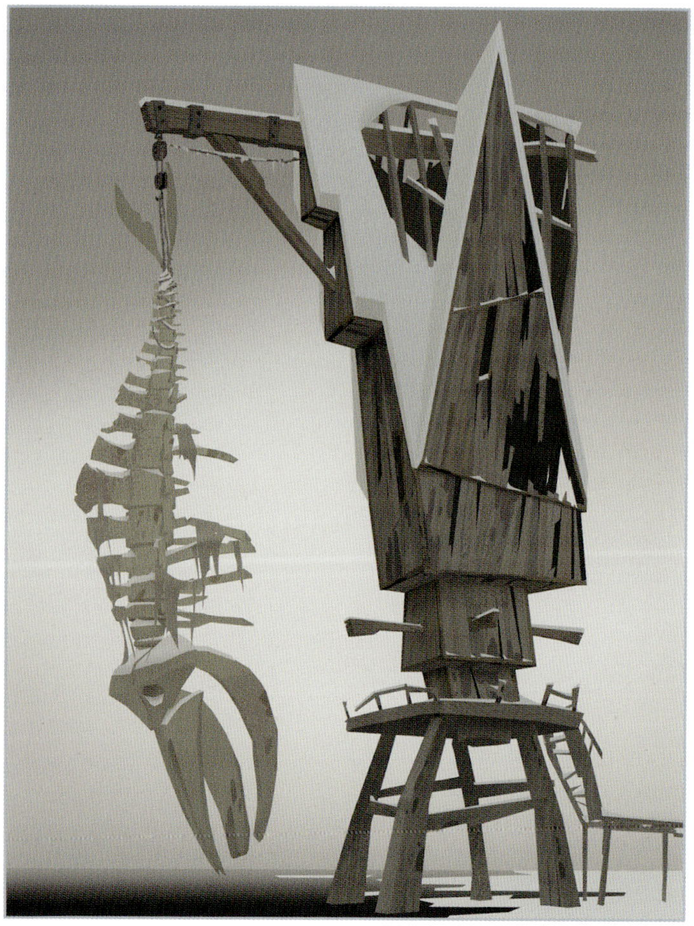

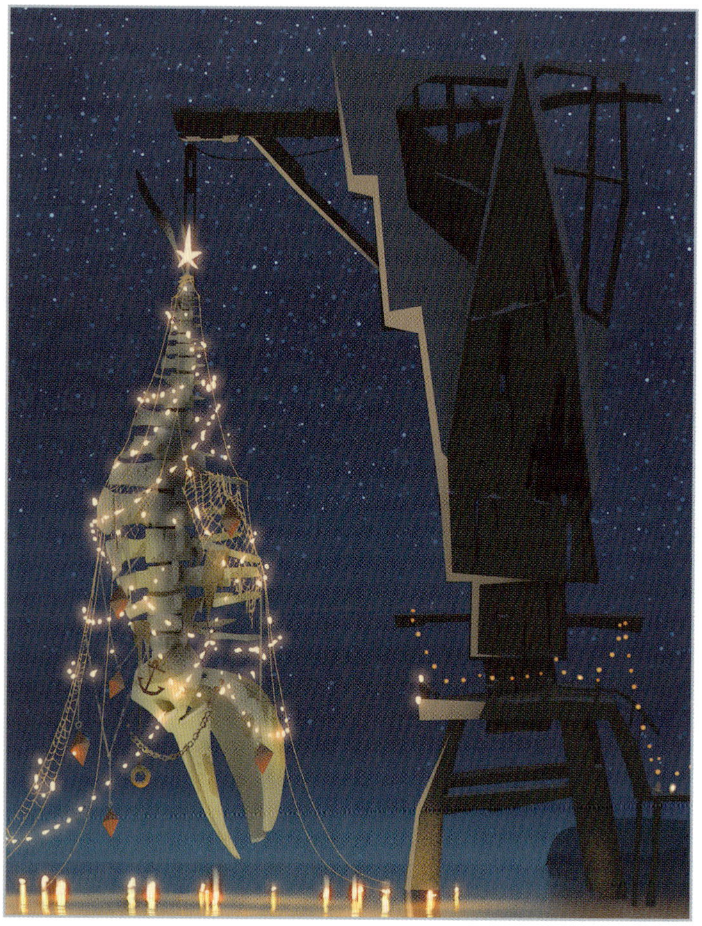

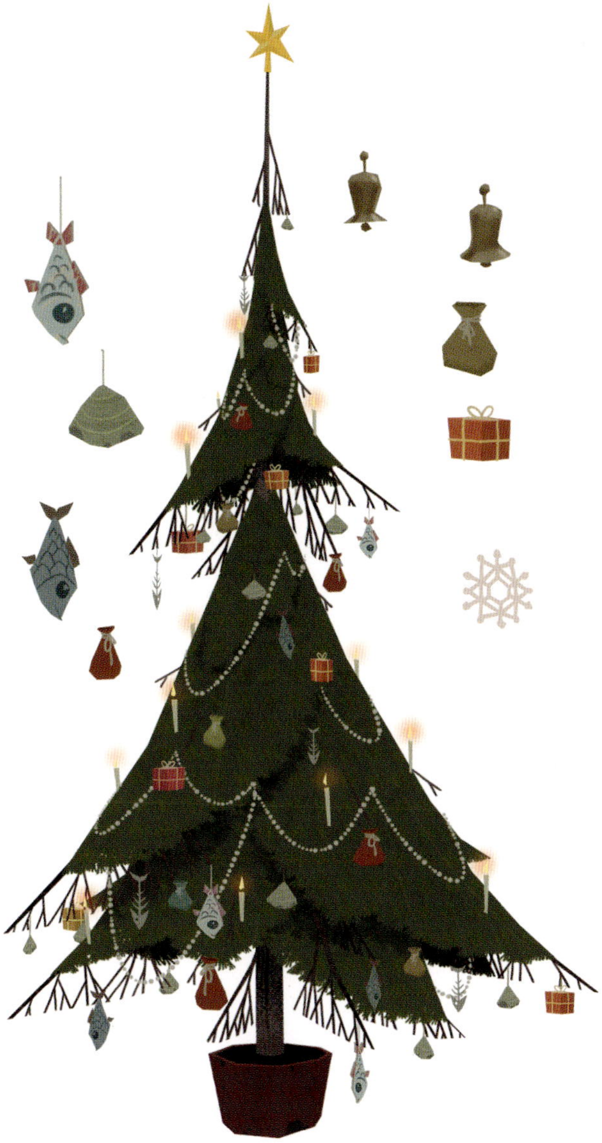

THIS PAGE: (ABOVE) Artwork by Szymon Biernacki. (BELOW) Color key by Samuel Smith.

Another strategy involved avoiding parallel lines and accentuating diagonals and triangles. "This is a place where Jesper doesn't feel comfortable at first. These sharp edges echo the state of mind of the people in the town as well, who are constantly fighting," says Biernacki. "However, we see the town transform into a kinder place as the plot unfolds. So we wanted to show how, as a result of Jesper's actions, the town also begins to change. So we see Smeerensburg transform as well and, by the final reel, it has turned into this beautiful Scandinavian village, bursting with colors and warmth."

As Jesper's plans are finally realized, the spirit of generosity and kindness takes over the whole community. Not only are the characters themselves transformed by their own good deeds, Smeerensburg also undergoes a visible change. There are smiles on the residents' faces, and bursts of color everywhere in the previously drab and harsh rooms and buildings.

"In the movie, the theme is phrased as 'a true act of kindness always sparks another,'" recalls Pablos. "That's essentially what Jesper learns. We are also treating kindness as a fast-spreading virus. First, a child receives a toy as a gift, which brings joy, and then a neighbor realizes that playing with a once-forbidden enemy is a lot more fun than fighting with them."

Pablos points out an interesting contrast between the conclusion of *Klaus* and those of typical animated family movies. "The classic ending for a villain in your typical animated movie is to be thrown off a cliff but, in our story, the worst thing that could happen was that our fighting clans would become in-laws!" says the director with a smile. "That means they become family with those they were taught to hate!"

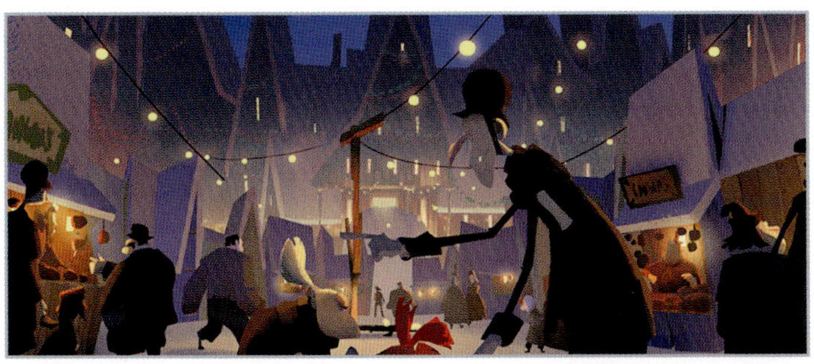

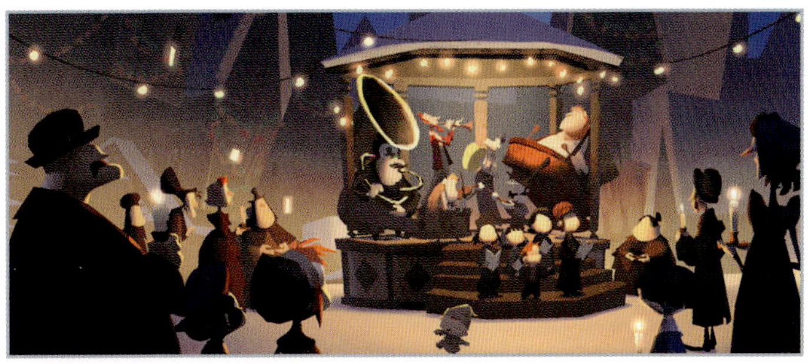

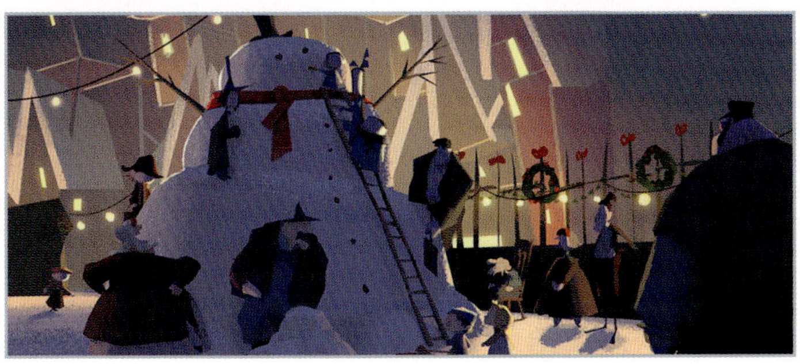

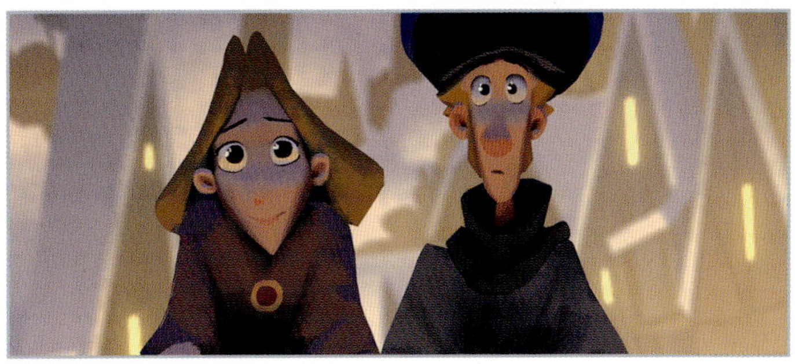

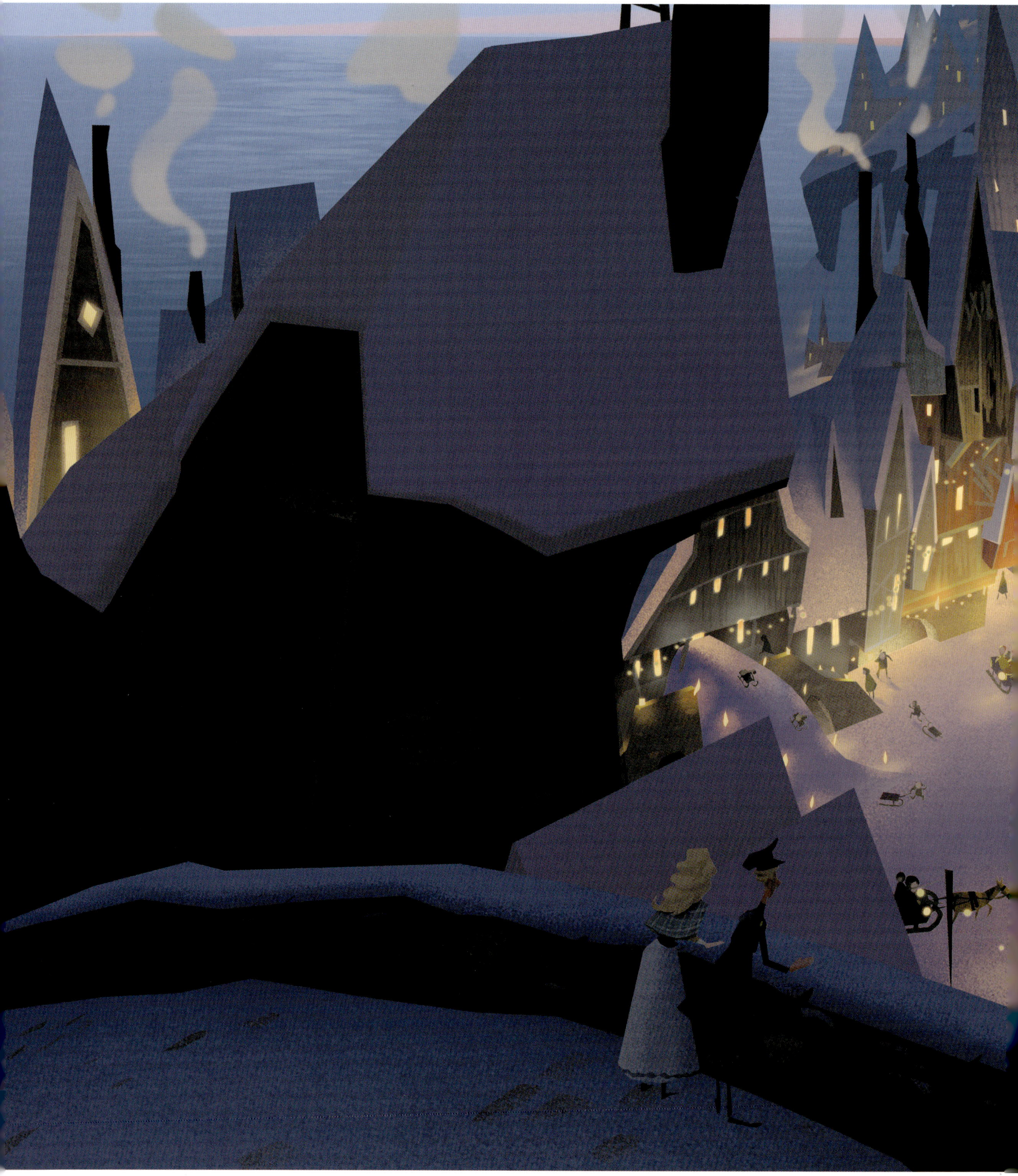

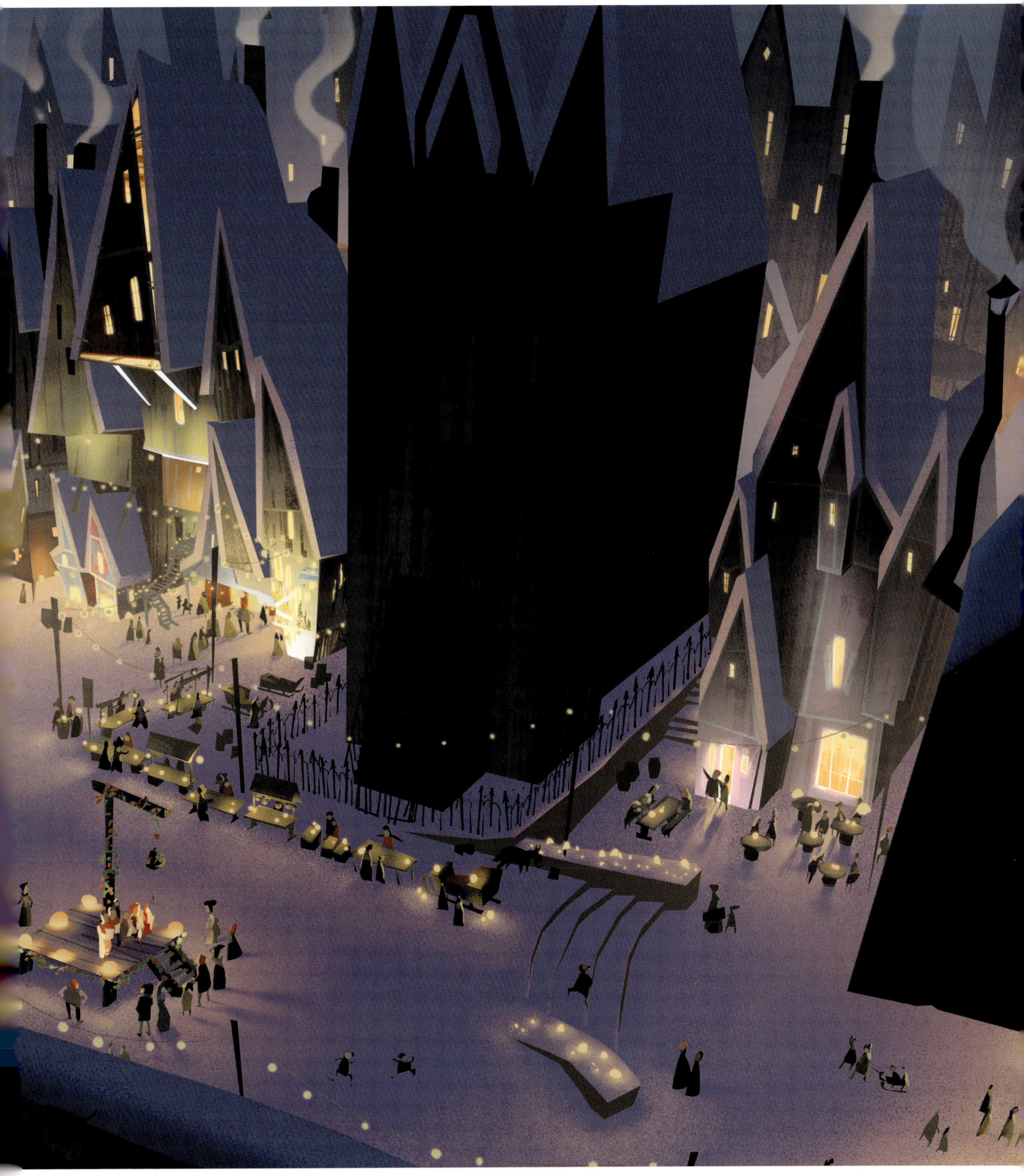

Alva

FROM FISHMONGER TO SCHOOLTEACHER

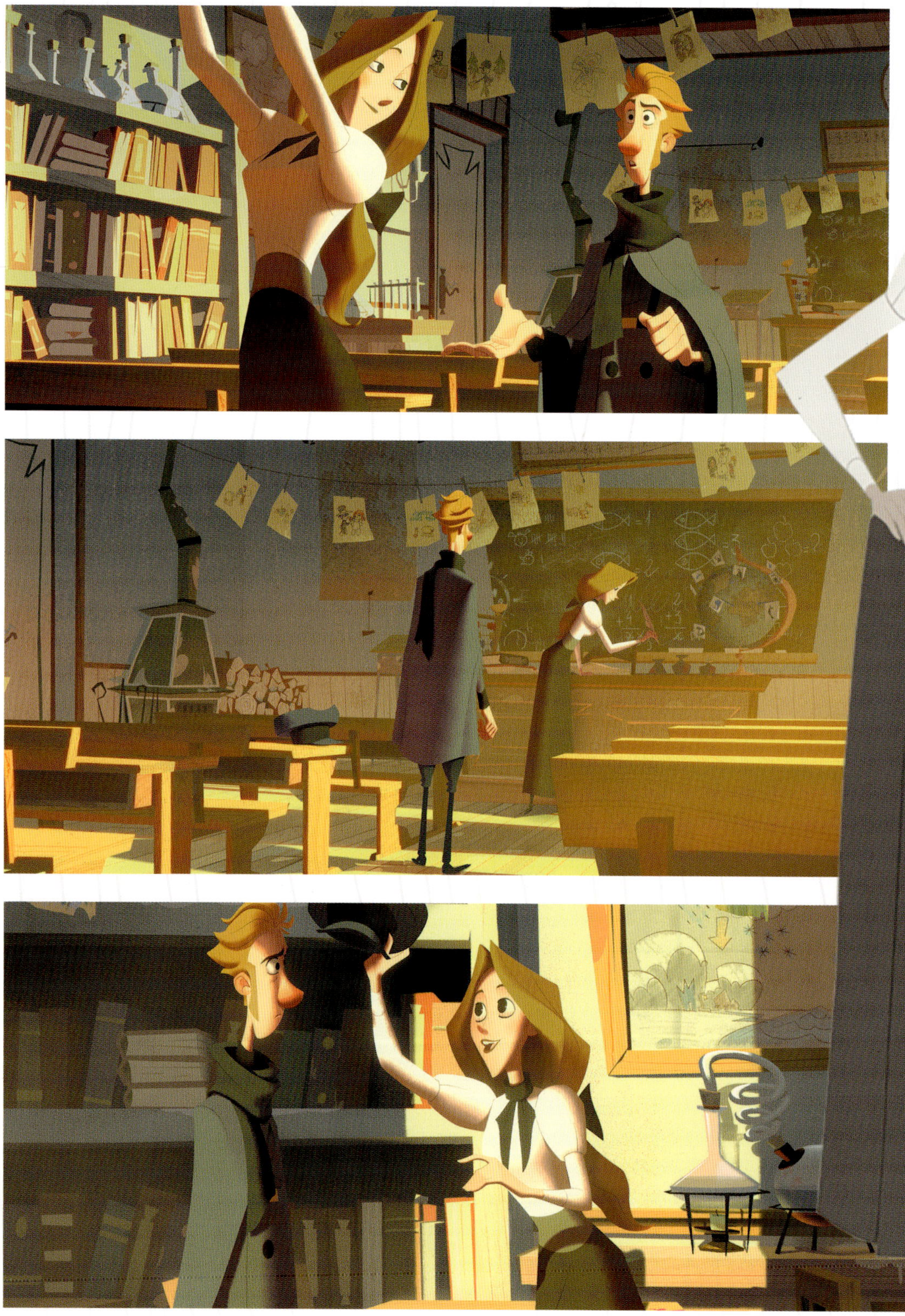

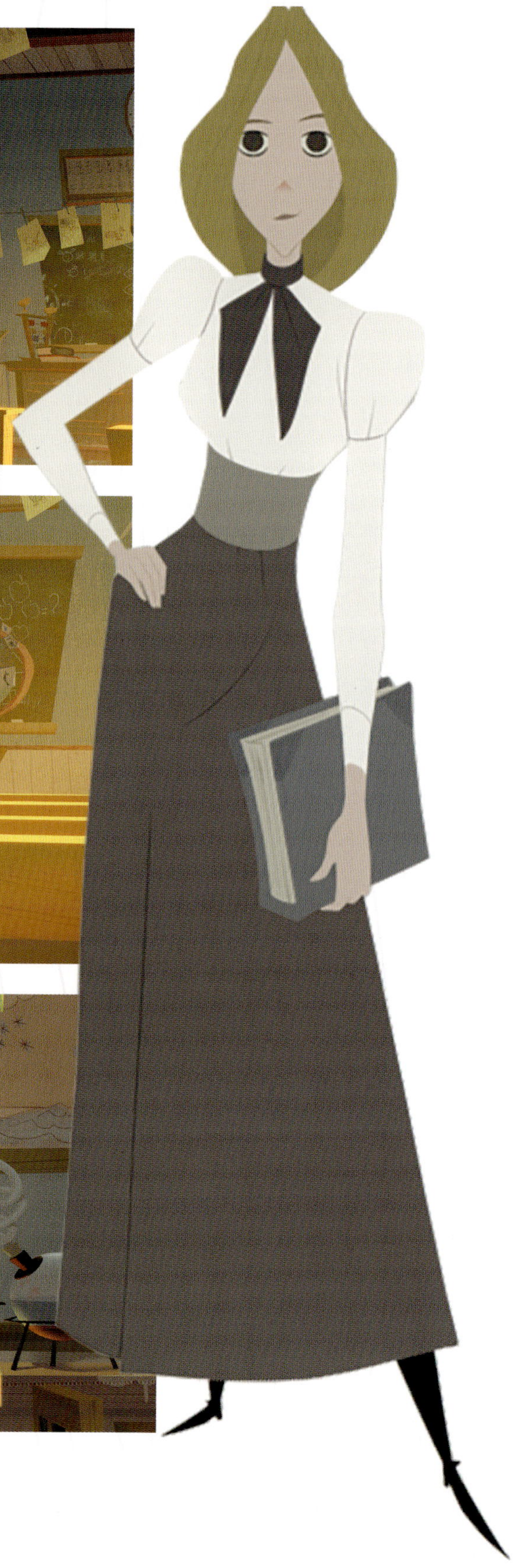

THIS PAGE: Alva, finally achieving her dream of being a schoolteacher.

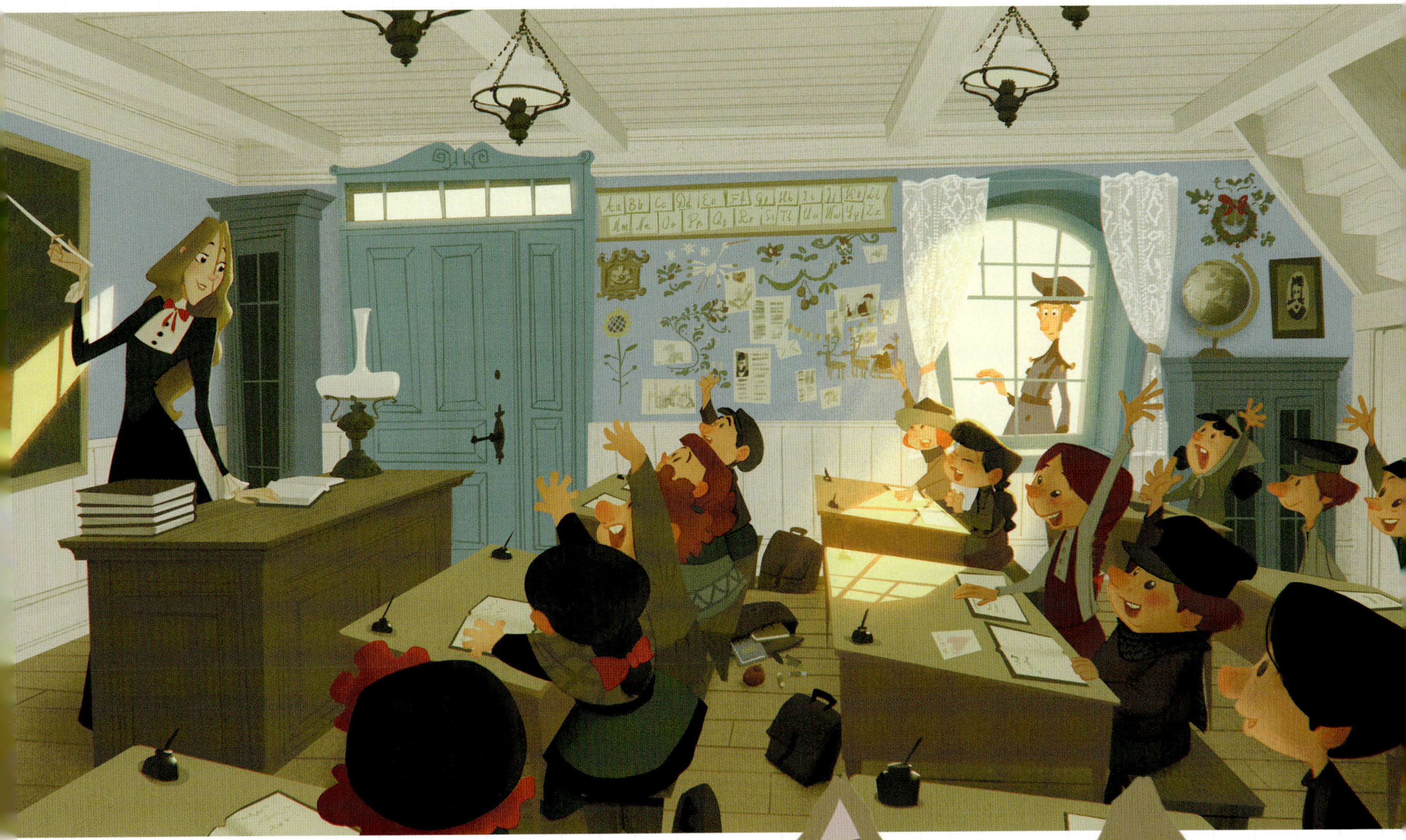

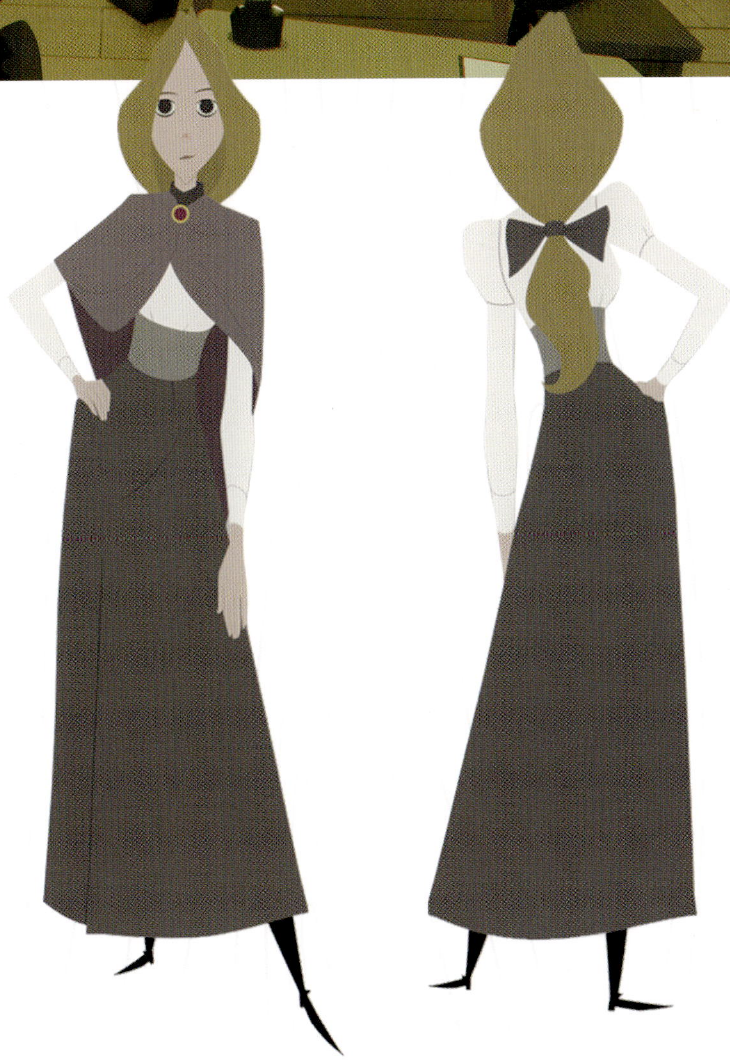

"Alva is one of the film's favorite characters because I think [her arc] is very interesting. She is very charming to look at as she re-evaluates her values, and there's something very powerful about her story."

Sergio Pablos, Writer-director

TOP: Artwork by Marcin Jakubowski and Juan Pablo Navas.

Schoolhouse

A TRANSFORMATION

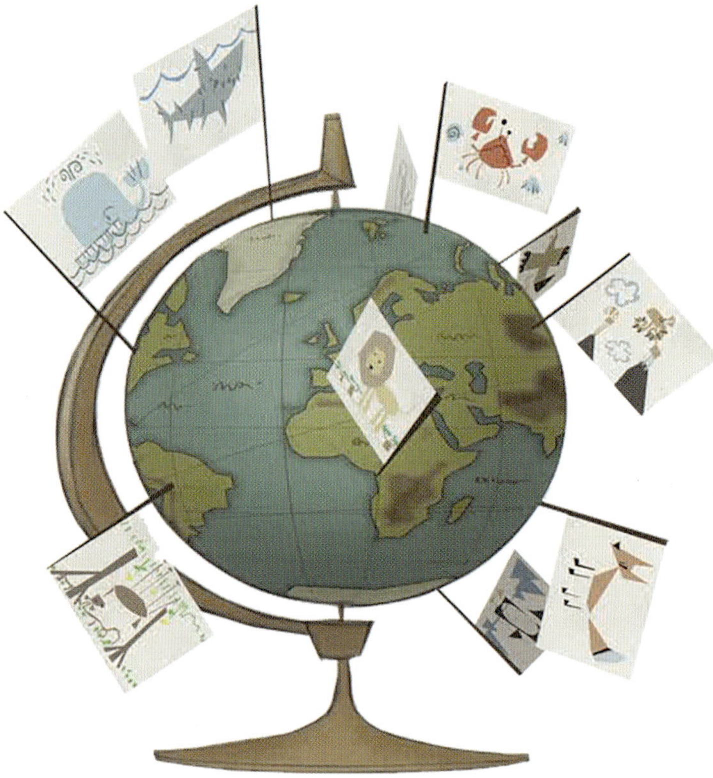

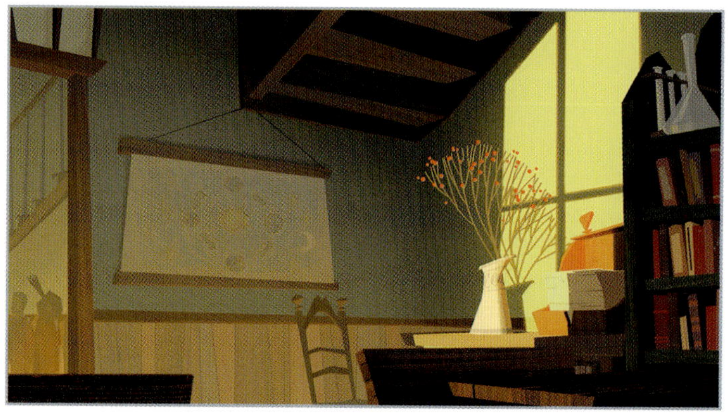

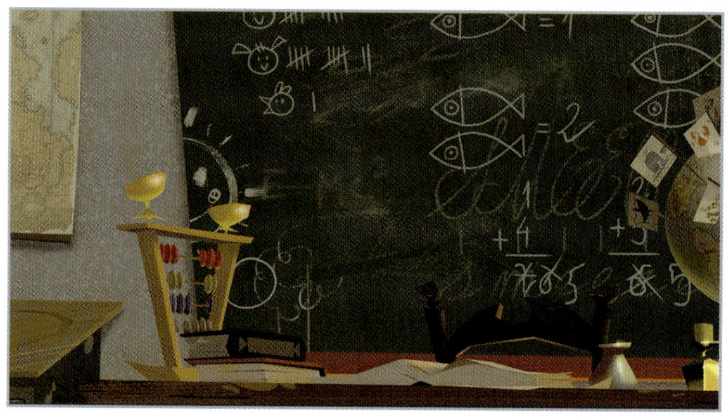

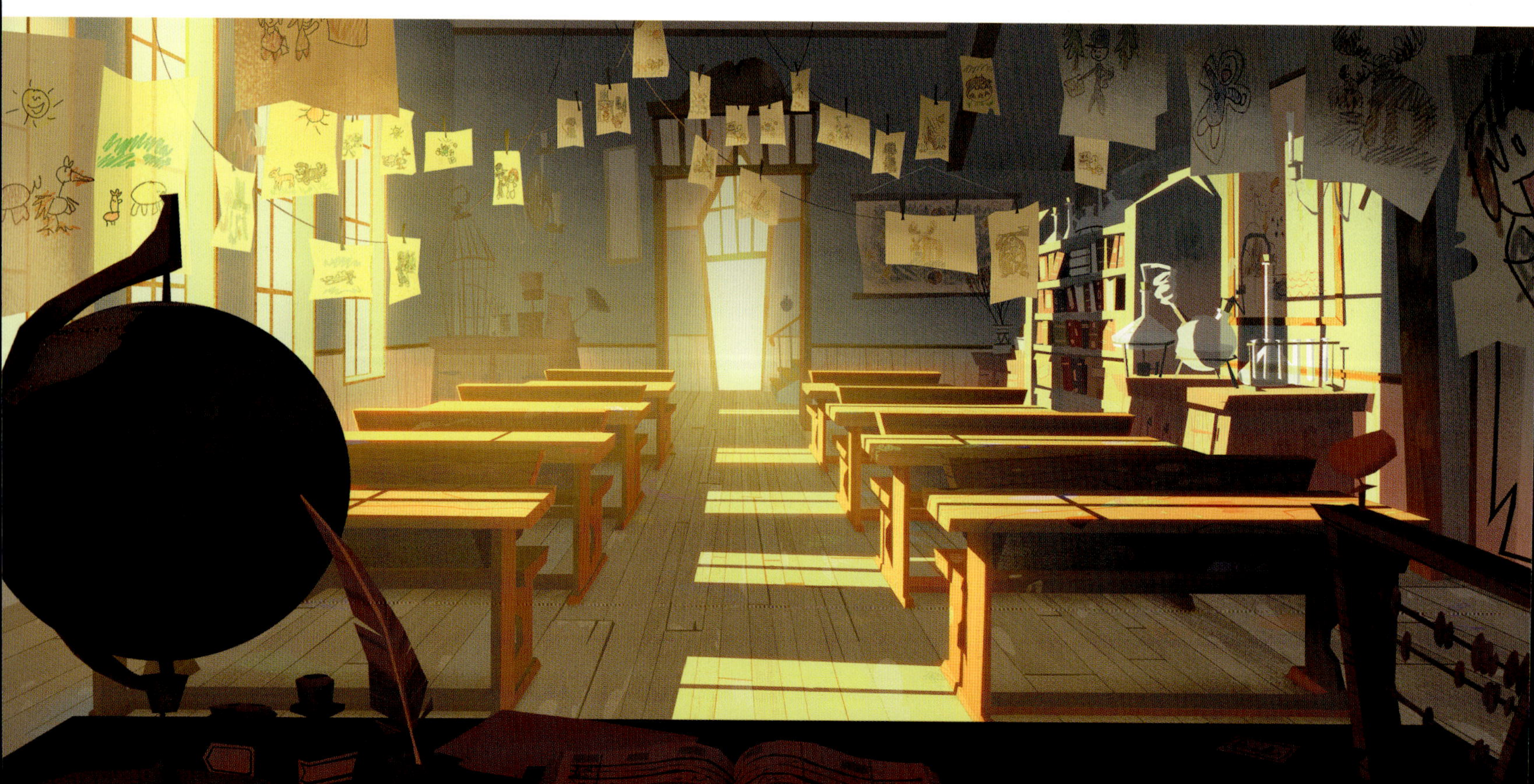

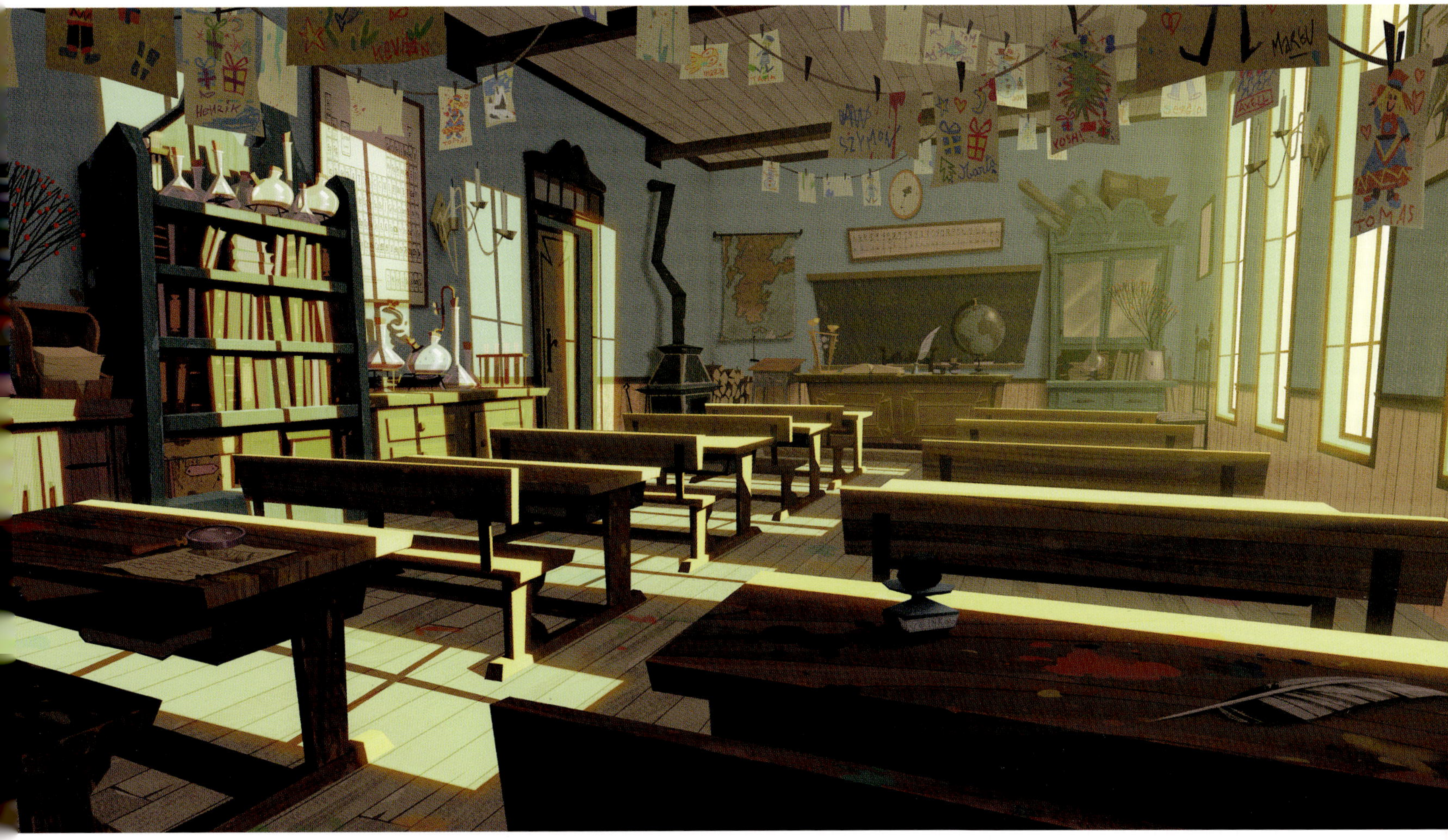

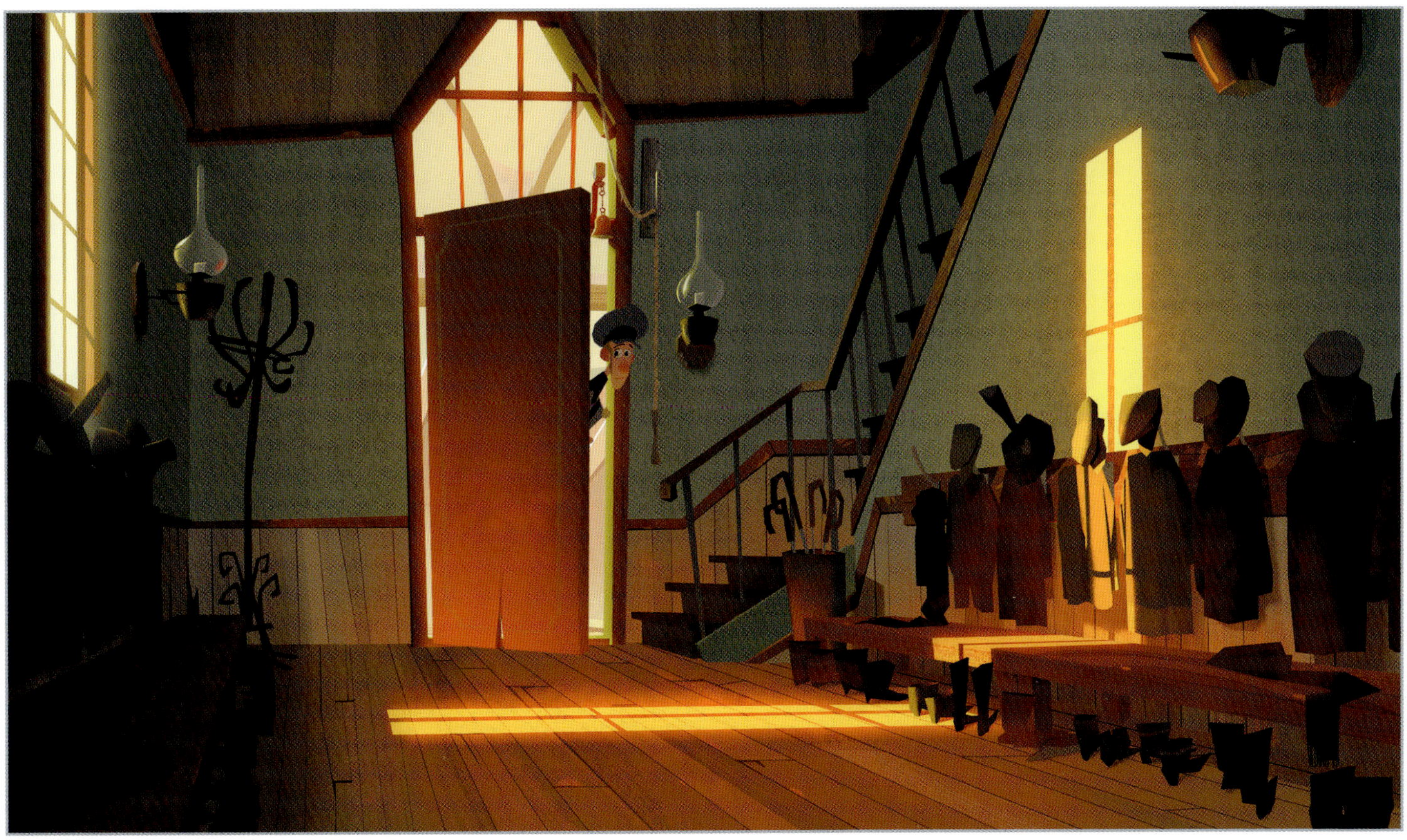

THIS SPREAD: Details of the transformed schoolhouse. Top right image by Arthus Pilorget.

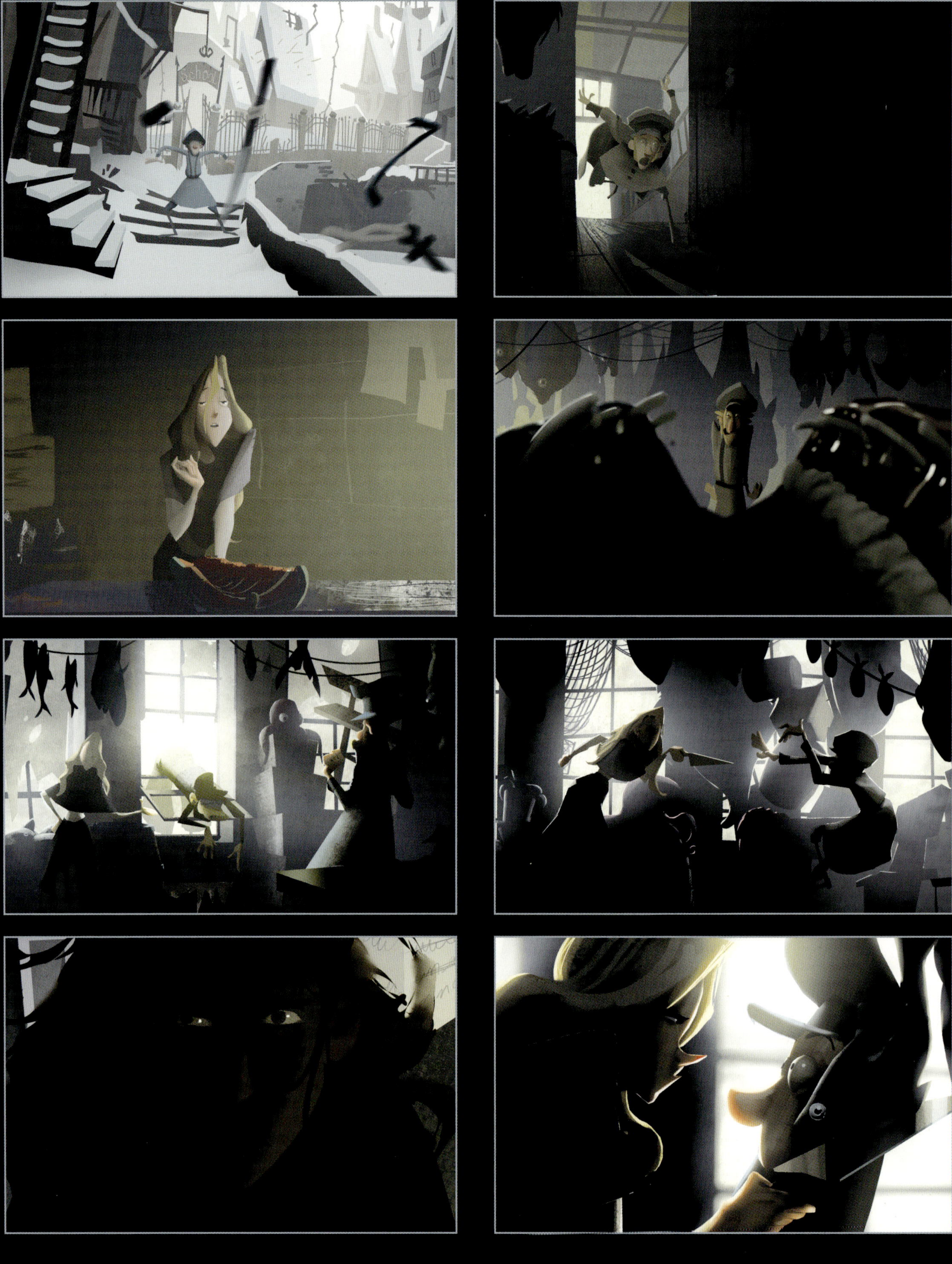

THIS SPREAD: Color keys by Samuel Smith.

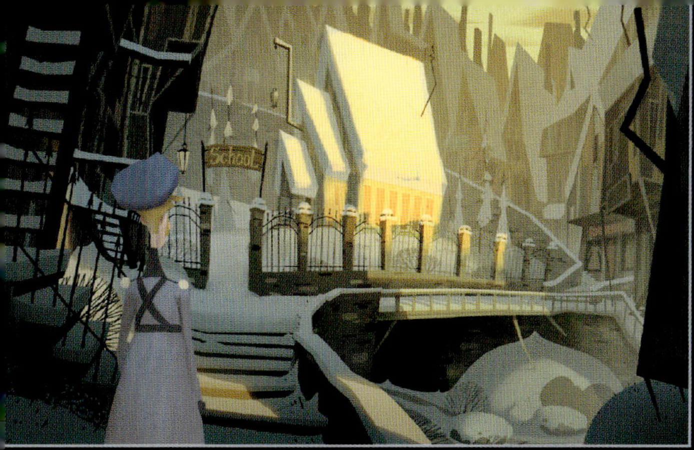
School
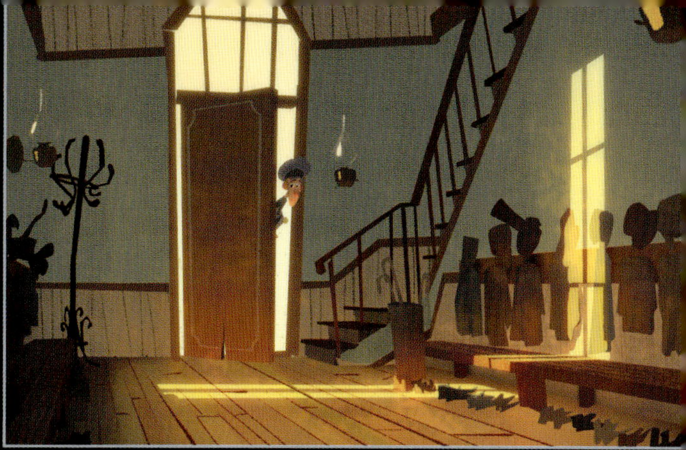
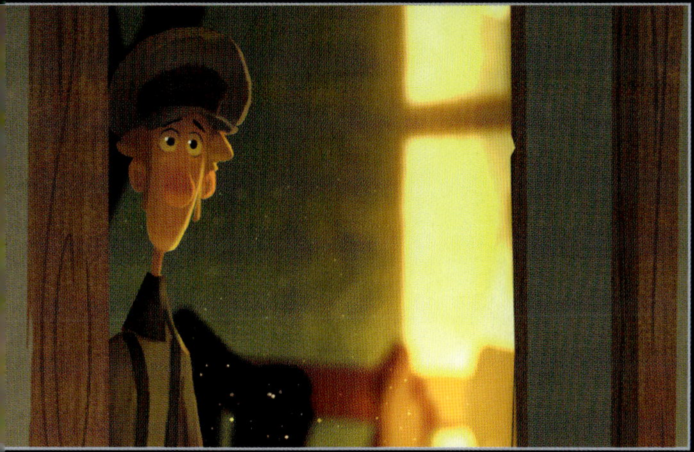
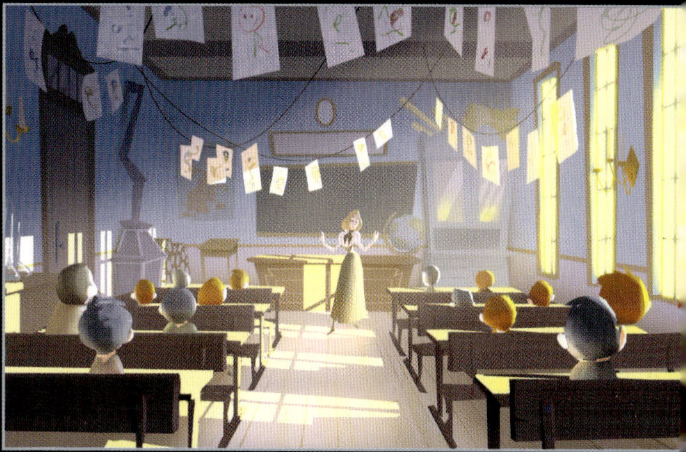
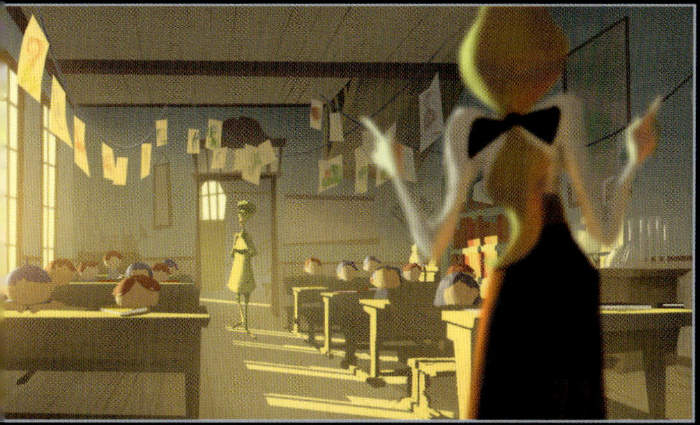
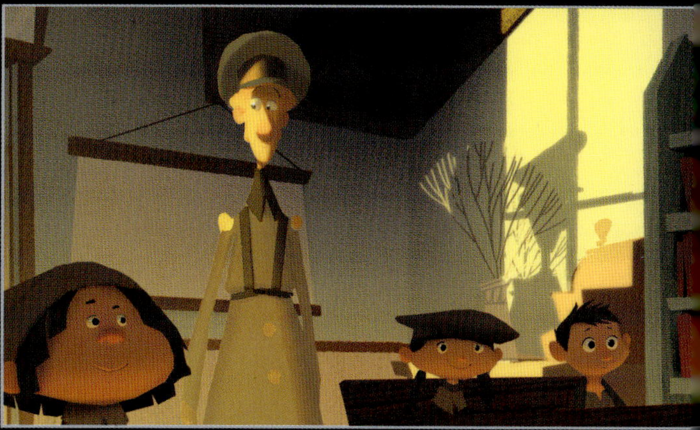
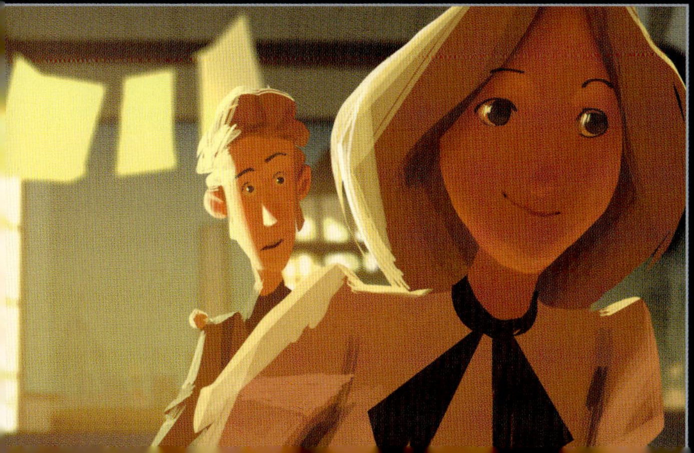
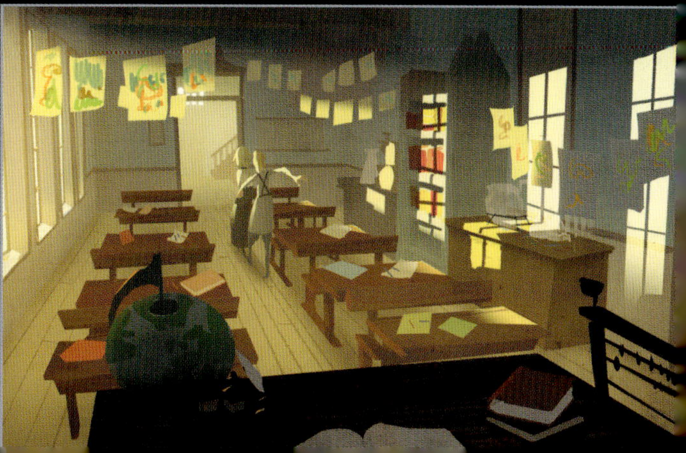

The Workshop

WHERE THE MAGIC HAPPENS

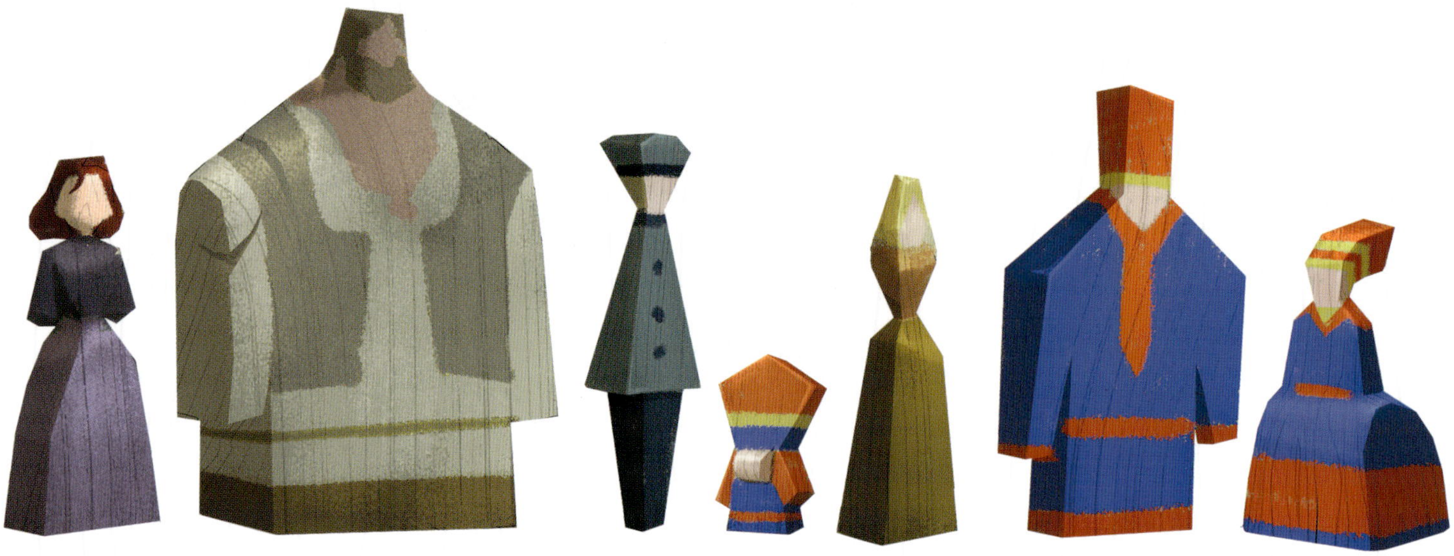

ABOVE: Artwork by Gabriel Gomez.

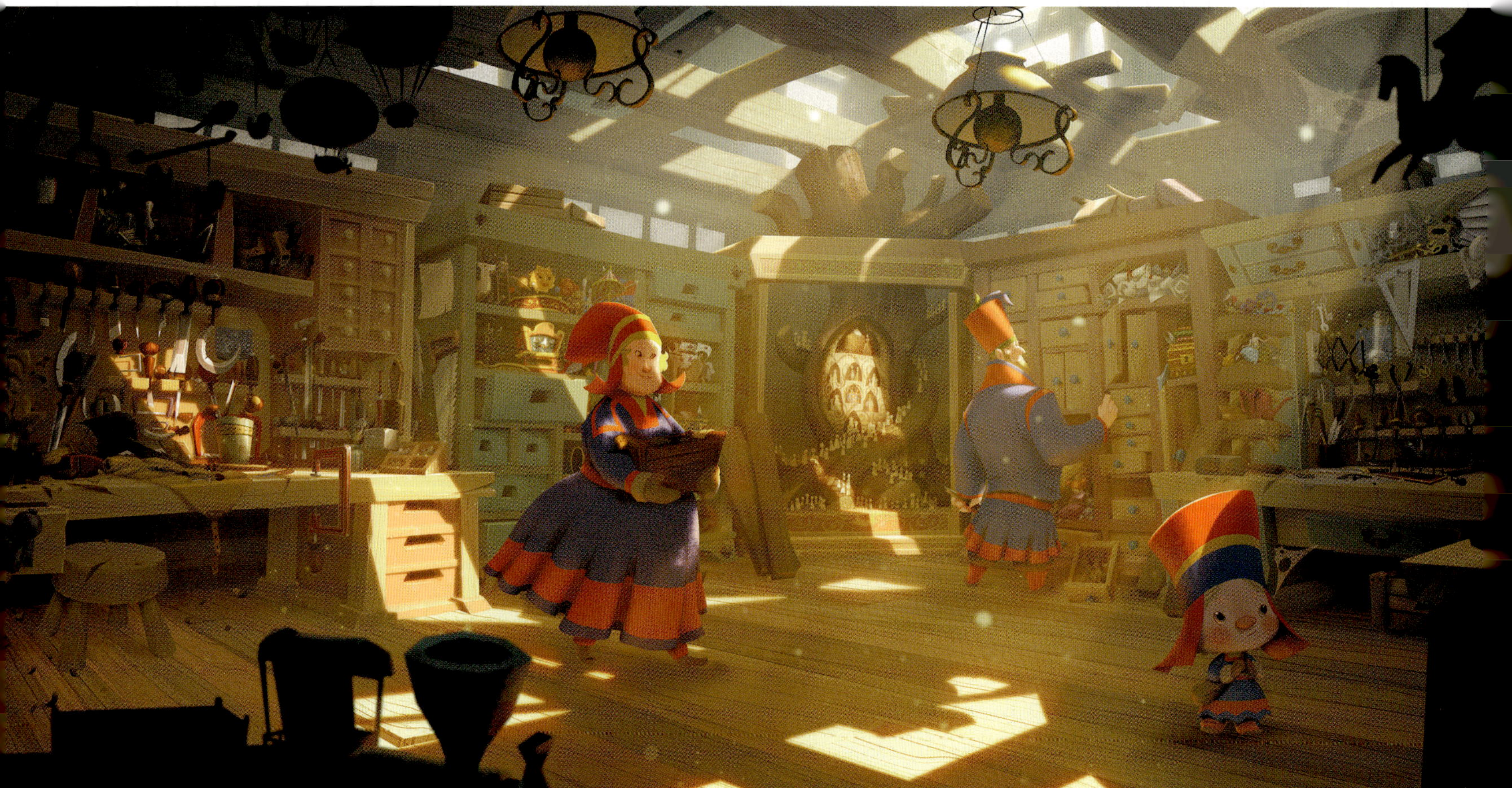

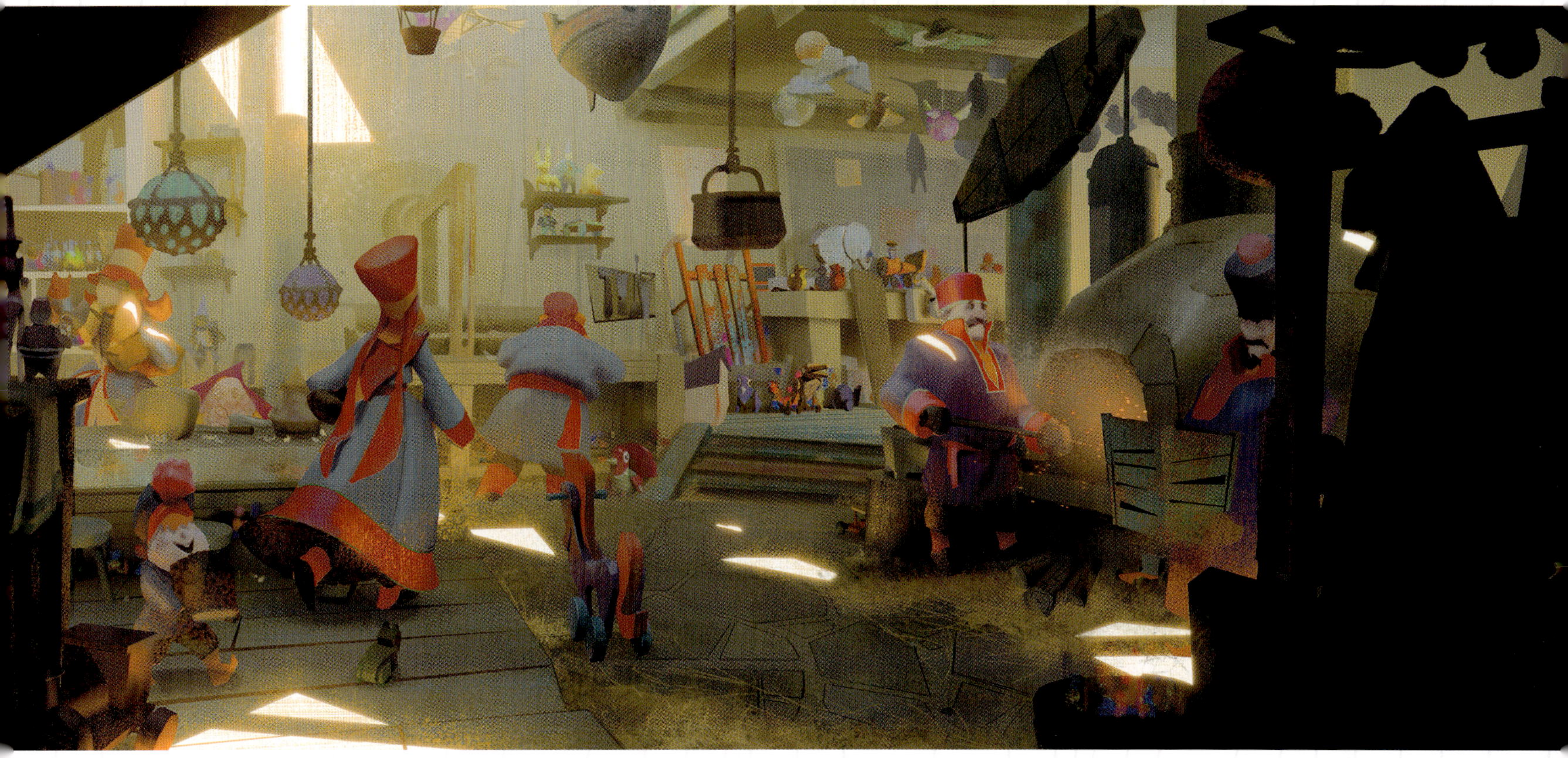

The workshop is described as one of the most vivid locations in the movie. "This is the place where the magic happens," notes production designer Marcin Jakubowski. "It symbolizes Klaus' heart. Before it transforms into a charming environment, we depicted it as a desolate, messy, and scary place. We had to design the interior and exterior in a way that could serve these contradictions. The main tool that allowed us to achieve this was the lighting. Initially, the light only seeps through small windows and cracks but, as the plot progresses, it becomes warmer and more present. Towards the end, when Klaus finds his true purpose, we shower the scenes with downpours of bright light, bounding around, radiating outwards and warming up dark corners and everyone in town."

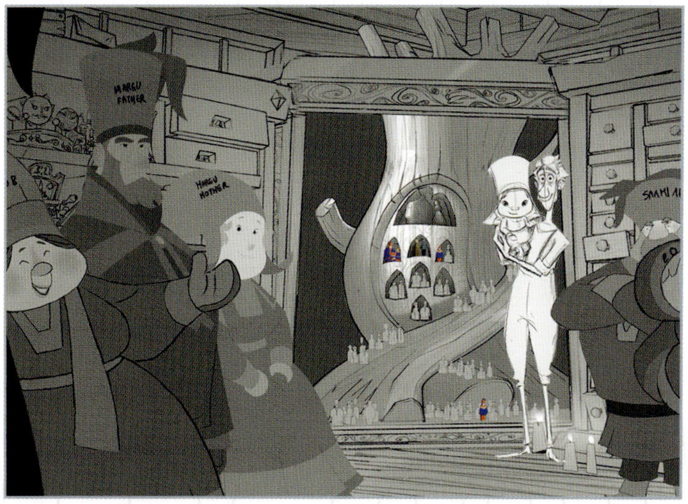

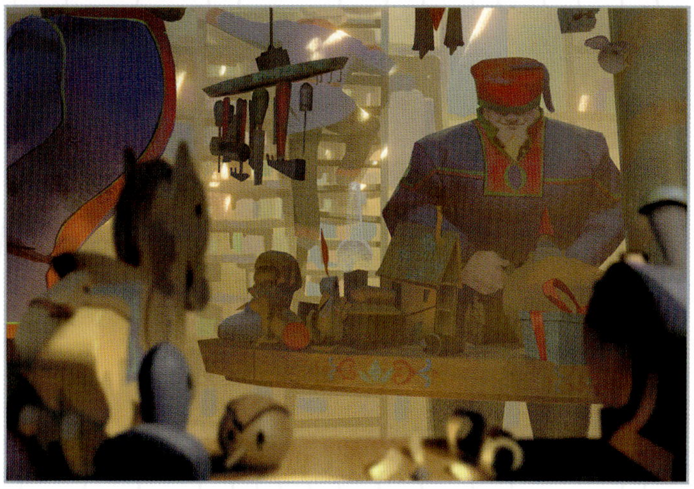

THIS PAGE: (TOP) Concept art by Kevin Le Moigne.

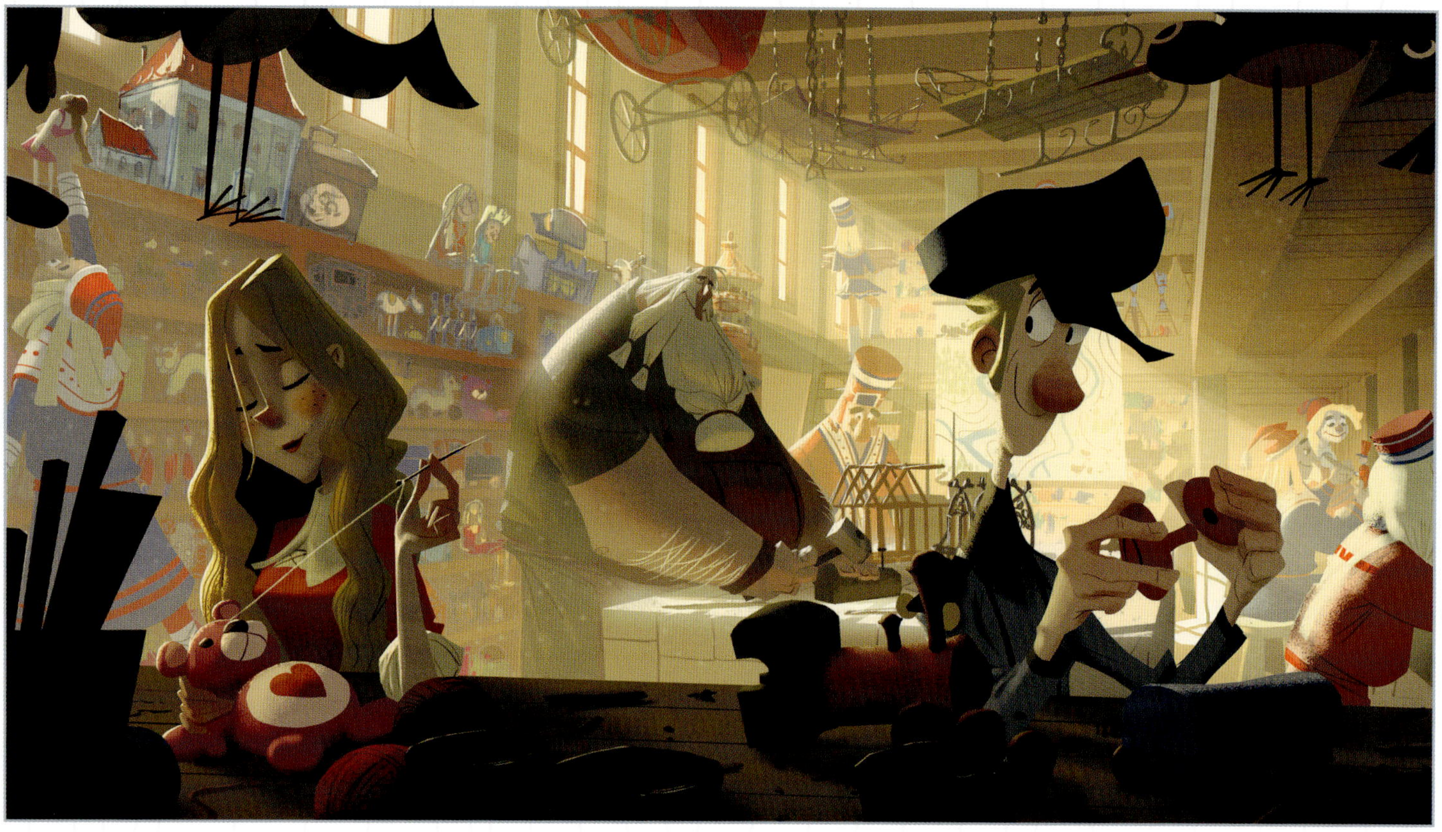

ABOVE: Artwork by Daniel Fernandez and Szymon Biernacki.

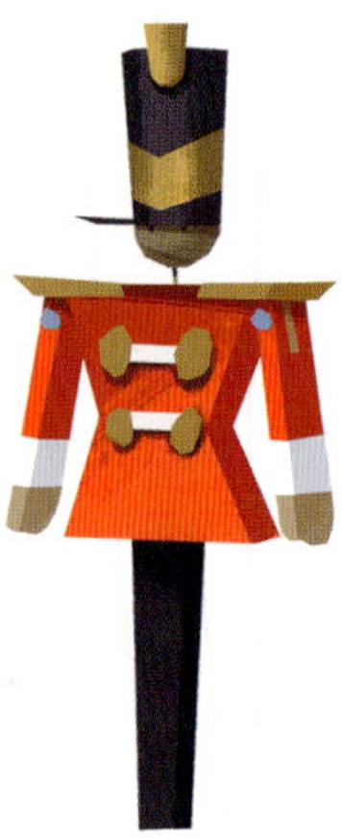

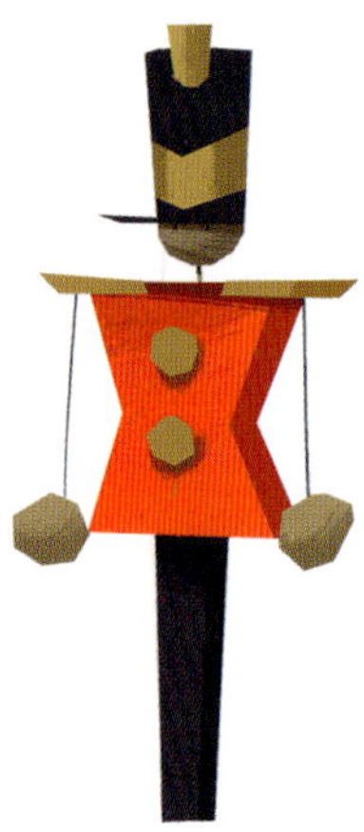

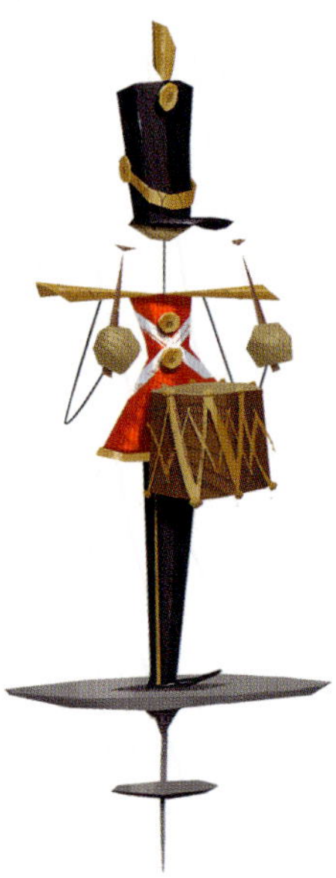

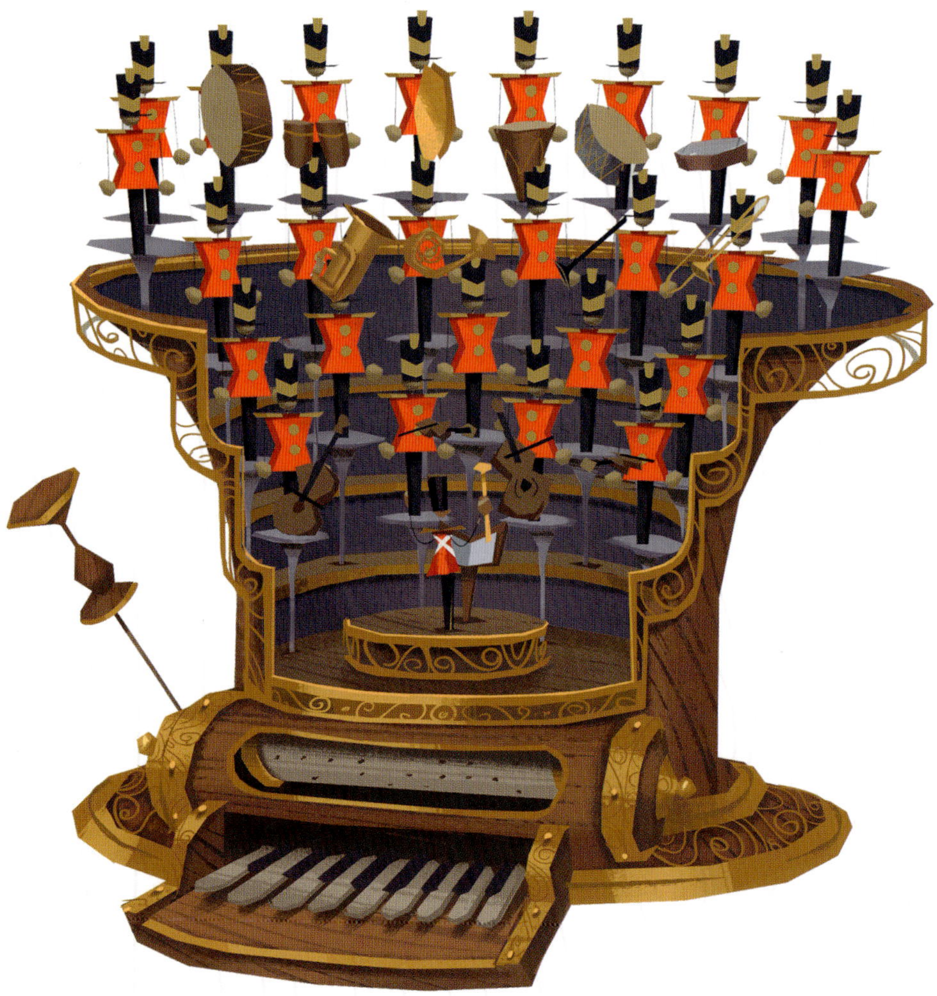

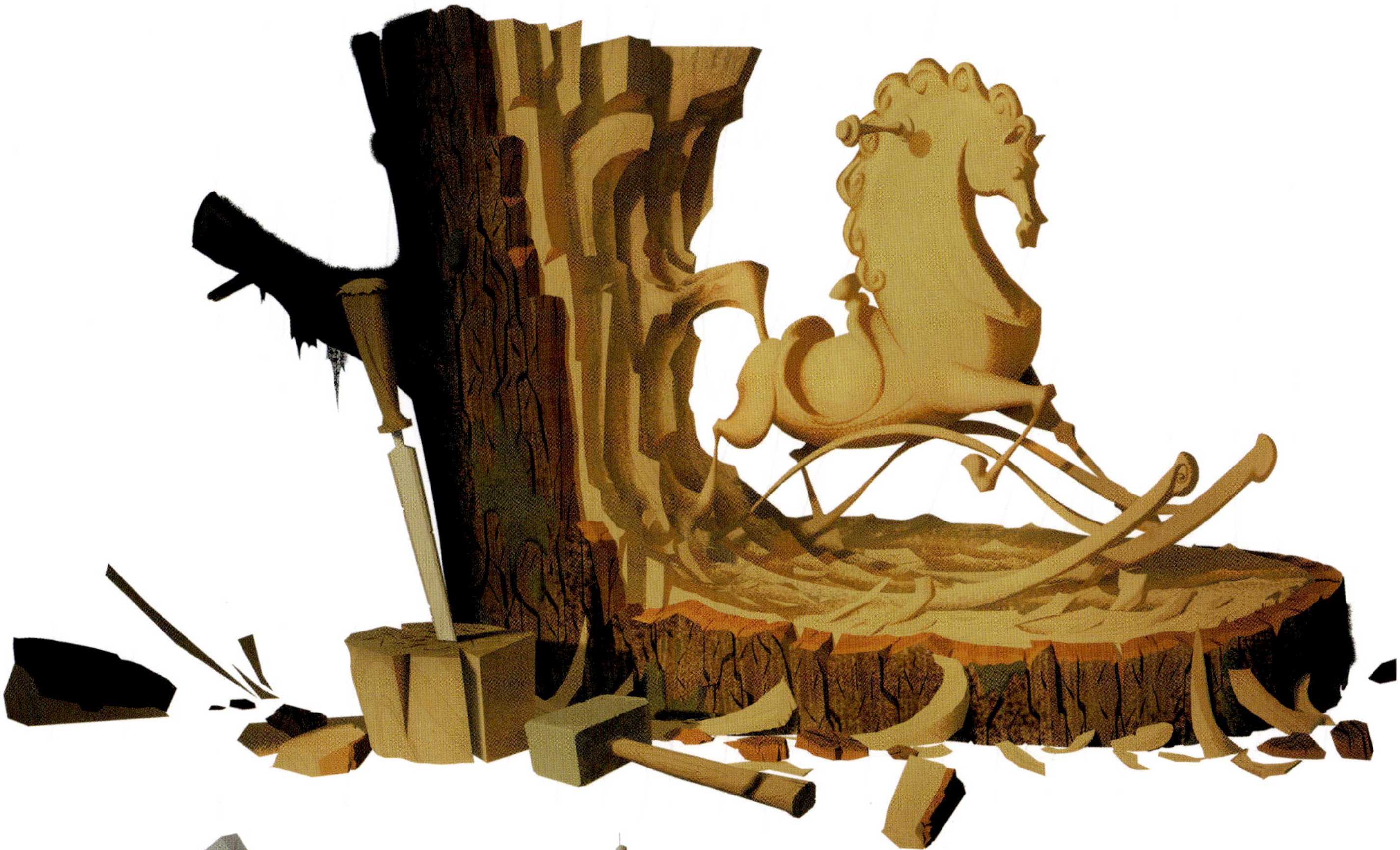

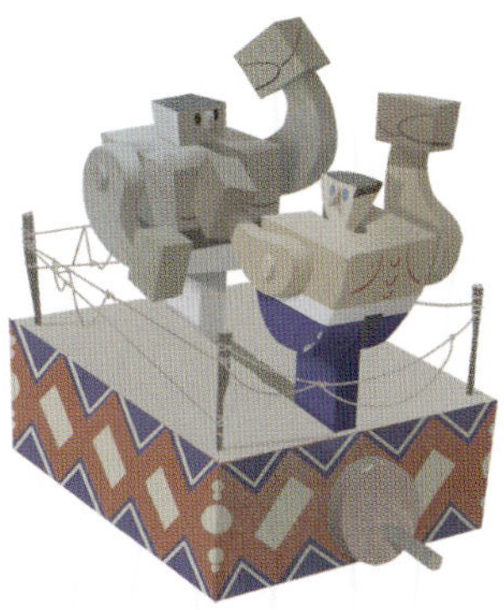

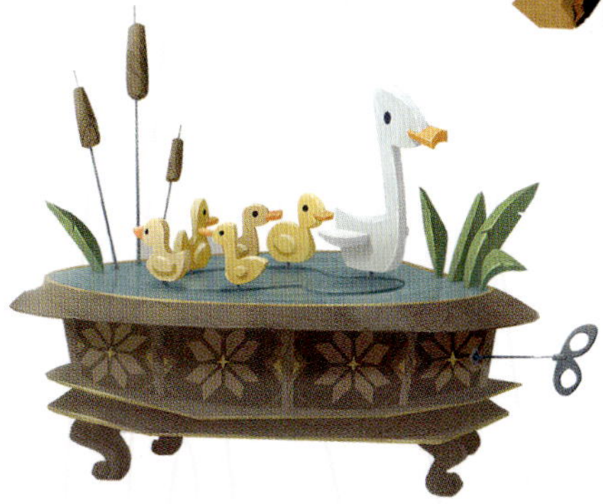

THIS SPREAD: Toy design by Betty Sourigues, Andres Arcos, Krzysztof Roslan, Szymon Biernacki, and Marcin Jakubowski; (BELOW) Artwork by Gabriel Gomez.

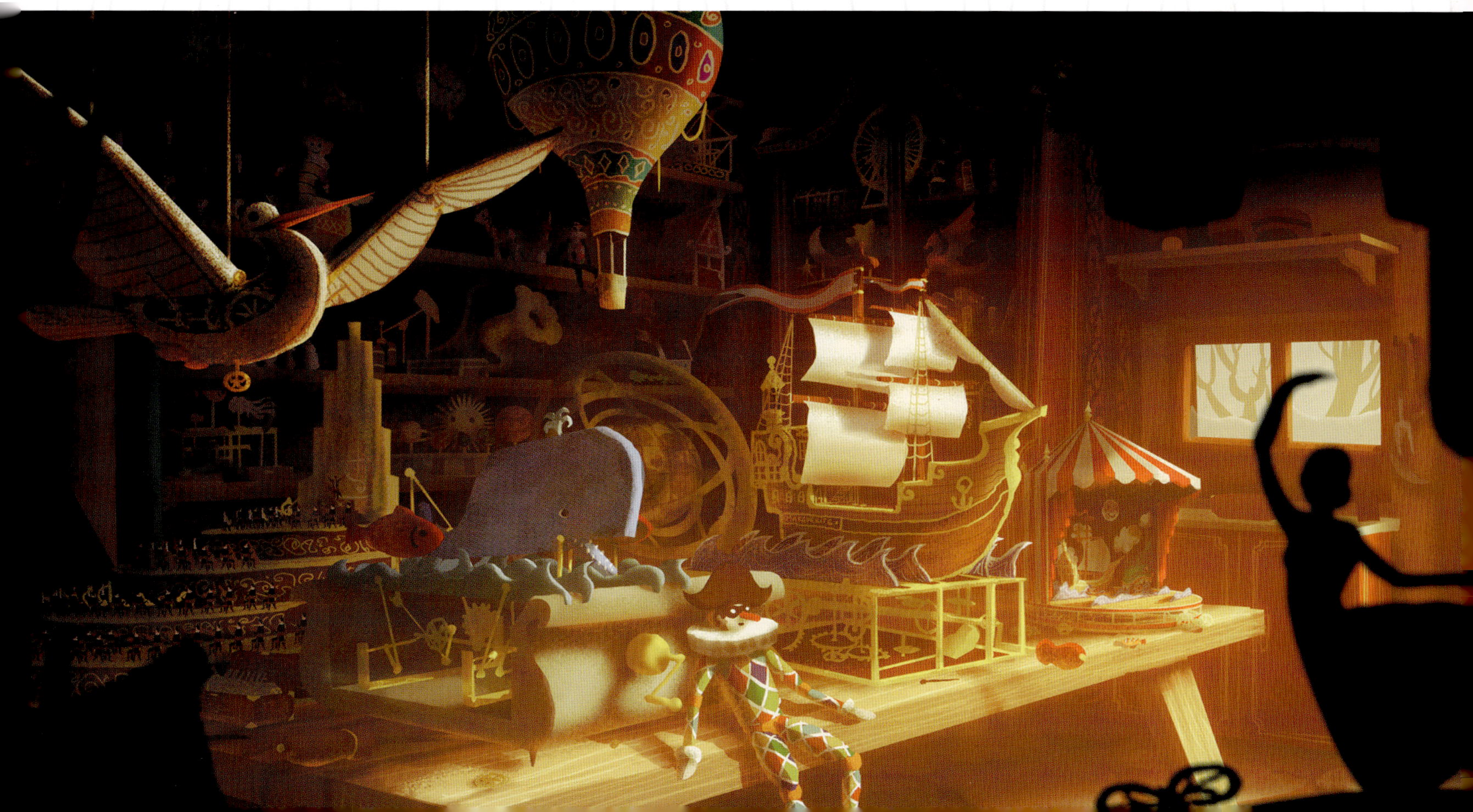

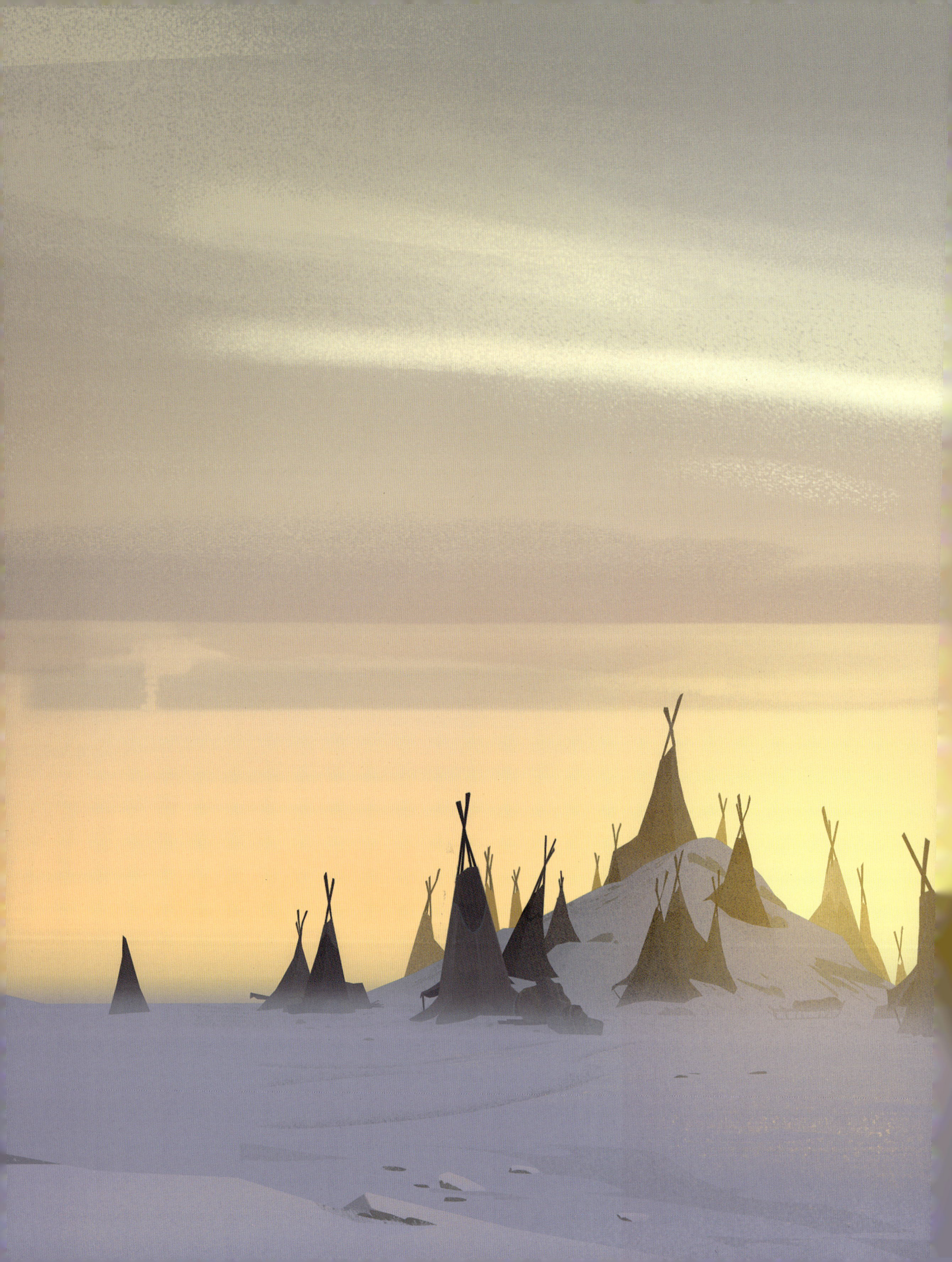

Learning From Others

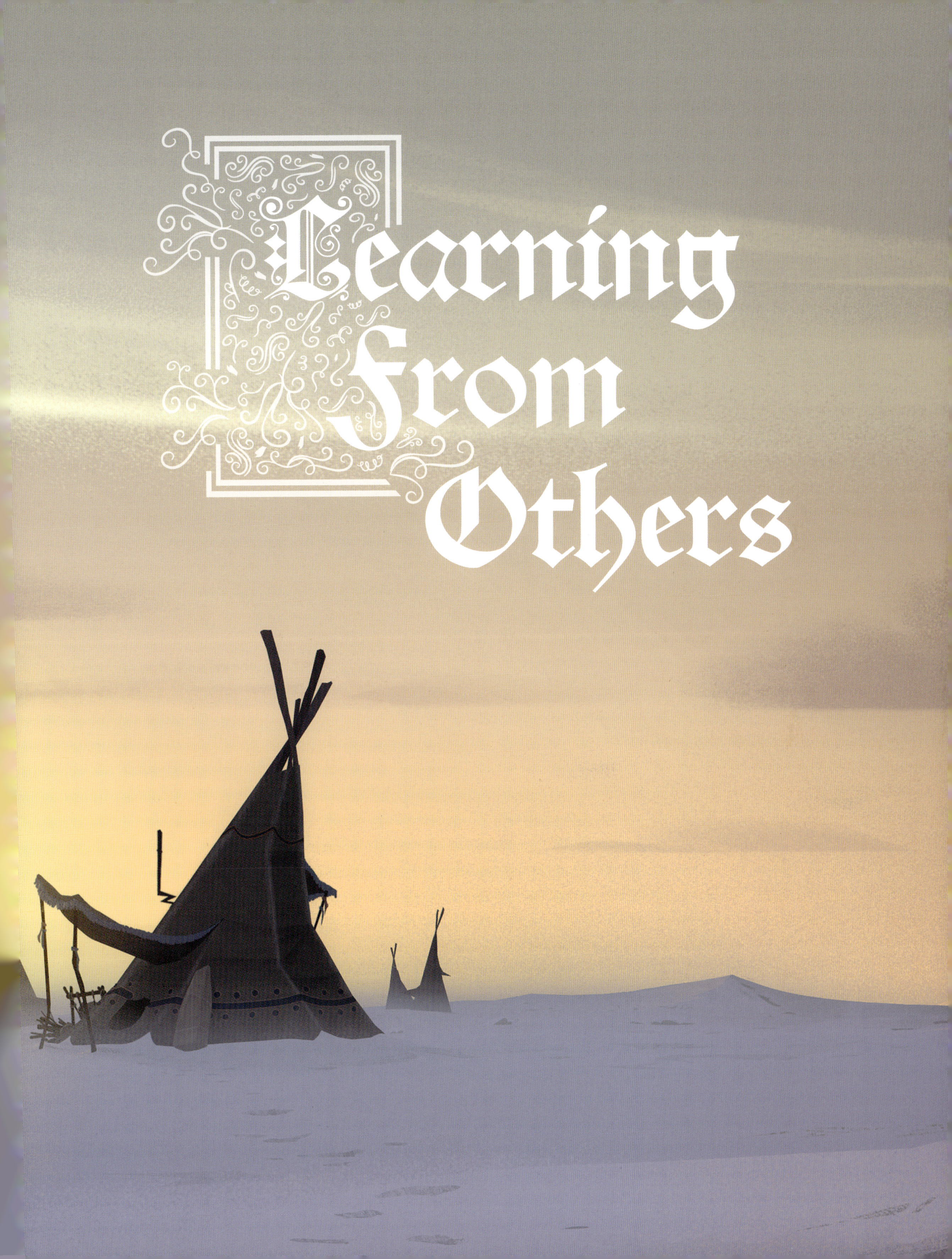

The Saami

LEARNING FROM OUTSIDERS

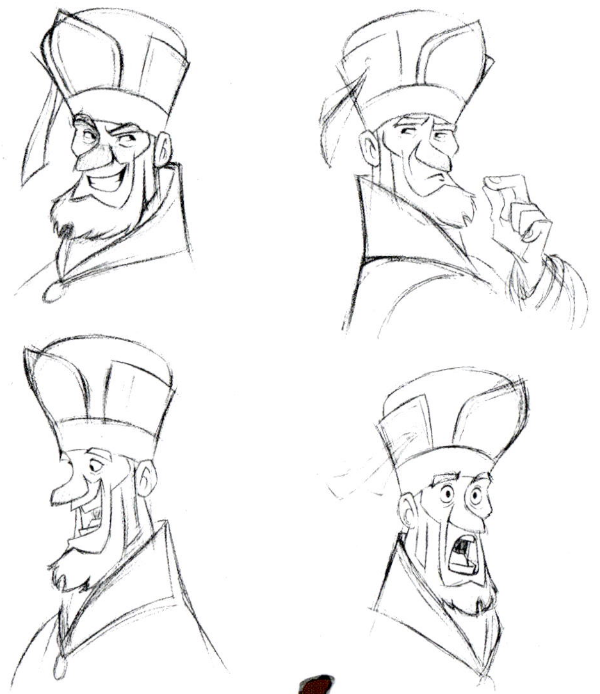

Pablos and his creative team knew that they wanted the Saami people of Scandinavia to play a major role in the movie. As they dove deep into their culture, these indigenous people and their part in the storyline began to develop further. Pablos talked about their role in the film, and the stunning visuals they provided. "The great thing was that the Saami wear these colorful outfits that really stand out against the white landscape, so they proved to be the perfect addition to this world."

PREVIOUS SPREAD: Concept artwork by Solene Chevaleyre.

THIS SPREAD: (BELOW) The Saami tribe by Daniel Fernandez; (TOP RIGHT) Character explorations by Torsten Schrank; (BOTTOM RIGHT) Concept artwork by Pascal Campion.

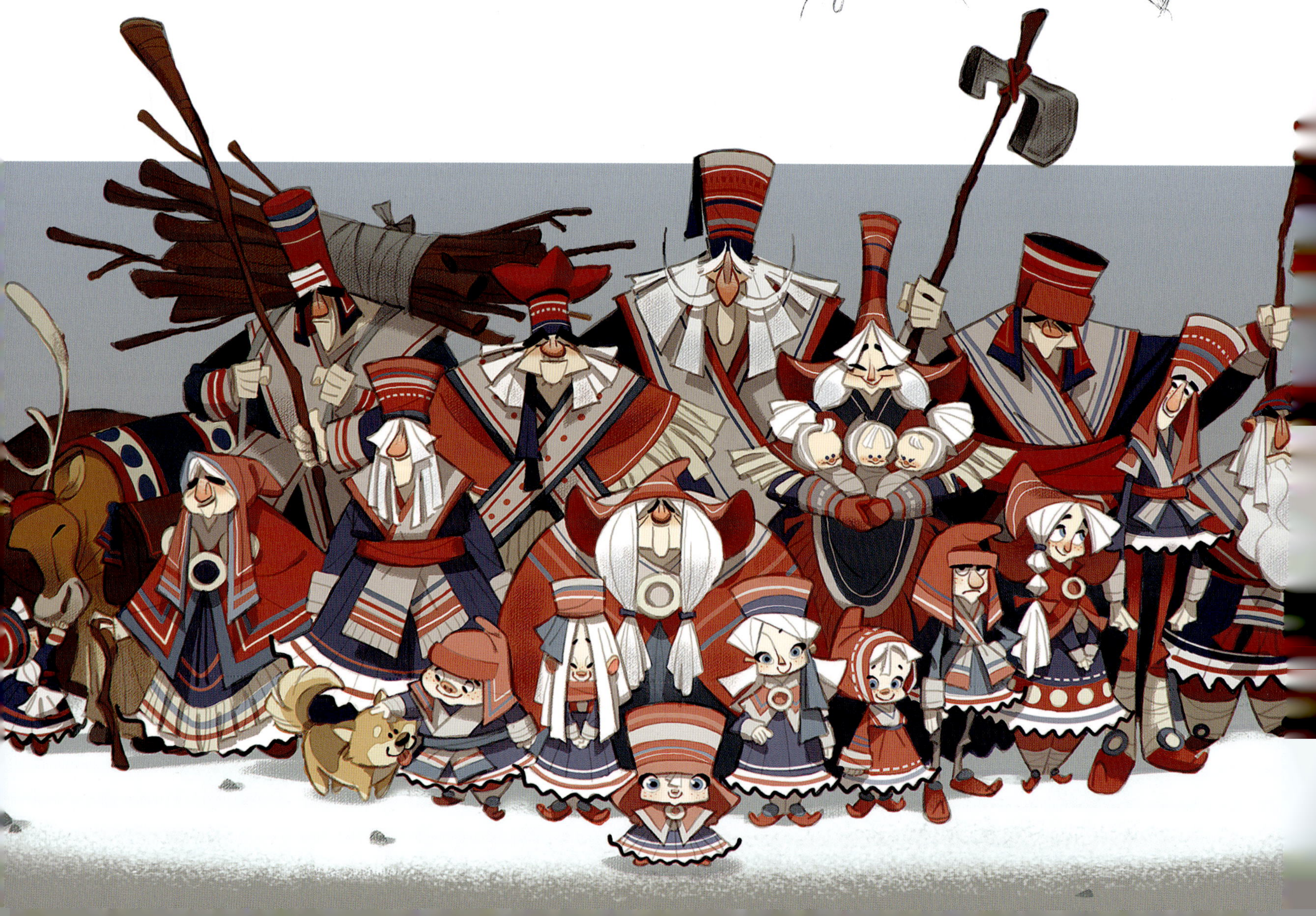

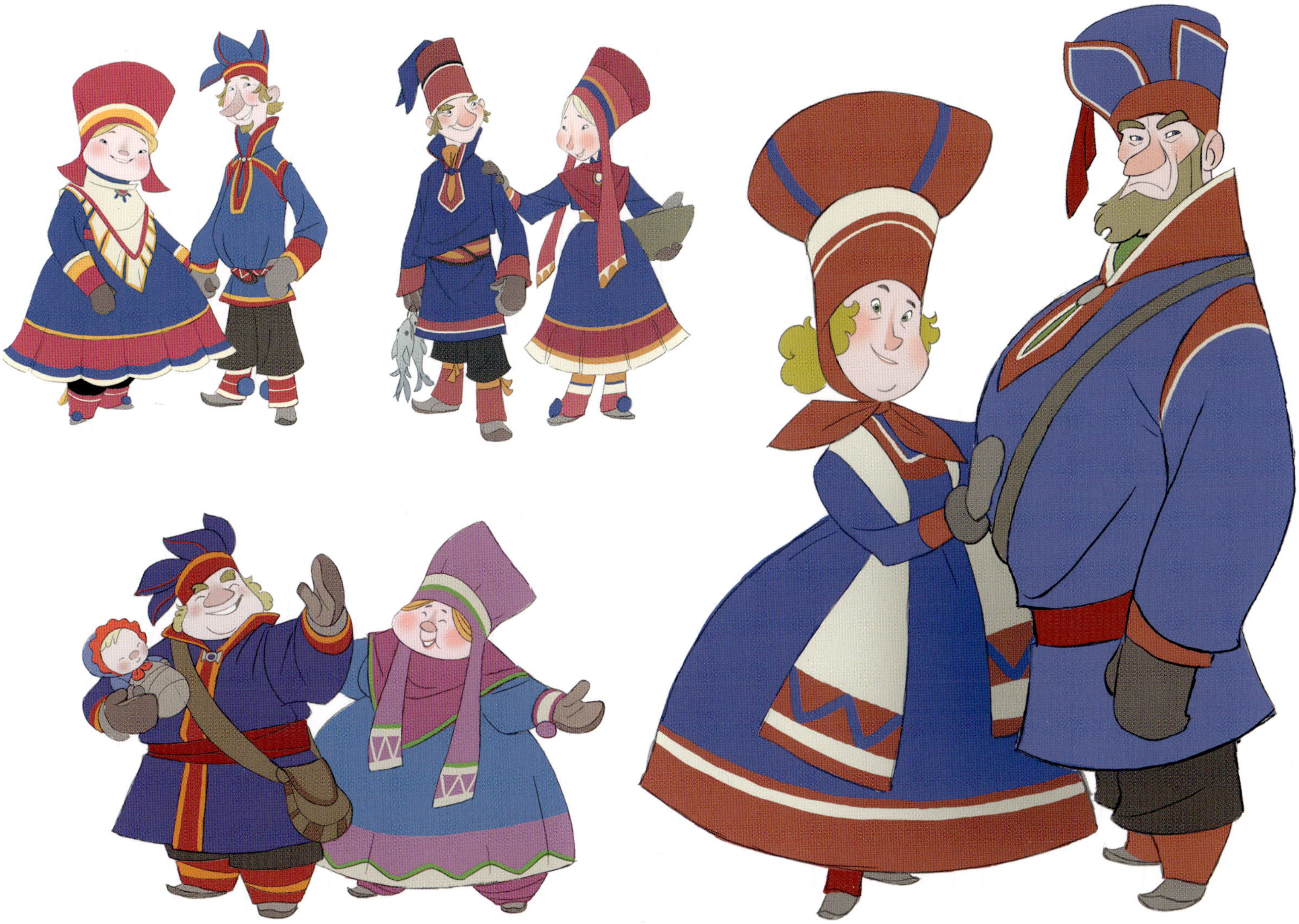

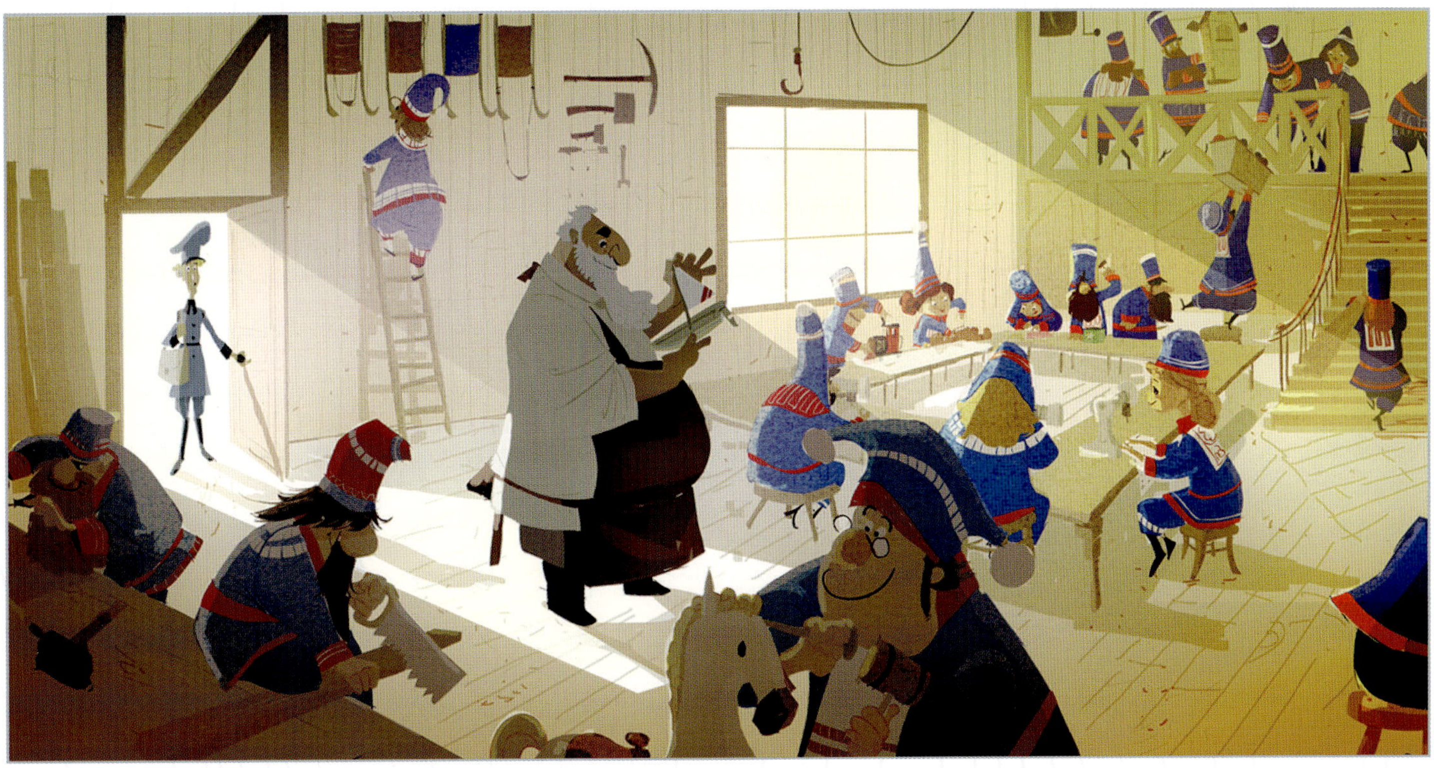

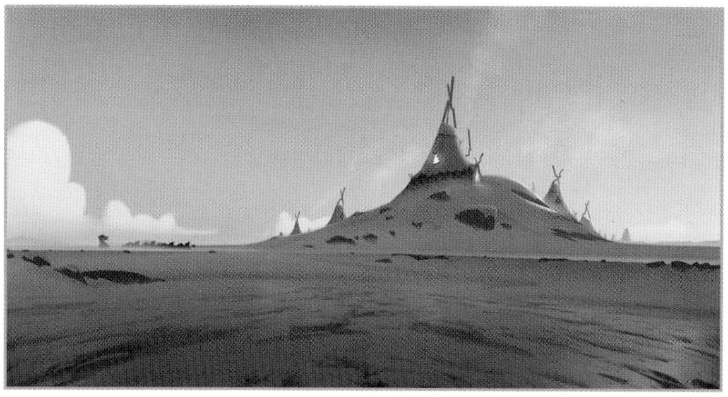

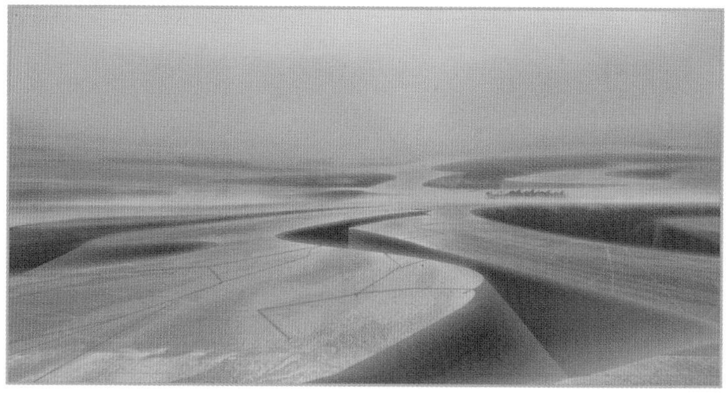

THIS SPREAD: The sprawling Nordic landscapes where the Saami tribe live. Concept art by Henrik Evensen.

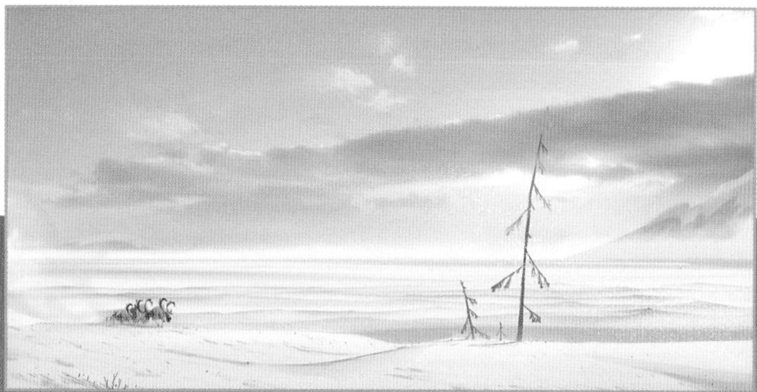

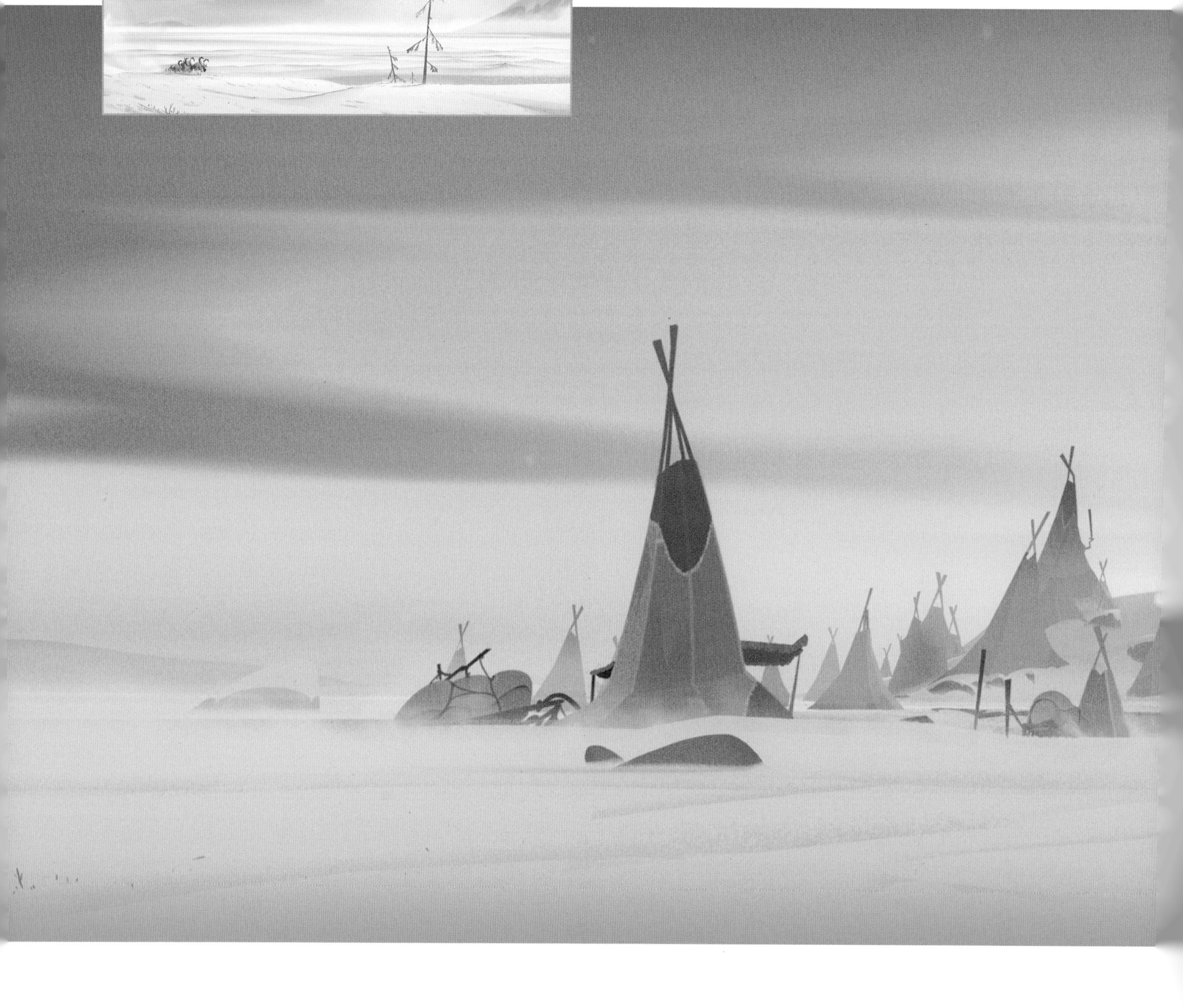

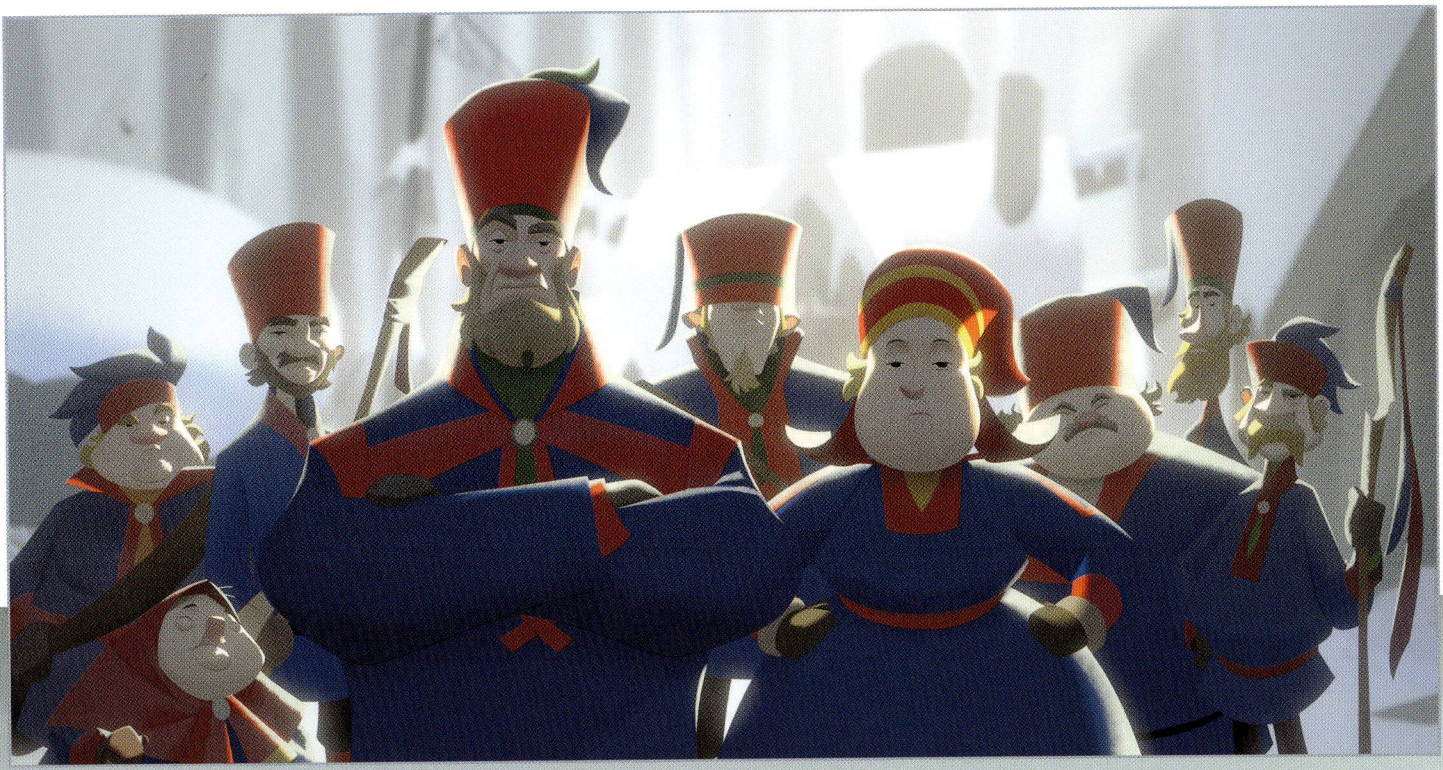

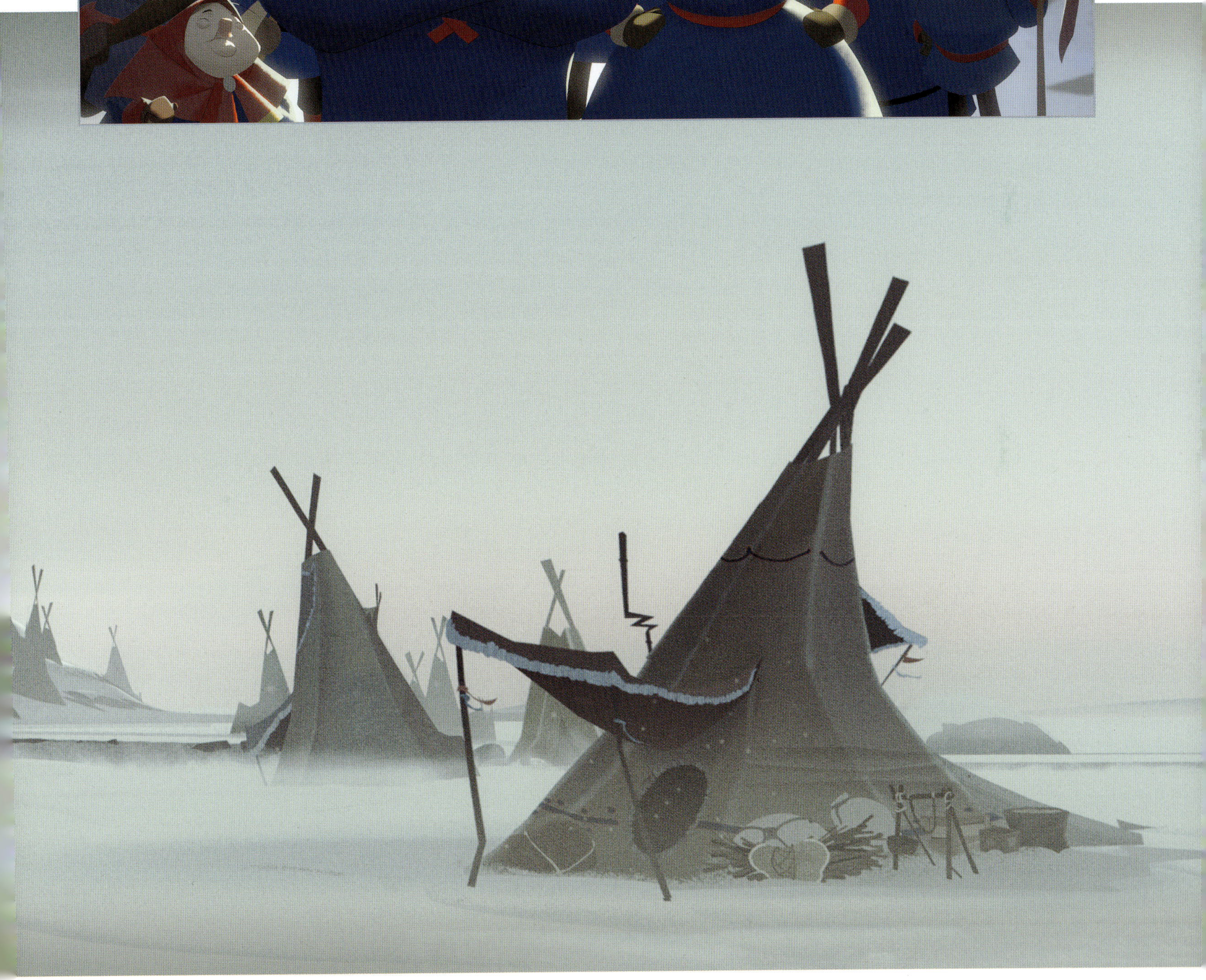

Margu

Margu, the adorable Saami girl who befriends Jesper and Alva, proved to be a wonderful choice. "Margu ended up being one of my favorite characters in the movie," Pablos says. "She is so cute, and everyone seems to really like her. The fact that she doesn't speak English is a major catalyst. Though Margu and Jesper can't understand each other verbally, they have a special connection that allows them to communicate without language."

To be as authentic as possible, Pablos set out to find a young native actress who could speak Saami correctly. "There are four different Saami dialects, but the most popular one is Northern Saami, and there are only about 15,000 speakers of this dialect worldwide," explains the director. "I knew that I could find a little girl who could also act. We were lucky to find Neda M. Labba, a young actress who had already acted in movies."

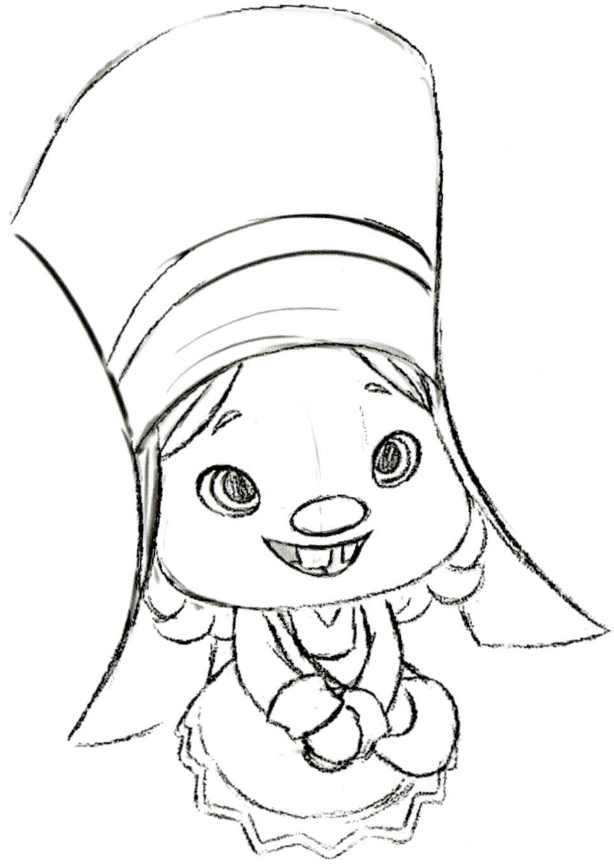

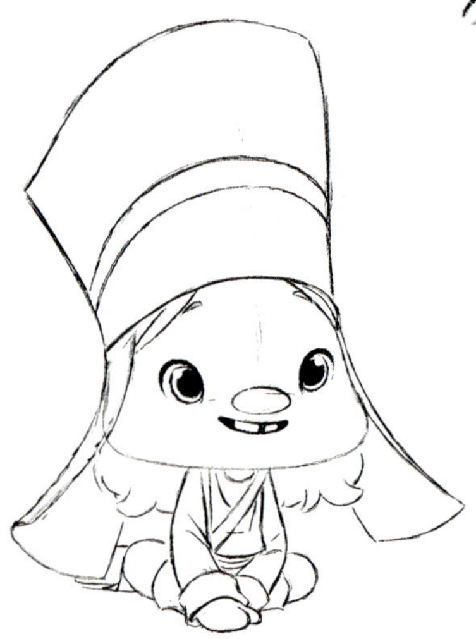

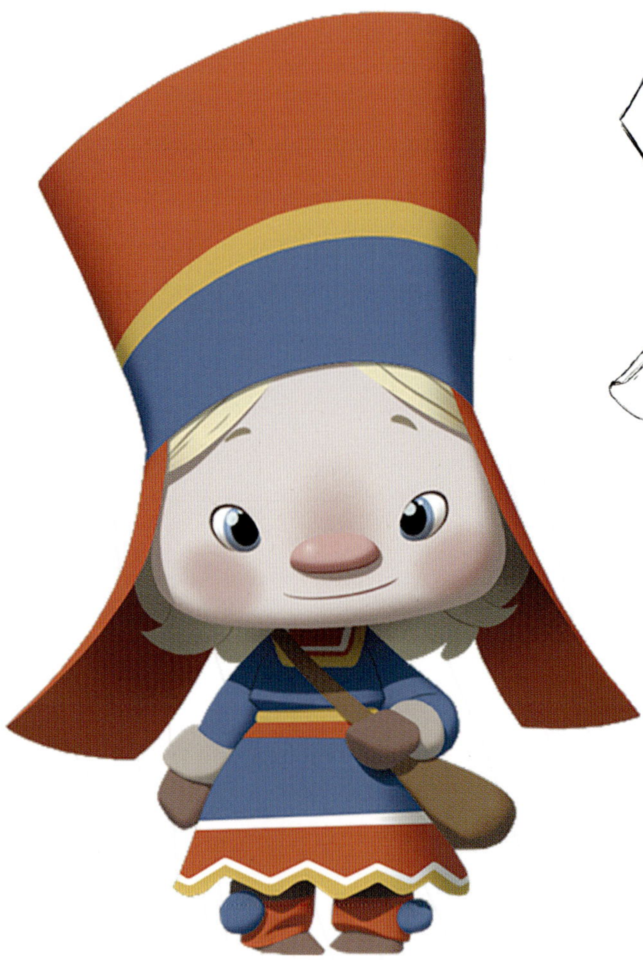

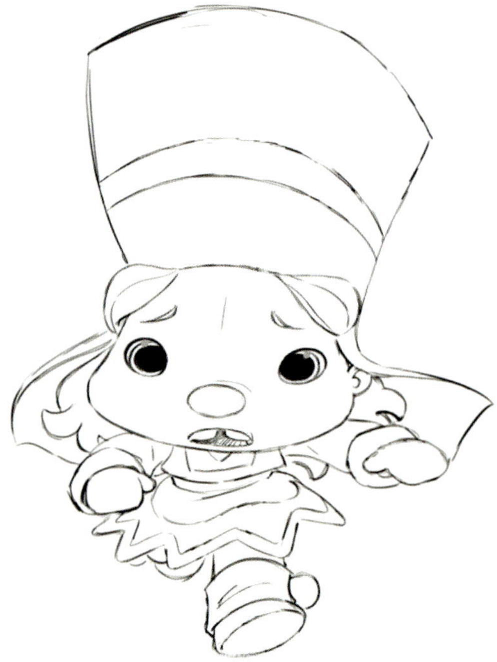

THIS PAGE: Sketches and final artwork for Margu by Slaven Reese.

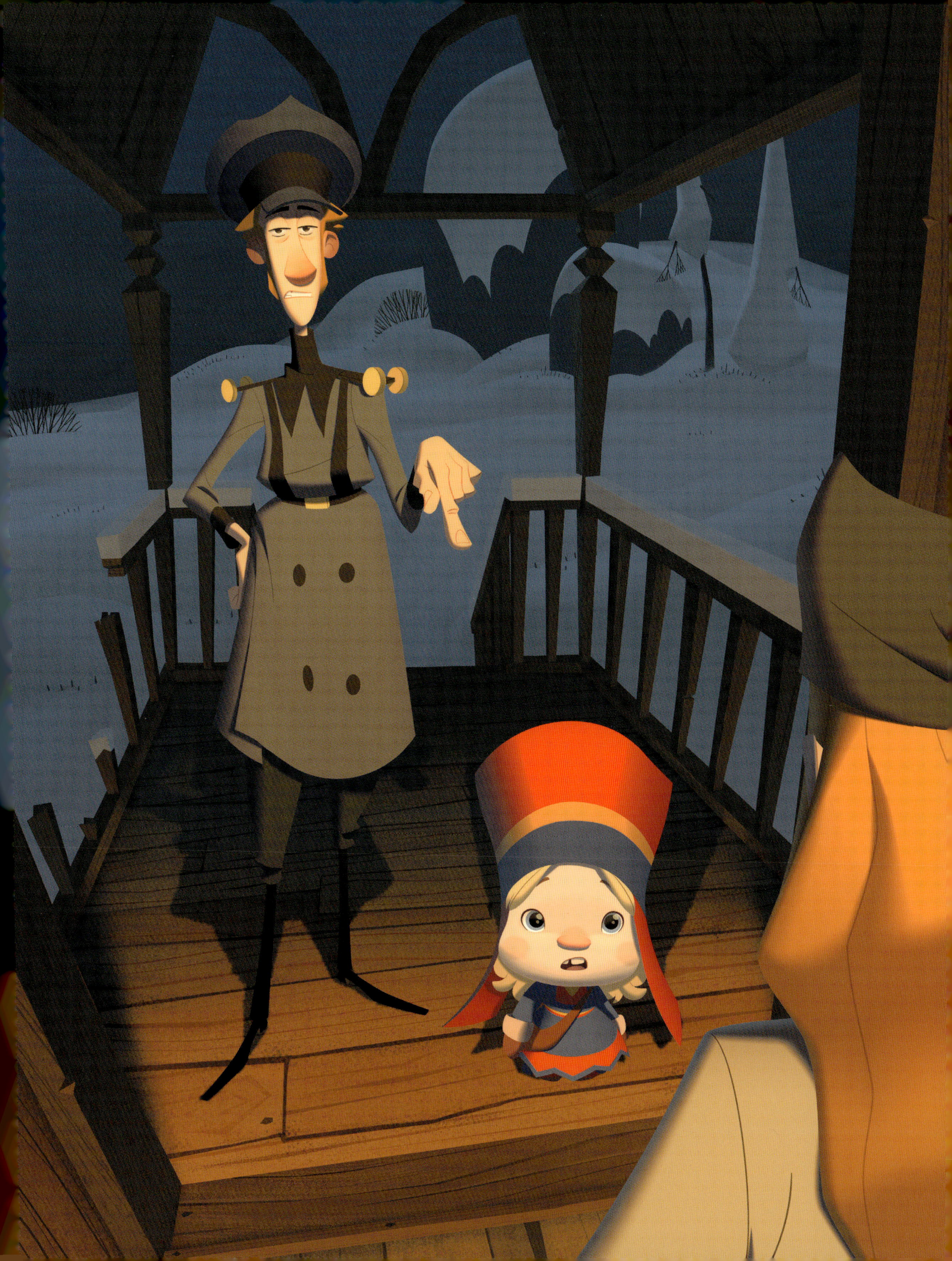

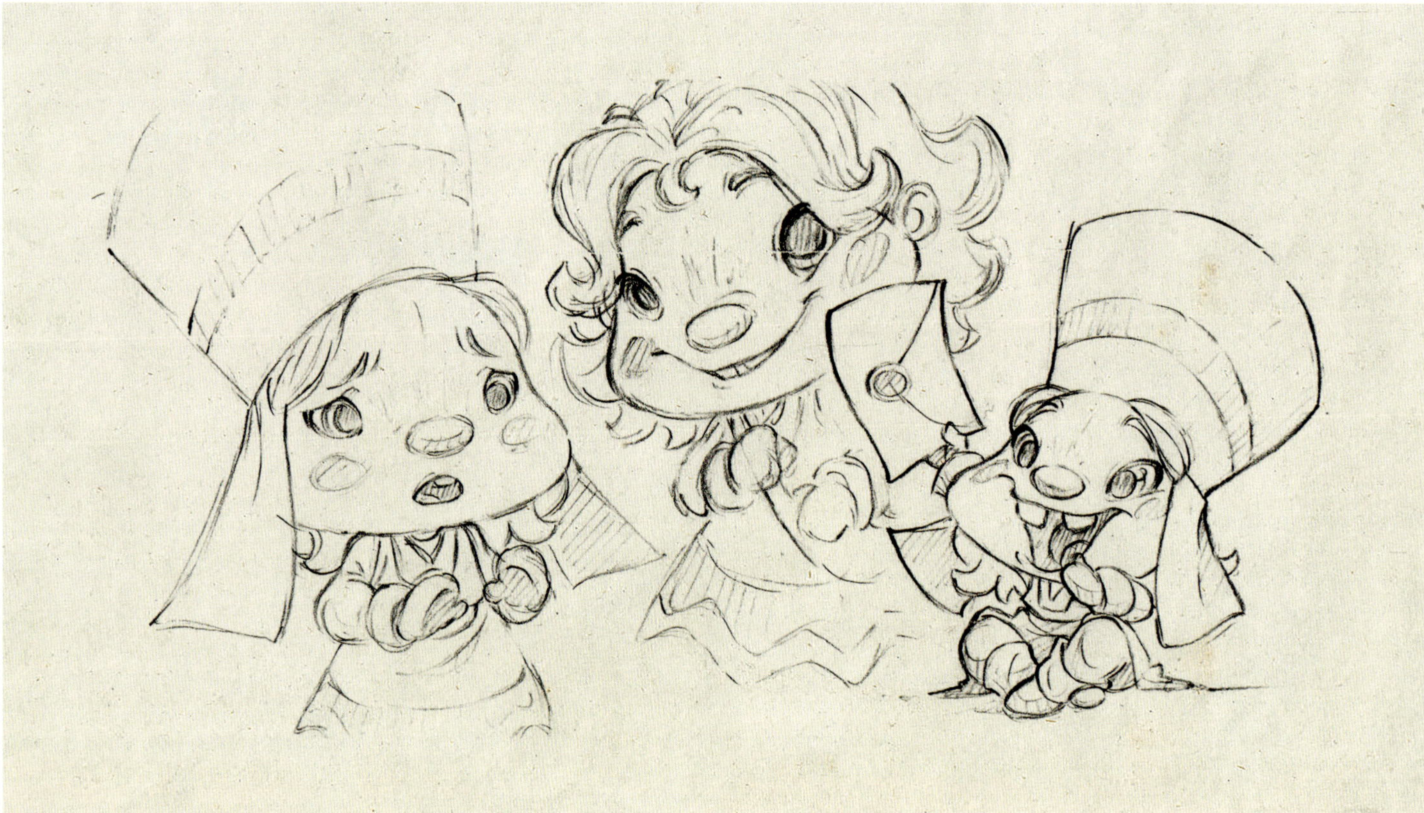

THIS PAGE: (ABOVE) A doodle of Margu, drawn by supervising animator Slaven Reese; (BELOW) Character exploration by Torsten Schrank.

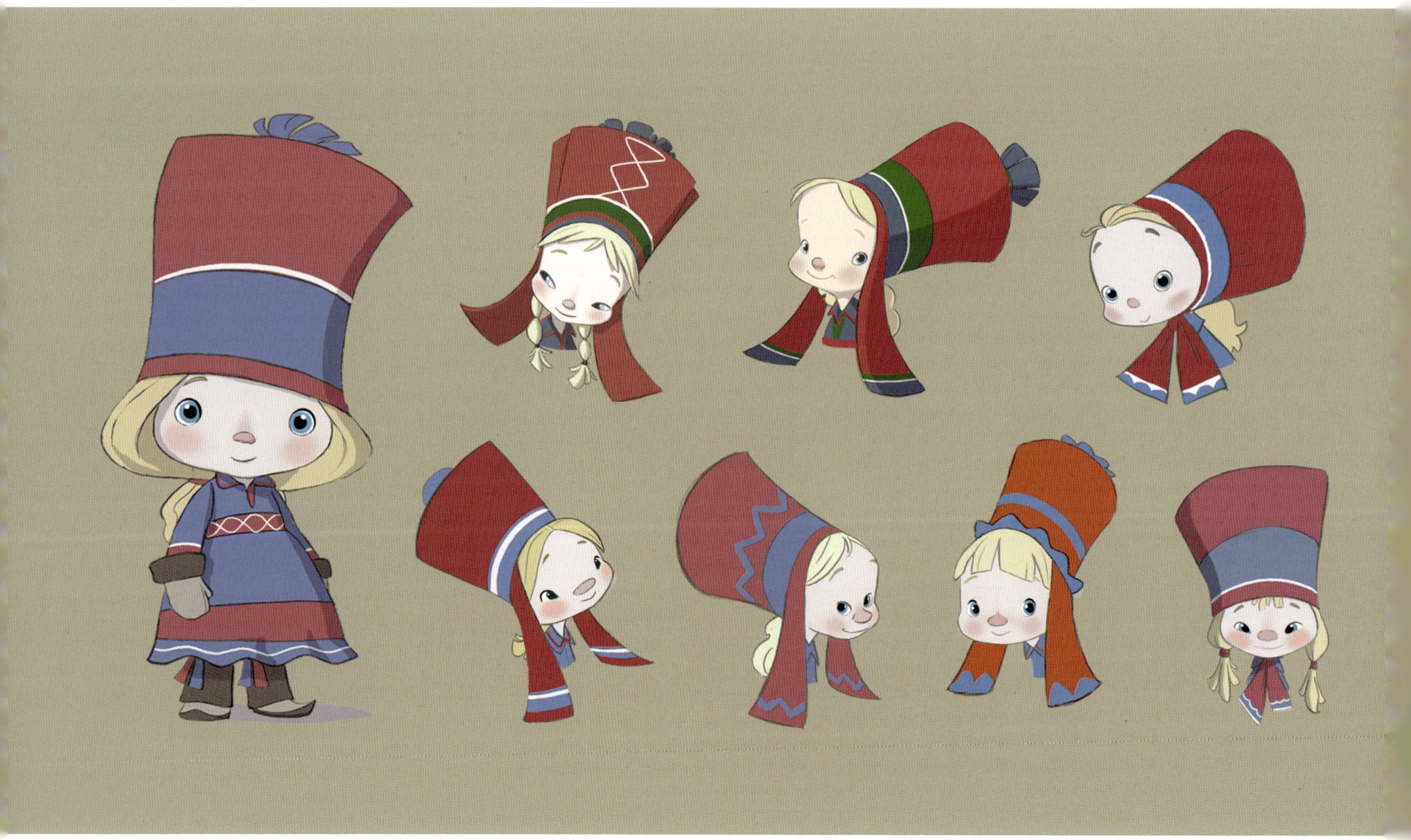

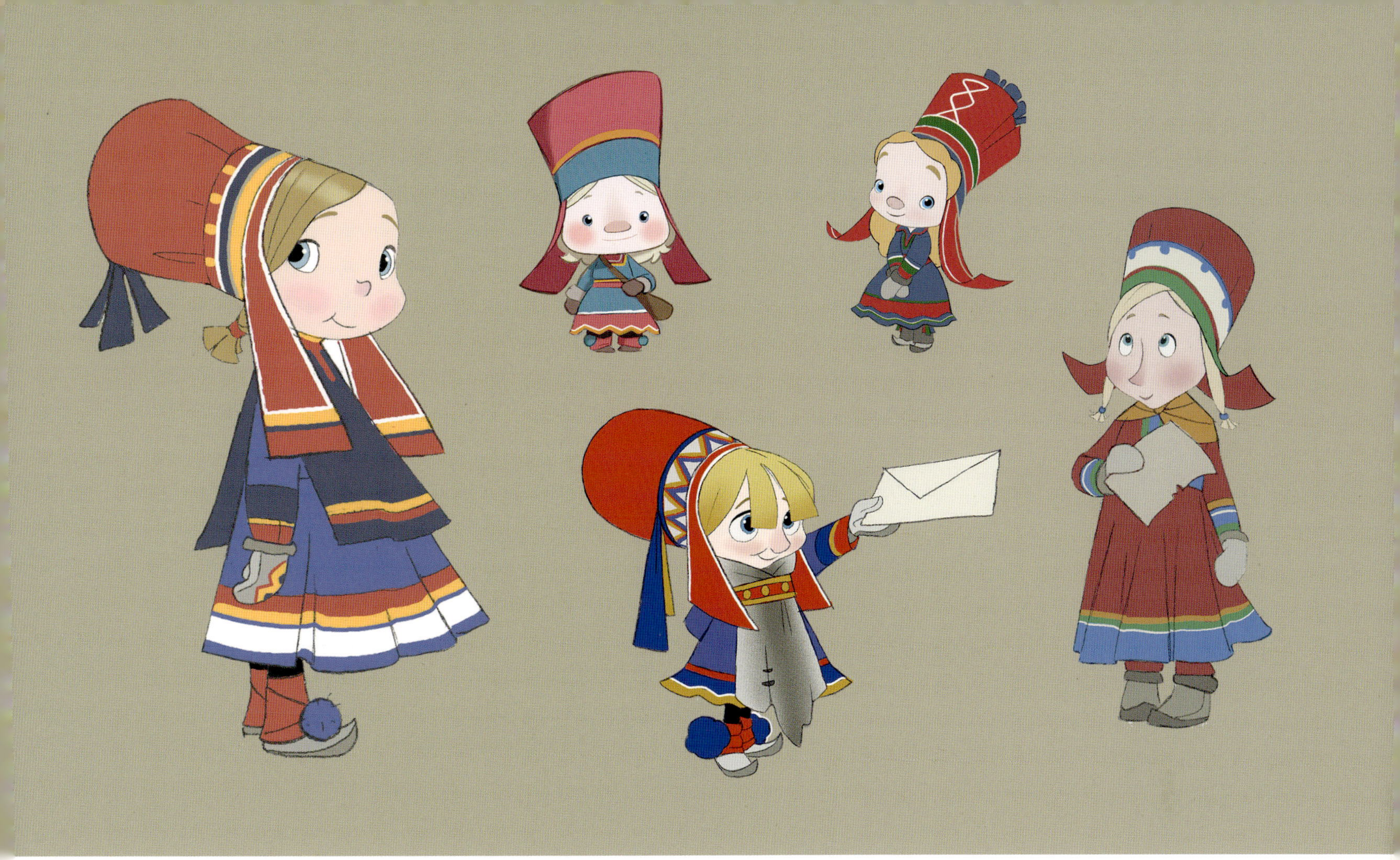

Some key members of the creative team traveled to Tromsø in Norway to record Neda. Along the way, they ended up learning a lot about the culture and traditions of the Saami. "I found out that they catch and release thousands of reindeer every year, and the whole trip to Norway was a valuable research experience," says Pablos. "At the end of the day, we sat down and had a traditional reindeer stew, right in front of all the reindeer, which was a bit odd, but still an amazing experience. We also enjoyed a performance of the traditional Saami a capella singing known as *yoik*, which I found very powerful and moving. This was all amazing material that really grounds the film in reality in a beautiful way."

Pablos says the part of Margu was quite challenging, because the audience needs to understand what she's saying just through context alone. "We knew that we didn't want to use subtitles for her, so it all relied on the way she said her lines," he notes. "You know there are grown-up actors that wouldn't be able to pull that off, but Neda did it beautifully. She is truly one of the most charming actors I've seen in a long time."

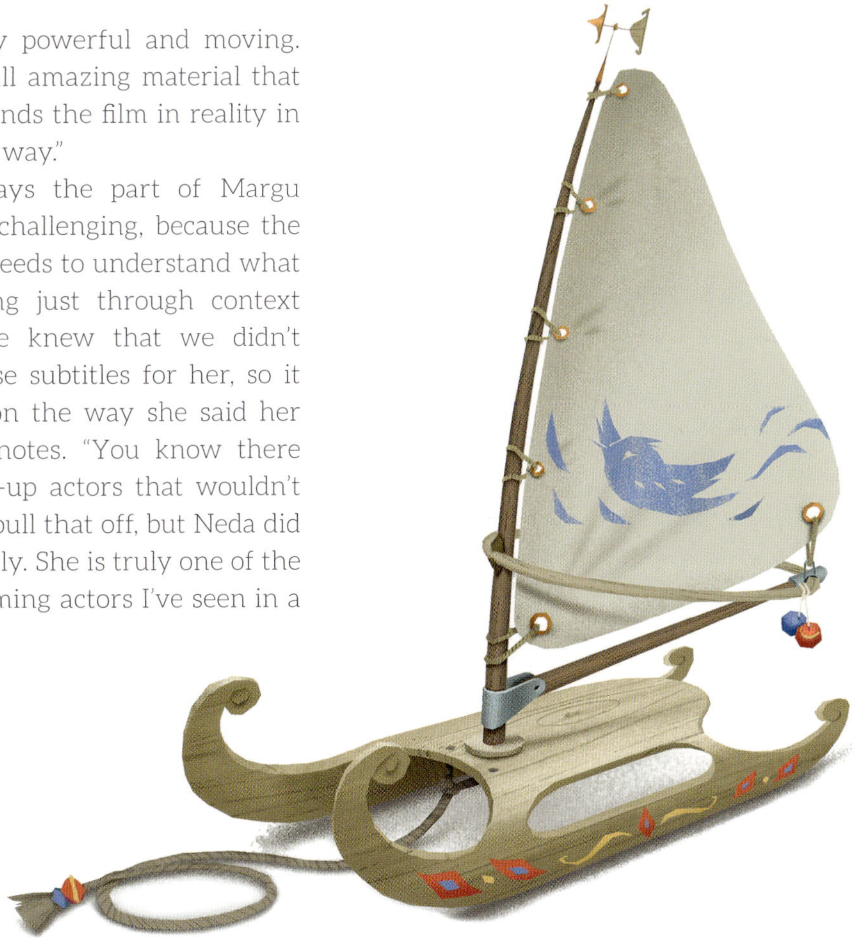

THIS PAGE: (TOP) Character exploration by Torsten Schrank; (BOTTOM RIGHT) Margu's sled, made for her by Klaus, designed by Krzysztof Roslan.

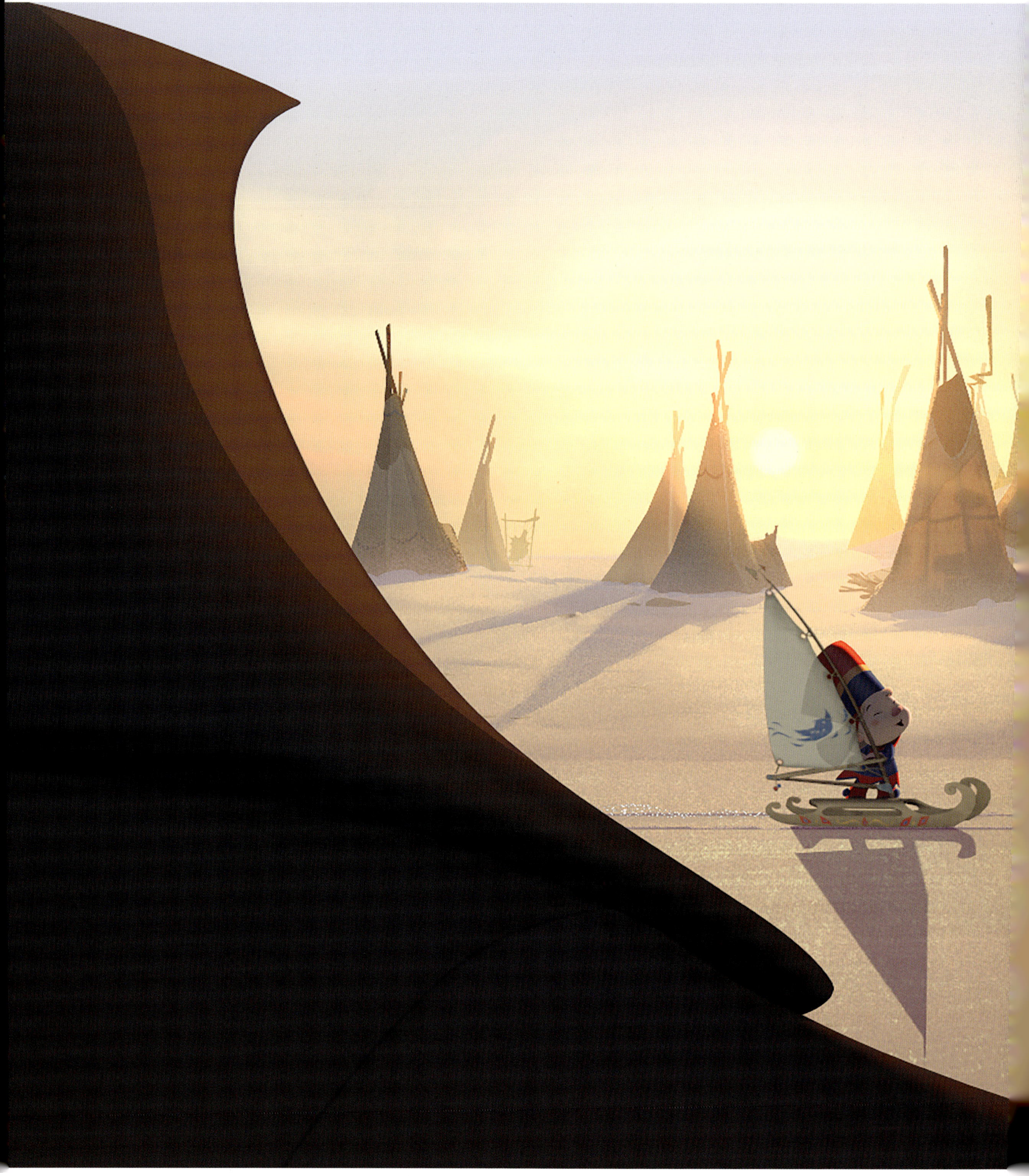

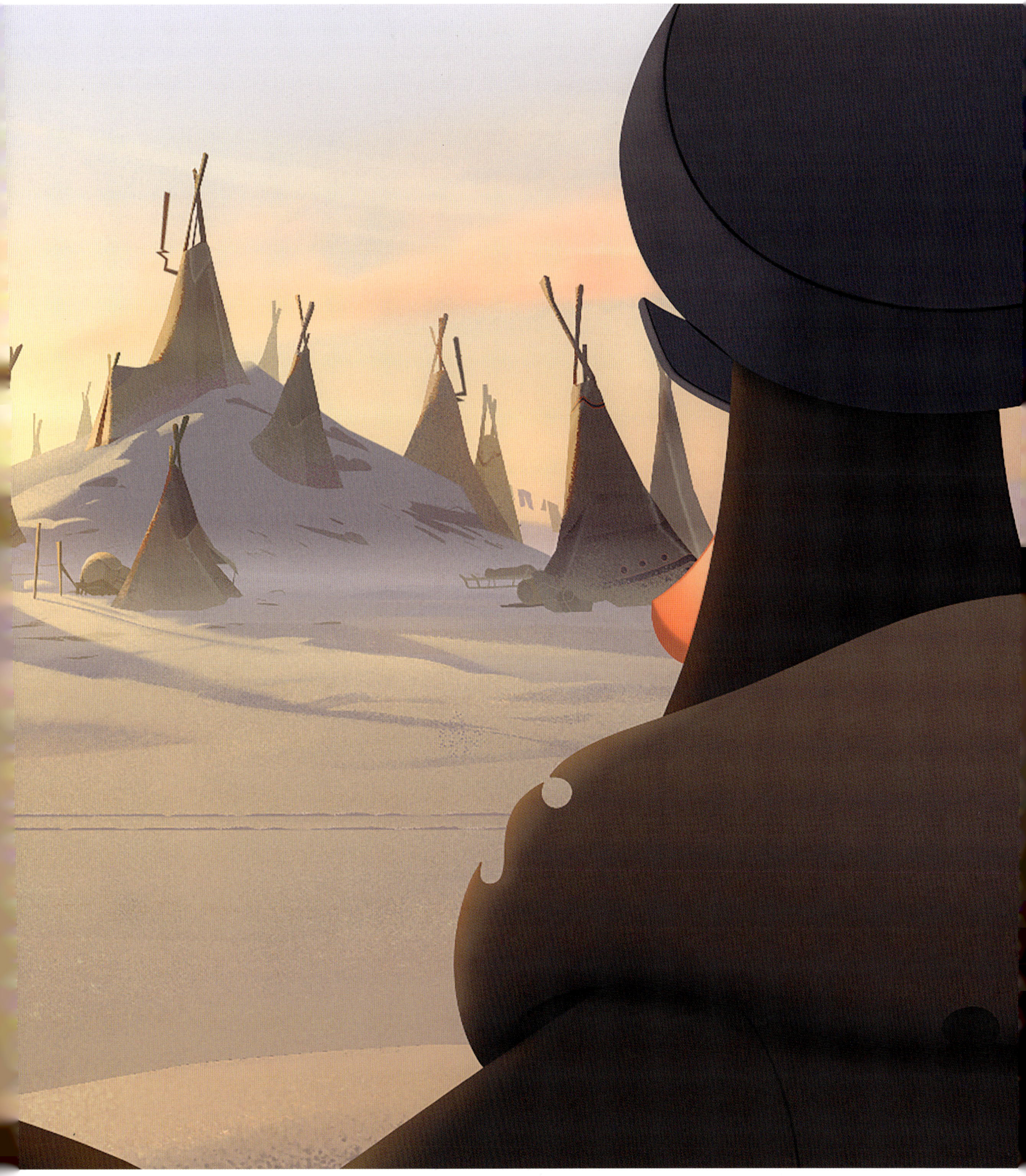

Klaus

NORDIC-INSPIRED DESIGN

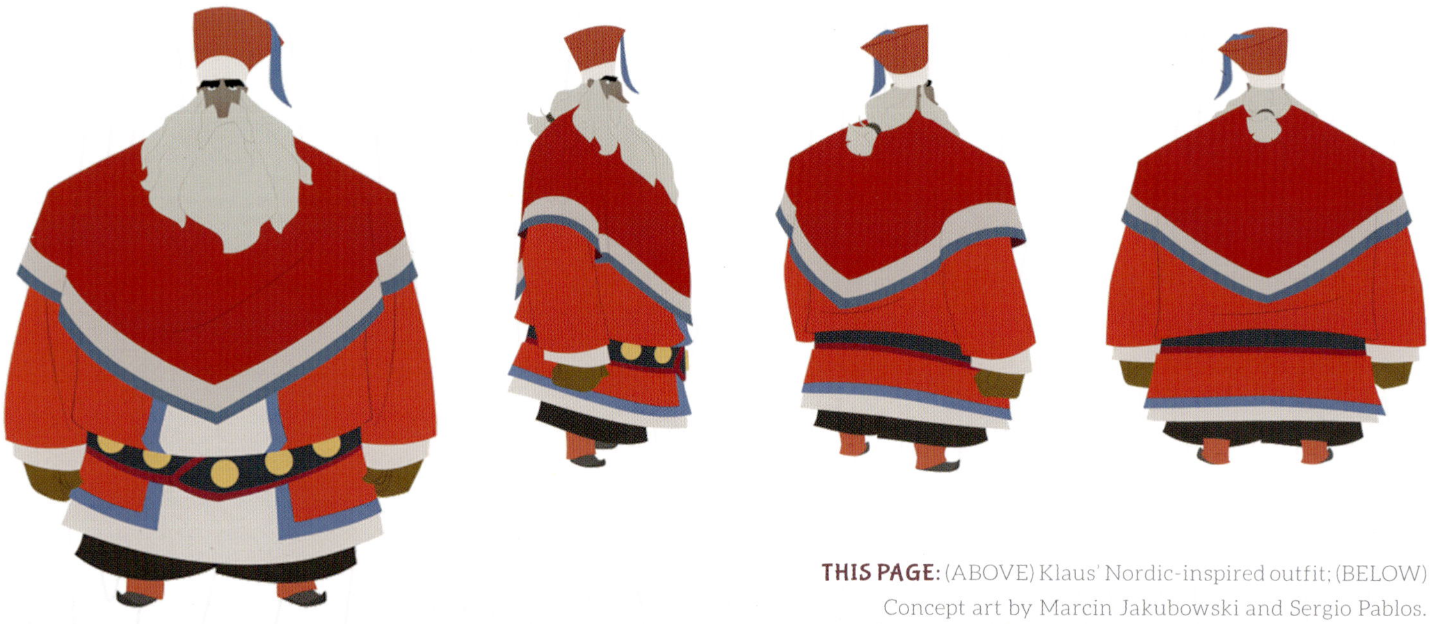

THIS PAGE: (ABOVE) Klaus' Nordic-inspired outfit; (BELOW) Concept art by Marcin Jakubowski and Sergio Pablos.

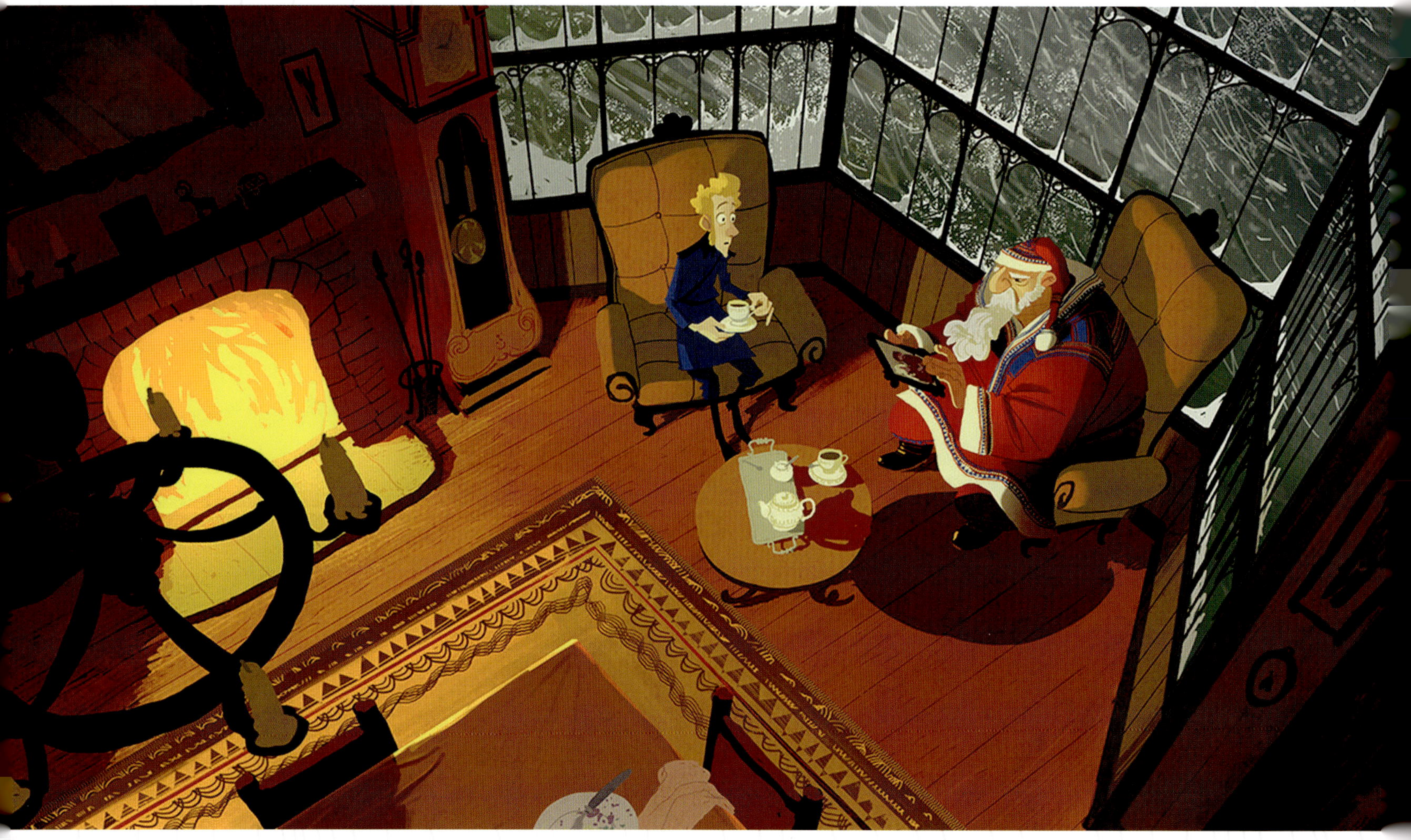

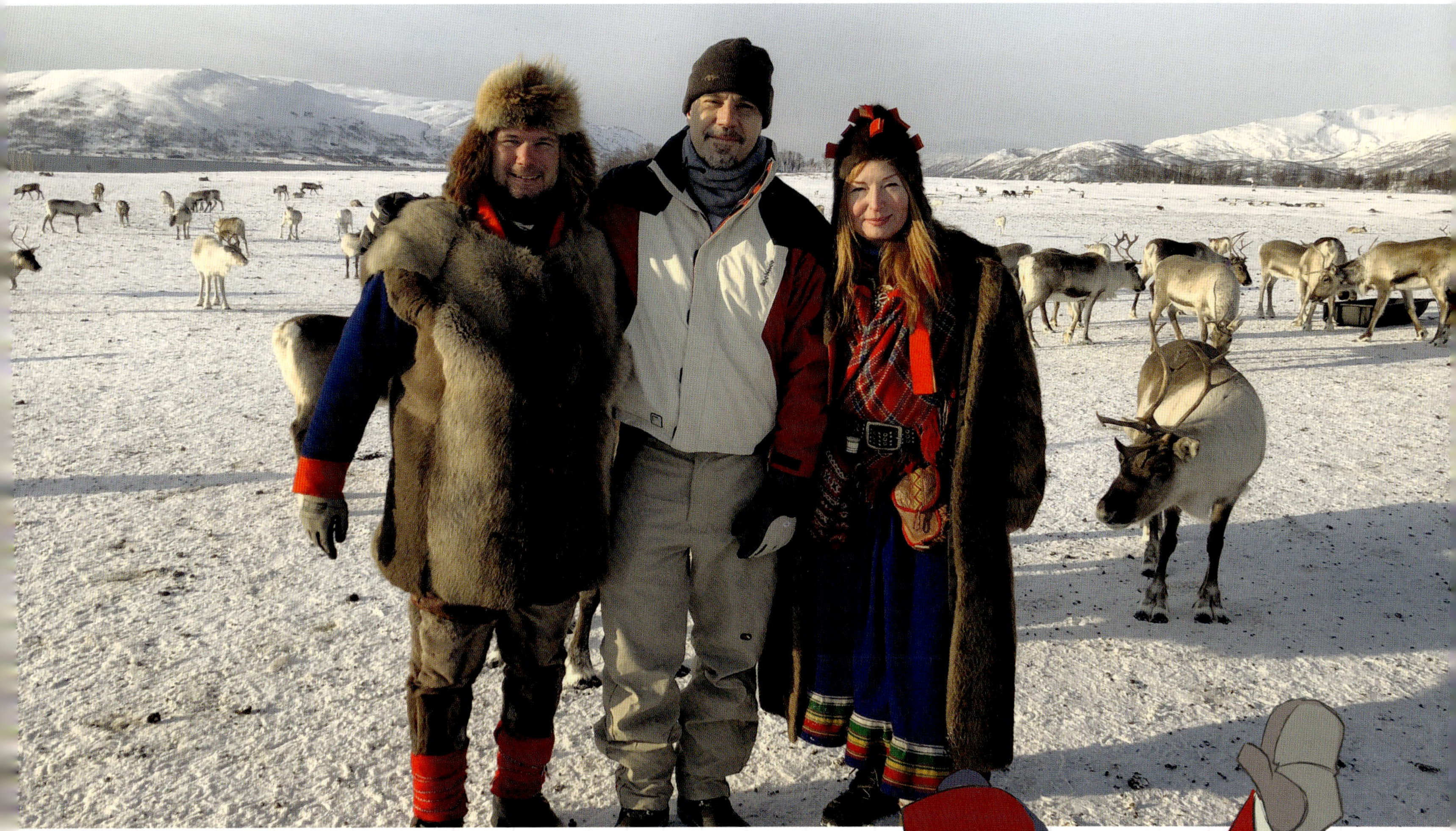

THIS PAGE: (ABOVE) Sergio Pablos with Saami people on a research trip; (RIGHT) Artwork by Torsten Schrank.

NEXT SPREAD: Concept art by Pascal Campion.

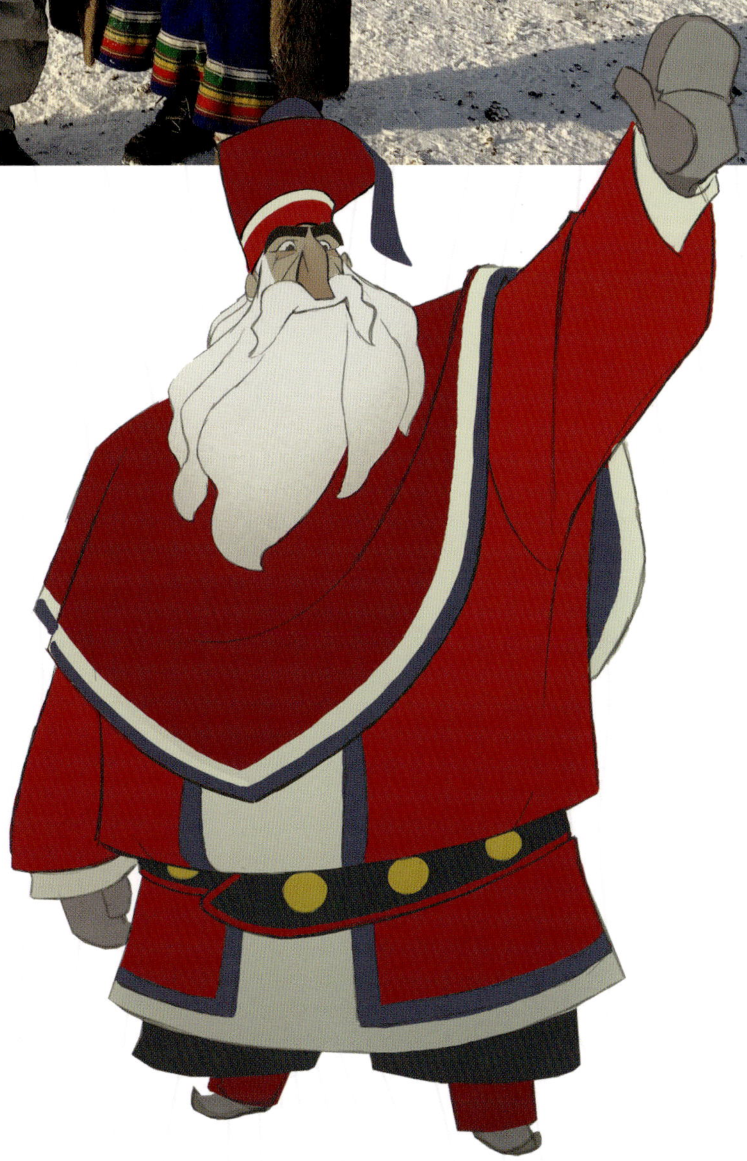

"Our art directors did such a great job of preparation and research for us, not only for creating the whole style of the movie, but also in gathering many photos about light, colors, snow, and also Nordic decorations and designs."

Guillem Ramisa de Soto, Pre-Compositing Supervisor

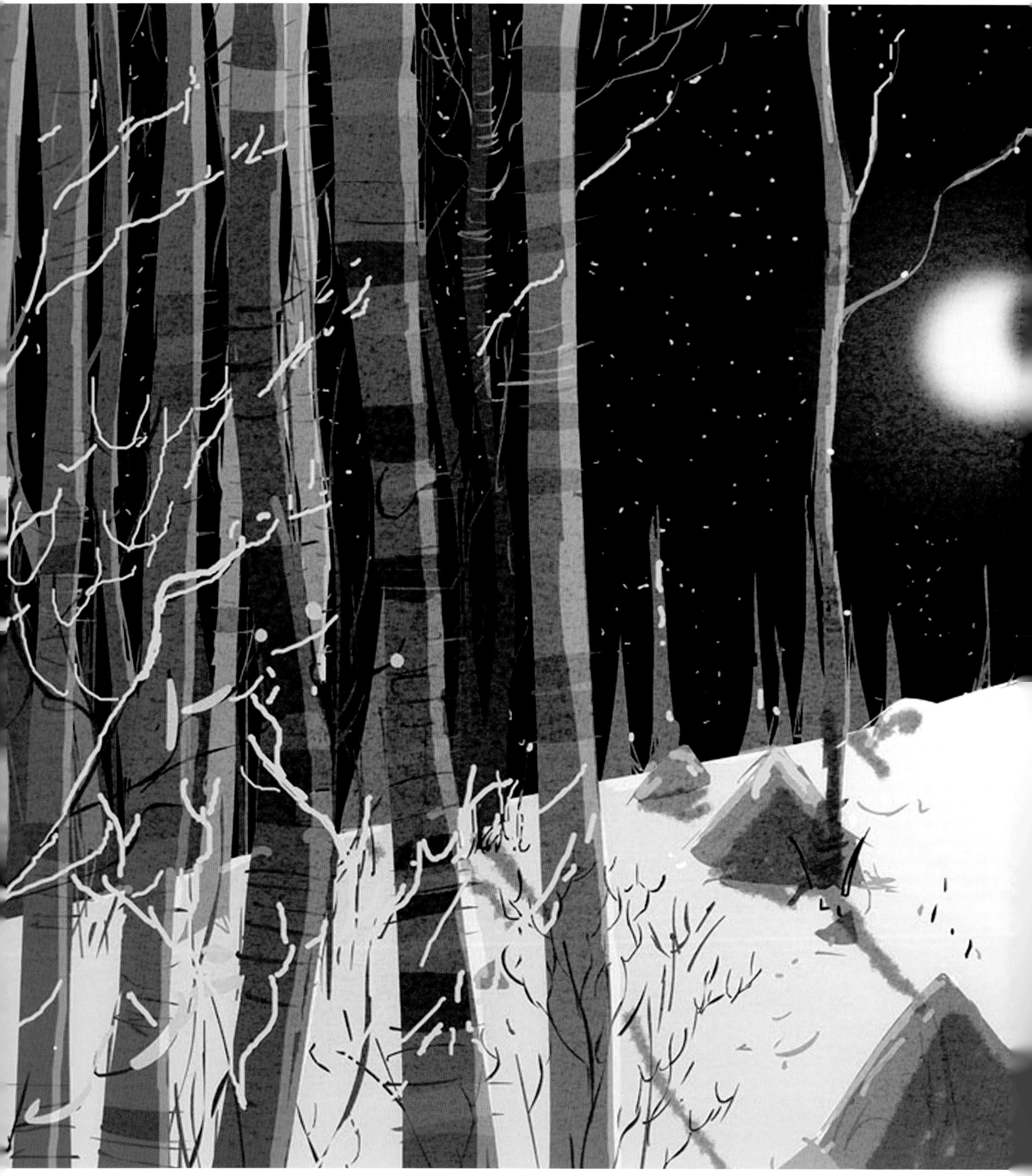

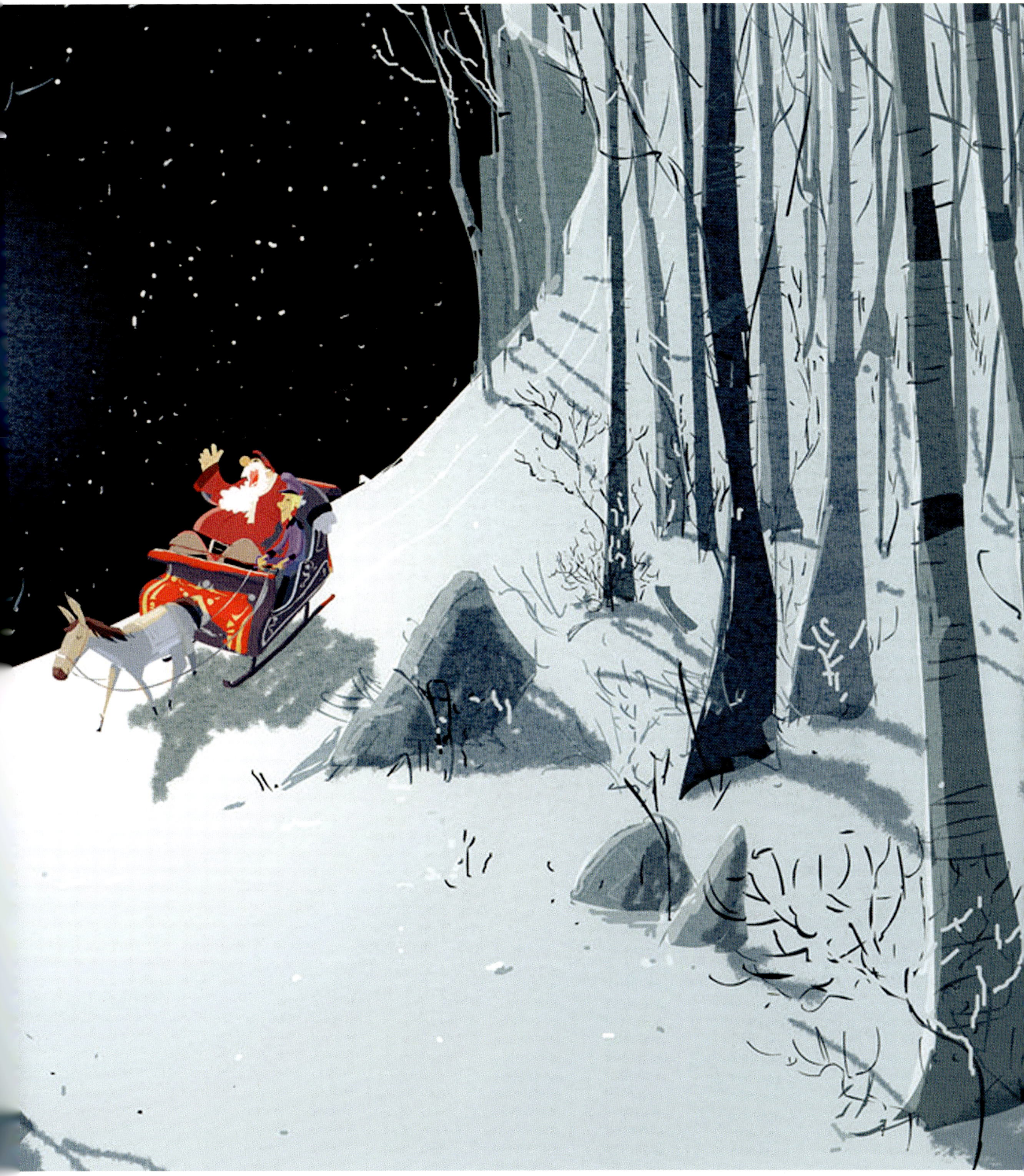

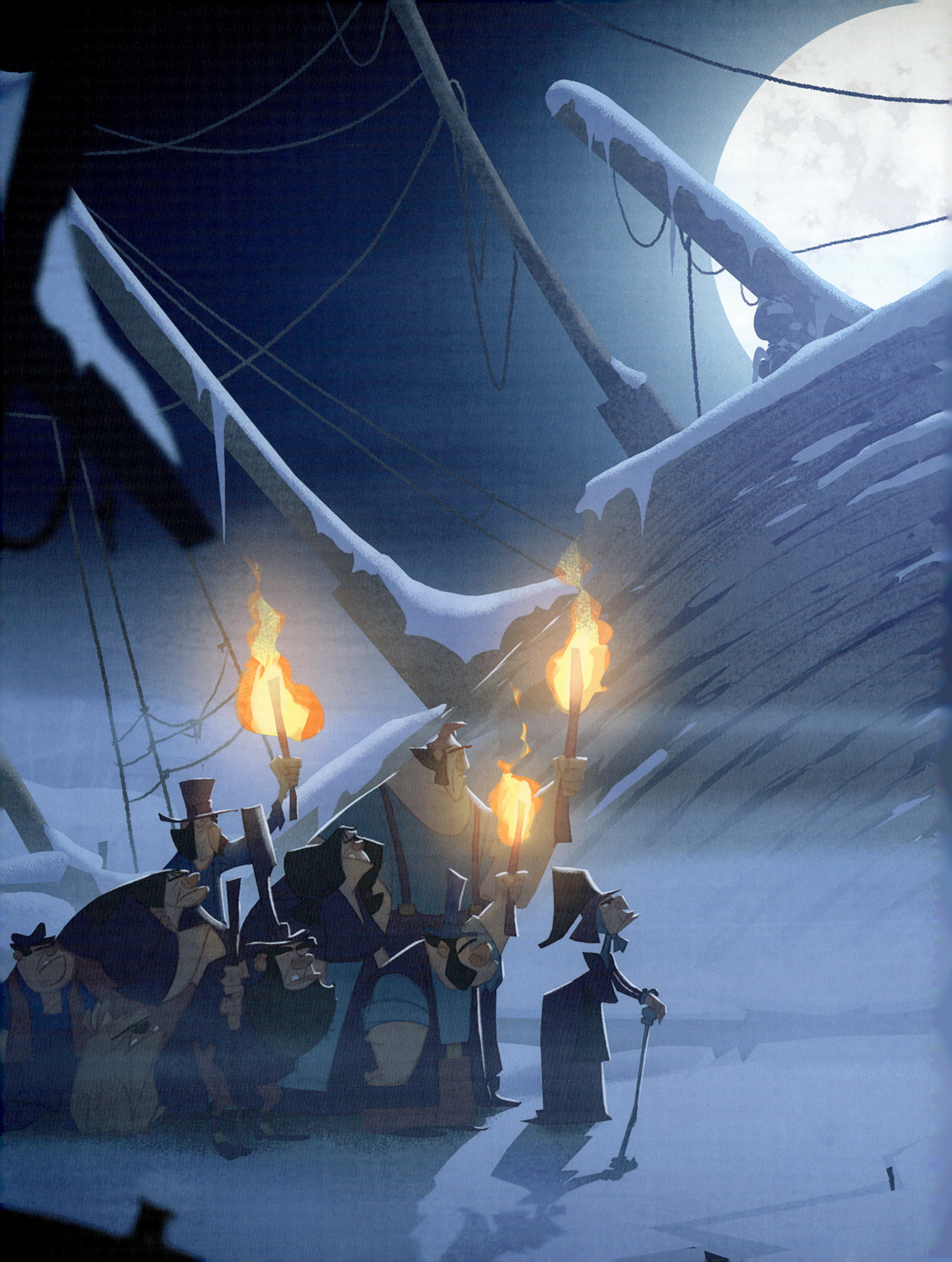

Calling a Truce

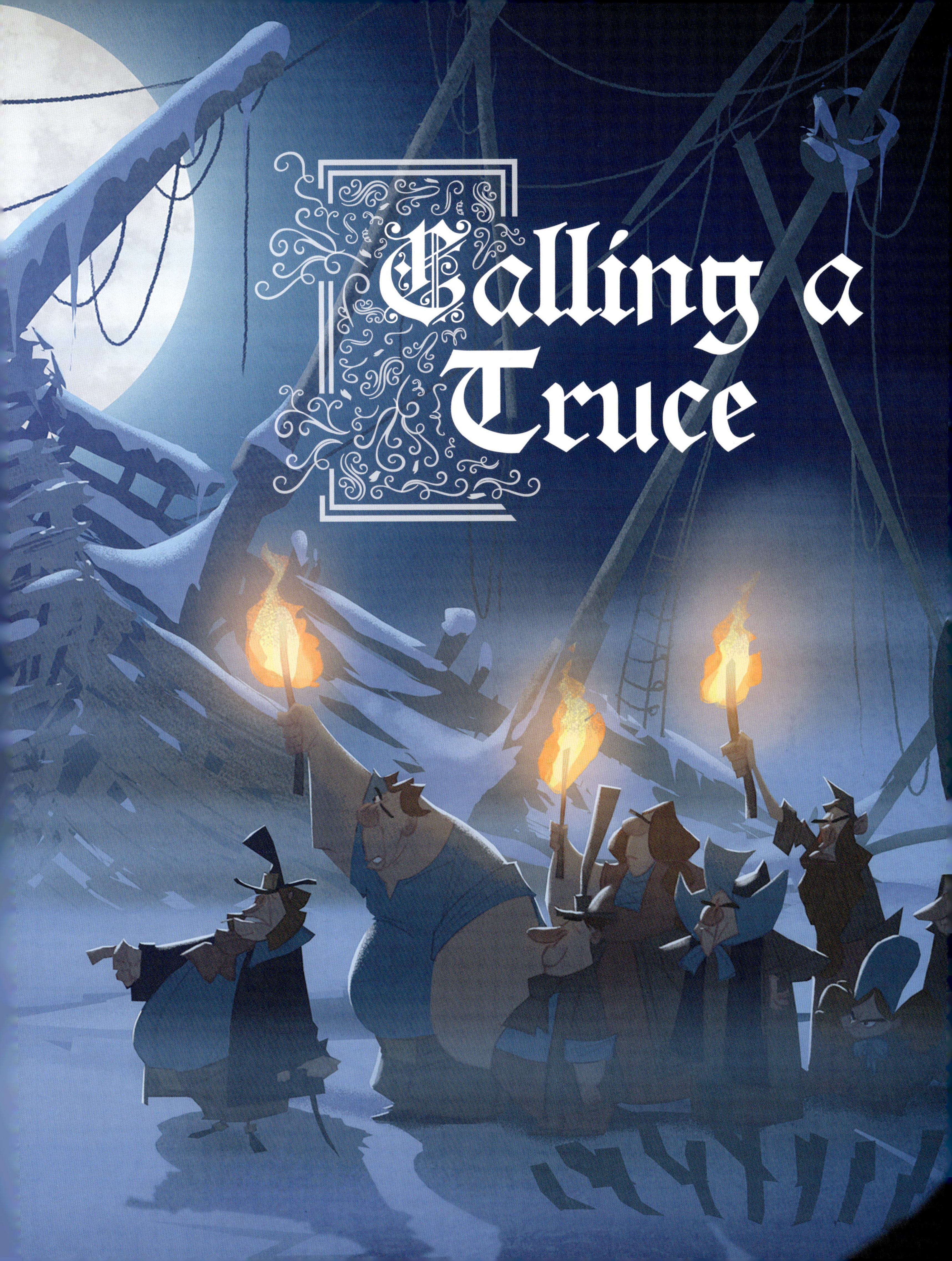

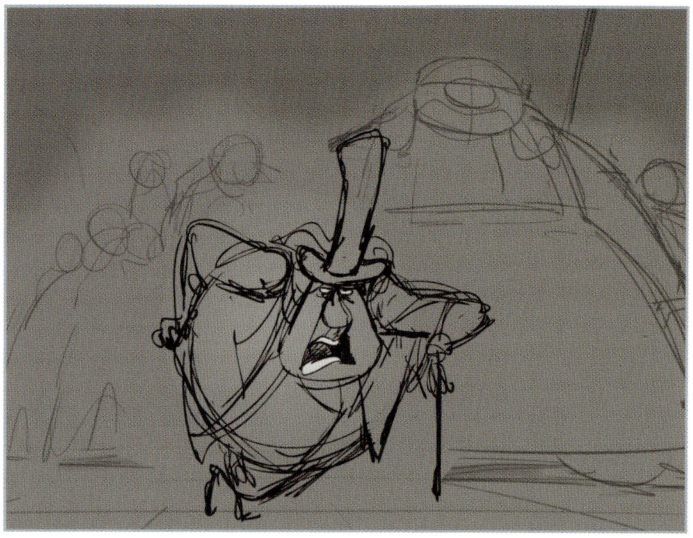

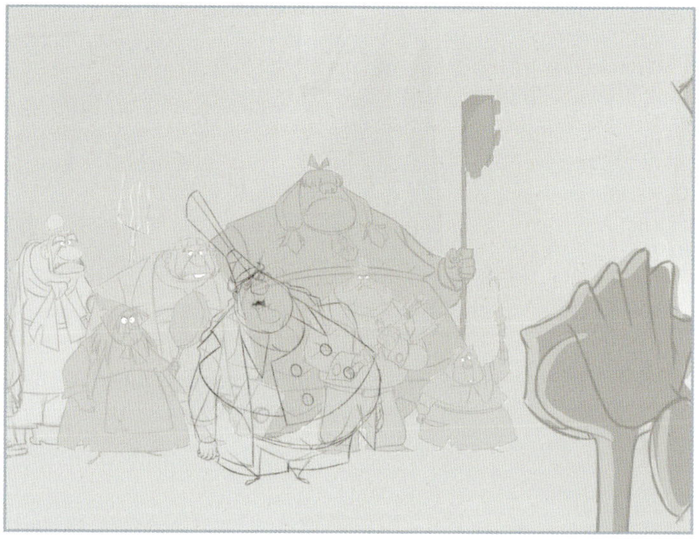

PREVIOUS SPREAD: Artwork by Szymon Biernacki and Juan Pablo Navas.

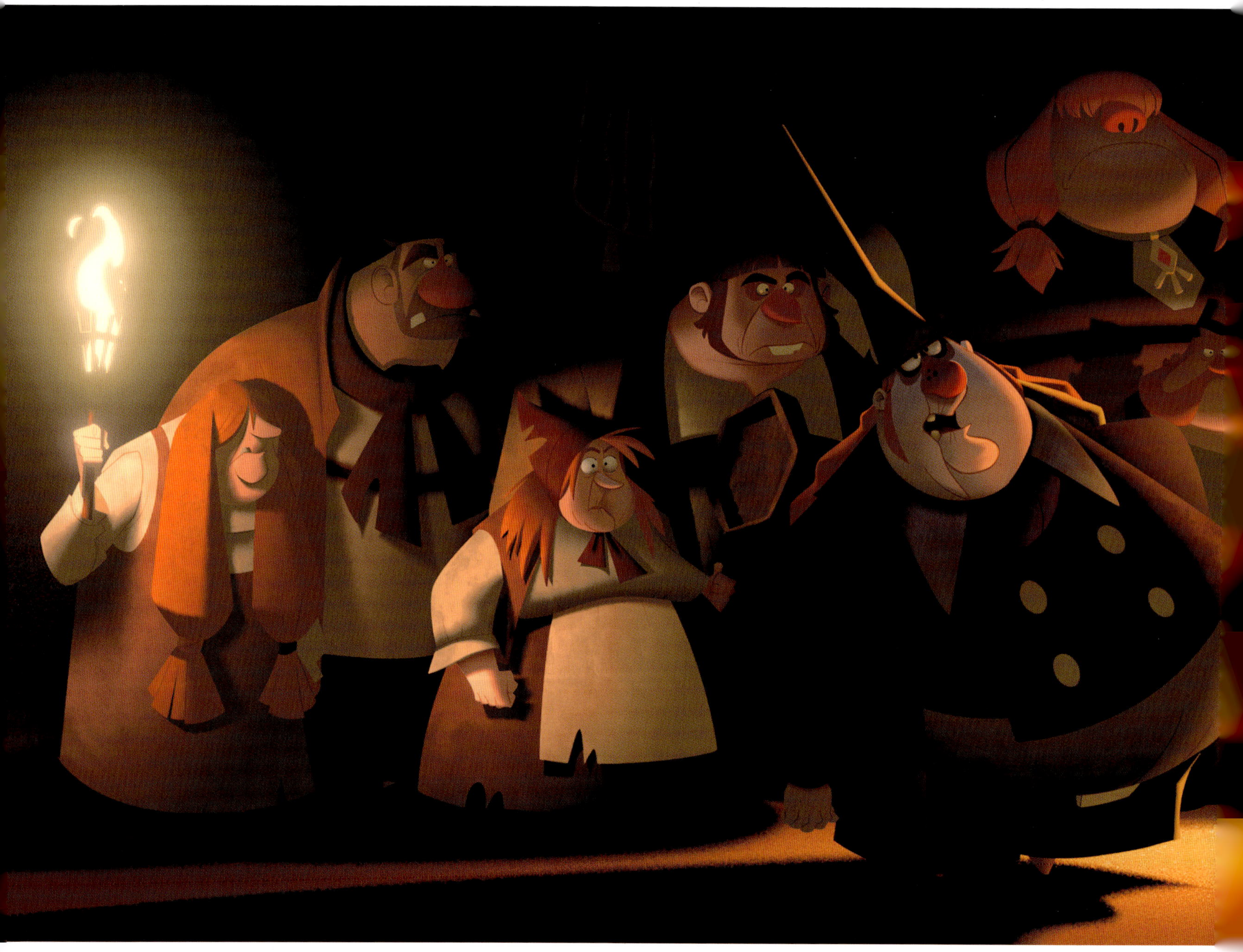

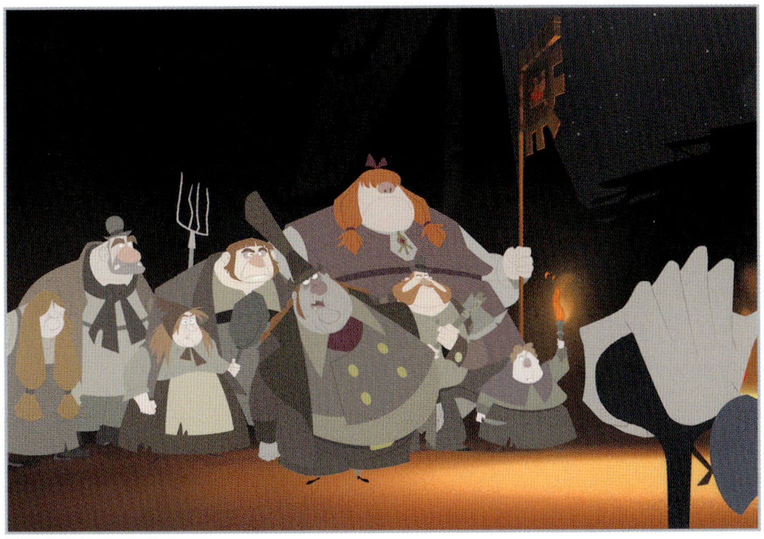

> "Our biggest mission was to support the story with the right design decisions and make a visual language that goes well with the tone of the story."
>
> Szymon Biernacki, Production Designer

THIS SPREAD: Shot breakdown, showing the Ellingboe/Krum truce.

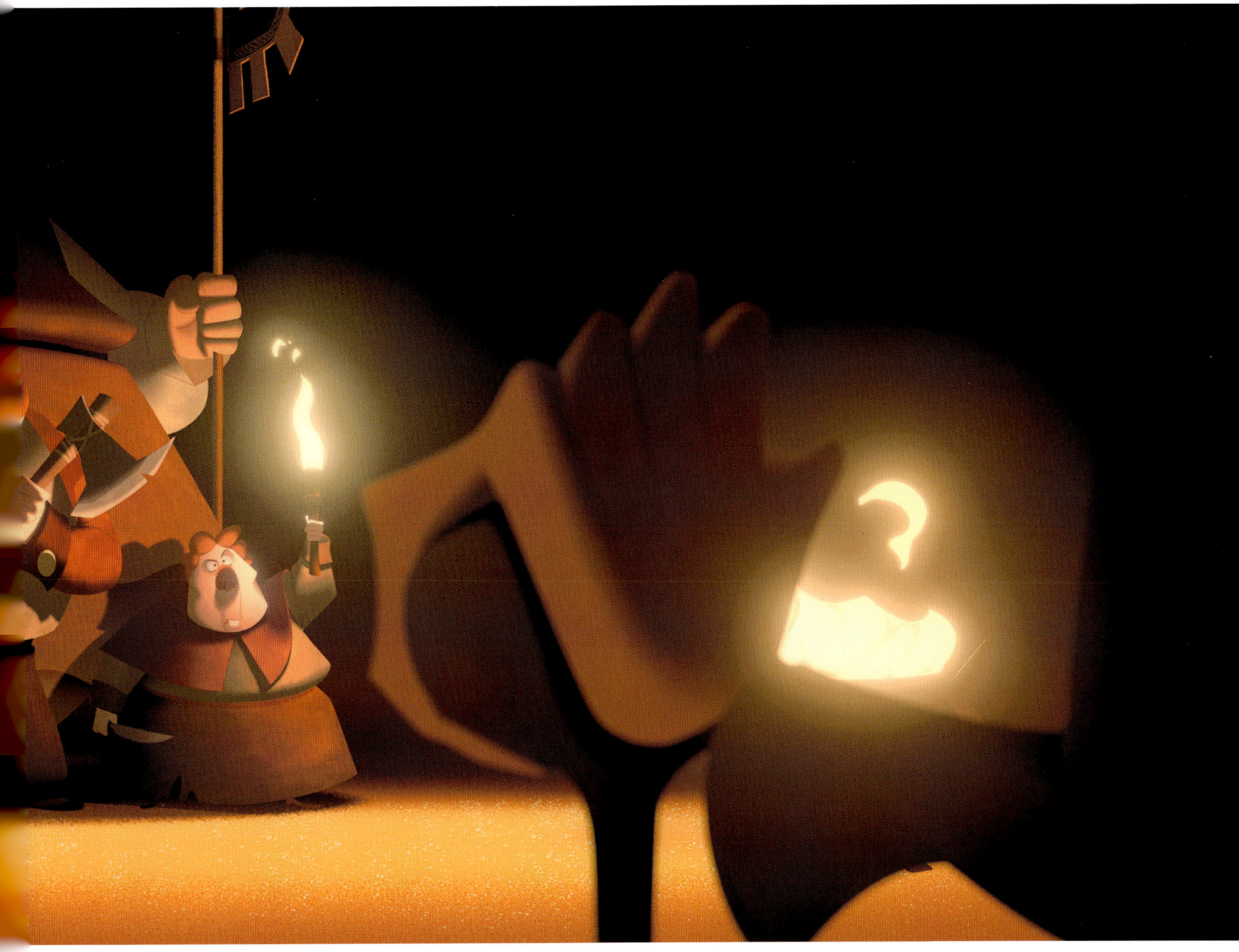

Olaf & Pumpkin

A FEUD–ENDING ROMANCE

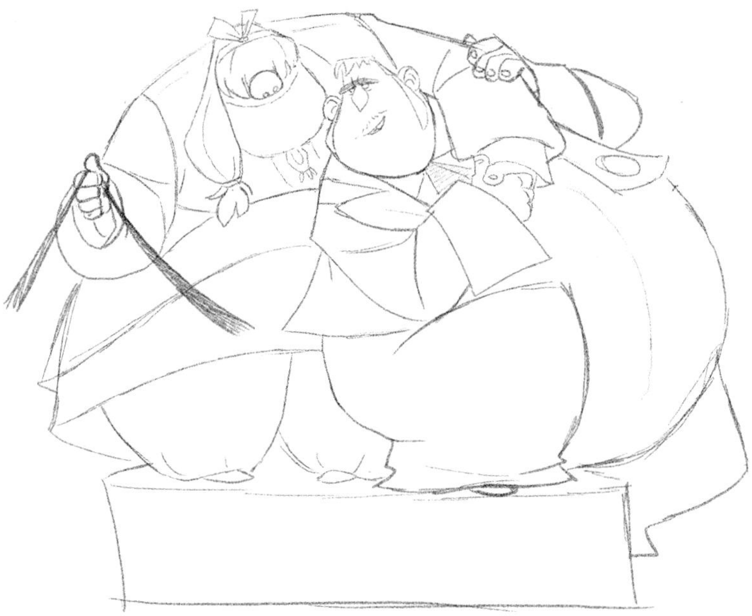

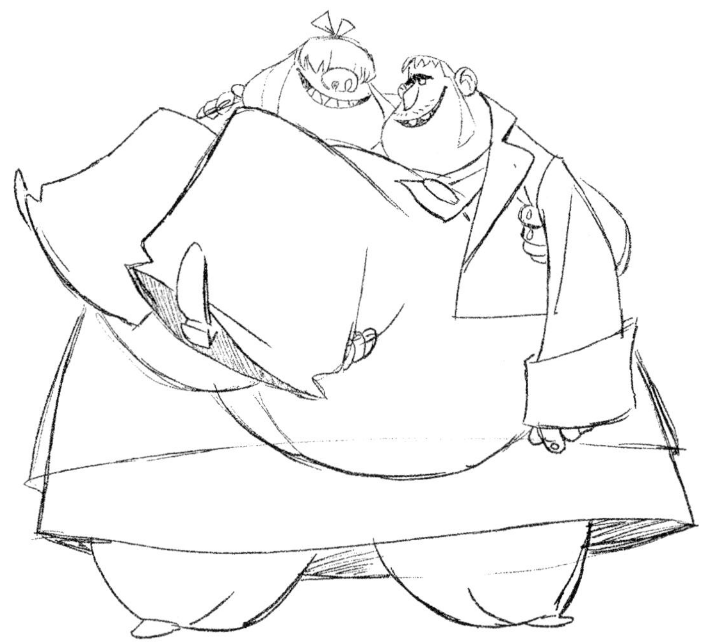

THIS SPREAD: Character exploration for Olaf and Pumpkin by Torsten Schrank and Charlie Bonifacio.

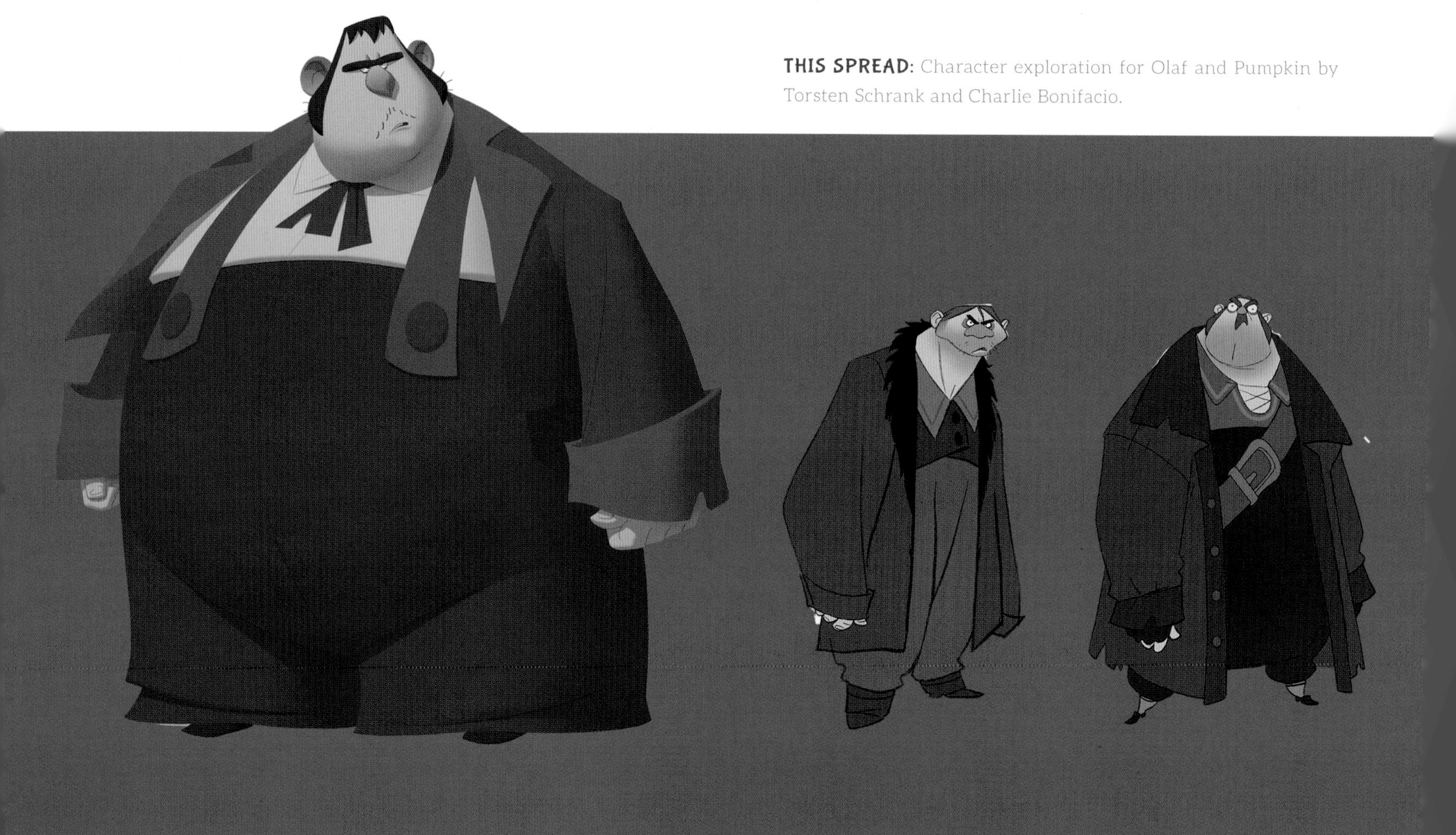

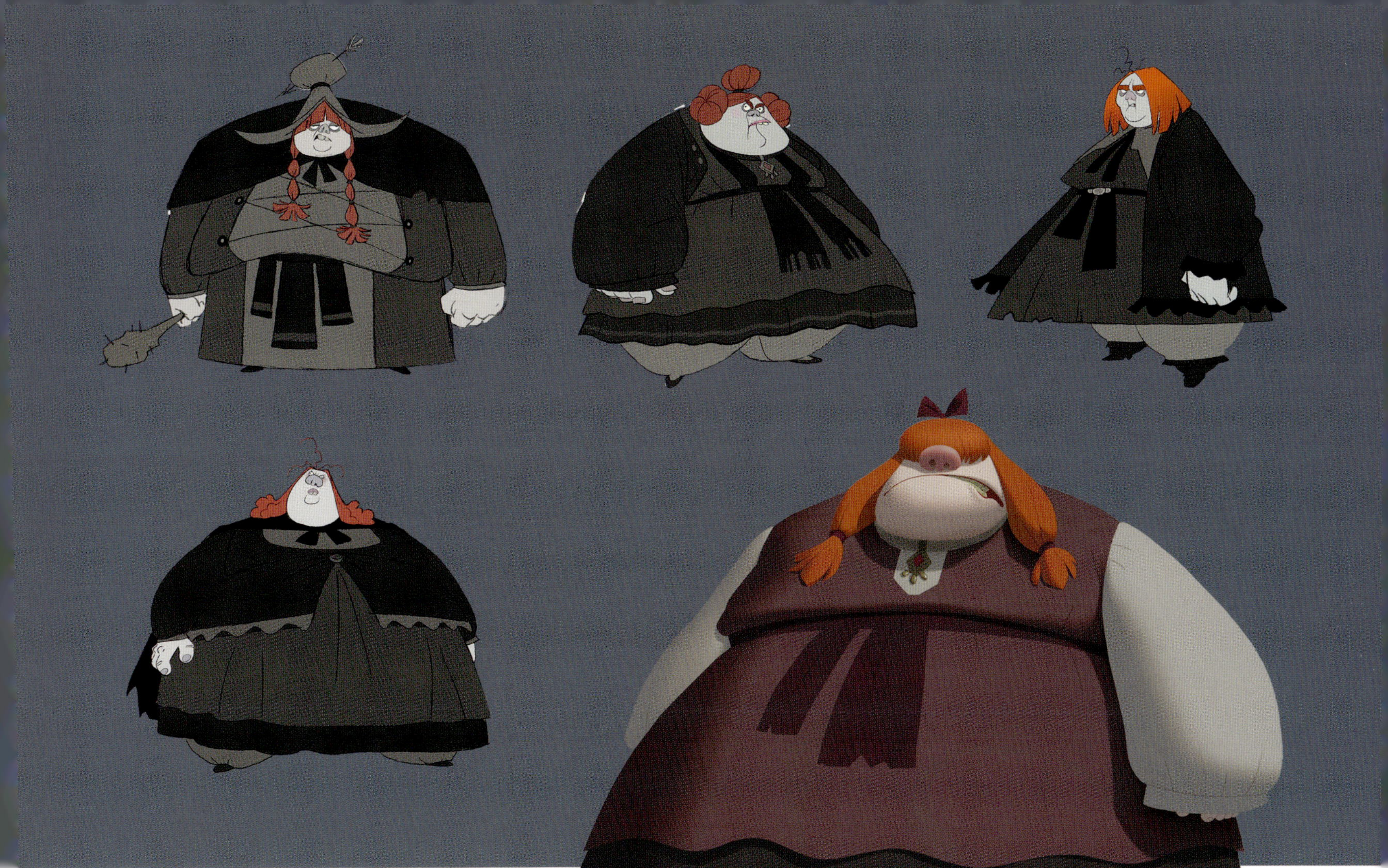

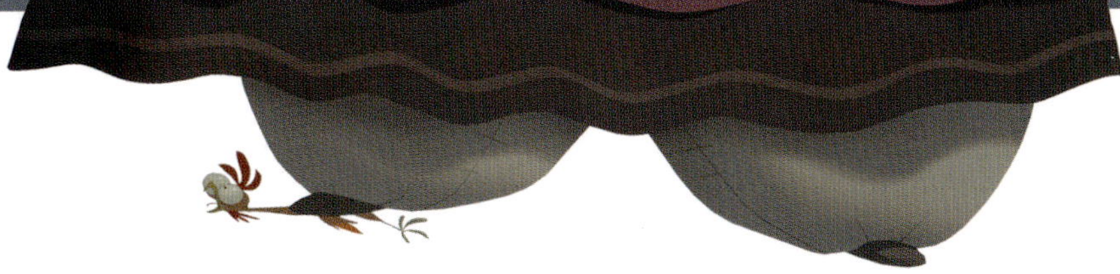

NEXT SPREAD: Artwork by Marcin Jakubowski.

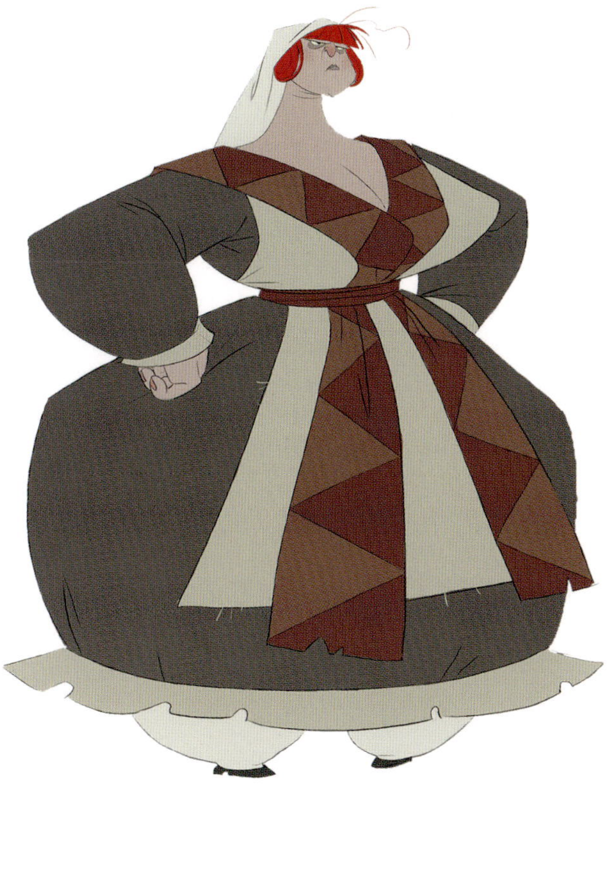

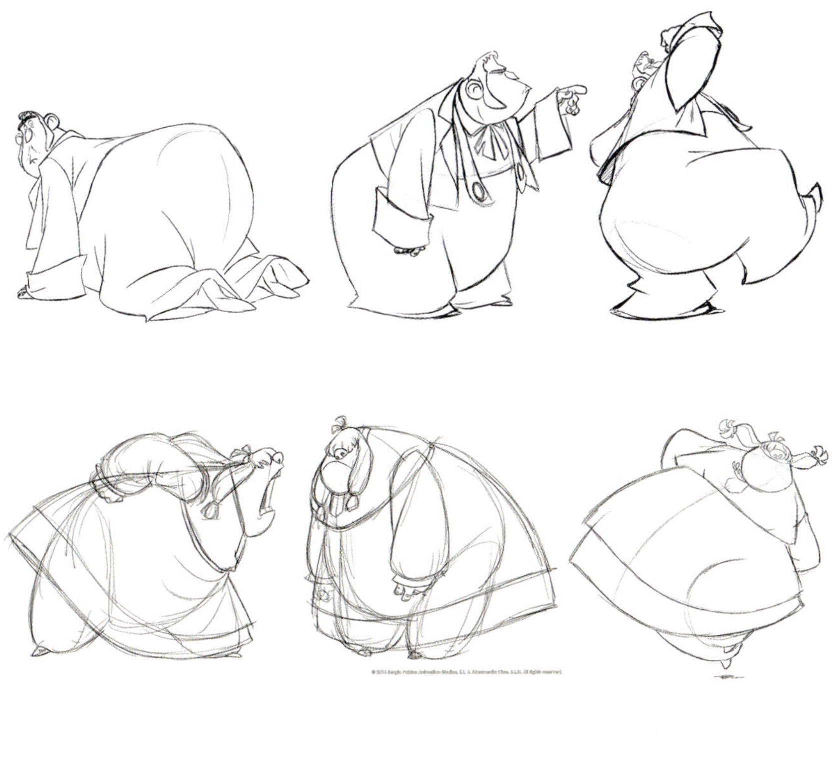

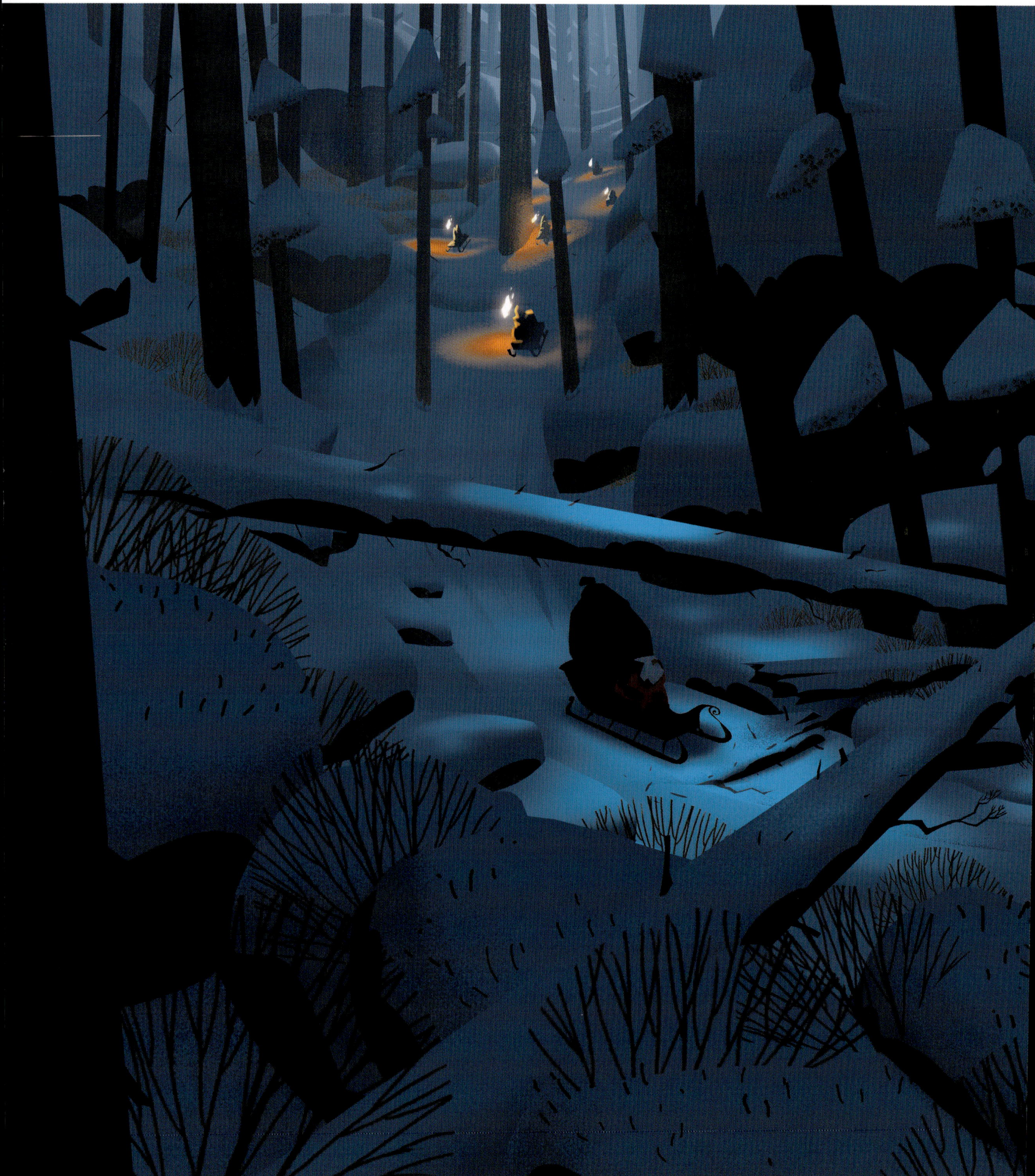

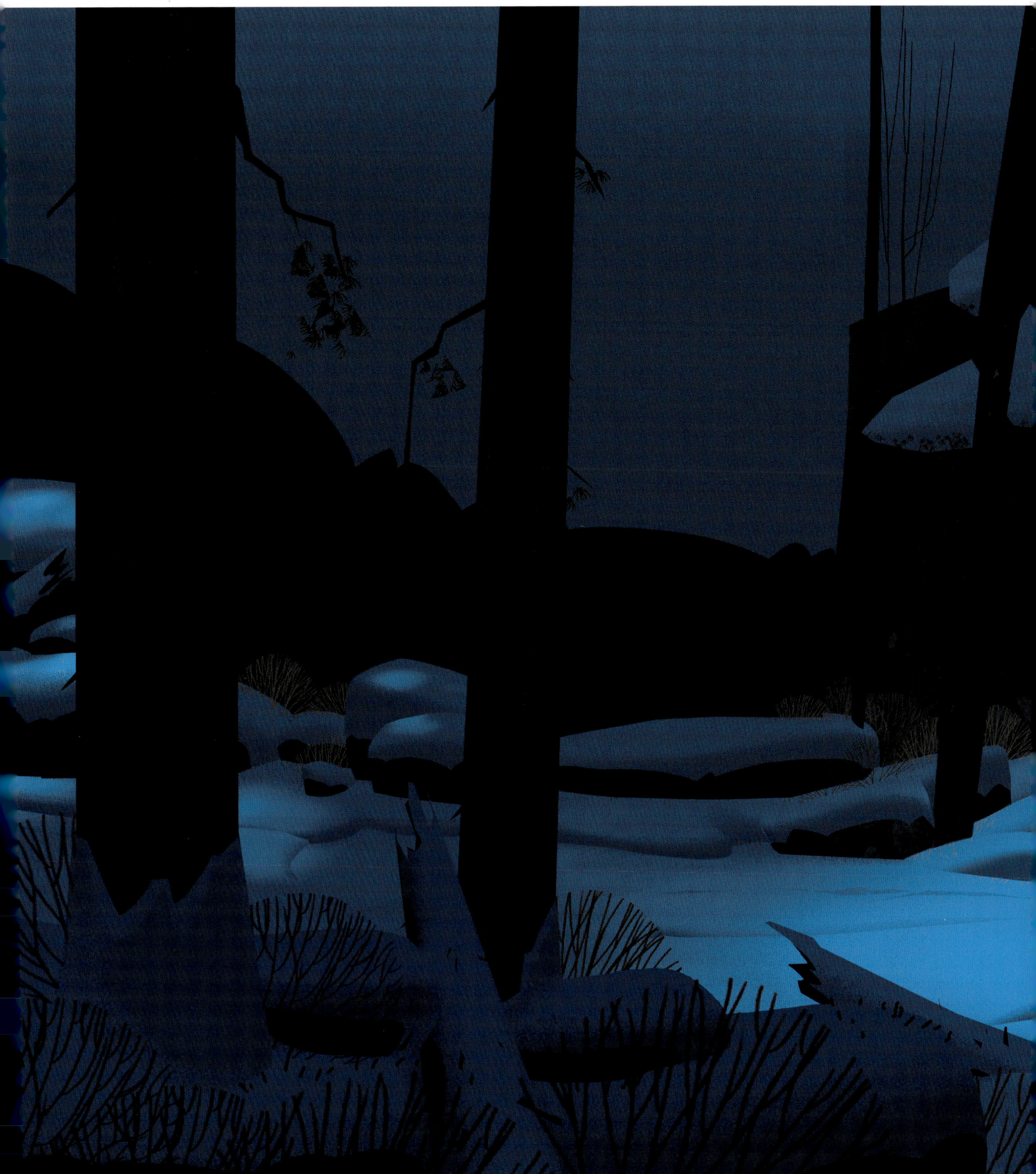

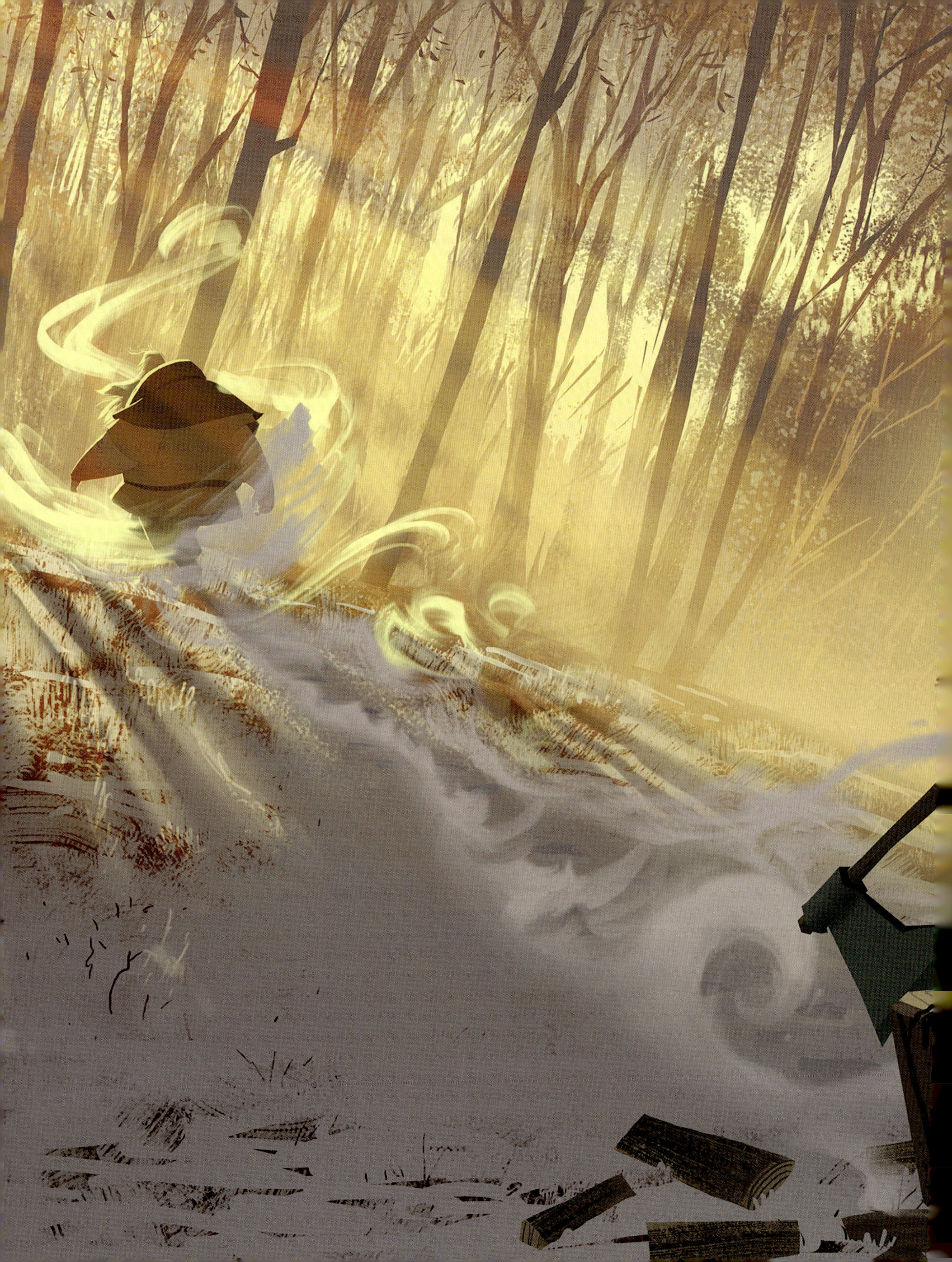

Into the Future

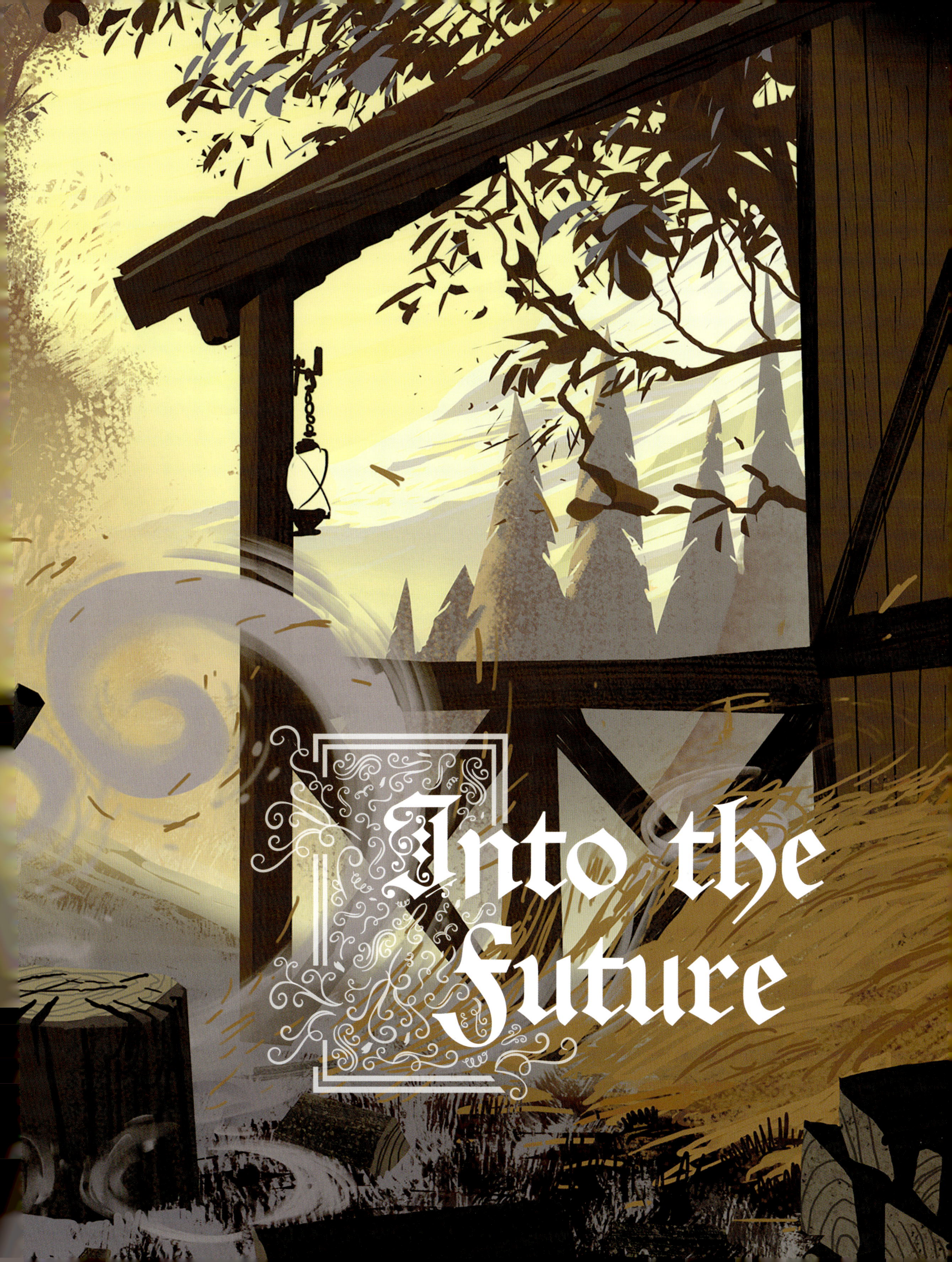

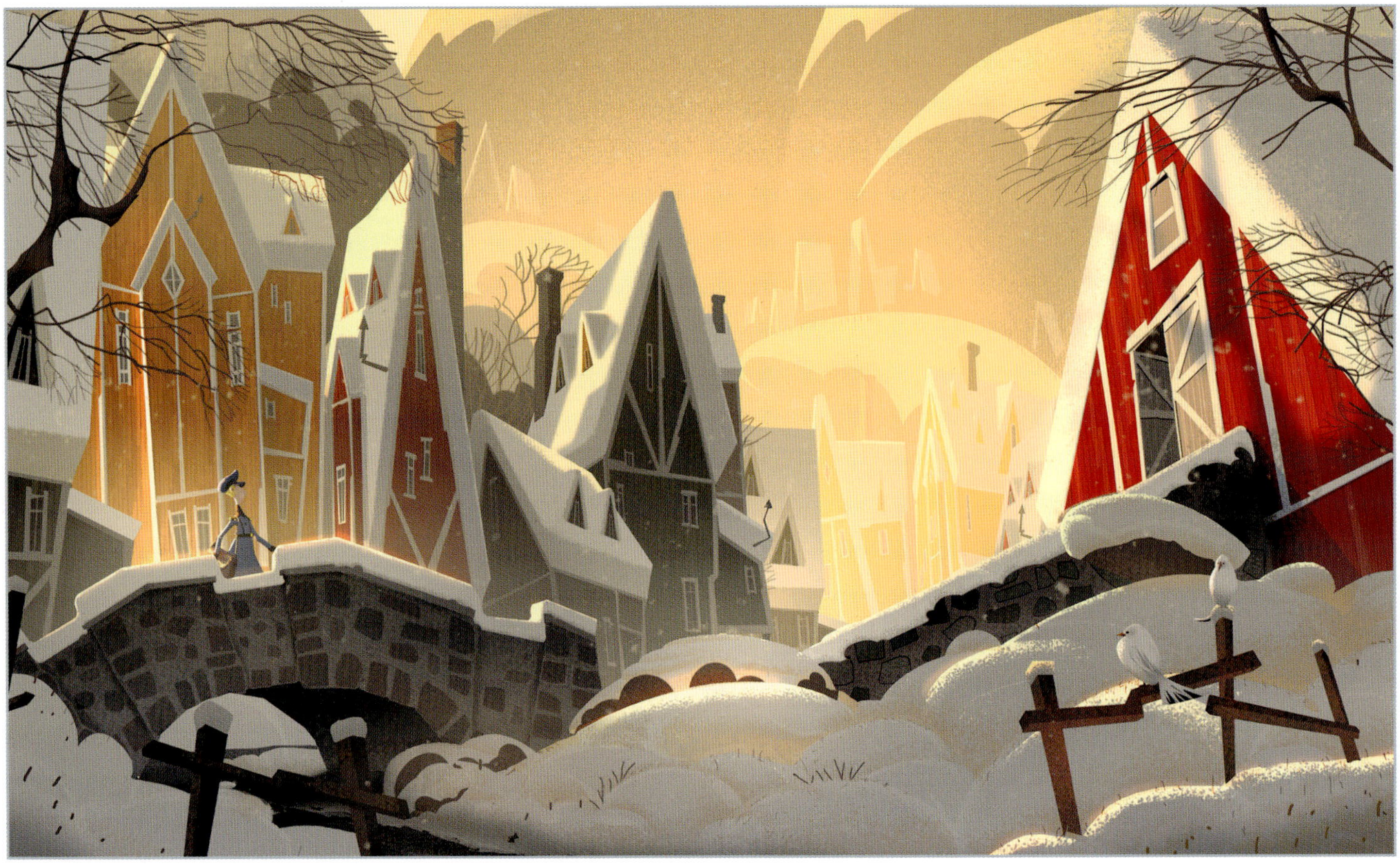

PREVIOUS SPREAD: Concept art by Marcin Jakubowski and Sergio Pablos.

NEXT SPREAD: Concept art by Pascal Campion.

THIS SPREAD: (ABOVE) Concept art by Henrik Evensen; (ABOVE RIGHT) Character exploration by Franco Spagnolo; (BELOW) Concept art by Marcin Jakubowski.

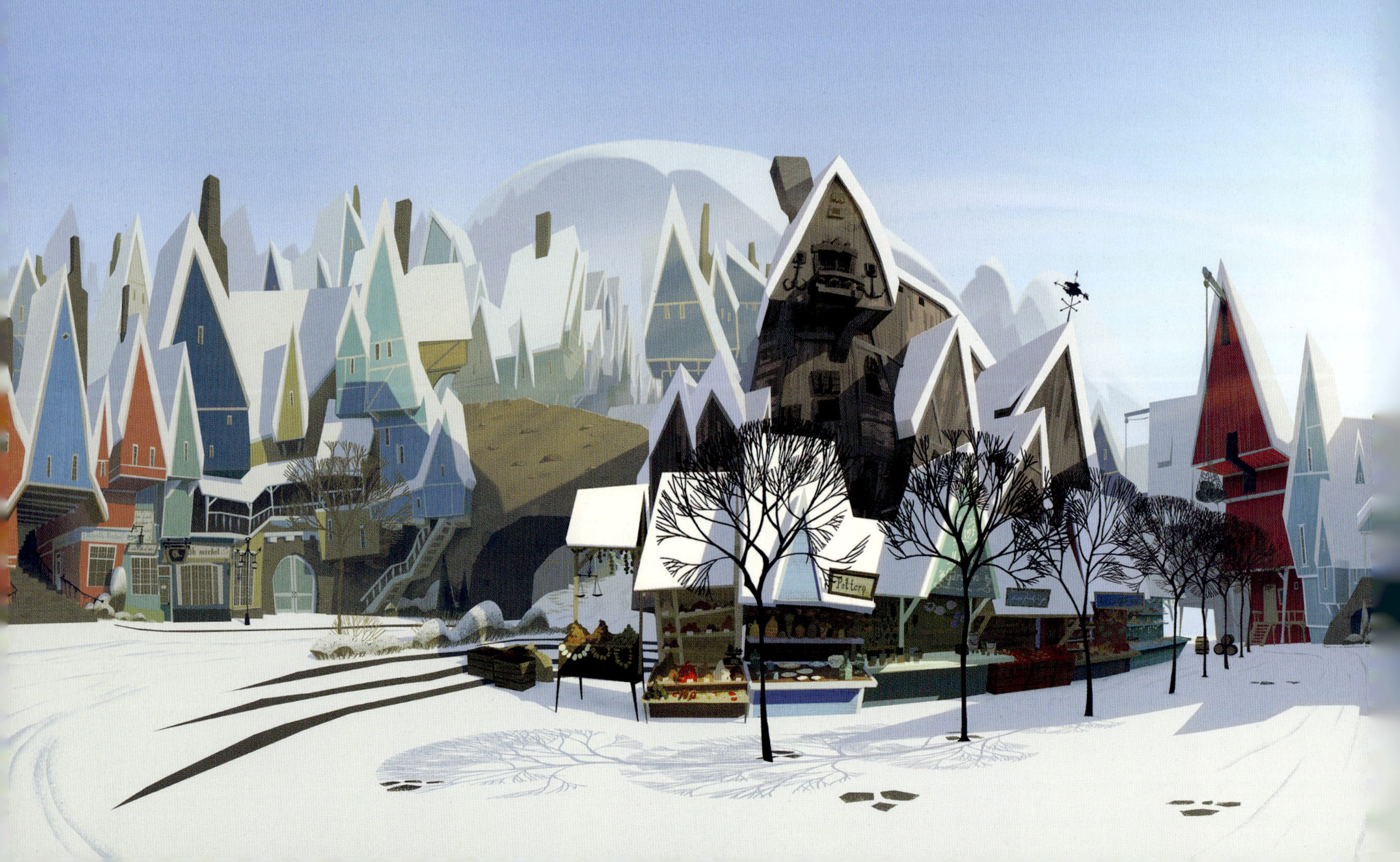

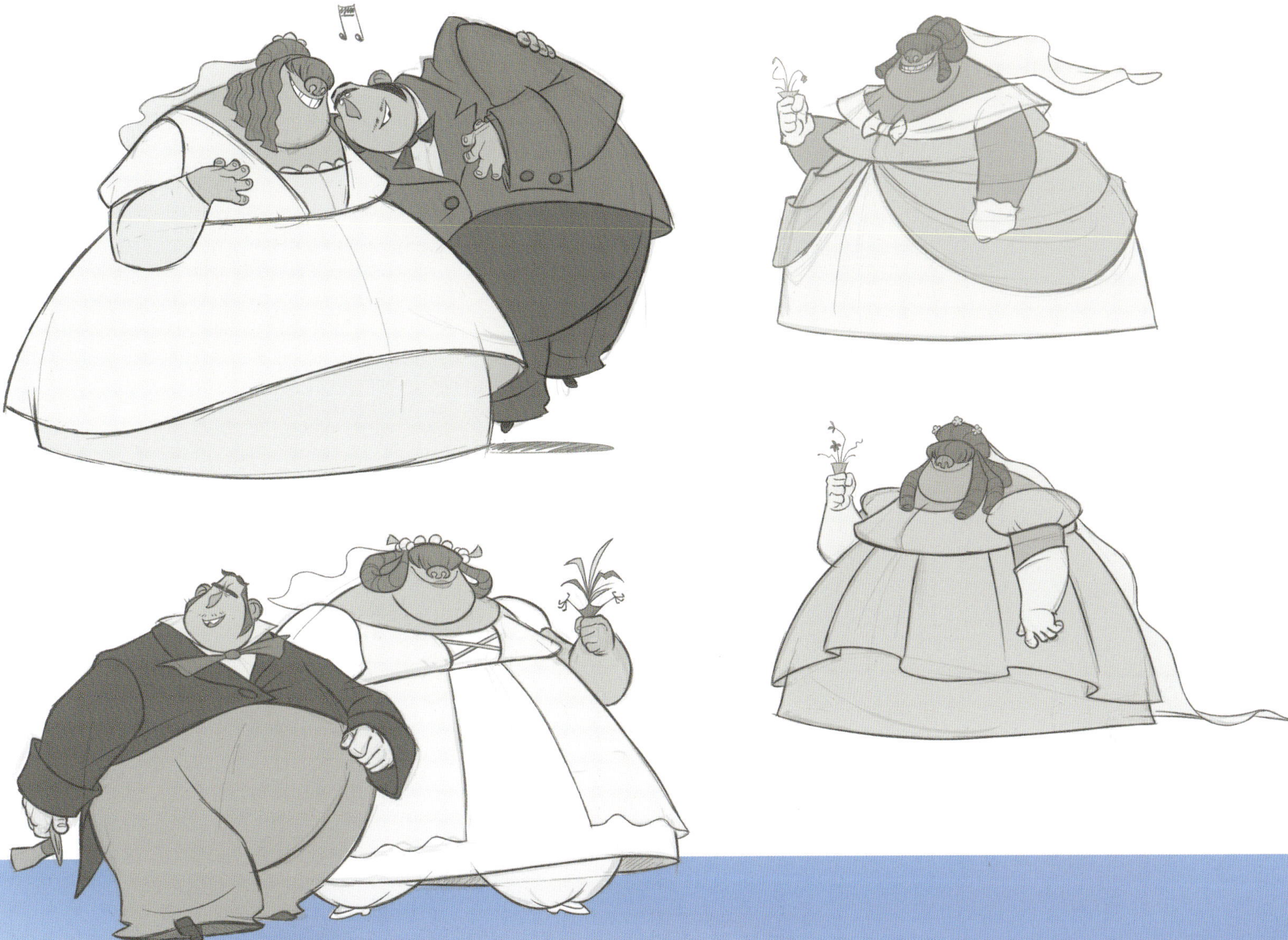

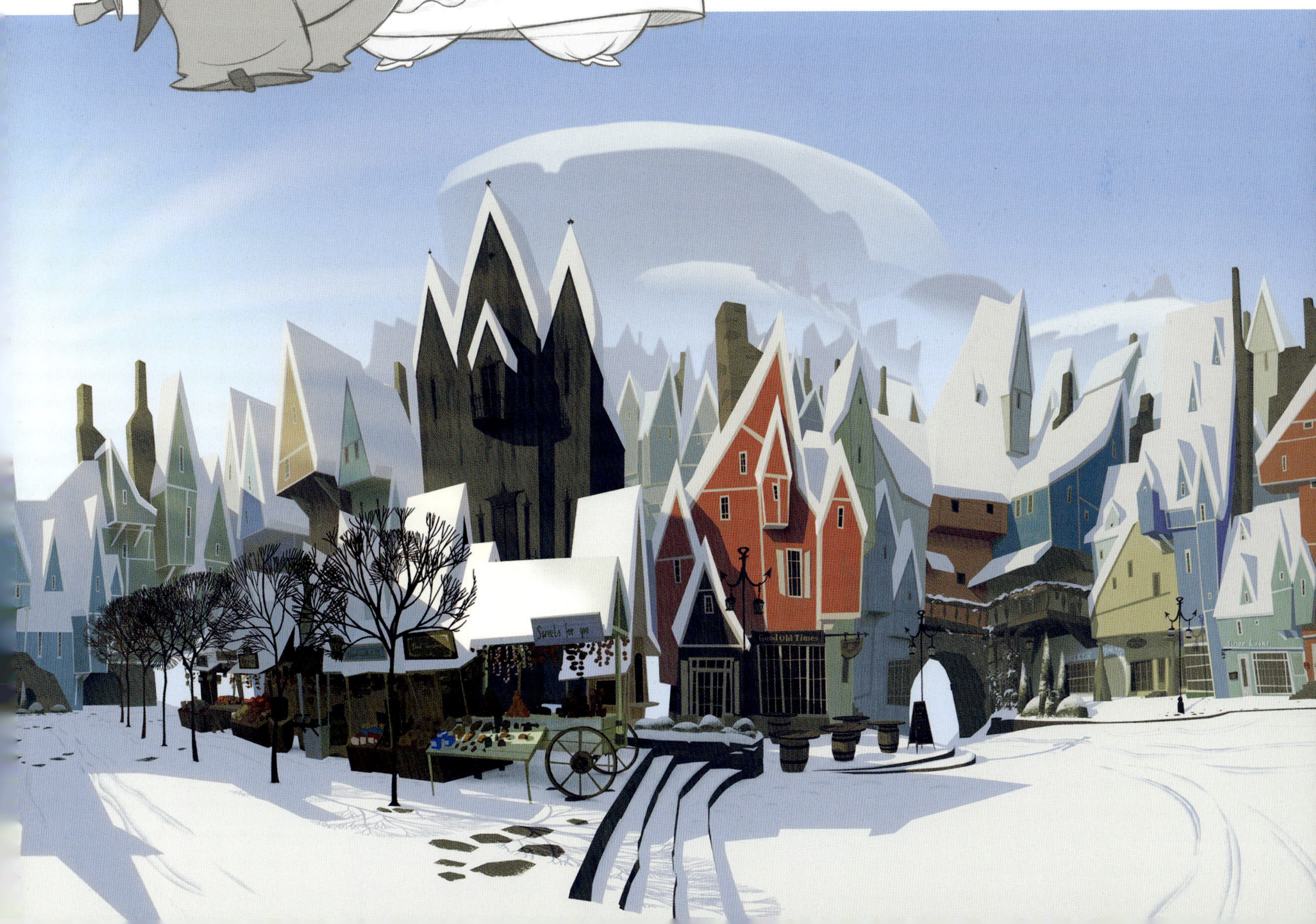
Sweets for you
Good Old Times

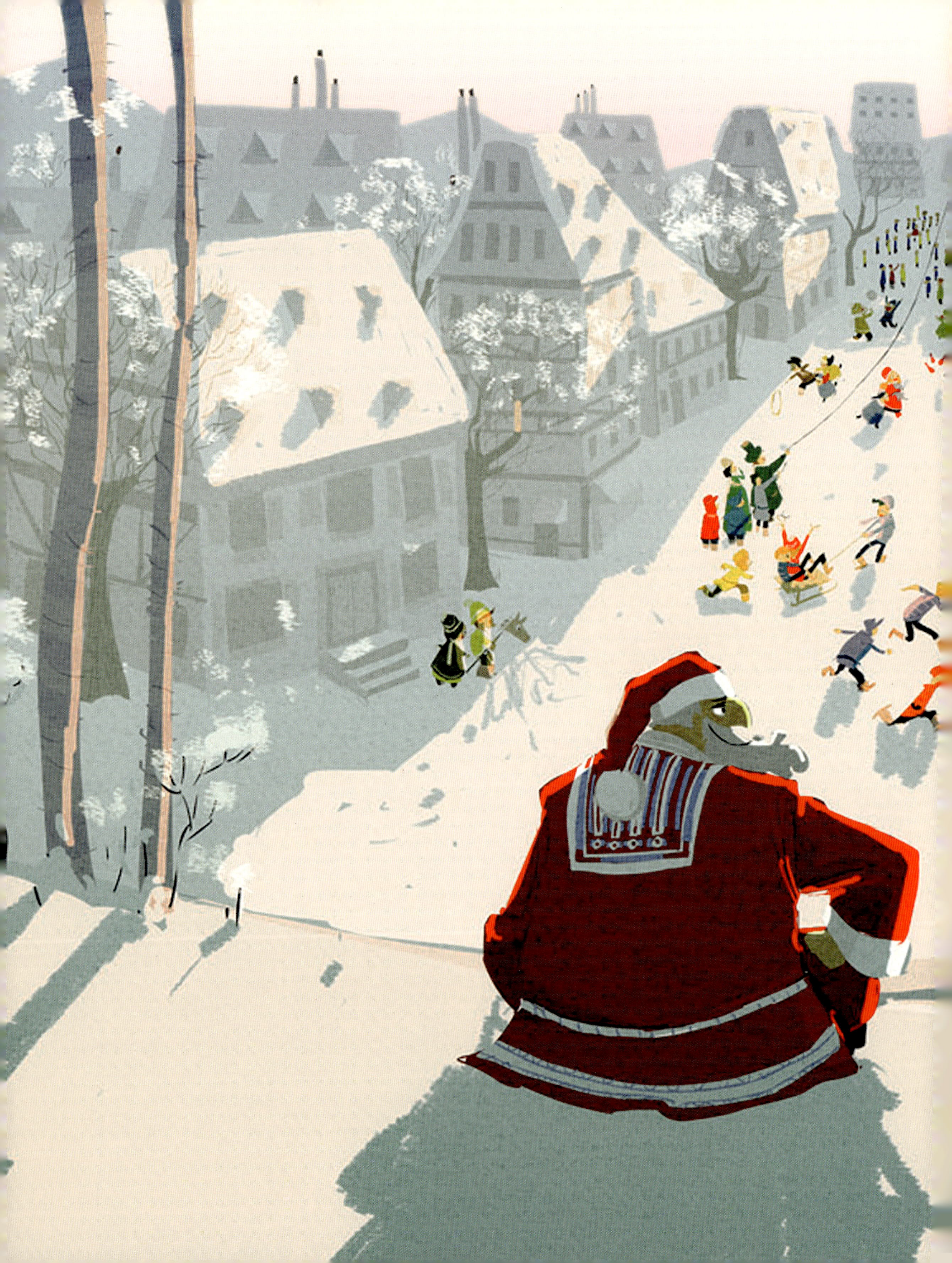

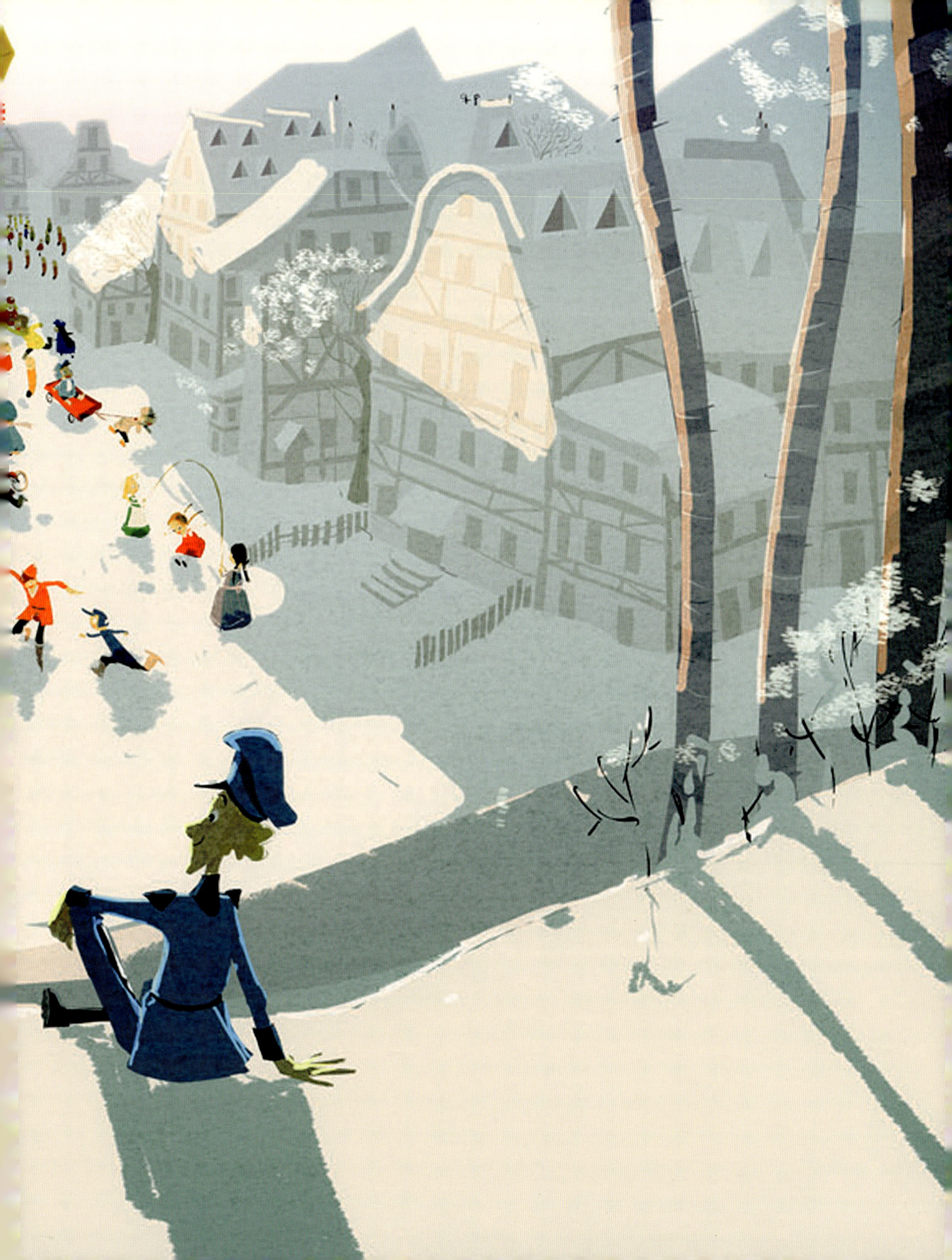

Something Special

The film's main character designer, Torsten Schrank (*Maya the Bee: The Honey Games, El Cid: The Legend*), says his goal was to add something special to every single one of the 200-plus characters he helped design. "Many times, graphic solutions can work well in one single drawing, but the animators had to track these through their animation and move them around," he explains. "Then, the lighting and shadow needed to find the right volumetric interpretation, too. Of course, all this needed to work from a visual point of view."

Schrank says it was crucial to make sure the shapes of the characters weren't overshadowing the characters' acting. "Shapes are very important in character design, but they should support the character the way good film music underlines a scene," he notes. "For me, the process of character design does not end with defining the look of the character. It starts with the first draft of the script, the very first sketch, goes through voice recording, animation, clean up, light and shadow, and ends up as the final result on screen. On *Klaus*, I had the fantastic opportunity to follow all these steps. It was a big challenge and a wonderful experience at the same time!"

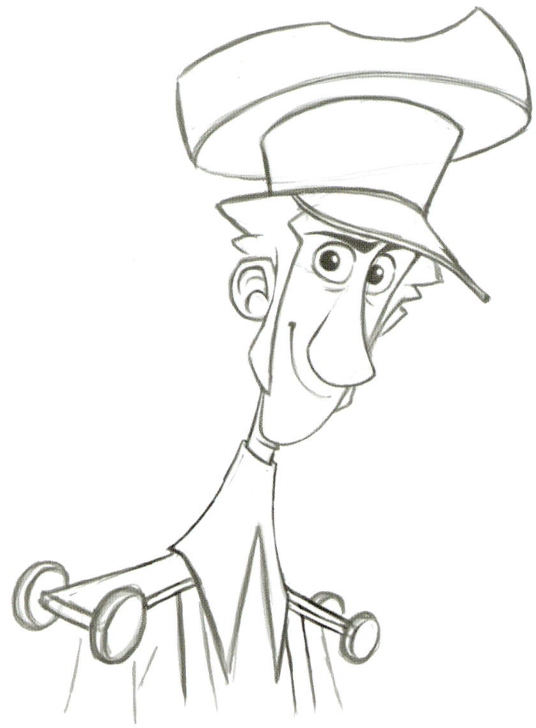

BELOW: Character designers had to work out the basic 'shape' of each character.

NEXT PAGE: Character lineups by Torsten Schrank.

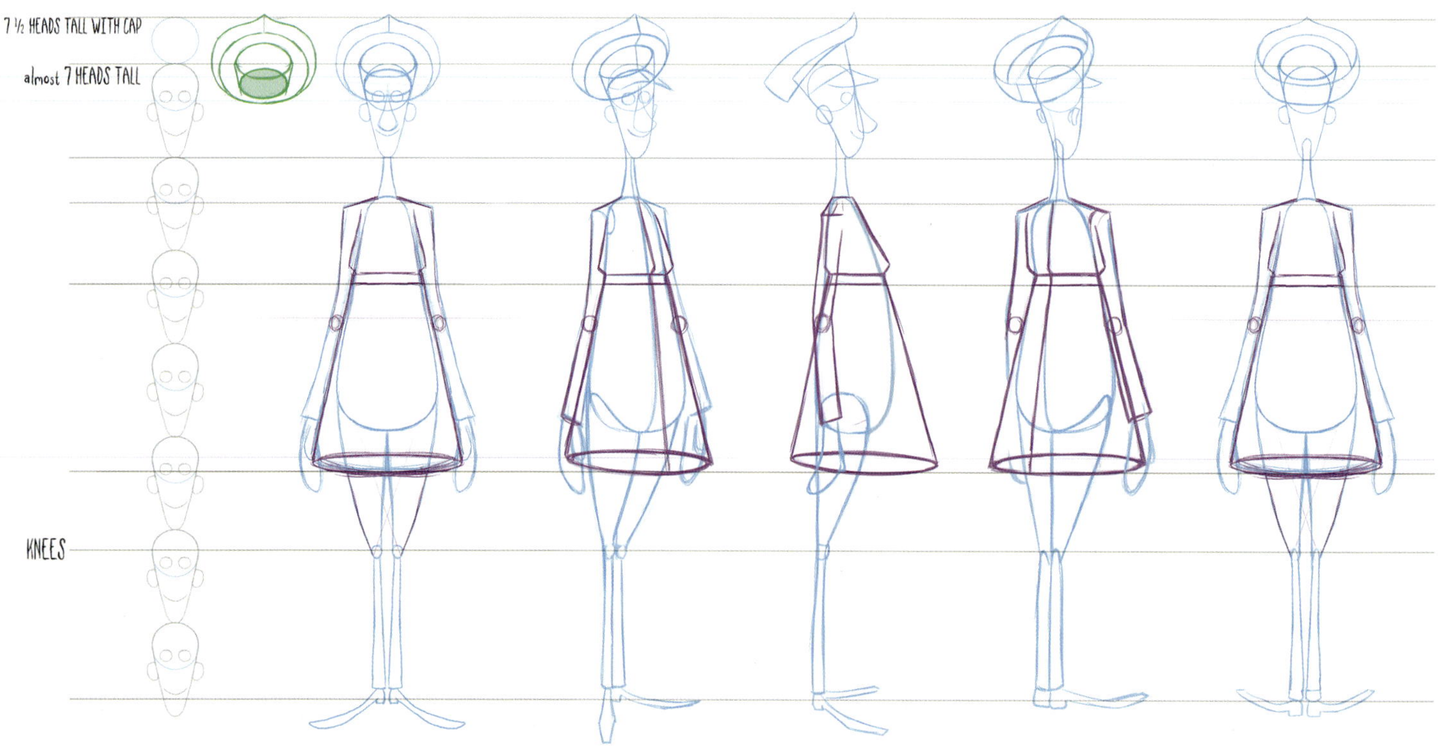

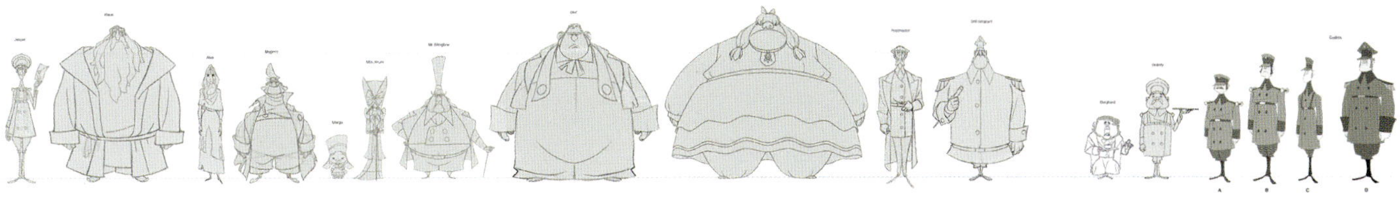

KIDS

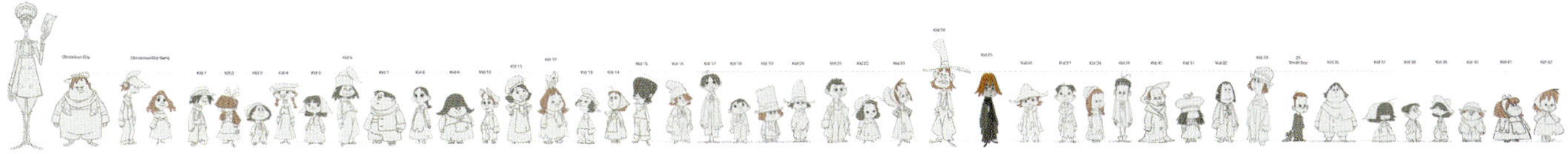

CLAN KRUM

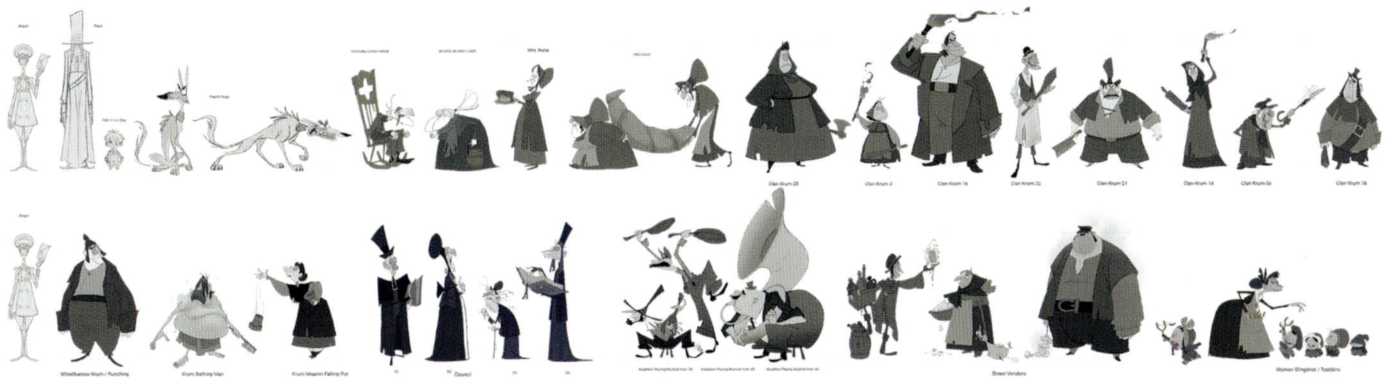

CLAN ELLINGBOE

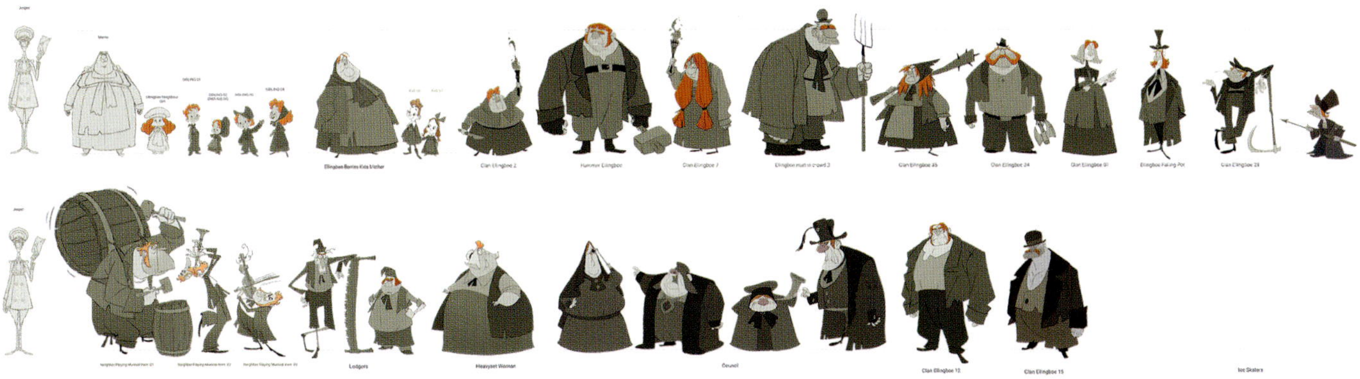

SAAMIS

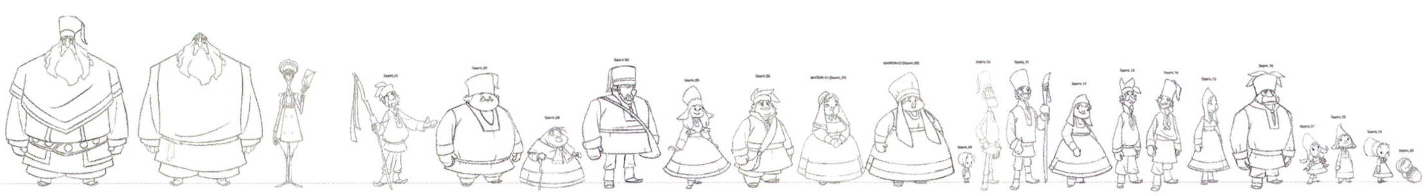

ANIMALS

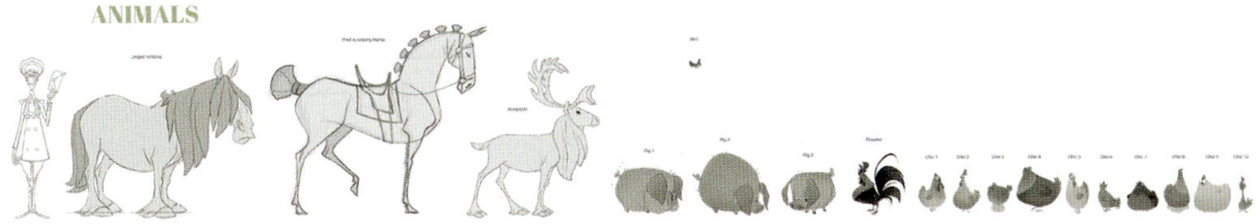

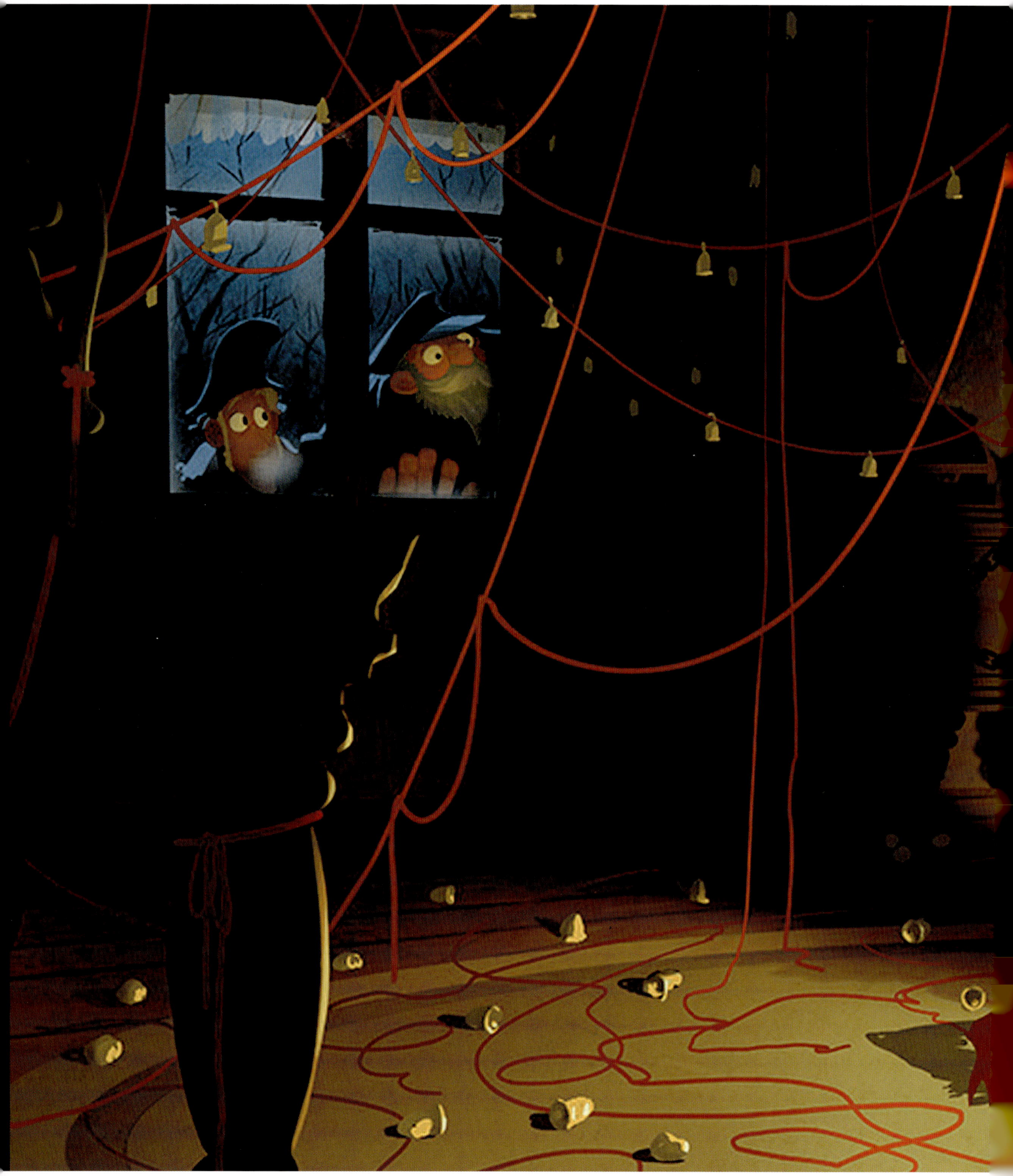

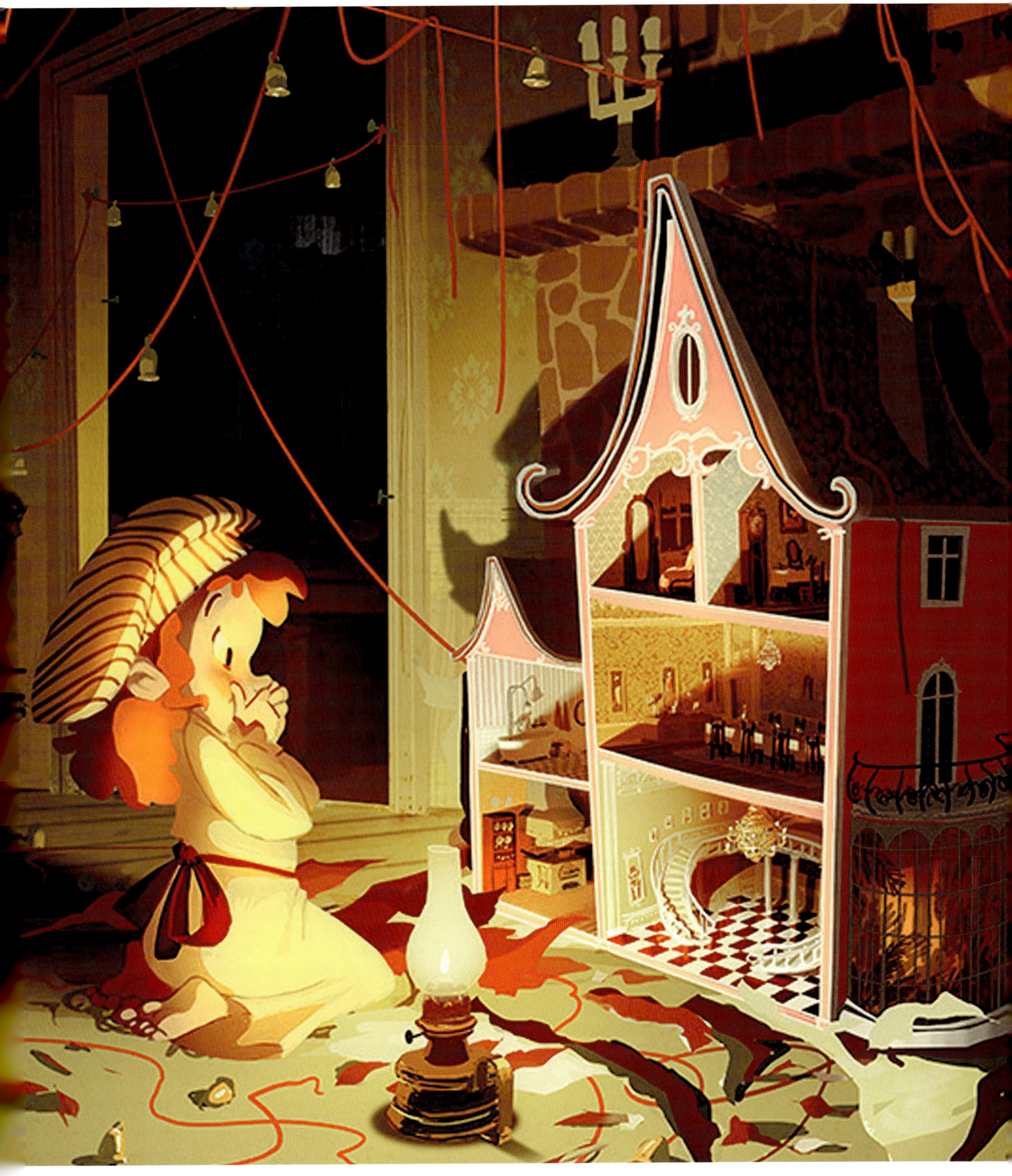

Anatomy of a Scene

THE CHRISTMAS PITCH

One of the key sequences and major turning points of the movie takes place about halfway through the script. The sequence begins with a few poetic and wordless images as we see Klaus chopping wood against the snow-covered landscape as the sun sets. It is here where we get a mystical sense of an otherworldly presence – the spirit of his late wife – looking after the old man. It's also a pivotal scene where Jesper comes up with the central conceit of the movie and tries to get Klaus onboard with his plan.

"It was a tricky scene in terms of storytelling, because we wanted to continue to develop the mystery of Klaus' past," recalls writer-director Sergio Pablos. "We also wanted to build this notion of the wind representing his wife's spirit. Meanwhile, we are at a place where we see Jesper trying to manipulate his friends and resorting to being the worst version of himself. It all had to come together in this sequence."

PREVIOUS SPREAD: Concept artwork by Marcin Jakubowski and Sergio Pablos.

THIS PAGE: Klaus is drawn back into the house by an otherworldly presence.

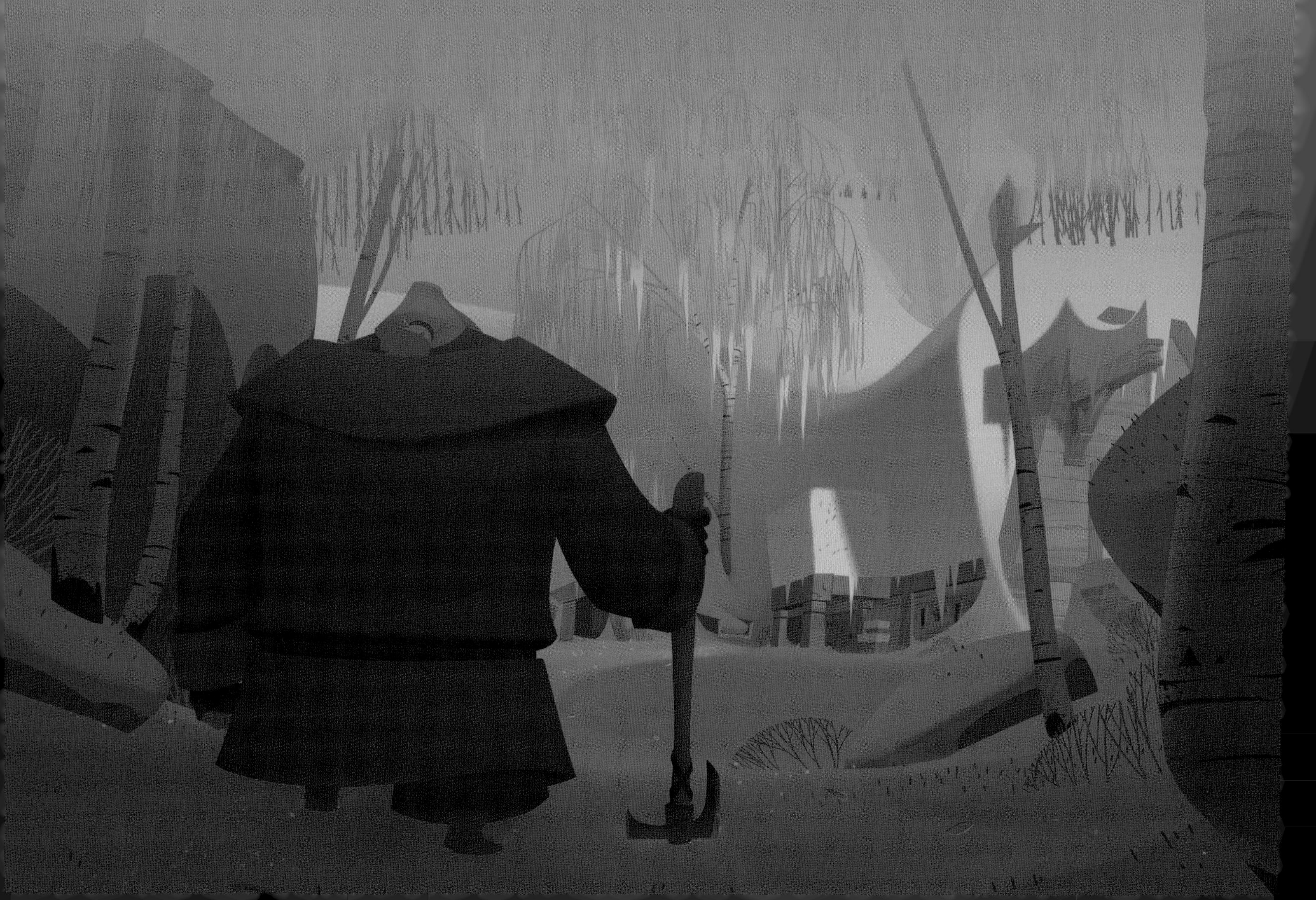

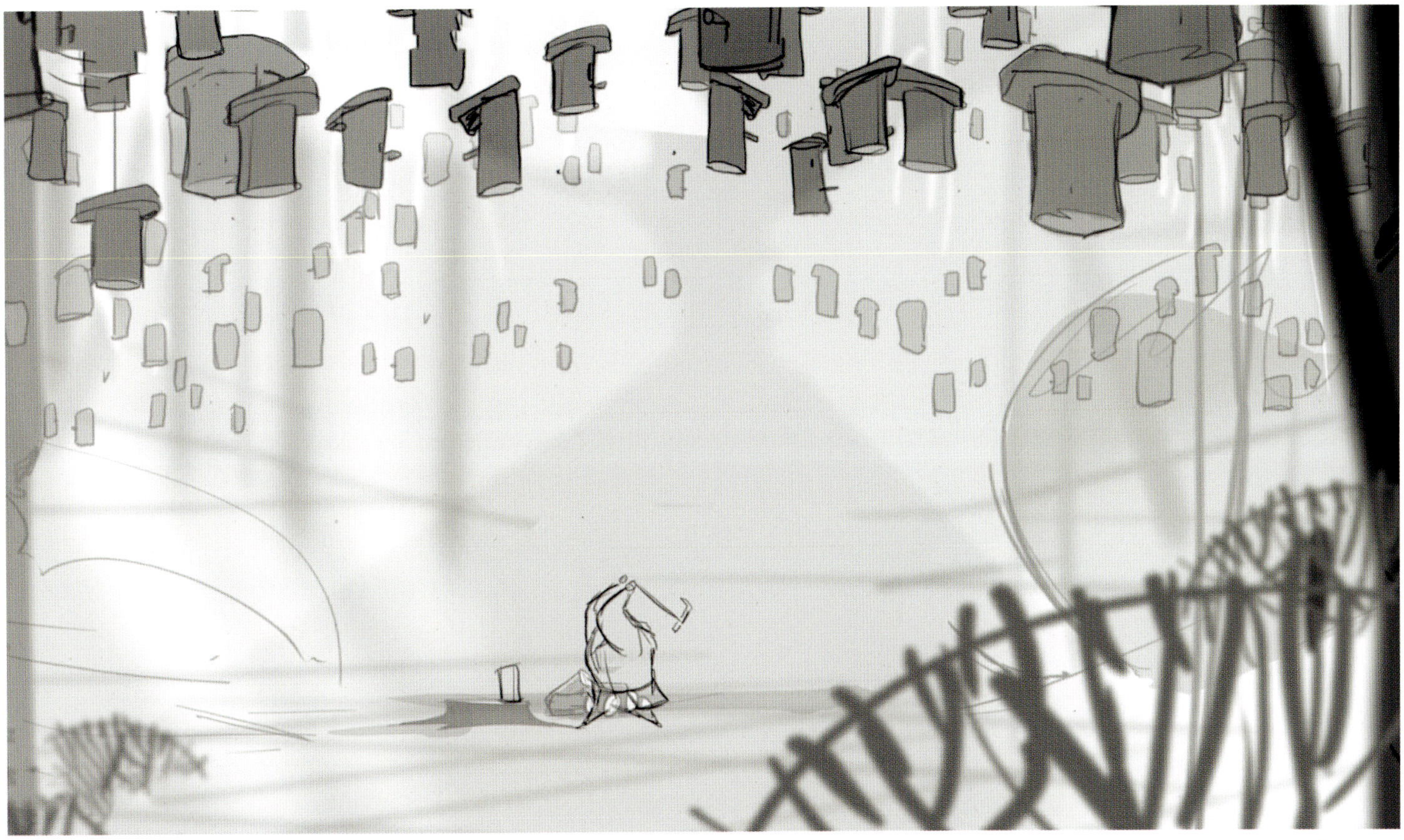

THIS PAGE: (ABOVE) Storyboard panel by Tom Sales; (BELOW) Color key by Daniel Merchán Ruiz.

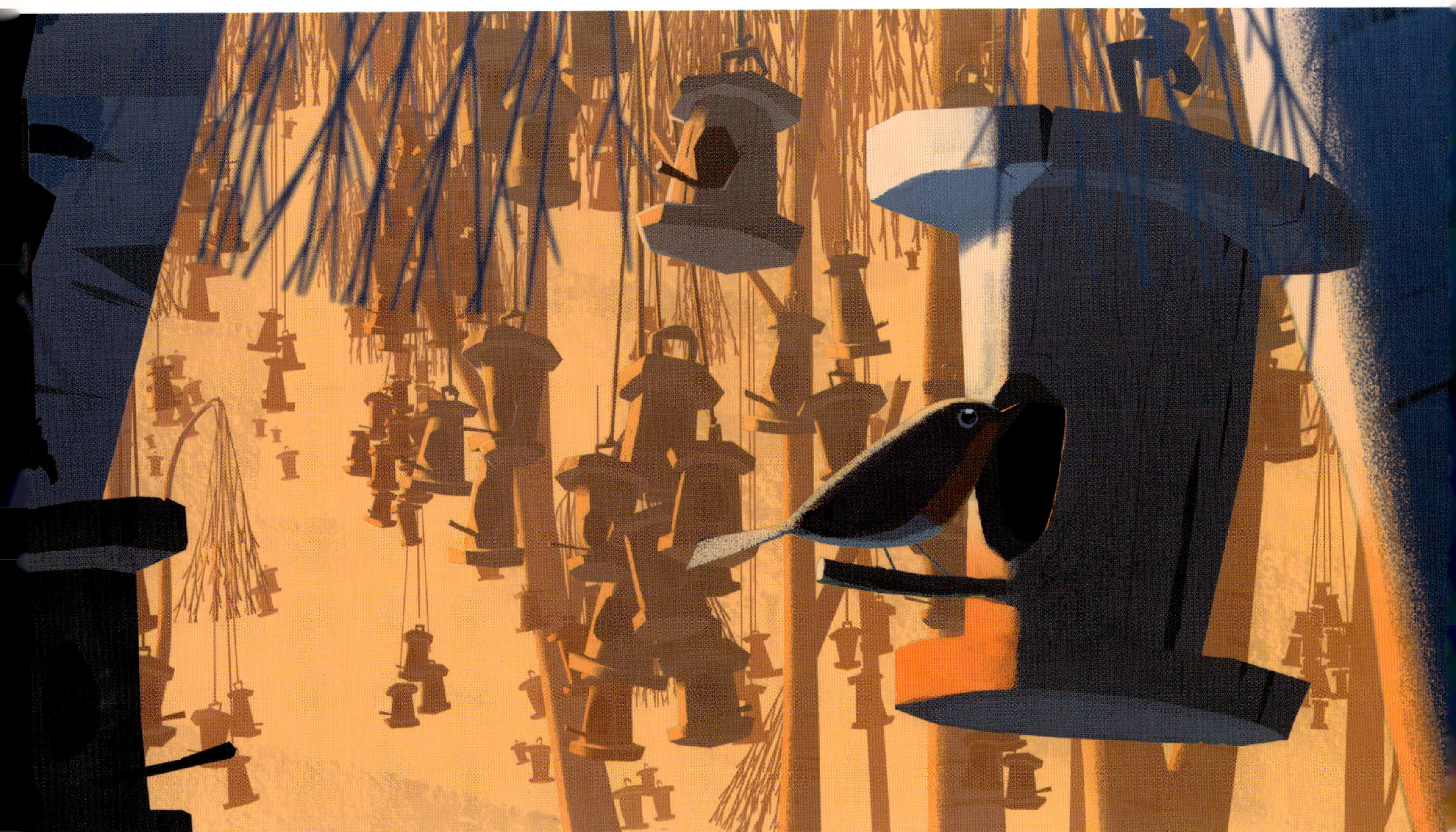

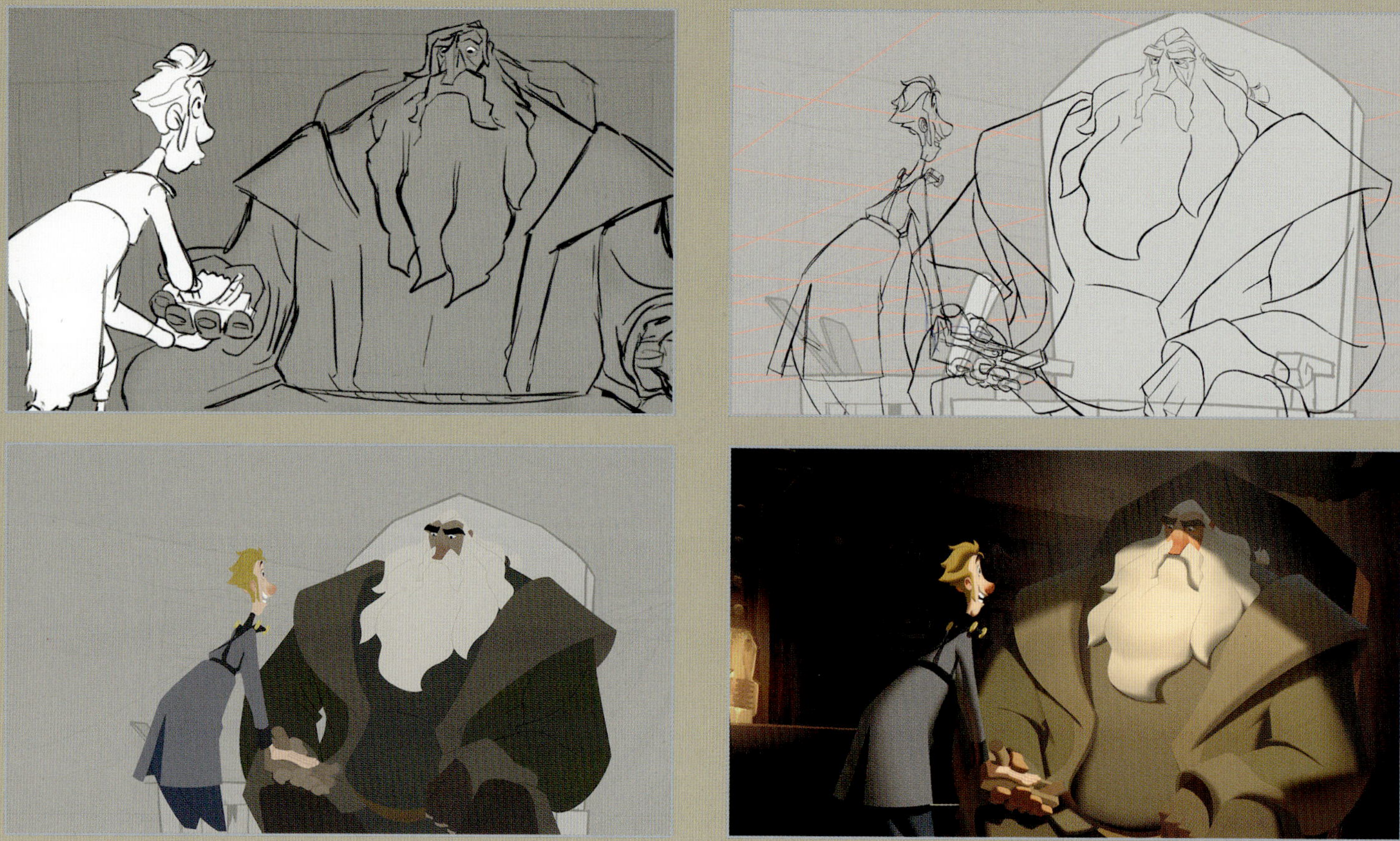

THIS PAGE: Multiple stages of one shot, where Jesper presents his pitch to Klaus.

Pablos says he is really proud of the way all the departments worked closely together to knock this sequence out of the park. "The animation, the lighting, the performances all came together. There is this richness and volumetric feeling that we only saw before in CG-animated movies," he points out. "You see the characters cross paths as they each develop within their own arcs. And you also begin to ask questions about Klaus' past... what happened to him that was so painful?"

As SPA's head of light and shadow Florian Aupetit explains, "This scene is a key point in the relationship between Klaus and Jesper, as it gives you a glimpse of Klaus' past. It's also a rollercoaster of emotions, as you go from hope, to happiness, then to anger and sadness in a very short period of time. We had to fine-tune the lighting on the characters, and our biggest challenge was determining the color keys and deciding the best mood for the Christmas pitch. We had to remove realistic logic in the scene, because it was more theatrical. The lighting came from the roof, and it needed to have this magical quality. Then, as Jesper acts in front of Klaus, showing his ideas for Christmas, we adapted the lighting to the story."

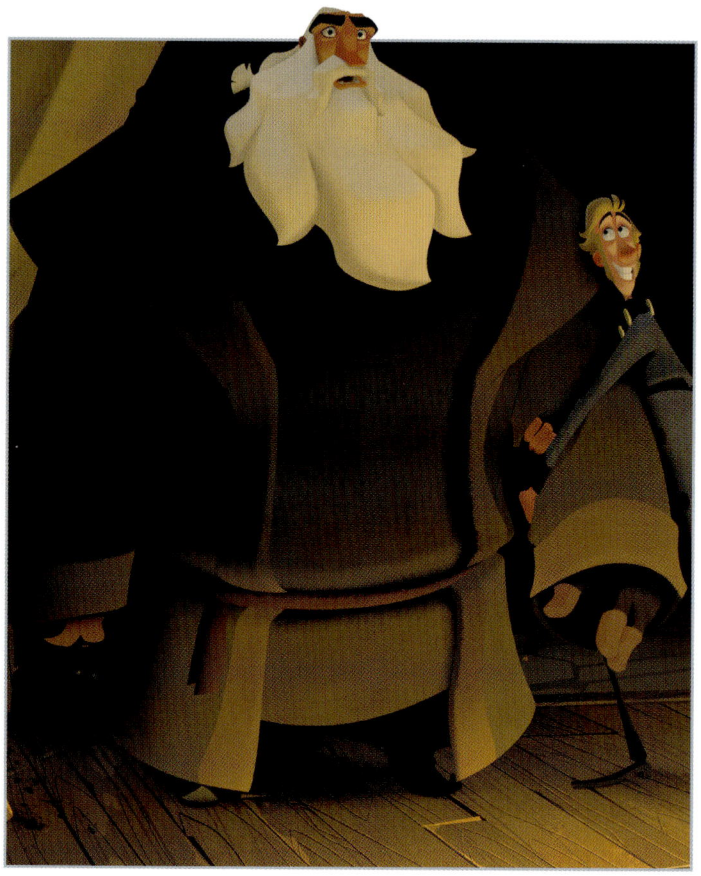

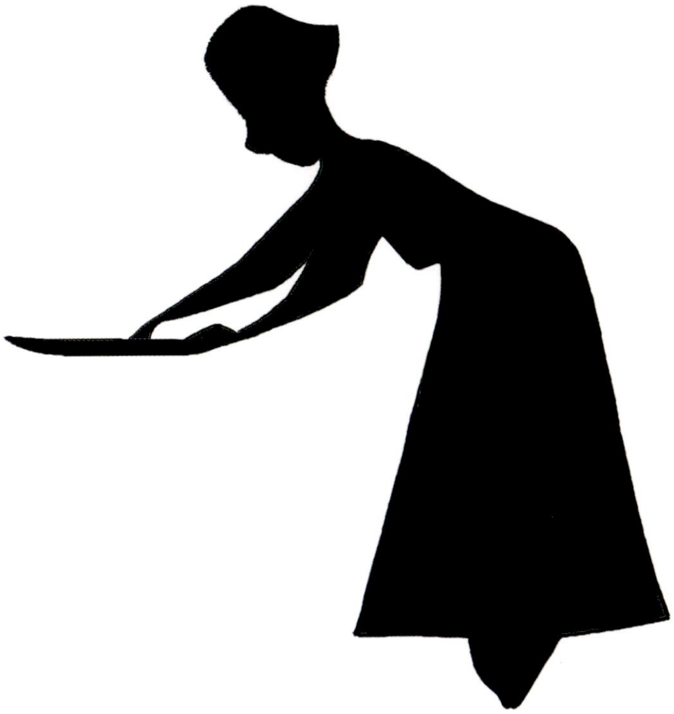

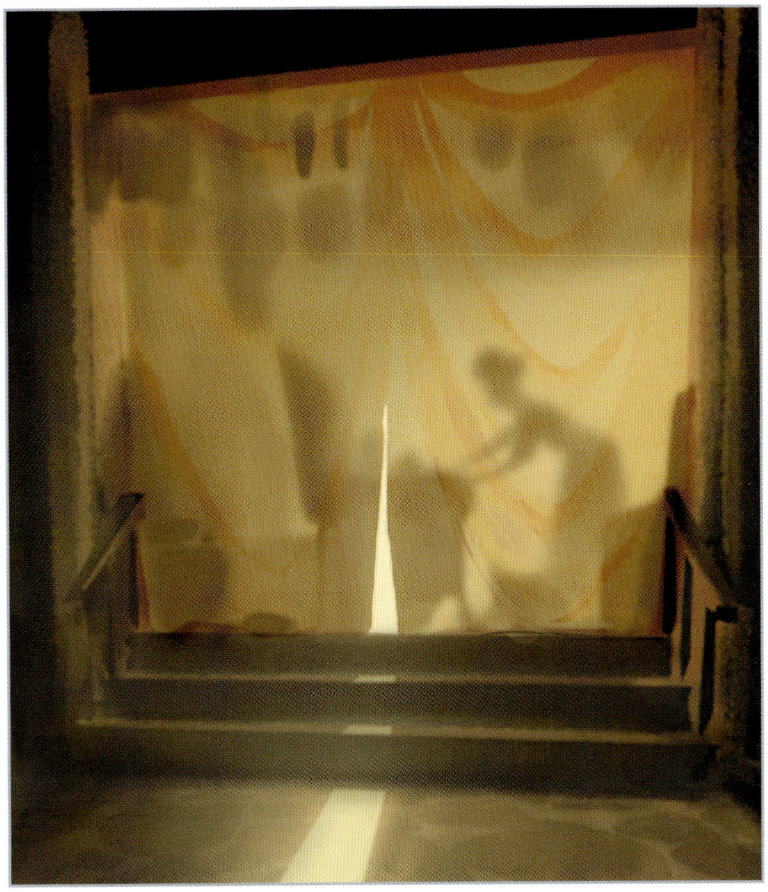

THIS PAGE: (ABOVE) Animators had to find an angle where Jesper's silhouette could be mistaken for Lydia's; (RIGHT) Artwork by Marcin Jakubowski; (BELOW) Jesper presents his Christmas pitch.

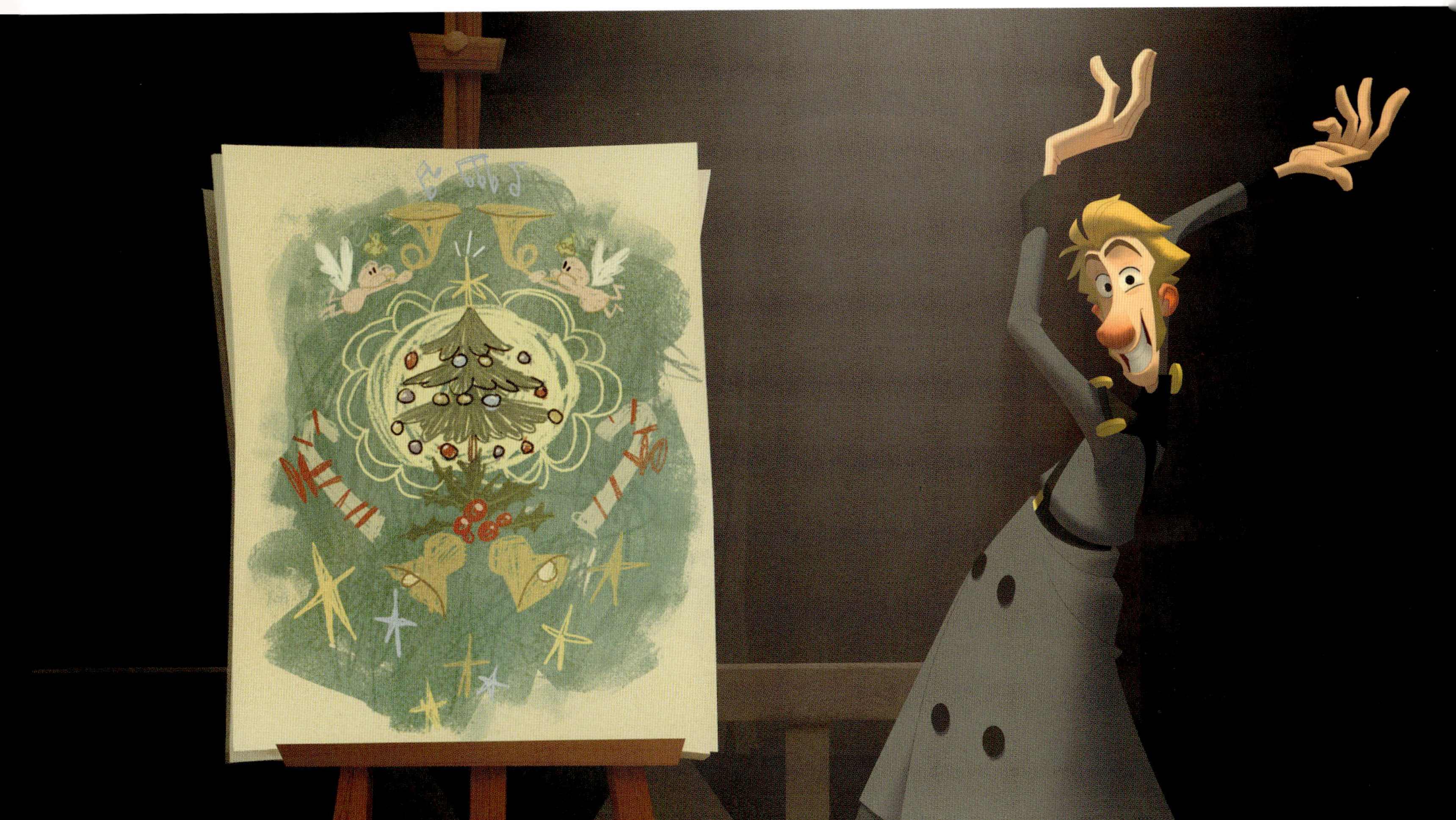

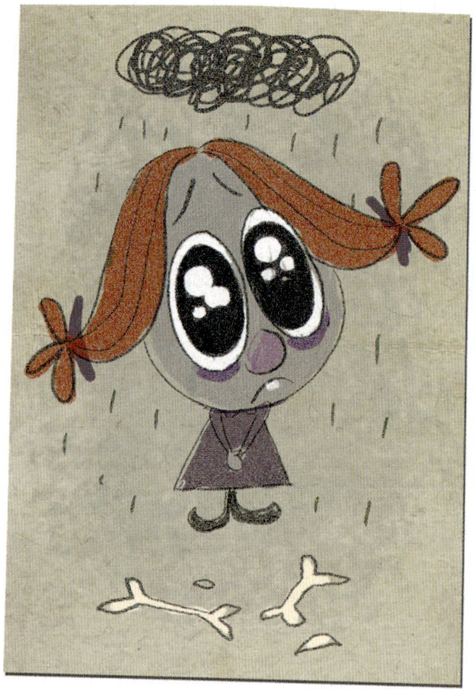

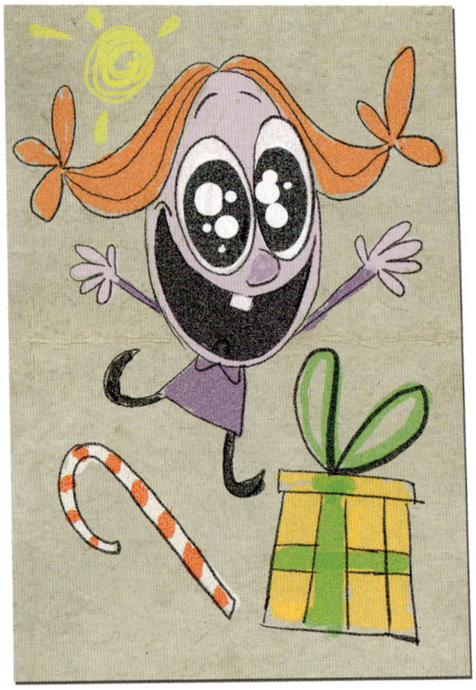

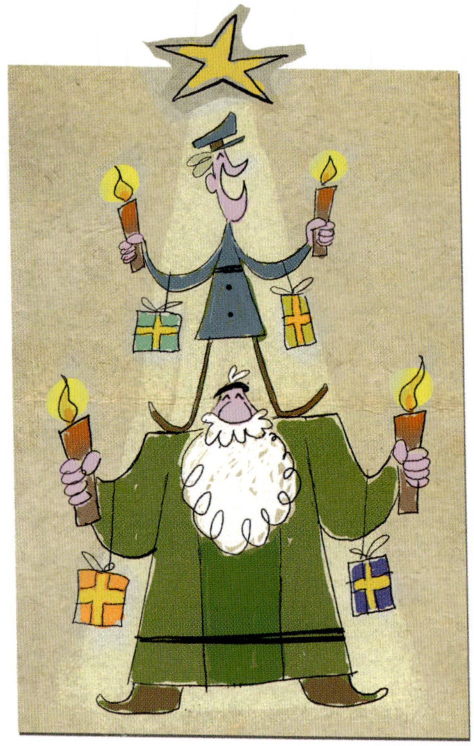

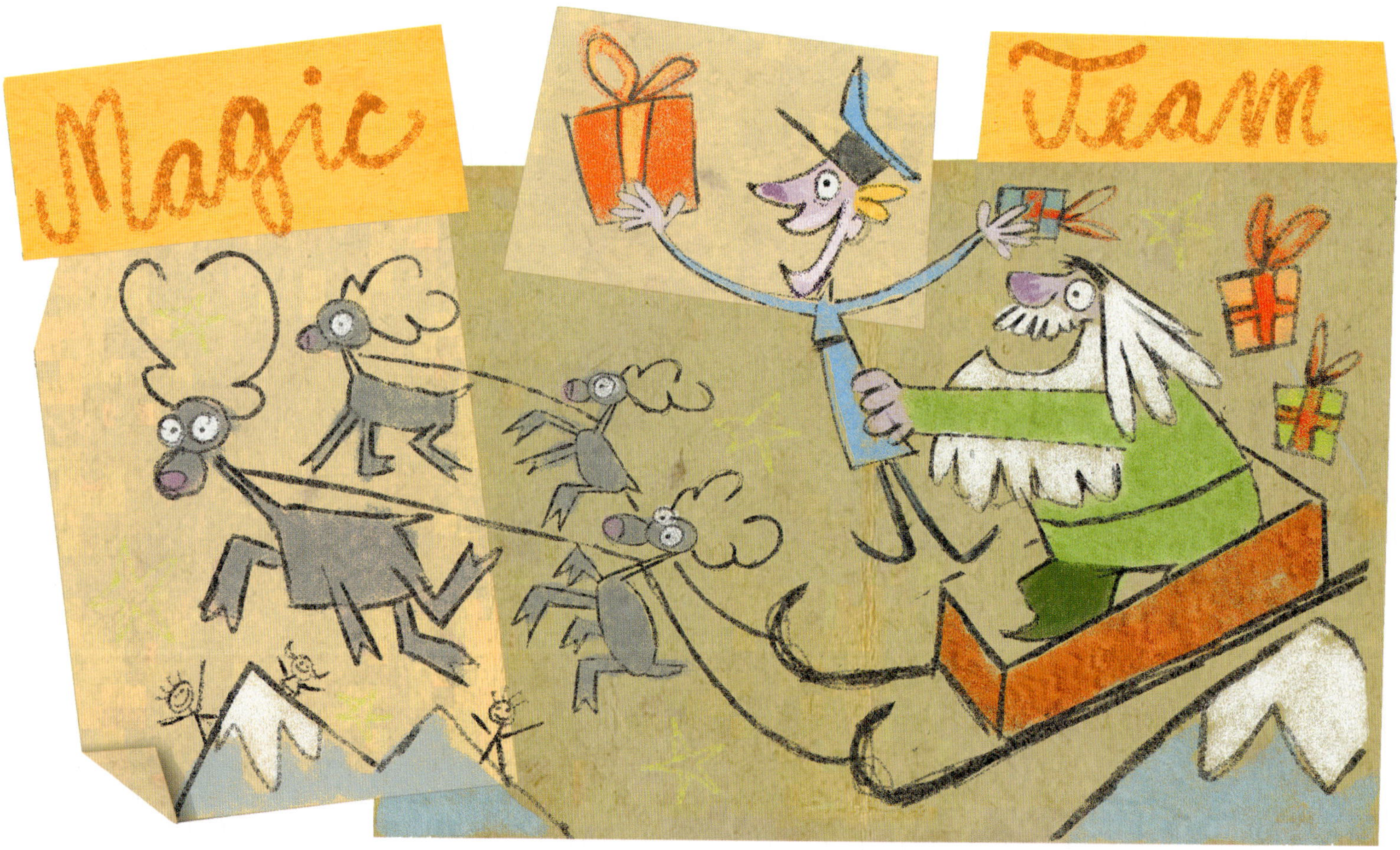

THIS PAGE: Drawings for Jesper's pitch by Torsten Schrank.

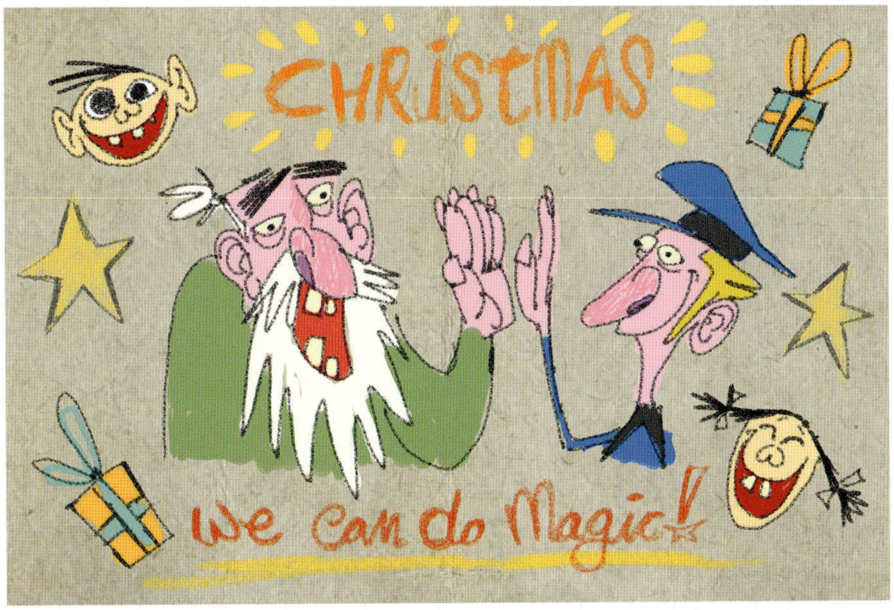
CHRISTMAS
we can do Magic!

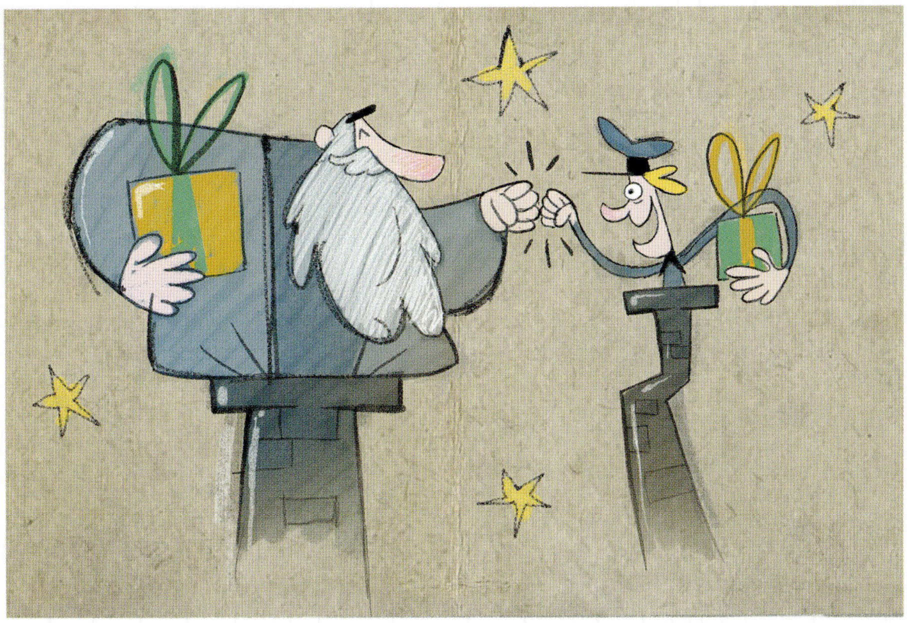

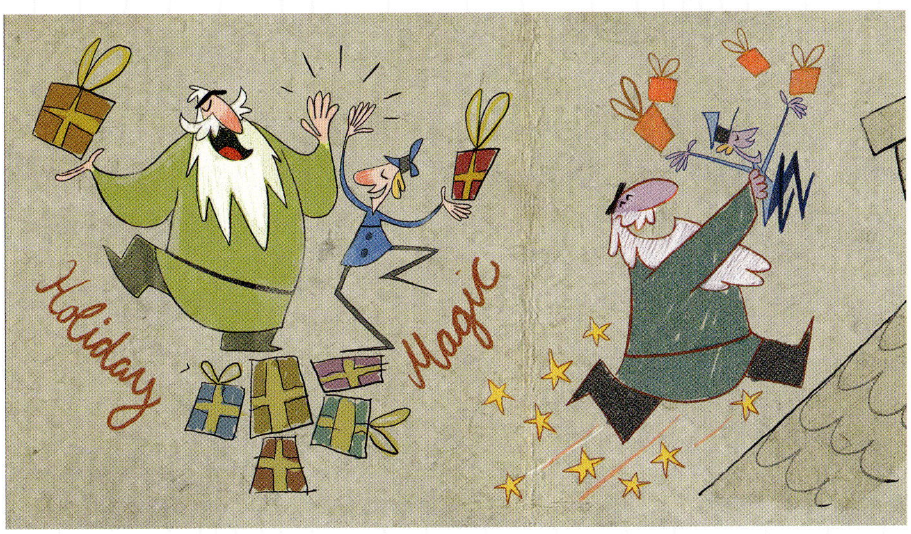
Holiday Magic

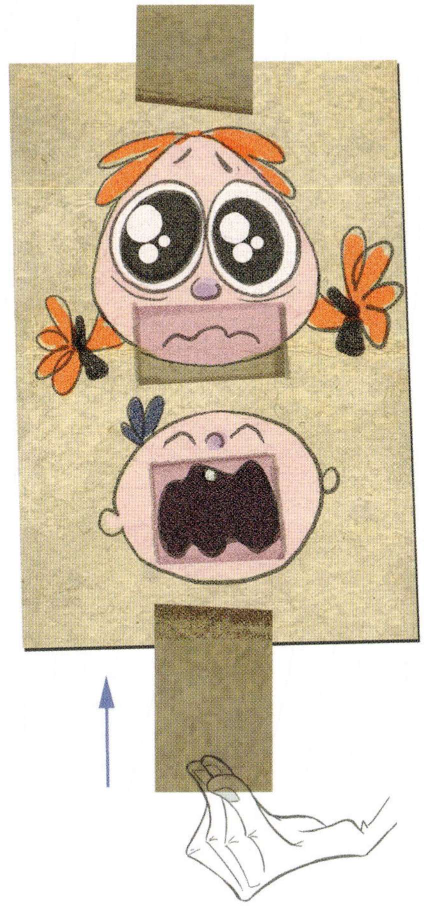

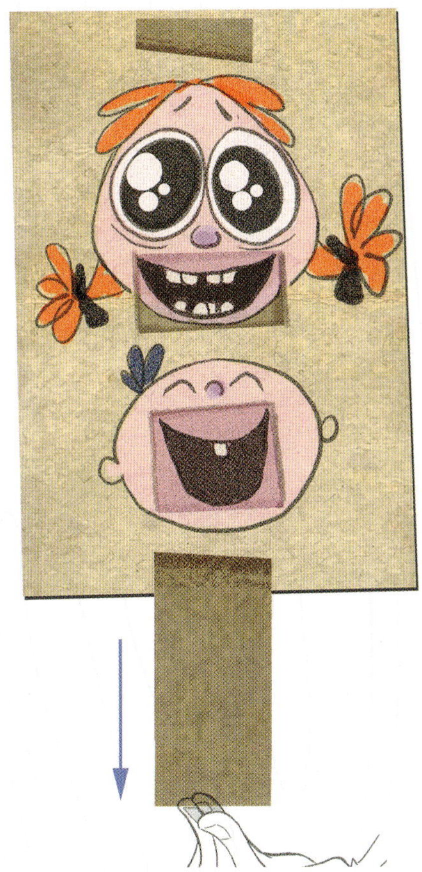

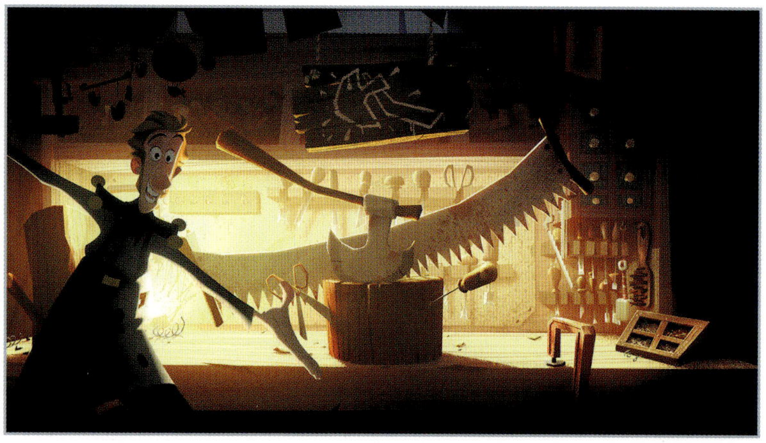

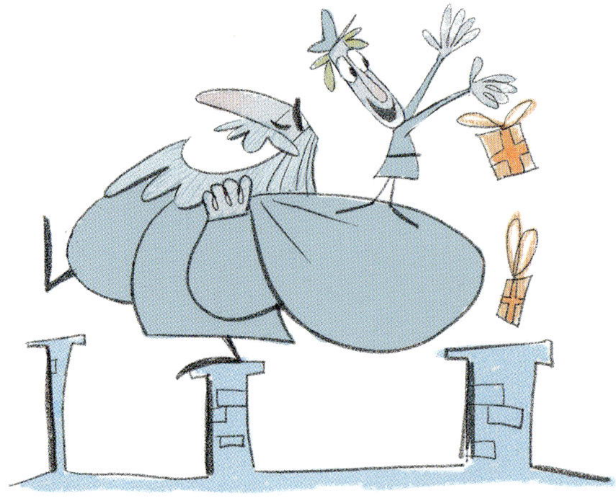

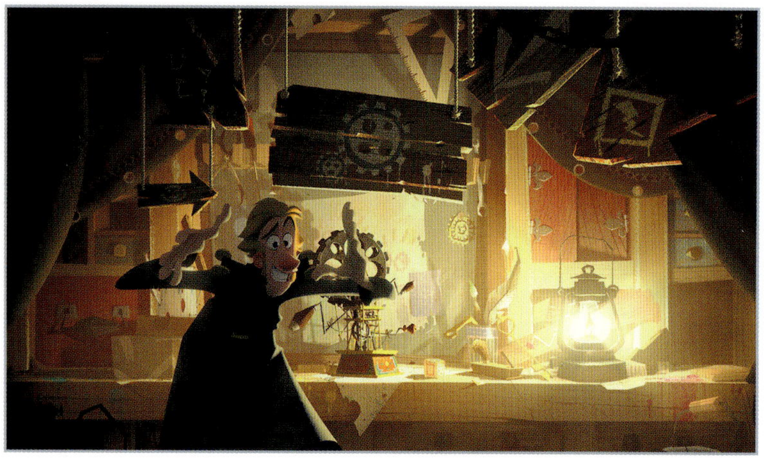

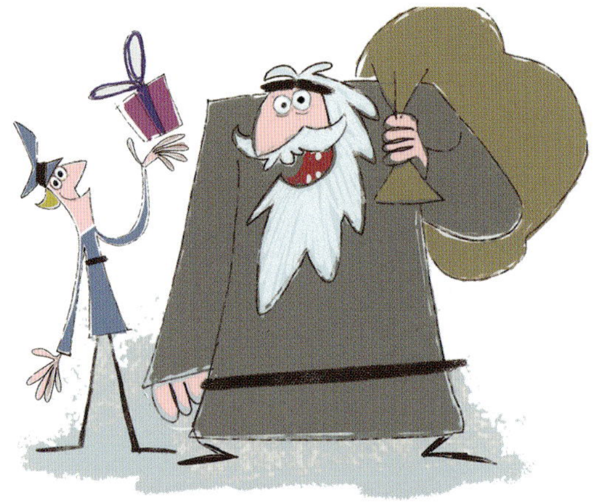

THIS PAGE: Klaus watches, bemused, as Jesper shows him his plans for a new workshop; (TOP RIGHT) Images by Torsten Schrank.

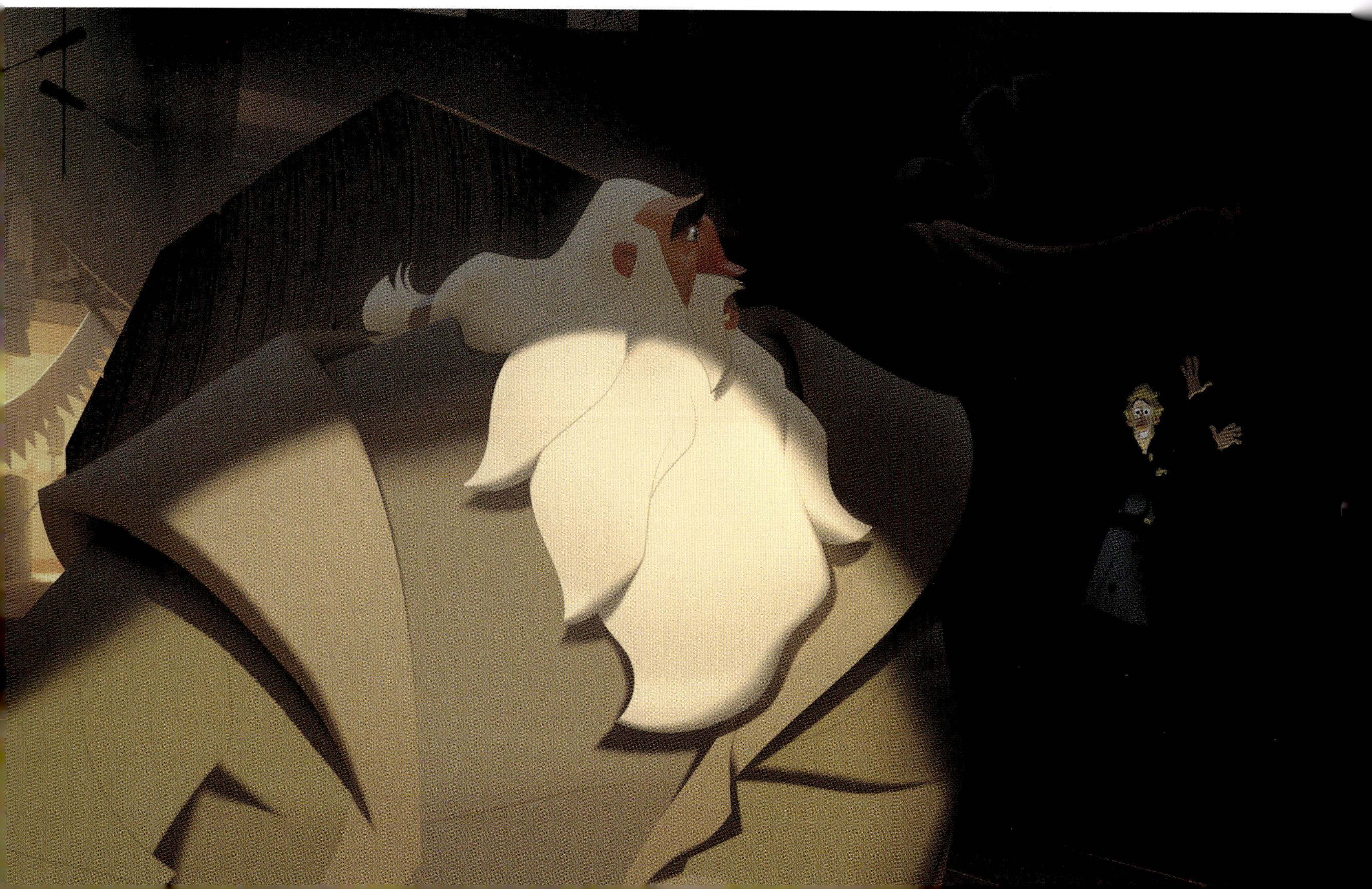

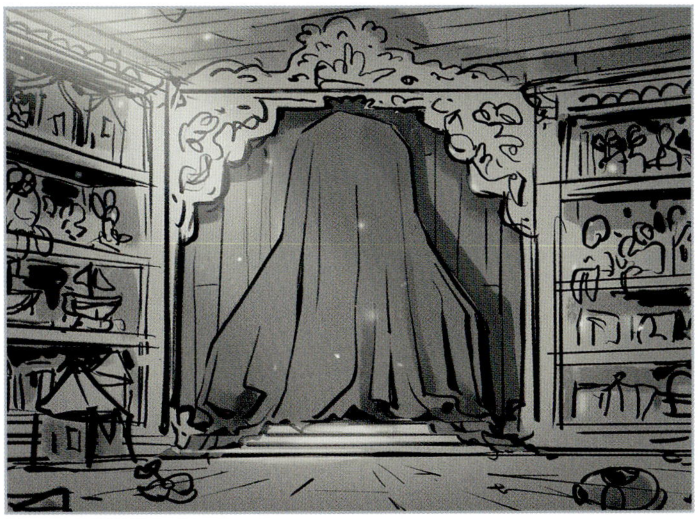

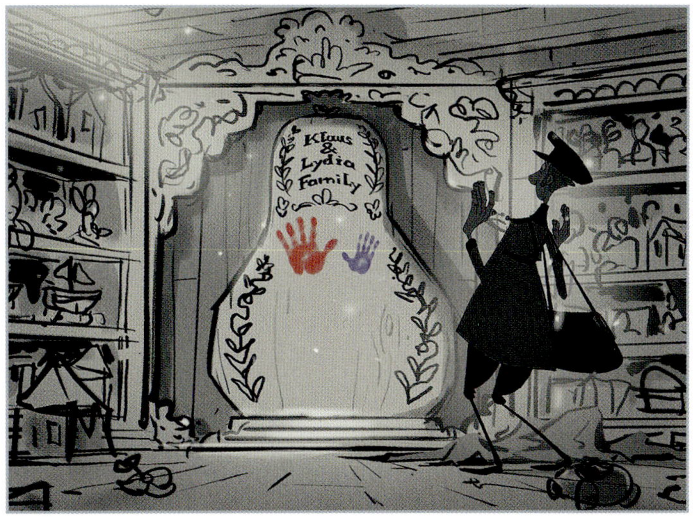

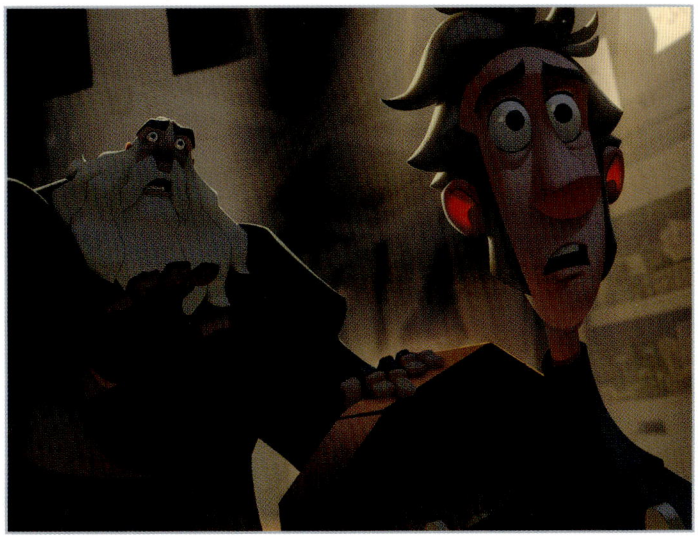

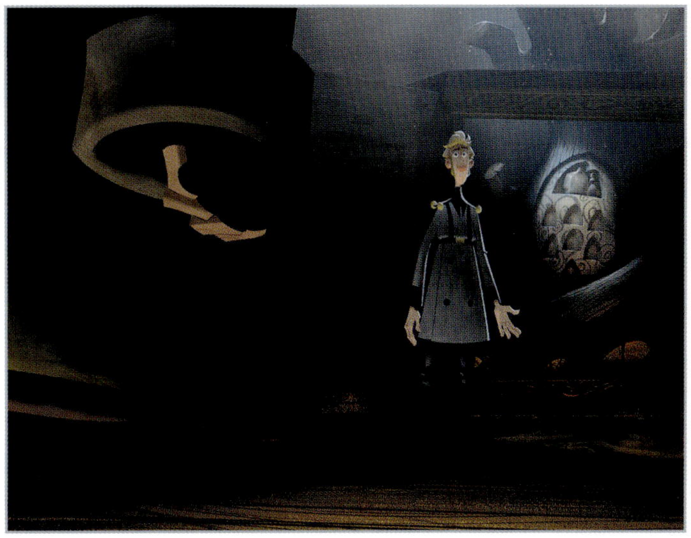

ABOVE: Jesper discovers the empty tree carving, to Klaus' dismay. Artwork by Arthus Pilorget.

The sequence involves three key locations – the chopping pit, the barn, and the interior of the barn. Each environment had to be designed and colored for the screen to create an atmosphere to furnish the specific needs of the narrative. As head of layout Armen Melkonian explains, "The sets were conformed and rearranged differently from other sequences that used the same locations to fit the story specifics. For example, Klaus' barn had to be redesigned to resemble a temple where he imagines a reunion with his deceased wife. The sets had to be colored, scaled, and lit in a way [that would] convince the audience when Klaus mistakes Jesper's silhouette for his wife's. The chopping pit was also reworked to create a sanctuary environment for Klaus. This was quite different from how it was presented in previous sequences."

For effects lead Silke Czarny, the scene had its share of challenges, one being how to visualize the ethereal quality of the wind blowing around Klaus. "Although the character interaction is at the center of this sequence, it all begins with the wind luring Klaus back to this house, and leading him to the encounter with Jesper," notes Czarny. "The difficulty with the wind is that it is a physical effect, but it is also magical. So, it has to have the appearance of intent, as if it has its own personality. Which is the case, because the wind is the medium through which the ghost of Klaus' wife, Lydia, can communicate with him."

Czarny says the hand-animated style of the film really helped the team deliver the mood they were searching for. "It gives it a light, ethereal feel by using soft brush strokes and then adding snow particles and leaves that get carried along with it," she notes. "The smooth flow of the wind was another very important part of the equation. Any movement that was too ragged would destroy the illusion of this natural motion. All of these details made the wind scenes some of the most time-consuming to animate for the effects team. But when you see the final product, you realize that it was all worth it."

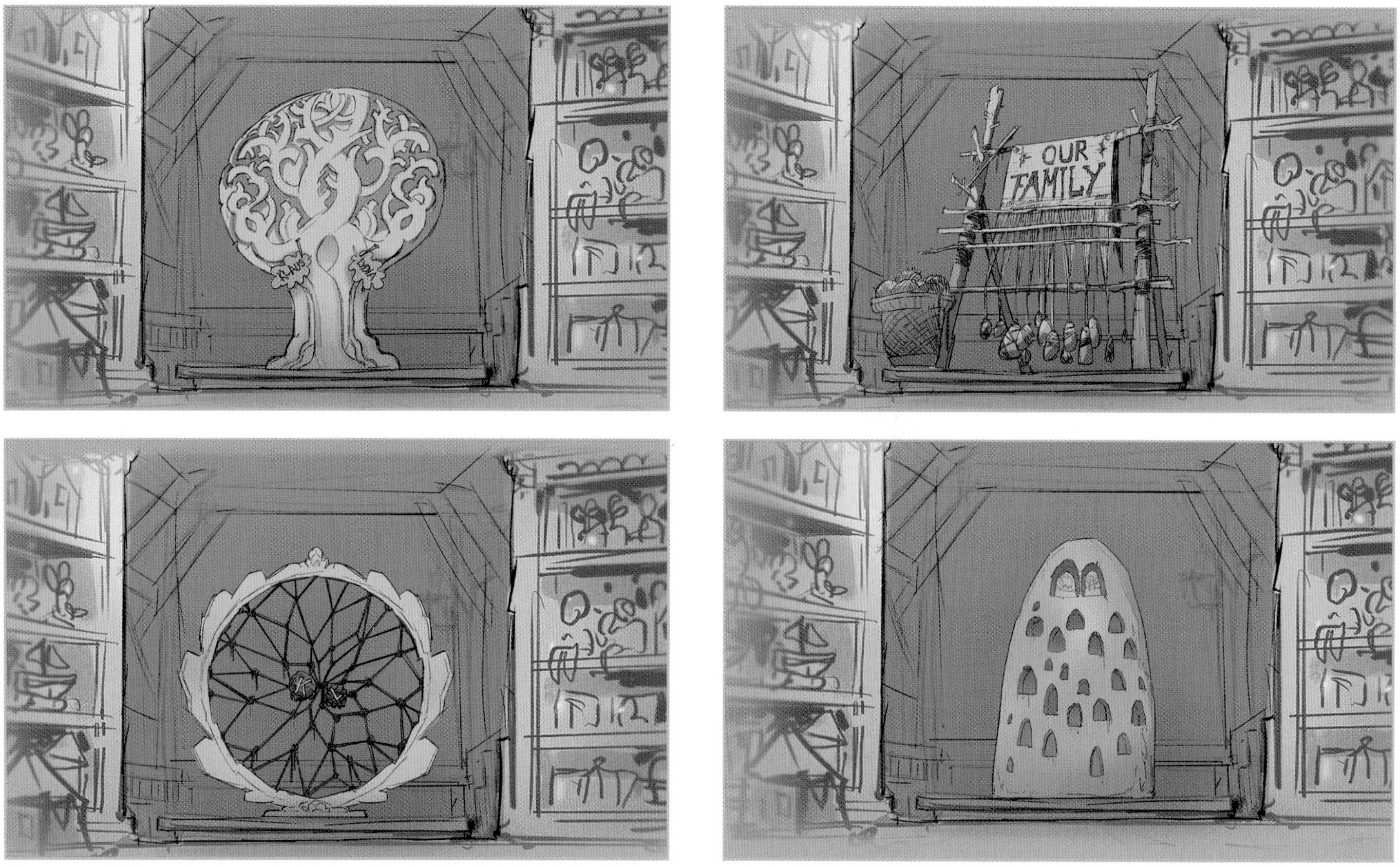

THIS PAGE: (ABOVE) Variant tree carvings by Tobi Trebeljahr; (BELOW) By Gabriel Gomez.

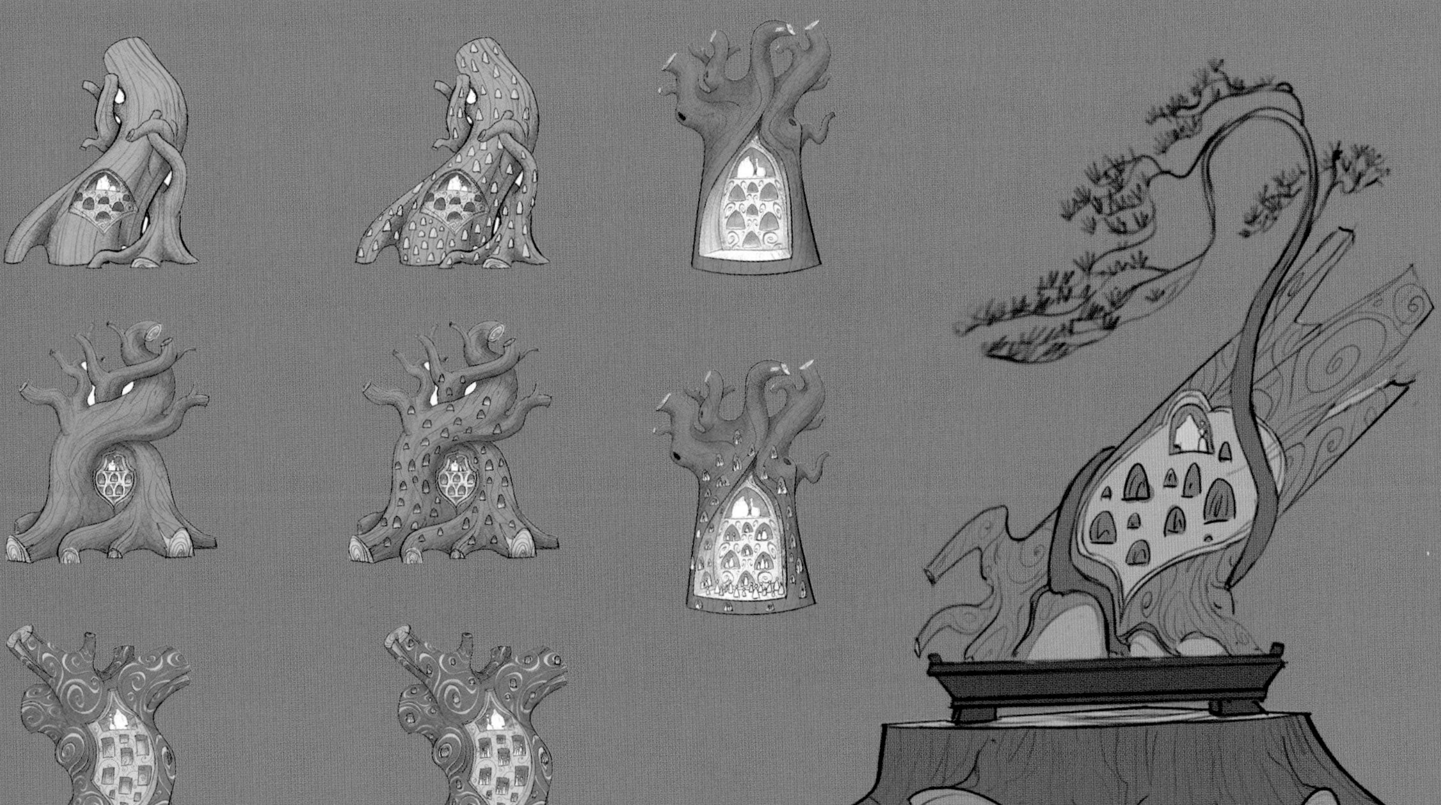

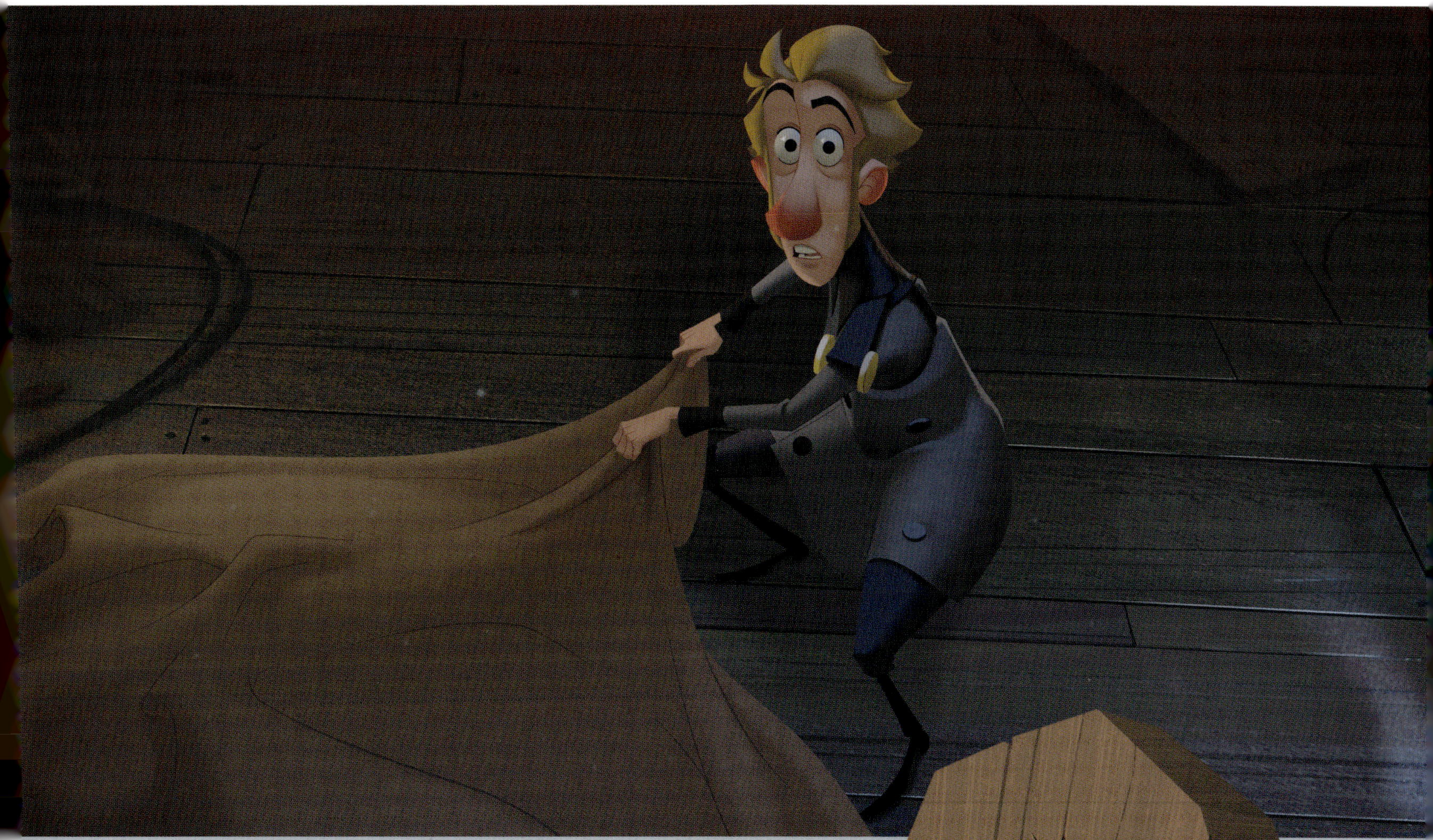

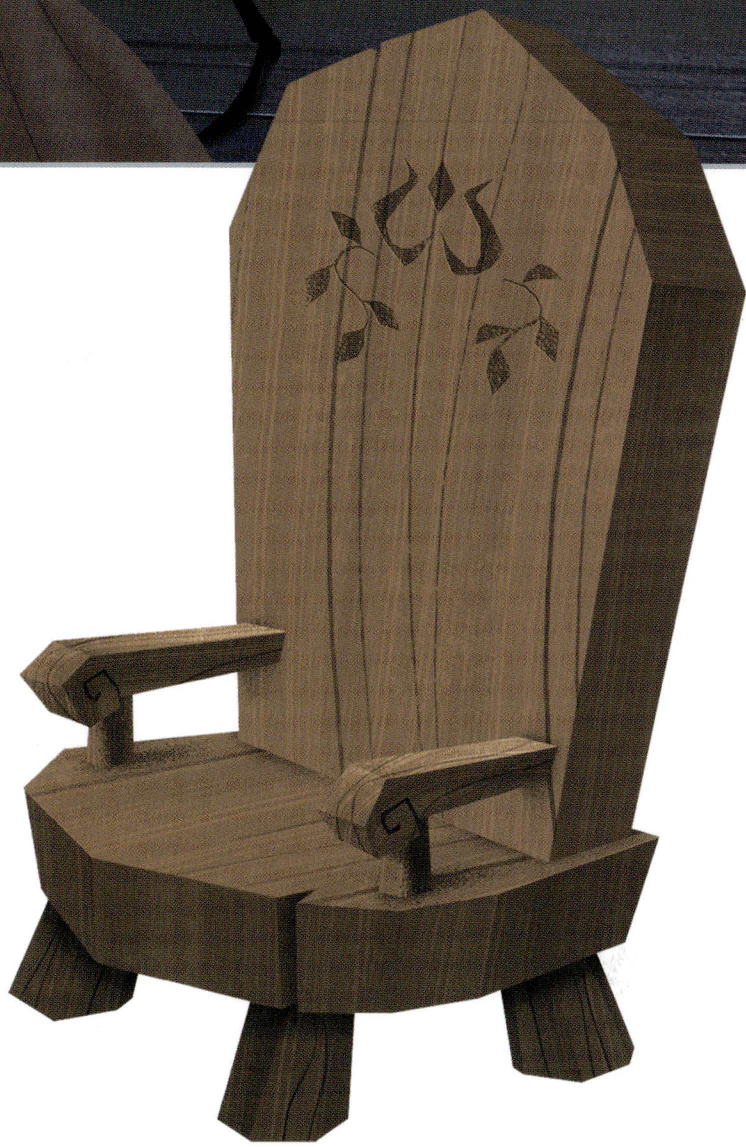

"One of our biggest challenges was determining the color keys and deciding the lighting and mood for the Christmas pitch. We had to remove the realistic logic we were following. The scene's lighting needed to feel theatrical and magical."

Florian Aupetit, Head of Lighting

THIS PAGE: Klaus' confusion and sadness turns to anger as Jesper discovers his empty wood carving.

SPA Studios

ADVANCING TRADITIONAL ANIMATION

Sergio Pablos and his team of 250 employees at SPA Studios were keen to pick up traditional animation where it had left off in the 1990s, when Disney, Pixar, and DreamWorks began to invest most of their creativity and innovation into developing a good-looking CG pipeline. "It was always the same pipeline and the same style, and it had stopped trying to evolve for a while," says Pablos. "I always felt like traditional animation should keep evolving, it should keep being pushed forward. So the aesthetic [of the movie] comes from discovering what we can add to the traditional animation pipeline by incorporating today's tools, ingenuity, and creativity to make it look different."

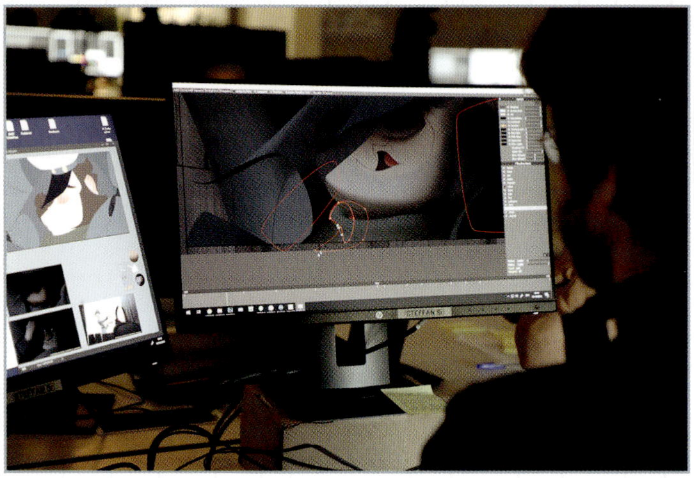

BELOW: Concept by Marcin Jakubowski.

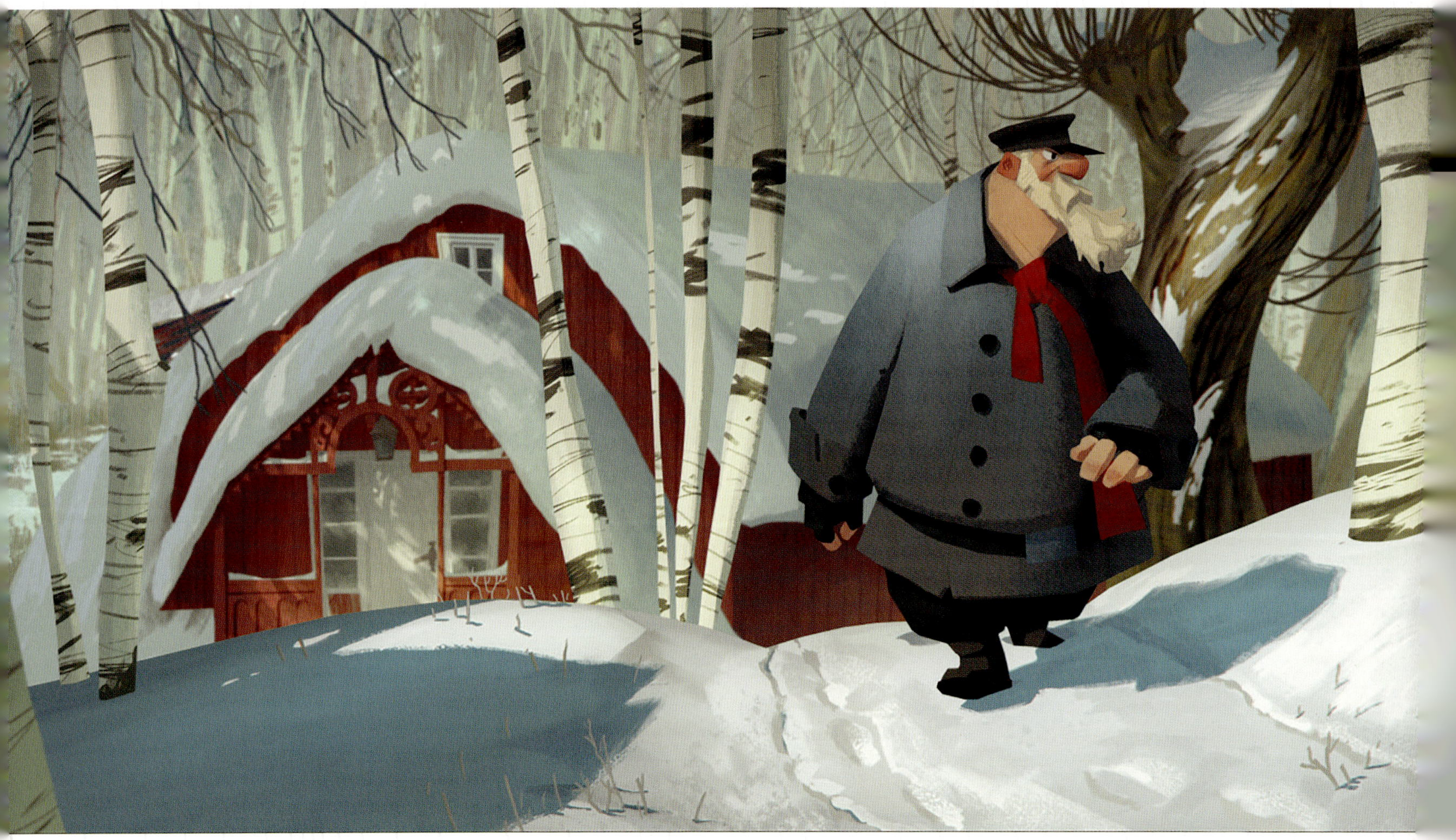

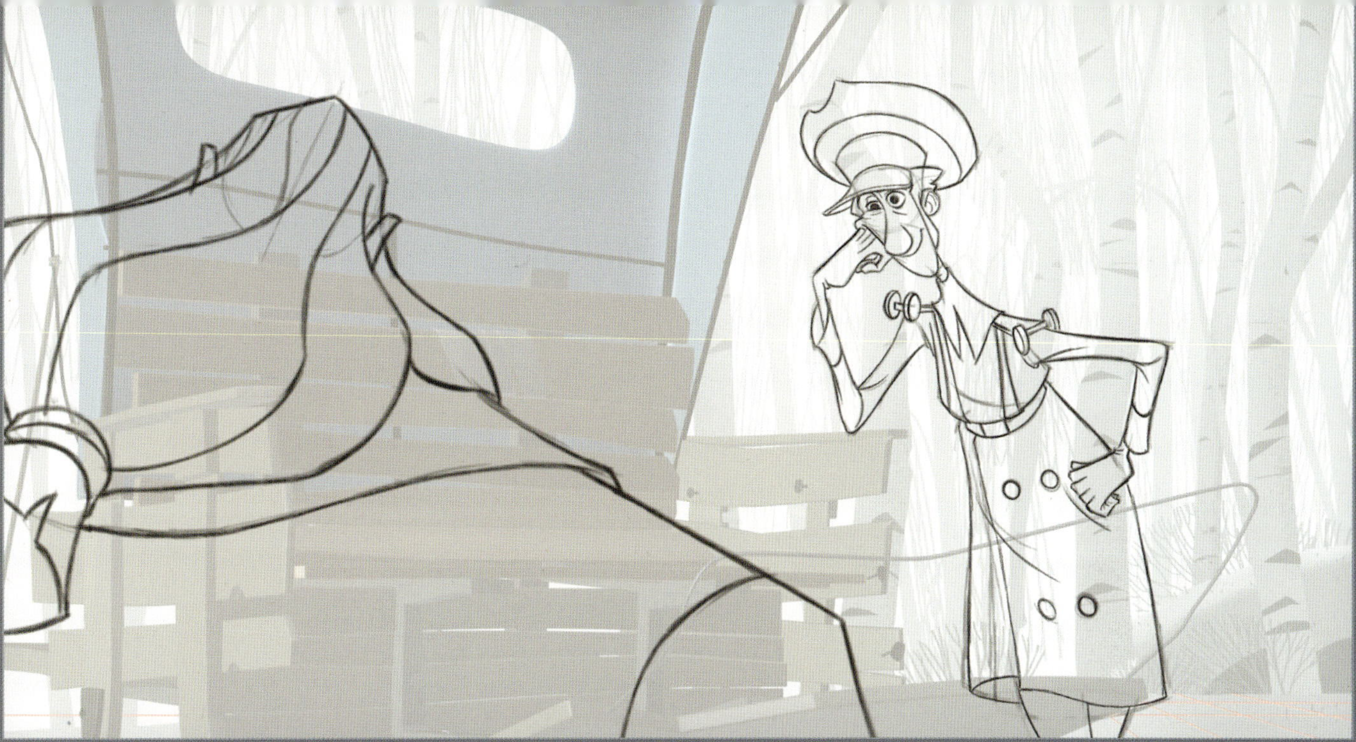

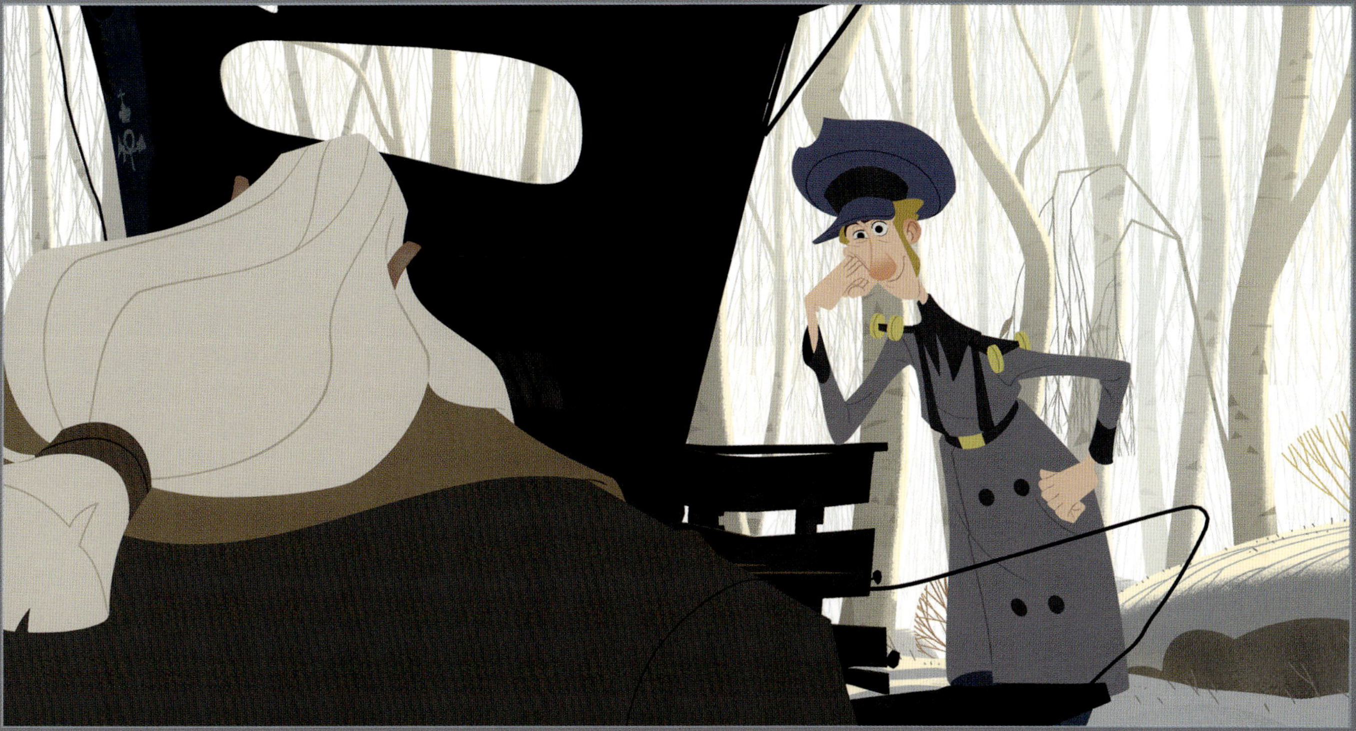

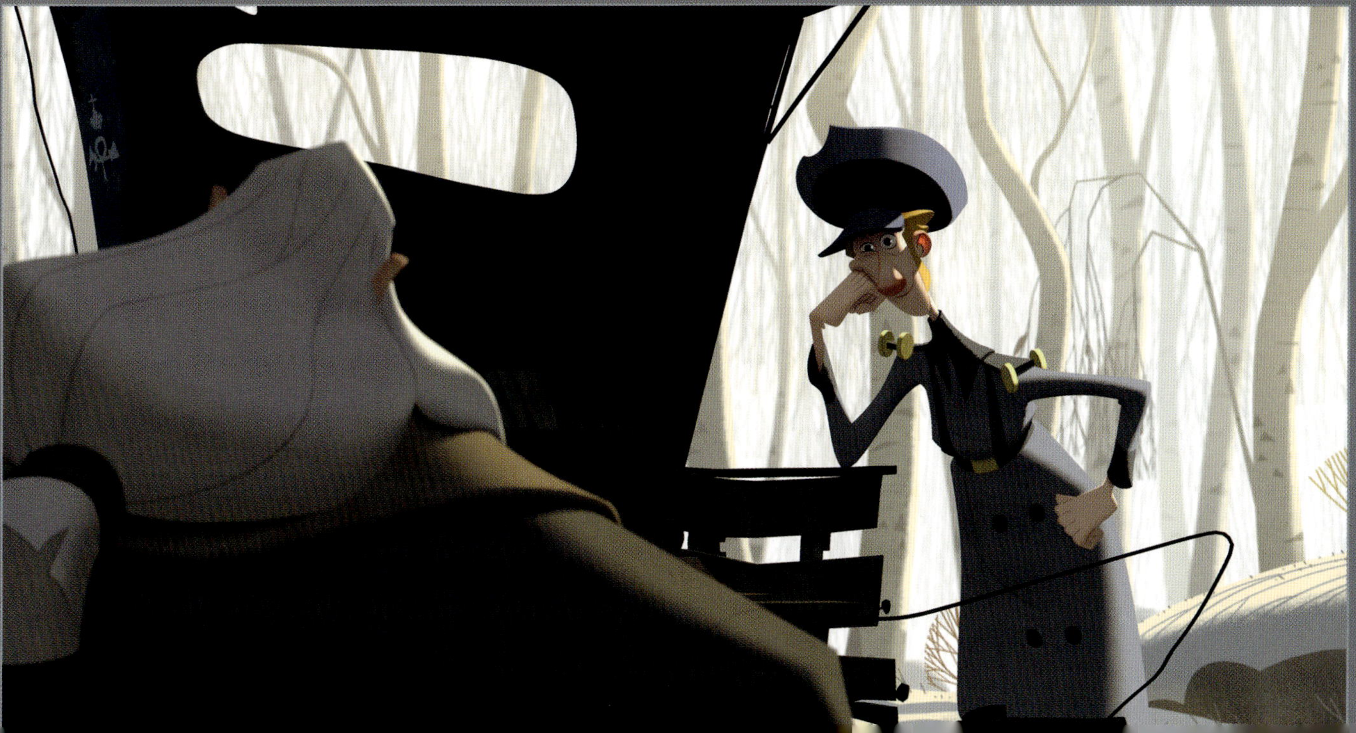

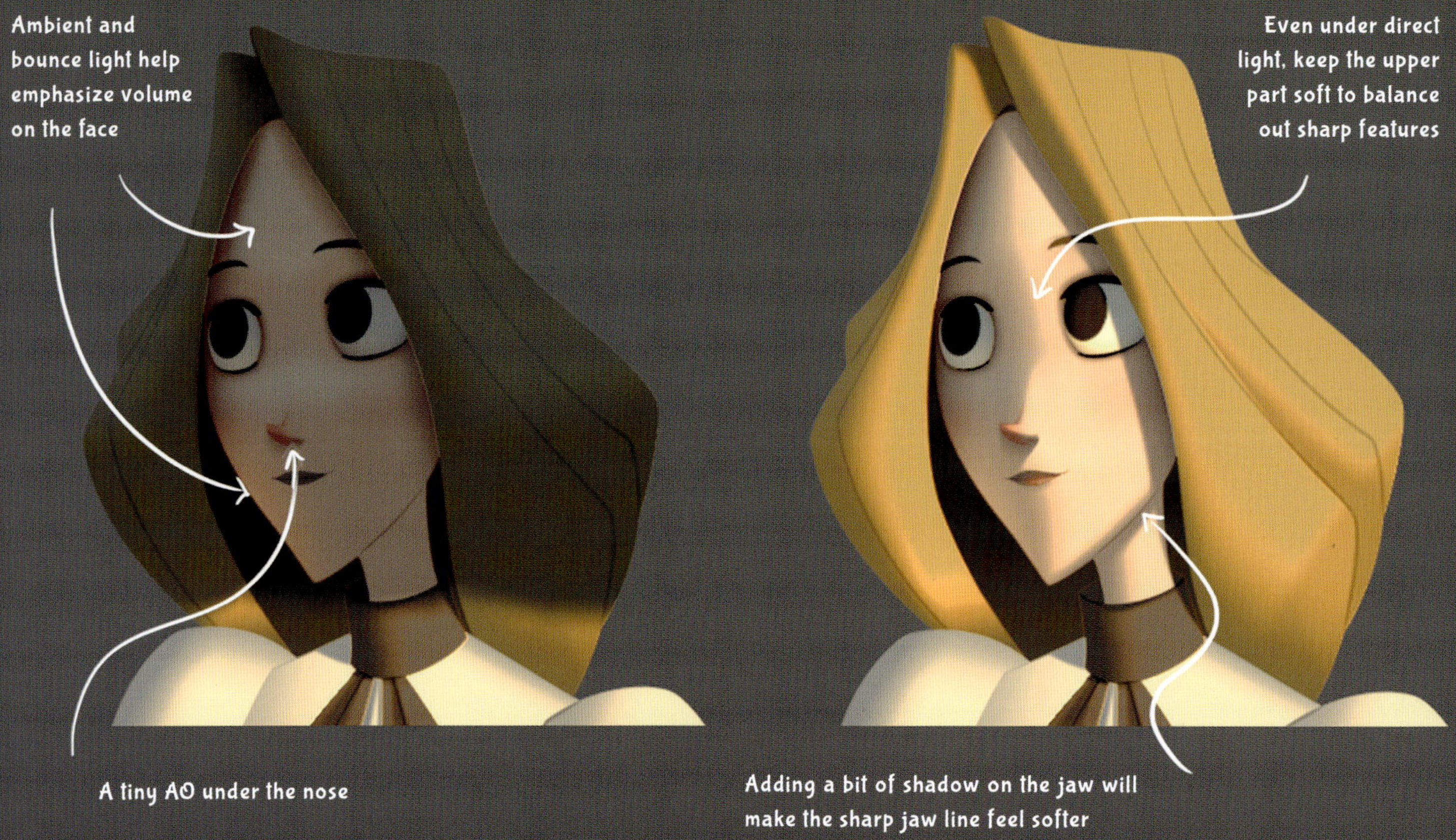
Ambient and bounce light help emphasize volume on the face
Even under direct light, keep the upper part soft to balance out sharp features
A tiny AO under the nose
Adding a bit of shadow on the jaw will make the sharp jaw line feel softer

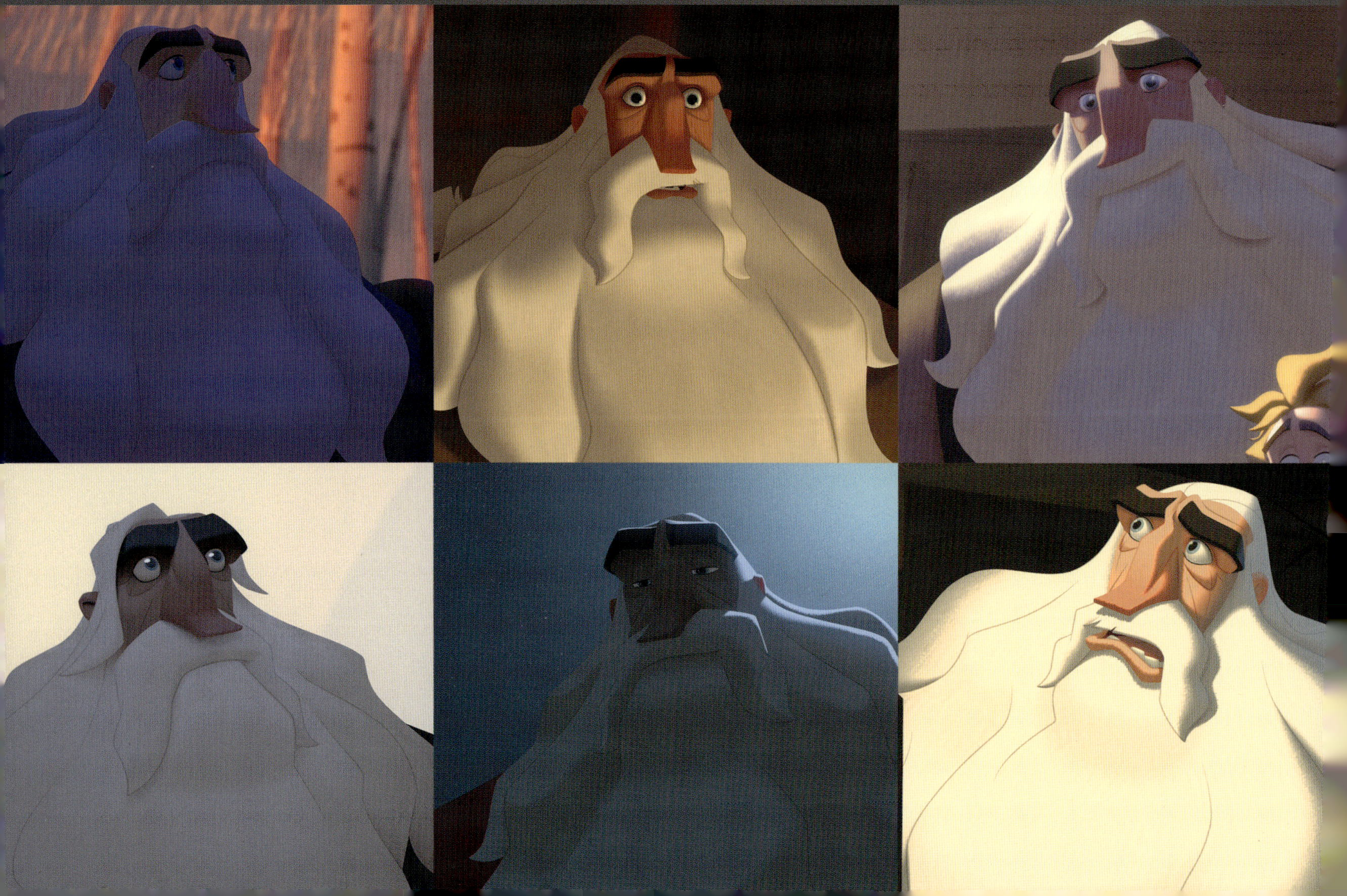

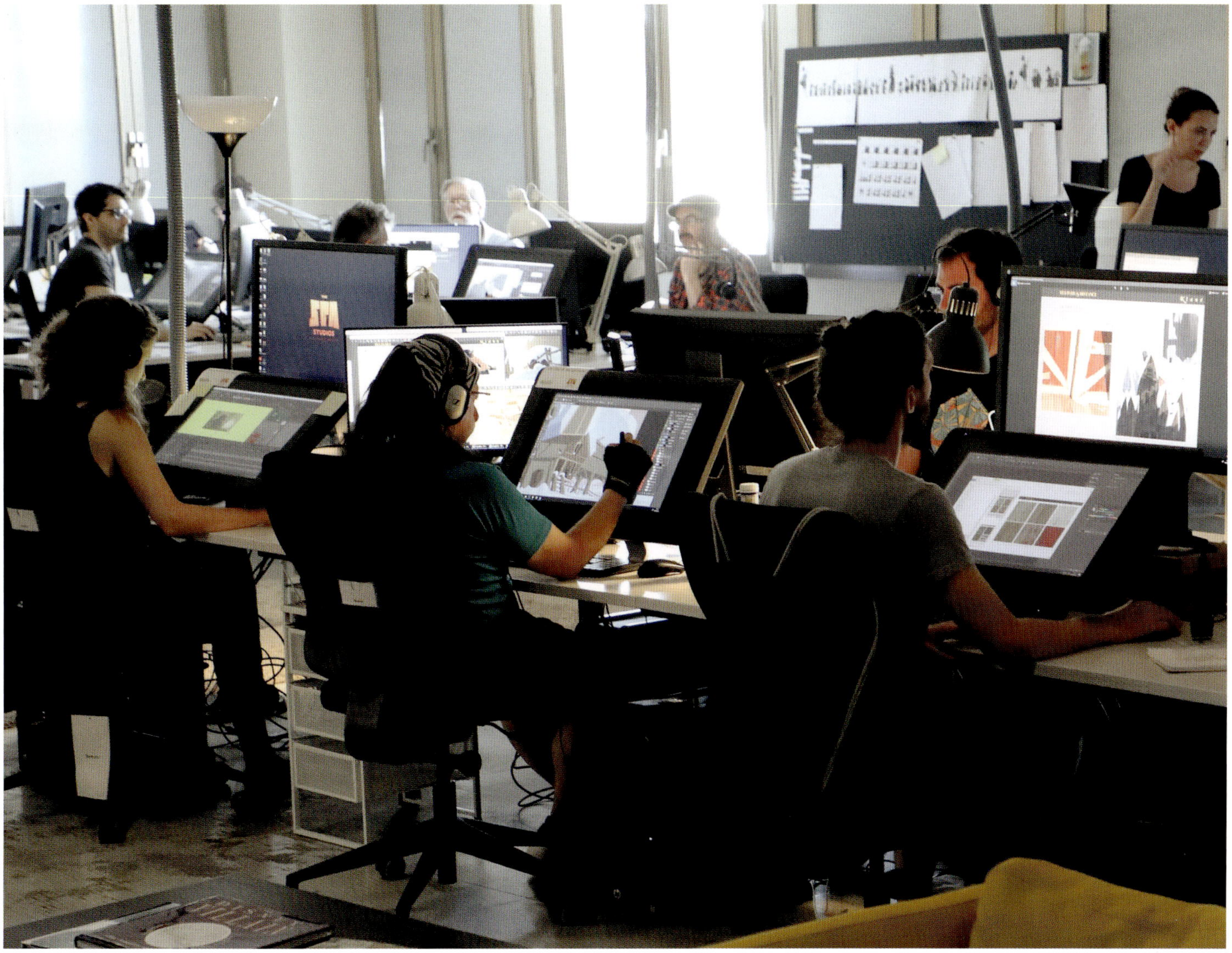

PREVIOUS PAGE: (TOP) Lighting guides by Renée Chio O'Shea.

THIS PAGE: SPA artists working on the film.

The SPA team set off to discover new ways to advance traditional animation for audiences in 2019 and beyond. After carefully analyzing the 2D pipeline, they came to the conclusion that they could make great progress in the ways they used light and color in the movie. "We decided to create tools to allow artists to effectively add volumetric lighting to drawings," says Pablos. "We looked at many different approaches but, in the end, we decided to go for a hand-crafted approach, which fits beautifully with the rest of the traditional animation process."

As a result, unlike many other traditionally animated movies, the characters and backgrounds look like they belong to the same world. "We're used to seeing 2D characters looking like stickers put on painted backgrounds," says Pablos. "I felt that we needed to feel like the same artists painted the whole world."

He mentions that, whenever he stepped into production departments in the past, he was impressed by the stunning artwork created by all the different artists who worked on the movie throughout the development process. "You see all this amazing art showcasing different sensibilities and styles," Pablos notes. "But once they are put through the pipeline, the art gets ground down to a standardized style. That always nagged at me that we weren't able to put any of the eclectic styles directly onto the screen."

To that end, the artists and technical innovators at SPA created a new system that allowed them to put visual development art into motion on the big screen, while preserving the original styles and details. As he points out, "We found that the best way was to start from traditional animation and try to add all the right bells and whistles to get the visuals right. As we like to [say], we're not bringing 2D back, we're bringing it forward!"

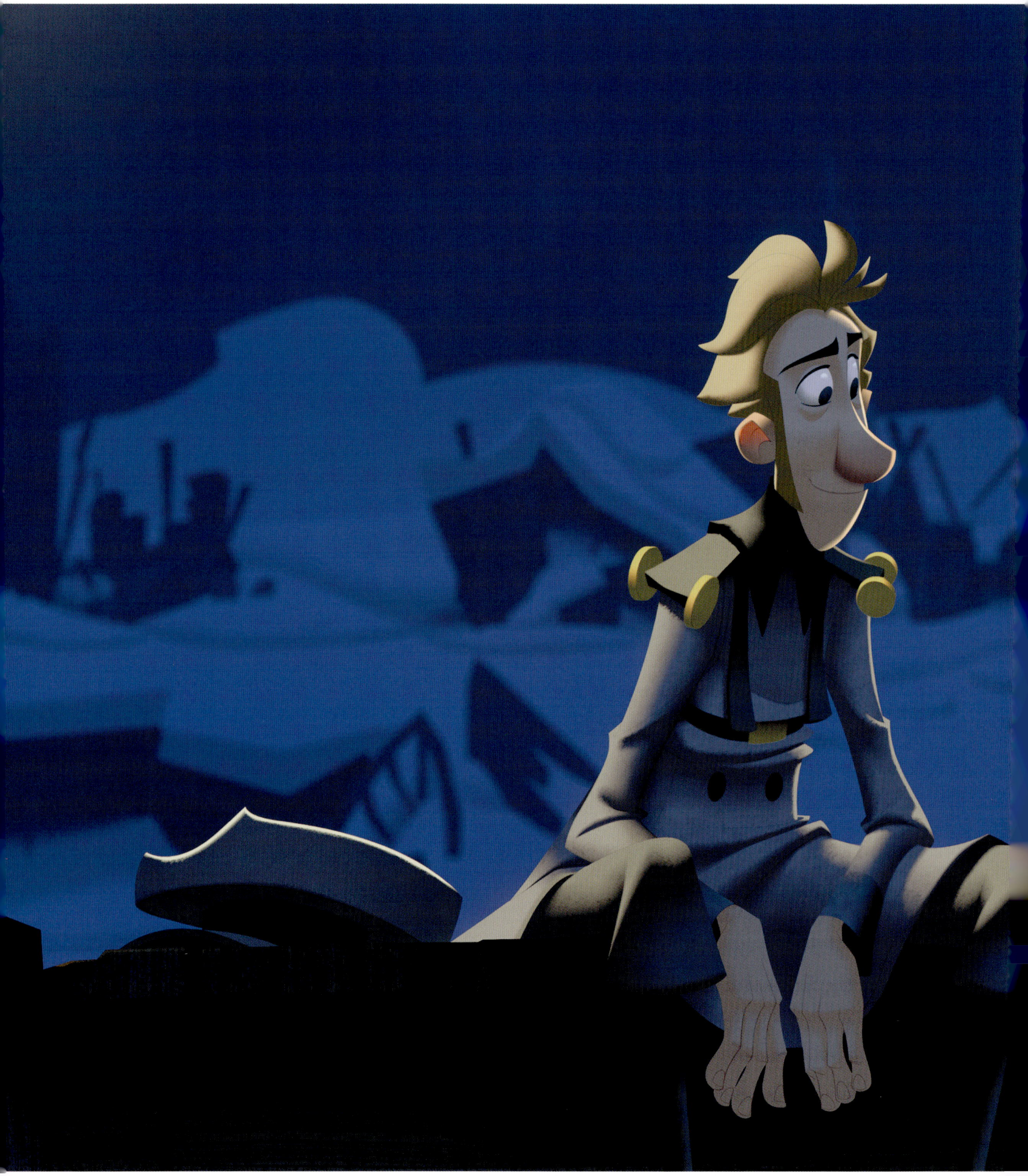

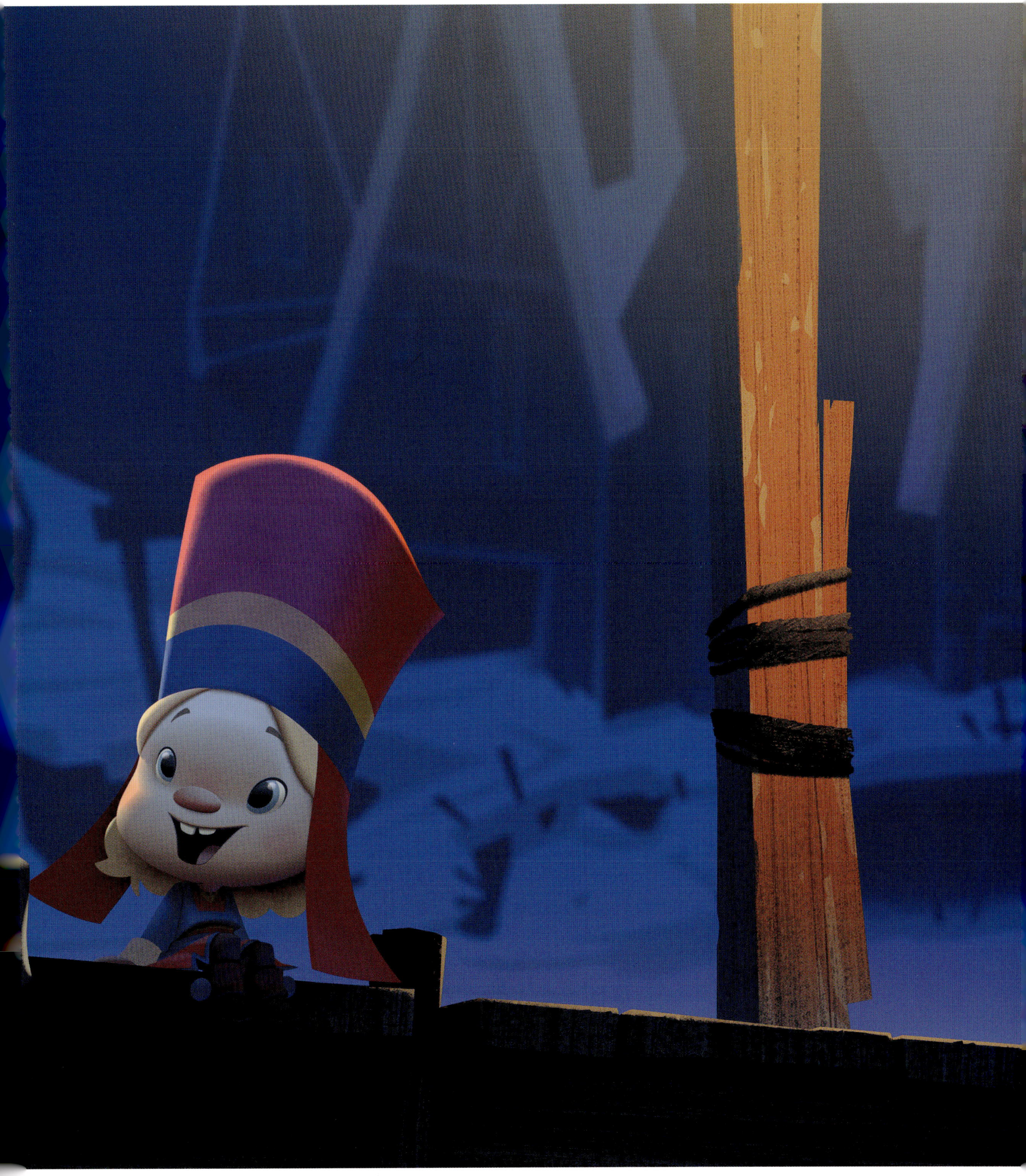

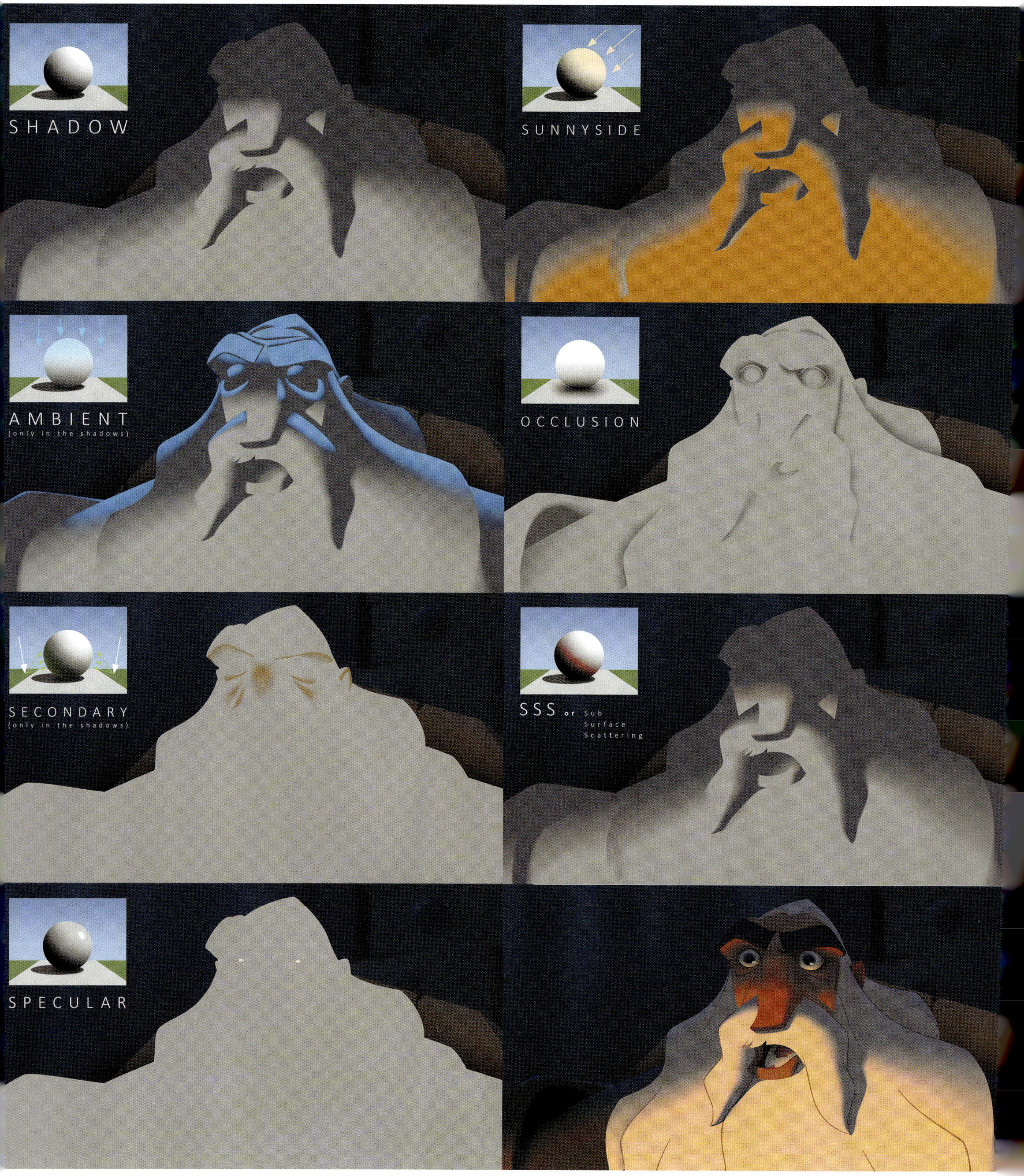
SHADOW
SUNNYSIDE
AMBIENT
(only in the shadows)
OCCLUSION
SECONDARY
(only in the shadows)
SSS or Sub Surface Scattering
SPECULAR

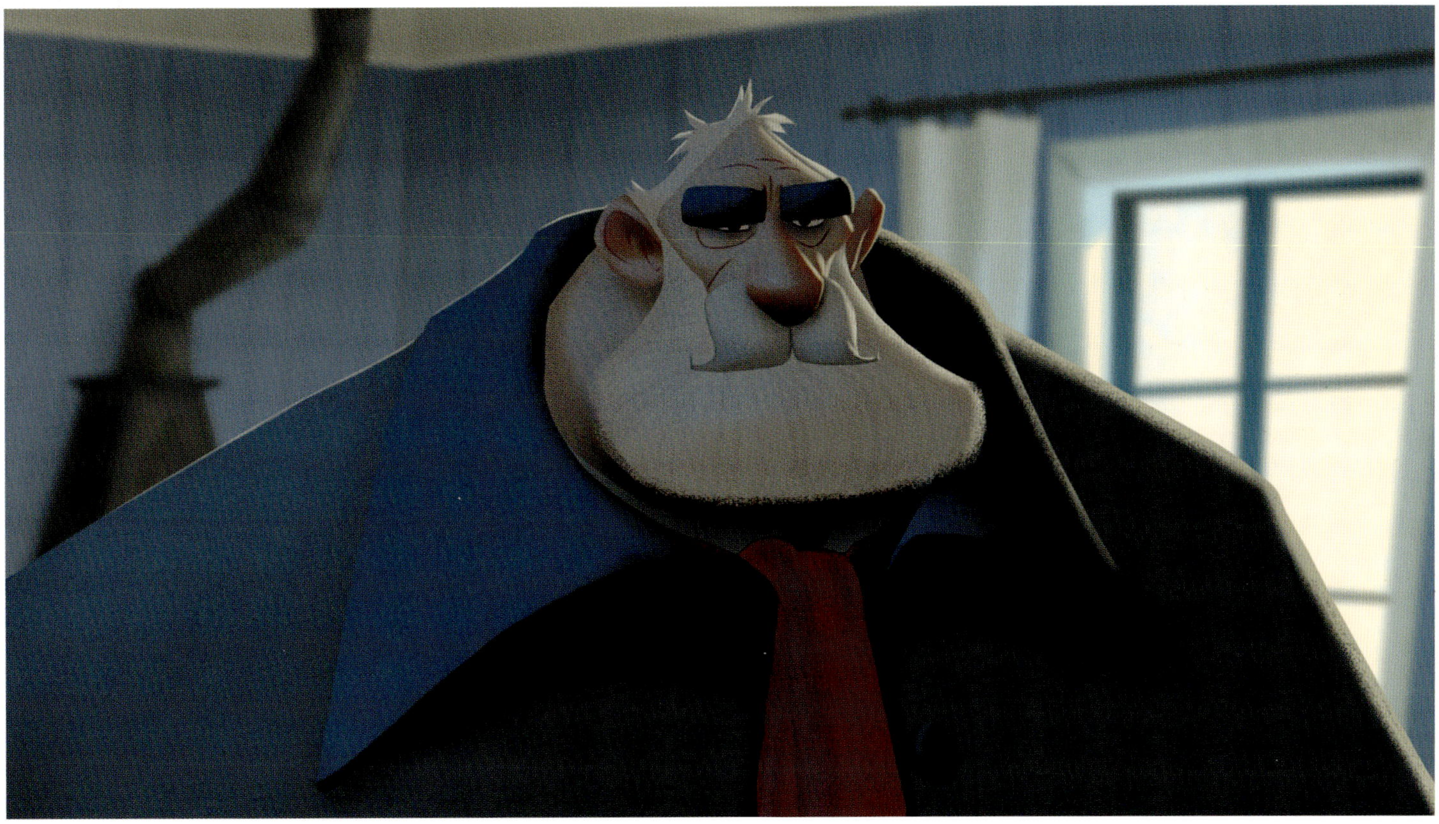

"We developed a new technique which allowed us to throw the light on top of the characters. This technique creates the sensation of volume and also helps integrate the characters with the backgrounds seamlessly."

Marcin Jakubowski, Production Designer

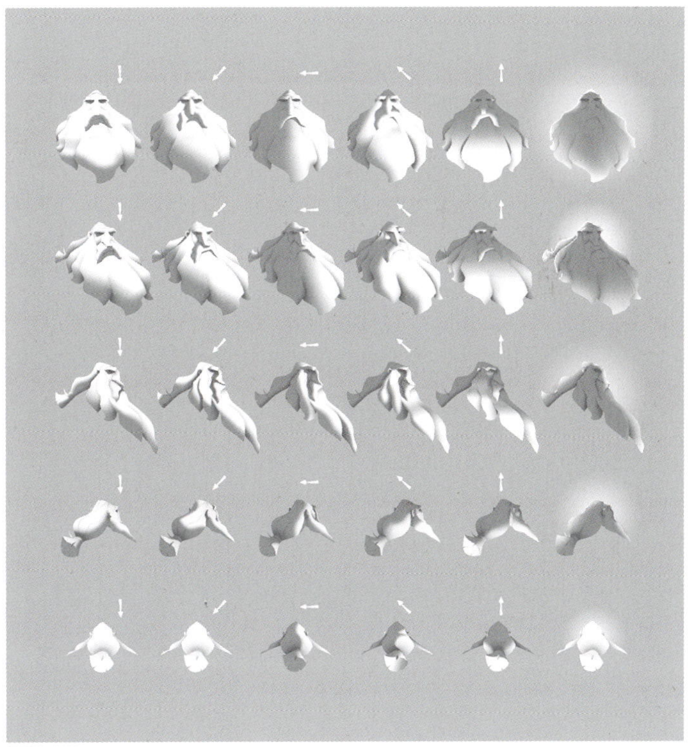

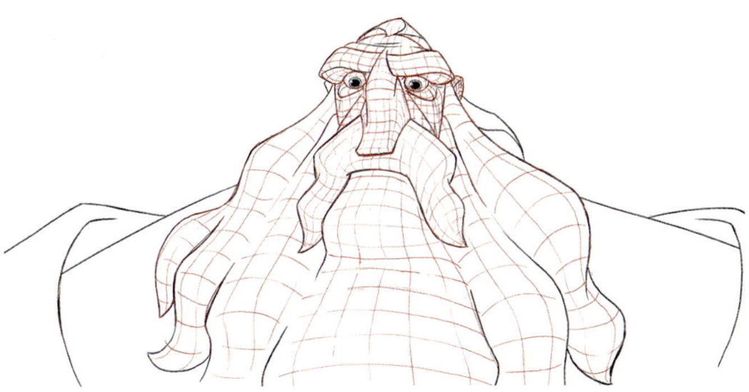

THIS SPREAD: Early lighting and shadowing tests done by the filmmakers while designing their new technique. Note the early character design above.

NEXT SPREAD: The SPA team behind *Klaus*.

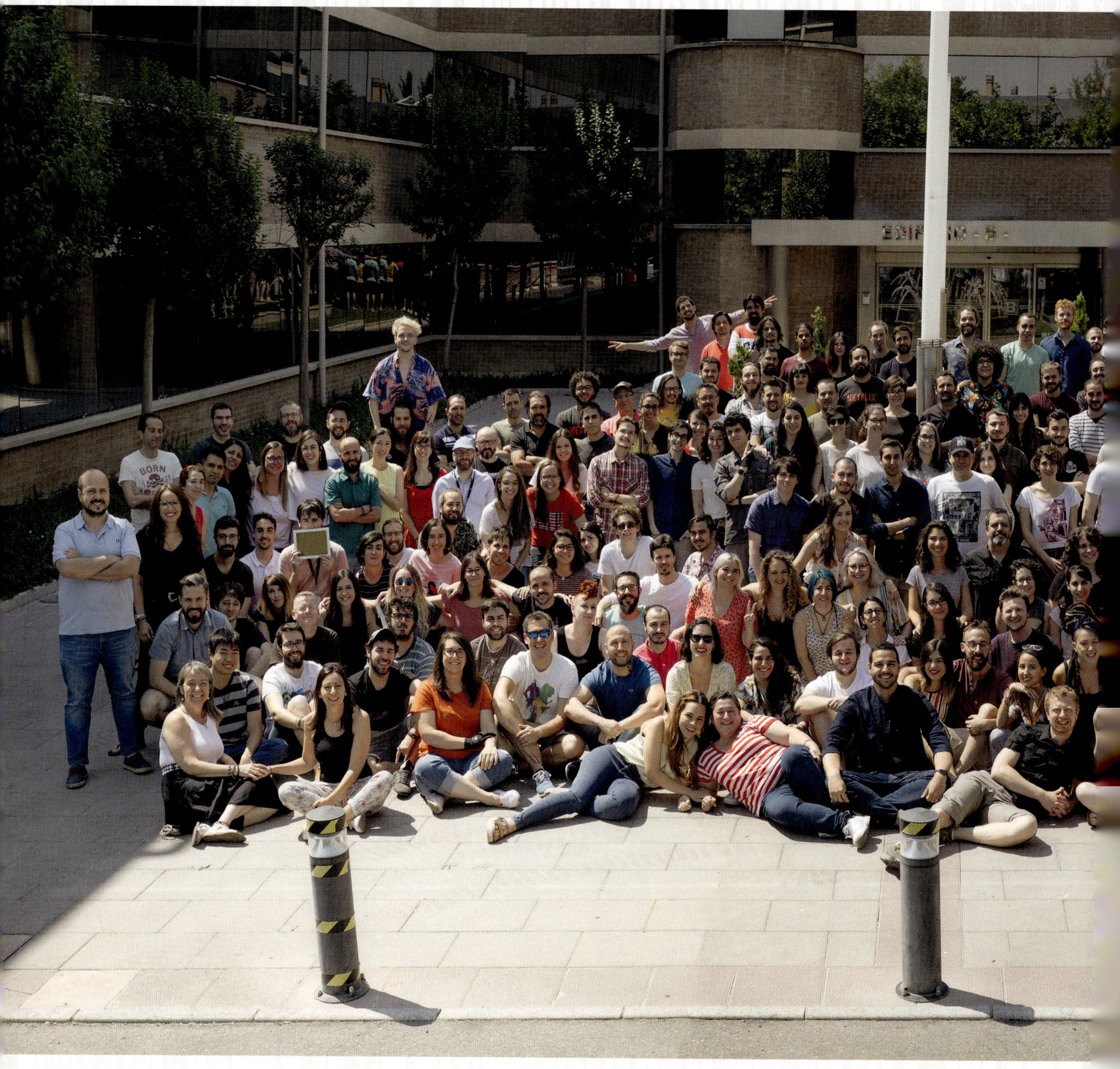
BORN
NETFLIX

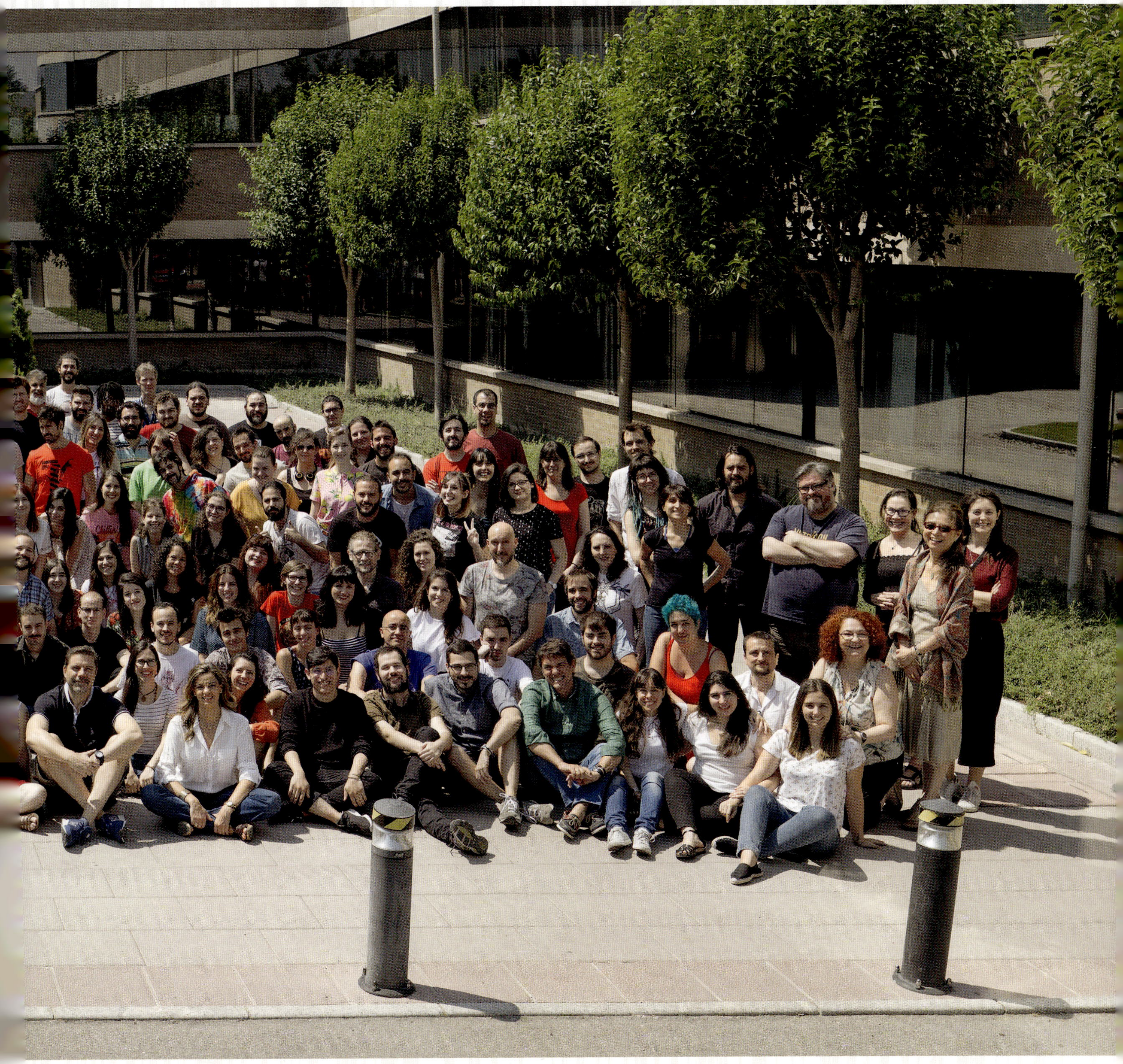

The Artistry

REAL-TIME SCULPTORS OF LIGHT

The team at SPA was already working with Les Films du Poisson Rouge, a studio based in Angoulême, France, to create the character textures for *Klaus*. SPA was looking to streamline the lighting system used in early tests, so they approached Anaël Seghezzi, head of technology for texture, light, and shadows at the French studio, who had been working on a 2D animation software called Houdoo for about a decade, and had developed a very effective in-betweening and tracking system. In addition, SPA and LFDPR collaborated to further develop the software to do light and shadow animation for *Klaus*.

THIS SPREAD: Concept art showing a transformed Smeerensburg, filled with light and warmth.

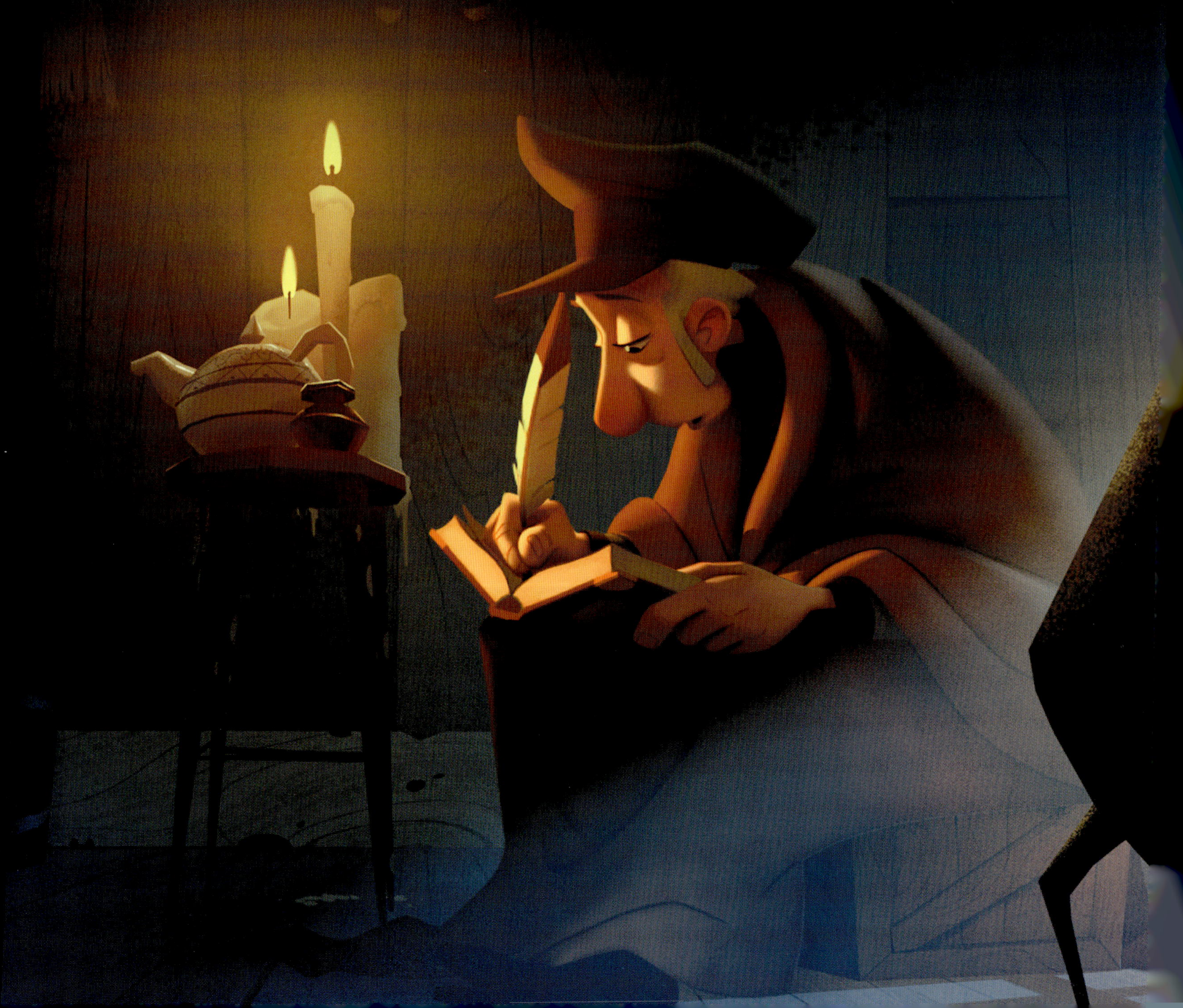

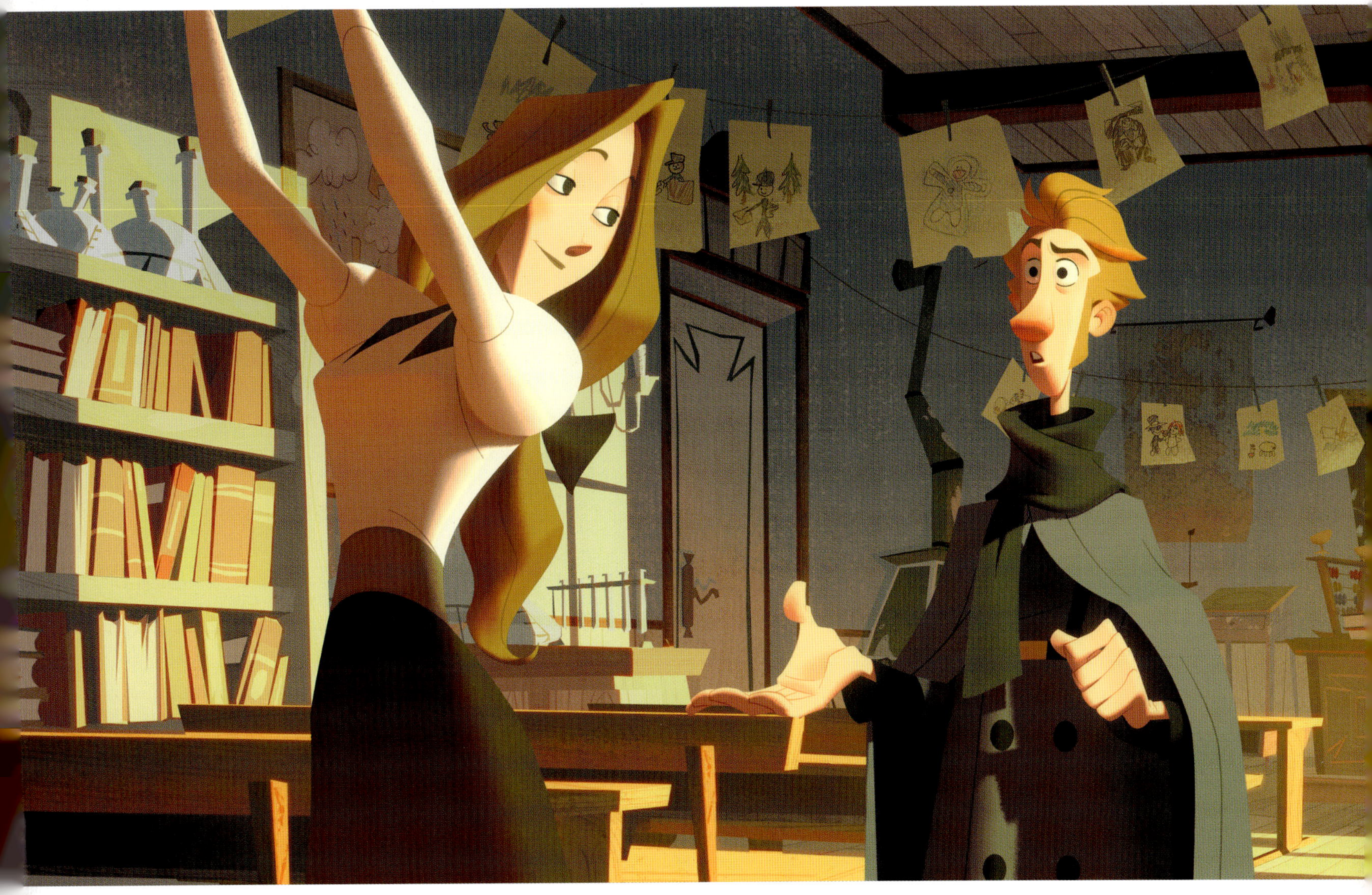

As Seghezzi explains, "Marcin [Jakubowski] and I talked about this technique and came up with a plan for a tool that would focus on automatic tracking and complete real-time rendering. It was late in pre-production and I had only three months to create a functioning prototype, so I used my existing software as the core and adapted Marcin's shader to work in real time. It worked surprisingly well, so I continued to improve it while I was working on the pipeline for texturing."

Seghezzi says the new tool enables artists to express the mood they want to convey without hidden layers and without any lag. "Lighting in traditional animation is often constrained by economy, and 3D lighting is generally bound by physics and long renders," he notes. "With this new tool, the lighting artists can work in real time, as painters and as sculptors of light."

After seeing how this technology had contributed to the overall look of *Klaus*, Seghezzi says he loves how it makes the concept art come alive in animation. "You can really feel the presence, the blood and sweat and hands of the people behind it," he says. "Of course, I'm very proud that we could do something new and original."

"The style had to work for both the darker moments and be effective in the transformations we see in the end, so that it could look positive, cheerful, and reminiscent of Christmas."

Szymon Biernacki, Production Designer

Conclusion

When Sergio Pablos and his driven, talented team at Madrid's SPA Studios set out to make a movie about the mysterious origins of Santa Claus, they knew that they had a challenging road ahead. They wanted to tell a fresh, emotional, and fascinating story that was both funny and poignant, and was suitable for family viewing. But they also wanted to use this opportunity to resurrect the power of 2D animation and use the latest digital technologies to restore the glory days of traditional animation.

Pablos is thrilled about the way the movie pushes 2D into a new era. "We're just starting to discover what we can do with this medium, and I feel we can do a lot more in the near future," he says. "Our team came together to create art that engages the audience and provokes a powerful emotional response. In addition, we leave the audience with this message of spreading joy and kindness, which is so important during these challenging times we live in."

Now, with *Klaus* available for streaming on Netflix this holiday season, they are finally able to share the fruits of their labor with audiences all over the world. "We went for the magic formula, which is 'make them laugh about thirty times and make them cry twice: first out of sorrow, and then out of joy,'" says Pablos. "I hope we got as close to that as possible."

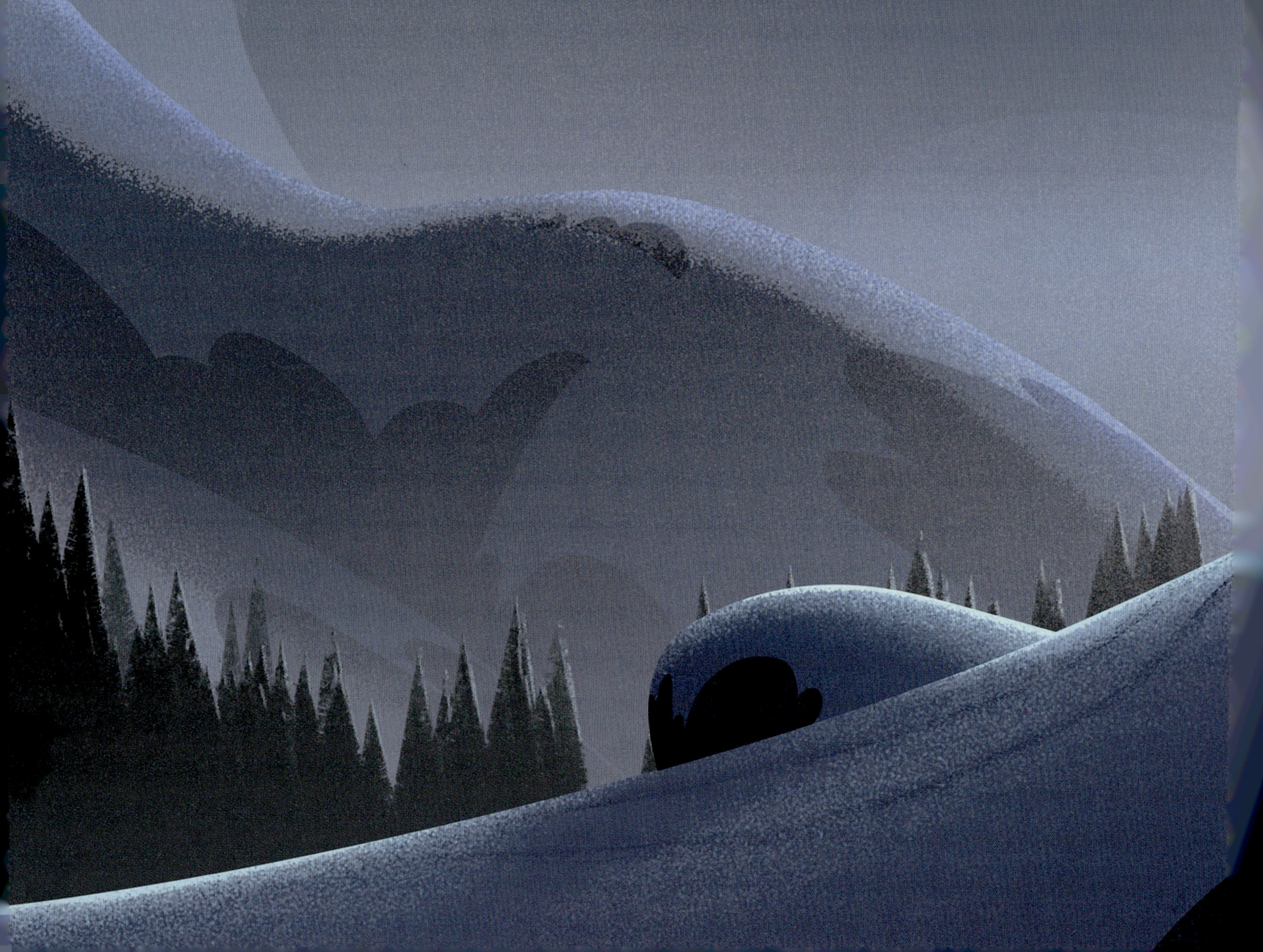

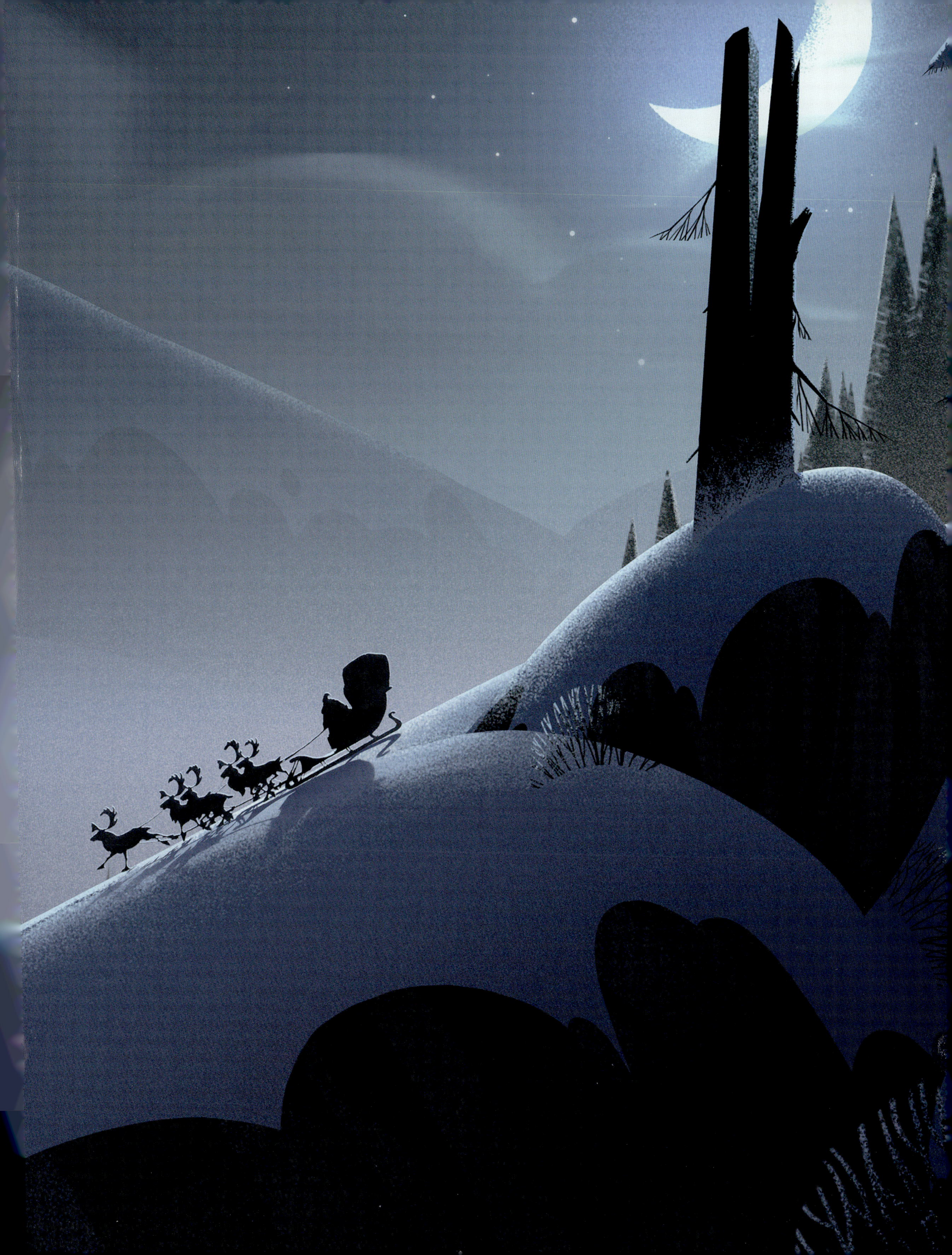

Acknowledgements

We would like to thank everyone who worked on *Klaus*. It was truly a herculean international effort, spanning the past nine years. We had artists come and work in Madrid from twenty-two countries, speaking over fifteen languages.

A huge thanks to the team at Netflix, including Matt Brodlie, Melissa Cobb, Damien de Froberville, Gregg Taylor, Olivier Mouroux, Sunny Park, and Paul Cichocki, for giving us this amazing opportunity and believing in us.

We would especially like to thank Ramin Zahed, Susie Rae, Natasha MacKenzie, Chris Gonzalez, Catherine Moller, Marcin Jakubowski, Szymon Biernacki, Sara Rodriguez Coca, Alfredo Jose Gutierrez, and all the people at Titan Books for creating this book practically overnight.

Our gratitude to James Baxter for writing the foreword and sharing his thoughts on bringing traditional animation forward.

From

Sergio Pablos,
Jinko Gotoh,
Marisa Roman, and
Matthew Teevan

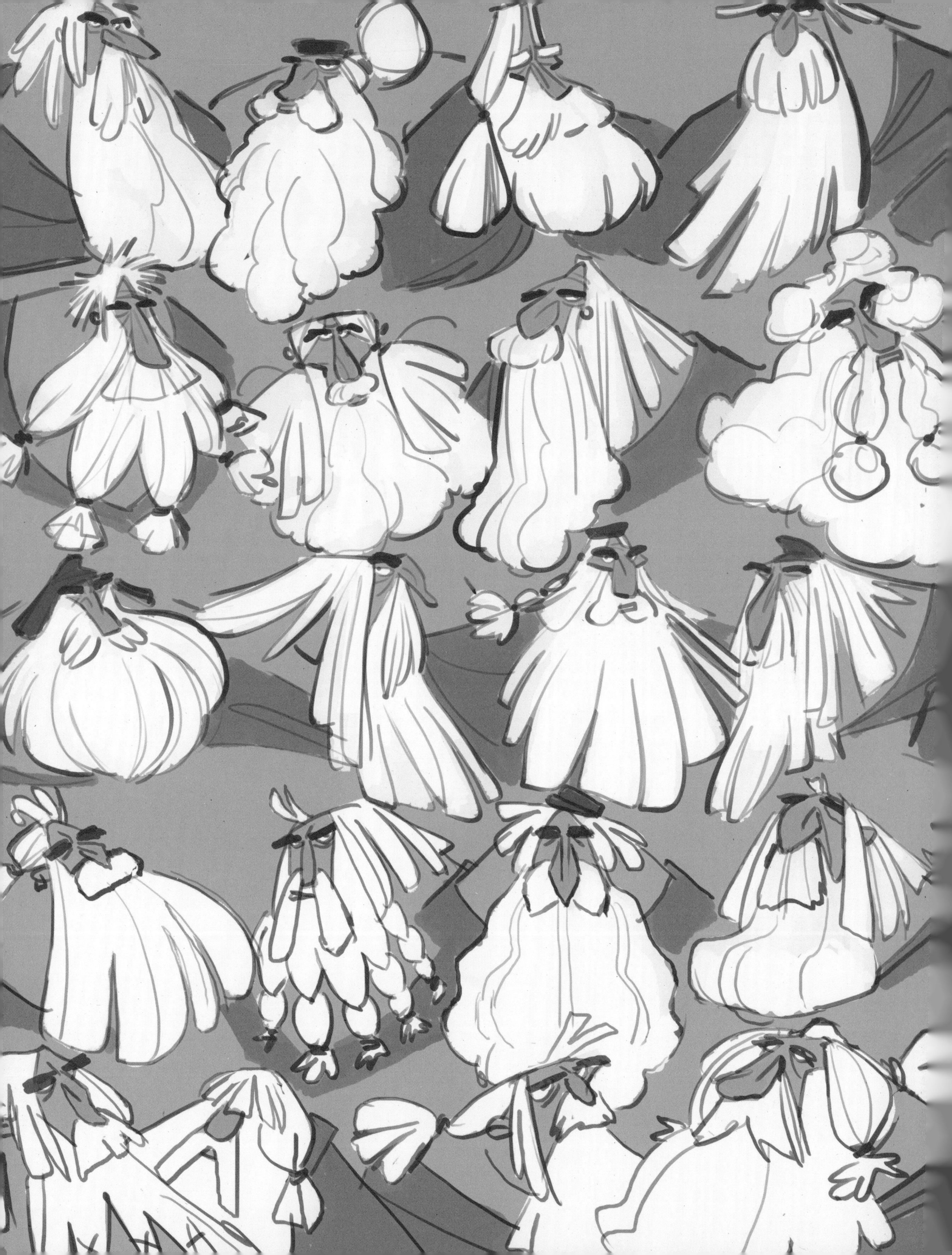